About the cover

Civil Rights March Past Brown Chapel in Selma, Alabama, March 1, 1965

The cover image presents a portion of the larger photograph, which appears below. When they explore American histories, scholars consider many different aspects of America's past and connect them for a rich, fresh synthesis. This photo of a civil rights march from Selma to Montgomery, Alabama, in 1965 offers a wider angle on the movement for racial equality that transformed the United States into the nation that exists today.

EXPLORING AMERICAN HISTORIES

A BRIEF SURVEY WITH SOURCES

Volume 2: Since 1865

Nancy A. Hewitt
Rutgers University

Steven F. Lawson
Rutgers University

Bedford/St. Martin's
Boston • New York

To Mary and Charles Takacs, Florence and Hiram Hewitt, Sarah and Abraham Parker, Lena and Ben Lawson, who made our American histories possible.

For Bedford/St. Martin's

Publisher for History: Mary V. Dougherty
Senior Executive Editor for History: William J. Lombardo
Director of Development for History: Jane Knetzger
Senior Developmental Editor: Sara Wise
Senior Production Editor: Christina M. Horn
Senior Production Supervisor: Jennifer Peterson
Senior Marketing Manager for U.S. History: Amy Whitaker
Associate Editor: Jennifer Jovin
Editorial Assistant: Arrin Kaplan
Production Assistant: Elise Keller
Copy Editor: Linda McLatchie
Map Editor: Charlotte Miller
Indexer: Leoni McVey
Cartography: Mapping Specialists, Ltd.
Photo Researcher: Naomi Kornhauser
Permissions Manager: Kalina K. Ingham

Senior Art Director: Anna Palchik
Text Designer: Jerilyn Bockorick
Cover Designer: Billy Boardman
Cover Art: Selma civil rights march: A march to Montgomery, Alabama, in front of Brown Chapel in Selma, Alabama, March 1, 1965. © Flip Schulke/CORBIS.
Composition: Cenveo Publisher Services
Printing and Binding: RR Donnelley and Sons

President, Bedford/St. Martin's: Denise B. Wydra
Presidents, Macmillan Higher Education: Joan E. Feinberg and Tom Scotty
Director of Marketing: Karen R. Soeltz
Production Director: Susan W. Brown
Associate Production Director: Elise S. Kaiser
Managing Editor: Elizabeth M. Schaaf

Manufactured in the United States

7 6 5
f   e   d

For information, write: Bedford/St. Martin's, 75 Arlington Street, Boston, MA 02116   (617-399-4000)

ISBN 978-0-312-40998-2 (Combined Edition)
ISBN 978-1-4576-4194-7 (Loose-leaf Edition)
ISBN 978-0-312-41000-1 (Volume 1)
ISBN 978-1-4576-4195-4 (Loose-leaf Edition, Volume 1)
ISBN 978-0-312-41001-8 (Volume 2)
ISBN 978-1-4576-4196-1 (Loose-leaf Edition, Volume 2)

Exploring American Histories is a new kind of U.S. history survey text. Unique among textbooks, its innovative format makes a broad and diverse American history accessible to a new generation of students and instructors interested in a more active learning and teaching style. To accomplish this, our book joins an inclusive yet brief narrative text with an integrated documents reader; together, these two elements create unsurpassed opportunities for exploring American history in ways best suited for the twenty-first-century classroom.

Format

Our extensive experience teaching American history in a wide variety of classrooms has led us to conclude that students learn history most effectively when they read historical narrative in conjunction with primary sources. Sources bring the past to life in ways that narrative alone cannot, while narrative offers the necessary framework, context, and chronology that documents by themselves do not typically provide. We believe that the most engaging entry to the past starts with individuals and how people in their daily lives connect to larger political, economic, cultural, and international developments. This approach makes the history relevant and memorable. The available textbooks left us unsatisfied, compelling us to assign additional books, readers, and documents we found on the Web. However, these supplementary texts raised costs for our students, and too often students had difficulty seeing how the different readings related to one another. Simply remembering what materials to bring to class became too unwieldy. So we decided to write our own book.

For *Exploring American Histories*, we sought to reconceive the relationship of the textbook and reader to create a mutually supportive set of course materials designed to help our students appreciate the diversity of America's history, to help instructors teach that primary sources are the building blocks of historical interpretation, and to encourage students to see that every past event can and should be considered from multiple perspectives. The people of the past experienced the events of their lifetimes in a variety of ways and from multiple vantage points, and historians debate continually among themselves and the general public about what actually happened and why it matters for us today. Consequently, there is no one story about the past; there are many stories, and so we wanted to emphasize these plural *Histories* in the book's title. Indeed, on the last day of our own survey classes, we measure our success by how well our students can demonstrate that they understand this rich complexity that is central to the discipline, and whether they can put the multiple stories they have come to understand into the context of the larger whole. Instructors at all types of schools share our goal, and we hope that *Exploring American Histories* will help them enrich their students' understanding of events of the past.

For *Exploring American Histories*, we have selected an extensive and diverse array of primary-source materials that highlight multiple perspectives, and we have integrated them at key points as teaching moments within the narrative text. Each chapter contains numerous featured primary sources with a distinctive pedagogy designed to help students make connections between the documents and the text's big themes. Every document is clearly cross-referenced within the narrative so that students can easily incorporate them into their reading as well as reflect on our interpretation. A specially selected set of interrelated documents placed at the end of each chapter addresses an important historical question related to the chapter.

Exploring American Histories also opens up a new dimension to the familiar textbook format by expanding beyond its printed pages to grant students and teachers access to a wealth of online tools and resources built specifically for our text to enhance reading comprehension and promote in-depth study. Of special note, every chapter includes an additional document set that instructors can order packaged with the book; each set of documents focuses on a particular theme and is available only online. Many of these projects incorporate multimedia sources such as audio and video files that until recently were unavailable to work with in class. In addition, *Exploring American Histories* features LearningCurve, an easy-to-assign adaptive learning tool that helps students rehearse the material in the narrative so that they come to class better prepared. Students receive access to LearningCurve, described more fully below, when they purchase a new copy of the book. And because textbook prices are a big concern, our "two-in-one" survey text—a combination of brief narrative plus reader—offers attractive cost savings for students.

Approach

During the last thirty years, scholarship in history has transformed our vision of the past, most notably by dramatically increasing the range of people historians study, and thus deepening and complicating traditional under-standings of change over time. Creating a story of the past was easier to do when it was limited to the study of great white men engaged in national politics and high-level diplomacy, but it was also stunted in its explanatory power and disconnected from the life experiences of nearly all our students. Over the last several decades, the historical profession itself has made huge strides in becoming more inclusive in membership, with teachers and scholars increasingly reflecting the diverse face of America. The range of new research has been vast, with a special focus on gender, race, ethnicity, and class, and histori-ans have produced landmark work in women's history, African American history, American Indian history, and labor history.

All of these changes in the historical profession have greatly influenced how the American history survey course is taught in two fundamental ways. First, many instructors now try to help their students see that ordinary people, from all walks of life, can and do affect the course of historical change. Second, many historians have become increasingly transparent about their methodology and have a strong desire to teach their students that history is an interpretive discipline and open to multiple perspectives. Since the 1970s, survey textbooks have changed in coverage, organization, and pedagogy, but they have struggled to get it right—becoming overwhelming in their scope, difficult to read, and losing the sense of story that makes the past accessible, engaging, and comprehensible. As more instructors have embraced teaching with documents, they have come to see these shortcomings in the available survey textbooks. Along with many of our colleagues, we came to the same conclusion ourselves. Many current texts are too long, so we've made ours brief. *Exploring American Histories* is comprehensive, but with a carefully selected amount of detail that is more in tune with what instructors can realistically expect their students to remember. Many texts include some documents, but the balance between narrative (too much) and primary sources (too few) was off-kilter, so we have included more documents and integrated them in creative ways that help students make the necessary connections and that spur them to think critically. But the most innovative aspect of *Exploring American Histories*, and what makes it a true alternative, is that its format introduces a unique textbook structure organized around the broad theme of *diversity*.

Diversity as a theme works in *Exploring American Histories* in several ways. First, diversity supports our presentation of an inclusive historical narrative, one that recognizes the American past as a series of interwoven stories made by a multiplicity of historical actors. We do this within a strong national framework that allows our readers to see how the various stories fit together and to understand why they matter. Our narrative is comple-mented by a wide variety of documents that challenge students to consider multiple points of view. In chapter 4, students hear from both a woman accused of witchcraft and a minister who defended the Salem witch trials. In chapter 25, we ask our readers to contrast an idyllic, inviting depiction of 1950s suburbia with a racially restrictive covenant of the same period.

Second, our theme of diversity allows us to foreground the role of individual agency as we push readers to consider the reasons behind historical change. Each chapter opens with a pair of American Histories, biographies that showcase indi-viduals who experienced and influenced events in a particular period, and then returns to them throughout the chapter to strengthen the connections and highlight their place in the bigger picture. These biographies cover both well-known Americans—such as Daniel Shays, Frederick Douglass, Andrew Carnegie, and Eleanor Roosevelt—and those who never gained fame or fortune—such as the activist Amy Kirby Post, organizer Luisa Moreno, and World War II internee Fred Korematsu. Introducing such a broad range of biographical subjects illuminates the many ways that individuals shaped and were shaped by historical events. This strategy also works to make visible throughout the chapter the intersections where history from the top down meets history from the bottom up and to connect social and political histories to their relation-ships with economic, cultural, and diplomatic developments. We work to show that events at the national level, shaped by elite political and economic leaders, have a direct impact on the lives of ordinary people; at the same time, we demonstrate that actions at the local level often have a significant influence on decisions made at the centers of national government and commerce. The discussions of the interrelationship among international, national, and local theaters and actors incorpo-rate the pathbreaking scholarship of the last three decades, which has focused on gender, race, class, and ethnicity in North America and the United States, and on colonization, empire, and globalization in the larger world.

Primary Sources

The heart of *Exploring American Histories* is its primary sources, and in every chapter we supply students with numer-ous and carefully selected documents from which they can evaluate the text's interpretations and construct their own versions of history. These firsthand accounts include maps, drawings, material artifacts, paintings, speeches, sermons, letters, diaries, memoirs, newspaper articles, political cartoons, laws, wills, court cases, petitions, advertisements, photographs, and blogs. In selecting documents, we have provided multiple perspectives on critical issues, including both well-known sources and those that are less familiar. But our choices were also influenced by the kinds of primary sources that exist. For some periods of American history and some topics, the available primary sources are limited and fragmentary.

For other eras and issues, the sources are varied and abundant, indeed sometimes overwhelming, especially as we move into the twentieth century. In all time periods, some groups of Americans are far better represented in primary sources than others. Those who were wealthy, well educated, and politically powerful produced and preserved many sources about their lives. And their voices are well represented in this textbook. But we have also provided documents by American Indians, enslaved Africans, colonial women, rural residents, immigrants, working people, and young people. Moreover, the lives of those who left few sources of their own can often be illuminated by reading documents written by elites to see what information they yield, intentionally or unintentionally, about less well-documented groups.

Individual documents are embedded throughout every chapter and connected to the narrative text with **Explore** prompts, and within each chapter these documents are treated in the following three ways:

- Each chapter has one annotated textual or visual source, with questions in the margins to help students consider a specific phrase or feature and analyze the source as a whole. These questions and annotations are intended to train students in historical habits of mind. A **Put It in Context** question prompts students to consider the source in terms of the broad themes of the chapter.
- Each chapter contains **Two Views**, a paired set of documents that show contrasting perspectives. Two Views documents are introduced by a single headnote and are followed by **Interpret the Evidence** and **Put It in Context** questions that prompt students to analyze and compare both items and place them in a larger historical framework.
- Each chapter also presents one or more additional documents consisting of excerpts or images of classic or lesser-known sources. These are provided to encourage more practice working with sources and to offer additional perspectives to compare with the narrative. These documents are accompanied by informative headnotes and conclude with **Interpret the Evidence** and **Put It in Context** questions.

A **Document Project** at the end of every chapter is the capstone of our integrated primary-sources approach. Each Document Project is a collection of five or six documents focused on a critical issue central to that chapter. It is introduced by a brief overview and ends with interpretive questions that ask students to draw conclusions based on what they have learned in the chapter and read in the sources.

We understand that the instructor's role is crucial in teaching students how to analyze primary-source materials and develop interpretations. Teachers can use the documents to encourage critical thinking and also to measure students' understanding and assess their progress. The integration of the documents in the narrative should prompt students to read more closely than they usually do, as they will see more clearly the direct connection between the two. We have organized the documents to give instructors the flexibility to use them in many different ways—as in-class discussion prompts, for take-home writing assignments, and even as the basis for exam questions—and also in different combinations, as the documents throughout the chapter can be compared and contrasted with one another. An instructor's manual for *Exploring American Histories* provides a wealth of creative suggestions for using the documents program effectively (see the Versions and Supplements description on pages xiii–xvi for more information on all the available instructor resources).

More Help for Students

We know that students often need help making sense of their reading. As instructors, all of us have had students complain that they cannot figure out what's important in the textbooks we assign. For many of our students, especially those just out of high school, their college history survey textbook is likely the most difficult book they have ever encountered. We understand the challenges that our students face, so in addition to the extensive document program, we have included the following pedagogical features designed to aid student learning:

- **Review and Relate** questions help students focus on main themes and concepts presented in each major section of the chapter.
- **Key terms** in boldface highlight important content. All terms are defined in a glossary at the end of the book.
- Clear **conclusions** help students summarize what they've read.
- A full-page **Chapter Review** lets students review key terms, important concepts, and notable events.

In addition, the book includes access to **LearningCurve**, an online adaptive learning tool that promotes engaged reading and focused review. Cross-references at the end of every major section and chapter in the text prompt students to log in and rehearse their understanding of the material they have just read. Students move at their own pace and accumulate points as they go, giving the interaction a game-like feel. Feedback for incorrect responses explains why the answer is incorrect and directs students back to the text to review before they attempt to answer the question again. The end result is a better understanding of the key elements of the text. See the inside front cover for more details.

We imagine *Exploring American Histories* as a new kind of American history textbook, one that not only offers a strong, concise narrative but also challenges students to construct their own interpretations through primary-source analysis. We are thrilled that our hopes have come to fruition, and we believe that our textbook will provide a thought-provoking and highly useful foundation for every U.S. history survey course and will benefit students and faculty alike. The numerous opportunities provided for active learning will allow teachers to engage students in stimulating ways and help them experience the past in closer connection to the present. After all, active learning is the basis for active citizenship, and teaching the survey course is our chance as historians, whose work is highly specialized, to reach the greatest number of undergraduates. We hope not only to inspire the historical imaginations of those who will create the next generation of American histories but also to spur them to consider the issues of today in light of the stories of yesterday.

Acknowledgments

We wish to thank the talented scholars and teachers who were kind enough to give their time and knowledge to review the manuscript:

Benjamin Allen, *South Texas College*
Christine Anderson, *Xavier University*
Uzoamaka Melissa C. Anyiwo, *Curry College*
Anthony A. Ball, *Housatonic Community College*
Terry A. Barnhart, *Eastern Illinois University*
Edwin Benson, *North Harford High School*
Paul Berk, *Christian Brothers University*
Deborah L. Blackwell, *Texas A&M International University*
Thomas Born, *Blinn College*
Margaret Bramlett, *St. Andrews Episcopal High School*
Lauren K. Bristow, *Collin College*
Tsekani Browne, *Duquesne University*
Jon L. Brudvig, *Dickinson State University*
Dave Bush, *Shasta College*
Barbara Calluori, *Montclair State University*
Julia Schiavone Camacho, *The University of Texas at El Paso*
Jacqueline Glass Campbell, *Francis Marion University*
Amy E. Canfield, *Lewis-Clark State College*
Dominic Carrillo, *Grossmont College*
Mark R. Cheathem, *Cumberland University*
Laurel A. Clark, *University of Hartford*
Myles L. Clowers, *San Diego City College*
Hamilton Cravens, *Iowa State University*
Audrey Crawford, *Houston Community College*
John Crum, *University of Delaware*
Alex G. Cummins, *St. Johns River State College*
Susanne Deberry-Cole, *Morgan State University*
Julian J. DelGaudio, *Long Beach City College*

Patricia Norred Derr, *Kutztown University*
John Donoghue, *Loyola University Chicago*
Timothy Draper, *Waubonsee Community College*
David Dzurec, *University of Scranton*
Keith Edgerton, *Montana State University Billings*
Blake Ellis, *Lone Star College*
Christine Erickson, *Indiana University–Purdue University Fort Wayne*
Todd Estes, *Oakland University*
Gabrielle Everett, *Jefferson College*
Julie Fairchild, *Sinclair Community College*
Randy Finley, *Georgia Perimeter College*
Kirsten Fischer, *University of Minnesota*
Michelle Fishman-Cross, *College of Staten Island*
Jeffrey Forret, *Lamar University*
Kristen Foster, *Marquette University*
Susan Freeman, *Western Michigan University*
Nancy Gabin, *Purdue University*
Kevin Gannon, *Grand View University*
Benton Gates, *Indiana University–Purdue University Fort Wayne*
Bruce Geelhoed, *Ball State University*
Mark Gelfand, *Boston College*
Jason George, *The Bryn Mawr School*
Judith A. Giesberg, *Villanova University*
Sherry Ann Gray, *Mid-South Community College*
Patrick Griffin, *University of Notre Dame*
Aaron Gulyas, *Mott Community College*
Scott Gurman, *Northern Illinois University*
Melanie Gustafson, *University of Vermont*
Brian Hart, *Del Mar College*
Paul Hart, *Texas State University*
Paul Harvey, *University of Colorado Colorado Springs*
Woody Holton, *University of Richmond*
Vilja Hulden, *University of Arizona*
Colette A. Hyman, *Winona State University*
Brenda Jackson-Abernathy, *Belmont University*
Troy R. Johnson, *California State University–Long Beach*
Shelli Jordan-Zirkle, *Shoreline Community College*
Jennifer Kelly, *The University of Texas at Austin*
Kelly Kennington, *Auburn University*
Andrew E. Kersten, *University of Wisconsin–Green Bay*
Janilyn M. Kocher, *Richland Community College*
Max Krochmal, *Duke University*
Peggy Lambert, *Lone Star College*
Jennifer R. Lang, *Delgado Community College*
John S. Leiby, *Paradise Valley Community College*
Mitchell Lerner, *The Ohio State University*
Matthew Loayza, *Minnesota State University, Mankato*
Gabriel J. Loiacono, *University of Wisconsin Oshkosh*
John F. Lyons, *Joliet Junior College*
Lorie Maltby, *Henderson Community College*

Christopher Manning, *Loyola University Chicago*
Marty D. Matthews, *North Carolina State University*
Eric Mayer, *Victor Valley College*
Suzanne K. McCormack, *Community College of Rhode Island*
David McDaniel, *Marquette University*
J. Kent McGaughy, *Houston Community College, Northwest*
Alan McPherson, *Howard University*
Sarah Hand Meacham, *Virginia Commonwealth University*
Brian Craig Miller, *Emporia State University*
Brett Mizelle, *California State University Long Beach*
Mark Moser, *The University of North Carolina at Greensboro*
Jennifer Murray, *Coastal Carolina University*
Peter C. Murray, *Methodist University*
Steven E. Nash, *East Tennessee State University*
Chris Newman, *Elgin Community College*
David Noon, *University of Alaska Southeast*
Richard H. Owens, *West Liberty University*
David J. Peavler, *Towson University*
Laura A. Perry, *University of Memphis*
Wesley Phelps, *University of St. Thomas*
Merline Pitre, *Texas Southern University*
Eunice G. Pollack, *University of North Texas*
Kimberly Porter, *University of North Dakota*
Cynthia Prescott, *University of North Dakota*
Gene Preuss, *University of Houston*
Sandra Pryor, *Old Dominion University*
Rhonda Ragsdale, *Lone Star College*
Michaela Reaves, *California Lutheran University*
Peggy Renner, *Glendale Community College*
Steven D. Reschly, *Truman State University*
Barney J. Rickman, *Valdosta State University*
Pamela Riney-Kehrberg, *Iowa State University*
Paul Ringel, *High Point University*
Timothy Roberts, *Western Illinois University*
Glenn Robins, *Georgia Southwestern State University*
Alicia E. Rodriquez, *California State University Bakersfield*
Mark Roehrs, *Lincoln Land Community College*
Patricia Roessner, *Marple Newtown High School*
John G. Roush, *St. Petersburg College*
James Russell, *St. Thomas Aquinas College*
Eric Schlereth, *The University of Texas at Dallas*
Ronald Schultz, *University of Wyoming*
Stanley K. Schultz, *University of Wisconsin–Madison*
Sharon Shackelford, *Erie Community College*
Donald R. Shaffer, *American Public University System*
David J. Silverman, *The George Washington University*
Andrea Smalley, *Northern Illinois University*
Molly Smith, *Friends School of Baltimore*
David L. Snead, *Liberty University*
David Snyder, *Delaware Valley College*
Jodie Steeley, *Merced College*
Bryan E. Stone, *Del Mar College*

Emily Straus, *SUNY Fredonia*
Jean Stuntz, *West Texas A&M University*
Nikki M. Taylor, *University of Cincinnati*
Heather Ann Thompson, *Temple University*
Timothy Thurber, *Virginia Commonwealth University*
T. J. Tomlin, *University of Northern Colorado*
Laura Trauth, *Community College of Baltimore County–Essex*
Russell M. Tremayne, *College of Southern Idaho*
Laura Tuennerman-Kaplan, *California University of Pennsylvania*
Vincent Vinikas, *The University of Arkansas at Little Rock*
David Voelker, *University of Wisconsin–Green Bay*
Ed Wehrle, *Eastern Illinois University*
Gregory Wilson, *University of Akron*
Maria Cristina Zaccarini, *Adelphi University*
Nancy Zens, *Central Oregon Community College*
Jean Hansen Zuckweiler, *University of Northern Colorado*

We also appreciate the help the following scholars and students gave us in providing the information we needed at critical points in the writing of this text: Leslie Brown, Andrew Buchanan, Gillian Carroll, Susan J. Carroll, Paul Clemens, Dorothy Sue Cobble, Jane Coleman-Harbison, Alison Cronk, Elisabeth Eittreim, Phyllis Hunter, Tera Hunter, William Link, James Livingston, Julia Livingston, Gilda Morales, Vicki L. Ruiz, Susan Schrepfer, Bonnie Smith, Melissa Stein, Margaret Sumner, Jessica Unger, and Anne Valk. Jacqueline Castledine and Julia Sandy-Bailey worked closely with us in finding documents and creating the Document Projects. Without them, this would not be a docutext.

We would particularly like to applaud the many hardworking and creative people at Bedford/St. Martin's who guided us through the labyrinthine process of writing a textbook from scratch. No one was more important to us than the indefatigable and unflappable Sara Wise, our developmental editor. We are also deeply grateful to Patricia Rossi, who first persuaded us to undertake this project. Joan Feinberg had the vision that guided us through every page of this book. We could not have had a better team than Denise Wydra, Mary Dougherty, William Lombardo, Jane Knetzger, Christina Horn, Jennifer Jovin, Katherine Bates, Amy Whitaker, Jenna Bookin Barry, Daniel McDonough, and Arrin Kaplan. They also enlisted Naomi Kornhauser, Charlotte Miller, Linda McLatchie, Heidi Hood, Rob Heinrich, Shannon Hunt, John Reisbord, and Michelle McSweeney to provide invaluable service. Finally, we would like to thank our friends and family who have been asking us these past years, "When will you be finished?" We are very pleased to be able to respond, "The time is now."

Nancy A. Hewitt and Steven F. Lawson

Adopters of **Exploring American Histories** and their students have access to abundant resources, including documents, presentation and testing materials, volumes in the acclaimed Bedford Series in History and Culture, and much more. For more information on the offerings described below, visit the book's catalog site at bedfordstmartins.com/hewittlawson/catalog, or contact your local Bedford/St. Martin's sales representative.

Get the Right Version for Your Class

To accommodate different course lengths and course budgets, *Exploring American Histories* is available in several different formats, including three-hole punched loose-leaf Budget books versions and e-books, which are available at a substantial discount.

- Combined edition (chapters 1–29)—available in paperback, loose-leaf, and e-book formats
- Volume 1: To 1877 (chapters 1–14)—available in paperback, loose-leaf, and e-book formats
- Volume 2: Since 1865 (chapters 14–29)—available in paperback, loose-leaf, and e-book formats

Assign the online, interactive Bedford x-Book. With all the content of the print book—plus integrated LearningCurve and the 29 extra Document Projects, some with audio or video—the *x-Book for Exploring American Histories* features a robust search engine, navigation tools, easy ways to take and share notes, and interactive exercises. And with fast ways to rearrange chapters and add new pages, sections, or links, it lets teachers build just the right book for their course.

Let students choose their e-book format. Students can purchase the downloadable *Bedford e-Book to Go for Exploring American Histories* from our Web site or find other PDF versions of the e-book at our publishing partners' sites: CourseSmart, Barnes & Noble NookStudy; Kno; CafeScribe; or Chegg.

Assign LearningCurve So That Your Students Come to Class Prepared

As described in the preface and on the inside front cover, students purchasing new books receive access to Learning Curve for *Exploring American Histories*, an online learning tool designed to help students rehearse content at their own pace in a nonthreatening, game-like environment. The feedback for wrong answers provides instructional coaching and sends students back to the book for review. Students answer as many questions as necessary to reach a target score, with repeated chances to revisit material they haven't mastered. Assigning LearningCurve is easy for instructors, and the reporting features help instructors track overall class trends and spot topics that are giving students trouble.

Send Students to Free Online Resources

The book's companion site at bedfordstmartins.com/hewittlawson gives students a way to read, write, and study by providing plentiful quizzes and activities, study aids, and history research and writing help.

FREE Online Study Guide. Available at the companion site, this popular resource provides students with quizzes and activities for each chapter, including multiple-choice self-tests that focus on important concepts; flash cards that test students' knowledge of key terms; timeline activities that emphasize causal relationships; and map quizzes intended to strengthen students' geography skills. Instructors can monitor students' progress through an online Quiz Gradebook or receive email updates.

FREE Research, Writing, and Anti-plagiarism Advice. Available at the companion site, Bedford's **History Research and Writing Help** includes **History Research and Reference Sources**, with links to history-related databases, indexes, and journals; **More Sources and How to Format a History Paper**, with clear advice on how to integrate primary and secondary sources into research papers and how to cite and format sources correctly; **Build a Bibliography**, a simple Web-based tool known as The Bedford Bibliographer that generates bibliographies in four commonly used documentation styles; and **Tips on Avoiding Plagiarism**, an online tutorial that reviews the consequences of plagiarism and features exercises to help students practice integrating sources and recognize acceptable summaries.

Take Advantage of Instructor Resources

Bedford/St. Martin's has developed a rich array of teaching resources for this book and for this course. They range from lecture and presentation materials and assessment tools to course management options. Most can be downloaded or ordered at bedfordstmartins.com/hewittlawson/catalog.

HistoryClass for *Exploring American Histories*. *History-Class*, a Bedford/St. Martin's Online Course Space, puts the online resources available with this textbook in one convenient and completely customizable course space. There you and your students can access the interactive x-book; video clips, maps, images, documents, and links; chapter review quizzes; and research and writing help. In *HistoryClass* you can get all our premium content and tools, which you can assign, rearrange, and mix with your own resources. *HistoryClass* also includes LearningCurve, Bedford/St. Martin's adaptive tool for quizzing to learn, and the additional Document Project for each chapter. For more information, visit yourhistoryclass.com.

Instructor's Resource Manual. The instructor's manual offers both experienced and first-time instructors tools for preparing lectures and running discussions. It includes chapter-review material, teaching strategies, and a guide to chapter-specific supplements available for the text, plus suggestions on how to get the most out of LearningCurve.

Computerized Test Bank. The test bank includes a mix of carefully crafted multiple-choice, short-answer, and essay questions for each chapter. It also contains the Interpret the Evidence and Put It in Context questions from the textbook and model answers for each. All questions appear in Microsoft Word format and in easy-to-use test bank software that allows instructors to add, edit, re-sequence, and print questions and answers. Instructors can also export questions into a variety of formats, including WebCT and Blackboard.

The Bedford Lecture Kit: PowerPoint Maps, Images, Lecture Outlines, and i>clicker Content. Look good and save time with *The Bedford Lecture Kit*. These presentation materials are downloadable individually from the Instructor Resources tab at bedfordstmartins.com/hewittlawson/catalog and are available on *The Bedford Lecture Kit* Instructor's Resource CD-ROM. They provide ready-made and fully customizable PowerPoint multimedia presentations that include lecture outlines with embedded maps, figures, and selected images from the textbook and extra background for instructors. Also available are maps and selected images in JPEG and PowerPoint formats; content for i>clicker, a classroom response system, in Microsoft Word and PowerPoint formats; the Instructor's Resource Manual in Microsoft Word format; and outline maps in

PDF format for quizzing or handing out. All files are suitable for copying onto transparency acetates.

Make History—Free Documents, Maps, Images, and Web Sites. *Make History* combines the best Web resources with hundreds of maps and images, to make it simple to find the source material you need. Browse the collection of thousands of resources by course or by topic, date, and type. Each item has been carefully chosen and helpfully annotated to make it easy to find exactly what you need. Available at bedfordstmartins.com/makehistory.

America in Motion: Video Clips for U.S. History. Set history in motion with *America in Motion,* an instructor DVD containing dozens of short digital movie files of events in twentieth-century American history. From the wreckage of the battleship *Maine*, to FDR's fireside chats, to Oliver North testifying before Congress, *America in Motion* engages students with dynamic scenes from key events and challenges them to think critically. All files are classroom-ready, edited for brevity, and easily integrated with PowerPoint or other presentation software for electronic lectures or assignments. An accompanying guide provides each clip's historical context, ideas for use, and suggested questions.

Videos and Multimedia. A wide assortment of videos and multimedia CD-ROMs on various topics in U.S. history is available to qualified adopters through your Bedford/St. Martin's sales representative.

Package and Save Your Students Money

For information on free packages and discounts up to 50%, visit bedfordstmartins.com/hewittlawson/catalog or contact your local Bedford/St. Martin's sales representative.

Online Document Projects for *Exploring American Histories*. A complete set of additional 29 Document Projects—one per chapter—is available to provide students with more opportunities to work with primary sources. Each set mirrors the pedagogy in the text with overviews, headnotes, and Interpret the Evidence and Put It in Context questions, and many sets include audio and video sources. Topics include loyalists in the American Revolution, abolitionist debates, women's liberation, and the Reagan Revolution. Automatically available online to all students who purchase the x-Book or *HistoryClass* and free when packaged with the text.

The Bedford Series in History and Culture. More than 150 titles in this highly praised series combine first-rate scholarship, historical narrative, and important primary documents for undergraduate courses. Each book is brief, inexpensive, and focused on a specific topic or period. For a complete list of titles, visit bedfordstmartins.com/history/ series. Package discounts are available.

Rand McNally Historical Atlas of American History. This collection of more than 84 full-color maps illustrates key events and eras, from early exploration, settlement, expansion, and immigration to U.S. involvement in wars abroad and on U.S. soil. Introductory pages for each section include a brief overview, timelines, graphs, and photographs to quickly establish a historical context. Available for $3.00 when packaged with the print text.

Maps in Context: A Workbook for American History. Written by historical cartography expert Gerald A. Danzer (University of Illinois at Chicago), this skill-building workbook helps students comprehend essential connections between geographic literacy and historical understanding. Organized to correspond to the typical U.S. survey course, *Maps in Context* presents a wealth of map-centered projects and convenient pop quizzes that give students hands-on experience working with maps. Available free when packaged with the print text.

The Bedford Glossary for U.S. History. This handy supplement for the survey course gives students historically contextualized definitions for hundreds of terms—from *abolitionism* to *zoot suit*—that they will encounter in lectures, reading, and exams. Available free when packaged with the print text.

U.S. History Matters: A Student Guide to U.S. History Online. This resource, written by Kelly Schrum, Alan Gevinson, and the late Roy Rosenzweig (all of George Mason University), provides an illustrated and annotated guide to 250 of the most useful Web sites for student research in U.S. history as well as advice on evaluating and using Internet sources. This essential guide is based on the acclaimed "History Matters" Web site developed by the American Social History Project and the Center for History and New Media. Available free when packaged with the print text.

Trade Books. Titles published by sister companies Hill and Wang; Farrar, Straus and Giroux; Henry Holt and Company; St. Martin's Press; Picador; and Palgrave Macmillan are available at a 50% discount when packaged with Bedford/St. Martin's textbooks. For more information, visit bedfordstmartins.com/tradeup.

A Pocket Guide to Writing in History. This portable and affordable reference tool by Mary Lynn Rampolla, now also available as a searchable e-book, provides reading, writing, and research advice useful to students in all history courses. Concise yet comprehensive advice on approaching typical history assignments, developing critical-reading skills, writing effective history papers, conducting research, using and documenting sources, and avoiding plagiarism—enhanced with practical tips and examples throughout—have made this slim reference a best seller. Package discounts are available.

A Student's Guide to History. This complete guide to success in any history course provides the practical help students need to be effective. In addition to introducing students to the nature of the discipline, author Jules Benjamin teaches a wide range of skills from preparing for exams to approaching common writing assignments, and he explains the research and documentation process with plentiful examples. Package discounts are available.

Going to the Source: The Bedford Reader in American History. Developed by Victoria Bissell Brown and Timothy J. Shannon, this reader's strong pedagogical framework helps students learn how to ask fruitful questions in order to evaluate documents effectively and develop critical-reading skills. The reader's wide variety of chapter topics that complement the survey course and its rich diversity of sources—from personal letters to political cartoons—provoke students' interest as it teaches them the skills they need to successfully interrogate historical sources. Package discounts are available.

America Firsthand. With its distinctive focus on ordinary people, this primary documents reader, by Anthony Marcus, John M. Giggie, and David Burner, offers a remarkable range of perspectives on American history from those who lived it. Popular Points of View sections expose students to different perspectives on a specific event or topic, and Visual Portfolios invite analysis of the visual record. Package discounts are available.

Explore Other Docutexts from Bedford/St. Martin's

Bedford/St. Martin's has been a leader in pioneering new ways to bring primary sources into the undergraduate classroom, beginning with the Bedford Series in History and

Culture, described above. The "docutext" format of *Exploring American Histories,* which combines a brief narrative with themed collections of written and visual sources, represents another innovation in making documents accessible for students. Docutexts authored by leading historians are now available from Bedford for a variety of history courses.

World History Survey. Find out about *Ways of the World: A Brief Global History with Sources,* by Robert W. Strayer, at bedfordstmartins.com/strayersources/catalog.

African American History. Find out about *Freedom on My Mind: A History of African Americans, with Documents,* by Deborah Gray White, Mia Bay, and Waldo E. Martin Jr., at bedfordstmartins.com/graywhite/catalog.

U.S. Women's History. Find out about *Through Women's Eyes: An American History with Documents,* by Ellen Carol DuBois and Lynn Dumenil, at bedfordstmartins.com/duboisdumenil/catalog.

Native American History. Find out about *First Peoples: A Documentary Survey of American Indian History,* by Colin G. Calloway, at bedfordstmartins.com/calloway/catalog.

Twentieth-Century European History. Find out about *Europe in the Contemporary World, 1900 to the Present: A Narrative History with Documents,* by Bonnie G. Smith, at bedfordstmartins.com/smitheurope/catalog.

Brief Contents

Contents

14
Emancipations and Reconstructions
1863–1877   424

15
Frontier Encounters
1865–1896   458

26
The Liberal Consensus and Its Challengers
1960–1973   822

27
The Conservative Ascendancy
1968–1992   858

Maps, Figures, and Tables

Maps

Figures and Tables

How to Use This Book

Start by reading the narrative and using the chapter tools to help you focus on what's important.

LEARNINGCurve
Check what you know.
bedfordstmartins.com/hewittlawson/LC

Scan the **chapter outline** for a preview of the chapter's big topics and themes.

The Granger Collection, New York

The Granger Collection, New York

Sawmill in Terraville, South Dakota, 1888.

Shoe-factory worker in Lynn, Massachusetts, 1895.

As you read, pay attention to the **boldfaced key terms**, which highlight important concepts you'll likely see on an exam. All terms are defined in the glossary of Key Terms at the end of the book.

oslavery document. Some Garrisonians a
work of the **underground railroad**, a se
ivists who assisted fugitives fleeing ensla
In 1835 Sarah and Angelina Grimké j
d soon began lecturing for the organiza
rominent South Carolina planter, they

new leisure pursuits. Many joined colleagues at restaurants, the theater, or sporting events. They also attended plays and lectures with their wives, visited museums, and took their children to the circus.

REVIEW & RELATE

At the end of each major section, answer the **Review & Relate** questions to check your understanding of key concepts.

Why did American cities become larger and more diverse in the first half of the nineteenth century?

What values and beliefs did the emerging American middle class embrace?

LEARNINGCurve bedfordstmartins.com/hewittlawson/LC

Then log on to **LearningCurve** to review the section you've just read. LearningCurve lets you move at your own pace and earn points as you go.

Use the Chapter Review to draw connections across all the sections of the narrative and identify significant historical developments.

Return to **LearningCurve** to review chapter material.

Test your knowledge of important concepts from the **Key Terms** list. See if you can not only define each term but also describe its significance.

LEARNINGCurve
Check what you know.
bedfordstmartins.com/hewittlawson/LC

Chapter Review

Online Study Guide ▶ bedfordstmartins.com/hewittlawson

KEY TERMS

separate spheres (p. 331)
deskilling (p. 333)
nativists (p. 337)
Second Great Awakening (p. 339)
temperance (p. 340)
transcendentalism (p. 341)
utopian societies (p. 344)
Appeal . . . to the Colored Citizens (p. 346)
_____ ciety (AASS) (p. 346)
_____ 346)
_____ (p. 348)

Answer the **Review & Relate** questions, which repeat the chapter's end-of-section comprehension prompts.

REVIEW & RELATE

1. Why did American cities become larger and more diverse in the first half of the nineteenth century?

2. What values and beliefs did the emerging American middle class embrace?

3. How and why did American manufacturing change over the course of the first half of the nineteenth century?

4. How did Northerners respond to the hard times that followed the panic of 1837? How did responses to the crisis vary by class, ethnicity, and religion?

5. What impact did the Second Great Awakening have in the North?

6. What new religious organizations and viewpoints emerged in the first half of the nineteenth century, *outside* of Protestant evangelical denominations?

7. How did the temperance movement reflect the range of tactics and participants involved in reform during the 1830s and 1840s?

8. What connections can you identify between utopian communities and mainstream reform movements in the first half of the nineteenth century?

9. How did the American Anti-Slavery Society differ from earlier abolitionist organizations?

10. How did conflicts over gender and race shape the development of the abolitionist movement in the 1830s and 1840s?

TIMELINE OF EVENTS

1820–1850	Size, number, and diversity of northern cities grow; immigration surges
1823	Textile factory town built in Lowell, Massachusetts
1826	American Temperance Society founded
1827	First workingmen's political party founded
1829	David Walker publishes *Appeal . . . to the Colored Citizens*
1830	Joseph Smith publishes *The Book of Mormon*
September 1830	Charles Grandison Finney brings Second Great Awakening to Rochester, New York
1833	William Lloyd Garrison founds American Anti-Slavery Society (AASS)
1837–1842	Panic of 1837
1839	American Anti-Slavery Society splits over the role of women in the society
1840	Liberty Party formed
	World Anti-Slavery Convention, L_
1842	Amy Post helps found the Wester_ Anti-Slavery Society
1843	William Miller predicts Second Coming of Christ
1844	Congress funds construction of the first telegraph line
May 1844	Anti-immigrant violence rocks Philadelphia
1845	Frederick Douglass publishes *Narrative of the Life of Frederick Douglass*
	Margaret Fuller publishes *Woman in the Nineteenth Century*
1845–1846	Irish potato famine
1846	Henry David Thoreau publishes *Civil Disobedience*

Review the **Timeline of Events**, which shows the relationship among chapter events.

Visit the **free Online Study Guide**, which provides more quizzes and activities to help you master the chapter content.

Apply these principles to your analysis of the chapter's primary sources.

Democracy cannot be based upon coercion, democracy must be based on convergence. Converge and align with us at #NatGat #occupy #OANatGat.

What will they be able to say about the author? How will they interpret the meaning of these sentences? Will they understand the abbreviations that have become a part of our everyday language?

A tweet—like a blog, a speech on YouTube, or a video of a protest—is a primary source, an original document or artifact created at or near the time of an event by people participating in or observing it. Different types of primary sources exist from different periods of history. In the seventeenth century and earlier, drawings, paintings, stone carvings, and relics were as plentiful as written sources are today. Printed texts and handwritten letters became more available from the eighteenth century on, while photographs, newspapers, typewritten letters, and recordings are widely available from the mid-nineteenth century through the twentieth and twenty-first centuries.

Many primary sources are produced by official institutions, while others are created by ordinary people who wrote and kept diaries and letters, took pictures, participated in oral interviews, or sent e-mails. Some documents such as newspapers provide information from official sources alongside letters, interviews, articles, and opinions offered by editors and political cartoonists. As with future historians who try to decode Twitter, historians have always had to make sense of documents filled with abbreviations and peculiarities of language and to decipher handwriting styles as puzzling as digital shorthand.

Historians use a wealth of primary sources to build an interpretation of the past and to set that interpretation alongside the work of other scholars. History refers to both the uncovering of facts about the past and interpretations of it. Besides presenting facts, then, this textbook provides interpretations of American history constructed by the book's authors that are based on their own primary research as well as the work of other historians. But it also offers a large array of primary sources, described on the next several pages, from which you can create your own interpretations and compare them with those offered by the authors.

To guide your analysis, begin by asking several basic questions that can be succinctly thought of as the five Ws: Who? What? Where? When? Why?

- **Who** is the author of the document and who is the intended audience?
- **What** kind of source is it—written, visual, official, unofficial—and what are the main ideas or opinions presented?
- **Where** was it created and how might that shape its meaning?
- **When** was it produced and how close to the event being recorded?
- **Why** was it created and how does that influence your interpretation of it?

Because history is interpretive, the kind of questions you ask will help shape the answers you come up with. The more questions you explore, the richer the history you produce will be.

Keep in mind that this book's narrative text and documents work together, each reinforcing the other. While the narrative helps place the documents in a larger context, the documents provide for more active engagement with an event or issue. Rather than merely receiving a collection of information, you will be able to participate in shaping an account of the past. If you consider all the primary sources in a chapter together, including those in the Document Project, you can begin to understand how historians assess and piece together diverse sources of evidence to forge a larger narrative about American history. The next pages introduce you to the types of documents you will be working with in this book.

Get to work exploring the documents.

Individual documents are easy to find and well integrated into every chapter.

> Red **Explore** boxes tell you where to find the source and where to return to the text to continue the story.

the issue opposing the measure. John C. Calhoun, a proslavery senator from South Carolina, refused to support any compromise that allowed Congress to decide the fate of slavery in the western territories. Meanwhile William H. Seward, an antislavery Whig senator from New York, proclaimed that in all good conscience he could not support a compromise that forced Northerners to help hunt down fugitives from slavery. Daniel Webster, a Massachusetts Whig and an elder statesman, appealed to his fellow senators to support the compromise in order to preserve the Union, but Congress adjourned with the fate of California undecided.

Explore

See Document 12.2 for Calhoun's final attempt to reject a compromise.

Before the Senate reconvened in the fall of 1850, however, the political landscape changed in unexpected ways. Henry Clay retired in the spring of 1850, leaving the Capitol with his last great legislative effort unfinished. On March 31, Calhoun died; his absence from the Senate made compromise more likely. In July, President Taylor died unexpectedly, and his vice president, Millard Fillmore of Buffalo, New York, was elevated to the presidency. Fillmore then appointed Webster as secretary of state, removing him from the Senate as well.

In September 1850, with President Fillmore's support, a younger cohort of senators and representatives steered the **Compromise of 1850** through Congress, one clause at a time, thereby allowing legislators to support only those parts of the compromise they found palatable. In the end, all the provisions passed, and Fillmore quickly signed the bills into law. California entered the Union as a free state, and John C. Frémont entered Congress as one of that state's first two senators. The Compromise of 1850, like the Missouri Compromise thirty years earlier, fended off a sectional crisis, but it also signaled future problems. Would popular sovereignty prevail when later territories sought admission to the Union, and would Northerners abide by a fugitive slave law that called on them to aid directly in the capture of runaway slaves?

The Fugitive Slave Act Inspires Northern Protest

The fugitive slave laws of 1793 and 1824 mandated that all states aid in apprehending and returning runaway slaves to their owners. The **Fugitive Slave Act of 1850** was different in two important respects. First, it eliminated jury trials for alleged fugitives. Second, the law required individual citizens, not just state officials, to help return runaways or

---

DOCUMENT 12.2

John C. Calhoun | On the Compromise of 1850, 1850

California's application for statehood in 1849 prompted another crisis over slavery. Southerners feared that admitting California as a free state would tip the balance in Congress against them. Senator Henry Clay tried to broker a compromise that would admit California as a free state but toughen the fugitive slave law. Amid vigorous congressional debate, South Carolina senator John C. Calhoun insisted that slavery be preserved. A colleague read Calhoun's address for the aging and ill senator. Calhoun's death a few weeks later helped pave the way for final passage of the Compromise of 1850.

Explore

How can the Union be saved? To this I answer, there is but one way by which it can be, and that is, by adopting such measures as will satisfy the States belonging to the Southern section that they can remain in the Union consistently with their honor and their safety. . . .

. . . The South asks for justice, simple justice, and less she ought not to take. She has no compromise to offer but the Constitution, and no concession or surrender to make. She has already surrendered so much that she has little left to surrender. Such a settlement would go to the root of the evil, and remove all cause of discontent, by satisfying the South that she could remain honorably and safely in the Union, and thereby restore the harmony and fraternal feelings between the sections which existed anterior to the Missouri agitation. . . .

But can this be done? Yes, easily; not by the weaker party, for it can of itself do nothing—not even protect itself—but by the stronger. The North has only to will it to accomplish it—to do justice by conceding to the South an equal right in the acquired territory, and to do her duty by causing the stipulations relative to fugitive slaves to be faithfully fulfilled—to cease the agitation of the slave question, and to provide for the insertion of a provision in the Constitution, by an amendment, which will restore to the South in substance the power she possessed of protecting herself, before the equilibrium between the sections was destroyed by the action of this Government. There will be no difficulty in devising such a provision—one that will protect the South, and which at the same time will improve and strengthen the Government, instead of impairing and weakening it.

Source: *The Congressional Globe*, 31st Cong., 2nd Sess. (1850), 453, 455.

Interpret the Evidence

- Calhoun objects to the Compromise of 1850 because it does not sufficiently protect southern rights. Which rights does he think need protection, and why does he think those rights are in jeopardy?
- Calhoun wants to regain the "harmony and fraternal feelings" between the sections that existed before "the Missouri agitation." Why does he pinpoint the Missouri Compromise as the moment when sectional divisions took hold?

Put It in Context

What developments in the 1840s led Calhoun and other southern leaders to fear that the South was becoming weaker, at least politically, compared to the North? Would northern senators have agreed?

---

else risk being fined or imprisoned. The act angered many Northerners who believed that the federal government had gone too far in protecting the rights of slaveholders and thereby aroused sympathy for the abolitionist cause.

Before 1850, the most well-known individuals aiding fugitives were free blacks such as David Ruggles in New

York City; Jermaine Loguen in Syracuse, New York; and, after his own successful escape, Frederick Douglass in Rochester, New York. Their main allies in this work were white Quakers such as Amy and Isaac Post in Rochester; Thomas Garrett in Chester County, Pennsylvania; and Levi and Catherine Coffin in Newport, Indiana. The work was

> Two **Interpret the Evidence** questions help you analyze the source.

> A **Put It in Context** question helps you connect the primary source to the larger historical narrative.

Annotated documents help you examine sources closely by breaking them down into smaller components.

Annotations direct you to points of interest—either specific text passages or visual details—to help you analyze the document and to model what to look for when you approach similar types of documents on your own.

DOCUMENT 14.4

Sharecropping Agreement, 1870

Because Congress did not generally provide freedpeople with land, African Americans lacked the capital to start their own farms. At the same time, plantation owners needed labor to plant and harvest their crops for market. Out of mutual necessity, white plantation owners entered into sharecropping contracts with blacks to work their farms in exchange for a portion of the crop, such as the following contract between Willis P. Bocock and several of his former slaves. Bocock owned Waldwick Plantation in Marengo County, Alabama.

Explore

What are the farmers' responsibilities?

Why would Bocock want to clarify that his laborers would work equally hard throughout the year?

How might putting a lien on crops for debts owed create difficulties for the black farmer?

Contract made the 3rd day of January in the year 1870 between us the free people who have signed this paper of one part, and our employer, Willis P. Bocock, of the other part. We agree to take charge of and cultivate for the year 1870, a portion of land, say [left blank] acres or thereabouts, to be laid off to us by our employer on his plantation, and to tend the same well in the usual crops, in such proportions as we and he may agree upon. We are to furnish the necessary labor, say an average hand to every 15 acres in the crops, making in all average hands; and are to have all proper work done, ditching, fencing, repairing, etc., as well as cultivating and saving the crops of all kinds, so as to put and keep the land we occupy and tend in good order for cropping, and to make a good crop ourselves; and to do our fair share of job work about the place. . . . We are to be responsible for the good conduct of ourselves, our hands, and families, and agree that all shall be respectful to employer, owners, and manager, honest, industrious, and careful about every thing, and shall not interrupt any thing about the place, working as industriously the last part of the year as the first; and then our employer agrees that he and his manager shall treat us kindly, and help us to study our interest and do our duty. If any hand or family proves to be of bad character, or dishonest, or lazy, or disobedient, or any way unsuitable our employer or manager has the right, and we have the right, to have such turned off. . . .

For the labor and services of ourselves and hands rendered as above stated, we are to have one third part of all the crops, or their net-proceeds, made and secured, or prepared for market by our force. . . .

We are to be furnished by our employer through his manager with provisions if we call for them: not over one peck of meal or corn, and $3\frac{1}{2}$ pounds of meat or its equivalent per week, for every 15 acres of land or average hand, to be charged to us at fair market prices.

And whatever may be due by us, or our hands to our employer for provisions or any thing else, during the year, is to be a lien on our share of the crops, and is to be retained by him out of the same before we receive our part.

Source: Waldwick Plantation Records, 1834–1971, LPR174, box 1, folder 9, Alabama Department of Archives and History.

Put It in Context

Why would free blacks and poor whites be willing to enter into such a contract?

DOCUMENT 11.4

Drunkard's Home, 1850

Temperance societies undertook a variety of activities to publiciz~~e~~
and parades were popular venues, as were newspapers and boo~~ks~~
Temperance Offering, an 1850 publication of the Sons of Temper~~ance~~
1842, the Sons of Temperance was one of the oldest temperance~~~~
mutual aid society that offered members life insurance, funeral b~~enefits~~

Explore

How does the father's drinking seem to affect the family's economic situation?

In this illustration, what is the source of the father's violence?

How~~~~
me~~~~

The National Temperance Offering, and Sons and Daughters of Temperance Gift (PS1265.N3 1850), University of Virginia Library

All annotated documents conclude with **Put It in Context** questions that ask you to figure out how the document fits in—or doesn't fit in—with the narrative you're reading.

Put It in Context

What moral arguments did members of the temperance movement use to support their cause?

"Two Views" comparison documents present contrasting or complementary perspectives on a single topic so that you can form your own interpretation.

Life in the Mills: Two Views

In the 1820s, the textile mills of Lowell, Massachusetts, provided the daughters of local farmers a way to contribute to their family incomes and experience some adventure. Soon, however, a slowing economy led to reduced wages, longer hours, and demands for increased productivity. The Lowell workers organized to protest these changes and went on strike several times during the late 1820s and the 1830s. The first selection below is from an 1844 edition of *The Lowell Offering*, a magazine to which mill workers contributed stories and poems. Factory owners controlled the content of the magazine to ensure an idealized vision of life in the mills. Still, the letter from "Susan" below does highlight the physical toll of industrial labor. Susan was a pseudonym for Harriet Farley, a weaver and the editor of *The Lowell Offering*. The selection at right is by Harriet Robinson, who entered the mills at age ten in 1834. She published a memoir in 1898 in which she recalls the growing dissatisfaction of the women workers and her critical role in a strike in 1836.

Explore

11.1 Letter from a Lowell Factory Worker, 1844

It makes my feet ache and swell to stand so much, but I suppose I shall get accustomed to that too. The girls generally wear old shoes about their work, and you know nothing is easier; but they almost all say that when they have worked here a year or two they have to procure shoes a size or two larger than before they came. The right hand, which is the one used in stopping and starting the loom, becomes larger than the left; but in other respects the factory is not detrimental to a young girl's appearance. Here they look delicate, but not sickly; they laugh at those who are much exposed, and get pretty brown; but I, for one, had rather be brown than pure white. I never saw so many pretty looking girls as there are

here. Though the number of men is small in proportion there are many marriages here, and a great deal of courting. I will tell you of this last sometime. . . .

You ask if the work is not disagreeable. Not when one is accustomed to it. It tried my patience sadly at first, and does now when it does not run well; but, in general, I like it very much. It is easy to do, and does not require very violent exertion, as much of our farm work does.

You also ask how I get along with the girls here. Very well indeed.

and workingmen started joining forces throughout the North to advocate for principles of liberty and equality. Self-educated artisans like Thomas Skidmore of New York City argued for the redistribution of property and the abolition of inheritance to equalize wealth in the nation. However, most workingmen's parties focused on more practical proposals: government distribution of free land in the West, the abolition of compulsory militia service and imprisonment for debt, public funding for education, and the regulation of banks and corporations. Although the

Explore

11.2 Harriet Robinson | Reflections on the 1836 Lowell Mills Strike, 1898

My own recollection of this first strike (or "turn out" as it was called) is very vivid. I worked in a lower room, where I had heard the proposed strike fully, if not vehemently, discussed; I had been an ardent listener to what was said against this attempt at "oppression" on the part of the corporation, and naturally I took sides with the strikers. When the day came on which the girls were to turn out, those in the upper rooms started first, and so many of them left that our mill was at once shut down. Then, when the girls in my room stood irresolute, uncertain what to do, asking each other, "Would you?" or "Shall we turn out?" and not one of them having the courage to lead off, *I*, who began to think they would not go out, after all their talk, became impatient, and started on ahead, saying, with childish bravado, "I don't care what you do, I am going to turn out, whether any one else does or not"; and I marched out, and was followed by the others.

As I looked back at the long line that followed me, I was more proud than I have ever been since at any success I may have achieved, and more proud than I shall ever be again until my own beloved State gives to its women citizens the right of suffrage.

The agent of the corporation where I then worked took some small revenges on the supposed ringleaders; on the principle of sending the weaker to the wall, my mother [a landlady] was turned away from her boarding-house, that functionary saying, "Mrs. Hanson, you could not prevent the older girls from turning out, but your daughter is a child, and *her* you could control."

It is hardly necessary to say that so far as results were concerned this strike did no good. The dissatisfaction of the operatives subsided, or burned itself out, and though the authorities did not accede to their demands, the majority returned to their work, and the corporation went on cutting down the wages.

Source: Harriet H. Robinson, *Loom and Spindle; or, Life among the Early Mill Girls* (New York: Thomas Y. Crowell, 1898), 84–86.

Interpret the Evidence questions help you analyze the sources.

Interpret the Evidence
- How did life on the farm differ from life in the factory? How does "Susan" describe her own adjustment to industrial work?
- What connections does Robinson make between the strike and the larger social and political context of 1830s Massachusetts? How does she see herself and her actions?

Put It in Context
Were "Susan" and Robinson typical factory workers in this period? Why or why not?

Trades Union was established later that year, with delegates representing more than twenty-five thousand workers across the North. These organizations aided skilled workers but refused admission to women and unskilled men.

panic of 1837, the common plight of workers became clearer. But the economic crisis made unified action nearly impossible as individuals sought to hold on to what little they had by any means available.

A Document Project concludes each chapter.

Each project provides multiple perspectives on a particular issue or development along with an **introduction** and **questions** to guide you through the process of interpretation. The chapter itself offers the background material for your interpretation.

and grasses that would have kept the earth from eroding and turning into dust. Instead, dust storms brought life to a grinding halt, blocking out the midday sun. See Document Project 22: The Depression in Rural America, page 712.

As the storms continued through the 1930s, most residents—approximately 75 percent—remained on

Red **cross-references** at the relevant point in the chapter direct you to the chapter's Document Project.

DOCUMENT 22.6
The Life of a White Sharecropper, 1938

In 1936 workers in the WPA's Federal Writers Project began the Folklore Project. Interviewers spoke with thousands of ordinary individuals to document their home lives, education, occupations, political and religious views, and the impact of the Great Depression on their families. Folklore Project worker Claude Dunnagan collected the following story from a white sharecropping family in Longtown, North Carolina.

I guess we been hard luck renters all our lives—me and Morrison both. They was ten young'uns in my family, and I was next to the youngest. We had it awful hard. . . . We went to Yadkin County and rented an old rundown farm for a share of what we could raise. The crops wasn't any good that year, the landlord came and got what we had raised and had the auctioneers come and sell our tools and furniture. They was a bunch of people at the sale that day from all around. I was standin' there watchin' the man sell the things when I saw a good lookin' man in overalls lookin' toward me. He watched me all durin' the sale and I knew what he was thinkin'. That was the first time I ever saw Allison. I reckon he fell in love with me right off, for we was married a few days later. Allison didn't have no true father. His mother wasn't married, and he was raised up by his kin folks. Then we moved to a little farm near Longtown, about ten miles away. The owner said we could have three-fourths of what we raised. The first two years the crops turned out pretty good so we could pay off the landlord and buy a little furniture . . . a bed and table and some chairs. Then the first baby came on. That was Hildreth. He's out in the field workin' now, suckerin' [removing sprouts] tobacco. . . . By that time, we was able to get a cow, and that came in good, for the baby was awful thin and weak. . . .

Hildreth was only six, but he could help a lot, pullin' and tyin' the tobacco, and helpin' hang it in the barn. We got out more tobacco that year than any other, but when we took it to market in Winston, they wasn't payin' but about twelve cents a pound for the best grade, so when we give the landlord his share and paid the fertilizer bill, we didn't have enough left to pay the doctor and store bill. We didn't know what we was goin' to do durin' the winter. Allison had raised a few vegetables and apples, so we canned what we could and traded the rest for some cotton cloth up at the store so the children would have something to wear that winter. Allison got a job helpin' build a barn for a neighbor, but it didn't last but two days. The neighbor gave him two second hand pairs of overalls for the work. . . .

Things are a lot better for the renter today than in the past. It used to be we couldn't get enough to eat and wear. Now we got a cow, a hog, and some chickens. Allison bought a second-hand car and every Sunday afternoon we ride somewhere. It's the only time we ever get away from home.

The landlord gives us five-sixths of what we raise, so we get along pretty good when the crops are fair. Of course we have to furnish the fertilizer and livestock. This year we had seven barns of tobacco and four acres of corn. Wheat turned out pretty good, too. We raised forty-three bushels, and I hear the price is going to be fair at the roller mill. I canned about all our extra fruits and vegetables. I reckon we still got about a hundred cans in the pantry.

Source: Library of Congress, Manuscript Division, WPA Federal Writers Project Collection.

The Depression in Rural America

During the 1930s, rural Americans' lives were devastated by the twin disasters of the Great Depression and, in the Great Plains, the most sustained drought in American history. But both problems only deepened the already difficult lives of many farmers. Agriculture in the South had long been dominated by sharecropping, a system that hampered crop diversification and left many African American tenant farmers vulnerable to exploitation by white landowners. In the Midwest, farmers had spent decades overgrazing pastures and exhausting the soil through overproduction. Prices dropped dramatically throughout the 1920s, and farmers were the only group whose incomes fell during that decade.

When the depression hit, many farmers did not have the resources to stay on their land, and farm foreclosures tripled in the early 1930s. Sharecroppers, tenant farmers, and former farm owners left their homes to find better opportunities, and a million people left the Great Plains alone. Most ended up as migrant agricultural laborers in farms and orchards on the West Coast. Feeling overrun by refugees, California passed a law in 1937 making it a misdemeanor to bring into California any indigent person who was not a state resident. This law remained in effect until 1941.

Under the New Deal, the federal government acted in a number of ways to relieve the plight of farmers around the country. The Agricultural Adjustment Act attempted to raise crop prices and stabilize agricultural incomes by encouraging farmers to cut production. The Farm Credit Act helped some farmers refinance mortgages at a lower rate, the Rural Electrification Administration brought electricity to farm areas previously without it, and the Soil Conservation Service advised farmers on how to properly cultivate their hillsides. The report of the Great Plains Committee (Document 22.10), another Roosevelt creation, details additional recommendations for helping the agricultural economy in the Midwest.

The following documents on the lives of farmers, sharecroppers, migrants, and labor organizers during the 1930s shed light on many aspects of the Great Depression. Consider what they reveal about the challenges faced by rural Americans and how different individuals and groups responded to those problems.

DOCUMENT 22.5
Ann Marie Low | Dust Bowl Diary, 1934

When massive dust storms swept through the Midwest beginning in the early 1930s, they blew away the topsoil of a once productive farm region and created hazardous living conditions. Residents needed to clean and wash repetitively to perform even simple daily tasks. Ann Marie Low, a young woman living with her family in southeastern North Dakota, describes in her diary the monotony and difficulty of life in the Dust Bowl.

May 21, 1934, Monday . . .
Saturday Dad, Bud, and I planted an acre of potatoes. There was so much dirt in the air I couldn't see Bud only a few feet in front of me. Even the air in the house was just a haze. In the evening the wind died down, and Cap came to take me to the movie. We joked about how hard it is to get cleaned up enough to go anywhere.

The newspapers report that on May 10 there was such a strong wind the experts in Chicago estimated 12,000,000 tons of Plains soil was dumped on that city. By the next day the sun was obscured in Washington, D.C., and ships 300 miles out at sea reported dust settling on their decks.

Sunday the dust wasn't so bad. Dad and I drove cattle to the Big Pasture. Then I churned butter and baked a ham, bread, and cookies for the men, as no telling when Mama will be back.

May 30, 1934, Wednesday
Ethel got along fine, so Mama left her at the hospital and came to Jamestown by train Friday. Dad took us both home.

The mess was incredible! Dirt had blown into the house all week and lay inches deep on everything. Every towel and curtain was just black. There wasn't a clean dish or cooking utensil. There was no food. Oh, there were eggs and milk and one loaf left of the bread I baked the weekend before. I looked in the cooler box down the well (our refrigerator) and found a little ham and butter. It was late, so Mama and I cooked some ham and eggs for the men's supper because that was all we could fix in a hurry. It turned out they had been living on ham and eggs for two days.

Mama was very tired. After she had fixed starter for bread, I insisted she go to bed and I'd do all the dishes. It took until 10 o'clock to wash all the dirty dishes. That's not wiping them—just washing them. The cupboards had to be washed out to have a clean place to put them.

Saturday was a busy day. Before starting breakfast I had to sweep and wash all the dirt off the kitchen and dining room floors, wash the stove, pancake griddle, and dining room table and chairs. There was cooking, baking, and churning to be done for those hungry men. Dad is 6 feet 4 inches tall, with a big frame. Bud is 6 feet 3 inches and almost as big-boned as Dad. We say feeding them is like filling a silo.

Mama couldn't make bread until I carried water to wash the bread mixer. I couldn't churn until the churn was washed and scalded. We just couldn't do anything until something was washed first. Every room had to have dirt almost shoveled out of it before we could wash floors and furniture.

We had no time to wash clothes, but it was necessary. I had to wash out the boiler, wash tubs, and the washing machine before we could use them. Then every towel, curtain, piece of bedding, and garment had to be taken outdoors to wash as much dust as possible shaken out before washing. The cistern is dry, so I had to carry all the water we needed from the well.

Source: Ann Marie Low, *Dust Bowl Diary* (Lincoln: University of Nebraska Press, 1984), 96–97.

DOCUMENT 22.7
Share[cropp]ing Family in Washington County, Arkansas, 1935

The Resettlement Administration (later the Farm Security Administration) documented the plight of migrant farmworkers and sharecroppers in numerous photographs. The following photo, taken by the noted photojournalist Arthur Rothstein, depicts a sharecropper's wife and daughters in Washington County, Arkansas, in 1935.

DOCUMENT 22.9
Frank Stokes | Let the Mexicans Organize, 1936

While union organizers made some gains in the industrial sector, they made little headway in the agricultural fields of California. Frank Stokes was a citrus grower who broke with his fellow farmers to support migrant labor organizing. In the following selection, Stokes argues in favor of unionization among migrant Mexican farmworkers.

The Mexican is to agricultural California what the Negro is to the medieval South. His treatment by the vegetable growers of the Imperial Valley is well known. What has happened to him in the San Joaquin has likewise been told. But for a time at least it appeared that the "citrus belt" was different. Then came the strike of the Mexican fruit pickers in Orange County. In its wake came the vigilantes, the night riders, the strike-breakers, the reporters whose job it was to "slant" all the stories in favor of the packers and grove owners. There followed the State Motor Patrol, which for the first time in the history of strike disorders in California set up a portable radio broadcasting station "in a secret place" in the strike area "to direct law-and-order activities." And special deputy badges blossomed as thick as Roosevelt buttons in the recent campaign.

Sheriff Jackson declared bravely: "It was the strikers themselves who drew first blood so from now on we will meet them on that basis." "This is no fight," said he, "between orchardists and pickers. It is a fight between the entire population of Orange County and a bunch of Communists." However, dozens and dozens of non-Communist Mexican fruit pickers were jailed; 116 were arrested en masse while traveling in automobiles along the highway. They were charged with riot and placed under bail of $500 each. . . . After fifteen days in jail the hearing was finally held—and the state's witnesses were able to identify only one person as having taken part in the trouble. . . . Judge Ames of the Superior Court ordered the release of all but one identified prisoner and severely criticized the authorities for holding the Mexicans in jail for so long a time when they must have known it would not be possible to identify even a small portion of the prisoners.

For weeks during the strike newspaper stories described the brave stand taken by "law-abiding citizens." These stories were adorned with such headlines as "Vigilantes Battle Citrus Strikers in War on Reds." During all this time, so far as I know, only one paper—the Los Angeles *Evening News*—defended the fruit pickers. . . .

These Mexicans were asking for a well-deserved wage increase and free transportation to and from the widely scattered groves; they also asked that tools be furnished by the employers. Finally they asked recognition of their newly formed union. Recognition of the Mexican laboring man's union, his cooperative organization formed in order that he might obtain a little more for his commodity, which is labor—here was the crucial point. The growers and packers agreed to furnish tools; they agreed to furnish transportation to and from the groves. They even agreed to a slight wage increase, which still left the workers underpaid. But recognition of the Mexican workers' union? Never! . . .

Not only in the fields are the Mexican people exploited. Not only as earners but as buyers they are looked upon as legitimate prey—for old washing machines that will not clean clothes, for old automobiles that wheeze and let down, for woolen blankets made of cotton, for last season's shop-worn wearing apparel. Gathered in villages composed of rough board shanties or drifting with the seasons from vegetable fields of the Imperial Valley to the grape vineyards of the San Joaquin, wherever they go it is the same old, pathetic story. Cheap labor!

Source: Frank Stokes, "Let the Mexicans Organize," *The Nation*, December 19, 1936, 731–32.

DOCUMENT 22.10
Report of the Great Plains Committee, 1937

In 1936 President Roosevelt established the Great Plains Committee to investigate the causes of the Dust Bowl and possible solutions for the region. The committee's report, submitted the following year, outlined how federal, state, and local government agencies could work together to restore the Great Plains to economic health. One of the witnesses the committee called to testify was Otis Nation, an organizer for the Oklahoma Tenant Farmers' Union, whose testimony follows.

Much has been written of our droughts here in Oklahoma, and how they have driven the farmers from the land. But little has been said of the other tentacles that choke off the livelihood of the small owner and the tenant. We do not wish to minimize the seriousness of these droughts and their effects on the farming population. But droughts alone would not have permanently displaced these farmers. The great majority of migrants had already become share-tenants and sharecroppers. The droughts hastened a process that had already begun. We submit the following as the cases for migratory agricultural workers:

1. *High interest rates.* Often a farmer borrows money for periods of 10 months and is charged an interest rate of 10 percent. These rates are charged when crops are good and when they fail. Through such practices the farmer loses his ownership; he becomes a tenant, then a sharecropper, then a migrant.
2. *The tenant and sharecropping system.* When share tenants are charged $33\frac{1}{3}$ percent of all corn or feed crops and 25 percent or more on cotton, plus 10 percent on all money borrowed at the bank, when sharecroppers are charged 50 to 75 percent of all he produces to the landlords, plus 10 percent for the bank's share on money invested; when these robbing practices are carried on in a community or a State, is it surprising that 33,241 farm families have left Oklahoma in the past 5 years?
3. *Land exhaustion, droughts, soil erosion, and the one-crop system of farming.* Lacking capital and equipment, small farmers have been unable to terrace their land or conduct other soil-conservation practices. The tenant and sharecropping system is chiefly responsible for the one-crop system. The landlord dictates what crops are to be planted—invariably cotton—and the tenant either plants it or gets off.
4. *Unstable markets.* Approximately a month and a half before the wheat harvest this year the price for this product was 93 cents here in Oklahoma City. But at harvest time the farmer sold his wheat for 46 cents to 60 cents per bushel, depending on the grade. . . . Kaffir [a grain sorghum] was selling for $1.30 one month ago, and yesterday we sold some for 85 cents per hundred. . . .

It is obvious to all of us that farm prices are set by speculators. The farmer's losses at the market have contributed in no small part to the farmer losing his place on the land. Higher prices for farm products are quoted when the farmer has nothing to sell.

5. *Tractor farming.* In Creek County, Okla., we have the record of one land-owner purchasing 3 tractors and forcing 31 of his 34 tenants and croppers from the land. Most of these families left the State when neither jobs nor relief could be secured. This is over 10 families per machine, 10 families who must quit their profession and seek employment in an unfriendly, industrialized farming section of Arizona or California. Many of these families were even unable to become "Joads" [the fictional family in *The Grapes of Wrath*] in these other States, and had to seek relief from an unfriendly national administration and a more unfriendly State administration. . . .

At this hearing we will have all kinds of statistical material presented and arguments based on this material. But I am one of those who is more interested in the people, my people, than in mere figures. I do not agree with those who say "the no-good must always be weeded out." I say that all of these people, casually referred to in statistical sums, are 100-percent Americans. There are no more important problems facing us than the problem of stopping this human erosion and rehabilitating those unfortunates who have already been thrown off the land. Certainly it is un-American for Americans to be starved and dispossessed of their homes in our land of plenty. Those who seek to exploit and harass these American refugees, the migratory workers, are against our principles of democracy.

Source: U.S. Congress, House Select Committee to Investigate the Interstate Migration of Destitute Citizens (Washington: Government Printing Office, 1940–1941), 2102.

Interpret the Evidence

1. What does Ann Marie Low's description of a typical day suggest about the particular challenges women faced during the Dust Bowl era (Document 22.5)?
2. Compare the living conditions described by a white southern sharecropper (Document 22.6) to those of the migrant family described by John Steinbeck (Document 22.8). How does the poverty of the two families differ? How would you explain the differences you note?
3. Compare the sharecropper's story (Document 22.6) with the photograph of the Arkansas family (Document 22.7). Do the subjects seem to react to the Great Depression in the same way? Do they seem hopeful or hopeless?
4. According to Frank Stokes, how did the fruit packers and grove owners characterize their conflict with the Mexican farmworkers (Document 22.9)? In what ways did their characterization draw on more general conservative criticisms of the New Deal?
5. According to the Great Plains Committee testimony (Document 22.10), what role did human-caused factors play in producing the misery that accompanied the dust storms of the early 1930s?

Put It in Context

● What do these documents tell us about expectations regarding government help during the Great Depression?

background photos: pages 714 and 718, Library of Congress

EXPLORING AMERICAN HISTORIES

Getty Images

Freed slaves in Richmond, Virginia, c. 1865.

Culver Pictures/The Art Archive at Art Resource, Inc.

Jack and Abby Landlord, freed slaves from Savannah, Georgia, 1875.

14

Emancipations and Reconstructions

1863–1877

Schlesinger Library, Radcliffe Institute, Harvard University/The Bridgeman Art Library

Women voting in Wyoming, 1870.

AMERICAN HISTORIES

Jefferson Franklin Long spent his life improving himself and his race. Born a slave in Alabama in 1836, Long showed great resourcefulness in taking advantage of the limited opportunities available to him under slavery. His master, a tailor who moved his family to Georgia, taught him the trade, but Long taught himself to read and write. When the Civil War ended, he opened a tailor shop in Macon, Georgia. The measure of financial security he earned allowed him to turn his attention to politics and participate in the Republican Party. Elected as Georgia's first black congressman in 1870, Long was committed to fighting for the political rights of freed slaves. In his first appearance on the House floor, he spoke out against a bill that would allow former Confederate officials to return to Congress. He questioned their loyalty to the Union from which they had recently rebelled and noted that many belonged to secret societies, such as the Ku Klux Klan, that intimidated black citizens. Despite his pleas, the measure passed, and Long decided not to run for reelection.

By the mid-1880s, Long had become disillusioned with the ability of black Georgians to achieve their objectives within the electoral system. Instead, he counseled African Americans to turn to institution building as the best hope for social and economic advancement. Advocating "Christianity, morality, education, and industry," Long helped found the Union Brotherhood Lodge, a black mutual aid society, with branches throughout central Georgia, that provided social and economic services for its members. He died in 1901, during a time of political disfranchisement and racial segregation that swept through Georgia and the rest of the South. In fact, after Long, Georgia would not elect another black congressman for a hundred years.

Jefferson Long and Andrew Johnson shared many characteristics, but their views on race led them to support decidedly different programs following the Civil War. Whereas Long fought for the right of self-determination for African Americans, Johnson believed that whites alone could decide what was best for freedmen. Born in 1808 in Raleigh, North Carolina, Andrew Johnson grew up in poverty. At the age of thirteen or fourteen, Johnson became a tailor's apprentice, but he ran away before completing his contract. Johnson settled in Tennessee in 1826 and, like Long, opened a tailor shop. The following year, he married Eliza McCardle, who taught him how to write. He began to prosper, purchasing his own home, farm, and a small number of slaves.

As he made his mark in Greenville, Tennessee, Johnson moved into politics, following fellow Tennessean Andrew Jackson into the Democratic Party. Success followed success as he advanced to higher political positions, and by the time the Civil War broke out, he was a U.S. senator. During his early political career, Johnson, a social and political outsider, championed the rights of workers and small farmers against the power of the southern aristocracy.

Jefferson Franklin Long and Andrew Johnson

At the onset of the Civil War, Johnson remained loyal to the Union even when Tennessee seceded in 1861. As a reward for his loyalty, President Abraham Lincoln appointed Johnson as military governor of Tennessee. In 1864 the Republican Lincoln chose the Democrat Johnson to run with him as vice president, thereby constructing a successful unity ticket. Less than six weeks after their inauguration in March 1865, Johnson became president upon Lincoln's assassination.

Fate placed Reconstruction in the hands of Andrew Johnson. After four years, the brutal Civil War between the rebellious southern states that seceded from the Union and the northern states that fought to preserve the nation had come to a close. Yet the hard work of reunion remained. Toward this end, President Johnson oversaw the reestablishment of state legislatures in the former Confederate states. These reconstituted governments agreed to the abolition of slavery, but they passed measures that restricted black civil and political rights. Johnson accepted these results and considered the southern states as having fulfilled their obligations for rejoining the Union. Most Northerners reached a different conclusion. Having won the bloody war, they suspected that they were now losing the peace to Johnson and the defeated South. •

both photos: Library of Congress

THE AMERICAN HISTORIES of Andrew Johnson and Jefferson Long intersected in Reconstruction, the hard-fought battle to determine the fate of the postwar South and the meaning of freedom for newly emancipated African Americans. Would the end of slavery be little more than a legal technicality, as Johnson and many other white Southerners hoped, or would Long's vision of a deeper economic and racial transformation prevail? From 1865 to 1877, the period of Reconstruction, Americans of all races and from all regions participated in the resolution of this question.

Prelude to Reconstruction

Even before Andrew Johnson became president in 1865 and emancipation freed Jefferson Long, Reconstruction had begun on a small scale. During the Civil War, blacks remaining in Union-occupied areas, such as the Sea Islands, located off the coast of South Carolina, had some experience with freedom. When Union troops arrived and most southern whites fled, the slaves chose to stay on the land. Some farmed for themselves, but most were employed by northern whites who moved south to demonstrate the profitability of newly freed black labor. The return of former plantation owners after the war generated conflicts. Rather than work for whites, freedpeople preferred to establish their own farms; but if forced to work for whites, they insisted on negotiating their wages instead of simply accepting what whites offered. Wives and mothers often refused to labor for whites at all in favor of caring for their own families. These conflicts reflected the priorities that would shape the actions of freedpeople across the South in the immediate aftermath of the war. For freedom to be meaningful, it had to include economic independence, the power to make family decisions, and the right to have some control over community issues.

African Americans Embrace Emancipation

When U.S. troops arrived in Richmond, Virginia, in April 1865, it signaled to the city's enslaved African American population that the war was over and that freedom was, finally, theirs. African American men, women, and children took to the streets and crowded into churches to celebrate. They gathered to dance, sing, pray, and shout. Four days after Union troops arrived, 1,500 African Americans, including a large number of soldiers, packed First African Baptist, the largest of the city's black churches. During the singing of the hymn "Jesus My All to Heaven Is Gone," they raised their voices at the line "This is the way I long have sought." Elsewhere in Virginia, black schoolchildren sang "Glory Hallelujah," and house slaves snuck out of the dinner service to shout for joy in the slave quarters. As the news of the Confederacy's defeat spread, newly freed African Americans across the South experienced similar emotions. However, the news did not reach some isolated plantations in Georgia, Louisiana, South Carolina, and Texas for months. David Harris, a South Carolina planter, claimed that he did not hear about the emancipation edict until June 1865. He did not mention it to the slaves on his plantation until August, when Union troops stationed nearby made it impossible for him to keep it from his workers any longer. Whenever they discovered their freedom, blacks recalled the moment vividly. Many years later, Houston H. Holloway, a Georgia slave who had been sold three times before he was twenty years old, recalled the day of emancipation. "I felt like a bird out a cage," he reported. "Amen. Amen, Amen. I could hardly ask to feel any better than I did that day."

For southern whites, however, the end of the war brought fear, humiliation, and uncertainty. From their point of view, the jubilation of their former slaves was salt in their wounds. In many areas, blacks celebrated their release from bondage under the protection of Union soldiers. When the army moved out, freedwomen and freedmen suffered deeply for their enthusiasm. When troops departed the area surrounding Columbia, South Carolina, for example, a plantation owner and his wife vented their anger and frustration on a former slave. The girl had assisted Union soldiers in finding silverware, money, and jewelry hidden by her master and mistress. Her former owners hanged the newly emancipated slave. Other whites beat, whipped, raped, slashed, and shot blacks who they felt had been too joyous in their freedom or too helpful to the Yankee invaders. As one North Carolina freedman testified, the Yankees "tol' us we were free," but once the army left, the planters "would get cruel to the slaves if they acted like they were free."

Newly freed slaves also faced less visible dangers. During the 1860s, disease swept through the South and through the contraband camps that housed many former slaves; widespread malnutrition and poor housing heightened the problem. A smallpox epidemic that spread south from Washington, D.C., killed more than sixty thousand freedpeople.

Despite the danger of acting free, southern blacks eagerly pursued emancipation. They moved; they married; they attended school; they demanded wages; they refused to work for whites; they gathered up their families; they created black churches and civic associations; they held political meetings. Sometimes, black women and men acted on their own, pooling their resources to advance their freedom. At other times, they called on government agencies for assistance and support. The most important of these agencies was the newly formed Bureau of Refugees, Freedmen, and Abandoned Lands, popularly known as the **Freedmen's Bureau**. Created by Congress in 1865 and signed into law by President Lincoln, the bureau provided ex-slaves with economic and legal resources. Private organizations—particularly northern missionary and educational associations, most staffed by former abolitionists, free blacks, and evangelical Christians—also aided African Americans in their efforts to give meaning to freedom.

Reuniting Families Torn Apart by Slavery

The first priority for many newly freed blacks was to reunite families torn apart by slavery. Men and women traveled across the South to find spouses, children, parents, siblings, aunts, and uncles. Well into the 1870s and 1880s, parents ran advertisements in newly established black newspapers, providing what information they knew about their children's whereabouts and asking for assistance in finding them. They sought help in their quests from government officials, ministers, and other African Americans. Milly Johnson wrote to the Freedmen's Bureau in March 1867, after failing to locate the five children she had lost under slavery. In the end, she was able to locate three of her children, but any chance of discovering the whereabouts of the other two was lost when the records of the slave trader who purchased them burned during the war. Although such difficulties were common, thousands of slave children were reunited with their parents in the aftermath of the Civil War.

Husbands and wives, or those who considered themselves as such despite the absence of legal marriage under slavery, also searched for each other. Those who lived on nearby plantations could now live together for the first time. Those whose husband or wife had been sold to distant plantation owners had a more difficult time. They wrote (or had letters written on their behalf) to relatives and friends who had been sold with their mate; sought assistance from government officials, churches, and even their former masters; and traveled to areas where they thought their spouse might reside.

Many such searches were complicated by long years of separation and the lack of any legal standing for slave marriages. In 1866 Philip Grey, a Virginia freedman, located his wife, Willie Ann, and their daughter Maria, who had been sold away to Kentucky years before. Willie Ann was eager to reunite with her husband, but in the years since being sold, she had remarried and borne three

children. Her second husband had joined the Union army and was killed in battle. When Willie Ann wrote to Philip in April 1866, explaining her new circumstances, she concluded: "If you love me you will love my children and you will have to promise me that you will provide for them all as well as if they were your own. . . . I know that I have lived with you and loved you then and love you still." Other spouses finally located their partner, only to discover that the husband or wife was happily married to someone else and refused to acknowledge the earlier relationship.

Despite these complications, most former slaves who found their spouse sought to legalize their relationship. Ministers, army chaplains, Freedmen's Bureau agents, and teachers were flooded with requests to perform marriage ceremonies. In one case, a Superintendent for Marriages for the Freedmen's Bureau in northern Virginia reported that he gave out seventy-nine marriage certificates on a single day in May 1866. In another, four couples went right from the fields to a local schoolhouse, still dressed in their work clothes, where the parson married them.

Of course, some former slaves hoped that freedom would allow them to leave an unhappy relationship. Having never been married under the law, couples could simply separate and move on. Complications arose, however, if they had children. In Lake City, Florida, in 1866, a Freedmen's Bureau agent asked for advice from his superiors on how to deal with Madison Day and Maria Richards. They refused to legalize the relationship forced on them under slavery, but both sought custody of their three children, the oldest only six years old. As with white couples in the mid-nineteenth century, the father eventually was granted custody on the assumption that he had the best chance of providing for the family financially.

Free to Learn

Reuniting families was only one of the many ways that southern blacks proclaimed their freedom. Learning to read and write was another. The desire to learn was all but universal. Writing of freedpeople during Reconstruction, Booker T. Washington, an educator and a former slave, noted, "It was a whole race trying to go to school. Few were too young, and none too old, to make the attempt to learn." A newly liberated father in Mississippi proclaimed, "If I nebber does nothing more while I live, I shall give my children a chance to go to school, for I considers education [the] next best ting to liberty."

A variety of organizations opened schools for former slaves during the 1860s and 1870s. By 1870 nearly a quarter million blacks were attending one of the 4,300 schools established by the Freedmen's Bureau. Black and white

Information Wanted.

INFORMATION is wanted of my mother, whom I left in Fauquier county. Va., in 1844, and I was sold in Richmond. Va., to Saml. Copeland. I formerly belonged to Robert Rogers. I am very anxious to hear from my mother, and any information in relation to her whereabouts will be very thankfully received. My mother's name was Betty, and was sold by Col. Briggs to James French.— Any information by letter, addressed to the Colored Tennessean, Box 1150, will be thankfully received.
                          THORNTON COPELAND.
sept16-3m

Reuniting Families
Thornton Copeland, a former slave, placed this advertisement in the *Colored Tennessean* in Nashville in October 1865. Like other freedpeople, he was looking for relatives, in this case his mother, from whom he had been forcibly separated.   Courtesy of the Tennessee State Library and Archives

Wedding Day, 1866

A Freedmen's Bureau minister unites a black Union soldier and his bride in Vicksburg, Mississippi. Most postwar weddings of freedpeople were less formal, but *Harper's Weekly*, a political magazine published in New York City and an ally of the Republican Party, wanted to present black families as respectable.
Library of Congress

churches and missionary societies also launched schools. Even before the war ended, the American Missionary Association called on its northern members to take the freedpeople "by the hand, to guide, counsel and instruct them in their new life." This and similar organizations sent hundreds of teachers, black and white, women and men, into the South to open schools in former plantation areas. Their attitudes were often paternalistic and the schools were segregated, but the institutions they established offered important educational resources for African Americans.

The demand for education was so great that almost any kind of building was pressed into service as a schoolhouse. A mule stable in Helena, Arkansas; a billiard room on the Sea Islands; a courthouse in Lawrence, Kansas; and a former cotton shed on a St. Simon Island plantation all attracted eager students. In New Orleans, local blacks converted a former slave pen into a school and named it after the famous activist, orator, and ex-slave Frederick Douglass.

Parents worked hard to keep their children in school during the day. Children, as they gained the rudiments of

education, passed on their knowledge to mothers, fathers, and older siblings whose work responsibilities prevented them from attending school. Still, many freedpeople, having worked all day in fields, homes, or shops, then walked long distances in order to get a bit of education for themselves. In New Bern, North Carolina, where many blacks labored until eight o'clock at night, a teacher reported that they still insisted on spending at least an hour "in earnest application to study."

Freedmen and freedwomen sought education for a variety of reasons. Some, like the Mississippi father noted above, viewed it as a sign of liberation. Others knew that they must be able to read the labor contracts they signed if they were ever to be free of exploitation by whites. Some men and women were eager to correspond with relatives far away, others to read the Bible. Growing numbers hoped to participate in politics, particularly the public meetings organized by freedpeople in cities across the South following the end of the war. These gatherings met to set an agenda for the future, and nearly everyone demanded that state

Freedmen's Bureau School
This photograph of a one-room Freedmen's Bureau school in North Carolina in the late 1860s shows the large number and diverse ages of students who sought to obtain an education following emancipation. The teachers included white and black northern women sent by missionary and reform organizations as well as southern black women who had already received some education.   The Granger Collection, New York

legislatures immediately establish public schools for African Americans. Most black delegates agreed with A. H. Ransier of South Carolina, who proclaimed that "in proportion to the education of the people so is their progress in civilization."

Despite the enthusiasm of blacks and the efforts of the federal government and private agencies, schooling remained severely limited throughout the South. A shortage of teachers and of funding kept enrollments low among blacks and whites alike. The isolation of black farm families and the difficulties in eking out a living limited the resources available for education. Only about a quarter of African Americans were literate by 1880.

Black Churches Take a Leadership Role

One of the constant concerns freedpeople expressed as they sought education was the desire to read the Bible and other religious material. Forced under slavery to listen to white preachers who claimed that God had placed Africans and their descendants in bondage, blacks sought to interpret the Bible for themselves. Like many other churches, the African Methodist Episcopal Church, based in Philadelphia, sent missionaries and educators into the South. These church leaders were eager to open seminaries, such as Shaw University in Raleigh, North Carolina, to train southern black men for the ministry.

From the moment of emancipation, freedpeople gathered at churches to celebrate community events. Black Methodist and Baptist congregations spread rapidly across the South following the Civil War. In these churches, African Americans were no longer forced to sit in the back benches listening to white preachers claim that the Bible legitimated slavery. They were no longer punished by white church leaders for moral infractions defined by white masters. Now blacks filled the pews, hired black preachers, selected their own boards of deacons and elders, and invested community resources in purchasing land, building houses of worship, and furnishing them. Churches were the largest structures available to freedpeople in many communities and thus were used for a variety of purposes by a host of community organizations.

They often served as schools, with hymnals and Bibles used to teach reading. Churches also hosted picnics, dances, weddings, funerals, festivals, and other events that brought blacks together to celebrate their new sense of freedom, family, and community. Church leaders, especially ministers, often served as arbiters of community standards of morality.

One of the most important functions of black churches in the years immediately following the Civil War was as sites for political organizing. Some black ministers worried that political concerns would overwhelm spiritual devotions. Others agreed with the Reverend Charles H. Pearce of Florida, who declared, "A man in this State cannot do his whole duty as a minister except he looks out for the political interests of his people." Whatever the views of ministers, black churches were among the few places where African Americans could express their political views free from white interference.

REVIEW & RELATE

- What were freedpeople's highest priorities in the years immediately following the Civil War? Why?

- How did freedpeople define freedom? What steps did they take to make freedom real for themselves and their children?

 LEARNINGCurve bedfordstmartins.com/hewittlawson/LC

National Reconstructions

Presidents Abraham Lincoln and Andrew Johnson viewed Reconstruction as a process of national reconciliation. They sketched out terms by which the former Confederate states could reclaim their political representation in the nation without much difficulty. Southern whites, too, sought to return to the Union quickly and with as little change as possible. Congressional Republicans, however, had a more thorough-going reconstruction in mind. Like many African Americans, Republican congressional leaders expected the South to extend constitutional rights to the freedmen and to provide them with the political and economic resources to sustain their freedom. Over the next decade, these competing visions of Reconstruction played out in a hard-fought and tumultuous battle over the social, economic, and political implications of the South's defeat and of the abolition of slavery.

Abraham Lincoln Plans for Reunion

In December 1863, President Lincoln issued the **Proclamation of Amnesty and Reconstruction**. He believed that the southern states could not have constitutionally seceded from the Union and therefore only had to meet minimum standards before they regained their political and constitutional rights. Lincoln declared that defeated southern states would have to accept the abolition of slavery and that new governments could be formed when 10 percent of those eligible to vote in 1860 (which in practice meant white southern men but not blacks) swore an oath of allegiance to the United States. Lincoln's plan granted amnesty to all but the highest-ranking Confederate officials, and the restored voters in each state would elect members to a constitutional convention and representatives to take their seats in Congress. In the next year and a half, Arkansas, Louisiana, and Tennessee reestablished their governments under Lincoln's "Ten Percent Plan."

Republicans in Congress had other ideas. They argued that the Confederates had broken their contract with the Union when they seceded and should be treated as "conquered provinces" subject to congressional supervision. In 1864 Congress passed the Wade-Davis bill, which established much higher barriers for readmission to the Union than did Lincoln's plan. For instance, the Wade-Davis bill substituted 50 percent of voters for the president's 10 percent requirement. Lincoln put a stop to this harsher proposal by using a pocket veto—refusing to sign it within ten days of Congress's adjournment.

Although Lincoln and his fellow Republicans in Congress disagreed about many aspects of postwar policy, Lincoln was flexible, and his actions mirrored his desire both to heal the Union and to help southern blacks. For example, the president supported the **Thirteenth Amendment**, abolishing slavery, which passed Congress in January 1865 and was sent to the states for ratification. In March 1865, Lincoln signed the law to create the Freedmen's Bureau. That same month, the president also expressed his sincere wish for reconciliation between the North and the South. "With malice toward none, with charity for all," Lincoln declared in his second inaugural address, "let us strive on to finish the work . . . to bind up the nation's wounds." Lincoln would not, however, have the opportunity to shape Reconstruction with his balanced approach. When he was assassinated in April 1865, it fell to Andrew Johnson, a very different sort of politician, to lead the country through the process of national reintegration.

Andrew Johnson and Presidential Reconstruction

The nation needed a president who could transmit northern desires to the South with clarity and conviction and ensure that they were carried out. Instead, the nation got a president who substituted his own aims for those of the North, refused to engage in meaningful compromise even with sympathetic opponents, misled the South into believing that he could achieve restoration quickly, and subjected himself to political humiliation. Like his mentor, Andrew Jackson,

Andrew Johnson was a staunch Union man. He proved his loyalty by serving diligently as military governor of Union-occupied Tennessee from 1862 to 1864. In the 1864 election, Lincoln chose Johnson, a Democrat, as his running mate in a thinly veiled effort to attract border-state voters. The vice presidency was normally an inconsequential role, so it mattered little to Lincoln that Johnson, a southern Democrat, was out of step with many Republican Party positions.

As president, however, Johnson's views took on profound importance. Born into rural poverty, Johnson had no sympathy for the southern aristocracy. Johnson had been a slave owner himself for a time, so his political opposition to slavery was not rooted in moral convictions. Instead, it sprang from the belief that slavery gave plantation owners inordinate power and wealth, which came at the expense of the majority of white Southerners who owned no slaves. He saw emancipation as a means to "break down an odious and dangerous [planter] aristocracy," not to empower blacks. Consequently, he was unconcerned with the fate of African Americans in the postwar South. He saw no reason to punish the South or its leaders because he believed that the end of slavery would doom the southern aristocracy. He hoped to bring the South back into the Union as quickly as possible and then let Southerners take care of their own affairs.

Johnson's views, combined with a lack of political savvy and skill, left him unable to work constructively with congressional Republicans, even the moderates who constituted the majority, such as Senators Lyman Trumbull of Illinois, William Pitt Fessenden of Maine, and John Sherman of Ohio. Moderate Republicans shared the prevalent belief of their time that whites and blacks were not equal, but they argued that the federal government needed to protect newly emancipated slaves. Senator Trumbull warned that without national legislation, ex-slaves would "be tyrannized over, abused, and virtually reenslaved." They expected southern states, where 90 percent of African Americans lived, to extend basic civil rights to the freedpeople, including equal protection and due process of law, and the right to work and hold property.

Nearly all Republicans shared these positions. The Radical wing of the party, however, wanted to go still further. Led by Senator Charles Sumner of Massachusetts and Congressman Thaddeus Stevens of Pennsylvania, this small but influential group advocated suffrage, or voting rights, for African American men as well as the redistribution of southern plantation lands to freed slaves. Stevens called on the federal government to provide freedpeople "a homestead of forty acres of land," which would give them some measure of economic independence. Nonetheless, whatever disagreements the Radicals had with the moderates, all Republicans believed that Congress should have a strong voice in determining the fate of the former Confederate states. From May to December 1865,

with Congress out of session, they waited to see what Johnson's restoration plan would produce, ready to assert themselves if his policies deviated too much from their own.

At first, it seemed as if Johnson would proceed as they hoped. He appointed provisional governors to convene new state constitutional conventions and urged these conventions to ratify the Thirteenth Amendment abolishing slavery, revoke the states' ordinances of secession, and refuse to pay Confederate war debts, which the victorious North did not consider legitimate because repayment would benefit southern bondholders who financed the rebellion. He also allowed the majority of white Southerners to obtain amnesty and a pardon by swearing their loyalty to the U.S. Constitution, but he required those who had held more than $20,000 of taxable property—the members of the southern aristocracy—to petition him for a special pardon to restore their rights. Republicans expected him to be harsh in dealing with his former political foes. Instead, Johnson relished the reversal of roles that put members of the southern elite at his mercy. As the once prominent petitioners paraded before him, the president granted almost all of their requests for pardons.

By the time Congress convened in December 1865, Johnson was satisfied that the southern states had fulfilled his requirements for restoration. Moderate and Radical Republicans disagreed, seeing few signs of change or contrition in the South. As a result of Johnson's liberal pardon policy, many former leaders of the Confederacy won election to state constitutional conventions and to Congress. Indeed, Georgians elected Confederate vice president Alexander H. Stephens to the U.S. Senate. In addition, although most of the reconstituted state governments ratified the Thirteenth Amendment, South Carolina and Mississippi refused to repudiate the Confederate debt, and Mississippi rejected the Thirteenth Amendment.

Far from providing freedpeople with basic civil rights protection, the southern states passed a variety of **black codes** intended to reduce blacks to a condition as close to slavery as possible. Some laws prohibited blacks from bearing arms; others outlawed intermarriage and excluded blacks from serving on juries. Many of these laws were designed to ensure that white landowners had a supply of black labor now that slavery had ended. The codes made it difficult for blacks to leave plantations unless they proved they could support themselves. Many southern whites contended that they were acting no differently than their northern counterparts who used vagrancy laws to maintain control over workers.

Northerners viewed this situation with alarm. In their eyes, the postwar South looked very similar to the Old South, with a few cosmetic adjustments. If the black codes prevailed, one Republican proclaimed, "then I demand to know of what practical value is the amendment abolishing slavery?" Others wondered what their wartime sacrifices

Mourning at Stonewall Jackson's Gravesite, 1866

Many Northerners were concerned that the defeat of the Confederacy did not lessen white Southerners' devotion to the "Lost Cause" of a society based on the domination of African Americans. Women, who led the efforts to memorialize Confederate soldiers, are shown at the gravesite of General Stonewall Jackson in Lexington, Virginia. Virginia Military Institute Archives

had been for if the South admitted no mistakes, was led by the same people, and continued to oppress its black inhabitants. The *Chicago Tribune* declared that Northerners would not allow the black codes to "disgrace one foot of soil in which the bones of our soldiers sleep and over which the flag of freedom waves." **See Document Project 14: Testing and Contesting Freedom, page 449.**

Johnson and Congressional Resistance

Faced with growing opposition in the North, Johnson stubbornly held his ground. He insisted that the southern states had followed his plan and were entitled to resume their representation in Congress. Republicans objected, and in December 1865 they barred the admission of southern lawmakers, an action that Johnson denounced as illegitimate. Up to this point, it was still possible for Johnson and Congress to work together, if Johnson had been willing to compromise. He was not. Instead, Johnson pushed moderates into the Radical camp with a series of legislative vetoes that challenged the fundamental tenets of Republican policies toward African Americans and the South. In January 1866, the president

refused to sign a bill passed by Congress to extend the life of the Freedmen's Bureau for another two years. A few months later, he vetoed the Civil Rights Act, which Congress had passed to protect freedpeople in the South from the restrictions placed on them by the black codes. These bills represented a consensus among moderate and Radical Republicans on the government's responsibility toward former slaves.

> **Explore**
>
> See Documents 14.1 and 14.2 for two perspectives on the Freedmen's Bureau.

Johnson justified his vetoes on both constitutional and personal grounds. Along with Democrats, he contended that so long as Congress refused to admit southern representatives, it could not legally pass laws affecting the South. The chief executive also condemned the Freedmen's Bureau bill because it infringed on the rights of states to handle their internal affairs concerning education and economic matters. Johnson's vetoes exposed his racism and his lifelong belief that the evil of slavery lay in the harm it did to poor white Southerners, not to enslaved blacks. Johnson

DOCUMENTS 14.1 AND 14.2

Debating the Freedmen's Bureau: Two Views

From the start, the Freedmen's Bureau generated controversy. To its Republican supporters, it helped southern blacks make the transition from slavery to freedom. For most white Southerners and many northern Democrats, however, the bureau was little more than an expensive social welfare program that rewarded idleness in blacks. Both points of view are represented in the following documents. In a report written to the Congressional Joint Committee on Reconstruction, Colonel Eliphalet Whittlesey, the assistant head of the Freedmen's Bureau in North Carolina, outlined the bureau's initial accomplishments. The anti-bureau cartoon reprinted here was created during the height of the conflict over Reconstruction between the Republican Congress and President Andrew Johnson; it was intended to support the election of a Democratic candidate for governor of Pennsylvania, an ally of Johnson.

Explore

14.1 Colonel Eliphalet Whittlesey | Report on the Freedmen's Bureau, 1865

All officers of the bureau are instructed—

To aid the destitute, yet in such a way as not to encourage dependence.

To protect freedmen from injustice.

To assist freedmen in obtaining employment and fair wages for their labor.

To encourage education, intellectual and moral. Under these four divisions the operations of the bureau can best be presented. . . .

The statistical reports prepared by Captain Almy, commissary of subsistence, forwarded herewith, will show a steady and healthy decrease of the number of dependents from month to month.

July there were issued 215,285 rations, valued at $44,994.56; August there were issued 156,289 rations, valued at $32,664.40; September there were issued 137,350 rations, valued at $28,706.15.

Should no unforeseen trouble arise, the number will be still further reduced. But we have in our camps at Roanoke island and Newbern, many women and children, families of soldiers who have died in the service, and refugees from the interior during the war, for whom permanent provision must be made. . . . The reports prepared by Surgeon Hogan will show the condition of freedmen hospitals. In the early part of the summer much suffering and mortality occurred for want of medical attendance and supplies. This evil is now being remedied by the employment of surgeons by contract. . . .

Contrary to the fears and predictions of many, the great mass of colored people have remained quietly at work upon the plantations of their former masters during the entire summer. The crowds seen about the towns in the early part of the season had followed in the wake of the Union army, to escape from slavery. After hostilities ceased these refugees returned to their homes, so that but few vagrants can now be found. In truth, a much larger amount of vagrancy exists among the whites than among the blacks. It is the almost uniform report of officers of the bureau that freedmen are industrious.

The report is confirmed by the fact that out of a colored population of nearly 350,000 in the State, only about 5,000 are now receiving support from the government. Probably some others are receiving aid from kind-hearted men who have enjoyed the benefit of their services from childhood. To the general quiet and industry of this people there can be no doubt that the efforts of the bureau have contributed greatly.

Source: *The Reports of the Committees of the House of Representatives Made during the First Session, Thirty-ninth Congress, 1865–1866* (Washington, D.C.: Government Printing Office, 1866), 186–87, 189.

14.2 Democratic Flier Opposing the Freedmen's Bureau Bill, 1866

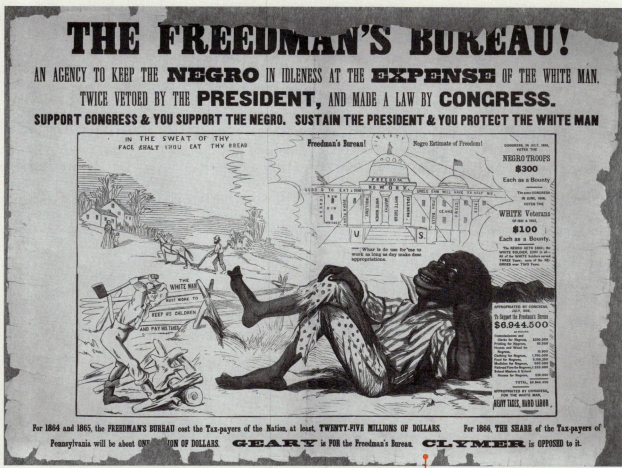

Library of Congress

Interpret the Evidence

- Why was there a need for the Freedmen's Bureau? How did Colonel Whittlesey measure its success?
- How is the Freedmen's Bureau portrayed in the poster? Why might its argument have appealed to some northern whites?

Put It in Context

How did prevailing racial assumptions shape both the cartoon and the report?

argued that these congressional bills discriminated against whites, who would receive no benefits under them, and put whites at a disadvantage with blacks who received government assistance. Johnson's private secretary recorded in his diary, "The president has at times exhibited a morbid distress and feeling against the Negroes," including those like Jefferson Long, who spoke out for their full civil rights.

Johnson's actions united moderates and Radicals against him. In April 1866, Congress repassed both the Freedmen's Bureau extension and Civil Rights Act over the president's vetoes. In June, lawmakers adopted the **Fourteenth Amendment**, which incorporated many of the provisions of the Civil Rights Act, and submitted it to the states for ratification (see Appendix). Reflecting its confrontational dealings with the president, Congress wanted to ensure more permanent protection for African Americans than simple legislation could provide. Lawmakers also wanted to act quickly, as the situation in the South seemed to be deteriorating rapidly. The previous month, a race riot had broken out in Memphis, Tennessee. For a day and a half, white mobs, egged on by local police, went on a rampage, during which they terrorized black residents of

the city and burned their houses and churches. "The late riots in our city," the editor of a Memphis newspaper asserted, "have satisfied all of one thing, that the *southern man* will not be ruled by the *negro*."

The Fourteenth Amendment defined citizenship to include African Americans, thereby nullifying the ruling in the *Dred Scott* case of 1857, which declared that blacks were not citizens. It extended equal protection and due process of law to all persons and not only citizens. The amendment repudiated Confederate debts, which some state governments had refused to do, and it barred Confederate office-holders from holding elective office unless Congress removed this provision by a two-thirds vote. Although most Republicans were upset with Johnson's behavior, at this point they were not willing to embrace the Radical position entirely. Rather than granting the right to vote to black males at least twenty-one years of age, the Fourteenth Amendment gave the states the option of excluding blacks and accepting a reduction in congressional representation if they did so.

Johnson remained inflexible. Instead of counseling the southern states to accept the Fourteenth Amendment, which would have sped up their readmission to the Union,

Memphis Race Riot

A skirmish between white policemen and black Union veterans on May 1, 1866, resulted in three days of rioting by white mobs that attacked the black community of Memphis, Tennessee. Before federal troops restored peace, numerous women had been raped, and forty-six African Americans and two whites had been killed. This illustration from *Harper's Weekly* depicts the carnage.   Courtesy of the Tennessee State Library and Archives

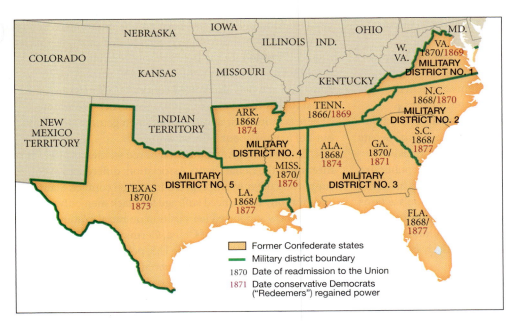

MAP 14.1 Reconstruction in the South

In 1867, Congress enacted legislation dividing the former Confederate states into five military districts. All the states were readmitted to the Union by 1870 and white, conservative Democrats (Redeemers) had replaced Republicans in most states by 1875. Only in Florida, Louisiana, and South Carolina did federal troops remain until 1877.

Map legend:
- Former Confederate states
- Military district boundary
- 1870 Date of readmission to the Union
- 1871 Date conservative Democrats ("Redeemers") regained power

he encouraged them to reject it. Ironically, Johnson's home state of Tennessee ratified the amendment, but the other states refused. In the fall of 1866, Johnson decided to take his case directly to northern voters before the midterm congressional elections. Campaigning for candidates who shared his views, he embarked on a swing through the Midwest. Clearly out of touch with northern public opinion, Johnson attacked Republican lawmakers and engaged in shouting matches with audiences. On election day, Republicans increased their majorities in Congress and now controlled two-thirds of the seats, providing them with greater power to override presidential vetoes.

Congressional Reconstruction

When the Fortieth Congress convened in 1867, Republican lawmakers charted a new course for Reconstruction. With moderates and Radicals united against the president, Congress intended to force the former Confederate states not only to protect the basic civil rights of African Americans but also to grant them the vote. Moderates now agreed with Radicals that unless blacks had access to the ballot, they would not be able to sustain their freedom. Extending the suffrage to African Americans also aided the fortunes of the Republican Party in the South by adding significant numbers of new black voters. By the end of March, Congress enacted three Military Reconstruction Acts. Together they divided ten southern states into five military districts, each under the supervision of a Union general and his troops (Map 14.1). The male voters of each state, regardless of race, were to elect delegates to a constitutional convention; only former Confederate officials were disfranchised.

The conventions were required to draft constitutions that guaranteed black suffrage and ratified the Fourteenth Amendment. Within a year, North Carolina, South Carolina, Florida, Alabama, Louisiana, and Arkansas had fulfilled these obligations and reentered the Union.

Having ensured congressional Reconstruction in the South, Republican lawmakers turned their attention to disciplining the president. Johnson continued to resist congressional policy and used his power as commander in chief to order generals in the military districts to soften the intent of congressional Reconstruction. In response, Congress passed the Command of the Army Act in 1867, which required the president to issue all orders to army commanders in the field through the General of the Army in Washington, D.C., Ulysses S. Grant. The Radicals had won over Grant and knew they could count on him to carry out their policies. Even more threatening to presidential power, Congress passed the **Tenure of Office Act**, which prevented Johnson from firing cabinet officers sympathetic to congressional Reconstruction. This measure barred the chief executive from removing from office any appointee that the Senate had ratified previously without returning to the Senate for approval.

Johnson sincerely believed that the Tenure of Office Act violated his presidential prerogative to remove subordinates he considered disloyal or incompetent. He may have had a legitimate constitutional point. However, the quick-tempered Johnson chose to confront the Radical Republicans directly rather than find a way to maneuver around a congressional showdown. In February 1868, Johnson fired Secretary of War Edwin Stanton, a Lincoln appointee and a Radical sympathizer, without Senate approval. In response, congressional Radicals prepared articles of impeachment on eleven counts of misconduct, including willful violation of the Tenure of Office Act.

In late February, the House voted 126 to 47 to impeach Johnson, the first president ever to be impeached, or charged with unlawful activity. The case then went to trial in the Senate, where the chief justice of the Supreme Court presided and a two-thirds vote was necessary for conviction and removal from office. After a six-week hearing, the Senate fell one vote short of convicting Johnson. Most crucial for Johnson's fate were the votes of seven moderate Republicans who refused to find the president guilty of violating his oath to uphold the Constitution, convinced that Johnson's actions were insufficient to merit the enormously significant step of removing a president from office. Although Johnson narrowly remained in office, Congress effectively ended his power to shape Reconstruction policy.

Not only did the Republicans restrain Johnson but they also won the presidency in 1868. Ulysses S. Grant, the popular Civil War Union general, ran against Horatio Seymour, the Democratic governor of New York. Although an ally of the Radical Republicans, Grant called for reconciliation with the South. He easily defeated Seymour, winning nearly 53 percent of the popular vote and 73 percent of the electoral vote.

The Struggle for Universal Suffrage

In February 1869, Congress passed the **Fifteenth Amendment** to protect black suffrage, which had initially been guaranteed by the Military Reconstruction Acts. A compromise between moderate and Radical Republicans, the amendment prohibited voting discrimination based on race, but it did not deny states the power to impose qualifications based on literacy, payment of taxes, moral character, or any other standard that did not directly relate to race. Subsequently, the wording of the amendment provided loopholes for white leaders to disfranchise African Americans and any other "undesirable" elements. The amendment did, however, cover the entire nation, including the North, where several states, such as Connecticut, Kansas, Michigan, New York, Ohio, and Wisconsin, still excluded blacks from voting.

The Fifteenth Amendment sparked serious conflicts not only within the South but also among old abolitionist allies. The American Anti-Slavery Society disbanded with abolition, but many members believed that important work still remained to be done to guarantee the rights of freedpeople. They formed the **American Equal Rights Association** immediately following the war. Members of this group divided over the Fifteenth Amendment.

Women's rights advocates, such as Elizabeth Cady Stanton and Susan B. Anthony, had earlier objected to the Fourteenth Amendment because it inserted the word *male* into the Constitution for the first time when describing citizens. Although they had been ardent abolitionists before the war, Stanton and Anthony worried that postwar policies intended to enhance the rights of southern black men would further limit the rights of women. Some African American activists also voiced concern. At a meeting of the Equal Rights Association in 1867, Sojourner Truth noted, "There is quite a stir about colored men getting their rights, but not a word about colored women."

The Fifteenth Amendment ignored women. At the 1869 meeting of the Equal Rights Association, differences over supporting the measure erupted into open conflict. Stanton and Anthony denounced suffrage for black men only, and Stanton now supported her position on racial grounds. She claimed that the "dregs of China, Germany, England, Ireland, and Africa" were degrading the U.S. polity and argued that white, educated women should certainly have the same rights as immigrant and African American men. Black and white supporters of the Fifteenth Amendment, including Frances Ellen Watkins Harper, Wendell Phillips, Abby Kelley, and Frederick Douglass, denounced Stanton's bigotry. Believing that southern black men urgently needed suffrage to protect their newly won freedom, they argued that the ratification of black men's suffrage would speed progress toward the achievement of suffrage for black and white women.

> **Explore**
>
> See Document 14.3 for one activist's views on ratifying suffrage for black men.

This conflict led to the formation of competing organizations committed to women's suffrage. The **National Woman Suffrage Association**, established by Stanton and Anthony, allowed only women as members and opposed ratification of the Fifteenth Amendment. The **American Woman Suffrage Association**, which attracted the support of women and men, white and black, supported ratification. Less than a year later, in the spring of 1870, the Fifteenth Amendment was ratified and went into effect. However, the amendment did not grant the vote to either white or black women. As a result, women suffragists turned to the Fourteenth Amendment to achieve their goal. In 1875 Virginia Minor, who had been denied the ballot in Missouri, argued that the right to vote was one of the "privileges and immunities" granted to all citizens under the Fourteenth Amendment. In *Minor v. Happersatt*, the Supreme Court ruled against her.

REVIEW & RELATE

- What was President Johnson's plan for reconstruction? How were his views out of step with those of most Republicans?

- What characterized congressional Reconstruction? What priorities were reflected in congressional Reconstruction legislation?

DOCUMENT 14.3

Frances Ellen Watkins Harper | On Suffrage, 1869

Born a free person of color in Baltimore, Maryland, Frances Ellen Watkins Harper distinguished herself as a poet, a teacher, and an abolitionist. After the Civil War, she became a staunch advocate of women's suffrage and a supporter of the Fifteenth Amendment, which set her at odds with the suffragists Susan B. Anthony and Elizabeth Cady Stanton. In this discussion at the May 1869 American Equal Rights Association meeting, she argues for ratification of the Fifteenth Amendment.

Explore

When it was a question of race, she [black women] let the lesser question of sex go. But the white women all go for sex, letting race occupy a minor position. She liked the idea of working women, but she would like to know if it was broad enough to take colored women? . . . [When I] was at Boston there were sixty women who left work because one colored woman went to gain a livelihood in their midst. If the nation could only handle one question, I would not have the black women put a single straw in the way, if only the men of the race could obtain what they wanted.

Source: Susan B. Anthony, Elizabeth Cady Stanton, and Matilda Joslyn Gage, eds., *History of Women's Suffrage, 1861–1876* (Rochester, NY: Susan B. Anthony, 1882), 2:391–92.

Frances Ellen Watkins Harper Image courtesy of Documenting the American South, The University of North Carolina at Chapel Hill Libraries

Interpret the Evidence

- According to Frances Harper, why do black and white women differ on support for black male suffrage?
- How does Harper's experience in Boston influence her opinion?

Put It in Context

Why was it important for black men to gain the right to vote even if it meant delaying women's suffrage?

Remaking the South

With President Johnson's power effectively curtailed, reconstruction of the South moved quickly. However, despite the fears of southern whites and their supporters in the North, the results were neither extreme nor revolutionary. Although African Americans for the first time participated extensively in electoral politics and made unprecedented gains, whites retained control of the majority of the region's wealth and political power. In contrast to revolutions and civil wars in other countries, only one rebel was executed for war crimes (the commandant of Andersonville Prison in Georgia); only one high-ranking official went to prison (Jefferson Davis); no official was forced into exile, though some fled voluntarily; very little land was confiscated and redistributed; and most rebels regained voting rights and the ability to hold office within seven years after the end of the rebellion.

Whites Reconstruct the South

During the first years of congressional Reconstruction, two groups of whites occupied the majority of elective offices in the South. A significant number of native-born Southerners joined Republicans in forming postwar constitutions and governments. Before the war, some had belonged to the Whig Party and opposed secession from the Union. Many mountain dwellers in Alabama, Georgia, North Carolina, and Tennessee had demonstrated a fiercely independent strain and had remained loyal to the Union. As a white resident of the Georgia mountains commented, "Now is the time for every man to come out and speak his principles publickly and vote for liberty as we have been in bondage long enough." Small merchants and farmers who detested large plantation owners also threw their lot in with the Republicans. Even a few ex-Confederates, such as General James A. Longstreet, decided that the South must change and allied with the Republicans. The majority of whites who continued to support the Democratic Party viewed these whites as traitors. They showed their distaste by calling them **scalawags**, an unflattering term meaning "scoundrels."

At the same time, northern whites came south to support Republican Reconstruction. They had varied reasons for making the journey, but most considered the South a new frontier to be conquered culturally, politically, and economically. Some had served in the Union army during the war, liked what they saw of the region, and decided to settle there. Some came to help provide education and assist the freedpeople in adjusting to a new way of

life. As a relatively underdeveloped area, the South also beckoned fortune seekers and adventurers who saw in the South an opportunity to get rich building railroads, establishing factories, and selling consumer goods. Southern Democrats denounced such northern interlopers as **carpetbaggers**, suggesting that they invaded the region with all their possessions in a satchel, seeking to plunder it and then leave. This characterization applied to some, but it did not accurately describe the motivations of most transplanted Northerners. While they did seek economic opportunity, they were acting as Americans always had in settling new frontiers and pursuing dreams of success. In dismissing them as carpetbaggers, their political enemies employed a double standard because they did not apply this demeaning label to those who traveled west—from both the North and the South—in search of economic opportunity at the expense of Indians and Mexicans settled there. Much of the negative feelings directed toward carpetbaggers resulted primarily from their attempts to ally with African Americans in reshaping the South.

Black Political Participation and Economic Opportunities

As much as the majority of southern whites detested scalawags and carpetbaggers, the primary targets of white hostility were African Americans who attempted to exercise their hard-won freedom. Blacks constituted a majority of voters in five states—Alabama, Florida, South Carolina, Mississippi, and Louisiana—while in Georgia, North Carolina, Texas, and Virginia they fell short of a majority. They did not use their ballots to impose black rule on the South as many white Southerners feared. Only in South Carolina did African Americans control the state legislature, and in no state did they manage to elect a governor. Nevertheless, for the first time in American history, blacks won a wide variety of elected positions. More than six hundred blacks served in state legislatures; another sixteen, including Jefferson F. Long, held seats in the U.S. House of Representatives; and two from Mississippi were chosen to serve in the U.S. Senate.

Officeholding alone does not indicate the enthusiasm that former slaves had for politics. African Americans considered politics a community responsibility, and in addition to casting ballots, they held rallies and mass meetings to discuss issues and choose candidates. Although they could not vote, women attended these gatherings and helped influence their outcome. Covering a Republican convention in Richmond in October 1867, held in the African First Baptist Church, the *New York Times* reported that "the entire colored population of Richmond" attended. Freedpeople also formed associations to promote education, economic advancement, and social welfare programs, all of which they saw as deeply intertwined with politics. These included organizations like Richmond's Mutual Benefit Society, a group formed by single mothers, and the Independent Order of St. Luke, a mutual aid society for black women and men. African American women led both.

The efforts of southern blacks to bolster their freedom included building alliances with sympathetic whites. The resulting interracial political coalitions produced considerable reform in the South. These coalitions created a public school system where none had existed before the war; provided funds for social services, such as poor relief and state hospitals; upgraded prisons; and rebuilt the South's transportation system by supporting railroads and construction projects. Moreover, the state constitutions that the Republicans wrote brought a greater measure of political democracy and equality to the South by extending the right to vote to poor white men as well as black men. Some states allowed married women greater control over their property and liberalized the criminal justice system. In effect, these Reconstruction governments brought the South into the nineteenth century.

Obtaining political representation was one way in which African Americans defined freedom. Economic independence constituted a second. Without government-sponsored land redistribution, however, the options for southern blacks remained limited. Lacking capital to start farms, they entered into various forms of tenant contracts with large landowners. **Sharecropping** proved the most common arrangement. Blacks and poor whites became sharecroppers for much the same economic reasons. They received tools and supplies from landowners and farmed their own plots of land on the plantation. In exchange, sharecroppers turned over a portion of their harvest to the owner and kept some for themselves. Crop divisions varied but were usually explained in detail on written agreements. To make this system profitable, sharecroppers concentrated on producing staple crops such as cotton and tobacco that they could sell for cash.

The benefits of sharecropping proved more valuable to black farmers in theory than in practice. To tide them over during the growing season, croppers had to purchase household provisions on credit from a local merchant, who was often also the farmers' landlord. At the mercy of store owners who kept the books and charged high interest rates, tenants usually found themselves in considerable debt at the end of the year. To satisfy the debt, merchants devised a crop lien system in which tenants pledged a portion of their yearly crop to satisfy what they owed. Most indebted tenants found themselves bound to the landlord because falling prices in agricultural staples during this period meant that they did not receive sufficient return on their produce to get out of debt. For many African Americans, sharecropping turned into a form of virtual slavery.

Explore

See Document 14.4 for an example of a sharecropping agreement.

The picture for black farmers was not all bleak, however. About 20 percent of black farmers managed to buy their own land. Through careful management and extremely hard work, black families planted gardens for household consumption and raised chickens for eggs and food. Despite its pitfalls, sharecropping provided a limited measure of labor independence and allowed some blacks to accumulate small amounts of cash.

Following the war's devastation, many of the South's white, small farmers known as yeomen also fell into sharecropping. Yet planters, too, had changed. Many sons of planters abandoned farming and became lawyers, bankers, and merchants. Despite these changes, one thing remained the same: White elites ruled over blacks and poor whites, and they kept these two economically exploited groups from uniting by fanning the flames of racial prejudice.

Economic hardship and racial bigotry drove many blacks to leave the South. In 1879 former slaves pooled their resources to create land companies and purchase property in Kansas on which to settle. They created black towns that attracted some 25,000 African American migrants from the South, known as **Exodusters**. Kansas was ruled by the Republican Party and had been home to the great antislavery martyr John Brown. As one hopeful freedman from Louisiana wrote to the Kansas governor in 1879, "I am anxious to reach your state . . . because of the sacredness of her soil washed in the blood of humanitarians for the cause of black freedom." Exodusters did not find the Promised Land, however, as poor-quality land and unpredictable weather made farming on the Great Plains a hard and often unrewarding experience. Nevertheless, for many African American migrants, the chance to own their own land and escape the oppression of the South was worth the hardships. In 1880 the census counted 40,000 blacks living in Kansas.

White Resistance to Congressional Reconstruction

Despite the Republican record of accomplishment during Reconstruction, white Southerners did not accept its legitimacy. They accused interracial governments of conducting a spending spree that raised taxes and encouraged corruption. Indeed, taxes did rise significantly, but mainly because of the need to provide new educational

DOCUMENT 14.4

Sharecropping Agreement, 1870

Because Congress did not generally provide freedpeople with land, African Americans lacked the capital to start their own farms. At the same time, plantation owners needed labor to plant and harvest their crops for market. Out of mutual necessity, white plantation owners entered into sharecropping contracts with blacks to work their farms in exchange for a portion of the crop, such as the following contract between Willis P. Bocock and several of his former slaves. Bocock owned Waldwick Plantation in Marengo County, Alabama.

Explore

What are the farmers' responsibilities?

Why would Bocock want to clarify that his laborers would work equally hard throughout the year?

How might putting a lien on crops for debts owed create difficulties for the black farmer?

Contract made the 3rd day of January in the year 1870 between us the free people who have signed this paper of one part, and our employer, Willis P. Bocock, of the other part. We agree to take charge of and cultivate for the year 1870, a portion of land, say [left blank] acres or thereabouts, to be laid off to us by our employer on his plantation, and to tend the same well in the usual crops, in such proportions as we and he may agree upon. We are to furnish the necessary labor, say an average hand to every 15 acres in the crops, making in all average hands; and are to have all proper work done, ditching, fencing, repairing, etc., as well as cultivating and saving the crops of all kinds, so as to put and keep the land we occupy and tend in good order for cropping, and to make a good crop ourselves; and to do our fair share of job work about the place. . . . We are to be responsible for the good conduct of ourselves, our hands, and families, and agree that all shall be respectful to employer, owners, and manager, honest, industrious, and careful about every thing, and shall not interrupt any thing about the place, working as industriously the last part of the year as the first; and then our employer agrees that he and his manager shall treat us kindly, and help us to study our interest and do our duty. If any hand or family proves to be of bad character, or dishonest, or lazy, or disobedient, or any way unsuitable our employer or manager has the right, and we have the right, to have such turned off. . . .

For the labor and services of ourselves and hands rendered as above stated, we are to have one third part of all the crops, or their net-proceeds, made and secured, or prepared for market by our force. . . .

We are to be furnished by our employer through his manager with provisions if we call for them: not over one peck of meal or corn, and $3\frac{1}{2}$ pounds of meat or its equivalent per week, for every 15 acres of land or average hand, to be charged to us at fair market prices.

And whatever may be due by us, or our hands to our employer for provisions or any thing else, during the year, is to be a lien on our share of the crops, and is to be retained by him out of the same before we receive our part.

Source: Waldwick Plantation Records, 1834–1971, LPR174, box 1, folder 9, Alabama Department of Archives and History.

Put It in Context

Why would free blacks and poor whites be willing to enter into such a contract?

Exodusters

This photograph of two black couples standing on their homestead was taken around 1880 in Nicodemus, Kansas. These settlers, known as Exodusters, had migrated to northwest Kansas following the end of Reconstruction. They sought economic opportunity free from the racial repression sweeping the South.   Library of Congress

and social services. Corruption, where building projects and railroad construction were concerned, was common during this time. Still, it is unfair to single out Reconstruction governments and especially black legislators as inherently depraved, as their Democratic opponents did. Economic scandals were part of American life after the Civil War. As enormous business opportunities arose and the pent-up energies that had gone into battles over slavery exploded into desires to accumulate wealth, many business leaders and politicians made unlawful deals to enrich themselves.

Most Reconstruction governments had only limited opportunities to transform the South. By the end of 1870, civilian rule had returned to all of the former Confederate states, and they had reentered the Union. Republican rule did not continue past 1870 in Virginia, North Carolina, and Tennessee and did not extend beyond 1871 in Georgia and 1873 in Texas. In 1874 Democrats deposed Republicans in Arkansas and Alabama; two years later, Democrats triumphed in Mississippi. In only three states—Louisiana, Florida, and South Carolina—did Reconstruction last until 1877.

The Democrats who replaced Republicans trumpeted their victories as bringing "redemption" to the South. Of course, these so-called **Redeemers** were referring to the white South. For black Republicans and their white allies, redemption meant defeat, not resurrection. Democratic victories came at the ballot boxes, but violence, intimidation, and fraud usually paved the way. It was not enough for Democrats to attack Republican policies. They also used racist appeals to divide poor whites from blacks and backed them up with force. In 1865 in Pulaski, Tennessee, General Nathan Bedford Forrest organized Confederate veterans into a social club called the **Knights of the Ku Klux Klan (KKK)**. The name came from the Greek word *kuklos*, meaning "circle." Spreading throughout the South, the KKK did not function as an ordinary social association; its followers donned robes and masks to hide their identities and terrify their victims. Ku Kluxers wielded rifles and guns and rode on horseback to the homes and

Visit of the Ku Klux Klan

This 1872 wood engraving by the noted magazine illustrator Frank Bellew appeared at the height of Ku Klux Klan violence against freed blacks in the South. This image depicts a black family seemingly secure in their home in the evening while masked Klansmen stand in their doorway ready to attack with rifles.   Library of Congress

churches of black and white Republicans to keep them from voting. When threats did not work, they murdered their victims. In 1871, for example, 150 African Americans were killed in Jackson County in the Florida Panhandle. A black clergyman lamented, "That is where Satan has his seat." Here and elsewhere, many of the individuals targeted had managed to buy property, gain political leadership, or in other ways defy white stereotypes of African American inferiority. Local rifle clubs, hunting groups, and other white supremacist organizations joined the Klan in waging a reign of terror. During the 1875 election in Mississippi, which toppled the Republican government, armed terrorists killed hundreds of Republicans and scared many more away from the polls.

To combat the terror unleashed by the Klan and its allies, Congress passed three Force Acts in 1870 and 1871. These measures empowered the president to dispatch officials into the South to supervise elections and prevent voting interference. Directed specifically at the KKK, one law barred secret organizations from using force to violate equal protection of the laws. In 1872 Congress established a joint committee to probe Klan tactics, and its investigations produced thirteen volumes of vivid testimony about the horrors perpetrated by the Klan. Elias Hill, a freedman

from South Carolina who had become a Baptist preacher and teacher, was one of those who appeared before Congress. He and his brother lived next door to each other. The Klansmen went first to his brother's house, where, as Hill testified, they "broke open the door and attacked his wife, and I heard her screaming and mourning [moaning]. . . . At last I heard them have [rape] her in the yard. She was crying and the Ku-Klux were whipping her to make her tell where I lived." When Klansmen finally discovered Elias Hill, they dragged him out of his house, accused him of preaching against the Klan, beat and whipped him, and threatened to kill him. On the basis of such testimony, the federal government prosecuted some 3,000 Klansmen. Only 600 were convicted, however. As the Klan disbanded in the wake of federal prosecutions, other vigilante organizations arose to take its place.

REVIEW & RELATE

What role did black people play in remaking southern society during Reconstruction?

How did southern whites fight back against Reconstruction? What role did terrorism and political violence play in this effort?

LEARNINGCurve bedfordstmartins.com/hewittlawson/LC

The Unmaking of Reconstruction

The violence, intimidation, and fraud perpetrated by Redeemers against black and white Republicans in the South does not fully explain the unmaking of Reconstruction. Although Republicans in Congress enacted legislation combating the KKK and racial discrimination in public facilities, by the early 1870s white Northerners had grown weary of the struggle to protect the rights of freedpeople. In the minds of many, white Northerners had done more than enough for black Southerners, and it was time to focus on other issues. Growing economic problems intensified this feeling. More and more northern whites came to believe that any debt owed to black people for northern complicity in the sin of slavery had been wiped out by the blood shed during the Civil War. By the early 1870s, burying and memorializing the Civil War dead emerged as a common concern among white Americans, in both the North and the South. White America was once again united, if only in the shared belief that it was time to move on, consigning the issues of slavery and civil rights to history.

The Republican Retreat

Most northern whites shared the racial views of their counterparts in the South. Although they had supported protection of black civil rights and suffrage, they still believed that African Americans were inferior to whites, and social integration was no more tolerable to them than it was to white Southerners. They began to sympathize with racist complaints voiced from the South that blacks were not capable of governing honestly and effectively.

In 1872 a group calling themselves **Liberal Republicans** challenged the reelection of President Grant, the Civil War general who had won the presidency on the Republican ticket in 1868. Financial scandals had racked the Grant administration. This high-level corruption reflected the get-rich-quick schemes connected to economic speculation and development following the Civil War. Outraged by these misdeeds and the rising level of immoral behavior in government and business, Liberal Republicans nominated Horace Greeley, editor of the *New York Tribune*, to run against Grant. They linked government corruption to the expansion of federal power that accompanied Reconstruction, and called for the removal of troops from the South and amnesty for former Confederates. They also campaigned for civil service reform in order to establish a merit system for government employment and for abolition of the "spoils system"—in which the party in power rewarded loyal supporters with political

appointments—that had been in place since the administration of Andrew Jackson.

The Democratic Party believed that Liberal Republicans offered the best chance to defeat Grant, and it endorsed Greeley. Despite the scandals that surrounded him, Grant remained popular. Moreover, the main body of Republicans "waved the bloody shirt," reminding northern voters that a ballot cast for the opposition tarnished the memory of brave Union soldiers who had died during the war. With the newly created national cemeteries, particularly the one established in Arlington, Virginia, providing a vivid reminder of the hundreds of thousands of soldiers killed, the "bloody shirt" remained a potent symbol. The president won reelection with an even greater margin than he had four years earlier. Nevertheless, the attacks against Grant foreshadowed the Republican retreat on Reconstruction. Among the Democrats sniping at Grant was Andrew Johnson. Johnson had returned to Tennessee, and in 1874 the state legislature chose the former president to serve in the U.S. Senate. He continued to speak out against the presence of federal troops in the South until his death in 1875.

Congressional and Judicial Retreat

By the time Grant began his second term, Congress was already considering bills to restore officeholding rights to former Confederates who had not yet sworn allegiance to the Union. Black representatives, such as Georgia congressman Jefferson Long, as well as some white lawmakers, remained opposed to such measures, but in 1872 Congress removed the penalties placed on former Confederates by the Fourteenth Amendment and permitted nearly all rebel leaders the right to vote and hold office. Two years later, for the first time since the start of the Civil War, the Democrats gained a majority in the House of Representatives and prepared to remove the remaining troops from the South.

Economic concerns increasingly replaced racial considerations as the top priority for northern Republican leaders. Northerners and Southerners began calling more loudly for national unity and reconciliation. In 1873 a financial panic resulting from the collapse of the Northern Pacific Railroad triggered a severe economic depression lasting late into the decade. Tens of thousands of unemployed workers across the country worried more about finding jobs than they did about blacks in the South. Businessmen, too, were plagued with widespread bankruptcy. As workers looked to labor unions for support, business leaders looked to the federal government for assistance. When strikes erupted across the country in 1877, most notably the Great Railway Strike, employers asked the U.S. government to remove troops from the

South and dispatch them against strikers in the North and the West.

While Northerners sought a way to extricate themselves from Reconstruction, the Supreme Court weakened enforcement of the civil rights acts. In 1873 the *Slaughterhouse* cases defined the rights that African Americans were entitled to under the Fourteenth Amendment very narrowly. Reflecting the shift from moral to economic concerns, the justices interpreted the amendment as extending greater protection to corporations in conducting business than that extended to blacks. As a result, blacks had to depend on southern state governments to protect their civil rights, the same state authorities that had deprived them of their rights in the first place. In *United States v. Cruikshank* (1876), the high court narrowed the Fourteenth Amendment further, ruling that it protected blacks against abuses only by state officials and agencies, not by private groups such as the Ku Klux Klan. Seven years later, the Court struck down the Civil Rights Act of 1875, which had extended "full and equal treatment" in public accommodations for persons of all races.

The Presidential Compromise of 1876

The presidential election of 1876 set in motion events that officially brought Reconstruction to an end. The Republicans nominated Rutherford B. Hayes, a Civil War officer and governor of Ohio. A supporter of civil service reform, Hayes was chosen, in part, because he was untainted by the corruption that plagued the Grant administration. The Democrats selected their own crusader against bribery and graft, Governor Samuel J. Tilden of New York, who had prosecuted political corruption in New York City.

The outcome of the election depended on twenty disputed electoral votes, nineteen from the South and one from Oregon. Tilden won 51 percent of the popular vote, but Reconstruction political battles in Florida, Louisiana, and South Carolina put the election up for grabs. In each of these states, the outgoing Republican administration certified Hayes as the winner, while the incoming Democratic regime declared for Tilden.

The Constitution assigns Congress the task of counting and certifying the electoral votes submitted by the states. Normally, this is merely a formality, but 1876 was different. Democrats controlled the House, Republicans controlled the Senate, and neither branch would budge on which votes to count. Hayes needed all twenty for victory; Tilden needed only one. To break the logjam, Congress created a fifteen-member **Joint Electoral Commission**, composed of seven Democrats, seven Republicans, and one independent (five members of the House, five U.S. senators, and five Supreme Court justices). As it turned out, the independent commissioner, Justice David Davis,

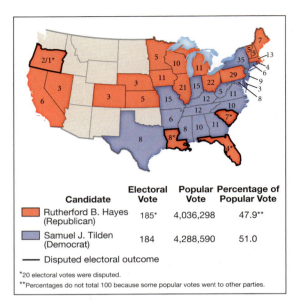

Candidate	Electoral Vote	Popular Vote	Percentage of Popular Vote
Rutherford B. Hayes (Republican)	185*	4,036,298	47.9**
Samuel J. Tilden (Democrat)	184	4,288,590	51.0
— Disputed electoral outcome			

*20 electoral votes were disputed.
**Percentages do not total 100 because some popular votes went to other parties.

MAP 14.2 The Election of 1876

The presidential election of 1876 got swept up in Reconstruction politics. Democrats defeated Republicans in Florida, Louisiana, and South Carolina, but both parties claimed the electoral votes for their candidates. A federal electoral commission set up to investigate the twenty disputed votes, including one from Oregon, awarded the votes and the election to the Republican, Rutherford B. Hayes.

resigned, and his replacement, Justice Joseph P. Bradley, voted with the Republicans to count all twenty votes for Hayes, making him president (Map 14.2).

Still, Congress had to ratify this count, and disgruntled southern Democrats in the Senate threatened a filibuster—unlimited debate—to block certification of Hayes. With the March 4, 1877, date for the presidential inauguration creeping perilously close and no winner officially declared, behind-the-scenes negotiations finally helped settle the controversy. A series of meetings between Hayes supporters and southern Democrats led to a bargain. According to the agreement, Democrats would support Hayes in exchange for the president appointing a Southerner to his cabinet, withdrawing the last federal troops from the South, and endorsing construction of a transcontinental railroad through the South. This **compromise of 1877** averted a crisis over presidential succession, underscored increased southern Democratic influence within Congress, and marked the end to strong federal protection for African Americans in the South.

REVIEW & RELATE

- Why did northern interest in Reconstruction wane in the 1870s?
- What common values and beliefs among white Americans were reflected in the compromise of 1877?

 LEARNINGCurve bedfordstmartins.com/hewittlawson/LC

Conclusion: The Legacies of Reconstruction

Reconstruction was, in many ways, profoundly limited. African Americans did not receive the landownership that would have provided them with the economic independence to bolster their freedom from the racist assaults of white Southerners. The civil and political rights that the federal government conferred did not withstand Redeemers' efforts to disfranchise and deprive the freedpeople of equal rights. The Republican Party shifted its priorities elsewhere, and Democrats gained enough political power nationally to short-circuit federal intervention, while numerous problems remained unresolved in the South. Northern support for racial equality did not run very deep, so white Northerners, who shared many of the prejudices of white Southerners, were happy to extricate themselves from further intervention in southern racial matters. Nor was there sufficient support to give women, white and black, the right to vote. Finally, federal courts, with growing concerns over economic rather than social issues, sanctioned Northerners' retreat by providing constitutional legitimacy for abandoning black Southerners and rejecting women's suffrage in court decisions that narrowed the interpretation of the Fourteenth and Fifteenth Amendments.

Despite all of this, Reconstruction did transform the country. As a result of Reconstruction, slavery was abolished, and the legal basis for freedom was enshrined in the Constitution. Indeed, blacks exercised a measure of political and economic freedom during Reconstruction that never entirely disappeared over the decades to come. In many areas, freedpeople, as exemplified by Congressman Jefferson Franklin Long among many others, asserted what they could never have during slavery—control over their lives, their churches, their labor, and their families. What they could not practice during their own time because of racial discrimination, their descendants would one day revive through the promises codified in the Fourteenth and Fifteenth Amendments.

African Americans transformed not only themselves; they transformed the nation. The Constitution became much more democratic and egalitarian through inclusion of the Reconstruction amendments. Reconstruction lawmakers took an important step toward making the United States the "more perfect union" that the nation's Founders had pledged to create. Reconstruction established a model for expanding the power of the federal government to resolve domestic crises that lay beyond the abilities of states and ordinary citizens. It remained a powerful legacy for those elected officials in the future who dared to invoke it. And Reconstruction transformed the South to its everlasting benefit. It modernized state constitutions, expanded educational and social welfare systems, and unleashed the repressed potential for industrialization and economic development that the preservation of slavery had restrained. Ironically, Reconstruction did as much for white Southerners as it did for black Southerners in liberating them from the past.

LEARNINGCurve
Check what you know.
bedfordstmartins.com/hewittlawson/LC

Chapter Review

Online Study Guide ▶ bedfordstmartins.com/hewittlawson

KEY TERMS

Freedmen's Bureau (p. 427)
Proclamation of Amnesty and Reconstruction (p. 431)
Thirteenth Amendment (p. 431)
black codes (p. 432)
Fourteenth Amendment (p. 436)
Tenure of Office Act (p. 437)
Fifteenth Amendment (p. 438)
American Equal Rights Association (p. 438)
National Woman Suffrage Association (p. 438)

American Woman Suffrage Association (p. 438)
scalawags (p. 440)
carpetbaggers (p. 440)
sharecropping (p. 441)
Exodusters (p. 441)
Redeemers (p. 443)
Knights of the Ku Klux Klan (KKK) (p. 443)
Liberal Republicans (p. 445)
Joint Electoral Commission (p. 446)
compromise of 1877 (p. 446)

REVIEW & RELATE

1. What were freedpeople's highest priorities in the years immediately following the Civil War? Why?

2. How did freedpeople define freedom? What steps did they take to make freedom real for themselves and their children?

3. What was President Johnson's plan for reconstruction? How were his views out of step with those of most Republicans?

4. What characterized congressional Reconstruction? What priorities were reflected in congressional Reconstruction legislation?

5. What role did black people play in remaking southern society during Reconstruction?

6. How did southern whites fight back against Reconstruction? What role did terrorism and political violence play in this effort?

7. Why did northern interest in Reconstruction wane in the 1870s?

8. What common values and beliefs among white Americans were reflected in the compromise of 1877?

TIMELINE OF EVENTS

1863   Lincoln issues Proclamation of Amnesty and Reconstruction

1865   Ku Klux Klan formed

Freedmen's Bureau established

Congress passes Thirteenth Amendment

April 1865   Lincoln assassinated; Andrew Johnson becomes president

May–December 1865   Presidential Reconstruction under Andrew Johnson

1866   Congress passes extension of Freedmen's Bureau and Civil Rights Act over Johnson's presidential veto

Congress passes Fourteenth Amendment

1867   Military Reconstruction Acts divide the South into military districts

Congress passes Command of the Army and Tenure of Office Acts

1868   Andrew Johnson impeached

1869   Congress passes Fifteenth Amendment

Women's suffrage movement splits over support of Fifteenth Amendment

1870   250,000 blacks attend schools established by the Freedmen's Bureau

Civilian rule reestablished in all former Confederate states

1870–1871   Jefferson Long serves as a Republican congressman from Georgia

1870–1872   Congress takes steps to curb KKK violence in the South

1872   Liberal Republicans challenge reelection of President Grant

1873   Financial panic sparks depression lasting until the late 1870s

1873–1883   Supreme Court limits rights of African Americans

1875   Congress passes Civil Rights Act outlawing discrimination in public accommodations, which the Supreme Court rules unconstitutional in 1883

1877   Republicans and southern Democrats reach compromise resulting in the election of Rutherford B. Hayes as president and the end of Reconstruction

1879   Black Exodusters migrate from South to Kansas

Testing and Contesting Freedom

Nine months after the Civil War ended in April 1865, twenty-seven states ratified the Thirteenth Amendment, abolishing slavery throughout the United States. Freedom, however, did not guarantee equal rights or the absence of racial discrimination. Immediately following the North's victory, white southern leaders enacted black codes, which aimed to prevent the former slaves from improving their social and economic status. Although Lincoln's successor, Andrew Johnson, himself a Southerner, did not support the codes, he did nothing to overturn them. An advocate of limited government, Johnson clashed repeatedly with Congress over Reconstruction, vetoing renewal of the Freedmen's Bureau bill and opposing ratification of the Fourteenth Amendment. In 1867 the Republican majority in Congress passed the Military Reconstruction Acts, which placed the South under military rule and forced it to extend equal political and civil rights to African Americans.

The Military Reconstruction Acts, followed by the ratification of the Fifteenth Amendment in 1870, extended suffrage to black men. In alliance with white Republicans, blacks won election to a variety of public offices, including seats on local and state governmental bodies. When these interracial legislatures provided funds for public education of blacks—for the first time in the South—and for black hospitals and other social services, their opponents attacked them for fraud, corruption, wasteful spending, and imposing "Black Rule." Opponents also created vigilante groups like the Ku Klux Klan to intimidate black and white Republicans through scare tactics backed up by violence and bloodshed. By 1877 the attempt of white southern Democrats, or Redeemers, had succeeded, leaving African Americans struggling to retain the freedom they had enjoyed during Reconstruction.

As you read the following documents, consider these general questions: How did blacks and whites view freedom? How essential was it for the federal government to supervise the movement from slavery to freedom? Why didn't southern whites accept the extension of civil rights for blacks, if only in a limited way? How did views about Reconstruction change over time?

Mississippi Black Code, 1865

Southern legislatures created black codes primarily to limit the rights of free blacks after emancipation and return them to a condition as close as possible to slavery. Mississippi was one of the first states to enact a black code. Although its laws did legalize marriage for blacks and allowed them to own property and testify in court, its primary intent was to limit freedpeople's mobility and economic opportunities. New vagrancy laws required blacks to provide written proof of residency and employment or else risk arrest, while other sections limited where they could live, restricted the terms of their employment, and banned intermarriage.

An Act to Confer Civil Rights on Freedmen, and for other Purposes

SECTION 1. All freedmen, free negroes and mulattoes may sue and be sued . . . in all the courts of law and equity of this State, and may acquire personal property, and choses in action [right to bring a lawsuit to recover chattels, money, or a debt], by descent or purchase, and may dispose of the same in the same manner and to the same extent that white persons may: Provided, That the provisions of this section shall not be so construed as to allow any freedman, free negro or mulatto to rent or lease any lands or tenements except in incorporated cities or towns, in which places the corporate authorities shall control the same.

SECTION 2. All freedmen, free negroes and mulattoes may intermarry with each other, in the same manner and under the same regulations that are provided by law for white persons: Provided, that the clerk of probate shall keep separate records of the same.

SECTION 3. All freedmen, free negroes or mulattoes who do now and have herebefore lived and cohabited together as husband and wife shall be taken and held in law as legally married, and the issue shall be taken and held as legitimate for all purposes; and it shall not be lawful for any freedman, free negro or mulatto to intermarry with any white person; nor for any person to intermarry with any freedman, free negro or mulatto; and any person who shall so intermarry shall be deemed guilty of felony, and on conviction thereof shall be confined in the State penitentiary for life; and those shall be deemed freedmen, free negroes and mulattoes who are of pure negro blood, and those descended from a negro to the third generation, inclusive, though one ancestor in each generation may have been a white person.

SECTION 4. In addition to cases in which freedmen, free negroes and mulattoes are now by law competent witnesses, freedmen, free negroes or mulattoes shall be competent in civil cases, when a party or parties to the suit, either plaintiff or plaintiffs, defendant or defendants; also in cases where freedmen, free negroes and mulattoes is or are either plaintiff or plaintiffs, defendant or defendants. They shall also be competent witnesses in all criminal prosecutions where the crime charged is alleged to have been committed by a white person upon or against the person or property of a freedman, free negro or mulatto. . . .

SECTION 5. Every freedman, free negro and mulatto shall, on the second Monday of January, one thousand eight hundred and sixty-six, and annually thereafter, have a lawful home or employment, and shall have written evidence thereof as follows, to wit: if living in any incorporated city, town, or village, a license from that mayor thereof; and if living outside of an incorporated city, town, or village, from the member of the board of police of his beat, authorizing him or her to do irregular and job work; or a written contract, as provided in SECTION 6 in this act; which license may be revoked for cause at any time by the authority granting the same.

Section 6. All contracts for labor made with freedmen, free negroes and mulattoes for a longer period than one month shall be in writing, and a duplicate, attested and read to said freedman, free negro or mulatto by a beat, city or county officer, or two disinterested white persons of the county in which the labor is to [be] performed, of which each party shall have one: and said contracts shall be taken and held as entire contracts, and if the laborer shall quit the service of the employer before the expiration of his term of service, without good cause, he shall forfeit his wages for that year up to the time of quitting. . . .

An Act to Amend the Vagrant Laws of the State . . .

Section 2. All freedmen, free negroes and mulattoes in this State, over the age of eighteen years, found on the second Monday in January, 1866, or thereafter, with no lawful employment or business, or found unlawful[ly] assembling themselves together, either in the day or night time, and all white persons assembling themselves with freedmen, free negroes or mulattoes, or usually associating with freedmen, free negroes or mulattoes, on terms of equality, or living in adultery or fornication with a freed woman, freed negro or mulatto, shall be deemed vagrants, and on conviction thereof shall be fined in a sum not exceeding, in the case of a freedman, free negro or mulatto, fifty dollars, and a white man two hundred dollars, and imprisonment at the discretion of the court, the free negro not exceeding ten days, and the white man not exceeding six months. . . .

Section 6. The same duties and liabilities existing among white persons of this State shall attach to freedmen, free negroes or mulattoes, to support their indigent families and all colored paupers; and that in order to secure a support for such indigent freedmen, free negroes, or mulattoes, it shall be lawful, and is hereby made the duty of the county police of each county in this State, to levy a poll or capitation tax on each and every freedman, free negro, or mulatto, between the ages of eighteen and sixty years, not to exceed the sum of one dollar annually to each person so taxed, which tax, when collected, shall be paid into the county treasurer's hands, and constitute a fund to be called the Freedman's Pauper Fund, which shall be applied by the commissioners of the poor for the maintenance of the poor of the freedmen, free negroes and mulattoes of this State, under such regulations as may be established by the boards of county police in the respective counties of this State.

Source: *Laws of the State of Mississippi, Passed at a Regular Session of the Mississippi Legislature, Held in the City of Jackson, October, November, and December, 1865* (Jackson, MS, 1866), 82–86, 165–67.

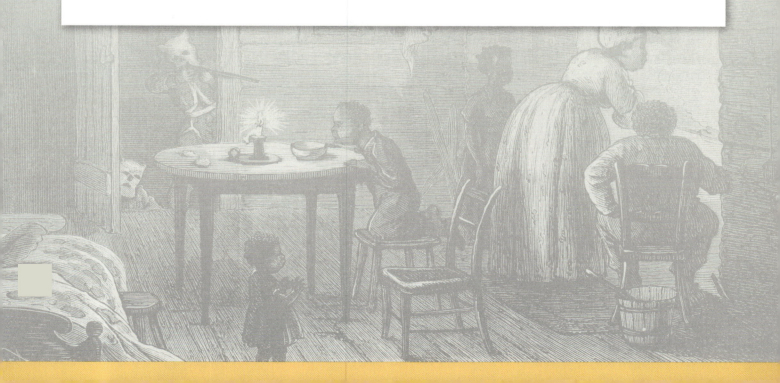

DOCUMENT 14.6

Richard H. Cain | Federal Aid for Land Purchase, 1868

Richard H. Cain, a free black minister raised in Ohio, went to South Carolina after the war and served as a Republican member of the U.S. House of Representatives for two terms in the 1870s. The following excerpt comes from a speech Cain made in 1868 as a representative to the South Carolina constitutional convention. Cain proposed that the convention petition Congress for a $1 million loan to purchase land that could be resold to freedmen at a reasonable price.

BELIEVE THE BEST MEASURE to be adopted is to bring capital to the State, and instead of causing revenge and unpleasantness, I am for even-handed justice. I am for allowing the parties who own lands to bring them into the market and sell them upon such terms as will be satisfactory to both sides. I believe a measure of this kind has a double effect: first, it brings capital, what the people want; second, it puts the people to work; it gives homesteads, what we need; it relieves the Government and takes away its responsibility of feeding the people; it inspires every man with a noble manfulness, and by the thought that he is the possessor of something in the State; it adds also to the revenue of the country. By these means men become interested in the country as they never were before. It was said that five and one-seventh acres were not enough to live on. If South Carolina, in its sovereign power, can devise any plan for the purchase of the large plantations in this State now lying idle, divide and sell them out at a reasonable price, it will give so many people work. I will guarantee to find persons to work every five acres. I will also guarantee that after one year's time, the Freedman's Bureau will not have to give any man having one acre of land anything to eat. This country has a genial clime, rich soil, and can be worked to advantage. The man who can not earn a living on five acres, will not do so on twenty-five.

I regret that another position taken by gentlemen in the opposition, is that they do not believe that we will get what we ask for. I believe that the party now in power in the Congress of the United States, will do whatever they can for the welfare of the people of this State and of the South. I believe that the noble men who have maintained the rights of the freedmen before and since their liberation, will continue to do everything possible to forward these great interests. I am exceedingly anxious, if possible, to allay all unpleasant feeling—I would not have any unpleasant feeling among ourselves.

I would not have any unpleasant feelings between the races. If we give each family in the State an opportunity of purchasing a home, I think they will all be better satisfied.

But it is also said that it will disturb all the agricultural operations in the State. I do not believe if the Congress of the United States shall advance one million of dollars to make purchase of lands, the laborers will abandon their engagement and run off. I have more confidence in the people I represent. I believe all who have made contracts will fulfill those contracts, and when their contracts have expired, they will go on their own lands, as all freemen ought to go.

Source: *Proceedings of the South Carolina Constitutional Convention of 1868* (Charleston, SC, 1868), 420–21.

DOCUMENT 14.7

Ellen Parton | Testimony on Klan Violence, 1871

In March 1871, white mobs killed some thirty African Americans in Meridian, Mississippi. Later that month, a joint committee of the Mississippi legislature held hearings on the violence, which included the following testimony by Ellen Parton of Mississippi, a former slave and domestic worker. The Klan suspected that Parton's husband was involved in the Union League, a southern affiliate of the Republican Party. Congress also conducted hearings on the vigilante violence against blacks throughout the South.

Ellen Parton, being sworn, states:

I reside in Meridian; have resided here nine years; occupation, washing and ironing and scouring; Wednesday night was the last night they came to my house; by "they" I mean bodies or companies of men; they came on Monday, Tuesday, and Wednesday. On Monday night they said that they came to do us no harm. On Tuesday night they said they came for the arms; I told them there was none, and they said they would take my word for it. On Wednesday night they came and broke open the wardrobe and trunks, and committed rape upon me; there were eight of them in the house; I do not know how many there were outside; they were white men; there was a light in the house; I was living in Marshal Ware's house; there were three lights burning. Mr. Ware has been one of the policemen of this town. He was concealed at the time they came; they took the claw hammer and broke open the pantry where he was lying; he was concealed in the pantry under some plunder, covered up well; I guess he covered himself up. A man said "here is Marshal's hat, where is Marshal?" I told him "I did not know"; they went then into everything in the house, and broke open the wardrobe; I called upon Mr. Mike Slamon, who was one of the crowd, for protection; I said to him "please protect me tonight, you have known me for a long time." This man covered up his head then; he had a hold of me at this time; Mr. Slamon had an oil-cloth and put it before his face, trying to conceal himself, and the man that had hold of me told me not to call Mr. Slamon's name any more. He then took me in the dining room, and told me that I had to do just what he said: I told him I could do nothing of that sort; that was not my way, and he replied "by God, you have got to," and then threw me down. This man had a black eye, where some one had beaten him; he had a black velvet cap on. After he got through with me he came through the house, and said that he was after the Union Leagues; I yielded to him because he had a pistol drawn; when he took me down he hurt me of course; I yielded to him on that account.

Source: *Report of the Joint Select Committee [of Congress] to Inquire into the Condition of Affairs in the Late Insurrectionary States, Mississippi* (Washington, D.C.: Government Printing Office, 1872), 1:38–39.

DOCUMENT 14.8
The Force Act, 1871

As testimony of antiblack violence mounted, Congress passed the Force Act (also known as the Ku Klux Klan Act) in April 1871. A federal response to stop the terror and intimidation of southern black and white Republicans by their opponents, the act provided both civil relief for damages and criminal penalties. It was rooted in the Fourteenth Amendment's guarantees of the rights and privileges of U.S. citizenship. The federal government dispatched troops to enforce the law and prosecuted hundreds of Klan members, often before predominantly black juries, resulting in the breakup of the Klan within a few years.

Be it enacted . . . That any person who, under color of any law, statute, ordinance, regulation, custom, or usage of any State, shall subject, or cause to be subjected, any person within the jurisdiction of the United States to the deprivation of any rights, privileges, or immunities secured by the Constitution of the United States, shall, any such law, statute, ordinance, regulation, custom, or usage of the State to the contrary notwithstanding, be liable to the party injured in any action at law, suit in equity, or other proper proceeding for redress; such proceeding to be prosecuted in the several district or circuit courts of the United States, with and subject to the same rights of appeal, review upon error, and other remedies provided in like cases in such courts, under the provisions of the [Civil Rights Act of 1866], and the other remedial laws of the United States which are in their nature applicable in such cases. . . .

Sec. 3. That in all cases where insurrection, domestic violence, unlawful combinations, or conspiracies in any State shall so obstruct or hinder the execution of the laws thereof, and of the United States, as to deprive any portion or class of the people of such State of any of the rights, privileges, or immunities, or protection, named in the Constitution and secured by this act, and the constituted authorities of such State shall either be unable to protect, or shall, from any cause, fail in or refuse protection of the people in such rights, such facts shall be deemed a denial by such State of the equal protection of the laws to which they are entitled under the Constitution of the United States; and in all such cases, or whenever any such insurrection, violence, unlawful combination, or conspiracy shall oppose or obstruct the laws of the United States or the due execution thereof, or impede or obstruct the due course of justice under the same, it shall be lawful for the President, and it shall be his duty to take such measures, by the employment of the militia or the land and naval forces of the United States, or of either, or by other means, as he may deem necessary for the suppression of such insurrection, domestic violence, or combinations. . . .

Sec. 6. That any person or persons, having knowledge that any of the wrongs conspired to be done and mentioned in the second section of this act are about to be committed, and having power to prevent or aid in preventing the same, shall neglect or refuse to do so, and such wrongful act shall be committed, such person or persons shall be liable to the person injured, or his legal representatives, for all damages caused by any such wrongful act which such first-named person or persons by reasonable diligence could have prevented.

Source: George P. Sanger, ed., *Statutes at Large and Proclamations of the United States of America from March 1871 to March 1873* (Boston: Little, Brown, 1873), 13–15.

DOCUMENT 14.9

Thomas Nast | Colored Rule in a Reconstructed (?) State, 1874

COLORED RULE IN A RECONSTRUCTED (?) STATE.—[See Page 242.]

(THE MEMBERS CALL EACH OTHER THIEVES, LIARS, RASCALS, AND COWARDS.)

COLUMBIA. "You are Aping the lowest Whites. If you disgrace your Race in this way you had better take Back Seats."

Thomas Nast began drawing for the popular magazine *Harper's Weekly* in 1859. Nast initially used his illustrations to rouse northern public sentiment for the plight of blacks in the South after the Civil War. By 1874, however, many Northerners had become disillusioned with federal efforts to enforce Reconstruction. Like them, Nash accepted the white southern point of view that "Black Reconstruction" was a recipe for corruption and immorality. This cartoon imagines a raucous scene in the South Carolina legislature, where black legislators have taken over the floor and call each other "thieves, liars, rascals, and cowards." Note the figure of Columbia (at the top right), who represents the nation, chastising black lawmakers with a switch. Nast highlights Columbia's message in the caption: "You are Aping the lowest Whites. If you disgrace your Race in this way you had better take Back Seats."

DOCUMENT 14.10

What the Centennial Ought to Accomplish, 1875

The following editorial appeared in the northern periodical *Scribner's Journal*. A year before the celebration of the nation's centennial, Northerners as well as Southerners were calling for national unity and reconciliation, and thus a true end to Reconstruction. Rather than dwelling on the "Lost Cause," the magazine's editors remind southern readers of the glories of the old nation as celebrated by former Confederate president Jefferson Davis in recalling the national unity during the victorious Mexican-American War.

WE ARE TO HAVE grand doings next year. There is to be an Exposition. There are to be speeches, and songs, and processions, and elaborate ceremonies and general rejoicings. Cannon are to be fired, flags are to be floated, and the eagle is expected to scream while he dips the tip of either pinion in the Atlantic and the Pacific, and sprinkles the land with a new baptism of freedom. . . .

. . . Before we begin our celebration of this event, would it not be well for us to inquire whether we have a nation? In a large number of the States of this country there exists not only a belief that the United States do not constitute a nation, but a theory of State rights which forbids that they ever shall become one. We hear about the perturbed condition of the Southern mind. We hear it said that multitudes there are just as disloyal as they were during the civil war. This, we believe, we are justified in denying. . . . They are not actively in rebellion, and they do not propose to be. They do not hope for the re-establishment of slavery. They fought bravely and well to establish their theory, but the majority was against them; and if the result of the war emphasized any fact, it was that *en masse* the people of the United States constitute a nation—indivisible in constituents, in interest, in destiny. The result of the war was without significance, if it did not mean that the United States constitute a nation which cannot be divided; which will not permit itself to be divided; which is integral, indissoluble, indestructible. . . . The great point with them is to recognize the fact that, for richer or poorer, in sickness and health, until death do us part,

these United States constitute a nation; that we are to live, grow, prosper, and suffer together, united by bands that cannot be sundered.

Unless this fact is fully recognized throughout the Union, our Centennial will be but a hollow mockery. If we are to celebrate anything worth celebrating, it is the birth of a nation. If we are to celebrate anything worth celebrating, it should be by the whole heart and united voice of the nation. If we can make the Centennial an occasion for emphasizing the great lesson of the war, and universally assenting to the results of the war, it will, indeed, be worth all the money expended upon and the time devoted to it. . . .

A few weeks ago, Mr. Jefferson Davis, the ex-President of the Confederacy, was reported to have exhorted an audience to which he was speaking to be as loyal to the old flag of the Union now as they were during the Mexican War. If the South could know what music there was in these words to Northern ears—how grateful we were to their old chief for them—it would appreciate the strength of our longing for a complete restoration of the national feeling that existed when Northern and Southern blood mingled in common sacrifice on Mexican soil. This national feeling, this national pride, this brotherly sympathy *must be restored*; and accursed be any Northern or Southern man, whether in power or out of power, whether politician, theorizer, carpet-bagger, president-maker, or plunderer, who puts obstacles in the way of such a restoration. Men of the South, we want you. Men of the South, we long for the restoration of your peace and your prosperity. We would see your cities thriving, your homes happy, your plantations teeming with plenteous harvests, your schools overflowing, your wisest statesmen leading you, and all causes and all memories of discord wiped out forever. You do not believe this? Then you do not know the heart of the North. Have you cause of complaint against the politicians? Alas! so have we. Help us, as loving and loyal American citizens, to make our politicians better. Only remember and believe that there is nothing that the North wants so much to-day, as your recognition of the fact that the old relations between you and us are forever restored—that your hope, your pride, your policy, and your destiny are one with ours. Our children will grow up to despise our childishness, if we cannot do away with our personal hates so far, that in the cause of an established nationality we may join hands under the old flag.

To bring about this reunion of the two sections of the country in the old fellowship, should be the leading object of the approaching Centennial. A celebration of the national birth, begun, carried on, and finished by a section, would be a mockery and a shame. The nations of the world might well point at it the finger of scorn. The money expended upon it were better sunk in the sea, or devoted to repairing the waste places of the war. Men of the South, it is for you to say whether your magnanimity is equal to your valor—whether you are as reasonable as you are brave, and whether, like your old chief, you accept that definite and irreversible result of the war which makes you and yours forever members of the great American nation with us. Let us see to it, North and South, that the Centennial heals all the old wounds, reconciles all the old differences, and furnishes the occasion for such a reunion of the great American nationality, as shall make our celebration an expression of fraternal good-will among all sections and all States, and a corner-stone over which shall be reared a new temple to national freedom, concord, peace, and prosperity.

Source: "What the Centennial Ought to Accomplish," *Scribner's Monthly*, August 1875, 509–10.

Interpret the Evidence

1. How did the black codes (Document 14.5) attempt to reimpose bondage on former slaves?
2. Why did African Americans consider property holding a fundamental right (see Document 14.6)?
3. Under what circumstances did the Force Act (Document 14.8) authorize federal prosecutions?
4. Contrast the image of South Carolina's black politicians as presented in Richard Cain's speech (Document 14.6) and Thomas Nast's cartoon (Document 14.9).
5. Despite Ku Klux Klan intimidation and the fear it produced in African Americans, what does the testimony of Ellen Parton (Document 14.7) reveal about black attempts to resist it?
6. What sources of unity existed between the North and the South that would bring Reconstruction to an end (see Document 14.10)?

Put It in Context

- How much did Reconstruction transform the South and the nation? What were its limitations?

background photo: page 451, Library of Congress

Private Collection/Peter Newark American Pictures/The Bridgeman Art Library

Library of Congress

Railroad construction crew, 1886.

Lone Wolf and his wife Etla, Kiowa Indians, c. 1860.

15
Frontier Encounters
1865–1896

Library of Congress

Nebraska family in front of sod house with cow on the hillside that forms the roof, 1887.

As an adult, Phoebe Ann Moses embodied the excitement and adventure of the mythical American West. Her childhood, however, was one of poverty and hardship. Born in 1860, Phoebe Ann grew up east of the Mississippi, seventy miles north of Cincinnati, Ohio. One of seven surviving children, she was sent to an orphanage at the age of nine, after her father died and her mother could not care for all her children. After working for a farm family, she ran away at the age of twelve and found a new home with a recently remarried widow. Over the next four years, Phoebe Ann learned to ride and hunt and became an expert shot with a rifle. At fifteen, she entered a shooting contest and defeated a professional marksman, Frank Butler. The competition sparked a romance, and the two married in 1876. Phoebe Ann changed her professional name to "Annie Oakley," and she and Butler went on tour throughout the Midwest in an act that featured precision shooting.

In 1884 Oakley and Butler met William F. "Buffalo Bill" Cody in New Orleans. Cody had been a buffalo hunter on the Great Plains and an army scout during the Indian wars of the 1870s. In 1883, as the western frontier began to recede and the U.S. government relocated Native Americans who lived there, Cody attempted to recapture and reinvent the frontier experience by staging "Wild West" shows. A year later, he hired Oakley, with Butler serving as her manager. For the next fifteen years, the diminutive Oakley was the star of the show. Wearing a fringed skirt, an embroidered blouse, and a broad felt hat emblazoned with a star, she stood atop her horse and shot the lights out of a revolving wheel of lit candles and took dead aim at other targets tossed in the air. Oakley toured Europe and fascinated heads of state and audiences alike with her version of "western authenticity." Fans at home and overseas displayed great nostalgia for a fast-diminishing era. When the census of 1890 reported that no open land was left to settle and thus no western frontier was left to conquer, Oakley's popularity soared. She continued performing in Wild West shows until her death in 1926.

While Annie Oakley portrayed the Wild West, Geronimo had lived it. Born to a Chiricahua Apache family in what was then northern Mexico (present-day Arizona and New Mexico), Geronimo led Apaches in a constant struggle against Spain, Mexico, and the United States. Driven to the hills of Arizona and New Mexico by Spanish conquistadors centuries before Geronimo was born, Apaches raided settlements to support themselves. In 1851 a band of Mexicans raided an Apache camp, murdering Geronimo's mother, wife, and three children. After fighting Mexicans, Geronimo clashed with U.S. troops and evaded capture until 1877, when an Indian agent arrested him in New Mexico. Sent to a reservation, Geronimo escaped and for eight years engaged in daring raids against his foes. In 1886 two Chiricahua scouts recruited by General Nelson Miles led the military to Geronimo. Against an army of five thousand soldiers, the Apache warrior, with a band of eighteen fighters and some women and children, finally surrendered and was eventually relocated by the U.S. government to Fort Sill, Oklahoma.

The once-elusive warrior decided to take advantage of his legendary reputation. With Buffalo Bill cashing in on America's fascination with the mythic West and "savage" Indians, Geronimo, like Annie Oakley, exploited this appeal. He sold photos of himself and pieces of his clothing; he appeared at the 1904 World's Fair in St. Louis, selling bows and arrows and autographs; and in 1905 he rode in President Theodore Roosevelt's inaugural parade as an example of a "tamed" Indian. Although he converted to Christianity, Geronimo, ever the rebel, was later expelled from his church for gambling. Crass commercialism and religious conversion aside, Geronimo never gave up the idea of returning to his birthplace. As long as the U.S. government prohibited him from going back to his ancestral lands in the Southwest, he considered himself a "prisoner of war." And so he remained until his death in 1909. •

photos: Beinecke Rare Book and Manuscript Library, Yale University; Library of Congres

AS PROFOUNDLY DIFFERENT as Annie Oakley's and Geronimo's individual histories were, they both contributed to the creation of a shared story, the myth of the American West. The West has great fascination in American culture. Stories about the frontier have romanticized both cowboys and Indians. These stories have also glorified individualism, self-help, and American ingenuity and minimized cooperation, organization, and the role of foreign influence in developing the West. As the American histories of Annie Oakley and Geronimo make clear, reality presents a more complicated picture of a diverse region initially inhabited by native peoples who were pushed aside by the arrival of white settlers and immigrants. In the areas known as the Great Plains and the far West, women took on new roles, and new cities emerged to accommodate the influx of miners, ranchers, and farmers.

Opening the West

The lands west of the Mississippi were not hospitable to farmers and other adventurers lured by the appeal of cheap land and a fresh start. These pioneers faced many challenges with rugged determination; however, they could not have settled the West on their own. Federal policy and foreign investment played a large role in encouraging and financing the development of the West. Railroads were essential in transforming the region (Map 15.1).

The Great Plains

In the mid-nineteenth century, the western frontier lay in the **Great Plains**. This region spreads through present-day North and South Dakota, Nebraska, Kansas, Oklahoma, Texas, Montana, Wyoming, Colorado, New Mexico, Idaho, Utah, Arizona, and Nevada. Lying on both sides of the Rocky Mountains, the Great Plains plateau was a semiarid territory with an average yearly rainfall of twenty inches, enough to sustain short grasslands but not many trees. Bison, pronghorn antelope, jack rabbits, and prairie dogs roamed over great distances to nourish themselves on the sparse vegetation that grew in this delicate ecosystem.

Grasshoppers and locusts periodically swarmed into the area. Indian hunters in the very dry central and southern plains—Apache, Arapaho, Cheyenne, Comanche, Kiowa—opened up these lands to human habitation and survived by hunting and cultivating the grasslands.

Prospects for sedentary farmers in this dry region did not appear promising. In 1878 geologist John Wesley Powell issued a report that questioned whether the land beyond the easternmost portion of the Great Plains could support small farming. Lack of rainfall, he argued, would make it difficult or even impossible for homesteaders to support themselves on family farms of 160 acres. Instead, he recommended that for the plains to prove economically sustainable, settlers would have to work much larger stretches of land, around 2,560 acres (4 square miles). This would provide ample room to raise livestock under dry conditions.

Powell's words of caution did little to diminish Americans' conviction, dating back to Thomas Jefferson, that small farmers would populate the territories brought under U.S. jurisdiction and renew democratic values as they ventured forth. Charles Dana Wilber, a booster of settlement in Nebraska, summed up the view of those who saw no barriers to the expansion of small farmers in the plains. Rejecting the idea that either a Divine Creator or nature had determined that these lands should remain a "perpetual desert," Wilber asserted that "in reality

MAP 15.1   The American West, 1860–1900

Railroads played a key role in the expansion and settlement of the American West. The network of railroads running throughout the West opened the way for extensive migration from the East and for the development of a national market. None of this would have been possible without the land grants provided to the railroads by the U.S. government.

there is no desert anywhere except by man's permission or neglect." Along with millions of others, he had great faith in Americans' ability to turn the Great Plains into a place where Jefferson's republican vision could take root and prosper.

Federal Policy and Foreign Investment

Despite the popular association of the West with individual initiative and self-sufficiency, the federal government played a huge role in facilitating the settlement of the West. National lawmakers enacted legislation offering free or cheap land to settlers and to mining, lumber, and railroad companies. The U.S. government also provided subsidies for transporting mail and military supplies, recruited soldiers to subdue the Indians who stood in the way of expansion, and appointed officials to govern the territories.

Along with federal policy, foreign investment helped fuel development of the West. Lacking sufficient funds of its own, the United States turned to Europe to finance the sale of public bonds and private securities. European financial houses held a majority ownership in the United States Mortgage Company and the Equitable Trust Company of New York, both of which bought and sold mortgages. European firms also invested in American mines, with the British leading the way. In 1872 an Englishman wrote that mines in Nevada were "more British than American." The development of the western cattle range—the symbol of the American frontier and the heroic cowboy—was also funded by overseas financiers. At the height of the cattle boom in the 1880s, British firms supplied some $45 million to underwrite ranch operations.

The largest share of money that flowed from Europe to the United States came with the expansion of the railroads, the most important ingredient in opening the West (Figure 15.1). The economist Joseph Schumpeter concluded that it was "primarily English (and other European) capital which took the responsibility for a great part of the $2 billion which are said to have been expended on American railroads from 1867 to 1873."

The **transcontinental railroad** became the gateway to the West. In 1862 the Republican-led Congress appropriated vast areas of land that railroad companies could use to lay their tracks or sell to raise funds for construction. The Central Pacific Company built from west to east, starting in Sacramento, California. The construction project attracted thousands of Chinese railroad workers, boosting the sparse population of the western territory. From the opposite direction, the Union Pacific Company began laying track in Council Bluffs, Iowa, and hired primarily Irish workers. In May 1869, the

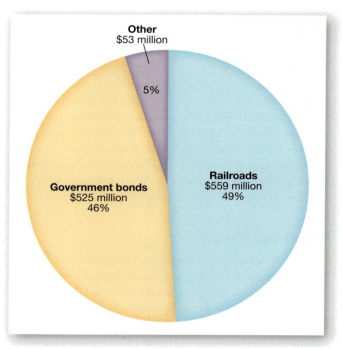

FIGURE 15.1 British Foreign Investment in the United States, 1876

British investment was an important source of funding for westward expansion following the Civil War. Nearly half of all British loans went toward financing railroad construction, which required large capital expenditures. The British also invested heavily in government bonds and to a lesser extent in cattle ranching and mining enterprises.

Source: Data from Mina Wilkins, *The History of Foreign Investment in the United States to 1914* (Cambridge, MA: Harvard University Press, 1989), 164.

Central Pacific and Union Pacific crews met at Promontory Point, Utah, amid great celebration. Workmen from the two companies drove a golden spike to complete the connection. For many Americans recovering from four years of brutal civil war and still embroiled in southern reconstruction (see chapter 14), the completion of the transcontinental railroad renewed their faith in the nation's ingenuity and destiny. A wagon train had once taken six to eight weeks to travel across the West. That trip could now be completed by rail in seven days. The railroad allowed both people and goods to move faster and in greater numbers than before. The West was now open not just to rugged pioneers but to anyone who could afford a railroad ticket.

The building of the railroads fostered corruption. Union Pacific promoters created a fake construction company called the Crédit Mobilier, which they used to funnel government bond and contract money into their own pockets. They also bribed congressmen to avoid investigation into their sordid dealings. Despite these efforts, in 1872 Congress exposed these wrongdoings.

Railroad Construction Crew
Chinese and other immigrant groups were instrumental in the construction of the transcontinental railroad. This Union Pacific construction crew includes a Chinese laborer standing in the center next to African American workers and a white foreman in the front left. The boulders in the rear show the massive rock formations and rugged terrain they had to blast through.   c 1870 (albumen print), Denver Public Library, Western History Collection/Bridgeman Images

REVIEW & RELATE

What role did the federal government play in opening the West to settlement and economic exploitation?

Explain the determination of Americans to settle in land west of the Mississippi River despite the challenges the region presented.

✔ *LEARNINGCurve* bedfordstmartins.com/hewittlawson/LC

Conquest of the Frontier

American pioneers may have thought they were moving into a wilderness, but the West was home to large numbers of American Indians. Before pioneers and entrepreneurs could go west to pursue their economic dreams, the U.S. government would have to remove this unwelcome obstacle to American expansion. Through treaties—most of which Americans broke—and war, white Americans conquered the Indian tribes inhabiting the Great Plains during the nineteenth century. After the native population was largely subdued, those who wanted to reform Indian policy focused on carving up tribal lands and forcing Indians to assimilate into American society.

Indian Civilizations

Long before white settlers appeared, the frontier was already home to diverse peoples. The many native groups who inhabited the West spoke distinct languages, engaged in different economic activities, and competed with one another for power and resources. The descendants of Spanish conquistadors had also lived in the Southwest and California since the late sixteenth century, pushing the boundaries of the Spanish empire northward from Mexico. Indeed, Spaniards established the city of Santa Fe as the territorial capital of New Mexico years before the English landed at Jamestown, Virginia, in 1607. The United States then acquired the New Mexican and California territories as spoils of the Mexican-American War in 1848.

By the end of the Civil War, around 350,000 Indians were living west of the Mississippi. They constituted the surviving remnants of the 1 million people who had occupied the land for thousands of years before Europeans set foot in America. Nez Percé, Ute, and Shoshone Indians lived in the Northwest and the Rocky Mountain region; Lakota, Cheyenne, Blackfoot, Crow, and Arapaho tribes occupied the vast expanse of the central and northern plains; and Apaches, Comanches, Kiowas, Navajos, and Pueblos made up the bulk of the population in the Southwest. Some of the tribes, such as the Cherokee, Creek, and Shawnee, had been forcibly removed from the East during Andrew

Jackson's presidency in the 1830s. The tribes each adapted in unique ways to the geography and climate of their home territories, spoke their own language, and had their own history and traditions. Some were hunters, others farmers; some nomadic, others sedentary. In New Mexico, the Apaches, including Geronimo, were expert horsemen and fierce warriors, while the Pueblo Indians built homes out of adobe and developed a flourishing system of agriculture. The lives of all Indian peoples were affected by the arrival of Europeans, but the consequences of cross-cultural contact varied considerably depending on the history and circumstances of each tribe (Map 15.2).

Given the rich assortment of Indian tribes, it is difficult to generalize about Indian culture and society. Pueblo Indians cultivated the land through methods of irrigation that foreshadowed modern practices. The Pawnees

periodically set fire to the land to improve game hunting and the growth of vegetation. Indians on the southern plains gradually became enmeshed in the market economy for bison robes, which they sold to American traders. Indians were not pacifists, and they engaged in warfare with their enemies in disputes over hunting grounds, horses, and honor. However, the introduction of guns by European and American traders had transformed Indian warfare into a much more deadly affair than had existed previously. And by the mid-nineteenth century, some tribes had become so deeply engaged in the commercial fur trade with whites that they had depleted their own hunting grounds.

Native Americans had their own approach toward nature and the land they inhabited. Most tribes did not accept private ownership of land, as white pioneers did. Indians recognized the concept of private property in

MAP 15.2   The Indian Frontier, 1870

Western migration posed a threat to the dozens of Indian tribes and the immense herds of bison in the region. The tribes had signed treaties with the U.S. government recognizing the right to live on their lands. The presence of U.S. forts did not protect the Indians from settlers who invaded their territories.

ownership of their horses, weapons, tools, and shelters, but they viewed the land as the common domain of their tribe, for use by all members. "The White man knows how to make everything," the Hunkpapa Lakota chieftain Sitting Bull remarked, "but he does not know how to distribute it." This communitarian outlook also reflected native attitudes toward the environment. They considered human beings not as superior to the rest of nature's creations, but rather as part of an interconnected world of animals, plants, and natural elements. Chief Joseph, leader of the Nez Percé Indians, explained to whites who tried to encroach on his land: "The country was made without lines of demarcation, and it's no man's business to divide it. . . . I see whites all over the country gaining wealth, and see their desire to give us lands that are worthless. . . . The earth and myself are of one mind. The measure of the land and the measure of our bodies are the same." According to this view, all plants and animals were part of a larger spirit world, which flowed from the power of the sun, the sky, and the earth.

The bison played a central role in Indian religion and society. By the mid-nineteenth century, approximately thirty million bison (commonly known as buffalo) grazed on the Great Plains. Before acquiring guns, Indians used a variety of means to hunt their prey, including bows and arrows and spears. Some rode their horses to chase bison and stampede them over cliffs. The meat from the buffalo provided food; its hide provided material to construct tepees and make blankets and clothes; bones were crafted into tools, knives, and weapons; even bison dung served a purpose—after it dried and hardened, "buffalo chips" became an excellent source of fuel. It is therefore not surprising that the Plains Indians dressed up in colorful outfits, painted their bodies, and danced to the almighty power of the buffalo and the spiritual presence within it.

Indian hunting societies contained gender distinctions, primarily around the use of horses to pursue bison. The task of riding horses to hunt bison became men's work; women waited for the hunters to return and then prepared the buffalo hides. Nevertheless, women refused to think of their role as passive: They saw themselves as sharing in the work of providing food, shelter, and clothing for the members of their tribe. Similarly, the religious belief that the spiritual world touched every aspect of the material world gave women an opportunity to experience this transcendent power without the mediation of male leaders, including the revered medicine men.

Changing Federal Policy toward Indians

The U.S. government started out by treating western Indians as autonomous nations, thereby recognizing their stewardship over the land they occupied. In 1851 the **Treaty of Fort Laramie** confined tribes on the northern plains to designated areas in an attempt to keep white

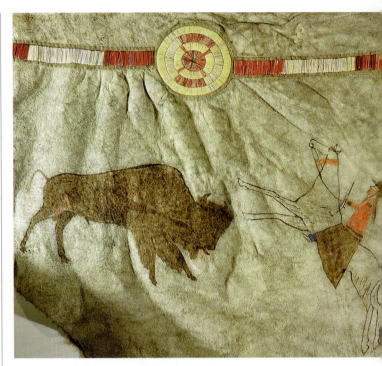

Buffalo Hunting

This pictograph from around 1875 depicts a Shoshone man on a buffalo hunt, affirming the personal connection between Indians and the buffalo. The successful hunter shows his skill as a horseman in this drawing made on his buffalo skin robe. The garment also includes a brightly ornamented quillwork strip at the top. © Werner Forman/TopFoto/The Image Works

settlers from encroaching on their land. A treaty two years later applied these terms to tribes on the southern plains. Indians kept their part of the agreement, but white miners racing to strike it rich did not. They roamed through Indian hunting grounds in search of ore and faced little government enforcement of the existing treaties. In fact, the U.S. military made matters considerably worse. On November 29, 1864, a peaceful band of 700 Cheyennes and Arapahos under the leadership of Chief Black Kettle gathered at Sand Creek, Colorado, supposedly under guarantees of U.S. protection. Instead, Colonel John M. Chivington and his troops launched an attack, despite a white flag of surrender hoisted by the Indians, and brutally scalped and killed some 270 Indians, mainly women and children. A congressional investigation later determined that the victims "were mutilated in the most horrible manner." Although there was considerable public outcry over the incident, as evidenced by the congressional investigation, the government did nothing to increase enforcement of its treaty obligations. In almost all disputes between white settlers and Indians, the government sided with the whites, regardless of the Indians' legal rights.

The duplicity of the U.S. government was not without consequences. The Sand Creek massacre unleashed Indian wars throughout the central plains, where the Lakota Sioux led the resistance from 1865 to 1868. In 1866 they killed eighty soldiers under the command of Captain William J. Fetterman in Wyoming. After two years of fierce fighting, both sides signed a second Treaty of Fort Laramie, which gave northern tribes control over the "Great Reservation" set aside in parts of present-day Montana, Wyoming, North Dakota, and South Dakota. Another treaty placed the southern tribes in a reservation carved out of western Oklahoma.

One of the tribes that wound up in Oklahoma was the Nez Percé. Originally settled in the corner where Washington, Oregon, and Idaho meet, the tribe was forced to sign a treaty ceding most of its land to the United States and to relocate onto a reservation. In 1877 Chief Joseph led the Nez Percé out of the Pacific Northwest, directing his people in an excruciating but daring march of 1,400 miles over mountains into Montana and Wyoming as federal troops pursued them. Intending to flee to Canada, the Nez Percé were finally intercepted in the mountains of northern Montana, just thirty miles from the border. Exhausted by the incredible journey, they surrendered. Subsequently, the government relocated these northwestern Indians to the southwestern territory of Oklahoma. In 1879 Chief Joseph pleaded with lawmakers in Congress to return his people to their home and urged the U.S. government to live up to the original intent of the treaties. His words carried some weight, and the Nez Percé returned under armed escort to a reservation in Washington.

The treaties did not produce a lasting peace. Though most of the tribes relocated onto reservations, some refused. The Apache chief Victorio explained why he would not resettle his people on a reservation. "We prefer to die in our own land under the tall cool pines," he declared. "We will leave our bones with those of our people. It is better to die fighting than to starve." General William Tecumseh Sherman, commander of the military forces against the Indians, issued orders to "push his measures for the utter destruction and subjugation of all who are outside the reservations in a hostile attitude." He went on to propose that the army "shall prosecute the war with vindictive earnestness against all hostile Indians till they are obliterated or beg for mercy." In November 1868, Lieutenant Colonel George Armstrong Custer took Sherman at his word and assaulted a Cheyenne village, killing more than one hundred Indians. Nearly a decade later, in 1876, the Indians, this time Lakota Sioux, exacted revenge by killing Custer and his troops at the **Battle of the Little Big Horn** in Montana. Yet this proved to be the final victory for the Lakota nation, as the army mounted an extensive and fierce offensive against them that shattered their resistance.

Among the troops that battled the Indians were African Americans. Known as "**buffalo soldiers**," a name given to them by the Indians but whose origin is unclear, they represented a cross section of the postwar black population looking for new opportunities that were now available after their emancipation. One enlisted man recalled: "I got tired of looking mules in the face from sunrise to sunset. Thought there must be a better livin' in this world." Some blacks enlisted to learn how to read and write; others sought to avoid unpleasant situations back home. Cooks, waiters, painters, bakers, teamsters, and farmers signed up for a five-year stint in the army at $13 a month. A few gained more glory than money. In May 1880, Sergeant George Jordan of the Ninth Cavalry led troops under his command to fend off Apache raids in Tularosa, New Mexico, for which he was awarded the Congressional Medal of Honor.

Indian Defeat

By the late 1870s, Indians had largely succumbed to U.S. military supremacy. The tribes, as their many victories demonstrated, contained agile horsemen and skilled warriors, but the U.S. army was backed by the power of an increasingly industrial economy. Telegraph lines and railroads provided logistical advantages in the swift deployment of U.S. troops and the ability of the central command to communicate with field officers. Although Indians had acquired firearms over the years from American traders as well as from defeated enemies on the battlefield, the army boasted an essentially unlimited supply of superior weapons. The diversity of Indians and historic rivalries among tribes also made it difficult for them to unite against their common enemy. The federal government exploited these divisions by hiring Indians to serve as army scouts against their traditional tribal foes.

In addition to federal efforts to subdue Indians, other disasters devastated native peoples in the second half of the nineteenth century. Even before the Civil War, many Indians had died of diseases such as smallpox, cholera, scarlet fever, and measles, for which they lacked the immunity that Europeans and white Americans had acquired. Moreover, Indian policy was fundamentally flawed by cultural misunderstanding. Even the most sensitive white administrators of Indian affairs considered Indians a degraded race, in accordance with the scientific thinking of the time. At most, whites believed that Indians could be lifted to a higher level of civilization, which in practice meant a withering away of their traditional culture and heritage. **See Document Project 15: American Indians and Whites on the Frontier, page 484**.

The wholesale destruction of the bison was the final blow to Indian independence. As railroads pushed their tracks beyond the Mississippi, they cleared bison from their path by sending in professional hunters with high-powered rifles to shoot the animals. Buffalo Bill Cody built his reputation by working as a crack sharpshooter for the Kansas Pacific Railroad. At the same time, buffalo products such as shoes, coats, and hats became fashionable in the East. By the mid-1880s, hunters had killed more than thirteen million bison. As a result of the relentless move of white Americans westward and conspicuous consumption back east, bison herds were almost annihilated.

Faced with decimation of the bison, broken treaties, and their opponents' superior military technology, Native Americans' capacity to wage war collapsed. Indians had little choice but to settle on shrinking reservations that the government established for them. The absence of war, however, did not necessarily bring them security. In the late 1870s, gold discoveries in the Black Hills of North Dakota ignited another furious rush by miners who swooped into the sacred lands supposedly guaranteed to the Lakota people. Rather than honoring its treaties, the U.S. government forced the tribes to relinquish still more land. Government officials continued to encourage western expansion by white settlers despite previous agreements with the Indians. General Custer's Seventh Cavalry was part of the military force trying to push Indians out of this mining region, when it was annihilated at the Little Big Horn in 1876. Elsewhere, Congress opened up a portion of western Oklahoma to white homesteaders in 1889. Although this land had not been assigned to specific tribes relocated in Indian Territory, more than eighty thousand Indians from various tribes lived there. This government-sanctioned land rush only added to the pressure from homesteaders and others to acquire more land at the expense of the Indians. A decade later, Congress officially ended Indian control of Indian Territory.

Reforming Indian Policy

As reservations continued to shrink under expansionist assault and government acquiescence, a movement arose to reform Indian policy. Largely centered in the East where few Indians lived, reformers came to believe that the future welfare of Indians lay not in sovereignty but in assimilation. In 1881 Helen Hunt Jackson published *A Century of Dishonor*, her exposé of the unjust treatment the Indians had received, including broken promises and fraudulent activities by government agents. Roused by this depiction of the Indians' plight, groups such as the Women's National Indian Association joined with ministers and philanthropists to advocate the transformation of native peoples into full-fledged Americans.

From today's vantage point, these well-intentioned reformers could be viewed as contributing to the demise of the Indians by trying to eradicate their cultural heritage. Judged by the standards of their own time, however, they truly wanted to save the Indians from the brutality and corrupt behavior they had endured, and they honestly believed they were acting in the Indians' best interests. The most advanced thinking among anthropologists at the time offered an approach that supported assimilation as the only alternative to extinction. The influential Lewis Morgan, author of *Ancient Society* (1877), concluded that all cultures evolved through three stages: savagery, barbarism, and civilization. Indians occupied the lower rungs, but reformers argued that by adopting white values they could become civilized. In effect, this would mean the cultural extermination of the Indians, but reformers such as Richard Henry Pratt, the founder of the Carlisle Indian School, stressed salvation as their motive. "Do not feed America to the Indian, which is tribalizing and not an Americanizing process," he wrote, "but feed the Indian to America, and America will do the assimilating and annihilate the problem."

Reformers such as Pratt faced opposition from white Americans who doubted that Indian assimilation was possible. For many Americans, secure in their sense of their own superiority, the decline and eventual extinction of the Indian peoples was an inevitable consequence of what they saw as Indians' innate inferiority. For example, a Wyoming newspaper predicted: "The same inscrutable Arbiter that decreed the downfall of Rome has pronounced the doom of extinction upon the red men of America." And it warned: "To pretend to defer this by mawkish sentimentalism . . . is unworthy of the age."

Reformers found their legislative spokesman in Senator Henry Dawes of Massachusetts. As legislative director of the Boston Indian Citizenship Association, Dawes shared Christian reformers' belief that becoming a true American would save both the Indians and the soul of the nation. "Soon I trust," Dawes remarked, "we will wipe out the disgrace of our past treatment and lift the [Indian] up into citizenship and manhood and cooperation with us to the glory of the country." A Republican who had served in Congress since the Civil War, Dawes had the same paternalistic attitude toward Indians as he had toward freed slaves. He believed that if both degraded groups worked hard and practiced thrift and individual initiative in the spirit of Dawes's New England Puritan forebears, they would succeed. The key for Dawes was private ownership of land.

Passed in 1887, the **Dawes Act** ended tribal rule and divided Indian lands into 160-acre parcels. The act allocated one parcel to each family head. The government held the lands in trust for the Indians for twenty-five years; at the end of this period, the Indians would receive American citizenship. In return, the Indians had to abandon their religious and cultural rites and practices, including storytelling and the use of medicine men. Whatever lands remained after this reallocation—and the amount was considerable—would be sold on the open market, and the profits from the sales would be placed in an educational fund for Indians.

Unfortunately, like most of the policies it replaced, the Dawes Act proved detrimental to Native Americans. Indian families received inferior farmlands and inadequate tools to cultivate them, while speculators reaped profits from the sale of the "excess" Indian lands. A little more than a decade after the Dawes Act went into effect, Indians controlled 77 million acres of land, down sharply from the 155 million acres they held in 1881. Additional legislation in 1891 forced Indian parents to send their children to boarding schools or else face arrest. At these educational institutions, Indian children were given "American" names, had their long hair cut, and wore uniforms in place of their native dress. The program for boys provided manual and vocational training and that for girls taught domestic skills, so that they could emulate the gender roles in middle-class American families. However, this schooling offered few skills of use in an economic world undergoing industrial transformation. The students "found themselves in a twilight world," one historian claimed. "They were not equipped or allowed to enter American society as equals, yet they had been subjected to sufficient change as to make returning to the reservations difficult and sometimes traumatic."

Indian Assimilation and Resistance

Not all Indians conformed to the government's attempt at forced acculturation. Some refused to abandon their traditional social practices, and others rejected the white man's version of private property and civilization. Many displayed more complicated approaches to survival in a world that continued to view Indians with prejudice. Geronimo and Sitting Bull participated in pageants and Wild West shows but refused to disavow their heritage. Ohiyesa, a Lakota also known as Charles Eastman, went to boarding school, graduated from Dartmouth College, and earned a medical degree from Boston University. He supported passage of the Dawes Act, believed in the virtues of an American education, and worked for the Bureau of Indian Affairs. At the same time, he spoke out against government corruption and fraud perpetrated against Indians. Reviewing his life in his later years, Eastman/Ohiyesa reflected: "I am an Indian and while I have learned much from civilization . . . I have never lost my Indian sense of right and justice."

Disaster loomed for those who resisted assimilation and held on too tightly to the old ways. In 1888 the prophet Wovoka, a member of the Paiute tribe in western Nevada, had a vision that Indians would one day regain control of the world and that whites would disappear. He believed that the Creator had provided him with a **Ghost Dance** that would make this happen. The dance spread to thousands of Lakota Sioux in the northern plains. Seeing the Ghost Dance as a sign of renewed Indian resistance, the army attempted to put a stop to the revival. On December 29, 1890, the Seventh Cavalry, Custer's old regiment, chased three hundred ghost dancers to Wounded Knee Creek on the Pine Ridge Reservation in present-day South Dakota. In a confrontation with the Lakota leader Big Foot, a gunshot accidentally rang out during a struggle with one of his followers. The cavalry then turned the full force of their weaponry on the Indians. When the hail of bullets ceased, about 250 Native Americans, many of them women and children, lay dead.

The message of the massacre at Wounded Knee was clear for those who raised their voices against Americanization. As Black Elk, a spiritual leader of the Oglala Lakota tribe, asserted: "A people's dream died there. . . . There is no center any longer, and the sacred tree is dead." It may not have been the policy of the U.S. government to exterminate the Indians as a people, but it was certainly U.S. policy to destroy Indian culture and society once and for all.

REVIEW & RELATE

How and why did federal Indian policy change during the nineteenth century?

Describe some of the ways that Indian peoples responded to federal policies. Which response do you think offered their greatest chance for survival?

LEARNINGCurve bedfordstmartins.com/hewittlawson/LC

The Mining Frontier

Among the settlers pouring into Indian Territory in the Rocky Mountains were miners in search of gold and silver. These prospectors envisioned instant riches that would come from a lucky strike. The vast majority found only backbreaking work, danger, and frustration. Miners continued to face hardship and danger as industrial mining operations took over from individual prospectors, despite the efforts of some miners to fight for better wages and working conditions. By 1900 the mining rush had peaked, and many of the boomtowns that had cropped up around the mining industry had emptied out.

The Business of Mining

The discovery of gold in California in 1848 had set this mining frenzy in motion. Over the next thirty years, successive waves of gold and silver strikes in Colorado, Nevada,

Washington, Idaho, Montana, and the Dakotas lured individual prospectors with shovels and wash pans. One of the biggest finds came with the **Comstock Lode** in the Sierra Nevada. All told, miners extracted around $350 million worth of silver from this source. Two of those who came to share in the wealth were Samuel Clemens and his brother Orion. Writing from Carson City, Nevada, Samuel described his new surroundings to his family: "The country is fabulously rich in gold, silver, copper, lead . . . thieves, murderers, desperadoes, ladies . . . lawyers, Christians, Indians, Chinamen, Spaniards, gamblers, sharpers, coyotes . . . poets, preachers, and jackass rabbits." He did not find his fortune in Nevada and soon turned his attention to writing, finally achieving success as the author called Mark Twain.

Like Twain, many of those who flocked to the Comstock Lode and other mining frontiers were men. Nearly half were foreign-born, many of them coming from Mexico or China. Using pans and shovels, prospectors could find only the ore that lay near the surface of the earth and water. Once these initial discoveries were played out, individual prospectors could not afford to buy the equipment needed to dig out the vast deposits of gold and silver buried deep in the earth. As a result, western mining operations became big businesses run by men with the financial resources necessary to purchase industrial mining equipment.

Explore

See Document 15.1 for a description of a gold rush town.

When mining became an industry, prospectors became wageworkers. In Virginia City, Nevada, miners labored for $4 a day, which was a decent wage for the time, but one that barely covered the monthly expenses of life in a mining boomtown. Moreover, the work was extremely dangerous. Mine shafts extended down more than a thousand feet, and working temperatures regularly exceeded 100 degrees Fahrenheit. Noxious fumes, fires, and floods of scalding water flowing through the shafts posed a constant threat. Between 1863 and 1880, at least three hundred miners died on the job, and accidents were a daily occurrence, leaving many men disabled and out of work with no compensation.

Struggling with low pay and dangerous work conditions, western miners sought to organize. In the mid-1860s, unions formed in the Comstock Lode areas of Virginia City and Gold Hill, Nevada. Although these unions had some success, they also provoked a violent backlash from mining companies determined to resist union demands. Companies hired private police forces to help break strikes. Such forces were often assisted by state militias deployed by elected officials with close ties to the companies. For example, in 1892 the governor of Idaho crushed an unruly strike by calling up the National Guard, a confrontation that resulted in the deaths of seven strikers. A year later, mine workers formed one of the most militant labor organizations in the nation, the Western Federation of Miners. Within a decade, it had attracted fifty thousand members. However, union solidarity did not extend to all races and ethnicities. The union was made up of members from Irish, English, Italian, Slavic, and Greek backgrounds but excluded Chinese, Mexican, and Indian workers from its ranks.

Life in the Mining Towns

Men worked the mines, but women flocked to the area as well. In Storey County, Nevada, the heart of the Comstock Lode, the 1875 census showed that women made up about half the population. Most employed women worked long hours as domestics in boardinghouses, hotels, and private homes. Prostitution, which was legal, accounted for the single largest segment of the female workforce. Most prostitutes were between the ages of nineteen and twenty-four, and they entered this occupation because few other well-paying jobs were available to them. The demand for their services remained high among the large population of unmarried men. Yet prostitutes faced constant danger, and many were victims of physical abuse, robbery, and murder.

Boomtowns like Virginia City sported a wild assortment of miners. They sought relief in taverns, brothels, and opium

Prostitution on the Frontier

Prostitution was one of the main sources of employment for women in frontier mining towns. A legal enterprise, it paid better than other work such as domestic service and teaching. In 1875 in the Comstock region of Nevada, 307 women plied their trade in brothels and saloons similar to the saloon shown here.

The Art Archive/Bill Manns/Art Resource, NY

DOCUMENT 15.1

Granville Stuart | Gold Rush Days, 1925

When the gold rush began in the West, Granville Stuart and his brother were among those who flooded into Montana in 1863 and struck it rich. News of their discovery set off a stampede of prospectors seeking their fortune. A second Virginia City sprang up in Montana to house the miners and the assortment of business people who served them. Gold dust, valued at $18 an ounce, became the medium of exchange. Stuart published his journals and reminiscences from his gold rush days sixty-two years later in 1925.

Explore

About the middle of January, 1864, a regular stampede craze struck Virginia City. The weather had been quite cold and work in the mines was temporarily suspended. A large number of idle men were about town and it required no more than one man with an imaginative mind to start half the population off on a wild goose chase. Somebody would say that somebody said, that somebody had found a good thing and without further inquiry a hundred or more men would start out for the reported diggings. . . .

Late in the evening on January 22, a rumor started that a big discovery had been made on Wisconsin creek, a distance of thirty miles from Virginia City. The report said that as much as one hundred dollars to the pan had been found; and

away the people flew all anxious to be first on the ground, where they could "just shovel up gold." Virginia City was almost deserted: men did not stop for horses, blankets, or provisions, the sole aim was to get there first and begin to shovel it out at the rate of one hundred to the pan. Fortunately the distance was not great and the weather was mild. Robert Dempsey had a ranch nearby and the stampeders got a supply of beef from him to last them back to town. It is needless to say that they found no diggings and all returned to Virginia [City] in a few days.

Source: Granville Stuart, *Forty Years on the Frontier as Seen in the Journals and Reminiscences of Granville Stuart, Gold-Miner, Trader, Merchant, Rancher, and Politician*, ed. Paul C. Phillips (Cleveland: Arthur H. Clark, 1925), 1:270–71.

Interpret the Evidence
- How did the expectations of newly arrived prospectors differ from reality?
- How would you characterize Stuart's attitude toward the scenes he describes?

Put It in Context

As western towns grew more crowded and the mining process became more complex, who profited from the frenzied atmosphere of mining regions?

dens. In Butte, Montana, miners frequented bars with such colorful names as "Bucket of Blood," "The Cesspool," and "Graveyard." They boarded in houses run by characters nicknamed "Mag the Rag," "Take-Five Annie," "Ellen the Elephant," and "The Racehorse." A folk tune described Butte's annual gala event, the "Hopheads' [drug addicts'] Ball":

All the junkies were invited
Yes every gink [skinny man] and muff [prostitute]
Not a single one was slighted
If they were on the stuff [opium].

Invitations were presented
To every hustler and her man.
They even sent up invites
To the hopheads in the can [jail].

As early as the 1880s, gold and silver discoveries had played out in the Comstock Lode. Boomtowns, which had sprung up almost overnight, now became ghost towns as gold and silver deposits dwindled. Even more substantial places like Virginia City, Nevada, experienced a severe decline as the veins of ore ran out. One revealing sign of the city's plummeting fortunes was the drop in the number of prostitutes, which declined by more than half by 1880. The mining frontier then shifted from gold and silver to copper, lead, and zinc, centered in Montana and Idaho. As with the early prospectors in California and Nevada, these miners eventually became wageworkers for giant consolidated mining companies. By the end of the nineteenth century, the Amalgamated Copper Company and the American Smelting and Refining Company dominated the industry.

Mining towns that survived, like Butte, became only slightly less rowdy places, but they did settle into more complex patterns of urban living. Though the population remained predominantly young and male, the young men were increasingly likely to get married and raise families. Residents lived in neighborhoods divided by class and ethnicity. For example, in Butte the west side of town became home to the middle and upper classes. Mine workers lived on the east side in homes subdivided into apartments and in boardinghouses. "The houses were almost skin to skin," one resident described the area, "and boy, there were kids all over in the neighborhood." The Irish lived in one section; Finns, Swedes, Serbs, Croatians, and Slovenes in other sections. Each group formed its own social, fraternal, and religious organizations to relieve the harsh conditions of overcrowding, poor sanitation, and discrimination. Residents of the east side relied on one another for support and frowned on those who deviated from their code of solidarity. "They didn't try to outdo the other one," one neighborhood woman remarked. "If you did, you got into trouble. . . . If they thought you were a little richer than they were, they wouldn't associate with you." Although western mining towns retained distinctive qualities, in their social and ethnic divisions they came to resemble older cities east of the Mississippi River.

REVIEW & RELATE

- How and why did the nature of mining in the West change during the second half of the nineteenth century?
- How did miners and residents of mining towns reshape the frontier landscape?

✓ *LEARNINGCurve* bedfordstmartins.com/hewittlawson/LC

Ranching and Farming Frontiers

Ranchers and farmers heading west also faced harsh realities. Cowboys worked long hours in tough but boring conditions on the open range. Farmers endured great hardships in trying to raise crops in an often inhospitable climate. Women played a critical role as pioneers, often setting out to acquire their own land or helping to run the family farm. Falling crop prices, however, led to soaring debt and forced many farmers into bankruptcy and off their land. Despite difficult physical and economic conditions, many of these women and men showed grit and determination not only in surviving but in improving their lives as well.

The Life of the Cowboy

There is no greater symbol of the frontier West than the cowboy. As portrayed in novels and film, the cowboy hero was the essence of manhood, an independent figure who fought for justice and defended the honor and virtue of women. Never the aggressor, he fought to protect law-abiding residents of frontier communities. Having helped tame some wild western town, the cowboy rode off into the sunset in search of new frontiers to challenge him.

This romantic image excited generations of American readers and later movie and television audiences. In reality, cowboys' lives were much more mundane. Cowpunchers worked for paltry monthly wages, put in long days herding cattle, and spent part of the night guarding them on the open range. Their major task was to make the 1,500-mile **Long Drive** along the Chisholm Trail. Beginning in the late 1860s, cowboys moved cattle from ranches in Texas through Oklahoma to rail depots in Kansas towns such as Abilene and Dodge City; from there, cattle were shipped by train eastward to slaughterhouses in Chicago. Life along the trail was monotonous, and riders had to contend with bad weather, dangerous work, and disease.

Numbering around forty thousand and averaging twenty-four years of age, the cowboys who rode through the Great Plains from Texas to Kansas came from diverse backgrounds. The majority, about 66 percent, were white, predominantly southerners who had fought for the South during the Civil War. Most of the rest were divided evenly between Mexicans, who had first tended cattle during Spanish rule in the Southwest, and African Americans, some of whom were former slaves and others Union veterans of the Civil War.

Explore

See Documents 15.2 and 15.3 for two depictions of cowboy life.

Besides experiencing rugged life on the range, black and Mexican cowboys faced racial discrimination. Jim Perry, an African American who rode for the three-million-acre XIT

Cowboy Myths and Realities: Two Views

William F. Cody, known as "Buffalo Bill," had been a real-life bison hunter in the American West and an army scout in the Indian wars of the 1860s and 1870s. Drawing on his authentic adventures and his heroism, Cody helped romanticize the figures that populated the American frontier, especially the cowboys, through his Wild West shows, a poster from which is shown here. The diary entries of George C. Duffield present a more mundane description of cowboy life. Duffield drove cattle on the open range in 1866 from Texas, where they were bred, to Iowa, where they went to market.

Explore

15.2
Buffalo Bill's Wild West Show, 1893

Explore

15.3 **George C. Duffield |**
Diary of a Real Cowboy, 1866

12th

Hard Rain & Wind. Big stampede & here we are among the Indians with 150 head of Cattle gone. Hunted all day & the Rain pouring down with but poor success. Dark days are these to me. Nothing but Bread & Coffee. Hands all Growling & Swearing—everything wet & cold. Beeves [steers] gone. Rode all day & gathered all but 35 mixed with 8 other Herds. Last Night 5000 Beeves stampeded at this place & a general mix up was the result.

13th

finished separating our Cattle & Moved up 4 miles. Very warm day—

14th

Last night there was a terrible storm. Rain poured in torrents *all* night & up to 12 AM today. Our Beeves left us in the night but for *once* on the whole trip we found them *all* together near camp at day break. *All* the other droves as far as I can hear are scattered to the four winds. Our Other Herd was all gone. We are now 25 Miles from Ark River & it is Very High. We are water bound by two creeks & but Beef & Flour to eat, am not Homesick but Heart sick. . . .

16th

Last night was a dark Gloomey night but we made it all right. Today it is raining & we have crossed Honey creek & am informed that there is another creek 6 miles ahead swimming. Twelve o clock today it rained one Hour so hard that a creek close by rose 20 ft in the afternoon. All wet.

Source: George C. Duffield, "Driving Cattle from Texas to Iowa, 1866," *Annals of Iowa* 14, no. 4 (1924): 253–54.

Interpret the Evidence

- What does the placement of Cody's portrait in the poster suggest about the role of white men in the West?
- How does Duffield's experience of the West differ from that conveyed in the poster?

Put It in Context

Why do you think Americans remember Buffalo Bill's version of the West rather than Duffield's?

Ranch in Texas for more than twenty years, complained: "If it weren't for my damned old black face I'd have been boss of one of these divisions long ago." Mexican *vaqueros*, or cowboys, earned one-third to one-half the wages of whites, whereas blacks were usually paid on a par with whites. Because the cattle kingdoms first flourished during Reconstruction, racial discrimination and segregation carried over into the Southwest. On one drive along the route to Kansas, a white boss insisted that a black cowboy eat and sleep separately from whites and shot at him when he refused to heed this order. Another white trail driver admitted that blacks "were usually called on to do the hardest work around the outfit." Nevertheless, the close proximity in which cowboys worked and the need for cooperation to overcome the pitfalls of the long drive made it difficult to enforce rigid racial divisions on the open range.

Large ranchers benefited the most from the cowboys' grueling work. Spaniards had originally imported cattle into the Southwest, and by the late nineteenth century some 5 million Texas longhorn steers grazed in the area. Cattle that could be purchased in Texas for $3 to $7 fetched a price of $30 to $40 in Kansas. The extension of railroads across the West opened up a quickly growing market for beef in the East. The development of refrigerated railroad cars guaranteed that slaughtered meat could reach eastern consumers without spoiling. With money to be made, the cattle industry rose to meet the demand. Fewer than 40 ranchers owned more than 20 million acres of land. One ranch in Texas spanned 200 miles and stocked 150,000 steers annually. Easterners and Europeans joined the boom and invested money in giant ranches. By the mid-1880s, approximately 7.5 million head of cattle roamed the western ranges, and large cattle ranchers became rich. Cattle ranching had become fully integrated into the national commercial economy.

Then the bubble burst. Ranchers who were already raising more cattle than the market could handle increasingly faced competition from cattle producers in Canada and Argentina. Prices spiraled downward. Another source of competition came from homesteaders who moved into the plains and fenced in their farms with barbed wire, thereby reducing the size of the open range. Yet the greatest disaster occurred from 1885 to 1887. Two frigid winters, together with a torrid summer drought, destroyed 90 percent of the cattle on the northern plains of the Dakotas, Montana, Colorado, and Wyoming. Under these conditions, outside capital to support ranching diminished, and many of the great cattle barons went into bankruptcy. This economic collapse consolidated the remaining cattle industry into even fewer hands. Some of those forced out of business turned to raising sheep, which require less water and grass than cattle to survive. The cowboy, never more than a hired hand, became a laborer for large corporations.

Farmers Head West

The federal government played a major role in opening up the Great Plains to the farmers who eventually clashed with cattlemen. The Republican Party of Abraham Lincoln had opposed the expansion of slavery in order to promote the virtues of free soil and free labor for white men and their families. During the Civil War, preoccupation with battle-field losses did not stop the Republican-controlled Congress from passing the **Homestead Act**. As an incentive for western migration, the act established procedures for distributing 160-acre lots to western settlers, on condition that they develop and farm their land. What most would-be settlers did not know, however, was that lots of 160 acres were not suitable to conditions on the Great Plains. As geologist John Wesley Powell would demonstrate, the intensive techniques needed to farm 160-acre plots simply would not work in the harsh, dry climate of the Great Plains.

Reality did not deter pioneers and adventurers. In fact, weather conditions in the region temporarily fooled them. The decade after 1878 witnessed an exceptional amount of rainfall west of the Mississippi. Though not precisely predictable, this cycle of abundance and drought had been going on for millennia. One settler, convinced that Providence was smiling on Americans, remarked about the sudden burst of rain: "The Lord knowed we needed more land an' He's gone and changed the climate." In addition, innovation and technology bolstered dreams of success. Farmers planted heartier strains of wheat imported from Russia that survived the fluctuations of dry and wet and hot and cold weather. Machines produced by industrial laborers in northern factories to the east allowed farmers to plow tough land and harvest its yield. Steel-tipped plows, threshers, combines, and harvesters expanded production greatly, and windmills and pumping equipment provided sources of power and access to scarce water.

The people who accepted the challenge of carving out a new life were a diverse lot. The Great Plains attracted a large number of immigrants from Europe, some two million by 1900. Minnesota and the Dakotas welcomed communities of settlers from Sweden and Norway. Nebraska housed a considerable population of Germans, Swedes, Danes, and Czechs. About one-third of the people who migrated to the northern plains came directly from a foreign country. Many of the rest, both native-born and foreign-born, had lived in towns and villages along the Mississippi River before they decided to seek new opportunities farther west.

Railroads and land companies lured settlers to the plains with tales of the fabulous possibilities that awaited their arrival. The federal government had given railroads generous grants of public land on which to build their tracks as well as parcels surrounding the tracks that they could sell off to raise revenue for construction. Western railroads advertised in both the United States and Europe, proclaiming that migrants to the plains would find "the garden spot of the world." The land "will grow anything that any other country will grow, and with less work," the Rock Island Railroad announced, "because it rains here more than any other place, and at just the right time."

Having lured prospective settlers with exaggerated claims, railroads offered bargain rates to transport them to their new homes. Families and friends often journeyed together and rented an entire car on the train, known as "the immigrant car," in which they loaded their possessions, supplies, and even livestock. Often migrants came to the end of the rail line before reaching their destination. They completed the trip by wagon or stagecoach.

Commercial advertising alone did not account for the desire to journey westward. Settlers who had made the trip successfully wrote to relatives and neighbors back east and in the old country about the chance to start fresh. Linda Slaughter, the wife of an army doctor in the Dakotas, gushed: "The farms which have been opened in the vicinity of Bismarck have proven highly productive, the soil being kept moist by frequent rains. Vegetables of all kinds are grown with but little trouble." Descriptions of abundance, combined with a spirit of adventure, inspired Lucy Goldthorpe to claim a homestead near Epping in the Dakota Territory. "Even if you hadn't inherited a bit of restlessness and a pioneering spirit from your ancestors," she asserted, "it would have been difficult to ward off the excitement of the boom which, like the atmosphere, involved every conversation."

Those who took the chance shared a faith in the future and a willingness to work hard and endure misfortune. They found their optimism and spirits sorely tested. Despite the company of family members and friends, settlers faced a lonely existence on the vast expanse of the plains. Homesteads were spread out, and a feeling of isolation became a routine part of daily life.

With few trees around, early settlers constructed sod houses. These structures let in little light but a good deal of moisture, keeping them gloomy and damp. A Nebraskan who lived in this type of house jokingly remarked: "There was running water in our sod house. It ran through the

Women Homesteaders in Nebraska

The Chrisman sisters—Lizzie, Lutie, Jennie Ruth, and Hattie—are shown outside their sod house in 1886. They are among the thousands of homesteaders who moved west in the late nineteenth century and built homes from the only natural resource the Great Plains had in abundance: sod.   AP Photo roof." Bugs, insects, and rodents, like the rain, often found their way inside to make living in such shelters even more uncomfortable.

If these dwellings were bleak, the climate posed even greater challenges. The plains did experience an unusual amount of rainfall in the late 1870s and early 1880s, but severe drought quickly followed. A plague of grasshoppers ravaged the northern plains in the late 1870s, destroying fruit trees and plants. Intense heat in the summer alternated with frigid temperatures in the winter. The Norwegian American writer O. E. Rolvaag, in *Giants in the Earth* (1927), his epic novel about Norwegian settlement in the Great Plains, described the extreme hardships that accompanied the fierce weather: "Blizzards from out of the northwest raged, swooped down and stirred up a greyish-white fury, impenetrable to human eyes. As soon as these monsters tired, storms from the northeast were sure to come, bringing more snow."

Women Homesteaders

The women of the family were responsible for making these houses more bearable. Mothers and daughters were in charge of household duties, cooking the meals, canning fruits and vegetables, and washing and ironing clothing. Despite the drudgery of this work, women contributed significantly to the economic well-being of the family by occasionally taking in boarders and selling milk, butter, and eggs.

In addition, a surprisingly large number of single women staked out homestead claims by themselves. Some were young, unmarried women seeking, like their male counterparts, economic opportunity. Others were widows attempting to take care of their children after their husband's death. One such widow, Anne Furnberg, settled a homestead in the Dakota Territory in 1871. Born in Norway, she had lived with her husband and son in Minnesota. After her husband's death, the thirty-four-year-old Furnberg moved with her son near Fargo and eventually settled on eighty acres of land. She farmed, raised chickens and a cow, and sold butter and eggs in town. The majority of women who settled in the Dakotas were between the ages of twenty-one and twenty-five, most had never been married, and a majority were native-born children of immigrant parents. A sample of nine counties in the Dakotas shows that more than 4,400 women became landowners. Nora Pfundheler, a single woman, explained her motivation: "Well I was 21 and had no prospects of doing anything. The land was there, so I took it."

Explore

See Document 15.4 for a description of one Norwegian homesteader's experience.

Once families settled in and towns began to develop, women, married and single, directed some of their energies to moral reform and extending democracy on the frontier. Because of loneliness and grueling work, some men turned to alcohol for relief. Law enforcement in newly established communities was often no match for the saloons that catered to a raucous and drunken crowd. In their roles as wives, mothers, and sisters, many women tried to remove the source of alcohol-induced violence that disrupted both family relationships and public decorum. In Kansas in the late 1870s, women flocked to the state's Woman's Christian Temperance Union, founded by Amanda M. Way. Although they did not yet have the vote, in 1880 these women vigorously campaigned for a constitutional amendment that banned the sale of liquor.

Temperance women also threw their weight behind the issue of women's suffrage. In 1884 Kansas women established the statewide Equal Suffrage Association, which delivered to the state legislature a petition with seven thousand signatures in support of women's suffrage. Their attempt failed, but in 1887 women won the right to vote and run for office in all Kansas municipal elections. By the end of the nineteenth century, fifteen women had held city offices throughout the state. Julia Robinson, who campaigned for women's suffrage in Kansas, recalled the positive role that some men played: "My father had always said his family of girls had just as much right to help the government as if we were boys, and mother and he had always taught us to expect Woman Suffrage in our day." Kansas did not grant equal voting rights in state and national elections until 1912, but women obtained full suffrage before then in many western states.

Farming on the Great Plains

Surviving loneliness, drudgery, and the weather still did not guarantee financial success for homesteaders. In fact, the economic realities of farming on the plains proved formidable. Despite the image of yeomen farmers—individuals engaged in subsistence farming with the aid of wives and children—most agriculture was geared to commercial transactions. Few farmers were independent or self-reliant. Farmers depended on barter and short-term credit. They borrowed from banks to purchase the additional land necessary to make agriculture economically feasible in the semiarid climate. They also needed loans to buy machinery to help increase production and to sustain their families while they waited for the harvest.

Instead of raising crops solely for their own use, farmers concentrated on the cash crops of corn and wheat.

DOCUMENT 15.4

Gro Svendsen | Letter from a Homesteader, 1863

Many of the settlers who moved to Minnesota and the Dakotas migrated from northern Europe. Most did not speak English, left behind family members, and experienced geographical and emotional isolation. Women played a significant role in running farms, as shown in the following letter that Gro Svendsen wrote to her family in Norway about her life as a homesteader in Minnesota in 1863. Svendsen offers a typical account of the challenges many settlers faced.

Explore

Dear Parents, Sisters, and Brothers (always in my thoughts):

I have often thought that I ought to tell you about life here in the New World. Everything is so totally different from what it was in our beloved Norway. You never will really know what it's like, although you no doubt try to imagine what it might be. Your pictures would be all wrong, just as mine were.

What emotions does Svendsen express about her life in America?

I only wish that I could be with you to tell you all about it. Even if I were to write you countless pages, I still could not tell you everything.

I remember I used to wonder when I heard that it would be impossible to keep the milk here as we did at home. Now I have learned that it is indeed impossible because of the heat here in the summertime. One can't make cheese out of the milk because of flies, bugs, and other insects. I don't know the names of all these insects, but this I do know: If one were to make cheese here in the summertime, the cheese itself would be alive with bugs. Toward late autumn it should be possible to keep the milk. The people who have more milk than they need simply feed it to the hogs.

It's difficult, too, to preserve the butter. One must pour brine over it or salt it; otherwise it gets full of maggots. Therefore it is best, if one is not too far from town, to sell the butter at once. This summer we have been getting from eight to ten cents a pound. Not a great profit. For this reason people around here do not have many cows—just enough to supply the milk needed for the household. It's not wise to have more than enough milk, because the flies are everywhere. Even the bacon must be preserved in brine, and so there are different ways of doing everything. . . .

What differences between life in Norway and life on the Great Plains does this letter indicate?

Why would Svendsen's relatives think she might be exaggerating?

I could tell you even more, but possibly many who read this letter may think I am exaggerating. I assure you that all that I have told you I have experienced myself. If they do not believe me, they should come over and find out for themselves.

Source: Gro Svendsen, *Frontier Mother: The Letters of Gro Svendsen*, ed. Pauline Farseth and Theodore Blegen (Northfield, MN: Norwegian-American Historical Association, 1950), 39–40.

Put It in Context

What particular challenges did homesteaders who emigrated from other countries face?

The price of these commodities depended on the impersonal economic forces of an international market that connected American farmers to growers and consumers throughout the world. When supply expanded and demand remained relatively stable during the 1880s and 1890s, prices fell. This deflation made it more difficult for farmers to pay back their loans, and banks moved to foreclose. Corn growers had a hedge against falling prices. By withholding some of their corn from market, they could feed it to their hogs, fatten them up, and sell them at higher prices. The reduction in the supply of corn caused prices to rise until it was worth selling corn again.

This "corn-hog cycle," however, did not benefit wheat growers. When prices plummeted, they had little choice but to raise more wheat in the hope that increased volume would yield more income. Instead, the expansion in supply, coming as it did from so many farmers, merely depressed prices further, leaving wheat farmers with debts they could not repay. Under these circumstances, almost half of the homesteaders in the Great Plains picked up and moved either to another farm or to a nearby city. Large operators bought up the farms they left behind and ran them like big businesses. As had been the case in mining and ranching, western agriculture was increasingly commercialized and consolidated over the course of the second half of the nineteenth century.

The federal government unwittingly aided this process of commercialization and consolidation, to the benefit of large companies. The government sought to make bigger plots of land available in regions where small farming had proven impractical. The Desert Land Act (1877) offered 640 acres to settlers who would irrigate the land, but it brought small relief for farmers because the land was too dry. These properties soon fell out of the hands of homesteaders and into those of cattle ranchers. The Timber and Stone Act (1878) allowed homesteaders to buy 160 acres of forestland at $2.50 an acre. Lumber companies hired "dummy entrymen" to file claims and then quickly transferred the titles and added the parcels to their growing tracts of woodland.

REVIEW & RELATE

How did market forces contribute to the boom and bust of the cattle ranching industry?

How did women homesteaders on the Great Plains in the late nineteenth century respond to frontier challenges?

LEARNINGCurve bedfordstmartins.com/hewittlawson/LC

Pushing Farther West

Some pioneers settled on the Great Plains or moved west for reasons beyond purely economic motives. The Mormons, for example, settled in Utah to find a religious home. The West Coast states of Washington, Oregon, and especially California, with their abundant resources and favorable climates, beckoned adventurers to travel beyond the Rockies and settle along the Pacific Ocean. The far West attracted many white settlers and foreign immigrants—especially Chinese—who encountered Spaniards and Mexicans already inhabiting the region. This encounter among diverse cultural groups sparked clashes that produced more oppression than opportunity for nonwhites.

Mormons Head West

Unlike miners, cowboys, and farmers, **Mormons** sought refuge in the West for religious reasons. By 1870 the migration of Mormons (members of the Church of Jesus Christ of Latter-Day Saints) into the Utah Territory had attracted more than 85,000 settlers, most notably in Salt Lake City. Originally traveling to Utah under the leadership of Brigham Young in the late 1840s, Mormons had come under attack from opponents of their religion and the federal government for several reasons. Most important, Mormons believed in polygamy (the practice of having more than one wife at a time), which violated traditional Christian standards of morality. Far from seeing the practice as immoral, Mormon doctrine held polygamy as a blessing that would guarantee both husbands and wives an exalted place in the afterlife. Non-Mormons denounced polygamy as a form of involuntary servitude, similar to African American slavery. In reality, only a small minority of Mormon men had multiple wives, and most of these polygamists had only two wives.

Mormons also departed from the mainstream American belief in private property. The church considered farming a communal enterprise. To this end, church elders divided land among their followers, so that, as Brigham Young explained, "each person perform[ed] his several duties for the good of the whole more than for individual aggrandizement." Mormon communities also displayed a tolerant attitude toward the Native American tribes they encountered, learning their languages in order to convert rather than destroy them.

In the 1870s, the federal government took increased measures to control Mormon practices. In *Reynolds v. United States* (1879), the Supreme Court upheld the criminal conviction of a polygamist Mormon man. Previously in 1862 and 1874, Congress had banned plural marriages in the Utah Territory, and the justices ruled that despite their religious convictions, Mormons possessed no constitutional right to violate federal law. Congress went further in 1882 by passing the Edmunds Act, which disfranchised men engaging in polygamy. In 1887 Congress aimed to slash the economic power of the church by limiting Mormon assets to $50,000 and seizing the rest for the federal Treasury. A few years later, under this considerable pressure, the Mormons officially abandoned polygamy.

Related to the attack on polygamy was the question of women's suffrage. In 1870 voters in Utah endorsed a referendum granting women the right to vote, which enfranchised more than seventeen thousand women. Emmeline B. Wells, a Mormon woman who defended both women's rights and polygamy, argued that women "should be recognized as . . . responsible being[s]," capable of choosing plural marriage of their own free will. Opponents of enfranchisement contended that as long as polygamy existed, extending the vote to "enslaved" Mormon women would only perpetuate the practice because they would vote the way their husbands did. This point of view prevailed, and the Edmunds-Tucker Act (1887) rescinded the right to vote for women in the territory. Only with the rejection of polygamy did Congress accept statehood for Utah in 1896. The following year, the state extended the ballot to women.

Californios

As with the nation's other frontiers, migrants to the West Coast did not find uninhabited territory. Besides Indians, the largest group that lived in California consisted of Spaniards and Mexicans. Since the eighteenth century, these *Californios* had established themselves as farmers and ranchers. The 1848 Treaty of Guadalupe Hidalgo, which ended the Mexican-American War, supposedly guaranteed the property rights of Californios and granted them U.S. citizenship, but reality proved different. Mexican American miners had to pay a "foreign miners tax," and Californio landowners lost their holdings to squatters, settlers, and local officials. Anglo politicians argued that the descendants of the original owners of Spanish land grants did not use them efficiently, and clever lawyers used the courts to deprive Californios of much of their property. By the end of the nineteenth century, about two-thirds of all land originally owned by Spanish-speaking residents had fallen into the hands of Euro-American settlers. By this time, many of these once proud and wealthy Californios had been forced into poverty and the low-wage labor force. The loss of land was matched by a diminished role in the region's government, as economic decline, ethnic bias, and the continuing influx of white migrants combined to greatly reduce the political influence of the Californio population.

Spaniards and Mexicans living in the Southwest met the same fate as the Californios. Although they battled to keep their landholdings, they did not receive the first-class citizenship promised by the Treaty of Guadalupe-Hidalgo. When Anglo cattle ranchers began forcing Mexican Americans off their land near Las Vegas, New Mexico, a rancher named Juan Jose Herrera assembled a band of masked night riders known as *Las Gorras Blancas* (The White Caps). In 1889 and 1890, as many as seven hundred White Caps burned Anglo fences, haystacks, barns, and homes. They also set fire to thousands of railroad ties when the Atchison, Topeka, and Santa Fe Railroad refused to increase wages for Hispanic workers. In the end, however, Spanish-speaking inhabitants could not prevent the growing number of whites from pouring onto their lands and isolating them politically, economically, and culturally.

Explore

See Document 15.5 for a list of demands from the White Caps.

The Chinese in the Far West

California and the far West also attracted a large number of Chinese immigrants. Migration to California and the West Coast was part of a larger movement in the nineteenth century out of Asia that brought impoverished Chinese to Australia, Hawaii, Latin America, and the United States. The Chinese migrated for several reasons in the decades after 1840. Internal conflicts in China sent them in search of refuge. Economic dislocation related to the British Opium Wars (1839–1842 and 1856–1860), along with bloody family feuds and a decade of peasant rebellion from 1854 to 1864, propelled migration. Faced with unemployment and starvation, the Chinese sought economic opportunity overseas. One man recounted the hardships that drove him to emigrate: "Sometimes we went hungry for days. My mother and [I] would go over the harvested rice fields of the peasants to pick the grains they dropped. . . . We had only salt and water to eat with the rice."

Chinese immigrants were attracted first by the 1848 gold rush and then by jobs building the transcontinental railroad. By 1880 the Chinese population had grown to 200,000, most of whom lived in the West. San Francisco became the center of the transplanted Chinese population, which congregated in the city's Chinatown. Under the leadership of a handful of businessmen, Chinese residents found jobs, lodging, meals, and social, cultural, and recreational outlets. Most of those who came were young unmarried men who intended to earn

DOCUMENT 15.5

White Caps Flier, 1890

Before the United States acquired California and the territories of Arizona and New Mexico in 1848, most of the people living in the area were of Spanish heritage. In New Mexico, Hispanic villagers farmed on communal land. In the 1880s, Anglo authorities enclosed the communal land with barbed wire to promote individual farming. In response, a group of frustrated residents known as *Las Gorras Blancas*, or "White Caps," burned barns and destroyed the fences of ranchers who enclosed common lands. In 1890 the White Caps posted fliers in the town of Las Vegas, New Mexico, in which they described a range of grievances.

Explore

NUESTRA PLATAFORMA— [Our Platform]

Our purpose is to protect the rights and interests of the people in general and especially those of the helpless classes.

We want the Las Vegas Grant settled to the benefit of all concerned, and this we hold is the entire community within the Grant.

We want no "land grabbers" or obstructionists of any sort to interfere. We will watch them.

We are not down on lawyers as a class, but the usual knavery and unfair treatment of the people must be stopped.

Our judiciary hereafter must understand that we will sustain it only when "Justice" is its watchword.

We are down on race issues, and will watch race agitators.

We favor irrigation enterprises, but will fight any scheme that tends to monopolize the supply of water sources to the detriment of residents living on lands watered by the same streams.

The people are suffering from the effects of partisan "bossism" and these bosses had better quietly hold their peace. The people have been persecuted and hauled about in every which way to satisfy their caprices.

We must have a free ballot and fair court and the will of the Majority shall be respected.

We have no grudge against any person in particular, but we are the enemies of bulldozers and tyrants.

If the old system should continue, death would be a relief to our suffering. And for our rights our lives are the least we can pledge.

If the fact that we are law-abiding citizens is questioned, come out to our houses and see the hunger and desolation we are suffering; and "this" is the result of the deceitful and corrupt methods of "bossism."

The White Caps 1,500 Strong and Gaining Daily

Source: *Las Vegas Daily Optic*, March 12, 1890, reprinted in *Foreigners in Their Native Land: Historical Roots of the Mexican Americans*, ed. David J. Weber (Albuquerque: University of New Mexico Press, 1973), 235–36.

Interpret the Evidence

- Whom do the White Caps claim to represent, and what are their grievances?
- How did the White Caps support their claim to be law-abiding citizens? How might Anglo authorities have responded to their claims?

Put It in Context

What kinds of difficulties did nonwhites face as white Americans moved westward during the nineteenth century?

enough money to return to China and start anew. The relatively few women who immigrated came as servants or prostitutes.

For many Chinese, the West proved unwelcoming. When California's economy slumped in the mid-1870s, many whites looked to the Chinese as scapegoats. White workingmen believed that the plentiful supply of Chinese laborers in the mines and railroads undercut their demands for higher wages. They contended that Chinese would work for less because they were racially inferior people who lived degraded lives. Anti-Chinese clubs mushroomed in California during the 1870s, and they soon became a substantial political force in the state. The Workingmen's Party advocated laws that restricted Chinese labor, and it initiated boycotts of goods made by Chinese people. Vigilantes attacked Chinese in the streets and set fire to factories that employed Asians. The Workingmen's Party and the Democratic Party joined forces in 1879 to craft a new state constitution that blatantly discriminated against Chinese residents. In many ways, these laws resembled the Jim Crow laws passed in the South that deprived African Americans of their freedom following Reconstruction (discussed in chapter 16).

Pressured by anti-Chinese sentiment on the West Coast, the U.S. government enacted drastic legislation to prevent any further influx of Chinese. The **Chinese Exclusion Act** of 1882 banned Chinese immigration into the United States and prohibited those Chinese already in the country from becoming naturalized American citizens. As a result, the Chinese remained a predominantly male, aging, and isolated population until World War II. The exclusion act, however, did not stop anti-Chinese assaults. In the mid-1880s, white mobs drove Chinese out of Eureka, California; Seattle and Tacoma, Washington; and Rock Springs, Wyoming.

Rock Springs Massacre

This engraving depicts the Rock Springs massacre in Wyoming. On September 3, 1885, a mob of white coal miners killed at least 28 Chinese miners, injured 15, and burned 75 homes of Chinese residents. The violence came after years of anti-Chinese sentiment in the western United States. White miners blamed the Chinese for working for lower wages and taking their jobs.   The Granger Collection, New York

REVIEW & RELATE

What migrant groups were attracted to the far West? What drew them there?

Explain the rising hostility to the Chinese and other minority groups in the late-nineteenth-century far West.

 LEARNINGCurve bedfordstmartins.com/hewittlawson/LC

Conclusion: The Ambiguous Legacy of the Frontier

The legacy of the pioneering generation of Americans has proven mixed. Men and women pioneers left their old lives behind and boldly pushed into uncharted territory to reinvent themselves. They encountered numerous obstacles posed by difficult terrain, forbidding climate, and unfamiliar inhabitants of the land they sought to harness. They built their homes, tilled the soil to raise crops, and mined the earth to remove the metals it contained. They developed cities that would one day rival those back east: San Francisco, Los Angeles, Seattle, and Denver. These pioneers served as the advance guard of America's expanding national and international commercial markets. As producers of staple crops and livestock and consumers of manufactured goods, they contributed to the expansion of America's factories, railroads, and telegraph communication system. The nation would memorialize their spirit as a model of individualism and self-reliance.

In fact, settlement of the West required more than individual initiative and self-determination. Without the direct involvement of the federal government, settlers would not have received free or inexpensive homesteads and military protection to clear native inhabitants out of their way. Without territorial governors and judges appointed by Washington to preside over new settlements,

there would have been even less law, order, and justice than appeared in the rough-and-tumble environment that attracted outlaws, con artists, and speculators. Railroads, mining, and cattle ventures all relied heavily on foreign investors. Moreover, all the individualism and self-reliance that pioneers brought would not have saved them from the harsh conditions and disasters they faced without banding together as a community and pitching in to create institutions that helped them collectively. Despite their desire to achieve success, various pioneers—farmers, prospectors, cowboys—mostly found it difficult to make it on their own and began working for larger farming, mining, and ranching enterprises, with many of them becoming wageworkers. And for an experience that has been portrayed as a predominantly male phenomenon, settlement of the West depended largely on women.

Pioneers did not fully understand the land and people they encountered. More from ignorance than design, settlers engaged in agricultural, mining, and ranching practices that depleted fragile grasses, eroded hillsides, and polluted rivers and streams with runoff wastes. The settlement of the West nearly wiped out the bison and left Native Americans psychologically demoralized, culturally endangered, and economically impoverished. Some Indians willingly adopted white ways, but most of them fiercely resisted acculturation. Other nonwhite minorities in the West, such as Mexicans and Chinese, experienced less extreme treatment, but they suffered nonetheless.

Panoramic landscape paintings often depicted glorious scenes of the Wild West, but the truth was more nuanced. Annie Oakley pleased audiences with daring exploits that glorified a West she had not experienced. Geronimo surrendered and spent the rest of his life exiled from his native lands. He, too, tried to follow the path of Oakley, but his public appearances could not hide the devastation that he and other Native Americans had experienced. The western frontier represented both opportunity and loss.

LEARNINGCurve
Check what you know.
bedfordstmartins.com/hewittlawson/LC

Chapter Review

Online Study Guide ▶ bedfordstmartins.com/hewittlawson

KEY TERMS

Great Plains (p. 461)
transcontinental railroad (p. 462)
Treaty of Fort Laramie (p. 465)
Battle of the Little Big Horn (p. 466)
buffalo soldiers (p. 466)
Dawes Act (p. 467)
Ghost Dance (p. 468)
Comstock Lode (p. 469)
Long Drive (p. 471)
Homestead Act (p. 474)
Mormons (p. 478)
Californios (p. 479)
Chinese Exclusion Act (p. 481)

REVIEW & RELATE

1. What role did the federal government play in opening the West to settlement and economic exploitation?

2. Explain the determination of Americans to settle in land west of the Mississippi River despite the challenges the region presented.

3. How and why did federal Indian policy change during the nineteenth century?

4. Describe some of the ways that Indian peoples responded to federal policies. Which response do you think offered their greatest chance for survival?

5. How and why did the nature of mining in the West change during the second half of the nineteenth century?

6. How did miners and residents of mining towns reshape the frontier landscape?

7. How did market forces contribute to the boom and bust of the cattle ranching industry?

8. How did women homesteaders on the Great Plains in the late nineteenth century respond to frontier challenges?

9. What migrant groups were attracted to the far West? What drew them there?

10. Explain the rising hostility to the Chinese and other minority groups in the late-nineteenth-century far West.

TIMELINE OF EVENTS

1848	Gold discovered in California
1851	First Treaty of Fort Laramie
1862	Homestead Act passed
1864	Sand Creek massacre
1865–1868	Lakota Sioux lead Indian resistance
Late 1860s	Large-scale cattle drives begin
1868	Second Treaty of Fort Laramie
1869	Transcontinental railroad completed
1870s	Gold discovered in Black Hills of North Dakota
1876	Battle of the Little Big Horn
1877	Desert Land Act
1878	John Wesley Powell questions suitability of Great Plains for small-scale farming
	Timber and Stone Act
1881	Helen Hunt Jackson publishes *Century of Dishonor*
1882	Edmunds Act passed
	Chinese Exclusion Act passed
1884	Annie Oakley joins William Cody's Wild West show
1885–1887	Cattle industry collapses
1886	Geronimo captured
1887	Dawes Act passed
	Kansas women win right to vote and run for office in municipal elections
1889–1890	Mexican American White Caps attack Anglo property
1890	Massacre at Wounded Knee
1893	Western Federation of Miners formed

American Indians and Whites on the Frontier

Views on the relationship between whites and American Indians varied widely in the late-nineteenth-century West. Some white Americans advocated exterminating the Indians, whereas others sought to assimilate them. These attitudes differed significantly by region. Whites who were most likely to encounter Indians were generally the least sympathetic. Government officials were also divided. The most notable differences were between civilians in the Interior Department who favored peaceful solutions and those in the War Department who were inclined to use military force to resolve conflicts. However, even white reformers did not always understand Indian culture; as a result, they developed policies that led to the decline of Indian tribal societies. On the other side, Indian attitudes ranged from fierce resistance to accommodation and, in rare cases, assimilation. Even those who eventually adapted to white society and gained a measure of fame within it, like Zitkala-Ša (Document 15.9), never fully abandoned their pride in Indian traditions.

The following documents speak to important recurring questions in American history: How do white Americans and their leaders deal with differences among people rooted in race and nationality? How do those considered minorities forge strategies to gain political and economic access while maintaining their own identities and heritage? And how well did the U.S. government in the late nineteenth century balance its commitment to the competing values of continental expansion and equal justice under the law?

DOCUMENT 15.6

James Michael Cavanaugh | Support for Indian Extermination, 1868

James Michael Cavanaugh was originally from Springfield, Massachusetts, but moved to Minnesota in 1854, where he served in Congress for one term. He subsequently moved to Colorado and then Montana and served in the House of Representatives as a Democrat from 1867 to 1871. In the following congressional speech, Cavanaugh explains his attitude toward Indians in a discussion about Indian appropriations with Republican representative Benjamin Butler of Massachusetts.

I WILL SAY THAT I like an Indian better dead than living. I have never in my life seen a good Indian (and I have seen thousands) except when I have seen a dead Indian. I believe in the Indian policy pursued by New England in years long gone. I believe in the Indian policy which was taught by the great chieftain of Massachusetts, Miles Standish. I believe in the policy that exterminates the Indians, drives them outside the boundaries of civilization, because you cannot civilize them. Gentlemen may call this very harsh language; but perhaps they would not think so if they had had my experience in Minnesota and Colorado. In Minnesota the almost living babe has been torn from its mother's womb; and I have seen the child, with its young heart palpitating, nailed to the window-sill. I have seen women who were scalped, disfigured, outraged. In Denver, Colorado Territory, I have seen women and children brought in scalped. Scalped why? Simply because the Indian was "upon the war-path," to satisfy his devilish and barbarous propensities. You have made your treaties with the Indians, but they have not been observed. General [William Tecumseh] Sherman went out a year ago to Colorado Territory. He made a treaty; and in less than twenty-four hours after the treaty was made the Indians were again "upon the war-path." The Indian will make a treaty in the fall, and in the spring he is

again "upon the war-path." The torch, the scalping-knife, plunder, and desolation follow wherever the Indian goes.

But, Mr. Chairman, I will answer the gentleman's question more directly. My friend from Massachusetts [Mr. Butler] has never passed the barrier of the frontier. All he knows about Indians (the gentleman will pardon me for saying it) may have been gathered, I presume, from the brilliant pages of the author of "The Last of the Mohicans," or from the lines of the poet Longfellow in "Hiawatha." The gentleman has never yet seen the Indian upon the war-path. He has never been chased, as I have been, by these red devils—who seem to be the pets of the eastern philanthropists.

Mr. Chairman, I regret that I have not prepared myself with statistics as to Indian atrocities. I desire to answer the gentleman from Massachusetts fairly. I repeat that the Indian policy of the Government from beginning to end is wrong. If the management of the Indians is to continue as a part of the civil service, then there ought to be a bureau of Indian affairs, under the charge of a Cabinet officer, who should be responsible for all matters connected with the management of the Indians.

Source: United States Congress, *The Congressional Globe: Containing the Debates and Proceedings of the Second Session of the Fortieth Congress*, May 28, 1868, 2638.

Thomas Nast |
"Patience until the Indian Is Civilized—So to Speak," 1878

Through his cartoons, artist Thomas Nast crusaded against political corruption and mistreatment of freedpeople in the South. Although generally sympathetic to the rights of American Indians, in this illustration he raises questions about what the federal government should do regarding conflicts between white settlers and Indians in the West. Nast depicts Secretary of the Interior Carl Schurz (left), an Indian reformer, counseling patience to western settlers.

Library of Congress

DOCUMENT 15.8

Helen Hunt Jackson | Challenges to Indian Policy, 1881

Helen Hunt Jackson's book *A Century of Dishonor* severely criticized U.S. policy toward Indians. Jackson sent a copy of her book to every member of Congress. Her handwritten inscription, intended to move lawmakers to action, contained the words of Benjamin Franklin: "Look upon your hands! They are stained with the blood of your relations." Despite her attack on the government's treatment of Indians and her advocacy of reform, Jackson believed that American Indians could not become citizens until they received proper training from enlightened white teachers.

There is not among these three hundred bands of Indians one which has not suffered cruelly at the hands either of the Government or of white settlers. The poorer, the more insignificant, the more helpless the band, the more certain the cruelty and outrage to which they have been subjected. This is especially true of the bands on the Pacific slope. These Indians found themselves of a sudden surrounded by and caught up in the great influx of gold-seeking settlers, as helpless creatures on a shore are caught up in a tidal wave. There was not time for the Government to make treaties; not even time for communities to make laws. The tale of the wrongs, the oppressions, the murders of the Pacific-slope Indians in the last thirty years would be a volume by itself, and is too monstrous to be believed.

It makes little difference, however, where one opens the record of the history of the Indians; every page and every year has its dark stain. The story of one tribe is the story of all, varied only by differences of time and place; but neither time nor place makes any difference in the main facts. Colorado is as greedy and unjust in 1880 as was Georgia in 1830, and Ohio in 1795; and the United States Government breaks promises now as deftly as then, and with an added ingenuity from long practice.

One of its strongest supports in so doing is the wide-spread sentiment among the people of dislike to the Indian, of impatience with his presence as a "barrier to civilization," and distrust of it as a possible danger. The old tales of the frontier life, with its horrors of Indian warfare, have gradually, by two or three generations' telling, produced in the average mind something like an hereditary instinct of unquestioning and unreasoning aversion which it is almost impossible to dislodge or soften. . . .

To assume that it would be easy, or by any one sudden stroke of legislative policy possible, to undo the mischief and hurt of the long past, set the Indian policy of the country right for the future, and make the Indians at once safe and happy, is the blunder of a hasty and uninformed judgment. The notion which seems to be growing more prevalent, that simply to make all Indians at once citizens of the United States would be a sovereign and instantaneous panacea for all their ills and all the Government's perplexities, is a very inconsiderate one. To administer complete citizenship of a sudden, all round, to all Indians, barbarous and civilized alike, would be as grotesque a blunder as to dose them all round with any one medicine, irrespective of the symptoms and needs of their diseases. It would kill more than it would cure. Nevertheless, it is true, as was well stated by one of the superintendents of Indian Affairs in 1857, that, "so long as they are not citizens of the United States, their rights of property must remain insecure against invasion. The doors of the federal tribunals being barred against them while wards and dependents, they can only partially exercise the rights of free government, or give to those who make, execute, and construe the few laws they are allowed to enact, dignity sufficient to make them respectable. While they continue individually to gather the crumbs that fall from the table of the United States, idleness, improvidence, and indebtedness will be the rule, and industry, thrift, and freedom from debt the exception. The utter absence of individual title to particular lands deprives every one among them of the chief incentive to labor and exertion—the very mainspring on which the prosperity of a people depends."

(continued on page 488)

All judicious plans and measures for their safety and salvation must embody provisions for their becoming citizens as fast as they are fit, and must protect them till then in every right and particular in which our laws protect other "persons" who are not citizens. . . .

Cheating, robbing, breaking promises—these three are clearly things which must cease to be done. One more thing, also, and that is the refusal of the protection of the law to the Indian's rights of property, "of life, liberty, and the pursuit of happiness."

When these four things have ceased to be done, time, statesmanship, philanthropy, and Christianity can slowly and surely do the rest. Till these four things have ceased to be done, statesmanship and philanthropy alike must work in vain, and even Christianity can reap but small harvest.

Source: Helen Hunt Jackson, *A Century of Dishonor: A Sketch of the United States Government's Dealings with Some of the Indian Tribes* (New York: Harper and Brothers, 1881), 337–38, 340–42.

DOCUMENT 15.9

Zitkala-Ša | Life at an Indian Boarding School, 1921

Gertrude Simmons Bonnin, who later took the Indian name Zitkala-Ša, lived on the Yankton Reservation in South Dakota, with her mother and brother until 1884, when missionaries recruited her to attend school so that she would become assimilated into Anglo-American culture. After attending a Quaker school in Wabash, Indiana, Zitkala-Ša briefly attended Earlham College and then taught at the Carlisle Indian Industrial School in Pennsylvania for two years. During that time, she experienced a reawakening of her American Indian heritage and consciousness and began publishing autobiographical accounts criticizing the educational practices of the schools she attended and at which she taught. In 1921 she recounted her own experiences in these Indian schools, including the incident she describes in the following selection.

THE FIRST DAY IN THE LAND of apples was a bitter-cold one; for the snow still covered the ground, and the trees were bare. A large bell rang for breakfast, its loud metallic voice crashing through the belfry overhead and into our sensitive ears. The annoying clatter of shoes on bare floors gave us no peace. The constant clash of harsh noises, with an undercurrent of many voices murmuring an unknown tongue, made a bedlam within which I was securely tied. And though my spirit tore itself in struggling for its lost freedom, all was useless.

A paleface woman, with white hair, came up after us. We were placed in a line of girls who were marching into the dining room. These were Indian girls, in stiff shoes and closely clinging dresses. The small girls wore sleeved aprons and shingled hair [haircut with the hair cut short from the back of the head to the nape of the neck]. As I walked noiselessly in my soft moccasins, I felt like sinking to the floor, for my blanket had been stripped from my shoulders. I looked hard at the Indian girls, who seemed not to care that they were even more immodestly dressed than I, in their tightly fitting clothes. While we marched in, the boys entered at an opposite door. I watched for the three young braves who came in our party. I spied them in the rear ranks, looking as uncomfortable as I felt.

A small bell was tapped, and each of the pupils drew a chair from under the table. Supposing this act meant they were to be seated, I pulled out mine and at once slipped into it from one side. But when I turned my head, I saw that I was the only one seated, and all the rest at our table remained standing. Just as I began to rise, looking shyly around to see how chairs were to be used, a second bell was sounded. All were seated at last, and I had to crawl back into my chair again. I heard a man's voice at one end of the hall, and I looked around to see him. But all the others hung their heads over their plates. As I glanced at the long chain of tables, I caught the eyes of a paleface woman upon me. Immediately I dropped my eyes, wondering why I was so keenly watched by the strange woman. The man ceased his mutterings, and then a third bell was tapped. Every one picked up his knife and fork and began eating. I began crying instead, for by this time I was afraid to venture anything more.

But this eating by formula was not the hardest trial in that first day. Late in the morning, my friend Judéwin gave me a terrible warning. Judéwin knew a few words of English; and she had overheard the paleface woman talk about cutting our long, heavy hair. Our mothers had taught us that only unskilled warriors who were captured had their hair shingled by the enemy. Among our people, short hair was worn by mourners, and shingled hair by cowards!

We discussed our fate some moments, and when Judéwin said, "We have to submit, because they are strong," I rebelled.

"No, I will not submit! I will struggle first!" I answered.

I watched my chance, and when no one noticed I disappeared. I crept up the stairs as quietly as I could in my squeaking shoes—my moccasins had been exchanged for shoes. Along the hall I passed, without knowing whither I was going. Turning aside to an open door, I found a large room with three white beds in it. The windows were covered with dark green curtains, which made the room very dim. Thankful that no one was there, I directed my steps toward the corner farthest from the door. On my hands and knees I crawled under the bed, and cuddled myself in the dark corner.

From my hiding place I peered out, shuddering with fear whenever I heard footsteps near by. Though in the hall loud voices were calling my name, and I knew that even Judéwin was searching for me, I did not open my mouth to answer. Then the steps were quickened and the voices became excited. The sounds came nearer and nearer. Women and girls entered the room. I held my breath and watched them open closet doors and peep behind large trunks. Some one threw up the curtains, and the room was filled with sudden light. What caused them to stoop and look under the bed I do not know. I remember being dragged out, though I resisted by kicking and scratching wildly. In spite of myself, I was carried downstairs and tied fast in a chair.

I cried aloud, shaking my head all the while until I felt the cold blades of the scissors against my neck, and heard them gnaw off one of my thick braids. Then I lost my spirit. Since the day I was taken from my mother I had suffered extreme indignities. People had stared at me. I had been tossed about in the air like a wooden puppet. And now my long hair was shingled like a coward's! In my anguish I moaned for my mother, but no one came to comfort me. Not a soul reasoned quietly with me, as my own mother used to do; for now I was only one of many little animals driven by a herder.

Source: Zitkala-Ša (Gertrude Bonnin), *American Indian Stories* (Washington, D.C.: Hayworth, 1921), 52–56.

DOCUMENT 15.10
Chief Joseph | Views on Indian Affairs, 1879

In 1877, following a string of treaties broken by the U.S. government, Chief Joseph led the Nez Percé on a 1,300-mile march from their tribal land in Oregon to Canada, in search of a home. Thirty miles from the Canadian border, they were surrounded by U.S. troops. Explaining "I am tired of fighting. . . . I will fight no more forever," Joseph was forced into negotiations with U.S. army general Nelson Miles. After his capture, Chief Joseph was taken to Washington, D.C., where he addressed a gathering of cabinet members and congressmen and tried to convince them to return tribal lands to the Nez Percé.

AT LAST I WAS GRANTED permission to come to Washington and bring my friend Yellow Bull and our interpreter with me. I am glad we came. I have shaken hands with a great many friends, but there are some things I want to know which no one seems able to explain. I can not understand how the Government sends a man out to fight us, as it did General Miles, and then breaks his word. Such a government has something wrong about it. I can not understand why so many chiefs are allowed to talk so many different ways, and promise so many different things. I have seen the Great Father Chief [President Rutherford B. Hayes], the next Great Chief [Secretary of the Interior], the Commissioner Chief [E. A. Hayt, Commissioner of Indian Affairs], the Law Chief [Congressman Benjamin Butler], and many other law chiefs [congressmen], and they all say they are my friends, and that I shall have justice, but while their mouths all talk right I do not understand why nothing is done for my people. I have heard talk and talk, but nothing is done. Good words do not last long unless they amount to something. Words do not pay for my dead people. They do not pay for my country, now overrun by white men. They do not protect my father's grave. They do not pay for all my horses and cattle. Good words will not give me back my children. Good words will not make good the promise of your War Chief General Miles. Good words will not give my people good health and stop them from dying. Good words will not get my people a home where they can live in peace and take care of themselves. I am tired of talk that comes to nothing. It makes my heart sick when I remember all the good words and all the broken promises. There has been too much talking by men who had no right to talk. Too many misrepresentations have been made, too many misunderstandings have come up between the white men about the Indians. If the white man wants to live in peace with the Indian he can live in peace. There need be no trouble. Treat all men alike. Give them all the same law. Give them all an even chance to live and grow. All men were made by the same Great Spirit Chief. They are all brothers. The earth is the mother of all people, and all people should have equal rights upon it. You might as well expect the rivers to run backward as that any man who was born a free man should be contented when penned up and denied liberty to go where he pleases. If you tie a horse to a stake, do you expect he will grow fat? If you pen an Indian up on a small spot of earth, and compel him to stay there, he will not be contented, nor will he grow and prosper. I have asked some of the great white chiefs where they get their authority to say to the Indian that he shall stay in one place, while he sees white men going where they please. They can not tell me.

I only ask of the Government to be treated as all other men are treated. If I can not go to my own home, let me have a home in some country where my people will not die so fast. I would like to go to Bitter Root Valley. There my people would be healthy; where they are now they are dying. Three have died since I left my camp to come to Washington.

When I think of our condition, my heart is heavy. I see men of my race treated as outlaws and driven from country to country, or shot down like animals.

I know that my race must change. We can not hold our own with the white men as we are. We only ask an even chance to live as other men live. We ask to be recognized as men. We ask that the same law shall work alike on all men. If the Indian breaks the law, punish him by the law. If the white man breaks the law, punish him also.

Let me be a free man—free to travel, free to stop, free to work, free to trade where I choose, free to choose my own teachers, free to follow the religion of my fathers, free to think and talk and act for myself—and I will obey every law, or submit to the penalty.

Whenever the white man treats the Indian as they treat each other, then we shall have no more wars. We shall all be alike—brothers of one father and one mother, with one sky above us and one country around us, and one government for all. Then the Great Spirit Chief who rules above will smile upon this land, and send rain to wash out the bloody spots made by brothers' hands from the face of the earth. For this time the Indian race are waiting and praying. I hope that no more groans of wounded men and women will ever go to the ear of the Great Spirit Chief above, and that all people may be one people.

Source: "An Indian's View of Indian Affairs," *North American Review*, April 1879, 431–33.

Interpret the Evidence

1. On what basis does James Michael Cavanaugh (Document 15.6) claim to be in a better position than Benjamin Butler to judge the best way to deal with Indians?

2. How does Thomas Nast's illustration (Document 15.7) compare with the arguments made by Congressman Cavanaugh?

3. What assumptions about Indians and their culture underlay the policy of assimilation advocated by reformers such as Helen Hunt Jackson (Document 15.8)?

4. What options did Indians have when confronted with white determination to eradicate their culture? What choice did Zitkala-Ša (Document 15.9) make? Why?

5. How did Chief Joseph's experience (Document 15.10) reflect the fundamental contradiction of federal policy toward Indians?

Put It in Context

- Imagine that you are an American president in the second half of the nineteenth century and can design Indian policy. Based on what you have read, what would you do, and why? What challenges might you face as you attempted to implement your policy?

The Granger Collection, New York

The Granger Collection, New York

Sawmill in Terraville, South Dakota, 1888.

Shoe-factory worker in Lynn, Massachusetts, 1895.

16
American Industry in the Age of Organization
1877–1900

The Granger Collection, New York

Duryea's Glen Cove Starch Works Factory, Glen Cove, New York.

AMERICAN HISTORIES

In 1848 Will and Margaret Carnegie left Scotland and sailed to America, hoping to find a better life for themselves and their two children. Once settled in Pittsburgh, Pennsylvania, the family went to work, including thirteen-year-old Andrew, who found a job in a textile mill. For $1.25 per week, he dipped spools into an oil bath and fired the factory furnace—tasks that left him nauseated by the smell of oil and frightened by the boiler. Nevertheless, like the hero of the rags-to-riches stories that were so popular in his era, Andrew Carnegie persevered, rising from poverty to great wealth through a series of jobs and clever investments. As a teenager, he worked as a messenger in a telegraph office and was soon promoted to telegraph operator. A superintendent of the Pennsylvania Railroad Company noticed Andrew's aptitude and made him his personal assistant and telegrapher. While in this position, Carnegie learned about the fast-developing railroad industry and purchased stock in a sleeping car company; the returns from that investment tripled his annual salary. Carnegie then became a railroad superintendent in western Pennsylvania, and by the time he was thirty-five, he had earned handsome returns on his investments in various industrial companies, as well as from oil investments he made just as that industry was emerging.

Andrew Carnegie eventually founded the greatest steel company in the world and became one of the wealthiest men of his time. In an era before personal and corporate income taxes, Carnegie earned hundreds of millions of dollars. He also became one of the era's

**Andrew Carnegie
and John Sherman**

greatest philanthropists, fulfilling his sense of community obligation by giving away a great deal of his fortune.

John Sherman also believed in public service, but for him it would come through politics. Sherman was born in Lancaster, Ohio, in 1823, a quarter of a century before the Carnegies set sail for the United States. Sherman became a lawyer like his father, an Ohio Supreme Court judge, and in 1844 he set up a practice with his older brother, William Tecumseh Sherman, the future Civil War general and Indian fighter (see chapter 15). Like Carnegie, Sherman made shrewd investments that made him a wealthy man, although not on the same scale as Carnegie.

Sherman decided to enter politics and in 1854 won election from Ohio to the House of Representatives as a member of the newly created Republican Party. He rose up the leadership ranks as Republicans came to national power with the election of Abraham Lincoln to the presidency in 1860. From 1861 to 1896, Sherman held a variety of major political positions, including U.S. senator from Ohio and secretary of the treasury under President Rutherford B. Hayes. After his term as treasury secretary ended, he returned to the Senate and wielded power as one of the top Republican Party leaders. Sherman, who had joined the Radical Republicans during Reconstruction (see chapter 14), did not hesitate to move with the Republican Party as its interests shifted from racial equality to promoting business and industry. With his background as chair of the Senate Finance Committee and as secretary of the treasury, Sherman was the most respected Republican of his time in dealing with monetary and financial affairs. Marcus Alonzo Hanna, a wealthy industrialist, considered the Ohio senator "our main dependence in the Senate for the protection of our business interests." Like Hanna, Sherman believed that government should serve business. His most famous accomplishment, the Sherman Antitrust Act, which authorized the government to break up organizations that restrained competition, embodied this belief. It enacted limited reforms without harming powerful business interests. ●

both photos: Library of Congress

WHILE THE AMERICAN HISTORIES

of Andrew Carnegie and John Sherman began very differently, both men played a prominent role in developing the government-business partnership that was crucial to the rapid industrialization of the United States. Carnegie's organization and management skills helped shape the formation of large-scale business. At the same time, Sherman and his fellow lawmakers provided support for that enterprise, using the power of government to reduce risks for businessmen and to increase incentives for economic expansion. In the view of men like Carnegie and Sherman, government's primary purpose was, in fact, to advance the agenda and interests of the business community—an agenda they were certain was in the best interests of the country as a whole.

The emphasis Carnegie and Sherman placed on the government-business alliance was, in part, a reaction to the extreme economic volatility of the late nineteenth century. The economy experienced painful depressions in the 1870s, 1880s, and 1890s, each accompanied by business failures and mass unemployment. Though recovery came in every instance and industrial output continued to soar, these financial fluctuations left businessmen ever more intent on stabilizing profits, wages, and prices. When faced with harsh economic realities and swift change, businessmen chose organization, cooperation, and government support as strategies to deal with the challenges they confronted.

America Industrializes

In this Age of Organization between 1870 and 1900, the United States grew into a global industrial power. Transcontinental railroads spurred this breathtaking transformation, linking regional markets into a national market for manufactured goods; at the same time, railroads themselves served as a massive new market for raw materials, new technologies, and, perhaps most important, steel. Building on advantages developed over the course of the nineteenth century, the Northeast and the Midwest led the way in the new economy, while efforts to industrialize the South met with uneven success. Men like Andrew Carnegie became both the heroes and the villains of their age. They engaged in ruthless practices that would lead some to label the new industrialists "robber barons," but they also created ingenious systems of industrial organization and corporate management that altered the economic landscape of the country and changed the place of the United States in the world.

The New Industrial Economy

The industrial revolution of the late nineteenth century originated in Europe. Great Britain was the world's first industrial power, but by the 1870s Germany had emerged as a major challenger for industrial dominance, increasing its steel production at a rapid rate and leading the way in the chemical and electrical industries. The dynamic economic growth stimulated by industrial competition quickly crossed the Atlantic. Eager and ambitious American entrepreneurs and engineers soon began applying the latest industrial innovations to U.S. enterprises.

Industrialization transformed the American economy. As industrialization took hold, the U.S. gross domestic product, the output of all goods and services produced annually, quadrupled—from $9 billion in 1860 to $37 billion in 1890. During this same period, the number of Americans employed by industry doubled, as American workers moved from farms to factories and immigrants flooded in from overseas to fill newly created industrial jobs. Moreover, the nature of industry itself changed, as small factories catering to local markets were displaced by large-scale firms producing for national and international markets. The midwestern cities of Chicago, Cincinnati, and St. Louis joined Boston, New York, and Philadelphia as centers of factory production, while the exploitation of the natural resources in the West took on an increasingly industrial character. Trains, telegraphs, and telephones connected the country in ways never before possible. In 1889 the respected economist David A. Wells marveled at

what had occurred over the past two decades: "An almost total revolution has taken place, and is yet in progress, in every branch and in every relation of the world's industrial and commercial system."

Wells did not exaggerate. From 1870 to 1913, the United States experienced an extraordinary rate of growth in industrial output: In 1870 American industries turned out 23.3 percent of the world's manufacturing production; by 1913 this figure had jumped to 35.8 percent. In fact, U.S. output in 1913 almost equaled the combined total for Europe's three leading industrial powers: Germany, the United Kingdom, and France. Of these European countries, only Germany experienced a slight rise in output from 1870 to 1913 (2.5 percent), while Britain's output dropped a precipitous 17.8 percent and France's declined 3.9 percent. By the end of the nineteenth century, the United States was surging ahead of northern Europe as the manufacturing center of the world.

At the heart of the American industrial transformation was the railroad. Large-scale business enterprises would not have developed without a national market for raw materials and finished products. A consolidated system of railroads crisscrossing the nation facilitated the creation of such a market (Figure 16.1). In addition, railroads were direct consumers of industrial products, stimulating the growth of a number of industries through their consumption of steel, wood, coal, glass, rubber, brass, and iron. For example, late-nineteenth-century railroads purchased more than 90 percent of the steel produced in U.S. factories. Finally, railroads contributed to economic growth by increasing the speed and efficiency with which products and materials were transported. One observer guessed that in 1890 if the country had to rely only on roads and waterways instead of trains to ship agricultural and industrial goods, the nation would have lost approximately $560 million, or 5 percent, of its gross national product.

Before railroads could create a national market, they had to overcome several critical problems. In 1877 railroad lines dotted the country in haphazard fashion. They primarily served local markets and remained unconnected at key points. This lack of coordination stemmed mainly from the fact that each railroad had its own track gauge (the width between the tracks), making shared track use impossible and long-distance travel extremely difficult.

The consolidation of railroads solved many of these problems. In 1886 railroad companies finally agreed to adopt a standard gauge. Railroads also standardized time zones, thus eliminating confusion in train schedules. During the 1870s, towns and cities each set their own time zone, a practice that created discrepancies among them. In 1882 the time in New York City and in Boston varied by 11 minutes and 45 seconds. The following year, railroads

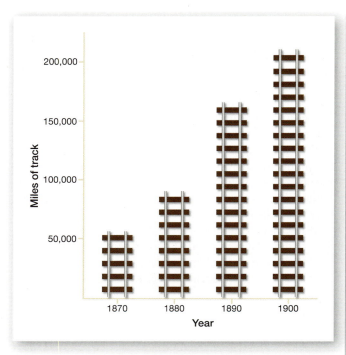

FIGURE 16.1   Expansion of the Railroad System, 1870–1900

The great expansion of the railroads in the late nineteenth century fueled the industrial revolution and the growth of big business. Connecting the nation from East Coast to West Coast, transcontinental railroads created a national market for natural resources and manufactured goods. The biggest surge in railroad construction occurred west of the Mississippi River and in the South.

agreed to coordinate times and divided the country into four standard time zones. Most cities soon cooperated, but not until 1918 did the federal government legislate the standard time zones that the railroads had first adopted.

Innovation and Inventions

As important as railroads were, they were not the only engine of industrialization. American technological innovation created new industries, while expanding the efficiency and productivity of old ones. Inventor Thomas Alva Edison began his career by devising ways to improve the telegraph and expand its uses. In 1866 a transatlantic telegraph cable connected the United States and Europe, allowing businessmen on both sides of the ocean to pursue profitable commercial ventures. New inventions also allowed business offices to run more smoothly: Typewriters were invented in 1868, carbon paper in 1872, adding machines in 1891, and mimeograph machines in 1892. As businesses grew, they needed more space for their operations. The construction of towering skyscrapers in the 1880s in cities such as Chicago and New York was made possible

by two innovations: structural steel, which had the strength to support tall buildings; and elevators, equipped with a safety device invented by Elisha Graves Otis in the 1850s.

Among the thousands of patents filed each year, Alexander Graham Bell's telephone revolutionized communications. By 1880 fifty-five cities offered local service and catered to a total of 50,000 subscribers, most of them business customers. A decade later, long-distance service connected New York, Boston, and Chicago, and by 1900 around 1.5 million telephones were in operation. Bell profited handsomely from his invention, created his own firm, and in 1885 established the giant American Telephone and Telegraph Company (AT&T).

Perhaps the greatest technological innovations that advanced industrial development in the late nineteenth century came in steel manufacturing. In 1859 Henry Bessemer, a British inventor, designed a furnace that burned the impurities out of melted iron and converted it into steel. The open-hearth process, devised by another Englishman, William Siemens, further improved the quality of steel by removing additional impurities from the iron. Railroads replaced iron rails with steel because it was lighter, stronger, and more durable than iron. Steel became the major building block of industry, furnishing girders and cables to construct manufacturing plants and office structures. As production became cheaper and more efficient, steel output soared from 13,000 tons in 1860 to 28 million tons in the first decade of the twentieth century.

Factory machinery needed constant lubrication, and the growing petroleum industry made this possible. A new drilling technique devised in 1859 tapped into pools of petroleum located deep below the earth's surface. In the post–Civil War era, new distilling techniques transformed this thick, smelly liquid into lubricating oil for factory machinery. This process of "cracking" crude oil also generated lucrative by-products for the home, such as kerosene and paraffin for heating and lighting. Robert A. Chesebrough discovered that a sticky oil residue could soothe cuts and burns, and in 1870 he began manufacturing a product he would soon trademark as Vaseline Petroleum Jelly. After 1900, the development of the gasoline-powered, internal combustion engine for automobiles opened up an even richer market for the oil industry.

Railroads also benefited from innovations in technology. Improvements included air brakes and automatic coupling devices to attach train cars to each other. Elijah McCoy, a trained engineer and the son of former slaves, was forced because of racial discrimination to work at menial railroad jobs shoveling coal and lubricating train parts every few miles to keep the gears from overheating. This grueling experience encouraged him to invent and patent an automatic lubricating device to improve efficiency.

Early innovations resulted from the genius of individual inventors, but by the late nineteenth century technological progress was increasingly an organized, collaborative effort. Thomas Edison and his team served as the model. In 1876 Edison set up a research laboratory in Menlo Park, New Jersey. Housed in a two-story, white frame building, Edison's "invention factory" was staffed by a team of inventors and craftsmen. Edison believed that "genius was 1 percent inspiration and 99 percent perspiration," and he devoted nearly every waking hour, often ignoring his family, to coordinating the invention process. In 1887 Edison opened another laboratory, ten times bigger than the one at Menlo Park, in nearby Orange, New Jersey. These facilities pioneered the research laboratories that would become a standard feature of American industrial development in the twentieth century.

Edison expected his research factories to produce "a minor invention every ten days and a big thing every six months or so." Edison and his crew largely succeeded. During his lifetime, Edison filed 1,093 U.S. patents; although he has received most of the credit, a good number of his inventions were the result of collaborative research. Out of his laboratory flowed inventions that revolutionized American business and culture. The phonograph and motion pictures changed the way people spent their leisure time. The electric lightbulb illuminated people's homes and made them safer by eliminating the need for candles and gas lamps, which were fire hazards. It also brightened city streets, making them available for outdoor evening activities, and lit up factories so that they could operate all night long.

Like his contemporaries who were building America's huge industrial empires, Edison cashed in on his workers' inventions. He joined forces with the Wall Street banker J. P. Morgan to finance the Edison Electric Illuminating Company, which in 1882 provided lighting to customers in New York City. Goods produced by electric equipment jumped in value from $1.9 million in 1879 to $21.8 million in 1890. In 1892, Morgan helped Edison merge his companies with several competitors and reorganized them as the General Electric Corporation, which became the industry leader.

Building a New South

Although the largely rural South lagged behind the North and the Midwest in manufacturing, industrial expansion did not bypass the region. Well aware of global economic trends and eager for the South to achieve its economic potential, southern business leaders and newspaper editors, especially the *Atlanta Constitution*'s editor Henry Grady, saw industrial development as the key to the creation of a **New South**. Attributing the Confederate defeat in the Civil War to the North's superior manufacturing output and

railroad supply lines, New South proponents hoped to modernize their economy in a similar fashion. One of those boosters was Richard H. Edmonds, the Virginia-born editor of the *Manufacturers' Record*. He extolled the virtues of the "real South" of the 1880s, characterized by "the music of progress—the whirr of the spindle, the buzz of the saw, the roar of the furnace, the throb of the locomotive." The South of Edmonds's vision would move beyond the regional separatism of the past and become fully integrated into the national economy.

Railroads were the key to achieving such economic integration, so after the Civil War new railroad tracks were laid throughout the South. Not only did this expanded railroad system create direct connections between the North and the South, but it also facilitated the growth of the southern textile industry. Seeking to take advantage of plentiful cotton, cheap labor, and the improved transportation system, investors built textile mills throughout the South, especially in the Carolinas and Georgia. Victims of falling prices and saddled with debt, sharecroppers and tenant farmers moved into mill towns in search of better employment. Mill owners preferred to hire girls and young women, who worked for low wages, to spin cotton and weave it on the looms. To do so, however, owners had to employ their entire family, for mothers and fathers would not let their daughters relocate without their supervision. Whatever attraction the mills offered applied only to whites. The pattern of white supremacy emerging in the post-Reconstruction South kept African Americans out of all but the most menial jobs.

Blacks contributed greatly to the construction of railroads in the New South, but they did not do so as free men. Convicts, most of whom were African American, performed the exhausting work of laying tracks through hills and swamps. Southern states used the **convict lease** system, in which blacks, usually imprisoned for minor offenses, were hired out to private companies to serve their time or pay off their fine. The convict lease system brought additional income to the state and supplied cheap labor to the railroads and planters, but it left African American convict laborers impoverished and virtually enslaved.

The South attracted a number of industries besides textile manufacturing. In the 1880s, James B. Duke established a cigarette manufacturing empire in Durham, North Carolina. Nearby tobacco fields provided the raw material that black workers prepared for white workers, who then rolled the cigarettes by machine. Acres of timber pines in the Carolinas, Florida, and Alabama sustained a lucrative lumber industry, one of the few to employ whites and blacks equally. Rich supplies of coal and iron in Alabama fostered the growth of the steel industry in Birmingham, which produced more than a million tons of steel at the turn of the twentieth century (Map 16.1).

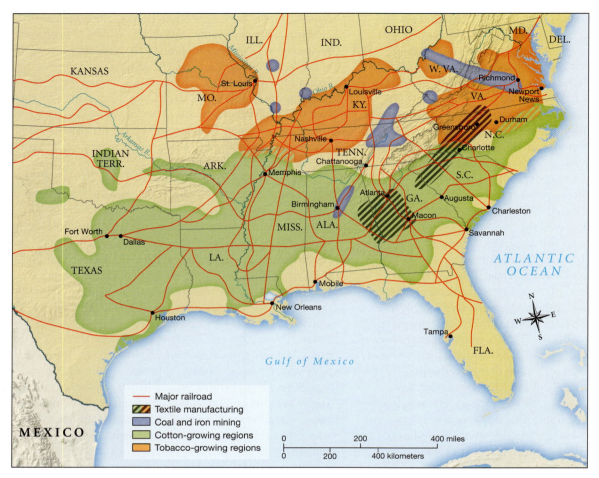

MAP 16.1   The New South, 1900
Although the South remained largely agricultural by 1900, it had made great strides toward building industries in the region. This so-called New South boasted an extensive railway network that provided a national market for its raw materials and manufactured goods, including coal, iron, steel, and textiles. Still, the southern economy in 1900 depended primarily on raising cotton and tobacco.

Despite this frenzy of industrial activity, the New South in many ways resembled the Old South. Southern entrepreneurs still depended on northern investors to supply much of the capital for investment. Investors were attracted by the low wages that prevailed in the South, but low wages also meant that southern workers remained poor and, in many cases, unable to buy the manufactured goods produced by industry. Efforts to diversify agriculture beyond tobacco and cotton were constrained by a sharecropping system based on small, inefficient plots. In fact, even though industrialization did make considerable headway in the South, the economy remained overwhelmingly agricultural. This suited many white southerners who wanted to hold on to the individualistic, agrarian values they associated with the Old South. In this way,

they sought to remain distinct from what they considered the acquisitive North. Yoked to old ideologies and a system of forced labor, modernization in the South could go only so far.

Industrial Consolidation

In both the North and the South, nineteenth-century industrialists strove to minimize or eliminate competition. To gain competitive advantages and increase profits, industrial entrepreneurs concentrated on reducing production costs, charging lower prices, and outselling the competition. Successful firms could then acquire rival companies that could no longer afford to compete, creating an industrial empire in the process.

Building such industrial empires was not easy, however, and posed creative challenges for business ventures. Heavy investment in machinery resulted in very high fixed costs (or overhead) that did not change much over time. Because overhead costs remained stable, manufacturers could reduce the per-unit cost of production by increasing the output of a product—what economists call "economy of scale." Manufacturers thus aimed to raise the volume of production and find ways to cut variable costs—for labor and materials, for example. Shaving off even a few pennies from the cost of making each unit could save millions of dollars on the total cost of production. Through such savings, a factory owner could sell his product more cheaply than his competitors and gain a larger share of the market.

A major organizational technique for reducing costs and underselling the competition was **vertical integration**. "Captains of industry," as their admirers called them, did not just build a business; they created a system—a network of firms, each contributing to the final product. Men like Andrew Carnegie controlled the various phases of production from top to bottom (vertical), extracting the raw materials, transporting them to the factories, manufacturing the finished products, and shipping them to market. In 1881, when Carnegie combined his operations with those of Henry Clay Frick of Pennsylvania, he gained not only a talented factory manager but also access to Frick's coal business. By using vertical integration, Carnegie eliminated middlemen and guaranteed regular and cheap access to supplies. He also avoided duplications in machinery, lowered inventories, and gained increased flexibility by shifting segments of the labor force to areas where they were most needed. This integrated system demanded close and careful management of the overall operation, which Carnegie provided. He manufactured steel with improved efficiency and cut costs. His credo became "Watch the costs and the profits will take care of themselves."

Businessmen also employed another type of integration—**horizontal integration**. This approach focused on gaining greater control over the market by acquiring firms that sold the same products. John D. Rockefeller, the founder of the mammoth Standard Oil Company, specialized in this technique. In the mid-1870s, he brought a number of key oil refiners into an alliance with Standard Oil to control four-fifths of the industry. At the same time, the oil baron ruthlessly drove out or bought up marginal firms that could not afford to compete with him. One such competitor testified to a congressional committee in 1879 about how Standard Oil had squeezed him out: "[Rockefeller] said that he had facilities for freighting and that the coal-oil business belonged to them; and any concern that would start in that business, they had sufficient money to lay aside a fund and wipe them out."

Horizontal integration was also a major feature in the telegraph industry. By 1861 Western Union had strung 76,000 miles of telegraph line throughout the nation. Founded in 1851, the company had thrived during the Civil War by obtaining most of the federal government's telegraph business. The firm had 12,600 offices housed in railroad depots throughout the country and strung its lines adjacent to the railroads. In the eight years before Cornelius Vanderbilt bought Western Union in 1869, the value of its stock jumped from $3 million to $41 million. Seeing an opportunity to make money, Wall Street tycoon Jay Gould set out to acquire Western Union. In the mid-1870s, Gould, who had obtained control over the Union Pacific Railway, financed companies to compete with the giant telegraph outfit. Gould did not succeed until 1881, when he engineered a takeover of Western Union by combining it with his American Union Telegraph Company. Gould made a profit of $30 million on the deal. On February 15, the day after the agreement, the *New York Herald Tribune* reported: "The country finds itself this morning at the feet of a telegraphic monopoly," a business that controlled the market and destroyed competition.

Bankers played a huge role in engineering industrial consolidation. No one did it more skillfully than John Pierpont Morgan. In the 1850s, Morgan started his career working for a prominent American-owned banking firm in London, and in 1861 he created his own investment company in New York City. Unlike the United States, Great Britain had a surplus of capital that bankers sought to invest abroad. Morgan played the central role in channeling funds from Britain to support the construction of major American railroads. During the 1880s and 1890s, Morgan orchestrated the refinancing of several ailing railroads, including the Baltimore & Ohio and the Southern Railroad. To maintain control over these enterprises, the Wall Street financier placed his allies on their boards of directors and selected the companies' chief operating officers. Morgan then turned his talents for organization to the steel industry. In 1901 he was instrumental in merging Carnegie's company with several competitors in which he had a financial interest. United States Steel, Morgan's creation, became the world's largest industrial corporation, worth $1.4 billion. By the end of the first decade of the twentieth century, Morgan's investment house held more than 340 directorships in 112 corporations, amounting to more than $22 billion in assets, the equivalent of $608 billion in 2012, all at a time when there was no income tax.

The Growth of Corporations

With economic consolidation came the expansion of **corporations**. Before the age of large-scale enterprise, the predominant form of business ownership was the partnership. Unlike partnerships, corporations provided investors with "limited liability." This meant that if the corporation went bankrupt, shareholders could not lose more than they had invested. Limited liability encouraged investment by keeping the shareholders' investment in the corporation separate from their other assets. In addition, corporations provided "perpetual life." Partnerships dissolved on the death of a partner, whereas corporations continued to function despite the death of any single owner. This form of ownership brought stability and order to financing, building, and perpetuating what was otherwise a highly volatile and complex business endeavor.

Capitalists devised new corporate structures to gain greater control over their industries. Rockefeller's Standard Oil Company led the way by creating the trust, a monopoly formed through consolidation. To evade state laws against monopolies, Rockefeller created a petroleum trust. He combined other oil firms across the country with Standard Oil and placed their owners on a nine-member board of trustees that ran the company. Subsequently, Rockefeller fashioned another method of bringing rival businesses together. Through a holding company, he obtained stock in a number of other oil companies and held them under his control.

The movement to create trusts, Rockefeller boasted, "was the origin of the whole system of modern economic administration." Statistics backed up his assessment. Between 1880 and 1905, more than three hundred mergers occurred in 80 percent of the nation's manufacturing firms. Great wealth became heavily concentrated in the hands of a relatively small number of businessmen. Around two thousand businesses, a tiny fraction of the total number, dominated 40 percent of the nation's economy.

Explore

See Document 16.1 for one cartoonist's interpretation of Rockefeller's power.

In their drive to consolidate economic power and shield themselves from risk, corporate titans generally had the courts on their side. In *Santa Clara County v. Southern Pacific Railroad Company* (1886), the Supreme Court decided that under the Fourteenth Amendment, which originally dealt with the issue of federal protection of African Americans' civil rights, a corporation was considered a "person." In effect, this ruling gave corporations the same right of due process that the framers of the amendment had meant to give to former slaves. In the 1890s, a majority of the Supreme Court embraced this interpretation. The right of due process shielded corporations from prohibitive government regulation of the workplace, including the passage of legislation reducing the number of hours in the workday.

Yet trusts did not go unopposed. In 1890 Congress passed Senator Sherman's Antitrust Act, which outlawed monopolies that prevented free competition in interstate commerce. The bill passed easily with bipartisan support because it merely codified legal principles that already existed. Sherman and his colleagues never intended to stifle large corporations, which through efficient business practices came to dominate the market. Rather, the lawmakers attempted to limit underhanded actions that destroyed competition. The judicial system further bailed out corporate leaders. In *United States v. E.C. Knight Company* (1895), a case against the "sugar trust," the Supreme Court rendered the Sherman Act virtually toothless by ruling that manufacturing was a local activity within a state and that, even if it was a monopoly, it was not subject to congressional regulation. This ruling left most trusts in the manufacturing sector beyond the jurisdiction of the **Sherman Antitrust Act**.

The introduction of managerial specialists, already present in European firms, proved the most critical innovation for integrating industry. With many operations controlled under one roof, large-scale businesses required a corps of experts to oversee and coordinate the various steps of production. Comptrollers and accountants pored over financial records to keep track of every penny spent and dollar earned. Traffic managers directed the movement of raw materials into plants and finished products out for distribution. Marketing executives were in charge of advertising goods and finding new markets. Efficiency experts sought to cut labor costs and make the production process operate more smoothly. Frederick W. Taylor, a Philadelphia engineer and businessman, developed the principles of scientific management. Based on his concept of reducing manual labor to its simplest components and eliminating independent action on the part of workers, managers introduced time-and-motion studies. Using a stopwatch, they calculated how to break down a job into simple tasks that could be performed in the least amount of time. From this perspective, workers were no different from the machines they operated.

Another vital factor in creating large-scale industry was the establishment of retail outlets that could sell the enormous volume of goods pouring out of factories. As consumer goods became less expensive, retail outlets sprang up to serve the growing market for household items, including watches, jewelry, sewing machines, cameras, and an assortment of rugs and furniture. Customers could shop at department stores—such as Macy's in New York City, Filene's in Boston, Marshall Field's in Chicago, Nordstrom's in Seattle, Gump's in San Francisco, Nieman Marcus in Dallas, Jacome's in Tucson, Rich's in Atlanta, and Burdine's in Miami—where they were waited on by a

DOCUMENT 16.1

Horace Taylor | What a Funny Little Government, 1900

As large firms merged with competitors to form giant companies that dominated the marketplace, opponents of such trusts decried the power that these enterprises wielded over the economy and the political system. Responding to such concerns, Congress passed the Sherman Antitrust Act in 1890, but the law proved weak and was loosely enforced. In the following illustration, cartoonist Horace Taylor, a Democrat, sought to make trusts an issue in the 1900 election by attacking John D. Rockefeller, whose Standard Oil Company embodied the evils of trusts for many critics.

Explore

How are the Capitol and Treasury depicted?

How does this illustration of Rockefeller emphasize the cartoonist's antitrust position?

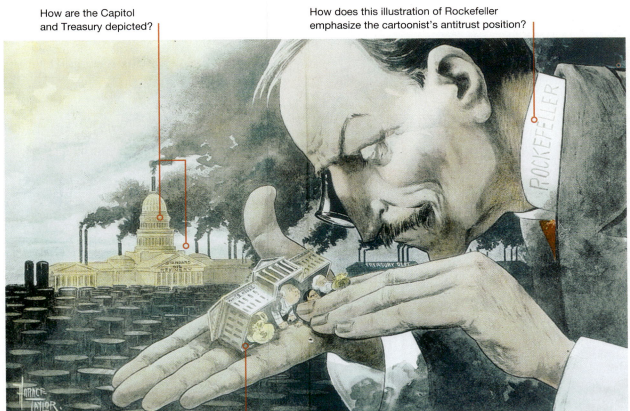

Collection of the New-York Historical Society

What is Rockefeller holding in his hand?

Put It in Context

What does this cartoon suggest about the relationship between big business and the federal government at the start of the twentieth century?

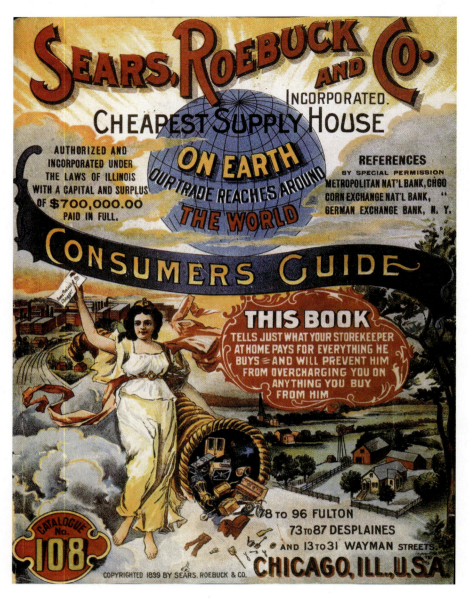

1899 Sears, Roebuck Catalog
The expansion of industrialization and completion of the transcontinental railroad created a national market for manufactured goods and led to the growth of consumer culture. The Chicago-based Sears, Roebuck used its mail-order catalog to attract customers throughout the United States and, as its cover suggests, the world. This colorful 1899 catalog offers the latest items in carpets, furniture, china, fashions, and photographic equipment and supplies.   The Granger Collection, New York

growing army of salesclerks. Or they could buy the cheaper items in Frank W. Woolworth's five and ten cent stores, which opened in towns and cities nationwide. Chain supermarkets—such as the Great Atlantic and Pacific Tea Company (A&P), founded in 1869—sold fruits and vegetables packed in tin cans. They also sold foods from the meatpacking firms of Gustavus Swift and Philip Armour, which shipped them on refrigerated railroad cars. Mail-order catalogs allowed Americans in all parts of the country to buy consumer goods without leaving their home. The catalogs of Montgomery Ward (established in 1872) and Sears, Roebuck (founded in 1886) offered tens of thousands of items. Rural free delivery (RFD), instituted by the U.S.

Post Office in 1891, made it even easier for farmers and others living in the countryside to obtain these catalogs and buy their merchandise without having to travel miles to the nearest post office. By the end of the nineteenth century, the industrial economy had left its mark on almost all aspects of life in almost every corner of America.

REVIEW & RELATE

What were the key factors behind the acceleration of industrial development in late-nineteenth-century America?

How did industrialization change the way American businessmen thought about their companies and the people who worked for them?

Free Markets and Rugged Individuals

American industrialization developed as rapidly as it did in large part because it was reinforced by traditional ideas and values. The notion that hard work and diligence would result in success meant that individuals felt justified, even duty-bound, to strive to achieve upward mobility and accumulate wealth. Churches, schools, intellectuals, and popular writers combined to buttress this doctrine of success. Those who succeeded believed that they had done so because they were more talented, industrious, and resourceful than others. Thus prosperous businessmen regarded competition and the free market as essential to the health of an economic world they saw based on merit. Yet these same businessmen also created trusts that destroyed competition, and they depended on the government for resources and protection. This obvious contradiction, along with the profoundly unequal distribution of wealth that characterized the late-nineteenth-century economy, generated a good deal of criticism of business tycoons and their beliefs.

The Doctrine of Success

Those at the top of the new industrial order justified their great wealth in a manner that most Americans could understand. The ideas of the Scottish economist Adam Smith, in *The Wealth of Nations* (1776), had gained popularity during the American Revolution. Advocating **laissez-faire** ("let things alone"), Smith contended that an "Invisible Hand," guided by natural law, guaranteed the greatest economic success if the government let individuals pursue their own self-interest unhindered by outside and artificial influences. In the late nineteenth century, businessmen and their conservative allies on the Supreme Court used Smith's doctrines to argue against restrictive government regulation. They equated their right to own and manage property with the personal liberty protected by the Fourteenth Amendment. Thus the Declaration of Independence, with its defense of "life, liberty, and the pursuit of happiness," and the Constitution, which enshrined citizens' political freedom, became instruments to guarantee unfettered economic opportunity and safeguard private property.

The view that success depended on individual initiative was reinforced in schools and churches. The McGuffey Readers, widely used to educate children, taught moral lessons of hard work, individual initiative, reliability, and thrift. The popular dime novels of Horatio Alger portrayed the story of young men, such as Ragged Dick, who rose through pluck and luck from "rags to riches." Americans could also hear success stories in houses of worship. Russell Conwell,

pastor of the Grace Baptist Church in Philadelphia, delivered a widely printed sermon entitled "Acres of Diamonds," which equated godliness with riches and argued that ordinary people had an obligation to strive for material wealth. "I say that you ought to get rich, and it is your duty to get rich," Conwell declared, "because to make money honestly is to preach the gospel." Conwell followed his own advice and became wealthy from the fees he earned delivering his popular sermon.

If economic success was a matter of personal merit, it followed that economic failure was as well. The British philosopher Herbert Spencer proposed a theory of social evolution based on this premise in his book *Social Statics* (1851). Imagining a future utopia, Spencer wrote, "Man was not created with an instinct for his own degradation, but from the lower he has risen to the higher forms. Nor is there any conceivable end to his march to perfection." In his view, those at the top of the economic ladder were closer

McGuffey Reader

Beginning in the mid-nineteenth century, McGuffey Readers became the most popular textbook for teaching elementary school pupils how to read. As this page from an edition first published in 1881 shows, the book included exercises that taught students moral lessons along with their readings. In emphasizing hard work and obedience, the readers instructed children in middle-class virtues.

to perfection than were those at the bottom. Any effort to aid the unfortunate would only slow the march of progress for society as a whole. Spencer's book proved extremely popular, selling nearly 400,000 copies in the United States by 1900. In recalling how Spencer's ideas influenced him, Carnegie wrote, "I remember that light came as in a flood and all was clear." Publication of Charles Darwin's landmark *On the Origin of Species* (1859) appeared to provide some scientific legitimacy for Spencer's view. The British naturalist argued that plants, animals, and humans progressed or declined because of their ability or inability to adapt favorably to the environment and transmit these characteristics to future generations. The connection between the two men's ideas has led some to label Spencer and his supporters "Social Darwinists." However, few defenders of laissez-faire principles in the late nineteenth century had actually read Darwin or referred to themselves as Social Darwinists, a term that came into widespread use only in the twentieth century.

Doctrines of success gained favor because they helped Americans explain the rapid economic changes that were disrupting their lives. Although most ordinary people would not climb out of poverty to middle-class respectability, let alone affluence, they clung to ideas that promised hope. After all, if a man like Carnegie could rise from poverty to become a multimillionaire, why not them? It mattered little that most of those who achieved extraordinary wealth did not emerge from the working class but rather came from the middle class. Ideas such as Spencer's that linked success with progress provided a way for those who did not do well to understand their failure and blame themselves for their own inadequacies. At the same time, the notion that economic success derived from personal merit legitimized the fabulous wealth of those who did rise to the top.

Capitalists such as Carnegie found a way to soften both the message of extreme competition and its impact on the American public. Denying that the government should help the poor, they proclaimed that men of wealth had a duty to furnish some assistance. In his famous essay **"The Gospel of Wealth"** (1889), Carnegie declared that "a man who died rich died disgraced." He argued that the rich should act as stewards of the wealth they earned. As trustees, they should administer their surplus income for the benefit of the community. Carnegie distinguished between charity (direct handouts to individuals), which he deplored, and philanthropy (building institutions that would raise educational and cultural standards), which he advocated. For example, Carnegie, Rockefeller, and railroad tycoons Leland Stanford and Cornelius Vanderbilt all gave endowments (and their names) to universities to provide education for those who worked hard to achieve it. Russell Conwell also gave away his fortune to various philanthropic enterprises, most

notably the founding of Temple University in Philadelphia, which opened its doors to poor men seeking a higher education. Carnegie was particularly generous in funding libraries (he provided the buildings but not the books) because they allowed people to gain knowledge through their own efforts.

Capitalists may have sung the praises of individualism and laissez-faire, but their actions contradicted their words. Successful industrialists in the late nineteenth century sought to destroy competition, not perpetuate it. Their efforts over the course of several decades produced giant corporations that measured the worth of individuals by calculating their value to the organization. As John D. Rockefeller, the master of consolidation, proclaimed, "The day of individual competition in large affairs is past and gone. **See Document Project 16: Debates about Laissez-Faire, page 517**.

Nor did capitalists strictly oppose government involvement. Although industrialists did not want the federal government to take any action that *retarded* their economic efforts, they did favor the use of the government's power to *promote* their enterprises and to stimulate entrepreneurial energies. Thus manufacturers pushed for congressional passage of high tariffs to protect goods from foreign competition and to foster development of the national marketplace. Industrialists demanded that federal and state governments dispatch troops when labor strikes threatened their businesses. They persuaded Washington to provide land grants for railroad construction and to send the army to clear Native Americans and bison from their tracks. They argued for state and federal courts to interpret constitutional and statutory law in a way that shielded property rights against attacks from workers. In large measure, capitalists succeeded not in spite of governmental support but because of it.

Challenges to Laissez-Faire

Proponents of government restraint and unbridled individualism did not go unchallenged. Critics of laissez-faire created an alternative ideology for those who sought to organize workers and expand the role of government as ways of restricting capitalists' power over labor and ordinary citizens.

Lester Frank Ward attacked laissez-faire in his book *Dynamic Sociology* (1883). A largely self-taught man who worked as a civil servant for the federal government, Ward did not disparage individualism but viewed the main function of society as "the organization of happiness." Contradicting Herbert Spencer, Ward maintained that societies progressed when government directly intervened to help citizens—even the unfortunate. Indeed, society could initiate "the systematic realization of its own interests, in the same manner that an intelligent and keen-sighted individual pursues his life-purposes." Rejecting laissez-faire, Ward argued that what people "really need is more government in its primary sense, greater protection from the rapacity of the favored few."

Some academics supported Ward's ideas. Most notably, economist Richard T. Ely applied Christian ethics to his scholarly assessment of capital and labor. He condemned the railroads for dragging "their slimy length over our country, and every turn in their progress is marked by a progeny of evils." In his book *The Labor Movement* (1886), Ely suggested that the ultimate solution for social ills resulting from industrialization lay in "the union of capital and labor in the same hands, in grand, wide-reaching, co-operative enterprises."

Two popular writers, Henry George and Edward Bellamy, added to the critique of materialism and greed. In *Progress and Poverty* (1879), George lamented: "Amid the greatest accumulations of wealth, men die of starvation." He blamed the problem on rent, which he viewed as an unjustifiable payment on the increase in the value of land, what he called "unearned increment." His remedy was to have government confiscate rent earned on land by levying a single tax on landownership. Though he advocated government intervention, he did not envision an enduring role for the state once it had imposed the single tax. By contrast, Bellamy imagined a powerful central government. In his novel *Looking Backward, 2000–1887* (1888), Bellamy scorned the "imbecility of private enterprise" and attacked industrialists who "maim and slaughter workers by thousands." In his view, the federal government should take over large-scale firms, administer them as workers' collectives, and redistribute wealth equally among all citizens.

Neither Bellamy, George, Ward, nor Ely endorsed the militant socialism of Karl Marx. The German philosopher predicted that capitalism would be overthrown and replaced by a revolutionary movement of industrial workers that would control the means of economic production and establish an egalitarian society. Although his ideas gained popularity among European labor leaders, they were not widely accepted in the United States during this period. George referred to Marx as "the prince of muddleheads." George and other critics believed that the American political system could be reformed without resorting to the extreme solution of a socialist revolution. They favored a cooperative commonwealth of capital and labor, with the government acting as an umpire between the two.

REVIEW & RELATE

In the late nineteenth century, how did many Americans explain individual economic success and failure?

How did the business community view the role of government in the economy at the end of the nineteenth century?

✓ LEARNINGCurve bedfordstmartins.com/hewittlawson/LC

Society and Culture in the Gilded Age

Wealthy people in the late nineteenth century used their fortunes to support lavish, indulgent lifestyles. For many of them, especially those with recent wealth, opulence rather than good taste was the standard of adornment. This tendency inspired writer Mark Twain and his collaborator Charles Dudley Warner to describe this era of wealth creation and vast inequality as the **Gilded Age**.

Twain and Warner had the very wealthy in mind when they coined the phrase, but others further down the social ladder found ways to participate in the culture of consumption. The rapidly expanding middle class enjoyed modest homes furnished with mass-produced consumer goods. Women played the central role in running the household, as most wives remained at home to raise children. Women and men often spent their free time attending meetings and other events sponsored by the many social, cultural, and political organizations that flourished during this era. Such prosperity was, however, largely limited to whites. For the majority of African Americans still living in the South, life proved much harder. In response to black aspirations for social and economic advancement, white politicians imposed a rigid system of racial segregation on the South. Although whites championed the cause of individual upward mobility, they restricted opportunities to achieve success to whites only.

Wealthy and Middle-Class Pleasures

In Chicago's Gold Coast, Boston's Back Bay, Philadelphia's Rittenhouse Square, San Francisco's Nob Hill, Denver's Quality Hill, and Cincinnati's Hilltop, urban elites lived lives of incredible material opulence. J. P. Morgan and John D. Rockefeller built lavish homes in New York City. William Vanderbilt constructed luxurious mansions along Fifth Avenue in Manhattan. High-rise apartment buildings also catered to the wealthy. Overlooking Central Park, the nine-story Dakota Apartments boasted fifty-eight suites, a banquet hall, and a wine cellar. Famous architects designed some of the finest of these stately homes, which their millionaire residents furnished with an eclectic mix of priceless art objects and furniture in a jumble of diverse styles. The rich and famous established private social clubs, sent their children to exclusive prep schools and colleges, and worshipped in the most fashionable churches.

Second homes, usually for use in the summer, were no less expensively constructed and decorated. Besides residences in Manhattan and Newport, Rhode Island, the Vanderbilts constructed a "home away from home" in the mountains of Asheville, North Carolina. The Biltmore, as they named it, contained 250 rooms, 40 master bedrooms, and an indoor swimming pool. Edward Julius Berwind of Philadelphia, who made his fortune in coal, constructed a magnificent summer residence in Newport. Modeled after a mid-eighteenth-century French chateau, The Elms cost $1.4 million (approximately $38.6 million in 2012) and was furnished with an assortment of Renaissance ceramics and French and Venetian paintings.

The wealthy also built and frequented opera houses, concert halls, museums, and historical societies as testimonies to their taste and sophistication. For example, the Vanderbilts, Rockefellers, Goulds, and Morgans financed the completion of the Metropolitan Opera House in New York City in 1883. When the facility opened, a local newspaper commented about the well-heeled audience: "The Goulds and the Vanderbilts and people of that ilk perfumed the air with the odor of crisp greenbacks." Upper-class women often traveled abroad to visit the great European cities and ancient Mediterranean sites.

Industrialization and the rise of corporate capitalism also brought an array of **white-collar workers** in managerial,

clerical, and technical positions. These workers formed a new, expanded middle class and joined the businesspeople, doctors, lawyers, teachers, and clergy who constituted the old middle class. More than three million white-collar workers were employed in 1910, nearly three times as many as in 1870.

Middle-class families decorated their residences with comfortable, mass-produced furniture, musical instruments, family photographs, books, periodicals, and a variety of memorabilia collected in their leisure time. They could relax in their parlors and browse through mass-circulation magazines like *Ladies' Home Journal* and *The Delineator*, a fashion and arts journal. They might also read a wide variety of popular newspapers that competed with one another with sensationalist stories. Or they could read some of the era's outpouring of fiction, including romances, dime novels, westerns, humor, and social realism, an art form that depicted working-class life.

Explore

See Document 16.2 for the cover of a popular women's magazine from 1900.

In the face of rapid economic changes, middle-class women and men joined a variety of social and professional organizations that were arising to deal with the problems accompanying industrialization (Table 16.1). During the 1880s, charitable organizations such as the American Red Cross were established to provide disaster relief. In 1892 the General Federation of Women's Clubs was founded to improve women's educational and cultural lives. Four years later, the National Association of Colored Women organized to help relieve suffering among the black poor, defend black women, and promote the interests of the black race. Many scholarly organizations were formed during this decade, including the American Historical Association, the Modern Language Association, and the American Mathematical Society.

During these swiftly changing times, adults became increasingly concerned about the nation's youth and sought to create organizations that catered to young people. Formed before the Civil War in England and expanded to the United States, the Young Men's Christian Association (YMCA) grew briskly during the 1880s as it erected buildings where young men could socialize, build moral character, and engage in healthy physical exercise. The Young Women's Christian Association (YWCA) provided similar

TABLE 16.1 An Age of Organizations, 1876–1896

Category	Year of Founding	Organization
Charitable	1881	American Red Cross
	1887	Charity Organization Society
	1889	Educational Alliance
	1893	National Council of Jewish Women
Sports/Fraternal	1876	National League of Baseball
	1882	Knights of Columbus
	1888	National Council of Women
	1892	General Federation of Women's Clubs
	1896	National Association of Colored Women
Professional	1883	Modern Language Association
	1884	American Historical Association
	1885	American Economic Association
	1888	American Mathematical Society

The Delineator, 1900

By 1900 *The Delineator* had become one of America's foremost women's magazines. On the surface, it appeared to cater to traditional gender norms, each month featuring stories on fashion, sewing, leisure, and home design. But the editors of *The Delineator* also called for women's rights and broader social reform. In 1907, for example, editor Theodore Dreiser organized a successful outreach program to find homes for abandoned and orphaned children.

Explore

THE DELINEATOR

In Guise of Summer

JULY, 1900.

PARIS, LONDON, NEW YORK

PUBLISHED MONTHLY BY THE BUTTERICK PUBLISHING CO. (LTD.)

SUBSCRIPTION PRICE, $1.00.   SINGLE COPY, 15 CENTS.

ENTERED AT THE POST-OFFICE, N. Y., AS SECOND-CLASS MAIL MATTER

© Sarah Fabian-Baddiel/Heritage-Images/The Image Works

Interpret the Evidence

- What does this woman's clothing and activity suggest about her background?
- Who do you think was the target audience for this magazine?

Put It in Context

What social and political trends during the late nineteenth century might account for the popularity of magazines like *The Delineator*?

opportunities for women. African Americans also partici-pated in "Y" activities through the creation of racially separate branches.

Changing Gender Roles

Middle-class wives generally remained at home, caring for the house and children, often with the aid of a servant. Whereas in the past farmers and artisans had worked from the home, now most men and women accepted as natural the separation of the workplace and the home caused by industrialization and urbanization. Although the birthrate and marriage rates among the middle class dropped during the late nineteenth century, wives were still expected to care for their husbands and family first to fulfill their feminine duties. Even though daughters increasingly attended colleges reserved for women, such as Smith, Radcliffe, Wellesley, and Mount Holyoke, their families viewed education as a means of providing refinement rather than a career. One physician aptly summed up the prevailing view that women could only use their brains "but little and in trivial matters" and should concentrate on serving as "the companion or ornamental appendage to man."

Middle-class women were now confronted with the new consumer culture. Department stores, chain stores, ready-made clothes, and packaged goods, from Jell-O and Kellogg's Corn Flakes to cake mixes, competed for the money and loyalty of female consumers. Hairdressers, cosmetic companies, and department stores offered a growing and ever-changing assortment of styles, even as they also provided new jobs to those unable to afford the latest fashions without a weekly paycheck. The expand-ing array of consumer goods did not, however, decrease women's domestic workload. They had more furniture to dust, fancier meals to prepare, changing fashions to keep up with, higher standards of cleanliness to maintain, and more time to devote to entertaining. Yet the availability of mass-produced goods to assist the housewife in her chores made her role as consumer highly visible, while making her role as worker nearly invisible.

For the more socially and economically independent young women—those who attended college or beauty and secretarial schools—new worlds of leisure opened up. Bicycling, tennis, and croquet became popular sports for women in the late nineteenth century. So, too, did playing basketball, both in colleges and through industrial leagues. Indeed, women's colleges made sports a requirement, to offset the stress of intellectual life and produce a more well-rounded woman. Young women who sought an air of sophistica-tion dressed according to the image of the Gibson Girl, the creation of illustrator Charles Dana Gibson. In the 1890s, the Gibson Girl became the model for the energetic, athletic "new woman," with her upswept hair, fancy hats, long skirts, flowing blouses, and disposable income.

Middle-class men enjoyed their leisure by joining fraternal organizations. Writing in the *North American Review* in 1897, W. G. Harwood commented that the late nineteenth century was the "Golden Age of Fraternity." Five and a half million men (of some 19 million adult men in the United States) joined fraternal orders, such as the Odd Fellows, Masons, Knights of Pythias, and Elks. These groups offered middle-class men a network of business contacts and gave them a chance to enjoy a commu-nal, masculine social environment otherwise lacking in their lives.

In fact, historians have referred to a "crisis of masculinity" afflicting a segment of middle- and upper-class men

Shopping in a Department Store
In cities around the country, department stores offered a variety of items appealing to middle-class consumers, especially women. In this photograph from 1893, shoppers interested in purchasing gloves receive personal attention from well-dressed salesclerks behind the counter of Rike's Department Store in Dayton, Ohio. © Bettmann/CORBIS

in the late nineteenth and early twentieth centuries. Middle-class occupations whittled away the sense of autonomy that men had experienced in an earlier era when they worked for themselves. The emergence of corporate capitalism had swelled the ranks of the middle class with organization men, who held salaried jobs in managerial departments. At the same time, the push for women's rights, especially the right to vote, and women's increasing involvement in civic associations threatened to reduce absolute male control over the public sphere.

Responding to this gender crisis, middle-class men sought ways to exert their masculinity and keep from becoming frail and effeminate. Psychologists like G. Stanley Hall warned that unless men returned to a primitive state of manhood, they risked becoming feminized and spiritually paralyzed. To avoid this, they should build up their bodies and engage in strenuous activities to improve their physical fitness. Edgar Rice Burroughs's *Tarzan of the Apes* (1912) extolled primitive manhood and contrasted its natural virtues with the vices of becoming overcivilized.

Men turned to sports to cultivate their masculinity. Besides playing baseball and football, they could attend various sporting events. Baseball became the national pastime, and men could root for their home team and establish a community with the thousands of male spectators who filled up newly constructed ballparks. These fields of dirt and grass were situated amid urban businesses, apartment buildings, and traffic and served as a metaphor for the preservation of an older, pastoral life alongside the hubbub of modern technology. Baseball, which had started as a game played by elites in New York City in the 1840s, soon became a commercially popular sport. It spread across the country as baseball clubs in different cities competed with each other. The sport came into its own with the creation of the professional National League in 1876 and the introduction of the World Series in 1903 between the winners of the National League and the American League pennant races.

Boxing also became a popular spectator sport in the late nineteenth century. Bare-knuckle fighting—without the protection of gloves—epitomized the craze to display pure masculinity. A boxing match lasted until one of the fighters was knocked out, leaving both fighters bloody and battered.

During the late nineteenth century, middle-class women and men also had increased opportunities to engage in different forms of sociability and sexuality. Gay men and lesbians could find safe havens in New York City's Greenwich Village and Chicago's North Side for their own entertainment. Although treated by medical experts as sexual "inverts" who might be cured by an infusion of "normal" heterosocial contact, gays and

lesbians began to emerge from the shadows of Victorian-era sexual constraints around the turn of the twentieth century. "Boston marriages" constituted another form of relationship between women. The term apparently came from Henry James's book *The Bostonians* (1886), which described a female couple living together in a monogamous, long-term relationship. This conjugal-style association appealed to financially independent women who did not want to get married. Many of these relationships were sexual, but some were not. In either case, they offered women of a certain class an alternative to traditional, heterosexual marriage.

Black America and Jim Crow

While wealthy and middle-class whites experimented with new forms of social behavior, African Americans faced greater challenges to preserving their freedom and dignity. In the South, where the overwhelming majority of blacks lived, post-Reconstruction southern governments adopted various techniques to keep blacks from voting. To circumvent the Fifteenth Amendment, southern states devised suffrage qualifications that they claimed were racially neutral, and the Supreme Court ruled in their favor. They instituted the poll tax, a tax that each person had to pay in order to cast a ballot. Poll taxes fell hardest on the poor, a disproportionate number of whom were African American. Disfranchisement reached its peak in the 1890s, as white southern governments managed to deny the vote to most of the black electorate (Map 16.2). Literacy tests officially barred the uneducated of both races, but they were administered in a manner that discriminated against blacks while allowing illiterate whites to satisfy the requirement. Many literacy tests contained a loophole called a "grandfather clause." Under this exception, men whose father or grandfather had voted in 1860—a time when white men but not black men, most of whom were slaves, could vote in the South—were excused from taking the test.

In the 1890s, white southerners also imposed legally sanctioned racial segregation on the region's black citizens. Commonly known as **Jim Crow** laws (named for a character in a minstrel show, where whites performed in black-face), these new statutes denied African Americans equal access to public facilities and ensured that blacks lived apart from whites. In 1883, when the Supreme Court struck down the 1875 Civil Rights Act (see chapter 14), it gave southern states the freedom to adopt measures confining blacks to separate schools, public accommodations, seats on transportation, beds in hospitals, and sections of graveyards. In 1896 the Supreme Court sanctioned Jim Crow, constructing the constitutional rationale for legally keeping the races apart. In ***Plessy v. Ferguson***, the high court ruled

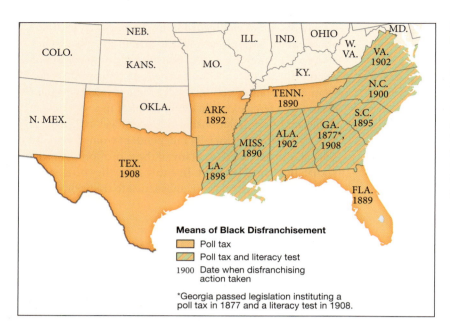

MAP 16.2   Black Disfranchisement in the South, 1889–1908

After Reconstruction, black voters posed a threat to the ruling Democrats by occasionally joining with third-party insurgents. To repel these challenges, Democratic Party leaders made racial appeals to divide poor whites and blacks. Chiefly in the 1890s and early twentieth century, white leaders succeeded in disfranchising black voters (and some poor whites), mainly by adopting poll tax and literacy requirements.

that a Louisiana law providing for "equal but separate" accommodations for "whites" and "coloreds" on railroad cars did not violate the equal protection clause of the Fourteenth Amendment. In its decision, the Court concluded that civil rights laws could not change racial destiny. "If one race be inferior to the other socially," the justices explained, "the Constitution of the United States cannot put them on the same plane." In practice, however, white southerners obeyed the "separate" part of the equation but never provided equal services. If blacks tried to overstep the bounds of Jim Crow in any way that whites found unacceptable, they risked their lives. Between 1884 and 1900, nearly 1,700 blacks were lynched in the South. Victims were often subjected to brutal forms of torture before they were hanged or shot.

In everyday life, African Americans carried on as best they could. Segregation provided many African Americans with opportunities to build their own businesses, control their own churches, develop their own schools staffed by black teachers, and form their own civic associations and fraternal organizations. Segregation, though harsh and unequal, did foster a sense of black community, promoted a rising middle class, and created social networks that enhanced racial pride. Founded in 1898, the North Carolina Life Insurance Company, one of the leading black-owned and black-operated businesses, employed many African Americans in managerial and sales positions. Burial societies ensured that their members received a proper funeral when they died. As with whites, black men joined lodges such as the Colored Masons and the Colored Odd Fellows, while women participated in the YWCA and the National Association of Colored Women. A small

percentage of southern blacks resisted Jim Crow by migrating to the North, where blacks still exercised the right to vote, more jobs were open to them, and segregation was less strictly enforced.

REVIEW & RELATE

- What role did consumption play in the society and culture of the Gilded Age?

- How did industrialization contribute to heightened anxieties about gender roles and race?

LEARNINGCurve bedfordstmartins.com/hewittlawson/LC

National Politics in the Era of Industrialization

Politicians such as John Sherman played an important role in the expanding industrial economy that provided new opportunities for the wealthy and the expanding middle class. For growing companies and corporations to succeed, they needed a favorable political climate that would support their interests. Businessmen frequently looked to Washington for assistance at a time when politicians were held in low repute. During this era, the office of the president was a weak and largely administrative post, and corporate leaders were unconcerned with the quality of the mind and character of presidents, legislators, and judges so long as these officials furthered their economic objectives. For much of this period, the two national political parties battled to a standoff, which resulted in congressional gridlock with little accomplished. Yet spurred by fierce partisan competition, political participation grew among the electorate.

Why Great Men Did Not Become President

James Bryce, a British observer of American politics, devoted a chapter of his book *The American Commonwealth* (1888) to "why great men are not chosen presidents." He acknowledged that the office of president "is raised far above all other offices [and] offers too great a stimulation to ambition." Yet he believed that the White House attracted mediocre occupants because the president functioned mainly as an executor. The stature of the office had shrunk following the impeachment of Andrew Johnson and the reassertion of congressional power during Reconstruction (see chapter 14). Presidents considered themselves mainly as the nation's top administrator. They did not see their roles as formulating policy or intervening on behalf of legislative objectives. Presidents had only a small White House staff to assist them, which reflected the meager demands placed on their office, especially in times of peace, which prevailed until 1898. The Civil Service Act of 1883 had reduced even further the political patronage the president had at his disposal. With the office held in such low regard, Bryce asserted, "most of the ablest men for thought, planning, and execution in America, go into the business of developing the national resources of the country." During the Age of Organization, great men became corporate leaders, not presidents.

Perhaps aware that they could expect little in the way of assistance or imagination from national leaders, voters refused to give either Democrats or Republicans solid support. No president between Ulysses S. Grant and William McKinley won back-to-back elections or received a majority of the popular vote. The only two-time winner, the Democrat Grover Cleveland, lost his bid for reelection in 1888 before triumphing again in 1892. Republicans scored victories in four out of six presidential contests from 1876 to 1896, but the vote tallies were extremely close.

Explore

See Documents 16.3 and 16.4 for two views on presidential greatness.

Nevertheless, the presidency attracted accomplished individuals. Rutherford B. Hayes (1877–1881), James A. Garfield (1881), and Benjamin Harrison (1889–1893) all had served ably in the Union army as commanding officers during the Civil War and had prior political experience.

The nation greatly mourned Garfield following his assassination in 1881 by Charles Guiteau, a disgruntled applicant for federal patronage. Upon Garfield's death, Chester A. Arthur (1881–1885) became president. He had served as a quartermaster general during the Civil War, had a reputation as sympathetic to African American civil rights, and had run the New York City Customs House effectively. Grover Cleveland (1885–1889, 1893–1897) first served as mayor of Buffalo and then as governor of New York. All of these men, as even Bryce admitted, worked hard, possessed common sense, and were honest. However, they were uninspiring individuals who lacked qualities of leadership that would arouse others to action.

Congressional Inaction

Character alone did not diminish the power of the president. More important was the structure of Congress, which prevented the president from providing vigorous leadership. Throughout most of this period, Congress remained narrowly divided. Majorities continually shifted from one party to the other. For all but two terms, Democrats controlled the House of Representatives, while Republicans held the majority in the Senate. Divided government meant that during his term in office no late-nineteenth-century president had a majority of his party in both houses of Congress. Turnover among congressmen in the House of Representatives, who were elected every two years, was quite high, and there was little power of incumbency. For example, of the twenty-one congressmen from Ohio elected in 1882, only ten had served in the previous session, and only four of the ten won reelection two years later. The Senate, however, provided more continuity and allowed senators, with six-year terms of office, to amass greater power than congressmen could, as evidenced by John Sherman serving six terms in the upper chamber.

For all the power that Congress wielded, it failed to govern effectively or efficiently. Contemporary observers lamented the dismal state of affairs in the nation's capital. A cabinet officer in 1869 complained: "You can't use tact with a Congressman! A Congressman is a hog! You must take a stick and hit him on the snout!"

Although both the House and the Senate contained men of great talent, fine speaking ability, and clever legislative minds, the rules of each body turned orderly procedure into chaos. In the House, measures did not receive adequate attention on the floor because the Speaker did not have the power to control the flow of systematic debate. Committee chairmen held a tight rein over the introduction and consideration of legislation and competed with one another for influence in the chamber. Congressmen showed little decorum as they conducted business on

The Making of a Great President: Two Views

The British traveler James Bryce admired the United States and toured the country in the late 1880s. His book *The American Commonwealth* (1888), though flattering of U.S. traditions and accomplishments, found its political leaders lacking in greatness—an opinion that many subsequent historians have shared, although Bryce and more recent historians might differ in their definition of greatness. In the following passage from his book, Bryce comments on the ordinariness of most American presidents. Contrast Bryce's assessment with the excerpt from the obituary of President Grover Cleveland published in the *New York Times*.

Explore

16.3 James Bryce | Why Great Men Are Not Chosen Presidents, 1888

Europeans often ask, and Americans do not always explain, how it happens that this great office, the greatest in the world, unless we except the Papacy, to which any man can rise by his own merits, is not more frequently filled by great and striking men? In America, which is beyond all other countries the country of a "career open to talents," a country, moreover, in which political life is unusually keen and political ambition widely diffused, it might be expected that the highest place would always be won by a man of brilliant gifts. But since the heroes of the Revolution died out with Jefferson and Adams and Madison some sixty years ago, no person except General Grant has reached the chair whose name would have been remembered had he not been President, and no President except Abraham Lincoln has displayed rare or striking qualities in the chair. Who now knows or cares to know anything about the personality of James K. Polk or Franklin

Pierce? The only thing remarkable about them is that being so commonplace they should have climbed so high. . . .

. . . Besides, the ordinary American voter does not object to mediocrity. He has a lower conception of the qualities requisite to make a statesman than those who direct public opinion in Europe have. He likes his candidate to be sensible, vigorous, and, above all, what he calls "magnetic," and does not value, because he sees no need for, originality or profundity, a fine culture or a wide knowledge. Candidates are selected to be run for nomination by knots of persons who, however expert as party tacticians, are usually commonplace men; and the choice between those selected for nomination is made by a very large body, an assembly of over eight hundred delegates from the local party organizations over the country, who are certainly no better than ordinary citizens.

Source: James Bryce, *The American Commonwealth* (London: Macmillan, 1888), 1:100, 102–3.

the House floor. Representatives chatted with each other, their voices drowning out the speakers at the podium, or they ignored the business at hand and instead answered correspondence and read newspapers.

The Senate, though more manageable in size and more stable in membership (only one-third of its membership stood for reelection every two years), did not function much more smoothly. Despite party affiliations, senators thought very highly of their own judgments and very little of the value of party unity. The position of

majority leader, someone who could impose discipline on his colleagues and design a coherent legislative agenda, had not yet been created. An exasperated Woodrow Wilson, who favored the British system of parliamentary government, attributed the problem to the failure to place trust in somebody "to assume final responsibility and blame." Wilson, the author of *Congressional Government* (1885) and a future president, concluded: "Our government is defective as it parcels out power and confuses responsibility." Under these circumstances, neither the

16.4 Obituary of Grover Cleveland, 1908

As a public man, considering the splendid record that he made, he will be put in the same class with Washington and Lincoln—one of the three great Presidents that this country has had. His greatness was justified by his exceptionally strong character and his many intellectual gifts. He was a man of great moral strength, and having the advantage of a fine intellect he thought seriously and deeply upon all subjects, and, having reached a conclusion, particularly as to a principle of morals or religion, or public weal [welfare], he was uncompromising. He agreed with David Crockett that the first thing was to determine what was right and then to do that thing.

What he was in public life he was equally in private life; strong in his views, tolerant in method, but uncompromising in principle. Most of his time was spent in promoting education and philanthropy—work which entailed sacrifices of his time and personal convenience, without fee or hope of reward beyond the desire to do that which was useful and good. These occupied, when not in public life, most of his time, so that when we look over his career, though he reached the proverbial three score and ten years, it is not to be measured by years alone, but by his splendid deeds and lofty ideals which affected all who came within the range of his influence.

Source: "All Washington Mourns, All Flags at Half Staff in Tribute to Dead Statesman," *New York Times*, June 25, 1908, 5.

Interpret the Evidence

- What qualities was Bryce surprised to find missing in American presidents? How might Bryce have characterized the values and beliefs of the typical American voter?
- What does the obituary of Grover Cleveland tell you about the qualities many Americans associated with "greatness"? What qualities do you think make a president "great"?

Put It in Context

What role did late-nineteenth-century presidents play in the great economic growth of the United States?

president nor Congress governed efficiently or responsibly.

An Energized and Entertained Electorate

Despite all the difficulties of the legislative process, political candidates eagerly pursued office and conducted extremely heated campaigns. The electorate considered politics a form of entertainment. Political parties did not stand for clearly

stated issues or offer innovative solutions; instead, campaigns took on the qualities of carefully staged performances. Candidates crafted their oratory to arouse the passions and prejudices of their audiences, and their managers handed out buttons, badges, and ceramic and glass plates stamped with the candidates' faces and slogans.

Partisanship helped fuel high political participation. During this period, voter turnout in presidential elections was much higher than at any time in the twentieth century. Region, as well as historical and cultural allegiances,

1892 Presidential Campaign Plate

Before radio, television, and the Internet, political parties advertised candidates in a variety of colorful ways, including banners, buttons, ribbons, and ceramic and glass plates. Voters, who turned out in record numbers during the late nineteenth century, coveted these items. This plate shows the 1892 Democratic presidential ticket of Grover Cleveland and Adlai Stevenson, who lost the election.   Collection of Steven F. Lawson

could be shaped to eradicate ignorance and vice. These Protestants were more likely to cast their ballots for Republicans, except in the South, where regional loyalty to the Democratic Party trumped religious affiliation.

Some people went to the polls because they fiercely disliked members of the opposition party. Northern white workers in New York City or Cincinnati, Ohio, for example, might vote against the Republican Party because they viewed it as the party of African Americans. Other voters cast their ballots against Democrats because they identified them as the party of Irish Catholics, intemperance, and secession.

Although political parties commanded fierce loyalties, the parties remained divided internally. For example, the Republicans pitted "Stalwarts" against "Half Breeds." Led by Senators Roscoe Conkling and Chester Arthur of New York, Zachariah Chandler of Michigan, and John Logan of Illinois, the Stalwarts presented themselves as the "Old Guard" of the Republican Party, what they called the "Grand Old Party" (GOP). The Half Breeds, a snide name given to them by the Stalwarts, tended to be younger Republicans and were represented by Senators James G. Blaine, John Sherman, and James A. Garfield of Ohio and George Frisbie Hoar of Massachusetts. This faction claimed to be more open to new ideas and less wedded to the old

replaced ideology as the key to party affiliation. The wrenching experience of the Civil War had cemented voting loyalties for many Americans. After Reconstruction, white southerners tended to vote Democratic; northerners and newly enfranchised southern blacks generally voted Republican. However, geographic region alone did not shape political loyalties; a sizable contingent of Democratic voters remained in the North, and southern whites and blacks periodically abandoned both the Democratic and Republican parties to vote for third parties.

Religion played an important role in shaping party loyalties during this period of intense partisanship. The Democratic Party tended to attract Protestants of certain sects, such as German Lutherans and Episcopalians, as well as Catholics. These faiths emphasized religious ritual and the acceptance of personal sin. They believed that the government should not interfere in matters of morality, which should remain the province of Christian supervision on Earth and divine judgment in the hereafter. By contrast, other Protestant denominations, such as Baptists, Congregationalists, Methodists, and Presbyterians, highlighted the importance of individual will and believed that the law

causes that the Republican Party promoted, such as racial equality. In the end, however, the differences between the two groups had less to do with ideas than with which faction would have greater power within the Republican Party.

Overall, the continuing strength of party loyalties produced equilibrium as voters cast their ballots primarily along strict party lines. The outcome of presidential elections depended on key "undecided" districts in several states in the Midwest and in New York and nearby states, which swung the balance of power in the electoral college. Indeed, from 1876 to 1896 all winning candidates for president and vice president came from Ohio, Indiana, Illinois, New York, and New Jersey.

REVIEW & RELATE

What accounted for the inefficiency and ineffectiveness of the federal government in the late nineteenth century?

How would you explain the high rates of voter turnout and political participation in an era of uninspiring politicians and governmental inaction?

Conclusion: Industry in the Age of Organization

From 1877 to 1900, American businessmen demonstrated a zeal for organization. Prompted by new technology that opened up national markets of commerce and communication, business entrepreneurs created large-scale corporations that promoted industrial expansion. Borrowing from European investors and importing and improving on European technology, by 1900 U.S. industrialists had surpassed their overseas counterparts.

Capitalists made great fortunes and lived luxurious lifestyles, emulating the fashions of European elites. Most corporate leaders did not rise from poverty but instead came from the upper middle class and had access to education and connections. Those like Andrew Carnegie, who rose from rags to riches, were the exceptions. The wealthy explained their success as the result of individual effort and hard work. This idea was reinforced in schoolbooks such as the McGuffey Readers, the novels of Horatio Alger, and religious sermons, like those of Russell Conwell.

Although most working Americans did not achieve much wealth in the Age of Organization, they had faith in the possibility of improving their economic position. Members of the middle class lived less extravagantly than did the wealthy; nonetheless, they enjoyed the comforts of the growing consumer economy. Although Jim Crow restricted the black middle class and a heightened sense of masculinity inhibited opportunities available to white women, both groups managed to carve out ways to lift themselves economically and socially.

In gaining success, the wealthy exchanged individualism for organization, competition for consolidation, and laissez-faire for government support. Without pro-business policies from Washington lawmakers and favorable decisions from the Supreme Court, big business would not have developed as rapidly as it did in this era. To prosper, corporations needed sympathetic politicians—whether to furnish free land for railroad expansion, enact tariffs to protect manufacturers, or protect private property. Even when a public outcry led to the regulation of trusts, the pro-business senator John Sherman shaped the legislation so as to minimize damage to corporate interests. In general, national politicians avoided engaging in fierce ideological conflicts, but they, too, organized. The political parties they fashioned encouraged a high level of political participation among voters.

It remained for those who did not share in the glittering wealth of the Gilded Age to find ways to resist corporate domination. The next chapter explores the efforts of workers and farmers to remedy the economic, social, and political ills that accompanied industrialization.

**John McLuckie and
Mary Elizabeth Lease**

1892 revealed that workers were vastly out-matched in their struggle with management.

Mary Elizabeth Clyens was the daughter of Irish Catholic parents who came to the United States as part of the great wave of Irish immigration that began in the 1840s. The sixth of eight children, Mary was raised in western Pennsylvania but moved to Kansas in 1870 to teach at a Catholic girls' school. There she met and married Charles L. Lease, a pharmacist turned farmer. The couple, however, could not support themselves and their four children through farming, and in 1883 the Leases moved to Wichita, where Charles returned to his original profession. In Wichita, Mary found a much wider scope to express her interests and beliefs than she had on the farm. She joined a variety of organizations and worked in support of Irish independence, women's suffrage, and movements to advance the cause of industrial workers and farmers exploited by big business, railroads, and banks.

Lease entered state and national politics through the Populist Party, which formed in 1890 to challenge the power of large corporations and their political allies, promote the interests of small farmers, and create an alliance between farmers and industrial workers. A mesmerizing speaker, she urged her audiences, according to reporters, to "raise less corn and more hell." In her book *The Problem of Civilization Solved* (1895), Lease offered a variety of remedies for late-nineteenth-century America's economic and political ills, including nationalizing railroad and telegraph lines, increasing the currency supply, and expanding popular democracy. She briefly served as president of the Kansas State Board of Charities when the Populists came to power in 1893, but her tendency to "raise hell" with elected officials in her party led to her removal from office. Following the collapse of the Populist Party in 1896, Lease and her family moved to New York City. She worked as a journalist, divorced her husband, and remained active as a speaker for educational reform and birth control until her death in 1931. ●

bottom photo: Kansas State Historical Society

THE AMERICAN HISTORIES of John McLuckie and Mary Elizabeth Lease were linked by the economic and political forces that shaped the lives of both factory workers and farmers in industrialized America. Even though the culture of rural America was quite different from that of the nation's industrial towns and cities, farmers and workers faced many of the same problems. Over the course of the late nineteenth century, both groups had seen control over the nature and terms of their work pass from the individual worker or farmer to large corporations and financial institutions. Both groups felt marginalized, dependent, and devalued. McLuckie and Lease were part of a larger effort by laborers and farmers to fight for their own interests against the concentrated economic and political power of big business and to regain control of their lives and their work.

Working People Organize

Industrialists were not the only ones who built organizations to promote their economic interests. Like their employers, working men and women also saw the benefits of organizing to increase their political and economic leverage. Determined to secure decent wages and working conditions, workers joined labor unions, formed political parties, and engaged in a variety of collective actions, including strikes. However, because workers' organizations were beset by internal conflicts over occupational status, race, ethnicity, and gender and were no match for the powerful alliance between corporations and the federal government, they failed to become a lasting national political force. Workers fared better in their own communities, where family, neighbors, and local businesses were more likely to come to their aid.

The Industrialization of Labor

The industrialization of the United States described in chapter 16 transformed the workplace, bringing together large numbers of laborers under difficult conditions. In 1870 few factories employed 500 or more workers. Thirty years later, more than 1,500 companies had workforces of this size, including General Electric, International Harvester, Pullman Palace Car Company, and U.S. Steel. Just after the Civil War, manufacturing employed 5.3 million workers; thirty years later, the figure soared to more than 15.1 million. Most of these new industrial workers came from two main sources. First, farmers like the Leases who could not make a decent living from the soil moved to nearby cities in search of factory jobs. Although mostly white, this group also included blacks who sought to escape the oppressive conditions of sharecropping. Between 1870 and 1890, some 80,000 African Americans journeyed from the rural South to cities in the South and the North to search for employment. Second, the economic opportunities in America drew millions of immigrants from Europe over the course of the nineteenth century. Immigrant workers initially came from northern Europe, mainly from England, Ireland, Germany, and Scandinavia. However, by the end of the nineteenth century, the number of immigrants from southern and eastern European countries, such as Austria-Hungary, Greece, Italy, and Russia, had surpassed those coming from northern Europe.

Inside factories, **unskilled workers**, those with no particular skill or expertise, encountered a system undergoing critical changes, as small-scale manufacturing gave way to larger and more mechanized operations. Immigrants, who made up the bulk of unskilled laborers, had to adjust both to a new country and to unfamiliar, unpleasant, and often dangerous industrial work. A traveler from Hungary who visited a steel mill in Pittsburgh that employed many Hungarian immigrants compared the factories to penitentiaries. "In making a tour of these prisons," he wrote, "wherever the heat is most insupportable, the flames most choking, there we are certain to find compatriots bent and wasted with toil." Nor were any government benefits—such as workers' compensation or unemployment insurance—available to industrial laborers who were hurt in accidents or laid off from their jobs.

Skilled workers, who had particular training or abilities and were more difficult to replace, were not immune to the changes brought about by industrialization and the creation of large-scale business enterprises. In the early days of manufacturing, skilled laborers operated as independent craftsmen. They provided their own tools, worked at their own pace, and controlled their production output. This approach to work enhanced their sense of personal dignity, reflected their notion of themselves as free citizens, and distinguished them from the mass of unskilled laborers. Mechanization, however, undercut their autonomy by dictating both the nature and the speed of production through practices of scientific management (see chapter 16). Instead of producing goods, skilled workers increasingly applied their craft to servicing machinery and keeping it running smoothly. One example of workers' resistance to this loss of independence on the shop floor occurred in Lowell, Massachusetts. Responding to a new regulation requiring all employees to report to their jobs in work clothes at the opening bell and to remain there with the door locked until the closing bell, a machinist promptly packed his tools, quit, and told his boss that he had not "been brought up under a system of slavery." While owners reaped the benefits of the mechanization and regimentation of the industrial workplace, many skilled workers saw such "improvements" as a threat to their freedom.

Explore

See Document 17.1 for one worker's opinion on mechanization.

Still, most workers did not oppose the technology that increased their productivity and resulted in higher wages. Compared to their mid-nineteenth-century counterparts, industrial laborers now made up a larger share of the general population, earned more money, and worked fewer hours. During the 1870s and 1880s, the average industrial worker's real wages (actual buying power) increased by 20 percent. At the same time, the average workday declined from ten and a half hours to ten hours. From 1870 to 1890, the general price index dropped 30 percent, allowing consumers to benefit from lower prices.

Yet workers were far from content, and the lives of industrial workers remained extremely difficult. Although workers as a group saw improvements in wages and hours, they did not earn enough income to support their families adequately. Also, there were widespread disparities based on job status, race, ethnicity, sex, and region. Skilled workers earned more than unskilled workers. Whites were paid more than African Americans, who were mainly shut out of better jobs. Immigrants from northern Europe, who had settled in the United States before southern Europeans, tended to hold higher-paying skilled positions. Southern factory workers, whether in textiles, steel, or armaments, earned less than their northern counterparts. And women, an increasingly important component of the industrial workforce, earned less than men. On average, women earned only 25 percent of what men did.

Between 1870 and 1900, the number of female wage-workers grew by 66 percent, accounting for about one-quarter

DOCUMENT 17.1

John Morrison | Testimony on the Impact of Mechanization, 1883

Like other skilled laborers, New York City machinist John Morrison saw the introduction of machinery that accompanied industrialization as a threat to his identity as a craftsman. Though highly paid compared with unskilled workers, craftsmen led the way in organizing unions and engaging in strikes against big business. In the following excerpt from his testimony before a U.S. Senate committee investigating conflicts between capital and labor, Morrison discusses the source of many skilled workingmen's discontent.

Explore

Question: Is there any difference between the conditions under which machinery is made now and those which existed ten years ago?

Answer: A great deal of difference.

Question: State the differences as well as you can.

Answer: Well, the trade has been subdivided and those subdivisions have been again subdivided, so that a man never learns the machinist's trade now. Ten years ago he learned, not the whole of the trade, but a fair portion of it. Also, there is more machinery used in the business, which again makes machinery. In the case of making the sewing-machine, for instance, you find that the trade is so subdivided that a man is not considered a machinist at all. Hence it is merely laborers' work and it is laborers that work at that branch of our trade. The different branches of the trade are divided and subdivided so that one man may make just a particular part of a machine and may not know anything whatever about another part of the same machine. In that way machinery is produced a great deal cheaper than it used to be formerly, and in fact, through this system of work,

100 men are able to do now what it took 300 or 400 men to do fifteen years ago. By the use of machinery and the subdivision of the trade they so simplify the work that it is made a great deal easier and put together a great deal faster. There is no system of apprenticeship, I may say, in the business. You simply go in and learn whatever branch you are put at, and you stay at that unless you are changed to another. . . .

Question: Are the machinists here generally contented, or are they in a state of discontent and unrest?

Answer: There is mostly a general feeling of discontent, and you will find among the machinists the most radical workingmen, with the most revolutionary ideas. You will find that they don't so much give their thoughts simply to trade unions and other efforts of that kind, but they go far beyond that; they only look for relief through the ballot or through a revolution, a forcible revolution.

Source: *Report of the Committee of the Senate upon the Relations between Labor and Capital*, 48th Cong. (1885), 755–59.

Interpret the Evidence

- How does Morrison explain the subdivision of labor in the modern factory?
- How does Morrison characterize the mood of skilled laborers?

Put It in Context

How did the introduction of machinery affect skilled workers?

of all nonfarm laborers. The majority of employed women, including those working in factories, were single and between the ages of sixteen and twenty-four. Overall, only 5 percent of married women worked outside the home, although 30 percent of African American wives were employed. Women workers were concentrated in several areas. White and black women continued to serve as maids and domestics. Others took over jobs that were once occupied by men. They

became teachers, nurses, clerical workers, telephone operators, and department store salesclerks. Although these jobs were initially seen as opening up new opportunities for women, they soon became identified as "women's work," which meant lower pay and less potential for professional advancement. Other women toiled in manufacturing jobs requiring fine eye-hand coordination, such as cigar rolling and work in the needle trades and textile industry.

Women also turned their homes into workplaces. In crowded apartments, they sewed furs onto garments, made straw hats, prepared artificial flowers, and fashioned jewelry. Earnings from piecework (work that pays at a set rate per unit) were even lower than factory wages, but they allowed married women with young children to contribute to the family income. When sufficient space was available, families rented rooms to boarders, and women provided meals and housekeeping for the lodgers. Some female workers found other ways to balance work with the needs and constraints of family life. To gain greater autonomy in their work, black laundresses began cleaning clothes in their own homes, rather than their white employers' homes, so that they could control their own work hours. In 1881 black washerwomen in Atlanta conducted a two-week strike to secure higher fees from white customers.

Manufacturing also employed many child workers. By 1900 about 10 percent of girls and 20 percent of boys between the ages of ten and fifteen worked, and at least 1.7 million children under the age of sixteen held jobs. Employers often exposed children to dangerous and unsanitary conditions. Although some children got fresh air working as newsboys, shining shoes, and collecting junk, most worked long, hard hours breathing in dust and fumes as they labored in textile mills, tobacco plants, print shops, and coal mines. In Indiana, young boys worked the night shift in dark, windowless glass factories. One of the adults working in a Rhode Island textile mill lamented: "Poor, puny weak little children are kept at work the entire year without intermission or even a month for schooling." Children under the age of ten, known as "breaker boys," climbed onto filthy coal heaps and picked out unprocessed material. Working up to twelve-hour days, these children received less than a dollar a day.

Women and children worked because the average male head of household could not support his family on his own pay, despite the increase in real wages. As Carroll D. Wright, director of the Massachusetts Bureau of the Statistics of Labor, reported in 1882, "A family of workers can always live well, but the man with a family of small children to support, unless his wife works also, has a small chance of living properly." For example, in 1883 in Joliet, Illinois, a railroad brakeman tried to support his wife and eight children on $360 a year. They rented a three-room house for $5 per month and ate mainly bread and potatoes. A state investigator described the way they lived: "Clothes ragged, children half dressed and dirty. They all sleep in one room regardless of sex. The house is devoid of furniture, and the entire concern is as wretched as could be imagined." Although not all laborers lived in such squalor, many wageworkers barely lived at subsistence level.

Although the average number of working hours dropped during this era, many laborers put in more than 10 hours a day on the job. In 1890 bakers worked more than 65 hours a week, steelworkers more than 66, and

canners 77. In the steel industry, blast-furnace operators toiled 12 hours a day, 7 days a week. They received a day off every 2 weeks, but only if they worked a 24-hour shift. Given the long hours and backbreaking work, it is not surprising that accidents were a regular feature of industrial life. Each year tens of thousands were injured on the job, and thousands died as a result of mine cave-ins, train wrecks, explosions in industrial plants, and fires at textile mills and garment factories. Railroad employment was especially unsafe—accidents ended the careers of one in six workers.

Agricultural refugees who flocked to cotton mills in the South also faced dangerous working conditions. Working twelve-hour days breathing the lint-filled air from the processed cotton posed health hazards, especially for the very young and the elderly. Textile workers also had to place their hands into heavy machinery to disentangle threads, making them extremely vulnerable to serious injury. Wages scarcely covered necessities, and on many occasions families did not know where their next meal was coming from. North Carolina textile worker J. W. Mehaffry complained that the mill owners "were slave drivers" who "work their employees, women, and children from 6 a.m. to 7 p.m. with a half hour for lunch." The company supplied houses, but the occupants had "very little furniture, just a couple of beds.

Chinese American Telephone Operator

The invention of the telephone brought jobs to many Americans, especially women. Yet not all operators were women, as this photograph shows. San Francisco's Chinatown employed workers from its own community, and in this photo a Chinese man works as a telephone operator while a child in a school uniform and an adult stand by him.　© CORBIS

Just enough to get by on is about all we had." Their meals usually consisted of potatoes, cornbread, and dried beans cooked in fat. This diet, without dairy products and fresh meat, led to outbreaks of pellagra, a debilitating disease caused by niacin (vitamin B3) deficiency.

Although wages and working hours improved slightly for some workers, employers kept the largest share of the increased profits that resulted from industrialization. In 1877 John D. Rockefeller collected dividends at the rate of at least $720 an hour, roughly double what his average employee earned in a year. Despite some success stories, prospects for upward mobility for most American workers remained limited. Unskilled workers might climb up the economic ladder during their lifetime, but usually not more than one rung. A manual worker might rise into the ranks of the semiskilled but would not make it into the middle class. And to achieve even this small upward mobility required putting the entire family to work and engaging in rigorous economizing, what one historian called "ruthless underconsumption." The Horatio Alger "rags to riches" stories (see chapter 16) proved a myth for nearly all workers. Despite their best efforts, most Americans remained part of the working class.

Women in the Knights of Labor

Under the leadership of Terence Powderly, the Knights of Labor admitted women in 1881. Four years later, the Knights established the Women's Work Department, directed by Leonora Barry, a married garment worker in Philadelphia. This photograph shows women delegates to the 1886 Knights of Labor convention, one of whom holds her infant child.   © Bettmann/CORBIS

Organizing Unions

Faced with improving but inadequate wages and hazardous working conditions, industrial laborers sought to counter the concentrated power of corporate capitalists by joining forces. They attempted to organize **unions**—groups of workers seeking rights and benefits from their employers through their collective efforts. Union organizing was prompted by attitudes that were common among employers. Most employers were convinced that they and their employees shared identical interests, and they believed that they were morally and financially entitled to establish policies on their workers' behalf. They refused to engage in negotiations with labor unions (a process known as **collective bargaining**) and rejected unions as illegitimate organizations. Although owners appreciated the advantages of companies banding together to eliminate competition or to lobby for favorable regulations, similar collective efforts by workers struck them as unfair, even immoral. It was up to the men who supplied the money and the machines—rather than the workers—to determine what was a fair wage and what were satisfactory working conditions. In 1877 William H. Vanderbilt, the son of transportation tycoon Cornelius Vanderbilt, explained this way of thinking: "Our men feel that although I . . . may have my millions and they the rewards of their daily toil, still we are about equal in the end. If they suffer, I suffer, and if I suffer they cannot escape." Needless to say, many workers disagreed. One of labor's central demands was the institution of the eight-hour workday. The idea came from Great Britain, which had industrialized earlier in the nineteenth century. In 1817 the British socialist Robert Owen had summarized this demand as "Eight hours labor, Eight hours recreation, Eight hours rest." This goal had not yet been achieved in Britain or the rest of industrial Europe when American labor activists picked it up in the 1860s, spreading the message through parades and rallies sponsored by Eight-Hour Leagues.

A growing number of working people failed to see the relationship between employer and employee as mutually beneficial. Increasingly, they considered labor unions to be the best vehicle for communication and negotiation between workers and owners. Though not the first national workers' organization, the **Noble Order of the Knights of Labor**, founded by Uriah Stephens in 1869, initiated the most extensive and successful campaign after the Civil War to unite workers and challenge the power of corporate capitalists. "There is no mutuality of interests . . . [between] capital and labor," the Massachusetts chapter of the Knights proclaimed. "It is the iron heel of a soulless monopoly, crushing the manhood out of sovereign citizens." In fact, the essential premise of the Knights was that *all* workers shared common interests that were very different from those of owners. Thus the union excluded only those it believed preyed on citizens both economically and morally—lawyers, bankers, saloon-keepers, and professional gamblers.

The Knights did not enjoy immediate success. Their participation in the Great Railroad Strike of 1877 (see chapter 14) drew some attention to the union, but the Knights did not really begin to flourish until Terence V. Powderly replaced Stephens as Grand Master of the organization in 1879. Powderly advocated the eight-hour workday, the abolition of child labor, and equal pay for women. Under his leadership, the Knights accepted African Americans, immigrants, and women as members, though they excluded Chinese immigrant workers, as did other labor unions. As a result, the Knights experienced a surge in membership from 9,000 in 1879 to nearly a million in 1885 (including John McLuckie), about 10 percent of the industrial workforce.

Rapid growth proved to be a mixed blessing. As membership grew, Powderly and the national organization exercised less and less control over local chapters. In fact, local chapters often defied the central organization by engaging in strikes, a labor tactic Powderly had officially disavowed. Nonetheless, with Powderly standing mainly on the sidelines, members of the Knights struck successfully against the Union Pacific Railroad and the Missouri Pacific Railroad in 1885. The following year, on May 1, 1886, local assemblies of the Knights joined a nationwide strike to press for an eight-hour workday, again without Powderly's approval. However, this strike was soon overshadowed by events in Chicago that would prove to be the undoing of the Knights (Figure 17.1).

For months before the general strike, the McCormick Harvester plant in Chicago had been at the center of an often violent conflict over wages and work conditions. On May 3, 1886, police killed two strikers in a clash between union members and strikebreakers who tried to cross the picket lines. In response, a group of anarchists led by the German-born activist August Spies called for a rally in **Haymarket Square** to protest police violence. Consisting mainly of foreign-born radicals, anarchists believed that government represented the interests of capitalists and stifled freedom for workers. Anarchists differed among themselves, but they generally advocated tearing down government authority, restoring personal freedom, and forming worker

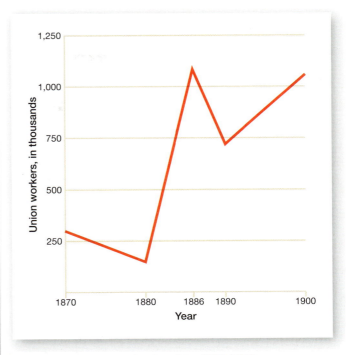

FIGURE 17.1   Union Membership, 1870–1900

Union membership fluctuated widely in the late nineteenth century. After reaching a low point in 1880, the number of union members rebounded after organizing by the Knights of Labor. Membership plummeted in the years after the Haymarket Square incident of 1886 but soared again in the 1890s through the efforts of the American Federation of Labor and western miners.   Source: Data from Richard B. Freeman, "Spurts in Union Growth: Defining Moments and Social Processes" (working paper 6012, National Bureau of Economic Research, Cambridge, MA, 1997).

communes to replace capitalism. To achieve their goals, anarchists like Spies advocated the violent overthrow of government.

The Haymarket rally began at 8:30 in the evening of May 4 and attracted no more than 1,500 people, who listened to a series of speeches as rain fell. By 10:30 p.m., when the crowd had dwindled to some 300 people, 180 policemen decided to break it up. As police moved into the square, someone set off a bomb. The police fired back, and when the smoke cleared, seven policemen and four protesters lay dead. Most of the fatalities and injuries resulted not from the bomb but from the police crossfire after the explosion. A subsequent trial convicted eight anarchists of murder, though there was no evidence that any of them had planted a bomb or used weapons; four of them, including August Spies, were executed. Although Powderly and other union leaders denounced the anarchists and the bombing, the incident greatly tarnished the labor movement. Capitalists and their allies in the press attacked labor unionists as radicals prone to violence and denounced strikes as un-American. Following the Haymarket incident, the membership rolls of the Knights plunged to below 500,000. By the mid-1890s, the Knights had fewer than 20,000 members.

As the fortunes of the Knights of Labor faded, the **American Federation of Labor (AFL)** grew in prominence, offering an alternative vision of unionization. Instead of one giant industrial union that included all workers, skilled and unskilled, the AFL organized only skilled craftsmen—the labor elite—into trade unions. In 1886 Samuel Gompers, a British-born cigar maker, became president of the AFL. Gompers considered trade unions "the business organizations of the wage earners to attend to the business of the wage earners" and favored the use of strikes. No social reformer, the AFL president concentrated on obtaining better wages and hours for workers so that they could share in the prosperity generated by industrial capitalism. By 1900 the AFL had around a million members. It achieved these numbers by recruiting the most independent, highest-paid, and least replaceable segment of the labor force—white male skilled workers. Unlike the Knights, the AFL had little or no place for women and African Americans in its ranks.

As impressive as the AFL's achievement was, the union movement as a whole experienced only limited success in the late nineteenth century. Only about one in fifteen industrial workers belonged to a union in 1900. Union membership was low for a variety of reasons. First, the political and economic power of corporations and the prospects of retaliation made the decision to sign up for union membership a risky venture. Second, the diversity of workers made organizing a difficult task. Foreign-born laborers came from many countries and were divided by language, religion, ethnicity, and history. Moreover, European immigrants quickly adopted native-born whites' racial prejudices against African Americans. Third, despite severe limitations in social mobility, American workers generally retained their faith in the benefits of the capitalist system. The pervasive doctrine of success defined workers not as laborers locked into the lower class but as businessmen on the rise, each with the potential to become a Rockefeller or a Carnegie. Finally, the government used its legal and military authority to side with employers and suppress militant workers.

Southern workers were the most resistant to union organizing. The agricultural background of mill workers left them with a heightened sense of individualism and isolation. In addition, their continued connection to family and friends in the countryside offered a potential escape route from industrial labor. Finally, employers' willingness to use racial tensions to divide working-class blacks and whites prevented them from joining together to further their common economic interests.

Clashes between Workers and Owners

Despite the difficulties of organizing workers, labor challenged some of the nation's largest industries in the late nineteenth century. Faced with owners' refusal to recognize or negotiate with unions, workers marshaled their greatest source of power: withholding their labor and going on strike. Employers in turn had powerful weapons at their command to break strikes. They could recruit strikebreakers and mobilize private and public security forces to protect their businesses. That workers went on strike against such odds testified to their desperation and courage.

Workers in the United States were not alone in their efforts to combat industrial exploitation. In England, laborers organized for better wages and working conditions. In 1888 in London, young women who worked as matchmakers staged a walkout to protest the exorbitant fines that employers imposed on them for arriving even one minute late to work. With community support, they won their demands. From 1888 to 1890, the number of strikes throughout Europe grew from 188 to 289. In 1890 thousands of workers in Budapest, Hungary, rose up to protest unsafe working conditions. European workers also campaigned for the right to vote, which unlike white male American workers, they were denied on economic grounds.

In the United States in the 1890s, labor mounted several highly publicized strikes. Perhaps the most famous was the 1892 **Homestead strike**. Steelworkers at Carnegie's Homestead, Pennsylvania, factory lived seven miles east of Pittsburgh and, like John McLuckie, played an active role in local politics and civic affairs. Residents generally believed that Andrew Carnegie's corporation paid decent wages that allowed them to support their families and buy their own homes. In 1892 craftsmen earned $180 a month, and they appeared to have Carnegie's respect. Others, like McLuckie, earned less than half that amount, and unskilled workers made even less.

In 1892, with steel prices falling, Carnegie decided to replace some of his skilled craftsmen with machinery, cut wages, save on labor costs, and bust McLuckie's union, the Amalgamated Association of Iron and Steel Workers, with which he had voluntarily negotiated in the past. Knowing that his actions would provoke a strike and seeking to avoid the negative publicity that would result, Carnegie left the country and went to Scotland, leaving his plant manager, Henry Clay Frick, in charge.

Fiercely anti-union, Frick prepared for the strike by building a three-mile, fifteen-foot-high fence, capped with barbed wire and equipped with searchlights, around three sides of the Homestead factory. A hated symbol of the manager's hostility, the fence became known as "Fort Frick." Along the fourth side of the factory flowed the Monongahela

River. Frick had no intention of negotiating seriously with the union on a new contract, and on July 1 he ordered a lockout. Only employees who rejected the union and accepted lower wages could return to work. The small town rallied around the workers, and the union members won a temporary victory. On July 6, barge-loads of armed Pinkerton detectives, hired by Frick to protect the plant, set sail toward the factory entrance alongside the Monongahela. McLuckie, the head of the Amalgamated, denounced the Pinkertons as "a band of cutthroats, thieves, and murderers in the employ of unscrupulous capital for the oppression of honest labor." From the shore, union men shot at the barges and set fire to a boat they pushed toward the Pinkertons. When the smoke cleared, the Pinkertons surrendered and hastily retreated onshore as women and men chased after them.

This triumph proved costly for the union. The battle left nine strikers and three Pinkerton detectives dead. Although community officials were on the workers' side, Frick convinced the governor of Pennsylvania to send in state troops to protect the factory and the strikebreakers. On July 23, Alexander Berkman, an anarchist who had no connection with the union, entered Frick's office and shot the steel executive in the neck, leaving him wounded but alive. The resulting unfavorable publicity, together with the state's prosecution of the union, broke the strike. Subsequently, steel companies blacklisted the union leaders for life, and McLuckie fled Pennsylvania and wound up nearly penniless in Arizona. Ever the philanthropist, when Carnegie heard of McLuckie's plight in 1900, he tried to give his former adversary some money anonymously. The proud and still defiant McLuckie declined the offer, but a friend of Carnegie's arranged for an Arizona railroad to hire him as a machinery-repair superintendent.

Explore

See Document 17.2 for an anarchist's account of the Homestead strike.

Like Andrew Carnegie, George Pullman considered himself an enlightened employer who took good care of the men who worked in his luxury sleeping railcar factory outside Chicago. However, also like the steel titan, Pullman placed profits over personnel. In 1893 a severe economic depression prompted Pullman to cut wages without correspondingly reducing the rents that his employees paid for living in company houses. This dual blow to worker income and purchasing power led to a fierce strike the following year. The Pullman workers belonged to the American Railway Union, headed by Eugene V. Debs, who believed that labor organizing was an integral part of a worker's rights of political and economic citizenship. After George Pullman refused to negotiate, the union voted to go on strike.

In the end, the **Pullman strike** was broken not by the Pullman company but by the federal government. The railroad managers association persuaded President Grover Cleveland's attorney general, Richard Olney, a former railroad lawyer, that strikers were interfering with delivery of the U.S. mail transported by train. Cleveland ordered federal troops to get the railroads operating, but the workers still refused to capitulate. Olney then obtained an injunction (a court order) from the federal courts to restrain Debs and other union leaders from continuing the strike. The government used the Sherman Antitrust Act to punish unions for conspiring to restrain trade, something it had rarely done with respect to large corporations. Refusing to comply, Debs and other union officials were charged with contempt, convicted under the Sherman Antitrust Act, and sent to jail. The strike collapsed. See Document Project 17: The Pullman Strike of 1894, page 550.

Debs remained unrepentant. After serving his jail sentence, he became even more radical. In 1901 he helped establish the Socialist Party of America. German exiles who came to the United States following revolutions in Europe in 1848 had brought with them the revolutionary ideas of the German philosopher Karl Marx. Marx argued that capital and labor were engaged in a class struggle that would end in a victory for the proletariat, the abolition of private property, and socialist rule. This revolution would come about through the violent overthrow of capitalist government and its replacement by communism. Marxist ideas attracted a small following in the United States, mainly among the foreign-born population. By contrast, other types of European socialists, including the German Social Democratic Party, which Marx denounced, appealed for working-class support by advocating the creation of a more just and humane economic system through the ballot box, not by violent revolution. Debs, born and raised in Terre Haute, Indiana, favored this nonviolent, democratic brand of socialism and managed to attract a broader base of supporters by articulating socialist doctrines in the language of cooperation and citizenship that many Americans shared. Debsian socialism appealed not only to industrial workers but also to dispossessed farmers and miners in the Southwest and Midwest.

Western miners had a history of labor activism, and by the 1890s they were ready to listen to radical ideas. Shortly after the Homestead strike ended in 1892, silver miners in Coeur d'Alene, Idaho, walked out after owners slashed their wages by 15 percent. Employers refused to recognize any union, obtained an injunction against the strike, imported strikebreakers to run the mines, and persuaded Idaho's governor to impose martial law, in which the military took over the normal operation of civilian affairs. The work stoppage lasted four months, resulting in the arrest of six hundred strikers, including their leader, Ed Boyce.

DOCUMENT 17.2

Emma Goldman | Reflections on the Homestead Strike, 1931

Emma Goldman was one of the most prominent radicals of the late nineteenth and early twentieth centuries. Goldman argued for sexual freedom and women's liberation. In addition, as an anarchist, she initially advocated the overthrow of capitalism through violent attacks. To this end, during the Homestead strike Goldman's lover, Alexander Berkman, attempted unsuccessfully to assassinate Henry Clay Frick, the manager of Carnegie's steel plant. In this passage from her autobiography, Goldman describes the events that led to the assassination attempt.

Explore

A few days after our return to New York the news was flashed across the country of the slaughter of steel-workers by Pinkertons. Frick had fortified the Homestead mills, built a high fence around them. Then, in the dead of night, a barge packed with strike-breakers, under protection of heavily armed Pinkerton thugs, quietly stole up the Monongahela River. The steel-men had learned of Frick's move. They stationed themselves along the shore, determined to drive back Frick's hirelings. When the barge got within range, the Pinkertons had opened fire, without warning, killing a number of Homestead men on the shore, among them a little boy, and wounding scores of others.

The wanton murders aroused even the daily papers. Several came out in strong editorials, severely criticizing Frick. He had gone too far; he had added fuel to the fire in the labour ranks and would have himself to blame for any desperate acts that might come.

We were stunned. We saw at once that the time for our manifesto had passed. Words had lost their meaning in the face of the innocent blood spilled on the banks of the Monongahela. Intuitively each felt what was surging in the heart of the others. Sasha [Alexander Berkman] broke the silence. "Frick is the responsible factor in this crime," he said; "he must be made to stand the consequences." It was the psychological moment for an *Attentat* [political violence]; the whole country was aroused, everybody was considering Frick the perpetrator of a cold-blooded murder. A blow aimed at Frick would re-echo in the poorest hovel, would call the attention of the whole world to the real cause behind the Homestead struggle. It would also strike terror in the enemy's ranks and make them realize that the proletariat of America had its avengers.

Source: Emma Goldman, *Living My Life* (New York: Alfred Knopf, 1931), 86–87.

Interpret the Evidence

- How does Goldman characterize the Pinkerton detectives?
- What did Goldman think the assassination of Frick would achieve?

Put It in Context

Why do you think public perception turned against militant labor activism in the aftermath of Homestead and other strikes during the late nineteenth century?

Although the workers lost, the following year they succeeded in forming the Western Federation of Miners, a radical union that continued their fight.

The **Industrial Workers of the World (IWW)**, which emerged largely through the efforts of the Western Federation of Miners, sought to raise wages, improve working conditions, and gain union recognition for the most exploited segments of American labor. The IWW, or "Wobblies" as they were popularly known, offered an alternative to Samuel Gompers's American Federation of Labor by attempting to unite all skilled and unskilled workers in an effort to overthrow capitalism. The

Wobblies favored strikes and direct-action protests rather than collective bargaining or mediation. At their rallies and strikes, they often encountered government force and corporation-inspired mob violence. Nevertheless, the IWW had substantial appeal among lumberjacks in the Northwest, dockworkers in port cities, miners in the West, farmers in the Great Plains, and textile workers in the Northeast. Of their 150 strikes, the most successful ones involved miners in Goldfield, Nevada (1906–1907); textile workers in Lawrence, Massachusetts (1912); and silk workers in Paterson, New Jersey (1913).

Even though industrialists usually had state and federal governments as well as the media on their side, workers continued to press for their rights. Workers used strikes as a last resort when business owners refused to negotiate or recognize their demands to organize themselves into unions. Although most late-nineteenth-century strikes failed, striking unionists nonetheless called for collective bargaining, higher wages, shorter hours, and improved working conditions—an agenda that unions and their political allies would build on in the future.

Working-Class Leisure in Industrial America

Despite the economic hardships and political repression that industrial laborers faced in the late nineteenth century, workers carved out recreational spaces over which they had control and that offered relief from their backbreaking toil. Time clocks, often viewed as an annoying part of scientific management, nevertheless clearly emphasized the difference between working and nonworking hours. For many, Sunday became a day of rest that took on a secular flavor.

Working-class leisure patterns varied by gender, race, and region. Women did not generally attend spectator sporting events, such as baseball and boxing matches, which catered to men. Nor did they find themselves comfortable in union halls and saloons, where men found solace in drink. Working-class wives preferred to gather to prepare for births, weddings, and funerals or to assist neighbors who lost their homes because of fire, death, or greedy landlords.

Once employed, working-class daughters found a greater measure of independence and free time by living in rooming houses on their own. Women's wages were only a small fraction of men's earnings, so working women rarely made enough money to support a regular social life along with paying for rent, food, and clothes. Still, they found ways to enjoy their free time. Some single women went out in groups, hoping to meet men who would pay for drinks, food, or a vaudeville show. Others dated so that they knew they would be taken care of for the evening. Some of the men who "treated" on a date assumed a right to sexual favors in return, and some of these women then expected men to provide them with housing and gifts in exchange for an ongoing sexual relationship. Thus emotional and economic relationships became intertwined in complicated ways.

Around the turn of the twentieth century, dance halls flourished as one of the mainstays of working-class communities throughout the nation. Huge dance palaces that held three thousand to five thousand people were built in the entertainment districts of most large cities. They made their money by offering music with lengthy intermissions for the sale of drinks and refreshments. Women and men also attended cabarets, some of which were racially integrated. In so-called red-light districts of the city, prostitutes earned money entertaining their clients with a variety of sexual pleasures.

Not all forms of leisure were strictly segregated along class lines. A number of forms of cheap entertainment appealed not only to working-class women and men but also to their middle-class counterparts. By the turn of the twentieth century, most large American cities featured amusement parks. Brooklyn's Coney Island stood out as the most spectacular of these sprawling playgrounds of fun and excitement. In 1884 the world's first roller coaster was built at Coney Island, providing thrills to those brave enough to ride it. Chicago residents could enjoy the Ferris wheel, which appeared at the 1893 World's Columbian Exposition. Designed by George Ferris, who operated a firm specializing in structural steel, the wheel rose 250 feet in the air, was propelled by two 1,000-horsepower steam engines, and accommodated 1,440 riders at a time.

Vaudeville houses—with their minstrel shows (whites in blackface) and comedians, singers, and dancers—brought howls of laughter to working-class audiences. Nickelodeons charged five cents to watch short films. Live theater generally attracted more wealthy patrons; however, the Yiddish theater, which flourished on New York's Lower East Side, and other immigrant-oriented stage productions appealed mainly to working-class audiences.

Southern workers also enjoyed music in their leisure time. Cheap banjoes and fiddles were mass-produced by the end of the nineteenth century. Pianos also became readily available, and one mountain boy, on hearing a piano for the first time, commented that it was the "beautifullest thing he had ever heard."

Itinerant musicians entertained audiences throughout the South. Lumber camps, which employed mainly

Trocadero Music Hall, 1893

The Trocadero Music Hall in Chicago opened in 1893 to attract people attending the city's upcoming World's Fair. It provided a mix of classical music and exotic European variety acts, as shown above, but drew really huge audiences with the appearance of Eugene Sandow, a body builder who exhibited feats of great physical strength.   Library of Congress

African American men, offered a popular destination for these musicians. Each camp contained a "barrelhouse," also called a "honky tonk" or a "juke joint." Besides showcasing music, the barrelhouse also gave workers the opportunity to "shoot craps, dice, drink whiskey, dance, every modern devilment you can do," as one musician who played there recalled. From the Mississippi delta emerged a new form of music—the blues. W. C. Handy, "the father of the blues," discovered this music in his travels through the delta, where he observed that southern blacks "sang about everything. Trains, steamboats, steam whistles, sledge hammers, fast women, mean bosses, stubborn mules." They performed these songs of woe accompanying themselves with anything that would make a "musical sound or rhythmical effect, anything from a harmonica to a washboard." Meanwhile in New Orleans, an amalgam of black musical forms evolved into jazz. Musicians such as "Jelly Roll" Morton experimented

with a variety of sounds, putting together African and Caribbean rhythms with European music, mixing pianos with clarinets, trumpets, and drums. Blues and jazz spread throughout the South, appearing in juke joints in Atlanta and Memphis, where men and women danced the night away.

In mountain valley mill towns, southern white residents preferred "old time" music, but with a twist. Originally enjoyed by British settlers, traditional ballads and folk songs concerned the deeds of kings and princes; rural southerners modified the lyrics to extol the exploits of outlaws and adventurers. Country music, which combined romantic ballads and folk tunes to the accompaniment of guitars, banjoes, and organs, emerged as a distinct brand of music by the twentieth century. As with African Americans, in the late nineteenth century working-class and rural whites found new and exciting types of music to entertain them in their leisure. Religious music also appealed to both white and black audiences and drew crowds to evangelical revivals held in tents on acres of grass fields.

Mill workers also amused themselves by engaging in social, recreational, and religious activities. Women visited each other and exchanged confidences, gossip, advice on child rearing, and folk remedies. Men from various factories organized baseball teams that competed in leagues with one another. Managers of a mill in Charlotte, North Carolina, admitted that they "frequently hired men better known for their batting averages than their work records."

REVIEW & RELATE

How did industrialization change the American workplace? What challenges did it create for American workers?

How did workers resist the concentrated power of industrial capitalists in the late nineteenth century, and why did such efforts have only limited success?

 LEARNINGCurve bedfordstmartins.com/hewittlawson/LC

Farmers Organize

Like industrial workers, farmers experienced severe economic hardships and a loss of political power in the face of rapid industrialization. The introduction of new machinery such as the combine harvester, introduced in 1878, led to substantial increases in the productivity of American farms. Soaring production, however, led to a decline in agricultural prices in the late nineteenth century, a trend that was accelerated by increased agricultural production around the world. Faced with an economic crisis caused by falling prices and escalating debt, farmers fought back, creating new organizations to champion their collective economic and political interests.

Farmers Unite

From the end of the Civil War to the mid-1890s, increased production of wheat and cotton, two of the most important American crops, led to a precipitous drop in the price these crops fetched on the open market. Falling prices created a debt crisis for many farmers. Most American farmers were independent businessmen who borrowed money to pay for land, seed, and equipment. When their crops were harvested and sold, they repaid their debts with the proceeds. As prices fell, farmers increased production in an effort to cover their

debts. This tactic led to a greater supply of farm produce in the marketplace and even lower prices. Unable to pay back loans, many farmers lost their property in foreclosures to the banks that held their mortgages and furnished them credit.

To make matters worse, farmers lived isolated lives. Spread out across vast acres of rural territory, farmers had few social and cultural diversions to enliven the long, hard days they worked from sunup to sundown. As the farm economy declined, more and more of their children left the monotony of rural America behind and headed for cities in search of new opportunities and a better life.

Early efforts to organize farmers were motivated by a desire to counteract the isolation of rural life by creating new forms of social interaction and cultural engagement. In 1867, Oliver H. Kelly, who worked as a clerk in the Department of Agriculture, founded the Patrons of Husbandry to brighten the lonely existence of rural Americans through educational and social activities, including lectures, agricultural fairs, and picnics. Known as **Grangers** (from the French word for "granary"), the association grew rapidly in the early 1870s, especially in the Midwest and the South. Between 1872 and 1874, approximately fourteen thousand new Grange chapters were established.

In addition to helping to alleviate rural isolation, Grangers formed farm cooperatives to sell their crops at higher prices and pool their purchasing power to buy finished goods at wholesale prices. The Grangers' interest in promoting the collective economic interests of farmers led to their increasing involvement in politics. Rather than forming a separate political party, Grangers endorsed candidates who favored their cause. Perhaps their most important objective was the regulation of shipping and grain storage prices. In many areas, individual railroads had monopolies on both of these services and, as a result, were able to charge farmers higher-than-usual rates to store and ship their crops. By electing sympathetic state legislators, Grangers managed to obtain regulations that placed a ceiling on the prices railroads and grain elevators could charge. The Supreme Court temporarily upheld these victories in *Munn v. Illinois* (1877) by affirming the constitutionality of state regulation of private property that benefited the public interest. In 1886, however, in *Wabash v. Illinois* the Supreme Court reversed itself and struck down these state regulatory laws as hindering the free flow of interstate commerce.

Another apparent victory for regulation came in 1887 when Congress passed the Interstate Commerce Act, establishing the **Interstate Commerce Commission (ICC)** to regulate railroads. Although big businessmen could not prevent occasional government regulation, they

Granger Movement, 1876

As the farmer's central placement in this lithograph implies, farmers were the heart of the Granger movement. The title is a variation on the movement's motto, "I Pay for All." A farmer with a plough and two horses stands at the center of the scene providing food for all, while other occupational types positioned around him echo a similar refrain based on their profession. Note the attitude toward the broker implied by the label "I Fleece You All."   Library of Congress

managed to render it largely ineffective. Large railroad lines found it easier to influence decisions of the ICC than those of agencies at the state level, which were more inclined to support local farmers and other shippers. In time, railroad advocates came to dominate the ICC and enforced the law in favor of the railway lines rather than the shippers. Implementation of the Sherman Antitrust Act (see chapter 16) also favored big business. From the standpoint of most late-nineteenth-century capitalists, national regulations often turned out to be more of help than a hindrance.

By the late 1880s, the Grangers had abandoned electoral politics and once again devoted themselves strictly to social and cultural activities. A number of factors explain the Grangers' return to their original mission. First, prices began to rise for some crops, particularly corn, relieving the economic pressure on midwestern farmers. Second, the passage of regulatory

legislation in a number of states convinced some Grangers that their political goals had been achieved. Finally, a lack of marketing and business experience led to the collapse of many agricultural collectives.

The withdrawal of the Grangers from politics did not, however, signal the end of efforts by farmers to form organizations to advance their economic interests. While farmers in the midwestern corn belt experienced some political success and an economic upturn, farmers farther west in the Great Plains and in the Lower South fell more deeply into debt, as the price of wheat and cotton on the international market continued to drop. In both of these regions, farmers organized **Farmers' Alliances**. In the 1880s, Milton George formed the Northwestern Farmers' Alliance. At the same time, Dr. Charles W. Macune organized the much larger Southern Farmers' Alliance, which boasted more than 4 million members. Southern black farmers, excluded from the

Southern Farmers' Alliance by prevailing white suprem- acist sentiment, created a parallel Colored Farmers' Alliance, which attracted approximately a quarter of a million supporters. The Alliances formed a network of recruiters to sign up new members. No recruiter was more effective than Mary Elizabeth Lease, who excited farm audiences with her forceful and colorful rhetoric, delivering 160 speeches in the summer of 1890 alone. Not only did Lease urge farmers and workers to unite against capitalist exploitation, but she also agitated for women's rights and voiced her determination "to place the mothers of this nation on an equality with the fathers."

The Southern Farmers' Alliance advocated a sophisticated plan to solve the farmers' problem of mounting debt. Macune devised a proposal for a **sub- treasury system**. Under this plan, the federal govern- ment would locate offices near warehouses in which farmers could store nonperishable commodities. In return, farmers would receive federal loans for 80 percent of the current market value of their produce. In theory, temporarily taking crops off the market would decrease supply and, assuming demand remained stable, lead to increased prices. Once prices rose, farmers would return to the warehouses, redeem their crops, sell them at the higher price, repay the government loan, and leave with a profit. Of the many recommendations proposed by the Alliances, the subtreasury system came closest to suggesting a realistic solution to the problem of chronic farm debt.

The first step toward creating a nationwide farmers' organization came in 1889, when the Northwestern and Southern Farmers' Alliances agreed to merge. Alliance leaders, including Lease, saw workers as fellow victims of industrialization, and they invited the Knights of Labor to join them. They also attempted to lower prevailing racial barriers by bringing the Colored Farmers' Alliance into the coalition. The following year, the National Farmers' Alliance and Industrial Union held its conven- tion in Ocala, Florida. The group adopted resolutions endorsing the subtreasury system, as well as recommen- dations that would promote the economic welfare of farmers and extend political democracy to "the plain people." These proposals included tariff reduction, government ownership of banks and railroads, a con- stitutional amendment creating direct election of U.S. senators, adoption of the secret ballot, and provisions for state and local referenda to allow voters to initiate and decide public issues.

Finally, the Alliance pressed the government to increase the money supply by expanding the amount of silver coinage in circulation. In the Alliance's view, such

a move would have two positive, and related, conse- quences. First, the resulting inflation would lead to higher prices for agricultural commodities, putting more money in farmers' pockets. Second, the real value of farmers' debts would decrease, since the debts were contracted in pre-inflation dollars and would be paid back with inflated currency. Naturally, the eastern bankers who supplied farmers with credit opposed such a policy. In fact, in 1873 Congress, under the leadership of Senator John Sherman, had halted the purchase of silver by the Treasury Department, a measure that helped reduce the money supply. Investment bankers, such as J. P. Morgan, opposed a bimetallic monetary standard that added silver to gold coinage. They believed that only the use of gold would preserve the faith that foreign investors had in U.S. currency. Under the Sherman Silver Purchase Act (1890), the government resumed buying silver, but the act placed limits on its purchase and did not guarantee the creation of silver coinage by the Treasury. In the past, some members of the Alliance, including Lease, had favored expanding the money supply with greenbacks (paper money). However, to attract support from western silver miners, Alliance delegates emphasized the free and unlimited coinage of silver. Alliance supporters met with bitter disappoint- ment, though, as neither the Republican nor the Demo- cratic Party embraced their demands. Rebuffed, farmers took an independent course and became more directly involved in national politics through the formation of the Populist Party.

Populists Rise Up

In 1892 the National Farmers' Alliance moved into the electoral arena as a third political party. The People's Party of America, known as the **Populists**, held its first nominating convention in Omaha, Nebraska, in 1892. In addition to incorporating the Alliance's Ocala planks into their platform, they adopted recommendations to broaden the party's appeal to industrial workers. Popu- lists endorsed a graduated income tax, which would impose higher tax rates on higher income levels. They also favored the eight-hour workday, a ban on using Pinkerton "mercenaries" in labor disputes, and immigra- tion restriction, which stemmed from the unions' desire to keep unskilled workers from glutting the market and depressing wages. Reflecting the influence of women such as Mary Lease, the party endorsed women's suf- frage. Although African Americans contributed to the founding of the Populists, the party did not offer specific proposals to prohibit racial discrimination or segrega- tion. Rather, the party focused on remedies to relieve the economic plight of impoverished white and black farmers in general.

Explore

See Documents 17.3 and 17.4 to compare the central tenets of the Grange and the Populists.

In 1892 the Populists nominated for president former Union Civil War general James B. Weaver. Although Weaver came in third behind the Democratic victor, Grover Cleveland, and the Republican incumbent, Benjamin Harrison, he managed to win more than one million popular votes and 22 electoral votes. For a third

DOCUMENTS 17.3 AND 17.4

Farmers and Workers Organize: Two Views

Farmers in the Midwest and the South organized to address the problems they faced as a result of industrialization and the growth of big business. The Patrons of Husbandry (the Grange) in the 1860s and 1870s and the Populists in the 1880s and 1890s both tried to deal with various social and economic issues. Compare the following pronouncement of the Grange with an excerpt from the Populist Party platform, adopted on July 4, 1892, in Omaha, Nebraska.

Explore

17.3 The Ten Commandments of the Grange, 1874

1. Thou shalt love the Grange with all thy heart and with all thy soul and thou shalt love thy brother granger as thyself.
2. Thou shalt not suffer the name of the Grange to be evil spoken of, but shall severely chastise the wretch who speaks of it with contempt.
3. Remember that Saturday is Grange day. On it thou shalt set aside thy hoe and rake, and sewing machine, and wash thyself, and appear before the Master in the Grange with smiles and songs, and hearty cheer. On the fourth week thou shalt not appear empty handed, but shalt thereby bring a pair of ducks, a turkey roasted by fire, a cake baked in the oven, and pies and fruits in abundance for the Harvest Feast. So shalt thou eat and be merry, and "frights and fears" shall be remembered no more.
4. Honor thy Master, and all who sit in authority over thee, that the days of the Granges may be long in the land which Uncle Sam hath given thee.
5. Thou shalt not go to law[yers].
6. Thou shalt do no business on tick [time]. Pay as thou goest, as much as in thee lieth.
7. Thou shalt not leave thy straw but shalt surely stack it for thy cattle in the winter.
8. Thou shalt support the Granger's store for thus it becometh thee to fulfill the laws of business.
9. Thou shalt by all means have thy life insured in the Grange Life Insurance Company, that thy wife and little ones may have friends when thou art cremated and gathered unto thy fathers.
10. Thou shalt . . . surely charter thine own ships, and sell thine own produce, and use thine own brains. This is the last and best commandment. On this hang all the law, and profits, and if there be any others they are these.

    Choke monopolies, break up rings, vote for honest men, fear God and make money. So shalt thou prosper and sorrow and hard times shall flee away.

Source: "The Ten Commandments of the Grange," *Oshkosh Weekly Times*, December 16, 1874, reprinted in *Rich Harvest: A History of the Grange, 1876–1900*, by D. Sven Nordin (Jackson: University Press of Mississippi, 1974), 240.

party competing for the presidency for the first time, this was a noteworthy accomplishment.

At the state level, Populists performed even better. They elected 10 congressional representatives, 5 U.S. senators, 3 governors, and 1,500 state legislators. Two years later, the party made even greater strides by increasing its total vote by 42 percent and achieving its greatest strength in the South. This electoral momentum positioned the Populists to make an even stronger run in the next presidential election. The economic depression that began in 1893 and the political discontent it generated further enhanced Populist chances for success.

17.4 Populist Party Platform, 1892

FINANCE—We demand a national currency, safe, sound, and flexible issued by the general government. . . .

1. We demand free and unlimited coinage of silver and gold at the present legal ratio of 16 to 1. . . .
3. We demand a graduated income tax.
4. We believe that the money of the country should be kept as much as possible in the hands of the people, and hence we demand that all State and national revenues shall be limited to the necessary expenses of the government, economically and honestly administered. . . .

TRANSPORTATION—Transportation being a means of exchange and a public necessity, the government should own and operate the railroads in the interest of the people. The telegraph and telephone . . . should be owned and operated by the government in the interest of the people.

LAND—The land, including all the natural sources of wealth, is the heritage of the people, and should not be monopolized for speculative purposes, and alien ownership of land should be prohibited. All land now held by railroads and other corporations in excess of their actual needs, and all lands now owned by aliens should be reclaimed by the government and held for actual settlers only.

EXPRESSION OF SENTIMENTS

1. Resolved, That we demand a free ballot, and a fair count in all elections . . . without Federal intervention, through the adoption by the States of the . . . secret ballot system.
2. Resolved, That the revenue derived from a graduated income tax should be applied to the reduction of the burden of taxation now levied upon the domestic industries of this country. . . .
4. Resolved, That we condemn the fallacy of protecting American labor under the present system, which opens our ports to [immigrants including] the pauper and the criminal classes of the world and crowds out our [American] wage-earners; and we . . . demand the further restriction of undesirable immigration.
5. Resolved, That we cordially sympathize with the efforts of organized workingmen to shorten the hours of labor. . . .
6. Resolved, That we regard the maintenance of a large standing army of mercenaries, known as the Pinkerton system, as a menace to our liberties, and we demand its abolition. . . .
9. Resolved, That we oppose any subsidy or national aid to any private corporation for any purpose.

Source: "People's Party Platform," *Omaha Morning World-Herald*, July 5, 1892.

Interpret the Evidence

- What do the language and tone of these two documents tell you about the organizations that created them?
- What measures did the Populists propose that the Grangers did not? What issues did both address?

Put It in Context

How did both the Grangers and the Populists respond to the shifts in economic and political power that occurred at the end of the nineteenth century?

REVIEW & RELATE

- Why was life so difficult for American farmers in the late nineteenth century?
- What were the similarities and differences between farmers' and industrial workers' efforts to organize in the late nineteenth century?

 LEARNINGCurve bedfordstmartins.com/hewittlawson/LC

The Depression of the 1890s

When the Philadelphia and Reading Railroad went bankrupt in early 1893, it set off a chain reaction that pushed one-quarter of American railroads into insolvency. As a result, on May 5, 1893, "Black Friday," the stock market collapsed in a panic, triggering the **depression of 1893**. Making this situation worse, England and the rest of industrial Europe had experienced an economic downturn several years earlier. As a result, in the early 1890s foreign investors began selling off their American stocks, leading to a flow of gold coin out of the country and further damage to the banking system. Hundreds of banks failed, which hurt the business people and farmers who relied on a steady flow of bank credit to keep their enterprises afloat. By the end of 1894, some 3 million people, nearly 12 percent of the American workforce, remained unemployed. Tens of thousands of homeless people wandered the streets of major American cities. The depression became the chief political issue of the mid-1890s and resulted in a realignment of power between the two major parties. Rather than capitalizing on depression discontent, however, the Populist Party split apart and collapsed.

Depression Politics

President Grover Cleveland's handling of the depression only made a bad situation worse. Railroad executive James J. Hill warned the president, "Business is at a standstill and the people are becoming thoroughly aroused. Their feeling is finding expression about as it did during the War of the Rebellion [Civil War]." With talk of civil war in the air, the Cleveland administration faced protest marches and labor strife. In the spring of 1894, Jacob Coxey, a wealthy businessman and Populist reformer from Ohio, and his associate, Carl Browne, led a march on Washington, D.C., demanding that Cleveland and Congress initiate a federal public works program to provide jobs for the unemployed. Coxey had previously supported the Greenback Party, which advocated inflating the money supply with paper currency to stimulate the economy and help those in distress. Though highly critical of the favored few who dominated the federal government, Coxey had faith that if "the people . . . come in a body like this, peaceably to discuss their grievances and demanding immediate relief, Congress . . . will heed them and do it quickly." For him, "relief" meant both creating jobs and increasing the money supply. After traveling for a month from Ohio, Coxey led a parade of some five hundred unemployed people into the nation's capital. Attracting thousands of spectators, **Coxey's army** attempted to mount their protest on the grounds of the Capitol building. In response, police broke up the demonstration and arrested Coxey for trespassing. Cleveland turned a deaf ear to Coxey's demands for federal relief and also disregarded protesters participating in nearly twenty other marches on Washington.

In the coming months, Cleveland's political stock plummeted further. He responded to the Pullman strike in the summer of 1894 by obtaining a federal injunction against the strikers and dispatching federal troops to Illinois when the workers disobeyed it. The president's action won him high praise from the railroads and conservative business interests, but it showed millions of American workers that the Cleveland administration did not have a solution for ending the suffering caused by the depression. From the outset of his term, the president had made his intentions about government assistance clear: "While the people should patriotically and cheerfully support their Government, its functions do not include the support of the people." In normal times, these words reflected the prevailing philosophy of self-help that most Americans shared, but in the midst of a severe depression they sounded heartless.

Making matters worse, Cleveland convinced Congress to repeal the Sherman Silver Purchase Act. This angered western miners, who relied on strong silver prices, along with farmers in the South and Great Plains who were swamped by mounting debt. At the same time, the removal of silver as a backing for currency caused private investors to withdraw their gold deposits from the U.S. Treasury. To keep the government financially solvent, Cleveland worked out an agreement with a syndicate led by J. P. Morgan to help sell government bonds, a deal that netted the businessmen a huge profit. In the midst of economic suffering, this deal looked like a corrupt bargain between government and the rich designed to ensure that the rich got richer as the poor got poorer.

Explore

See Document 17.5 for one cartoonist's depiction of the debt crisis.

DOCUMENT 17.5

Walter Huston | "Here Lies Prosperity," 1895

The "money question" became a focus of American politics in the first half of the 1890s and was exacerbated by the depression of 1893. Those who supported the gold standard believed that it provided the basis for a sound and stable economy. Proponents of the unlimited coinage of silver, especially Populists and Democrats such as William Jennings Bryan, asserted that expansion of the money supply would liberate farmers and workers from debt and bring prosperity to more Americans. The following cartoon illustrates the "free silver" point of view.

Explore

Why does the cartoonist use the phrases "enslaved," "stabbed in the back," "assassinated," and "traitors"? Whom does he accuse of these misdeeds?

According to this cartoon, what is the cause of poverty?

What burden keeps the working man in chains?

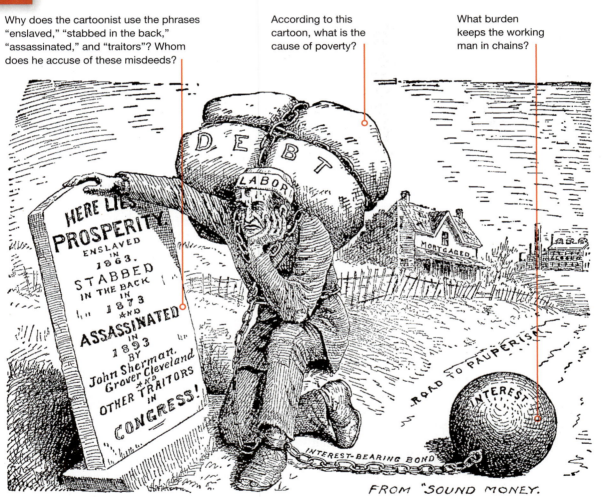

"The Situation: The Result of Interest Bearing Bonds and Sherman," in *Sound Money* (Massillon, OH), August 22, 1895. Reproduced from Worth Robert Miller, *Populist Cartoons: An Illustrated History of the Third Party Movement in the 1890s* (Kirksville, MO: Truman State University Press, 2011).

Put It in Context

How did the depression of 1893 affect the economic situation of farmers and working people? Whom did debt affect more?

In 1894 Congress also passed the Wilson-Gorman Act, which raised tariffs on imported goods. Intended to protect American businesses by keeping the price of imported goods high, it also deprived foreigners of the necessary income with which to buy American exports. This drop in exports did not help economic recovery. The Wilson-Gorman Act did include a provision that the Populists and other reformers endorsed: a progressive income tax of 2 percent on all annual earnings over $4,000. No federal income tax existed at this time, so even this mild levy elicited cries of "socialism" from conservative critics, who challenged the tax in the courts. They found a receptive audience in the Supreme Court. In *Pollack v. Farmers Loan and Trust* (1895), the justices, who had already struck down a number of attempts to regulate business, declared the income tax unconstitutional and denounced it as the opening wedge in "a war of the poor against the rich; a war constantly growing in intensity and bitterness."

With Cleveland's legislative program in shambles and his inability to solve the depression abundantly clear, the Democrats suffered a crushing blow at the polls. In the congressional elections of 1894, the party lost an astonishing 120 seats in the House. This defeat offered a preview of the political shakeup that loomed ahead.

Political Realignment in the Election of 1896

The presidential election of 1896 marked a turning point in the political history of the nation, one that would shape national politics for the next thirty-six years. Democrats nominated William Jennings Bryan of Nebraska, a farmers' advocate who favored silver coinage. When he vowed that he would not see Republicans "crucify mankind on a cross of gold," the Populists endorsed him as well. Bryan was the first major party nominee for the White House since 1868 who did not come from Ohio, Indiana, or New York.

Republicans nominated William McKinley, the governor of Ohio and a supporter of the gold standard and high tariffs on manufactured and other goods. While Bryan barnstormed around the country, McKinley remained at his home in Canton, Ohio, to conduct his campaign from his front porch. His campaign manager, Marcus Alonzo Hanna, an ally of Ohio senator John Sherman, raised an unprecedented amount of money, about $16 million, mainly from wealthy industrialists who feared that the free and unlimited coinage of silver would debase the U.S. currency. Hanna saturated the country with pamphlets, leaflets, and posters, many of them written in the native languages of immigrant groups. He also hired a platoon of speakers to fan out across the country

denouncing Bryan's free silver cause as financial madness. Republican Theodore Roosevelt, who would later become president himself, remarked that Hanna advertised McKinley "as if he were patent medicine." By contrast, Bryan raised about $1 million and had to travel around the country making personal appearances, in part to compensate for his campaign's lack of funds.

The outcome of the election transformed the Republicans into the majority party in the United States. McKinley won 51 percent of the popular vote and 61 percent of the electoral vote, making him the first president since Grant in 1872 to win a majority of the popular vote. More important than this specific contest, however, was that the election proved critical in realigning the two parties. Voting patterns shifted with the 1896 election, giving Republicans the edge in party affiliation among the electorate not only in this contest but also in presidential elections over the next three decades (Map 17.1).

What happened to produce this critical realignment in electoral power? The main ingredient was Republicans' success in fashioning a coalition that included both corporate capitalists and their workers. Although Bryan made sincere appeals for the votes of urban dwellers and industrial workers along class lines, they generally fell on deaf ears. Many of these voters took out their anger on Cleveland's Democratic Party and Bryan as its standard-bearer for failing to end the depression. In addition, Bryan, who hailed from Nebraska and reflected

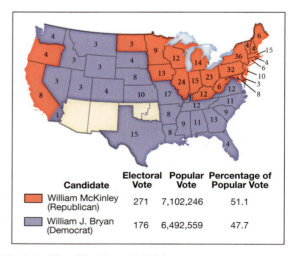

Candidate	Electoral Vote	Popular Vote	Percentage of Popular Vote
William McKinley (Republican)	271	7,102,246	51.1
William J. Bryan (Democrat)	176	6,492,559	47.7

MAP 17.1   The Election of 1896

William McKinley's election in 1896 resulted in a realignment of political power in the United States that lasted until 1932. Republicans became the nation's majority party by forging a coalition of big business and urban industrial workers from the Northeast and Midwest. Democratic strength was confined to the South and small towns and rural areas of the Great Plains and Mountain states.

small-town agricultural America and its values, could not win over the swelling numbers of urban immigrants who considered Bryan's world alien to their experience. A great orator, Bryan nevertheless sounded anti-urban, and his defeat signaled the decline of rural America in presidential politics. His campaign was the last serious effort to win the White House with mostly farm and small-town votes.

The election of 1896 broke the political stalemate in the Age of Organization. The core of Republican backing came from industrial cities of the Northeast and Midwest. Republicans won support from their traditional constituencies of Union veterans, businessmen, and African Americans and added to it the votes of a large number of urban wageworkers. The campaign persuaded voters that the Democratic Party represented the party of depression and that Republicans stood for prosperity and progress. Another factor helping the Republicans was that in 1897 the depression finally ended, largely as a result of gold discoveries in Alaska, which helped increase the money supply, and foreign crop failures, which raised American farm prices. Democrats managed to hold on to the South as their solitary political base.

The Decline of the Populists

The year 1896 also marked the end of the Populists as a national force, as the party was torn apart by internal divisions over policy priorities and electoral strategy. Populist leaders such as Tom Watson of Georgia did not want the Populist Party to emphasize free silver above the rest of its reform program. Other northern Populists, who either had fought on the Union side during the Civil War or had close relatives who did, such as Mary Lease, could not bring themselves to join the Democrats, the party of the old Confederacy. Nevertheless, the Populist Party officially backed Bryan, but to retain its identity, the party nominated Watson for vice president on its own ticket. After McKinley's victory, the Populist Party collapsed.

Losing the presidential election alone did not account for the disintegration of the Populists. Several problems plagued the third party. The nation's recovery from the depression removed one of the Populists' prime sources of electoral attraction. Despite appealing to industrial workers, the Populists were unable to capture their support. The free silver plank attracted silver miners in Idaho and Colorado, but the majority of workers failed to identify with a party composed mainly of farmers. As consumers of agricultural products, industrial laborers did not see any benefit in raising farm prices. Populists also failed to create a stable, biracial

coalition of dispossessed farmers. Most southern white Populists did not truly accept African Americans as equal partners, even though both groups had mutual economic interests. Southern white Populists framed their arguments around class as the central issue driving the exploitation of farmers and workers by wealthy planters and industrialists. However, in the end, they succumbed to racial prejudice.

To eliminate Populism's insurgent political threat, southern opponents found ways to disfranchise black and poor white voters. During the 1890s, southern states inserted into their constitutions voting requirements that virtually eliminated the black electorate and greatly diminished the white electorate. Seeking to circumvent the Fifteenth Amendment's prohibition against racial discrimination in the right to vote, conservative white lawmakers adopted regulations based on wealth and education because blacks were disproportionately poor and had lower literacy rates. They instituted poll taxes, which imposed a fee for voting, and literacy tests, which asked tricky questions designed to trip up would-be black voters (see chapter 16). In 1898 the Supreme Court upheld the constitutionality of these voter qualifications in *Williams v. Mississippi*. Recognizing the power of white supremacy, the Populists surrendered to its appeals.

Tom Watson provides a case in point. He started out by encouraging racial unity but then switched to divisive politics. In 1896 the Populist vice presidential candidate, who had assisted embattled black farmers in his home state of Georgia, called on citizens of both races to vote against the crushing power of corporations and railroads. By whipping up racial antagonism against blacks, his Democratic opponents appealed to the racial pride of poor whites to keep them from defecting to the Populists. Chastened by the outcome of the 1896 election and learning from the tactics of his political foes, Watson embarked on a vicious campaign to exclude blacks from voting. "What does civilization owe the Negro?" he bitterly asked. "Nothing! Nothing! NOTHING!!!" Only by disfranchising African Americans and maintaining white supremacy, Watson and other white reformers reasoned, would poor whites have the courage to vote against rich whites.

Nevertheless, even in defeat the Populists left an enduring legacy. Many of their political and economic reforms—direct election of senators, the graduated income tax, government regulation of business and banking, and a version of the subtreasury system (called the Commodity Credit Corporation, created in the 1930s)—became features of reform in the twentieth century. Populists also foreshadowed other attempts at

SMITH WANTS FAIR DIVISION OF PIE!

(OVER)

ISAAC SMITH

C.H. JOHNSON

PIE

Norman E. Jennett

DEBATE IN THE LEGISLATURE ON THE ELECTION LAW.

Isaac Smith, Republican Leader, to C. H. Johnson, Populist Leader—"That's the way you Populists have done my race. We have elected them to good fat offices; we've made them Governor, and now you turn and tell us we ought never to have been allowed to vote, anyhow."

Populists and Race
The relationship between the Populists and African Americans was complex, but after 1896 the political connection between the two shattered. In this cartoon, Isaac Smith, a black Republican, chides C. H. Johnson, a Populist leader, for supporting a North Carolina election law that disfranchised blacks. Smith reminds Johnson that Populists had campaigned for African American votes in the past, and accuses him of walking off without sharing any of the pie.   North Carolina Collection, University of North Carolina Library at Chapel Hill

creating farmer-labor parties in the 1920s and 1930s. Perhaps their greatest contribution, however, came in showing farmers that their old individualist ways would not succeed in the modern industrial era. Rather than re-creating an independent political party, most farmers looked to organized interest groups, such as the Farm Bureau, to lobby on behalf of their interests. Whatever their approach, farmers both reflected and contributed to the Age of Organization.

REVIEW & RELATE

- How did the federal government respond to the depression of 1893?

- What were the long-term political consequences of the depression of 1893?

✓ **LEARNINGCurve** bedfordstmartins.com/hewittlawson/LC

Conclusion: A Passion for Organization

From 1877 to 1900, industrial workers and farmers joined the march toward organization led by the likes of Carnegie, Rockefeller, and Morgan. These wealthy titans of industry and finance had created the large corporations that transformed the rhythms and meanings of factory labor and farm life. Working people such as John McLuckie met

the challenges of the new industrial order by organizing unions. Lacking the power of giant companies, which was reinforced by the federal government, labor unions nevertheless carved out sufficient space for workers to join together in their own defense to resist absolute corporate rule. At the same time, farmers, perhaps the most individualistic workers, and their advocates, such as Mary Elizabeth Lease, created organizations that proposed some of the most forward-looking solutions to remedy the ills accompanying industrialization. Though the political fortunes of the Grangers and Populists declined, their message persisted: Resourceful and determined workers and farmers could, and should, join together to ensure survival not just of the fittest but of the neediest as well.

Under the pressure of increased turmoil surrounding industrialization and a brutal economic depression, the political system reached a crisis in the 1890s. Despite the historic shift in party loyalties brought about by the election of William McKinley, it remained to be seen whether political party realignment could furnish the necessary leadership to address the problems of workers and farmers. Industrialization had proven painful and disorienting for millions of Americans. The events of the 1890s convinced many Americans, including many in the middle class, that the hands-off approach to social and economic problems that had prevailed in the past was no longer acceptable. In cities and states across the country, men and women took up the cause of reform. They had to wait for national leaders to catch up to them.

LEARNINGCurve
Check what you know.
bedfordstmartins.com/hewittlawson/LC

Chapter Review

Online Study Guide ▶ bedfordstmartins.com/hewittlawson

KEY TERMS

unskilled workers (p. 529)
skilled workers (p. 529)
unions (p. 532)
collective bargaining (p. 532)
Noble Order of the Knights of Labor (p. 532)
Haymarket Square (p. 533)
American Federation of Labor (AFL) (p. 534)
Homestead strike (p. 534)
Pullman strike (p. 535)
Industrial Workers of the World (IWW) (p. 536)
Grangers (p. 539)
Interstate Commerce Commission (ICC) (p. 539)
Farmers' Alliances (p. 540)
subtreasury system (p. 541)
Populists (p. 541)
depression of 1893 (p. 544)
Coxey's army (p. 544)

REVIEW & RELATE

1. How did industrialization change the American workplace? What challenges did it create for American workers?

2. How did workers resist the concentrated power of industrial capitalists in the late nineteenth century, and why did such efforts have only limited success?

3. Why was life so difficult for American farmers in the late nineteenth century?

4. What were the similarities and differences between farmers' and industrial workers' efforts to organize in the late nineteenth century?

5. How did the federal government respond to the depression of 1893?

6. What were the long-term political consequences of the depression of 1893?

TIMELINE OF EVENTS

1865–1895	U.S. manufacturing jobs jump from 5.3 million to 15.1 million
1867	Patrons of Husbandry (Grange) founded
1869	Noble Order of the Knights of Labor founded
1870–1900	Number of female wageworkers increases by 66 percent
1877	Great Railroad Strike
1879	Terence Powderly becomes leader of Knights of Labor
1880s	Northwestern, Southern, and Colored Farmers' Alliances formed
1886	Haymarket Square violence
	American Federation of Labor founded
1887	Interstate Commerce Act passed
1889	Northwestern and Southern Farmers' Alliances merge
1890	Sherman Silver Purchase Act passed
1890s	Southern states strip blacks of the right to vote
1892	Homestead steelworkers' strike
	Populist Party established
1893	Depression triggered by stock market collapse
1894	Pullman strike
	Coxey's army marches to Washington
	Sherman Silver Purchase Act repealed
1896	Populists back William Jennings Bryan for president
1897	Depression ends
	Populist Party declines
1901	Eugene Debs establishes Socialist Party of America

The Pullman Strike of 1894

Late-nineteenth-century industrialists exercised massive power over workers and the conditions of labor. Yet this power was not absolute. Workers organized into unions to secure higher wages, shorter hours, improved safety, and a fairer measure of control of the labor process. Even those corporate owners who were considered sympathetic to the needs of laborers and their families, such as railcar magnate George Pullman, assumed the right to manage their businesses as they saw fit. Though Pullman had constructed a model town with clean housing and parks for his employees, he refused to heed workers' economic complaints after the depression of 1893 began.

When the American Railway Union (ARU), headed by Eugene V. Debs, launched a nationwide strike against the Pullman company in May 1894 to improve economic conditions and gain recognition for the union, Pullman refused to negotiate. Rebuffed by Pullman, the union coordinated strike activities across the country from its headquarters in Chicago. Workers refused to operate trains with Pullman cars attached, and when the railroads hired strikebreakers, some 260,000 strikers brought rail traffic to a halt. In response, U.S. Attorney General Richard Olney, a member of many railroad boards, obtained a federal injunction ordering strikers back to work, but without success. At Olney's recommendation, President Grover Cleveland ordered federal troops into Chicago to enforce the injunction. Their clash with strikers resulted in thirteen deaths, more than fifty injuries, hundreds of thousands of dollars in property damages, and the spread of violence to twenty-six states. After the government arrested union leaders, including Debs, for disobeying the injunction, the strike collapsed in July 1894, and the Supreme Court upheld Debs's imprisonment.

The following documents reveal the points of view from four major combatants in the labor struggle. As you read these documents, consider the larger questions raised by this episode: Why have organizations been essential to advancing the rights of individuals in an industrialized society? Why was organized labor not more successful in gaining a larger share of power from capital? How did gender influence labor conflict and organizing? And what role should the government play in shaping the outcome of conflicts between labor and capital?

DOCUMENT 17.6

George Pullman | Testimony before the U.S. Strike Commission, 1894

In July 1894, President Grover Cleveland appointed a Commission to Investigate the Chicago (Pullman) Strike. Although the Cleveland administration played a major role in ending the strike to the detriment of the American Railway Union, the president selected Carroll D. Wright, the U.S. commissioner of labor, to chair the commission. Wright had significant experience investigating labor conditions and collecting statistical data, and he was sympathetic to the plight of workers. George Pullman appeared before the commission to explain his position on the strike.

COMMISSIONER WRIGHT . . . State generally what the idea was of establishing the town [of Pullman] in connection with your manufacturing plant. . . .

PULLMAN [reading from a statement] The object in building Pullman was the establishment of a great manufacturing business on the most substantial basis possible, recognizing, as we did, and do now, that the working people are the most important element which enters into the successful operation of any manufacturing enterprise. We decided to build, in close proximity to the shops, homes for workingmen of such character and surroundings as would prove so attractive as to cause the best class of mechanics to seek that place for employment in preference to others. We also desired to establish the place on such a basis as would exclude all baneful [harmful] influences, believing that such a policy would result in the greatest measure of success, both from a commercial point of view, and also, what was equally important, or perhaps of greater importance, in a tendency toward continued elevation and improvement of the conditions not only of the working people themselves, but of their children growing up about them. . . .

If any lots had been sold in Pullman it would have permitted the introduction of the baneful elements which it was the chief purpose to exclude from the immediate neighborhood of the shops, and from the homes to be erected about them. The plan was to provide homes in the first place for all people who should desire to work in the shops, at reasonable rentals, with the expectation that as they became able and should desire to do so, they would purchase lots and erect homes for themselves within convenient distances, or avail themselves of the opportunity to rent homes from other people who should build in that vicinity. As a matter of fact, at the time of the strike 563 of the shop employees owned their homes, and 461 of that number are now employed in the shops; 560 others at the time of the strike lived outside; and, in addition, an estimated number from 200 to 300 others employed at Pullman were owners of their homes. . . .

Due attention was paid to the convenience and general well-being of the residents by the erection of stores and markets, a church, public schools, a library, and public halls for lectures and amusements; also a hotel and boarding houses. The basis on which rents were fixed was to make a return of 6 percent on the actual invest-ment, which at that time, 1881, was a reasonable return to be expected from such an investment; and in calculating what, for such a purpose, was the actual investment in the dwellings on the one hand and the other buildings on the other, an allowance was made for the cost of the streets and other public improvements, just as it has to be considered in the valuation of any property for renting anywhere, all public improvements having to be paid for by the owner of a lot, either directly or by special assessment, and by him considered in the valuation. The actual operations have never shown a net return of 6 percent, the amount originally con-templated. The investment for several years returned a net revenue of about 4½ percent, but during the last two years additional taxes and heavier repairs have brought the net revenue down to 3.82 percent. . . .

(continued on page 552)

COMMISSIONER NICOLAS WORTHINGTON   I wanted to know what you had in mind at the time you made the statement that "it was very clear that no prudent man could submit to arbitration in this matter" when you were referring to your daily losses as a reason why any prudent man could not submit to arbitration?

PULLMAN   The amount of the losses would not cut any figure; it was the principle involved, not the amount that would affect my views as to arbitration.

WORTHINGTON   Then it was not the amount of losses that the company was then sustaining, but it was the fact that a continuance of the business at the rates that had been paid would entail loss upon the company?

PULLMAN   It was the principle that that should not be submitted to a third party. That was a matter that the company should decide for itself. . . .

WORTHINGTON   Now, let me ask you if, taking all the revenues of the Pullman company for the last year, so far as you are advised, if the company has lost money or made money during the last year?

PULLMAN   The company has made money during the last year.

Source: *Executive Documents of the Senate of the United States*, 53rd Cong. (1894–1895), 529–30, 553.

DOCUMENT 17.7

Eugene V. Debs | On Radicalism, 1902

American Railway Union leader Eugene Debs served six months in jail after leading the Pullman strike. This experience moved him in more radical directions politically, and he established the Socialist Party. He ran as the party's presidential candidate five times, and in 1905 Debs helped form the Industrial Workers of the World, an organization interested in uniting all workers and challenging the capitalist system. In 1902 he described to the readers of the *Comrade*, a New York socialist newspaper, his thoughts on the Pullman strike and how he became a socialist.

In 1894 the American Railway Union was organized and a braver body of men never fought the battle of the working class.

Up to this time I had heard but little of Socialism, knew practically nothing about the movement, and what little I did know was not calculated to impress me in its favor. I was bent on thorough and complete organization of the railroad men and ultimately the whole working class, and all my time and energy were given to that end. My supreme conviction was that if they were only organized in every branch of the service and all acted together in concert they could redress their wrongs and regulate the conditions of their employment. The stockholders of the corporation acted as one, why not the men? It was such a plain proposition—simply to follow the example set before their eyes by their masters—surely they could not fail to see it, act as one, and solve the problem. . . .

Next followed the final shock—the Pullman strike—and the American Railway Union again won, clear and complete. The combined corporations were paralyzed and helpless. At this juncture there [was] delivered, from wholly unexpected quarters, a swift succession of blows that blinded me for an instant and then opened wide my eyes—and in the gleam of every bayonet and the flash of every rifle *the class struggle was revealed.* This was my first practical lesson in Socialism, though wholly unaware that it was called by that name.

An army of detectives, thugs, and murderers [was] equipped with badge and beer and bludgeon and turned loose; old hulks of cars were fired; the alarm bells tolled; the people were terrified; the most startling rumors were set afloat; the press volleyed and thundered, and over all the wires sped the news that Chicago's white throat was in the clutch of a red mob; injunctions flew thick and fast, arrests followed, and our office and headquarters, the heart of the strike, was sacked, torn out, and nailed up by the "lawful" authorities of the federal government; and when in company with my loyal comrades I found myself in Cook county jail at Chicago, with the whole press screaming conspiracy, treason, and murder. . . .

Acting upon the advice of friends we sought to employ John Harlan, son of the Supreme Justice, to assist in our defense—a defense memorable to me chiefly because of the skill and fidelity of our lawyers, among whom were the brilliant Clarence Darrow and the venerable Judge Lyman Trumbull, author of the thirteenth amendment to the Constitution, abolishing slavery in the United States.

Mr. Harlan wanted to think of the matter over night; and the next morning gravely informed us that he could not afford to be identified with the case, "for," said he, "you will be tried upon the same theory as were the anarchists, with probably the same result." That day, I remember, the jailer, by way of consolation, I suppose, showed us the blood-stained rope used at the last execution and explained in minutest detail, as he exhibited the gruesome relic, just how the monstrous crime of lawful murder is committed.

But the tempest gradually subsided and with it the bloodthirstiness of the press and "public sentiment." We were not sentenced to the gallows, nor even to the penitentiary—though put on trial for conspiracy—for reasons that will make another story.

The Chicago jail sentences were followed by six months at Woodstock [the Illinois jail where Debs was imprisoned] and it was here that Socialism gradually laid hold of me in its own irresistible fashion. Books and pamphlets and letters from socialists came by every mail and I began to read and think and dissect the anatomy of the system in which workingmen, however organized, could be shattered and battered and splintered at a single stroke. . . .

The American Railway Union was defeated but not conquered—overwhelmed but not destroyed. It lives and pulsates in the Socialist movement, and its defeat but blazed the way to economic freedom and hastened the dawn of human brotherhood.

Source: Eugene V. Debs, *Debs: His Life, Writings, and Speeches* (Chicago: Charles Kerr, 1908), 81–84.

DOCUMENT 17.8

Jennie Curtis | Testimony before the U.S. Strike Commission, 1894

During the Pullman strike, seamstress Jennie Curtis was president of the American Railway Union Local 269, known as the "girls' union." Following a stirring speech by Curtis at an ARU convention, the union agreed to support workers striking against Pullman. In the following excerpt, Curtis explains to Carroll D. Wright, chairman of the congressional commission that later investigated the strike, the dire economic situation employees faced as the company cut back wages and raised rents.

COMMISSIONER WRIGHT   State your name, residence, and occupation.

CURTIS   Jennie Curtis; reside at Pullman; have been a seamstress for the Pullman company in the repair shops sewing room; worked for them five years.

WRIGHT   Are you a member of any labor organization?

CURTIS   Yes, sir; I am a member of the American Railway Union.

WRIGHT   How long have you been a member of that union?

CURTIS   Since about the 8th day of last May.

WRIGHT   Do you hold any position in the union?

CURTIS   I am president of the girls' union, local, No. 269, at Pullman.

WRIGHT   Did you have anything to do with the strike at Pullman, which occurred on the 11th of May, 1894?

CURTIS   No, sir.

WRIGHT   Had you anything to do with any of the efforts to avoid the strike, or to settle the difficulties?

CURTIS   I had not, further than being on a committee which called to see Mr. Pullman and Mr. Wickes, the general manager of the company, to ask for more wages, asking to arbitrate, and such as that.

WRIGHT   Were you on those committees, or some of them?

CURTIS   Yes, sir; I was.

WRIGHT   State briefly what you did as a member serving upon those committees.

CURTIS   I was on a committee that went from Pullman to speak for the girls in May before the strike, to ask for more wages. . . .

WRIGHT   State what took place at the first interview.

CURTIS   We went there and asked, as the men did, for more wages; we were cut lower than any of the men's departments throughout the works; in 1893 we were able to make 22 cents per hour, or $2.25 per day, in my department, and on the day of the strike we could only earn, on an average, working as hard as we possibly could, from 70 to 80 cents a day.

COMMISSIONER JOHN D. KERNAN   Can you give us how the wages changed from month to month?

CURTIS   Whenever the men were cut in their wages the girls also received a cut. We were cut twice inside of a week in November, 1893, and in January our wages were cut again; that was the last cut we received, and we worked as hard as we possibly could and doing all we could, too. The most experienced of us could only make 80 cents per day, and a great many of the girls could only average 40 to 50 cents per day. . . .

WRIGHT   Do you pay rent in Pullman?

CURTIS   No, sir; not now.

WRIGHT   You pay board?

CURTIS   Yes, sir. My father worked for the Pullman company for thirteen years. He died last September, and I paid the rent to the Pullman company up to the time he died; I was boarding at the time of my father's death. He being laid off and sick for three months, owed the Pullman company $60 at the time of his death for back rent, and the company made me, out of my small earnings, pay that rent due from my father.

KERNAN   How did they make you do it?

CURTIS   The contract was that I should pay $3 on the back rent every pay day; out of my small earnings I could not give them $3 every pay day, and when I did not do so I was insulted and almost put out of the bank by the clerk for not being able to pay it to them. My wages were cut so low that I could not pay my board and give them $3 on the back rent, but if I had $2 or so over my board I would leave it at the bank on the rent. On the day of the strike I still owed them $15, which I am afraid they never will give me a chance to pay back.

Source: *Executive Documents of the Senate of the United States*, 53rd Cong. (1894–1895).

DOCUMENT 17.9

Report from the Commission to Investigate the Chicago Strike, 1895

The commission appointed by President Grover Cleveland to investigate the Pullman strike concluded that strikes were wasteful, disruptive, and unlawful. Blaming both capital and labor for the strike, the commission believed that the Pullman trouble originated because neither the public nor the government had taken adequate measures to control monopolies and corporations and had failed "to reasonably protect the rights of labor and redress its wrongs."

Committee Recommendations Following Investigation of the Chicago Strike

I.

(1) That there be a permanent United States strike commission of three members, with duties and powers of investigation and recommendation as to disputes between railroads and their employees similar to those vested in the Interstate Commerce Commission as to rates, etc.

a. That, as in the interstate commerce act, power be given to the United States courts to compel railroads to obey the decisions of the commission, after summary hearing unattended by technicalities, and that no delays in obeying the decisions of the commission be allowed pending appeals.

b. That, whenever the parties to a controversy in a matter within the jurisdiction of the commission are one or more railroads upon one side and one or more national trade unions, incorporated under chapter 567 of the United States Statutes of 1885–86, or under State statutes, upon the other, each side shall have the right to select a representative, who shall be appointed by the President to serve as a temporary member of the commission in hearing, adjusting, and determining the particular controversy. . . .

c. That, during the pendency of a proceeding before the commission inaugurated by national trade unions, or by an incorporation of employees, it shall not be lawful for the railroads to discharge employees belonging thereto except for inefficiency, violation of law, or neglect of duty; nor for such unions or incorporation during such pendency to order, unite in, aid, or abet strikes or boycotts against the railroads complained of; nor, for a period of six months after a decision, for such railroads to discharge any such employees in whose places others shall be employed, except for the causes aforesaid; nor for any such employees, during a like period, to quit the service without giving thirty days' written notice of intention to do so, nor for any such union or incorporation to order, counsel, or advise otherwise. . . .

II.

(1) The commission would suggest the consideration by the States of the adoption of some system of conciliation and arbitration like that, for instance, in use in the Commonwealth of Massachusetts. That system might be reenforced by additional provisions giving the board of arbitration more power to investigate all strikes, whether requested so to do or not, and the question might be considered as to giving labor organizations a standing before the law, as heretofore suggested for national trade unions.

(2) Contracts requiring men to agree not to join labor organizations or to leave them, as conditions of employment, should be made illegal, as is already done in some of our States.

III.

(1) The commission urges employers to recognize labor organizations; that such organizations be dealt with through representatives, with special reference to conciliation and arbitration when difficulties are threatened or arise. It is satisfied that employers should come in closer touch with labor and should recognize that, while the interests of labor and capital are not identical, they are reciprocal.

(2) The commission is satisfied that if employers everywhere will endeavor to act in concert with labor; that if when wages can be raised under economic conditions they be raised voluntarily, and that if when there are reductions reasons be given for the reduction, much friction can be avoided. It is also satisfied that if employers will consider employees as thoroughly essential to industrial success as capital, and thus take labor into consultation at proper times, much of the severity of strikes can be tempered and their number reduced.

Source: *Report on the Chicago Strike of June–July, 1894 by the United States Strike Commission* (Washington, D.C.: Government Printing Office, 1895), LII–LIV.

DOCUMENT 17.10

Grover Cleveland | Reflections on the Pullman Strike, 1904

After Grover Cleveland left the White House in 1897, he became a trustee of Princeton University. He delivered several addresses as part of a lecture series on public affairs that was established in his honor. In 1904, a decade after the Pullman strike, he discussed his administration's role in dealing with the strike in an article in the popular magazine *McClure's*.

I N THE LAST DAYS OF JUNE, 1894, a very determined and ugly labor disturbance broke out in the City of Chicago. Almost in a night it grew to full proportions of malevolence and danger. Rioting and violence were its early accompaniments; and it spread so swiftly that within a few days it had reached nearly the entire Western and Southwestern sections of our country. Railroad transportation was especially involved in its attacks. The carriage of United States mails was interrupted, interstate commerce was obstructed, and railroad property was riotously destroyed.

This disturbance is often called "The Chicago Strike." It is true that its beginning was in that city; and the headquarters of those who inaugurated it and directed its operations were located there; but the name thus given to it is an entire misnomer so far as it applies to the scope and reach of the trouble. Railroad operations were more or less affected in twenty-seven states and territories; and in all these the interposition of the General Government was to a greater or less extent invoked. . . .

The employees of the Pullman Palace Car Company could not on any reasonable and consistent theory be regarded as eligible to membership in an organization devoted to the interests of railway employees; and yet, during the months of March, April, and May, 1894, it appears that nearly 4,000 of these employees were enrolled in the American Railway Union. This, to say the least of it, was an exceedingly unfortunate proceeding, since it created a situation which implicated in a comparatively insignificant quarrel between the managers of an industrial establishment and their workmen, the large army of the Railway Union. It was the membership of these workmen in the Railway Union and the Union's consequent assumption of their quarrel, that gave it the proportions of a tremendous disturbance, paralyzing the most important business interests, obstructing the functions of the Government, and disturbing social peace and order. . . .

I shall not enter upon an enumeration of all the disorders and violence, the defiance of law and authority, and the obstructions of national functions and duties, which occurred in many localities as a consequence of this labor contention, thus tremendously reinforced and completely under way. It is my especial purpose to review the action taken by the Government for the maintenance of its own authority and the protection of the special interests intrusted to its keeping, so far as they were endangered by this disturbance; and I do not intend to especially deal with the incidents of the strike except in so far as a reference to them may be necessary to show conditions which not only justified but actually obliged the Government to resort to stern and unusual measures in the assertion of its prerogatives. . . .

Owing to the enforced relationship of Chicago to the strike which started within its borders, and because of its importance as a center of railway traffic, Government officials at Washington were not surprised by the early and persistent complaints of mail and interstate commerce obstructions which reached them from that city. It was from the first anticipated that this would be the seat of the most serious complications, and the place where the strong arm of the law would be most needed. In these circumstances it would have been a criminal neglect of duty if those charged with the protection of Governmental agencies and the enforcement of orderly obedience and submission to Federal authority, had been remiss in preparations for any emergency in that quarter.

. . . The Attorney-General, in making suggestions concerning legal proceedings, wrote: "It has seemed to me that if the rights of the United States were vigorously asserted in Chicago, the origin and center of the demonstration, the result would be to make it a failure everywhere else, and to prevent its spread over the entire country," and in that connection he indicated that it might be advisable, instead of relying entirely upon warrants issued under criminal statutes, against persons actually guilty of the offense of obstructing United States mails, that the courts should be asked to grant injunctions which would restrain and prevent any attempt to commit such offense.

Source: "The Government in the Chicago Strike of 1894," *McClure's Magazine*, July 1904, 227–29, 231–32.

Interpret the Evidence

1. Why does George Pullman (Document 17.6) think he has treated his workers fairly? Why might workers have disagreed with him?

2. According to Eugene V. Debs (Document 17.7), what was the purpose of labor activism? How did the Pullman strike teach Debs about socialism?

3. How did being a woman affect Jennie Curtis's experiences as a Pullman worker (see Document 17.8)?

4. How do you think Pullman and Debs would have responded to the report on the Pullman strike issued by the Commission to Investigate the Chicago Strike (Document 17.9)?

5. What do you think of Grover Cleveland's belief that the Pullman employees had no business joining the American Railway Union (see Document 17.10)?

Put It in Context

- What do these documents reveal about the complex relationship among labor, management, and government at the close of the nineteenth century?

LEARNINGCurve
Check what you know.
bedfordstmartins.com/hewittlawson/LC

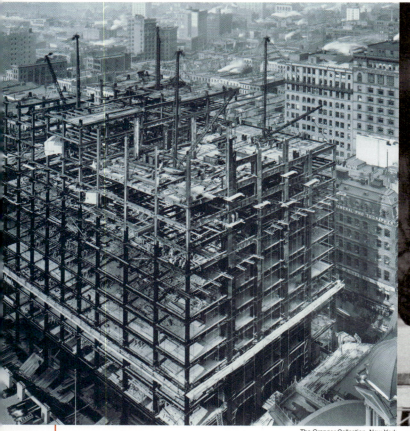

The Granger Collection, New York

The Woolworth Building under construction, New York City, 1912.

Private Collection/Peter Newark American Pictures/The Bridgeman Art Library

An Italian family on the ferry from Ellis Island to New York City, 1905.

18
Cities, Immigrants, and the Nation

1880–1914

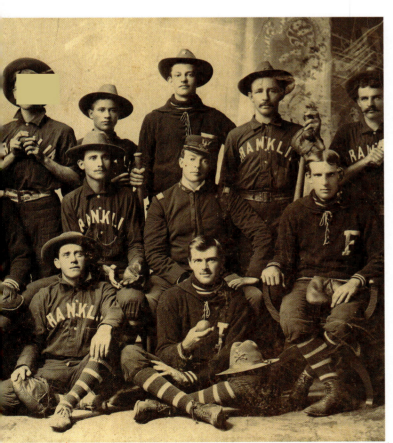

Virginia Historical Society, Richmond, Virginia, USA/The Bridgeman Art Library

Baseball team, Franklin, Virginia.

AMERICAN HISTORIES

In the fall of 1905, Beryl Lassin faced a difficult choice. Living in the *shtetl* (a Jewish town) of Borrisnov in western Russia, Lassin had few if any opportunities as a young locksmith. Beryl and his wife, Lena, lived at a dangerous time in Russia. Jews were subject to periodic pogroms, state-sanctioned outbreaks of anti-Jewish violence carried out by local Christians. Beryl also faced a discriminatory military draft that required conscripted Jews to serve twenty-year terms in the army, far longer than their Christian countrymen. His wife's brother had already left Russia for the United States, and the couple decided that Beryl should follow his brother-in-law's example before the draft caught up with him. The couple couldn't afford two steamship tickets, so with the understanding that his wife would follow as soon as possible, Beryl set sail for America alone on the steamship *Zeeland*, which sailed from Antwerp, Belgium, on October 7, 1905. He was crammed into the steerage belowdecks with hundreds of other passengers, most of them fellow Jews. Ten days later, his ship chugged into New York harbor, where Beryl found a less than hospitable greeting. Disembarking at Ellis Island, the processing center for immigrants, he stood in long lines and underwent a strenuous medical examination, including a painful eye inspection, to ensure that he was fit to enter the country. He also had to prove that he had someplace to go, in his case the apartment of his brother-in-law on New York City's Lower East Side. With no money, Beryl boarded a ferry across the Hudson that took him to a new life in the United States.

Less than a year later, Lena joined her husband. Over the next decade, the couple had five children. Shortly after the youngest girl was born, Lena died of cancer. Her death threw the family into turmoil, as Beryl, now called Ben, had to place two of the three youngest children in the Hebrew Children's Home and the other in foster care. The children were reunited with their father when Ben remarried, but life was still difficult. Ben was injured at his job as a mechanic and did not work full-time again. To make ends meet, his three eldest boys dropped out of school and went to work. Still, like many other immigrants, Ben's family managed to leave the crowded Lower East Side, following a trail blazed by earlier Jewish immigrants to Harlem and then the Bronx. Ben preferred to speak in Yiddish and never learned to read English. Nor did he become an American citizen, and after World War I, as an alien, he had to register annually with the federal government. His children, however, were all citizens because they had been born in the United States.

On June 8, 1912, another immigrant followed a similar route that took her on a different journey. Seventeen years old and unmarried, Maria Vik decided to leave her home in the small village of Kiestyderocz, Hungary. As a Catholic, Maria did not experience the religious persecution that Beryl did. Like many other Hungarians who ventured to the United States at this time, Maria, the oldest daughter, left to help support her family back in the old country. She had an aunt living in the United States, and she came across with a Hungarian couple who escorted young women for domestic service in America. Her sea voyage began in Hamburg, Germany, aboard the ship *Amerika*, and unlike Beryl she had a cabin in second class.

Maria, too, landed at Ellis Island and passed the rigorous entry exams. Soon she boarded a train for Rochester in western New York. There she worked as a cook for a German physician, learned English, and led an active social life within the local Hungarian community. In Rochester, she met and fell in love with Karoly (Charles) Takacs, a cabinetmaker from Hungary, who,

Beryl Lassin and
Maria Vik Takacs

like Beryl Lassin, had come to avoid the military draft. Charles became a citizen in May 1916. By marrying him, Mary, as she was now called, became a citizen as well.

The couple moved forty-five miles west of Rochester to Middleport and purchased a small farm in a neighborhood filled with Hungarian immigrants. Because so many Hungarians lived in the area, Mary spoke mainly Hungarian and began to speak more English only when the oldest of her four children entered kindergarten.

The American histories of Beryl Lassin and Maria Vik Takacs took one to the urban bustle of New York City, the other to a quiet, rural village in western New York State. The Lassins, who rented walk-up apartments in five-story buildings and whose children had to drop out of school, did not fare as well economically as did the Takacses, who owned property and sent their three daughters to college. However, as different as their lives in America were, neither Beryl nor Maria regretted their choice to leave Europe for the United States. Like millions of other immigrants at the turn of the twentieth century, they had come to America to build better lives for themselves and their families, and both saw their children and grandchildren succeed in ways that they could have only dreamed of in their native countries. Indeed, Ben Lassin changed his surname to Lawson, and his son Murray married Ceil Puchowitzky (Parker), the daughter of another Russian-Jewish immigrant. Mary and Charles's daughter Irene married Robert Hewitt, whose family arrived from northern Europe in the nineteenth century. Murray's son, Steven F. Lawson, and Irene's daughter, Nancy A. Hewitt—the grandchildren of Beryl and Maria, respectively—became historians, got married, and wrote this textbook. The experiences of the Lawson and Hewitt families, like countless others, reflect the complicated ways that immigrants were transformed into Americans at the same time that the United States was forever changed by the new additions to its population. ●

THE LASSINS AND the Takacses were part of a flood of immigrants who entered the United States from 1880 to the outbreak of World War I in 1914. Unlike the majority of earlier immigrants, who had come from northern Europe, most of the more than 20 million people who arrived during this period came from southern and eastern Europe. They entered the United States mainly through seaports in the Northeast, but some came through ports in New Orleans, Louisiana, and Key West and Tampa, Florida, in the South; across the Texas and California borders from Mexico; and through ports in San Francisco and Seattle on the West Coast. Though many moved to small towns and rural villages, most remained in cities, which experienced enormous population growth as a result. In these large urban areas, impoverished immigrants entered the political mainstream of American life, welcomed by political bosses and their machines, who saw in them a chance to gain the allegiance of millions of new voters. At the same time, their coming upset many middle- and upper-class city dwellers who blamed these new arrivals for lowering the quality of urban life.

A New Wave of Immigrants

For more than three hundred years following the settlement of the North American colonies, the majority of white immigrants to America were northern European Protestants. Black Americans were brought forcibly from Africa, mainly by way of the West Indies and the Caribbean. Although African Americans originally followed their own religious practices, most eventually converted to Protestantism. By the end of the nineteenth century, however, a new pattern of immigration had emerged, one that included much greater ethnic and religious diversity. These new immigrants often encountered hostility from those whose ancestors had arrived generations earlier, and faced the difficult challenge of retaining their cultural identities while becoming assimilated as Americans.

Immigrants Arrive from Many Lands

Immigration to the United States was part of a worldwide phenomenon. In addition to the United States, European immigrants also journeyed to other countries in the Western Hemisphere, especially Canada, Argentina, Brazil, and Cuba. Others left China, Japan, and India and migrated to Southeast Asia and Hawaii. From England and Ireland, migrants ventured to other parts of the British empire, including Australia, New Zealand, and South Africa. As with those who came to the United States, these immigrants left their homelands to find new job opportunities or to obtain land to start their own farms. In countries like Australia, New Zealand, and South Africa, white settlers often pushed aside native peoples—Aborigines in Australia, Maori in New Zealand, and blacks in South Africa—to make communities for themselves. Whereas most immigrants chose to relocate voluntarily, some made the move bound by labor contracts that limited their movement during the terms of the agreement. Chinese, Mexican, and Italian workers made up a large portion of this group.

The late nineteenth century saw a shift in the country of origin of immigrants to the United States: Instead of coming from northern and western Europe, many now came from southern and eastern European countries, most notably Italy, Greece, Austria-Hungary, Poland, and Russia. In 1882 around 789,000 immigrants entered the United States, 87 percent of whom came from northern and western Europe. By contrast, twenty-five years later in 1907,

SS *Zeeland*

The SS *Zeeland* was a British and Belgian ocean liner first launched in 1901. Four years later, like thousands of other immigrants, Beryl Lassin made the journey from Russia to Antwerp, where he boarded this ship, and finally landed at Ellis Island. Traveling in steerage, the cheapest fare, he ate poor meals and suffered from overcrowding and poor sanitation. Photograph courtesy of the Peabody Essex Museum, Salem, Massachusetts of the 1,285,000 newcomers who journeyed to America, 81 percent originated from southern and eastern Europe.

Most of those settling on American shores after 1880 were Catholic or Jewish and hardly knew a word of English. They tended to be even poorer than immigrants who had arrived before them, coming mainly from rural areas and lacking suitable skills for a rapidly expanding industrial society. In the words of one historian, who could easily have been describing Beryl Lassin's life: "Jewish poverty [in Russia] is a kind of marvel for . . . it has origins in fathers and grandfathers who have been wretchedly poor since time immemorial." Even after relocating to a new land and a new society, such immigrants struggled to break patterns of poverty that were, in many cases, centuries in the making.

Immigrants came from other parts of the world as well. From 1860 to 1924, some 450,000 Mexicans migrated to the U.S. Southwest. Many traveled to El Paso, Texas, near the Mexican border, and from there hopped aboard one of three railroad lines to jobs on farms and in mines, mills, and construction. Cubans, Spaniards, and Bahamians traveled to the Florida cities of Key West and Tampa, where they established and worked in cigar factories. Tampa grew from a tiny village of a few hundred people in 1880 to a city of 16,000 in 1900. Although Congress had excluded Chinese immigration after 1882, it did not close the door to migrants from Japan. Unlike the Chinese, the Japanese had not competed with white workers for jobs on railroad and other construction projects. Moreover, Japan had emerged as a major world power in the late nineteenth century and gained some grudging respect from American leaders by defeating Russia in the Russo-Japanese War of 1904–1905. Some 260,000 Japanese arrived in the United States during the first two decades of the twentieth century. Many of them first settled in Hawaii and then moved to the West Coast states of California, Oregon, and Washington, where they worked as farm laborers and gardeners and established businesses catering to a Japanese clientele. Nevertheless, like the Chinese before them, Japanese immigrants were considered part of an inferior "yellow race" and encountered discrimination in their West Coast settlements.

This wave of immigration changed the composition of the American population. By 1910 one-third of the population was foreign-born or had at least one parent who came from abroad. Foreigners and their children made up more than three-quarters of the population of New York City, Detroit, Chicago, Milwaukee, Cleveland, Minneapolis, and San Francisco. Immigration, though not as extensive in the South as in the North, also altered the character of southern cities. About one-third of the population of Tampa, Miami, and New Orleans consisted of foreigners and their descendants. The borderland states of Texas, New Mexico, Arizona, and southern California contained similar percentages of immigrants, most of whom came from Mexico.

These immigrants came to the United States largely for economic, political, and religious reasons. Nearly all were poor and expected to find ways to make money in America. U.S. railroads and steamship companies advertised in Europe and recruited passengers by emphasizing economic opportunities in the United States. Early immigrants wrote to relatives back home extolling the virtues of what they had found, perhaps exaggerating their success. However, for people barely making a living, or for those subject to religious discrimination and political repression, what did it matter if they arrived in America and the streets were not paved in gold, as legend had it? In fact, if many of the streets were not paved at all, at least the immigrants could get jobs paving them!

The importance of economic incentives in luring immigrants is underscored by the fact that millions returned to their home countries after they had earned sufficient money to establish a more comfortable lifestyle. Of the more than 27 million immigrants from 1875 to 1919, 11 million returned home (Table 18.1). One immigrant from Canton, China, accumulated a small fortune as a merchant on Mott Street, in New York City's Chinatown. According to residents of his hometown in China, "[Having] made his wealth among the barbarians this man had faithfully returned to pour it out among his tribesmen, and he is living in our village now very happy." Jews, Mexicans, Czechs, and Japanese had the lowest rates of return. Immigrant groups facing religious or political persecution in their homeland were the least likely to return. It is highly doubtful that a poor Jewish immigrant like Beryl Lassin would have received a warm welcome home in his native Russia, if he had been allowed to return at all.

TABLE 18.1 Percentage of Immigrant Departures versus Arrivals, 1875–1914

Year	Arrivals	Departures	Percentage of Departures to Arrivals
1875–1879	956,000	431,000	45%
1880–1884	3,210,000	327,000	10%
1885–1889	2,341,000	638,000	27%
1890–1894	2,590,000	838,000	32%
1895–1899	1,493,000	766,000	51%
1900–1904	3,575,000	1,454,000	41%
1905–1909	5,533,000	2,653,000	48%
1910–1914	6,075,000	2,759,000	45%

Creating Immigrant Communities

Immigrants were processed at their port of entry, and the government played no role in their relocation in America. New arrivals were left to search out transplanted relatives and other countrymen on their own. In cities such as New York, Boston, and Chicago, immigrants occupied neighborhoods that took on the distinct ethnic characteristics of the groups that inhabited them. A cacophony of different languages echoed in the streets as new residents continued to communicate in their mother tongues. The neighborhoods of immigrant groups often were clustered together, so residents were as likely to learn phrases in their neighbors' languages as they were to learn English.

The formation of **ghettos**—neighborhoods dominated by a single ethnic, racial, or class group—eased immigrants' transition into American society. Without government assistance or outside help, these communities assumed the burden of meeting some of the challenges that immigrants faced in adjusting to their new environment. Living within these ethnic enclaves made it easier for immigrants to find housing, hear about jobs, buy food, and seek help from those with whom they felt most comfortable. **Mutual aid societies** sprang up to provide social welfare benefits, including insurance payments and funeral rites. "A *landsman* died in the factory," a founder of one such Jewish association explained, and the worker was buried in an unmarked grave. When his Jewish neighbors heard about it, "his body [was] dug up, and the decision taken to start our organization with a cemetery." Group members established social centers where immigrants could play cards or dominoes, chat and gossip over tea or coffee, host dances and benefits, or just relax among people who shared a common heritage. In San Francisco's Chinatown, the largest Chinese community in California, such organizations usually consisted of people who had come from the same towns in China. These groups performed a variety of services, including finding jobs for their members, resolving disputes, campaigning against anti-Chinese discrimination, and sponsoring parades and other cultural activities. One society member explained: "We are strangers in a strange country. We must have an organization to control our country fellows and develop our friendship."

The same impulse to band together occurred in immigrant communities throughout the nation. On the West Coast, Japanese farmers joined *kenjinkai*, which not only provided social activities but also helped first-generation immigrants locate jobs and find housing. In Ybor City, Tampa's cigar-making section, mutual aid organizations rose to meet the needs of Spaniards, Cubans, Afro-Cubans, and Italians. El

El Centro Español

This 1912 postcard shows El Centro Español in Ybor City, the cigar-making district of Tampa, Florida. This facility served the Spanish community as a social club and mutual aid society. Immigrants attended dances, plays, and concerts and took English lessons, which eased their adaptation to a new homeland. Courtesy of the State Archives of Florida

Centro Español sponsored dances catering to Spaniards, only to be outdone by the rival El Centro Asturiano, which constructed a building that contained a 1,200-seat theater with a 27-by-80-foot stage, "$4,000 worth of modern lighting fixtures, a *cantina*, and a well stocked *biblioteca* (library)." Cubans constructed their own palatial $60,000 clubhouse, El Circulo Cubano, with lovely stained-glass windows, a pharmacy, a theater, and a ballroom. Less splendid and more economical, La Union Martí-Maceo became the home away from home for Tampa's Afro-Cubans. Besides the usual attractions, the club sponsored a baseball team that competed against other Latin teams. The establishment of such clubs and cultural centers speaks to the commitment of Tampa's immigrant groups to enhance their communities—a commitment backed up with significant financial expenditures.

Besides family and civic associations, churches and synagogues provided religious and social activities for ghetto dwellers. The number of Catholic churches nationwide more than tripled—from 3,000 in 1865 to 10,000 in 1900. Churches celebrated important landmarks in their parishioners' lives—births, baptisms, weddings, and deaths—in a far warmer and more personal manner than did clerks in city hall. Like mutual aid societies, churches offered food and clothing to those who were ill or unable to work and fielded sports teams to compete in recreational leagues. Immigrants altered the religious practices and rituals in their churches to meet their own needs and expectations, many times over the objections of their clergy. Various ethnic groups challenged the orthodox practices of the Catholic Church and insisted that their parishes adopt religious icons that they had worshipped in the old country. These included patron saints or protectresses from Old World towns, such as the Madonna del Carmine, whom Italian Catholics in New

York's East Harlem celebrated with an annual festival that their priests considered a pagan ritual. Women played the predominant role in running these street festivities. German Catholics challenged Vatican policy by insisting that each ethnic group have its own priests and parishes. Some Catholics, like Mary Vik, who lived in rural areas that did not have a Catholic church in the vicinity, attended services with local Christians from other denominations.

Religious worship also varied among Jews. German Jews had arrived in the United States in an earlier wave of immigration than their eastern European coreligionists. By the early twentieth century, they had achieved some measure of economic success and founded Reform Judaism, with Cincinnati, Ohio, as its center. This brand of Judaism relaxed strict standards of worship, including absolute fidelity to kosher dietary laws, and allowed prayers to be said in English. By contrast, eastern European Jews, like Beryl Lassin, observed the traditional faith and went to *shul* (synagogue) on a regular basis, maintained a kosher diet, and prayed in Hebrew.

With few immigrants literate in English, foreign-language newspapers proliferated to inform their readers of local, national, and international events. Between the mid-1880s and 1920, 3,500 new foreign-language newspapers came into existence. These newspapers helped sustain ethnic solidarity in the New World as well as maintain ties to the Old World. Newcomers could learn about social and cultural activities in their communities and keep abreast of news from their homeland. German-language tabloids dominated the field and featured such dailies as the *New Yorker Staatszeitung,* the *St. Louis Anzeiger des Westens,* the *Cincinnati Volksblatt,* and the *Wisconsin Banner.*

Like other communities with poor, unskilled populations, immigrant neighborhoods bred crime. Young men joined gangs based on ethnic heritage and battled with those of other immigrant groups to protect their turf. Adults formed underworld organizations—some of them tied to international criminal syndicates, such as the Mafia—that trafficked in prostitution, gambling, robbery, and murder. Tongs (secret organizations) in New York City's and San Francisco's Chinatowns, which started out as mutual aid societies, peddled vice and controlled the opium trade, gambling, and prostitution in their communities. A survey of New York City police and municipal court records from 1898 concluded that Jews "are prominent in their commission of forgery, violation of corporation ordinance, as disorderly persons (failure to support wife or family), both grades of larceny, and of the lighter grade of assault."

Crime was not the only social problem that plagued immigrant communities. Newspapers and court records reported husbands abandoning their wife and children, engaging in drunken and disorderly conduct, or abusing

their family. Boarders whom immigrant families took into their homes for economic reasons also posed problems. Cramped spaces created a lack of privacy, and male boarders sometimes attempted to assault the woman of the house while her husband and children were out to work or in school. Finally, generational conflicts within families began to develop as American-born children of immigrants questioned their parents' values. Daughters born in America sought to loosen the tight restraints imposed by their parents. If they worked outside the home, young women were expected to turn their wages over to their parents. A young Italian woman, however, displayed her independence after receiving her first paycheck. "I just went downtown first and I spent a lot, more than half of my money," she admitted. "I just went hog wild." Thus the social organizations and mutual aid societies that immigrant groups established were more than a simple expression of ethnic solidarity and pride. They were also a response to the very real problems that challenged the health and stability of immigrant communities.

Explore

See Document 18.1 for a depiction of one immigrant family's intergenerational conflict.

Hostility toward Recent Immigrants

On October 28, 1886, the United States held a gala celebration for the opening of the Statue of Liberty in New York harbor, a short distance from Ellis Island. French sculptors Frédéric-Auguste Bartholdi and Alexandre-Gustave Eiffel had designed the 151-foot-tall monument, *Liberty Enlightening the World,* to appear at the Centennial Exposition in Philadelphia in 1876. Ten years overdue, the statue arrived in June 1885, but funds were still needed to finish construction of a base on which the sculpture would stand. Ordinary people dipped into their pockets for spare change, contributing to a campaign that raised $100,000 so that Lady Liberty could finally hold her uplifted torch for all to see. In 1903 the inspiring words of Emma Lazarus, a Jewish poet, were inscribed on the pedestal welcoming new generations of immigrants.

> Give me your tired, your poor,
> Your huddled masses yearning to breathe free,
> The wretched refuse of your teeming shore,
> Send these, the homeless, tempest-tossed to me,
> I lift my lamp beside the golden door!

Despite the welcoming inscription on the Statue of Liberty, many Americans whose families had arrived before the 1880s considered the influx of immigrants from southern and eastern Europe at best a necessary evil and at

DOCUMENT 18.1

Anzia Yerzierska | Immigrant Fathers and Daughters, 1925

Anzia Yerzierska, a Jewish immigrant who came to the United States from Poland around 1890, wrote about the struggles of immigrant families in adjusting to their new world. Her novel *Bread Givers* focuses on the conflict of a Jewish daughter, Sara Smolinski, patterned after herself, and the girl's father, Reb Smolinski, a Talmudic scholar. Intent on taking advantage of new opportunities in America, Sara resists her father's attempts to impose his Old World beliefs about the traditional duties of a subservient female.

Explore

As I came through the door with my bundle, Father caught sight of me. "What's this?" he asked. "Where are you going?"

"I'm going back to work, in New York."

"What? Wild-head! Without asking, without consulting your father, you get yourself ready to go? Do you yet know that I want you to work in New York? Let's first count out your carfare to come home every night. Maybe it will cost so much there wouldn't be anything left from your wages."

"But I'm not coming home!"

"What? A daughter of mine, only seventeen years old, not home at night?"

"I'll go to Bessie or Mashah."

"Mashah is starving poor, and you know how crowded it is by Bessie."

"If there's no place for me by my sisters, I'll find a place by strangers."

"A young girl, alone, among strangers? Do you know what's going on in the world? No girl can live without a father or a husband to look out for her. It says in the Torah, only through a man has a woman an existence. Only through a man can a woman enter Heaven."

"I'm smart enough to look out for myself. It's a new life now. In America, women don't need men to boss them."

"*Blut-und-Eisen!* ["blood and iron"] They ought to put you in a madhouse till you're cured of your crazy nonsense!" . . .

Wild with all that was choked in me since I was born, my eyes burned into my father's eyes. "My will is as strong as yours. I'm going to live my own life. Nobody can stop me. I'm not from the old country. I'm American!"

"You blasphemer!" His hand flung out and struck my cheek. "Denier of God! I'll teach you respect for the law!"

I leaped back and dashed for the door. The Old World had struck its last on me.

Source: Anzia Yerzierska, *Bread Givers* (New York: Persea Books, 1975), 136–38.

Interpret the Evidence

- How does Sara's father view the father-daughter relationship? How does Sara see it?
- Why does Sara's father object to her working in the city? What role does religion play in shaping his point of view?

Put It in Context

What values and beliefs does Sara associate with the Old World? What new values does she associate with America?

worst a menace. Industrialists counted on immigrants to provide the cheap labor that performed backbreaking work in their factories. Not surprisingly, existing industrial workers saw the newcomers as a threat to their economic livelihoods. In their view, the arrival of large numbers of immigrants could only result in greater competition for jobs and lower wages. Moreover, even though most immigrants came to America to find work and improve the lives of their families, a small portion antagonized and frightened capitalists and middle-class Americans with their radical calls for the reorganization of society and the overthrow of the government. Of course, the vast majority of immigrants were not radicals, but a large proportion of radicals were recent immigrants. During times of labor-management strife (see chapter 17), this fact made it easier for businessmen and their spokesmen in the press to advance the notion that anti-American radicalism was a chronic immigrant disease.

Anti-immigrant fears linked to ideas about race and ethnicity had a long history in the United States. In 1790 Congress passed a statute restricting citizenship to those deemed white:

> Any Alien being a free white person, who shall have resided within the limits and under the jurisdiction of the United States for the term of two years, may be admitted to become a citizen thereof on application to any common law Court of record in any one of the States wherein he shall have resided for the term of one year at least, and making proof to the satisfaction of such Court that he is a person of good character, and taking the oath or affirmation prescribed by law to support the Constitution of the United States.

This standard excluded American Indians, who were regarded as savages, and African Americans, most of whom were slaves at the time. In 1857 the Supreme Court ruled that even free blacks were not citizens. From the very beginning of the United States, largely Protestant lawmakers debated whether Catholics and Jews qualified as whites. Although lawmakers ultimately included Catholics and Jews within their definition of "white," over the next two centuries Americans viewed racial categories as not simply matters of skin color. Ethnicity (country or culture of origin) and religion became absorbed into and intertwined with racial categories. A sociological study of Homestead, Pennsylvania, published in 1910 broke down the community along the following constructed racial lines: "Slav, English-speaking European, native white, and colored." Russian Jewish immigrants such as Beryl Lassin were recorded as Hebrews rather than as Russians, suggesting that Jewishness was seen by Christian America as a racial identity.

Scores of races were presumed to exist based on perceived shades of skin color. In 1911 a congressional commission on immigration noted that Poles are "darker than the Lithuanians" and "lighter than the average Russian." These were not neutral judgments, however. Natural scientists and social scientists had given credence to the idea that some races and ethnic groups were superior and others were inferior. Based on Darwin's theory of evolution (see chapter 16), biologists and anthropologists constructed measures of racial hierarchies, placing descendants of northern Europeans with lighter complexions—Anglo-Saxons, Teutonics, and Nordics—at the top of the evolutionary scale. Those with darker skin were deemed inferior "races," with Africans and Native Americans at the bottom. Scholars attempting to

make disciplines such as history more "scientific" accepted these racial classifications. At Johns Hopkins University, the leading center of academic training in the social sciences in the 1880s, historian Herbert Baxter Adams argued that the influx of southern European immigrants threatened the capacity for self-government developed in the United States by early settlers originating from Great Britain and Germany. The prevailing sentiment of this era reflected demeaning images of many immigrant groups: Irish as drunkards, Chicanos and Cubans as lazy, Italians as criminals, Hungarians as ignorant peasants, Jews as cheap and greedy, and Chinese as drug addicts. These characteristics resulted supposedly from inherited biological traits, rather than from extreme poverty or other environmental conditions.

Newer immigrants, marked as racially inferior, became a convenient target of hostility. Skilled craftsmen born in the United States viewed largely unskilled workers from abroad who would work for low wages as a threat to their attempts to form unions and keep wages high. Middle-class city dwellers blamed urban problems on the rising tide of foreigners. In addition, Protestant purists felt threatened by Catholics and Jews and believed these "races" incapable or unworthy of assimilation into what they considered to be the superior white, Anglo-Saxon, and Protestant culture. In 1890 social scientist Richard Mayo Smith wrote, "It is scarcely probable that by taking the dregs of Europe, we shall produce a people of high social intelligence and morality."

Nativism—the belief that foreigners pose a serious danger to one's native society and culture—arose as a reactionary response to immigration. New England elites, such as Massachusetts senator Henry Cabot Lodge and writer John Fiske, argued that southern European, Semitic, and Slavic races did not fit into the "community of race" that had founded the United States. In 1893 Lodge and fellow Harvard graduates established the Immigration Restriction League and lobbied for federal legislation that would exclude adult immigrants unable to read in their own language. In 1887 Henry F. Bowers of Clinton, Iowa, founded a similar organization, the American Protective Association, which claimed a total membership of 2.5 million at its peak. The group proposed restricting Catholic immigration, making English a prerequisite to American citizenship, and prohibiting Catholics from teaching in public schools or holding public offices. Obsessed with the supposed threat posed by Catholics, Bowers directed the expansion of the organization throughout the Midwest.

Explore

See Document 18.2 for a nativist perspective on immigration.

DOCUMENT 18.2

"The Stranger at Our Gate," 1899

Critics of late-nineteenth-century immigration often relied on the germ theory of disease in their arguments for stricter immigration laws. However, nativist objections to immigrants went far beyond issues of public health. According to nativists, immigrants were sources of both biological and cultural "contamination." In the following cartoon, "The Stranger at Our Gate," the "germs" carried by immigrants are not limited to those associated with disease.

Explore

What do the inscription on the gate and the caption below the cartoon tell us about the specific policies the cartoon supports?

How would you interpret Uncle Sam's body language in facing the would-be immigrant?

What does the cartoon suggest about the role of religion in anti-immigrant sentiment?

What specific "threats" does the immigrant appear to pose to the United States?

THE STRANGER AT OUR GATE.

EMIGRANT.—Can I come in?   UNCLE SAM.—I 'spose you can; there's no law to keep you out.

The Ohio State University Billy Ireland Cartoon Library & Museum

Put It in Context

What does this cartoon tell us about prevailing attitudes toward immigration at the end of the nineteenth century?

Proposals to restrict immigration, however, did nothing to deal with the millions of foreigners already in America. To preserve their status and power and increase the size of the native-born population, nativists embraced the idea of **eugenics**—a pseudo-science that advocated "biological engineering"—and supported the selective breeding of "desirable" races to counter the rapid population growth of "useless" races. Accordingly, eugenicists promoted the institutionalization of people deemed "unfit," sterilization of those considered mentally impaired, and the licensing and regulation of marriages to promote better breeding. In pushing for such measures, eugenicists believed that they were following the dictates of modern science and acting in a humane fashion to prevent those deemed unfit from causing further harm to themselves and to society. Alexander Graham Bell (see chapter 16), the inventor of the telephone, was one of the early champions of eugenics and immigration restriction.

Others took a less harsh approach. As had been the case with American Indians (see chapter 15), reformers stressed the need for immigrants to assimilate into the dominant culture, embrace the values of individualism and self-help, adopt American styles of dress and grooming, and exhibit loyalty to the U.S. government. They encouraged immigrant children to attend public schools, where they would learn to speak English and adopt American cultural rituals by celebrating holidays such as Thanksgiving and Columbus Day. In 1892 schools adopted the pledge of allegiance, written by Francis Bellamy, which recited American ideals of "liberty and justice for all" and affirmed loyalty to the nation and its flag. Educators encouraged adult immigrants to attend night classes to learn English. Ben Lassin tried this approach sporadically, but he did not prove to be an apt pupil. Like many immigrants, he made only limited progress toward assimilation.

The Assimilation Dilemma

If immigrants were not completely assimilated, neither did they remain the same people who had lived on the farms and in the villages of Europe, Asia, Mexico, and the Caribbean. Some sought to become full-fledged Americans, like Mary Vik, or at least see that their children did so. Writer Israel Zangwill, an English American Jew, portrayed this goal and furnished the enduring image of assimilation in his 1908 play *The Melting-Pot*. Zangwill portrayed people from distinct backgrounds entering the cauldron of American life, mixing together, and emerging as citizens identical to their native-born counterparts. This representation of the **melting pot** became the ideal as depicted in popular cartoons, ceremonies adopted by business corporations, and lessons presented in school classrooms.

However, the melting pot worked better as an ideal than as a mirror of reality. Immigrants during this period never fully lost the social, cultural, religious, and political identities they had brought with them. Even if all immigrants had sought full assimilation, which they did not, the anti-immigrant sentiment of many native-born Americans reinforced their status as strangers and aliens. The same year that Zangwill's play was published, Alfred P. Schultz, a New York physician, provided a dim view of the prospects of assimilation in his book *Race or Mongrel*. Schultz dismissed the melting pot theory that public schools could change the children of all races into Americans, which he found absurd. **See Document Project 18: "Melting Pot" or "Vegetable Soup"?, page 582**.

Thus most immigrants faced the dilemma of assimilating while holding on to their heritage. Sociologist W. E. B. Du Bois summed up this predicament for one of the nation's earliest transported groups. In his monumental *The Souls of Black Folk* (1903), Du Bois wrote that African Americans felt a "two-ness," an identity carved out of their African heritage together with their lives as slaves and free people in America. This "double-consciousness . . . two souls, two thoughts, two unreconciled strivings" also applies to immigrants at the turn of the twentieth century. Immigrants who entered the country after 1880 were more like vegetable soup—an amalgam of distinct parts within a common broth—than a melting pot.

REVIEW & RELATE

- What challenges did new immigrants to the United States face?
- What steps did immigrants take to meet these challenges?

✓ *LEARNINGCurve* bedfordstmartins.com/hewittlawson/LC

Becoming an Urban Nation

In the half century after the Civil War, the population of the United States quadrupled, but the urban population soared sevenfold. In 1870 one in five Americans lived in cities with a population of 8,000 or more. By 1900 one in three resided in cities of this size. In 1870 only Philadelphia and New York had populations over half a million. Twenty years later, in addition to these two cities, Chicago's population exceeded 1 million; St. Louis, Boston, and Baltimore had more than 500,000 residents; and Cleveland, Buffalo, San Francisco, and Cincinnati boasted populations over 250,000. Urbanization was not confined to the Northeast and Midwest. Denver's population jumped from 4,700 in 1870 to more than 107,000 in 1890. During that same period, Los Angeles grew nearly fivefold, from 11,000 to 50,000, and Birmingham leaped from 3,000 to 26,000. "We live in the age of great cities," the Reverend Samuel Lane Loomis, a Massachusetts schoolteacher, remarked in 1886. "Each successive year finds a stronger and more irresistible current sweeping in towards the centers of life." This phenomenal urban growth also brought remarkable physical changes to the cities, as tall buildings reached toward the skies, electric lights brightened the nighttime hours, and water and gas pipes, sewers, and subways snaked below the ground.

The New Industrial City

Urban growth in America was part of a long-term global phenomenon. Between 1820 and 1920, some 60 million people globally moved from rural to urban areas. Most of them migrated after the 1870s, and as noted earlier, millions journeyed from towns and villages in Europe to American cities. Yet the number of Europeans who migrated internally was greater than those who went overseas. As in the United States, Europeans moved from the countryside to urban areas in search of jobs. Many migrated to the city on a seasonal basis, seeking winter employment in cities and then returning to the countryside at harvest time. Whether as permanent or temporary urban residents, these migrants took jobs as bricklayers, factory workers, and cabdrivers.

Before the Civil War, commerce was the engine of growth for American cities. Ports like New York, Boston, New Orleans, and San Francisco became distribution centers for imported goods or items manufactured in small shops in the surrounding countryside. Cities in the interior of the country located on or near major bodies of water, such as Chicago, St. Louis, Cincinnati, and Detroit, served similar functions. As the extension of railroad transportation led to the development of large-scale industry (see chapter 16), these cities and others became industrial centers as well.

Industrialization contributed to rapid urbanization in several ways. It drew those living on farms, who either could not earn a satisfactory living or were bored by the isolation of rural areas, into the city in search of better-paying jobs and excitement. One rural dweller in Massachusetts complained: "The lack of pleasant, public entertainments in this town has much to do with our young people feeling discontented with country life." In 1891, a year after graduating from Kansas State University, the future newspaper editor William Allen White headed to Kansas City, enticed, as he put it, by the "marvels" of "the gilded metropolis." In addition, while the mechanization of farming increased efficiency, it also reduced the demand for farm labor. In 1896 one person could plant, tend, and harvest as much wheat as it had taken eighteen farmworkers to do sixty years before.

Industrial technology also made cities more attractive and livable places. Electricity extended nighttime entertainment and powered streetcars to convey people around town. Improved water and sewage systems provided more sanitary conditions, especially given the demands of the rapidly expanding population. Structural steel and electric elevators made it possible to construct taller and taller buildings, which gave cities such as Chicago and New York their distinctive skylines. Scientists and physicians made significant progress in the fight against the spread of contagious diseases, which had become serious problems in crowded cities.

Although immigrants increasingly accounted for the influx into the cities, before 1890 the rise in urban population came mainly from Americans on the move. In addition to young men like William Allen White, young women left the farm to seek their fortune. The female protagonist of Theodore Dreiser's novel *Sister Carrie* (1900) abandons small-town Wisconsin for the lure of Chicago. In real life, mechanization created many "Sister Carries" by making farm women less valuable in the fields. The possibility of purchasing mass-produced goods from mail-order houses such as Sears, Roebuck also left young women less essential as homemakers because they no longer had to sew their own clothes and could buy labor-saving appliances from catalogs.

Similar factors drove rural black women and men into cities. Plagued by the same poverty and debt that white sharecroppers and tenants in the South faced, blacks suffered from the added burden of racial oppression and violence in the post-Reconstruction period. From 1870 to 1890, the African American population of Nashville, Tennessee, soared from just over 16,000 to more than 29,000. In Atlanta, Georgia, the number of blacks jumped from slightly above 16,000 to around 28,000. Richmond, Virginia, and Montgomery, Alabama, followed suit, though the increase was not quite as high.

Economic opportunities were more limited for black migrants than for their white counterparts. African American migrants found work as cooks, janitors, and domestic servants. Work in cotton mills remained off-limits to blacks, but many found employment as manual laborers in manufacturing companies—including tobacco factories, which employed women and men; tanneries; and cottonseed oil firms—and as dockworkers. In 1882 the Richmond Chamber of Commerce applauded black workers as "easily taught" and "most valuable hand[s]." Although the overwhelming majority of blacks worked as unskilled laborers for very low wages, others opened small businesses such as funeral parlors, barbershops, and construction companies or went into professions such as medicine, law, banking, and education that catered to residents of segregated black

African American Family, 1900

Despite the rigid racial segregation and oppression that African Americans faced in the late nineteenth century, some black families found ways to achieve economic success and upward mobility. With its piano and fine furniture, the home of this African American family reflects middle-class conventions of the period. The father is a graduate of Hampton Institute, a historically black university founded after the Civil War to educate freedpeople.   Library of Congress

in a railroad yard. "The colored women like this work," she explained, because "we make more money . . . and we do not have to work as hard as at housework," which required working sixteen-hour days, six days a week.

Although many blacks found they preferred their new lives to the ones they had led in the South, the North did not turn out to be the promised land of freedom. Black newcomers encountered discrimination in housing and employment. Residential segregation confined African Americans to racial ghettos, such as the South Side of Chicago and New York City's Harlem. Black workers found it difficult to obtain skilled employment despite their qualifications, and women and men most often toiled as domestics, janitors, and part-time laborers.

Nevertheless, African Americans in northern cities built their own communities that preserved and reshaped their southern culture and offered a degree of insulation against the harshness of racial discrimination. A small black middle class appeared in Washington, D.C., Philadelphia, Chicago, and New York City consisting of teachers, attorneys, and small business people. In 1888 African Americans organized the Capital Savings Bank of Washington, D.C. Ten years later, two black real estate agents in New York City were worth more than $150,000 each, and one agent in Cleveland owned $100,000 in property. The rising black middle class provided leadership in the formation of mutual aid societies, lodges, and women's clubs. Newspapers such as the *Chicago Defender* and *Pittsburgh Courier* furnished local news to their subscribers and reported national and international events affecting people of color. As was the case in the South, the church was at the center of black life in northern cities. More than just religious institutions, churches furnished space for social activities and the dissemination of political information. The Baptist Church attracted the largest following among blacks throughout the country, followed by the African Methodist Episcopal (AME) Church. By the first decade of the twentieth century, more than two dozen churches had sprung up in Chicago alone. Whether housed in newly constructed buildings or in storefronts, black churches provided worshippers freedom from white control. They also allowed members of the northern black middle class to demonstrate what they considered to be respectability and refinement.

neighborhoods. Despite considerable individual accomplishments, by the turn of the twentieth century most blacks in the urban South had few prospects for upward economic mobility.

In 1890, although 90 percent of African Americans lived in the South, a growing number were moving to Northern cities to seek employment and greater freedom. Boll weevil infestations during the 1890s decimated cotton production and forced sharecroppers and tenants off farms. At the same time, blacks saw significant erosion of their political and civil rights in the last decade of the nineteenth century. Most black citizens in the South were denied the right to vote and experienced rigid, legally sanctioned racial segregation in all aspects of public life (see chapter 16). Between 1890 and 1914 approximately 485,000 African Americans left the South. By 1914 New York, Chicago, and Philadelphia each counted more than 100,000 African Americans among their population, and another twenty-nine northern cities contained black populations of 10,000 or more. An African American woman expressed her enthusiasm about the employment she found in Chicago, where she earned $3 a day working

This meant discouraging enthusiastic displays of "old-time religion," which celebrated more exuberant forms of worship. As the Reverend W. A. Blackwell of Chicago's AME Zion Church declared, "Singing, shouting, and talking [were] the most useless ways of proving Christianity." This conflict over modes of religious expression reflected a larger process that was under way in black communities at the turn of the twentieth century. As black urban communities in the North grew and developed, tensions and divisions emerged within the increasingly diverse black community, as a variety of groups competed to shape and define black culture and identity.

Cities Expand Upward and Outward

As the urban population increased, cities expanded both out and up. Before 1860, the dominant form of brick and stone construction prevented buildings from rising more than four or five stories. As late as 1880, church steeples usually remained the tallest structures in cities. However, as cities became much more populous, land values soared. During the 1870s and 1880s, one piece of property in Chicago rose in value from $160 to $800. In Denver, the value of a city block leaped from $6,500 to $205,000, and in New York City a lot that sold for $80 in 1840 fetched $8,000 forty years later. Steep prices prompted architects to make the most of small, expensive plots of land by finding ways to build taller structures. Architects began using cast-iron columns instead of the thick, heavy walls of brick that limited floor space. The resulting "cloudscrapers" raised the urban skyline to ten stories. The development of structural steel, which was stronger and more durable than iron, turned cloudscrapers into **skyscrapers**, which stretched some thirty stories into the air. With the development of the electric elevator and the radiator, which replaced fireplaces with hot water circulated through pipes, even taller skyscrapers came to loom over downtown business districts in major cities.

Cities also expanded horizontally, as new transportation technology made it possible for residents to move around a much larger urban landscape. In the mid-nineteenth century in cities such as Boston and Philadelphia, pedestrians could still walk from one end of the city to the other within an hour. If residents preferred to ride public conveyances, they could pay a fare and hop on board a horse-drawn railcar. These vehicles moved slowly and left tons of horse manure in the streets. To avoid such problems, in 1873 San Francisco, followed by Seattle and Chicago, installed a system of cable-driven trolley cars. Still,

Chicago Skyscraper, 1898

Chicago's Marshall Field and Company building rose up twelve stories and became the second-tallest department store in the world. This granite skyscraper was constructed in sections between 1892 and 1914, and it was the first department store to install escalators.   Courtesy Everett Collection

these trolleys proved slow and unreliable. By 1914, however, advances in transportation converted walking cities into riding cities.

Electricity provided the transportation breakthrough. In 1888 naval engineer Frank J. Sprague, who had once worked for inventor Thomas Edison, completed the first electric trolley line in Richmond, Virginia. Electric-powered streetcars traveled twice as fast as horses and left little mess on the streets. Subways could run underground without asphyxiating passengers and workmen with a steam engine's smoke and soot. Boston opened the first subway in 1897, followed by New York City in 1904.

Bridges spanning large rivers and waterways also helped extend the boundaries of the inner city. Railroad companies had originally worked out the details of constructing such bridges, but not until 1883 did they become the symbol of urban growth. In that year, the Brooklyn Bridge opened, connecting Manhattan with the city of Brooklyn. Designed and engineered by John Augustus Roebling, the bridge had taken thirteen years to complete and cost twenty men their lives. It stretched more than a mile across the East River and was broad enough for a footpath, two double carriage lanes, and two railroad lines. In addition, the bridge featured arches cut like giant cathedral windows. In looking up at its supporting cables, one observer marveled that they hung "like divine messages from above." During its first year in operation, more than 11 million people passed over the bridge; today, more than 51 million vehicles cross the bridge each year.

The electrification of public transportation and the construction of bridges made it feasible for some people to live considerable distances from their workplace. In the eighteenth and nineteenth centuries, middle- and upper-class merchants and professionals usually lived near their shops and offices in the heart of the city, surrounded by their employees. After 1880, the huge influx of immigration brought large numbers of impoverished workers to city centers. The resulting traffic congestion and overcrowded housing pushed wealthier residents to seek more open spaces in which to build houses. The new electric trolley lines allowed middle-class urbanites to move miles away from downtown areas. With an investment of $2,000 to $10,000, a considerable sum in those days, they built roomy homes filled with modern conveniences on leafy streets. In 1850 the Boston metropolis spread in a radius of two to three miles around the city and had a population of 200,000. In 1900 suburban Boston ringed the city in a ten-mile radius, with a population of more than 1 million. Increasingly, cities divided into two parts: an inner commercial and industrial core housing the working class, and outer communities occupied by a wealthier class of white, older-stock Americans.

How the Other Half Lived

As the middle and upper classes fled the industrial urban center for the suburbs, the working poor moved in to replace them. They lived in old factories and homes and in shanties and cellars. Because land values were higher in the city, the poorest people could least afford high rents. To make ends meet, families crowded into existing apartments, sometimes taking in boarders to help pay the rent. This led to increased population density and over-crowding in the urban areas where immigrants lived. On New York's Lower East Side, the population density was the highest in the world. In 1880, 47,000 people lived within the teeming area. Ten years later, the number had climbed to more than 57,000, a population density of 334,080 per square mile, about ten times the citywide average. Such overcrowding fostered communicable diseases and frustration, giving the area the nicknames "typhus ward" and "suicide ward."

Overcrowding combined with extreme poverty turned immigrant neighborhoods into slums, which were characterized by substandard housing. Impoverished immigrants typically lived in multiple-family apartment buildings called **tenements** (legally defined as containing more than three families). First constructed in 1850, these early dwellings often featured windowless rooms and little or no plumbing and heating. In 1879 a New York law reformed the building codes and required minimal plumbing facilities and that all bedrooms (but not all rooms) have a window. Constructed on narrow 25-by-100-foot lots, these five- and six-story buildings included four small apartments on a floor and had only two toilets off the hallway. Tenements stood right next to each other, with only an air shaft separating them. Although these dwellings marked some improvement in living conditions, they proved miserable places to live in—dark, damp, and foul smelling. In 1895 a federal government housing inspector observed that the air shafts provided "imperfect light and ventilation" and that "refuse matter or filth of one kind or another [was] very apt to accumulate at the bottom, giving rise to noxious odors." The air shafts also operated as a conduit for fires that moved swiftly from one tenement to another.

In fact, the density of late-nineteenth-century cities could turn individual fires into citywide disasters. The North Side of Chicago burned to the ground in 1871, and Boston and Baltimore suffered catastrophic fires as well. On April 18, 1906, an earthquake in San Francisco set the city ablaze, causing about 1,500 deaths and terrible destruction of businesses and homes. Such fires could, however, have long-term positive consequences. The great urban confla-grations encouraged construction of fireproof buildings made of brick and steel instead of wood. In addition, citizens organized fire watches and established municipal fire departments to replace volunteer companies. An unintended side effect, fires provided cities with a chance to rebuild. Chicago's skyscrapers and its system of urban parks were built on land cleared by fire.

Besides furnishing grossly inadequate housing, tenements stood out as eyesores, "scabs" on the landscape, especially for those who had lived in cities before the new wave of immigration began. In 1890 Jacob Riis, a Danish immigrant, newspaperman, and photographer, illustrated the brutal conditions endured by tenement families such as Beryl Lassin's on New York's Lower East Side. "In the stifling July nights," he wrote in *How the Other Half Lives*, "when the big barracks are like fiery furnaces, their very walls giving out absorbed heat, men and women lie in restless, sweltering rows, panting for air and sleep." Under these circumstances, Riis lamented, an epidemic "is excessively fatal among the children of the poor, by reason of the practical impossibility of isolating the patient in a tenement." Despite their obvious problems, tenements soon spread to other cities such as Cleveland, Cincinnati, and Boston, and one block might have ten of these buildings, housing as many as four thousand people.

With all the misery they spawned as places to live, tenements also functioned as workplaces. Czech immigrants made cigars in their apartments from six in the morning until nine at night, seven days a week, for about 6 cents an hour. By putting an entire family to work, they could make $15 a week and pay their rent of $12 a month. Clothing contractors in particular saw these tenement **sweatshops** as a cheap way to produce their products. By jamming two or three sewing machines into an apartment and paying workers a fixed amount for each item they produced, contractors kept their costs down and avoided factory regulations. Riis observed men, women, and children "bending over their machines, or ironing clothes at the window, half-naked. Proprieties do not count on the East Side."

Even when immigrants left sweatshop apartments and went to work in factories, they continued to face exploitation. The Jewish and Italian clothing workers who toiled in the **Triangle Shirtwaist Company**, located in New York City's Greenwich Village, worked long hours for little pay. In 1911 a fire broke out on the eighth story of the factory and quickly spread to the ninth and tenth floors. The fire engines' ladders could not reach that high, and one of the exits on the ninth floor was locked to keep workers from stealing material. More than 140 people died in the blaze—some by jumping out the windows, but most by getting trapped behind the closed exit door.

Explore

See Document 18.3 for one reaction to the Triangle Shirtwaist fire.

Slums compounded the potential for disease, poor sanitation, fire, congestion, and crime. Living on poor diets, slum dwellers proved particularly vulnerable to epidemics. Cholera and typhoid—as well as an outbreak of yellow fever in Memphis in the 1870s and in Tampa in the 1870s and 1880s—killed tens of thousands. Tuberculosis was even deadlier. An epidemic that began in a slum neighborhood could easily spread into more affluent areas of the city. Children suffered the most. Almost one-quarter of the children born in American cities in 1890 did not live to celebrate their first birthday.

Contributing to the outbreak of disease was faulty sewage disposal, a problem that vexed city leaders. Until the invention of the modern indoor flush toilet in the early twentieth century, people relied on outdoor toilets, with as many as eight hundred people using a single facility. All too often, cities dumped human waste into rivers that also supplied drinking water. In 1881 the exasperated mayor of Cleveland called the Cuyahoga River "an open sewer through the center of the city." Two years later, a group of Philadelphians complained that their water was "not only distasteful and unwholesome for drinking, but offensive for bathing purposes." At the same time, the great demand for water caused by the population explosion resulted in lower water pressure. Consequently, residents in the upper floors of tenements had to carry buckets of water from the lower floors. Until cities overcame their water and sanitation challenges, epidemics would continue to plague urban dwellers.

Urban crowding created other problems as well. Traffic moved slowly through densely populated cities. Pedestrians and commuters had to navigate around throngs of people walking on sidewalks and streets, peddlers selling out of pushcarts, and piles of garbage cluttering the walkways. Streets remained in poor shape. In 1889 the majority of Cleveland's 440 miles of streets consisted of sand and gravel. Chicago did not fare much better. In 1890 most road surfaces were covered with wooden blocks, and three-quarters of the city's more than 2,000 miles of streets remained unpaved. Rainstorms quickly made matters worse by turning foul-smelling, manure-filled streets into mud. Washington, D.C., solved much of the problem of clogged roads by covering them with asphalt. For the most part, only smaller cities like New Haven, Connecticut, could afford to pave the streets.

Poverty and overcrowding contributed to increased crime. The U.S. murder rate quadrupled between 1880 and 1900, at a time when the murder rates in most European cities were declining. In New York City, crime thrived in slums with the apt names of "Bandit's Roost" and "Hell's Kitchen," and groups of young hoodlums, such as the "Sewer Rats" and "Rock Gang," preyed on unsuspecting citizens. Poverty forced some of the poor to turn to theft or prostitution. One twenty-year-old prostitute, who supported her sickly mother and four brothers and sisters, lamented: "Let God Almighty judge who's to blame most, I that was driven, or them that drove me to the pass I'm in." Rising criminality led to the formation of urban police departments, though many law officers supplemented their incomes by collecting graft (illegal payments) for ignoring criminal activities.

REVIEW & RELATE

What factors contributed to rapid urban growth in the late nineteenth century?

How did the American cities of 1850 differ from those of 1900? What factors account for these differences?

DOCUMENT 18.3

Rose Schneiderman | The Triangle Shirtwaist Fire, 1911

On March 25, 1911, fire erupted in the Triangle Shirtwaist factory in lower New York City. Most of the company's six hundred garment workers were immigrant women. The building had inadequate fire escapes and blocked exits, which resulted in the high death toll of 146 workers. This catastrophe aroused many New Yorkers to rally around factory reforms. In the aftermath of the fire, Rose Schneiderman, a Polish Jewish immigrant who had led a strike at the Triangle Shirtwaist Company in 1909, addressed a memorial gathering at the Metropolitan Opera House.

Explore

I would be a traitor to those poor burned bodies if I were to come here to talk good fellowship. We have tried you good people of the public—and we have found you wanting.

The old Inquisition had its rack and its thumbscrews and its instruments of torture with iron teeth. We know what these things are today: the iron teeth are our necessities, the thumbscrews are the high-powered and swift machinery close to which we must work, and the rack is here in the firetrap structures that will destroy us the minute they catch fire.

This is not the first time girls have been burned alive in this city. Every week I must learn of the untimely death of one of my sister workers. Every year thousands of us are maimed. The life of men and women is so cheap and property is so sacred! There are so many of us for one job, it matters little if 140-odd are burned to death.

We have tried you, citizens! We are trying you now and you have a couple of dollars for the sorrowing mothers and brothers and sisters by way of a charity gift. But every time the workers come out in the only way they know to protest against conditions which are unbearable, the strong hand of the law is allowed to press down heavily upon us.

Public officials have only words of warning for us—warning that we must be intensely orderly and

Victims of the Triangle Shirtwaist Company Fire, 1911 © Bettmann/CORBIS

must be intensely peaceable, and they have the workhouse just back of all their warnings. The strong hand of the law beats us back when we rise— back into the conditions that make life unbearable.

I can't talk fellowship to you who are gathered here. Too much blood has been spilled. I know from experience it is up to the working people to save themselves. And the only way is through a strong working-class movement.

Source: Leon Stein, *The Triangle Fire* (New York: Carroll & Graf, 1962), 144–45.

Interpret the Evidence

- Why did Schneiderman reject the possibility of an alliance between the middle class and the working class?
- In Schneiderman's view, what role did the government play in the oppression of working-class people?

Put It in Context

What does this speech convey about working conditions for female laborers at the start of the twentieth century?

Urban Politics at the Turn of the Century

The problems that booming cities faced in trying to absorb millions of immigrants proved formidable and at times seemed insurmountable. From a governmental standpoint, cities had limited authority over their own affairs. They were controlled by state legislatures and needed state approval to raise revenues and pass regulations. For the most part, there were no zoning laws to regulate housing construction. Private companies owned public utilities, and competition among them produced unnecessary duplication and waste. The government services that did exist operated on a segmented basis, with the emphasis on serving wealthier neighborhoods at the expense of the city at large. Missing was a vision of the city as a whole, one that would view the distinct sections as part of a larger tapestry. Cities had become so large and complex that no one could stand back and see the entire picture.

Political Machines and City Bosses

City government in the late nineteenth century was fragmented. Mayors usually did not have much power, and decisions involving public policies such as housing, transportation, and municipal services often rested in the hands of private developers. For instance, by 1890 Chicago had eleven branches of government that were constantly at odds with one another. Bringing some order out of this chaos, the **political machine** functioned to give cities the centralized authority and services that they otherwise lacked. At the head of the machine was the political **boss**. Although the boss himself (and they were all men) held some public office, his real authority came from leadership of the machine. These organizations maintained a tight network of loyalists throughout city wards (districts), each of which contained designated representatives responsible for catering to the needs of their constituents. Whether Democratic or Republican, political machines did not care about philosophical issues; they were concerned primarily with staying in power.

The strength of political machines rested in large measure on immigrants. The organization provided a kind of public welfare when private charity could not cope satisfactorily with the growing needs of the poor. Machines doled out turkeys on holidays, furnished a load of coal for the winter, provided jobs in public construction, arranged for shelter and meals if tenement houses burned down, and intervened with the police and the courts when a constituent got into trouble. Bosses sponsored baseball clubs, held barbecues and picnics, and attended christenings, bar

Philadelphia, 1897

This photograph shows the hustle and bustle of Philadelphia, which along with other cities grew enormously in the late nineteenth century. Urban politicians had to grapple with the challenges posed by the incredible pace of change, including the rapid influx of immigrants. The presence in this scene of carts, a horse, and a streetcar shows a city in transition.　Library of Congress

mitzvahs, weddings, and funerals, sometimes all in a single day. As George Washington Plunkitt, a boss in New York City's Tammany Hall machine, reflected, it was a "strenuous life." For enterprising members of immigrant groups—and this proved especially true for the Irish during this period—the machine offered upward mobility out of poverty as they rose through its ranks.

The poor were not the only group that benefited from connections to political machines. The machine and its functionaries helped businessmen maneuver through the maze of contradictory and overlapping codes regulating building and licenses that impeded their routine course of activities. In addition to assisting legitimate businessmen, the machine facilitated the underworld commerce of vice, prostitution, and gambling by acting as an arbiter to keep this trade within established boundaries—all for a cut of the illegal profits.

In return for these services, the machine received the votes of grateful immigrants and a plentiful supply of funds from businessmen. When challenged by reformers or other political rivals, the machine readily engaged in corrupt election practices to maintain its power. Mobilizing the "graveyard vote," bosses took names from tombstones to pad lists of registered voters. They also hired "repeaters" to vote more than once under phony names and did not flinch from dumping whole ballot boxes into the river or using hired thugs to scare opponents from the polls.

Bosses enriched themselves through graft and corruption. They secured protection money from both legitimate and illegitimate business interests in return for their services. Boss William Marcy Tweed, the head of Tammany Hall in the 1860s and 1870s, swindled New York City out of a fortune while supervising the construction of a lavish three-story courthouse in lower Manhattan. The original budget for the building was $250,000, but the city spent more than $13 million on the structure, making out checks to Tweed's phony associates "T. C. Cash" and "Philip F. Dummey." The building remained unfinished in 1873, when Tweed was convicted on fraud charges and went to jail. In later years, Tammany Hall's Plunkitt distinguished this kind of "dishonest graft" from the kind

of "honest graft" that he practiced. If he received inside information about a future sale of city property, Plunkitt reasoned, why shouldn't he get a head start, buy it at a low price, and then sell it at a higher figure? As he delighted in saying, "I seen my opportunities and I took 'em." What could be more American?

Explore

See Documents 18.4 and 18.5 for opposing perspectives on machine politics.

Yet the services of political machines came at a high cost. Corruption and graft led to higher taxes on middle-class residents. Moreover, the image of the political boss as a modern-day Robin Hood who stole from the rich and gave to the poor is greatly exaggerated. Much of the proceeds of machine activities went into the private coffers of machine bosses and other functionaries and did not go to worthy public ventures. Trafficking in vice might have run more smoothly under the coordination of the machine, but the

DOCUMENTS 18.4 AND 18.5

Political Machines: Two Views

At the turn of the twentieth century, investigative journalism exposed what many saw as glaring inequalities in industrializing America. In *The Shame of the Cities*, journalist Lincoln Steffens wrote about the need for significant political reform in the city of Philadelphia. Machine bosses such as New York City's George Washington Plunkitt, however, challenged Steffens's observations about the role of political machines in urban government, presenting themselves as much more effective representatives of the people's interests than the reformers.

Explore

18.4 Lincoln Steffens | *The Shame of the Cities*, 1904

The honest citizens of Philadelphia have no more rights at the polls than the [N]egroes down South. Nor do they fight very hard for this basic privilege. You can arouse their Republican ire by talking about the black Republican votes lost in the Southern States by white Democratic intimidation, but if you remind the average Philadelphian that he is in the same position, he will look startled, then say, "That's so, that's literally true, only I never thought of it in just that way." And it is literally true.

The machine controls the whole process of voting, and practices fraud at every stage. The assessor's list is the voting list, and the assessor is the machine's man. . . . The assessor pads the list with the names of dead dogs, children, and non-existent persons. One newspaper printed the picture of a dog, another that of a little four-year-old [N]egro boy, down on such a list.

Source: Lincoln Steffens, *The Shame of the Cities* (New York: McClure, Phillips, 1904), 198–99.

safety and health of city residents hardly improved. Most importantly, although immigrants and the poor did benefit from an informal system of social welfare, the machine had no interest in resolving the underlying causes of their problems. As the dominant urban political party organization, the machine cared little about issues such as good housing, job safety, and sufficient wages. The British observer James Bryce, who toured America in the late 1880s and admired much of what he saw, nevertheless judged the machine-controlled municipal governments to be "the one conspicuous failure of the United States." It remained for others to provide alternative approaches to relieving the plight of the urban poor.

Urban Reformers

The men and women who criticized the political bosses and machines—and the corruption and vice they fostered—usually came from the ranks of the upper middle class and the wealthy. Their solutions to the urban crisis typically centered around toppling the political machine and replacing it with a civil service that would allow government to function on the basis of merit rather than influence peddling and cronyism. Both locally and nationally, they pushed for civil service reform. In 1883 Congress responded to this demand by passing the **Pendleton Civil Service Reform Act**, which required federal jobs to be awarded on the basis of merit, as determined by competitive examinations, rather than through political connections. As for the immigrants who supported machine politics, these reformers preferred to deal with them from afar and expected that through proper education they might change their lifestyles and adopt American ways.

Another group of Americans from upper- and middle-class backgrounds put aside whatever prejudices they might have held about working-class immigrants and dealt directly with newcomers to try to solve various social problems. These reformers—mostly young people, and many of them women and college graduates—took up residence in **settlement houses** located in urban slums. Settlement houses offered a variety of services to

---

Explore

18.5 George Washington Plunkitt | Confessions of a Political Boss, 1905

If a family is burned out I don't ask whether they are Republicans or Democrats, and I don't refer them to the Charity Organization Society, which would investigate their case in a month or two and decide they were worthy of help about the time they are dead from starvation. I just get quarters for them, buy clothes for them if their clothes were burned up, and fix them up till they get things runnin' again. It's philanthropy, but it's politics, too—mighty good politics. Who can tell how many votes one of these fires bring me? The poor are the most grateful people in the world, and, let me tell you, they have more friends in their neighborhoods than the rich have in theirs. . . .

I've been reading a book by Lincoln Steffens on *The Shame of the Cities*. Steffens means well but, like all reformers, he don't know how to make distinctions. He can't see no difference between honest graft and dishonest graft, and, consequent, he gets things all mixed up. There's the biggest kind of difference between political looters and politicians who make a fortune out of politics by keepin' their eyes wide open. The looter goes in for himself alone without considerin' his organization or his city. The politician looks after his own interests, the organization's interests, and the city's interests all at the same time.

Source: William L. Riordan, *Plunkitt of Tammany Hall* (New York: E. P. Dutton, 1963), 28–29.

Interpret the Evidence

- Why does Steffens claim that white urban voters are in a similar position as southern blacks?
- According to Plunkitt, what advantages does his form of community service have over that offered by reformers?

Put It in Context

What role did political machines play in the governance of cities?

community residents, including day care for children; cooking, sewing, and secretarial classes; neighborhood playgrounds; counseling sessions; and meeting rooms for labor unions. Settlement house organizers, pioneers of the social work profession, understood that immigrants gravitated to the political machine or congregated in the local tavern not because they were inherently immoral but because these institutions helped mitigate their suffering and, in some cases, offered concrete paths to advancement. Although settlement house workers wanted to Americanize immigrants, they also understood immigrants' need to hold on to remnants of their original culture.

By 1900 approximately one hundred settlement houses had been established in major American cities. Jane Addams, who founded Hull House in Chicago, contended that "the dependence of classes on each other is reciprocal" and insisted that "the things which make men alike are finer and better than the things that keep them apart." Other settlement houses reflecting a similar philosophy included the South End House in Boston, directed by Robert A. Woods, and the Henry Street Settlement in New York City, founded by Lillian Wald. Addams and Wald, as well as other social workers, preferred a hands-on approach. They actively mobilized neighborhood residents to engage in politics and to vote for candidates who understood their problems and would campaign for improved garbage collection, housing inspection, better schools, and other community improvements.

Religiously inspired reform provided similar support for slum dwellers. In contrast to clergy such as Russell Conwell (see chapter 16), who emphasized cash more than Christ, some Protestant ministers began to argue that immigrants' problems resulted not from chronic racial or ethnic failings but from their difficult environment. One of the best-known figures among this group was Washington Gladden, a minister who had lived in Springfield and Columbus, Ohio. Originally a defender of laissez-faire, by the mid-1880s Gladden had come to believe that unregulated private enterprise was "inequitable." He compared financial speculators to vampires "sucking the life-blood of our commerce." In books and from the pulpit, Gladden preached Christianity as a "social gospel," which included support for civil service reform, antimonopoly regulation, income tax legislation, factory inspection laws, and workers' right to strike.

Despite the efforts of social gospel advocates and the charitable organizations that arose to help relieve human misery, such as the Salvation Army, private attempts to combat the various urban ills, however well-meaning, proved insufficient. The problems were structural, not personal, and one group or even several operating together did not have the resources or power to make urban institutions more efficient, equitable, and humane. As Jane Addams noted, "Private beneficence is totally inadequate to deal with the vast numbers of the city's disinherited." If reformers were to succeed in tackling the most significant social problems and make lasting changes in American society and politics, they would have to enlist state and federal governments.

REVIEW & RELATE

What role did political machines play in late-nineteenth-century cities?

Who led the opposition to machine control of city politics, and what solutions and alternatives did they offer?

LEARNINGCurve bedfordstmartins.com/hewittlawson/LC

Conclusion: A Nation of Cities

Immigrants from southern and eastern Europe who came to the United States between the 1880s and 1914 survived numerous hardships as they strove to create a better life for their families. Like industrialists, workers, and farmers, they organized to advance collective interests. Immigrants joined together in neighborhood groups—houses of worship, fraternal organizations, burial societies, political machines, and settlement houses—to promote their own welfare. Some achieved success and returned to their homelands to live in relative splendor. Most of those who remained in the United States, like Mary Vik and Ben Lassin, struggled to earn a living but managed to pave the way for their children and grandchildren to obtain better education and jobs. Mary's granddaughter, Nancy A. Hewitt, earned a Ph.D. in history from the University of Pennsylvania, and Ben's grandson, Steven F. Lawson, earned a doctorate in history from Columbia University. They became university professors and in writing this book have tried to preserve their grandparents' legacy.

Immigrants were not the only group on the move in the late nineteenth century. African Americans migrated in search of political freedom and economic opportunity. They relocated from the rural South to the urban South and North, where they continued to encounter discrimination. Yet cities gave them more leeway to develop their own political, economic, cultural, and social institutions than they had before. Although they encountered segregation, African Americans in the North were allowed to vote, a tool they would use to gain equality in the future. Because of long-standing patterns of racism, supported by law, African Americans would struggle much longer than did white immigrants to obtain equality and justice.

Few public institutions attempted to aid immigrants or racial minorities as they made the difficult transition to urban and industrial life. Yet immigrants did participate in urban politics through the efforts of political bosses and their machines who sought immigrant votes. In return, political machines provided immigrants with rudimentary social and political services that they could rarely find anywhere else. Political machines, however, bred corruption, along with higher taxes to fund their extravagances. Dishonest government prompted middle- and upper-class urban dwellers to take up reform in order to sweep the political bosses out of office and diminish the power of their immigrant supporters, as we will see in the next chapter.

LEARNINGCurve
Check what you know.
bedfordstmartins.com/hewittlawson/LC

Chapter Review

Online Study Guide ▶ bedfordstmartins.com/hewittlawson

KEY TERMS

ghettos (p. 565)
mutual aid societies (p. 565)
nativism (p. 568)
eugenics (p. 570)
melting pot (p. 570)
skyscrapers (p. 573)
tenements (p. 574)
sweatshops (p. 575)
Triangle Shirtwaist Company (p. 575)
political machine (p. 577)
boss (p. 577)
Pendleton Civil Service Reform Act (p. 579)
settlement houses (p. 579)

REVIEW & RELATE

1. What challenges did new immigrants to the United States face?

2. What steps did immigrants take to meet these challenges?

3. What factors contributed to rapid urban growth in the late nineteenth century?

4. How did the American cities of 1850 differ from those of 1900? What factors account for these differences?

5. What role did political machines play in late-nineteenth-century cities?

6. Who led the opposition to machine control of city politics, and what solutions and alternatives did they offer?

TIMELINE OF EVENTS

1880–1914	Period of significant immigration to United States
1882	Chinese Exclusion Act passed
1883	Pendleton Civil Service Reform Act requires that federal jobs be awarded on the basis of merit
	Brooklyn Bridge opens
1886	Statue of Liberty opens in New York City
1887	American Protective Association formed to restrict immigration
1892	U.S. schools adopt pledge of allegiance
1893	Immigration Restriction League founded
1897	Boston opens first subway system in the United States
1903	W. E. B. Du Bois publishes *The Souls of Black Folk*
1906	San Francisco earthquake
1908	Israel Zangwill publishes *The Melting-Pot*
1911	Triangle Shirtwaist Company fire in New York City

DOCUMENT 18.7

"Be Just—Even to John Chinaman," 1893

The following cartoon appeared in the satirical magazine *Judge* the year after Congress renewed the Chinese Exclusion Act and added provisions requiring the Chinese already living in the United States to carry certificates of identity and residence. A caption (not shown) beneath the cartoon states: "Judge (to Miss Columbia)—'You allowed that boy to come into your school, it would be inhuman to throw him out now—it will be sufficient in the future to keep his brothers out.'" While the cartoon favors the Chinese Exclusion Act, it presents a more complex message. It accepts the presence of other immigrant groups and Native Americans, shown in stereotyped depictions, suggesting that schooling will turn them into true Americans. It also expresses some sympathy for the Chinese remaining in the country. The cartoon also proposes that some of these earlier immigrants harbored anti-Chinese feelings. Note the Irish American holding up a blackboard that says, "Kick Out the Heathen; He's Got No Vote."

BE JUST---EVEN TO JOHN CHINAMAN.

DOCUMENT 18.8

Alfred P. Schultz | The Mongrelization of America, 1908

Using the fall of Rome as his example, Alfred P. Schultz argued in *Race or Mongrel* that the mixing of races produced a mongrel civilization and inevitably led to the decay of a nation. As one reviewer noted at the time, the author's "apparent object is to check alien immigration into the United States." Like most opponents of the new immigrants, Schultz used arguments based on moral judgments and supposedly sound medical and scientific information.

The influx of these races cannot be without consequences. The surgeons at the ports of immigration observe that the present immigrants have a much higher percent of loathsome diseases, and that, in general physique, it is very much inferior to the immigration of thirty years ago. The history of the races now coming proves beyond doubt their mental inferiority to the races that immigrated before the advent of Slavs and Latins. If immigration is still a blessing, then the sturdy Northern races are in every way preferable to the Southern and Southeastern debris of races that have been. The free admission of these latter prevents the coming of the former, for if content to compete with Slavs and Latins, the Northerners need not migrate as far as the United States. Much more important than the economic effects of immigration are the racial effects of immigration. . . .

Up to the middle of the last century a distinct national character was developing in the United States, and certain distinctive traits were forming. The addition of millions of other races has caused a decomposition which prevented the endurance of these characteristics, and caused this development to cease. . . .

One cause only is sufficiently powerful to cause the decay of a nation. This cause is promiscuousness. A nation is decayed that consists of degenerates, and it consists of degenerates when it no longer constitutes a distinct race. A degenerated race is one that has no longer the same internal worth which it had of old, for the reason that incessant infusions of foreign blood have diluted and weakened the old blood. In other words, a nation is deteriorated that consists of individuals not at all related or very distantly related to the founders of the nation. . . .

The principle that all men are created equal is still considered the chief pillar of strength of the United States. It is a little declamatory phrase, and only one objection can be raised against it, that it does not contain one iota of truth. Every man knows that the phrase is a falsehood. The truth is that all men are created unequal. Even the men of one and the same race are unequal; the inequalities, however, are not greater than the inequalities existing between the individual leaves of one tree, for they are variations of one and the same type. The differences between individuals of distinct races are essential, and, as they are differences that exist between one species and another, they are lasting. The attempts at creating perfect man, man pure and simple, or "The American," by a fusion of all human beings, is similar to the attempt of creating the perfect dog by a fusion of all canine races. Every animal breeder knows that it cannot be done. . . .

The United States is not much less cosmopolitan today than imperial Rome was. The friends of universal uniformity and of eternal peace will say: "Well, as soon as we are equally worthless, we will not know it, and happiness and peace will prevail." The conclusion is false. The mongrels are equally worthless, but there is no harmony in the depraved lot. The instincts of the different races do not entirely disappear, but they cannot develop. The result is internal unhappiness as far as the individual is concerned, and discord, chronic civil war, as far as the state is concerned. Anarchy within the individual, anarchy in the state.

And why should promiscuousness in the United States have a different effect than it had in Rome and

(continued on page 586)

elsewhere? The opinion is advanced that the public schools change the children of all races into Americans. Put a Scandinavian, a German, and a Magyar boy in at one end, and they will come out Americans at the other end. Which is like saying, let a pointer, a setter, and a pug enter one end of a tunnel and they will come out three greyhounds at the other end.

Public schools are in our time not educational institutions, but information bureaus, and the cultivation of the memory predominates. The children of every race can be trained to the cultivation of memory, but they cannot all be educated alike. The instincts of the different races are too much out of harmony. It is for this reason that the schools give information, with very little education. Schools cannot accomplish the impossible. To express the same opinion biologically, "All animals cannot be fed with the same fodder." . . .

This is the truth: schools, political institutions, and environment are utterly incapable to produce anything. No man can ever become anything else than he is already potentially and essentially. Education and schools are favourable or detrimental to development. They cannot create. To express it differently, no man can ever learn anything or know anything that he does not know already potentially and essentially. . . . Biologically expressed, this sentence reads as follows: A young pug develops into nothing but an old pug, a young greyhound into nothing but an old greyhound; and never, in all the ages between the creation of the world and doomsday, does a pug develop into a greyhound, no matter what the education, the training, the political institutions, and the environment.

Source: Alfred P. Schultz, *Race or Mongrel* (Boston: L. C. Page, 1908), 254–55, 257–61, 266.

DOCUMENT 18.9

Randolph S. Bourne | Trans-national America, 1916

Not all Americans embraced the melting pot or disparaged immigrants. Randolph Bourne, a journalist and political activist, took a middle position on the issue dividing those calling for assimilation and those seeking to curtail immigration. In an essay that appeared in the *Atlantic Monthly*, Bourne argued for a "trans-national America," where instead of completely shedding their Old World cultures, immigrants retained the best of their cultural identities within the larger democratic American society.

We are all foreign-born or the descendants of foreign-born, and if distinctions are to be made between us they should rightly be on some other ground than indigenousness. The early colonists came over with motives no less colonial than the later. They did not come to be assimilated in an American melting-pot. They did not come to adopt the culture of the American Indian. They had not the smallest intention of "giving themselves without reservation" to the new country. They came to get freedom to live as they wanted to. They came to escape from the stifling air and chaos of the old world; they came to make their fortune in a new land. They invented no new social framework. Rather they brought over bodily the old ways to which they had been accustomed. Tightly concentrated on a hostile frontier, they were conservative beyond belief. Their pioneer daring was reserved for the objective conquest of material resources. In their folkways, in their social and political institutions, they were, like every colonial people, slavishly imitative of the mother-country. So that, in spite of the "Revolution," our whole legal and political system remained more English than the English, petrified and unchanging, while in England law developed to meet the needs of the changing times.

It is just this English-American conservatism that has been our chief obstacle to social advance. We have needed the new peoples—the order of the German and Scandinavian, the turbulence of the Slav and Hun—to save us from our own stagnation. I do not mean that the illiterate Slav is now the equal of the New Englander of pure descent. He is raw material to be educated, not into a New Englander, but into a socialized American along such lines as those thirty nationalities are being educated in the amazing schools of Gary [Indiana]. I do not believe that this process is to be one of decades of evolution. The spectacle of Japan's sudden jump from medievalism to post-modernism should have destroyed that superstition. We are not dealing with individuals who are to "evolve." We are dealing with their children, who, with that education we are about to have, will start level with all of us. Let us cease to think of ideals like democracy as magical qualities inherent in certain peoples. Let us speak, not of inferior races, but of inferior civilizations. We are all to educate and to be educated. These peoples in America are in a common enterprise. It is not what we are now that concerns us, but what this plastic next generation may become in the light of a new cosmopolitan ideal.

We are not dealing with static factors, but with fluid and dynamic generations. To contrast the older and the newer immigrants and see the one class as democratically motivated by love of liberty, and the other by mere money-getting, is not to illuminate the future. To think of earlier nationalities as culturally assimilated to America, while we picture the later as a sodden and resistive mass, makes only for bitterness and misunderstanding.

There may be a difference between these earlier and these later stocks, but it lies neither in motive for coming nor in strength of cultural allegiance to the homeland. . . .

What we emphatically do not want is that these distinctive qualities should be washed out into a tasteless, colorless fluid of uniformity. Already we have far too much of this insipidity—masses of people who are cultural half-breeds, neither assimilated Anglo-Saxons nor nationals of another culture. Each national colony in this country seems to retain in its foreign press, its vernacular literature, its schools, its intellectual and patriotic leaders, a central cultural nucleus. From this nucleus the colony extends out by imperceptible gradations to a fringe where national characteristics are all but lost. Our cities are filled with these half-breeds who retain their foreign names but have lost the foreign savor. This does not mean that they have actually been changed into New Englanders or Middle Westerners. It does not mean that they have been really Americanized. It means that, letting slip from them whatever native culture they had, they have substituted for it only the most rudimentary American—the American culture of the cheap newspaper, the "movies," the popular song, the ubiquitous automobile. The unthinking who survey this class call them assimilated, Americanized. The great American public school has done its work. With these people our institutions are safe. We may thrill with dread at the aggressive hyphenate [hyphenated American], but this tame flabbiness is accepted as Americanization. The same moulders of opinion whose ideal is to melt the different races into Anglo-Saxon gold hail this poor product as the satisfying result of their alchemy. . . .

. . . Let us face realistically the America we have around us. Let us work with the forces that are at work. Let us make something of this trans-national spirit instead of outlawing it. Already we are living this cosmopolitan America. What we need is everywhere a vivid consciousness of the new ideal. Deliberate headway must be made against the survivals of the melting-pot ideal for the promise of American life.

Source: Randolph S. Bourne, "Trans-national America," *Atlantic Monthly*, July 1916, 87–88, 90, 97.

DOCUMENT 18.10

Jacob Riis | The Color Line in New York, 1891

Jacob Riis is best known for writing about eastern European immigrants living in crowded tenements on New York's Lower East Side. However, his classic work of photojournalism, *How the Other Half Lives*, also provided a portrait of New York's African American residents, many of whom migrated from the South after the Civil War and lived on the Upper East Side of Manhattan in the neighborhoods of Yorkville and Harlem. As this passage demonstrates, Riis was a sharp observer of the forces of racial discrimination that placed blacks at a disadvantage compared to white immigrants.

The color line must be drawn through the tenements to give the picture its proper shading. The landlord does the drawing, does it with an absence of pretense, a frankness of despotism, that is nothing if not brutal. The Czar of all the Russias is not more absolute upon his own soil than the New York landlord in his dealings with colored tenants. Where he permits them to live, they go; where he shuts the door, stay out. By his grace they exist at all in certain localities; his ukase [order] banishes them from others. He accepts the responsibility, when laid at his door, with unruffled complacency. It is business, he will tell you. And it is. He makes the prejudice in which he traffics pay him well, and that, as he thinks it quite superfluous to tell you, is what he is there for. . . .

Cleanliness is the characteristic of the [N]egro in his new surroundings, as it was his virtue in the old. In this respect he is immensely the superior of the lowest of the whites, the Italians and the Polish Jews, below whom he has been classed in the past in the tenant scale. Nevertheless, he has always had to pay higher rents than even these for the poorest and most stinted rooms. The exceptions I have come across, in which the rents, though high, have seemed more nearly on a level with what was asked for the same number and size of rooms in the average tenement, were in the case of tumble-down rookeries in which no one else would live, and were always coupled with the condition that the landlord should "make no repairs." It can readily be seen that his profits were scarcely curtailed by his "humanity." The reason advanced for this systematic robbery is that white people will not live in the same house with colored tenants, or even

in a house recently occupied by [N]egroes, and that consequently its selling value is injured. The prejudice undoubtedly exists, but it is not lessened by the house agents, who have set up the maxim "once a colored house, always a colored house."

There is method in the maxim, as shown by an inquiry made last year by the *Real Estate Record*. It proved agents to be practically unanimous in the endorsement of the [N]egro as a clean, orderly, and "profitable" tenant. Here is the testimony of one of the largest real estate firms in the city: "We would rather have [N]egro tenants in our poorest class of tenements than the lower grades of foreign white people. We find the former cleaner than the latter, and they do not destroy the property so much. We also get higher prices. We have a tenement on Nineteenth Street, where we get $10 for two rooms which we could not get more than $7.50 for from white tenants previously." . . .

[Riis cites several similar instances of higher rents charged to black tenants.]

I have quoted these cases at length in order to let in light on the quality of this landlord despotism that has purposely confused the public mind, and for its own selfish ends is propping up a waning prejudice. It will be cause for congratulation if indeed its time has come at last. Within a year, I am told by one of the most intelligent and best informed of our colored citizens, there has been evidence, simultaneous with the colored hegira [flight] from the low downtown tenements, of a movement toward less exorbitant rents.

Source: Jacob Riis, *How the Other Half Lives: Studies among the Tenements of New York* (New York: Charles Scribner's and Sons, 1914), 148, 150–52.

Interpret the Evidence

1. According to Israel Zangwill, how will immigrants become "real Americans" (Document 18.6)?
2. What is Alfred Schultz's view of the melting pot (Document 18.8)? In his estimation, why is assimilation an impossible goal for America?
3. Why might other immigrant groups have supported Chinese exclusion (see Document 18.7)?
4. How does Randolph Bourne's vision of America's future differ from that of Zangwill? On what points might the two men have agreed?
5. What explanation does Jacob Riis offer for the high rents and poor accommodations that African Americans were forced to accept (Document 18.10)? What differences between the experiences of white immigrants and African Americans does Riis's description suggest?

Put It in Context

- What are the limitations of the melting pot metaphor for immigrant assimilation? What metaphor would you employ to describe the assimilation process? Why?

background photo: page 588, Library of Congress

Schlesinger Library, Radcliffe Institute, Harvard University/The Bridgeman Art Library

Library of Congress

The women's suffrage organization headquarters of Ohio, 1912.

Newsboys in Philadelphia, 1910.

19

Progressivism and the Search for Order

1900–1917

Library of Congress

Sewing class at Haines Normal and Industrial Institute, Augusta, Georgia.

AMERICAN HISTORIES

Gifford Pinchot grew up on a lavish Connecticut estate catered to by tutors and governesses and vacationing in rural areas, where Gifford learned to hunt, fish, and enjoy the splendor of nature. Yet Pinchot rejected a life of leisure and gentility. Like other affluent young men and women of his time, Pinchot sought to make his mark through public service, in his case by working to conserve and protect America's natural resources. In 1885, following his father's advice, Gifford entered Yale University to study forestry. However, the university did not offer a forestry program, reflecting the predominant view that the nation's natural resources were, for all practical purposes, unlimited. Pinchot cobbled together courses in various scientific fields at Yale, but he knew that after graduating his only option for further study was to travel to Europe, where forests were treated as crops that needed care and replenishing.

By the time Pinchot returned in 1890, many Americans had begun to see the need to conserve the nation's forests, waterways, and oil and mineral deposits and to protect its wild spaces. Drawing on his training as a scientist and his experiences in Europe, Pinchot advocated the use of natural resources by sportsmen and businesses under carefully regulated governmental authority. Appointed to head the Federal Division of Forestry in 1898, Pinchot found a vigorous ally in the White House when Theodore Roosevelt took office in 1901 after William McKinley's assassination. In 1907 Pinchot began to speak of the need for conservation, which he defined as "the use of the natural resources now existing on this continent for the benefit of the people who live here now." This use of resources included responsible business practices in industries such as logging and mining.

Not all environmentalists agreed. In contrast to Pinchot, author and nature photographer Geneva (Gene) Stratton-Porter focused her energies on *preservation*, the protection of public land from any private development and the creation of national parks. Born in 1863 in Wabash County, Indiana, Stratton-Porter spent her childhood on a farm roaming through fields, watching birds, and observing "nature's rhythms." After marrying in 1886,

Stratton-Porter took up photography and hiked into the wilderness of Indiana to take pictures of wild birds.

Stratton-Porter built a reputation as a nature photographer. She also published a series of novels and children's books that revealed her vision of the harmony between human beings and nature. She urged readers to preserve the environment for plant life and wildlife so that men and women could lead a truly fulfilling existence on Earth and not destroy God's creation. Of all the preservationists, Stratton-Porter reached the widest audience. Five of her books sold more than a million copies, and several were made into movies. ●

photos: Library of Congress; Indiana Historical Society P0391 (detail)

THE AMERICAN HISTORIES of Gifford Pinchot and Gene Stratton-Porter reveal the efforts of just two of the many individuals who searched for ways to control the damaging impact of modernization on the United States. From roughly 1900 to 1917, many Americans sought to bring some order out of the chaos accompanying rapid industrialization and urbanization. Despite the magnitude of the issues they targeted, those who believed in the need to combat the problems of industrial America possessed an optimistic faith—sometimes derived from religious principles, sometimes from a secular outlook—that they could relieve the stresses and strains that modern life brought. Such people were not bound together by a single, rigid ideology. Instead, they were united by faith in the notion that if people joined together and applied human intelligence to the task of improving the nation, progress was inevitable. So widespread was this hopeful conviction that we call this period the Progressive Era.

In pursuit of progress and stability, reformers tried to control the behavior of groups they considered a threat to the social order. Equating difference with disorder, many progressives tried to impose white middle-class standards of behavior on immigrant populations. Some

sought to eliminate the "problem" altogether by curtailing further immigration from southern and eastern Europe. Many white progressives, particularly in the South, supported segregation and disfranchisement, which limited opportunities for African Americans. At the same time, however, black progressives and their white allies created organizations dedicated to securing racial equality.

The Roots of Progressivism

At the turn of the twentieth century, many Americans believed that the nation was in dire need of reform. Two decades of westward expansion, industrialization, urbanization, and skyrocketing immigration had transformed the country in unsettling and, in the minds of many, dangerous ways. In the aftermath of the social and economic turmoil that accompanied the depression of the 1890s, many members of the middle and upper classes were convinced that unless they took remedial measures, the country would collapse under the weight of class conflict. Progressives advocated governmental intervention, yet they sought change without radically altering capitalism or the democratic political system. A progressive newspaper editor explained in 1912: "The world moves and we have to move with it. So with all that is going on with politics today. . . . It is evolution, and not revolution."

Progressive Origins

Progressives contended that old ways of governing and doing business did not address modern conditions. In one sense, they inherited the legacy of the Populist movement of the 1890s. Progressives attacked laissez-faire capitalism, and by regulating monopolies they aimed to limit the power of corporate trusts, which they saw as a threat to economic and political democracy. Like the Populists, progressive reformers advocated instituting an income tax as well as a variety of initiatives designed to give citizens a greater say in government. However, progressives differed from Populists in fundamental ways. Perhaps most important, progressives were interested primarily in urban and industrial America, while the Populist movement had emerged in direct response to the problems that plagued rural America in the late nineteenth century.

Progressives were heirs to the intellectual critics of the late nineteenth century who challenged laissez-faire and rejected Herbert Spencer's doctrine of the "survival of the fittest" (see chapter 16). **Pragmatism** greatly influenced progressives. Identified with Harvard psychologist and philosopher William James and philosopher John Dewey, pragmatists contended that the meaning of truth did not reside in some absolute doctrine but could only be discovered through experience. Ideas had to be measured by their practical consequences. From these critics, progressives derived a healthy skepticism toward rigid dogma and instead relied on human experience to guide social action.

Reformers also drew inspiration from the religious ideals of the **social gospel** (see chapter 18). In *Christianity and the Social Crisis* (1907), the Protestant clergyman Walter Rauschenbusch of Rochester, New York, urged Christians to embrace the teachings of Jesus on the ethical obligations for social justice and to put these teachings into action by working among the urban poor. Progressive leaders such as Theodore Roosevelt and Gifford Pinchot combined the moral fervor of the social gospel with the rationalism of the gospel of scientific efficiency.

Pragmatism and the social gospel appealed to members of the new middle class. Before the Civil War, the middle class had consisted largely of ministers, lawyers, physicians, and small proprietors. The growth of large-scale businesses during the second half of the nineteenth century expanded the middle class, which now included men whose professions grew out of industrialization, such as engineering, corporate management, and social work. The new middle class established organizations to promote their own professional goals and further the public interest. One of the most powerful groups, the American Medical Association (AMA), had originally formed in 1847 but grew rapidly at the turn of the century. The AMA raised qualifications to increase the level of education required to practice medicine, thus limiting access to the profession. Progressivism drew many of its most devoted adherents from this new middle class.

Muckrakers

The growing desire for reform at the turn of the century received a boost from investigative journalists known as **muckrakers**. Popular magazines such as *McClure's* and *Collier's* sought to increase their readership by publishing exposés of corruption in government and the shady operations of big business. Filled with details uncovered through

Ida M. Tarbell

Investigative journalist Ida Tarbell, shown in her home office in 1905, exposed the ruthless business practices that John D. Rockefeller used to create and run his Standard Oil Company. Tarbell was one of the Progressive Era's muckrakers, who published articles in popular magazines and wrote books that evoked public outrage and calls for reform.   The Ida M. Tarbell Collection, Pelletier Library, Allegheny College intensive research, these articles had a sensationalist appeal that both informed and aroused their mainly middle-class readers. In 1902 journalist Ida Tarbell lambasted the ruthless and dishonest business practices of the Rockefeller family's Standard Oil Company, the model of corporate greed. Lincoln Steffens wrote about machine bosses' shameful rule in cities such as Chicago, Cincinnati, Cleveland, Minneapolis, New York, St. Louis, and Philadelphia. Ida B. Wells, a Memphis journalist, wrote scathing articles and pamphlets condemning the lynching of African Americans. Other muckrakers exposed fraudulent practices in insurance companies, child labor, drug abuse, and prostitution.

Ironically, President Theodore Roosevelt coined the term *muckraker* in 1906 not as a compliment but as a sign of disgust for journalists he thought were more interested in making sensationalist charges than in carefully documenting their stories. He compared them to the character in John Bunyan's novel *Pilgrim's Progress* who was so absorbed in looking at the filth (muck) on the ground that he did not see a beautiful gift offered to him. Roosevelt feared that if muckraking became too sensational and unrestrained, it would threaten moderate reform and encourage more radical alternatives. Yet muckrakers did succeed in raising middle-class awareness and generated wide support for the political reforms that Roosevelt and other progressives proposed.

REVIEW & RELATE

- What late-nineteenth-century trends and developments influenced the progressives?
- Why did the progressives focus on urban and industrial America?

 **LEARNING**Curve bedfordstmartins.com/hewittlawson/LC

Humanitarian Reform

Humanitarian reformers focused on the plight of urban immigrants, African Americans, and the underprivileged. They tried mainly to improve housing and working conditions for impoverished city dwellers. Their motives were not always purely altruistic. Unless living standards improved, many reformers reasoned, immigrants and racial minorities would contaminate the cities' middle-class inhabitants with communicable diseases, escalating crime, and threats to traditional cultural norms. These reformers also supported suffrage for women, whose votes, they believed, would help purify electoral politics and elect candidates committed to social and moral reform.

Female Progressives and the Poor

Women played the leading role in efforts to improve the lives of the impoverished. Jane Addams, the daughter of a wealthy businessman, had toured Europe after graduating from a women's college in Illinois. The Toynbee Hall settlement house in London impressed her for its work in helping poor residents of the area. In 1889 Addams, after returning home to Chicago, and her friend Ellen Starr established **Hull House** as a center for social reform in the northwest neighborhood of the city. Hull House inspired a generation of young women to work directly in immigrant communities. Many were college-educated, professionally trained women who were shut out of jobs in male-dominated professions. Staffed mainly by women, settlement houses became all-purpose urban support centers. Not only did they provide recreational facilities, social activities, and educational classes for neighborhood residents, but they also became launching pads for campaigns aimed at improving living and working conditions for the urban poor. Calling on women to take up **civic housekeeping**, Addams maintained that women could protect their individual households from the chaos of industrialization and urbanization only by attacking the sources of that chaos in the community at large.

> **Explore**
>
> See Document 19.1 for a description of one civic housekeeping effort.

Settlement house and social workers occupied the front lines of humanitarian reform, but they found considerable support from women's clubs. Formed after the Civil War, these local groups provided protected spaces for middle-class women to meet, share ideas, and work on common projects. In 1890 these local associations were brought together under the umbrella of the General Federation of Women's Clubs, which by the end of the nineteenth century counted 495 chapters and 160,000 members. By 1900 these clubs—which had initially been devoted to discussions of religion, culture, and science—began to help the needy and lobby for social justice legislation. "Since men are more or less closely absorbed in business," one club woman remarked about this civic awakening, "it has come to pass that the initiative in civic matters has devolved largely upon women." Starting out in towns and cities, club women carried their message to state and federal governments and campaigned for legislation that would establish social welfare programs for working women and their children.

In an age of strict racial segregation, African American women formed their own clubs to undertake reform activities. They sponsored day care centers, kindergartens, and work and home training projects. The activities of black club women, like those of white club women,

DOCUMENT 19.1

Jane Addams | Civic Housekeeping, 1910

In the following excerpt from her memoir, *Twenty Years at Hull-House*, Jane Addams describes the activities of the Hull House Woman's Club, formed by the residents of the neighborhood served by the settlement house. In an effort to improve their surroundings, club women took it upon themselves to investigate the city's poor garbage collection service in their wards and its possible connection to high death rates in the area.

Explore

The Hull-House Woman's Club had been organized the year before by the resident kindergartner [teacher] who had first inaugurated a mothers' meeting. The new members came together, however, in quite a new way that summer when we discussed with them the high death rate so persistent in our ward. After several club meetings devoted to the subject, despite the fact that the death rate rose highest in the congested foreign colonies and not in the streets in which most of the Irish American club women lived, twelve of their number undertook in connection with the residents, to carefully investigate the condition of the alleys. During August and September the substantiated reports of violations of the law sent in from Hull-House to the health department were one thousand and thirty-seven. For the club woman who had finished a long day's work of washing or ironing followed by the cooking of a hot supper, it would have been much easier to sit on her doorstep during a summer evening than to go up and down ill-kept alleys and

get into trouble with her neighbors over the condition of their garbage boxes. It required both civic enterprise and moral conviction to be willing to do this three evenings a week during the hottest and most uncomfortable months of the year. Nevertheless, a certain number of women persisted, as did the residents, and three city inspectors in succession were transferred from the ward because of unsatisfactory services. Still the death rate remained high and the condition seemed little improved throughout the next winter. In sheer desperation, the following spring when the city contracts were awarded for the removal of garbage, with the backing of two well-known business men, I put in a bid for the garbage removal of the nineteenth ward. My paper was thrown out on a technicality but the incident induced the mayor to appoint me the garbage inspector of the ward.

Source: Jane Addams, *Twenty Years at Hull-House* (New York: Macmillan, 1910), 284–85.

Interpret the Evidence

- Why did Addams and the other club women decide to tackle the garbage problem in their neighborhood?
- What does this action suggest about the role that residents played in improving their own neighborhood?

Put It in Context

How does the women's investigation reflect the progressive notion of civic housekeeping?

reflected a class bias, and they tried to lift up poorer blacks to ideals of middle-class womanhood. In doing so, they challenged white supremacist notions that black women and men were incapable of raising healthy and strong families. By 1916 the National Association of Colored Women, whose motto was "lifting as we climb," boasted 1,000 clubs and 50,000 members.

White working-class women also organized, but because of employment discrimination there were few, if any, black female industrial workers to join them. Building on the settlement house movement and together with middle-class and wealthy women, working-class women founded the National Women's Trade Union League (WTUL) in 1903. The WTUL was dedicated to securing higher wages and

Children at Hull House, 1900

Child care was one of the many services that Hull House provided for immigrants on the west side of Chicago. Founded in 1889 by Jane Addams and Ellen Starr, Hull House also offered health care, job counseling, and English lessons. Settlement house workers also led campaigns to abolish child labor, support women's suffrage, and reform immigration.   Jane Addams Collection, Swarthmore College Peace Collection

Not all women believed in the idea of protective legislation for women. In 1898 Charlotte Perkins Gilman published *Women and Economics*, in which she argued against the notion that women were ideally suited for domesticity. She contended that women's accepted relationship to men was unnatural. "We are the only animal species in which the female depends on the male for food," Gilman wrote, "the only animal species in which the sex relation is also the economic relation." Emphasizing the need for economic independence, Gilman advocated the establishment of communal kitchens that would free women from household chores and allow them to compete on equal terms with men in the workplace. Emma Goldman, an anarchist critic of capitalism and middle-class sexual morality, also spoke out against the kind of marriage that made women "keep their mouths shut and their wombs open." She endorsed "free love," in which women and men enjoyed sex equally. These and a growing number of other women did not consider themselves reformers so much as radicals, and even feminists—women who aspire to reach their full potential and gain access to the same opportunities as men.

improved working conditions, and its slogan, "The Eight-Hour Day: A Living Wage; to Guard the Home," expressed its objectives. The WTUL recognized that many women needed to earn an income to help support their families, and it backed protective legislation based on women's specific needs.

Believing women to be physically weaker than men, most female reformers advocated special legislation to protect women in the workplace. They campaigned for state laws prescribing the maximum number of hours women could work, and they succeeded in 1908 when they won a landmark victory in the Supreme Court in *Muller v. Oregon*, which upheld an Oregon law establishing a ten-hour workday for women. These reformers also convinced lawmakers in forty states to establish pensions for mothers and widows. In 1912 their focus shifted to the federal government with the founding of the Children's Bureau in the Department of Commerce and Labor. Headed by Julia Lathrop, an Addams disciple from Illinois, the bureau attracted female reformers, collected sociological data, and devised a variety of publicly funded social welfare measures. In 1916 Congress enacted a law banning child labor under the age of fourteen (it was declared unconstitutional in 1918). In 1921 Congress passed the Shepherd-Towner Act, which allowed nurses to offer maternal and infant health care information to mothers.

Fighting for Women's Suffrage

Until 1910, women did not have the right to vote, except in a handful of western states (see chapter 15). The passage of the Fourteenth and Fifteenth Amendments had disappointed many campaigners for women's suffrage. Although the amendments extended citizenship to African Americans and protected the voting rights of black men, they left women, both white and black, ineligible to vote. The Fourteenth Amendment had underscored this distinction by specifically referring to "male inhabitants" in its provision dealing with voting for national officials (see chapter 14). Following Reconstruction, the two major organizations campaigning for women's suffrage at the state and national levels—Susan B. Anthony and Elizabeth Cady Stanton's National Woman Suffrage Association and Lucy Stone and Julia Ward Howe's American Woman Suffrage Association—failed to achieve major victories. In 1890 the two groups combined to form the National American Woman Suffrage Association, and by 1918 women could vote in fifteen states and the territory of Alaska (Map 19.1).

Suffragists included a broad coalition of supporters and based their campaign on a variety of arguments. Reformers such as Jane Addams stressed that suffrage for women would be an extension of "civic housekeeping." They attributed corruption in politics to the absence of women's maternal influence. In this way, mainstream suffragists couched their arguments within traditional conceptions of women as family nurturers. They claimed that men should not fear women's desire to vote; rather, they should see it as an expansion of traditional household duties into the public sphere. By contrast, suffragists such as Alice Paul rejected arguments stressing women's domesticity and their inherent difference from men. Paul, who had earned a Ph.D. from the University of Pennsylvania and two law degrees, asserted that women deserved the vote on the basis of their equality with men as citizens. She founded the National Woman's Party and in 1923 proposed that Congress adopt an Equal Rights Amendment to provide full legal equality to women.

Traditionalists, both male and female, fought against women's suffrage. They believed that women were best suited by nature to devote themselves to their families and leave the rough-and-tumble world of politics to men. Suffrage opponents insisted that extending the right to vote to women would destroy the home, lead to the moral degeneracy of children, and tear down the social fabric of the country.

Campaigns for women's suffrage did not apply to all women. White suffragists in the South often manipulated racial prejudice to support female enfranchisement. In the wake of the Populist Party's efforts to recruit black voters in the 1890s, most of the former Confederate states rewrote their constitutions or enacted statutes removing African Americans from the voter rolls through the use of poll taxes, literacy tests, and grandfather clause requirements (see chapter 17). Although they did not constitute a majority, outspoken white suffragists such as Rebecca Latimer Felton from Georgia, Belle Kearney from Mississippi, and Kate Gordon from Louisiana used white suprem- acist arguments to make a case for white women gaining the vote. As long as even a fraction of black men voted and the Fifteenth Amendment continued to exist, they contended that allowing southern white women to vote would preserve white supremacy by offsetting black men's votes. These arguments also had a class component. Poll taxes and literacy tests disfranchised poor, uneducated whites. Extending the vote to white women would benefit mainly those in the middle class who had some education and enough family income to satisfy restrictive literacy test and poll tax requirements.

Many middle-class women outside the South used similar reasoning, but they targeted newly arrived immigrants instead of African Americans. Many Protestant women and men viewed Catholics and Jews from southern and eastern Europe as racially inferior and spiritually

dangerous. They blamed such immigrants for the ills of the cities in which they congregated, and some suffragists believed that the vote of middle-class Protestant women would help clean up the mess the immigrants created. One supporter proclaimed that suffragists "had always recognized the usefulness of woman suffrage as a counterbalance to the foreign vote."

African American women challenged these racist arguments and mounted their own drive for female suffrage. If "white women needed the vote to acquire advantages and protection of their rights," Adella Hunt Logan of Tuskegee, Alabama, remarked, "then Black women needed the vote even more so." African American women had an additional incentive to press for enfran- chisement. As the target of white sexual predators during slavery and its aftermath, some black women saw the vote as a way to address this problem. Although they did not gain much support from the National American Woman Suffrage Association, by 1916 African American women worked through the National Association of Colored Women and formed suffrage clubs throughout the nation.

Explore

See Document 19.2 for an argument for suffrage for black women.

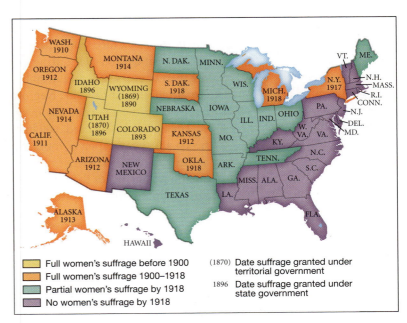

MAP 19.1   Women's Suffrage
Western states and territories were the first to approve women's suffrage. Yet even as western states enfranchised women, most placed restrictions on or excluded African American, American Indian, Mexican American, and Asian American women. States granting partial suffrage allowed women to vote only in certain contests, such as municipal or school board, primary, or presidential elections.

DOCUMENT 19.2

Nannie Helen Burroughs | Suffrage for Black Women, 1915

Nannie Helen Burroughs, a founder of the National Association of Colored Women, spoke out for black women's right to vote at a time when many white women's suffrage groups excluded African Americans. For Burroughs and other black suffragists, the right to vote was not just a civic duty but essential for eliminating racial discrimination and subservience. In the following excerpt that appeared in the *Crisis*, the magazine of the NAACP, Burroughs presents the case for suffrage for black women.

Explore

Why does Burroughs claim it is more important for black women than for black men to obtain and exercise the right to vote?

How does Burroughs characterize the role of black women in reform movements?

What does Burroughs mean when she says that the ballot is black women's "weapon of moral defense"?

When the ballot is put into the hands of the American woman the world is going to get a correct estimate of the Negro woman. It will find her a tower of strength of which poets have never sung, orators have never spoken, and scholars have never written.

Because the black man does not know the value of the ballot, and has bartered and sold his most valuable possession, it is no evidence that the Negro woman will do the same. The Negro woman, therefore, needs the ballot to get back, by the wise *use* of it, what the Negro man has lost by the *misuse* of it. She needs it to ransom her race. A fact worthy of note is that in every reform in which the Negro woman has taken part, during the past fifty years, she has been as aggressive, progressive, and dependable as those who inspired the reform or led it. The world has yet to learn that the Negro woman is quite superior in bearing moral responsibility. A comparison with the men of her race, in moral issues, is odious. She carries the burdens of the Church, and of the school and bears a great deal more than her economic share at home.

Another striking fact is that the Negro woman carries the moral destiny of two races in her hand. Had she not been the woman of unusual moral stamina that she is, the black race would have been made a great deal whiter, and the white race a great deal blacker during the past fifty years. She has been left a prey for the men of every race, but in spite of this, she has held the enemies of Negro female chastity at bay. The Negro woman is the white woman's as well as the white race's most needed ally in preserving an unmixed race.

The ballot, wisely used, will bring to her the respect and protection that she needs. It is her weapon of moral defense. Under present conditions, when she appears in court in defense of her virtue, she is looked upon with amused contempt. She needs the ballot to reckon with men who place no value upon her virtue, and to [mold] healthy public sentiment in favor of her own protection.

Source: Nannie Helen Burroughs, "Black Women and Reform," *The Crisis*, August 1915, 187.

Put It in Context

How do Burroughs's arguments differ from those of white suffragists?

The campaign for women's suffrage in the United States was part of an international movement. Victories in New Zealand (1893), Australia (1902), and Norway (1913) spurred on American suffragists. In the 1910s, radical American activists found inspiration in the militant tactics employed by some in the British suffrage movement. Activists such as Alice Paul conducted wide-ranging demonstrations in Washington, D.C., including chaining themselves to the gates of the White House. Although mainstream suffrage leaders denounced these new tactics, they gained much-needed publicity for the movement, which in turn aided the lobbying efforts of more moderate activists. In 1919 Congress passed the Nineteenth Amendment granting women the vote. The following year, the amendment was ratified by the states.

Progressivism and African Americans

As with the suffrage, social justice progressives faced huge barriers in the fight for racial equality. By 1900 white supremacists in the South had disfranchised almost all black voters and imposed a rigid system of segregation in education and all aspects of public life, and they enforced these measures with violence. From 1880 to 1900, white supremacists lynched thousands of African Americans, often because of perceived violations of racial norms. Antiblack violence also took the form of race riots that erupted in southern cities such as Wilmington, North Carolina, and Tampa, Florida, in 1898 and Atlanta in 1906. Farther north, in Springfield, Illinois, a riot broke out in 1908 when the local sheriff tried to protect two black prisoners, one accused of raping a white woman and the other charged with murdering a white man, from a would-be lynch mob. This confrontation triggered two days of white violence against blacks, some of whom fought back, leaving twenty-four businesses and forty homes destroyed and seven people (two blacks and five whites) dead.

As the situation for African Americans deteriorated, black leaders responded in several ways. Booker T. Washington espoused an approach that his critics called accommodation but that he defended as practical. Born a slave and emancipated at age nine, Washington attended Hampton Institute in his home state of Virginia. Run by sympathetic whites, the school considered moral training its top priority. In their view, because slavery had hindered black advancement, African Americans would first have to build up their character and accept the virtues of abstinence, thrift, and industriousness before seeking a more intellectual education. In 1881 Washington founded **Tuskegee Institute** in Alabama, which he modeled on Hampton. In 1895 white business and civic leaders invited Washington to deliver an address at a cotton exposition held in Atlanta. The black educator received an enthusiastic reception for his message urging African Americans to remain in the South, accept racial segregation, concentrate on moral and economic development, and avoid politics. At the same time, he called on white leaders to fulfill their part of the bargain by protecting blacks from the growing violence directed at them.

White leaders in both the South and the North embraced Washington, and he became the most powerful African American of his generation. He secured philanthropic contributions from white benefactors for Tuskegee and other schools he favored. He had considerable influence over leading black newspapers and in 1900 organized the National Negro Business League. Although he discouraged public protests against segregation, he emphasized racial pride and solidarity among African Americans. "We are a nation within a nation," he commented, and "[we must] see to it that in every wise and legitimate way our people are taught to patronize racial enterprises." Yet Washington was a complex figure, who secretly financed and supported court challenges to electoral disfranchisement, railroad segregation, jury discrimination, and peonage (forced labor to repay debt).

Washington's enormous power did not discourage opposing views among African Americans. Ida B. Wells, like Washington, had been born a slave. In 1878, at age sixteen, Wells lost her parents in a yellow fever epidemic that swept through her hometown in Mississippi. To support her five siblings, she took a job in Memphis as a teacher. Six years later, Wells sued the Chesapeake & Ohio Railroad for moving her from the first-class "Ladies Coach" to the segregated smoking car because she was black. She won her case in the lower court, but her victory was reversed by the Tennessee Supreme Court. Undeterred, she began writing for the *Free Speech* newspaper, in which she owned a one-third interest. When her articles exposing injustices in the Memphis school system got her fired from teaching, she took up journalism full-time.

Unlike Washington, Wells believed that black leaders had to speak out vigorously against racial inequality and lynching. From 1885 to 1900, approximately 2,500 people were lynched, most of them southern blacks. One lynching took place in Memphis on March 9, 1892, when three black men were murdered by a white mob. The victims had operated a grocery store that had become the target of hostility from white competitors, who forcibly tried to put it out of business. In response, the black businessmen resisted an assault by armed whites and shot three of them in self-defense. Wells applauded the black store owners' actions. As she wrote, "When the white man . . . knows he runs as great a risk of biting the dust every time his Afro-American victim does, he will have greater respect for Afro-American life." Subsequently arrested for their armed resistance, the three men were snatched from jail and lynched.

In response to Wells's articles about the Memphis lynching, a white mob burned down her newspaper's building. She fled to Chicago, where she continued to investigate the issue of lynching. In a report she published, she refuted the myth that the rape of white women by black men was the leading cause of lynching and asserted that evidence of such crimes was scarce. She concluded that racists used this brand of extralegal violence to ensure that African Americans would not challenge white supremacy. Wells took her campaign throughout the North and to Europe, where she gave lectures condemning lynching. She also joined the drive for women's suffrage, which she hoped would give black women a chance to use their votes to help combat racial injustice.

W. E. B. Du Bois also rejected Washington's accommodationist stance and urged blacks to demand first-class citizenship. In contrast to Washington and Wells, Du Bois had not experienced slavery. His ancestors were free blacks, and he grew up in Great Barrington, Massachusetts. Educated at Fisk University, a black institution, he transferred to Harvard and earned a Ph.D. in history. In 1899 he published *The Philadelphia Negro*, the first scientific study of the plight of blacks in urban America—a scholarly counterpart to the emerging investigative literature that fueled progressive reform. Du Bois

DOCUMENTS 19.3 AND 19.4

Addressing Inequality: Two Views

By the end of the nineteenth century, the former Confederate states had stripped most blacks of the right to vote and instituted legal forms of segregation. In the face of violence, hostility, and widespread discrimination, African American leaders Booker T. Washington and W. E. B. Du Bois developed two of the most influential approaches to the problem of racial inequality. Washington emphasized black economic self-development and accommodation within the existing social and political system, whereas Du Bois insisted that blacks must resist second-class citizenship in all forms.

Explore

19.3 Booker T. Washington | The Atlanta Compromise, 1895

The wisest among my race understand that the agitation of questions of social equality is the extremest folly, and that progress in the enjoyment of all the privileges that will come to us must be the result of severe and constant struggle rather than of artificial forcing. No race that has anything to contribute to the markets of the world is long in any degree ostracized. It is important and right that all privileges of the law be ours, but it is vastly more important that we be prepared for the exercise of those privileges. The opportunity to earn a dollar in a factory just now is worth infinitely more than the opportunity to spend a dollar in an opera house.

In conclusion, may I repeat that nothing in thirty years has given us more hope and encouragement, and drawn us so near to you of the white race, as this opportunity offered by the Exposition [a cotton exhibition held in Atlanta]; and here bending, as it were, over the altar that represents the results of the struggles of your race and mine, both starting practically empty-handed three decades ago, I pledge that, in your effort to work out the great and intricate problem which God has laid at the doors of the South, you shall have at all times the patient, sympathetic help of my race; only let this be constantly in mind that, while from representations in these buildings of the product of field, of forest, of mine, of factory, letters, and art, much good will come, yet far above and beyond material benefits will be that higher good, that, let us pray God, will come, in a blotting out of sectional differences and racial animosities and suspicions, in a determination to administer absolute justice, in a willing obedience among all classes to the mandates of law. This, coupled with our material prosperity, will bring into our beloved South a new heaven and a new earth.

Source: Booker T. Washington, *The Story of My Life and Work* (Cincinnati: W. W. Ferguson, 1900), 170–71.

agreed with Washington about advocating self-help as a means for advancement, but he did not believe this effort would succeed without a proper education and equal voting rights. In *The Souls of Black Folk* (1903), Du Bois argued that African Americans needed a liberal arts education, in the tradition of Fisk and Harvard, rather than the manual training and industrial arts curriculum at Tuskegee. Du Bois contended that a classical, humanistic education would produce a cadre of leaders, the "Talented Tenth," who would guide African Americans to the next stage of their development. Rather than forgoing immediate political rights, as Washington advocated, African American leaders should demand the universal right to vote. Only then, Du Bois contended, would African Americans gain equality, self-respect, and dignity as a race.

Explore

See Documents 19.3 and 19.4 for Washington's and Du Bois's responses to inequality.

Du Bois was an intellectual who put his ideas into action. In 1905 he spearheaded the creation of the Niagara

Explore

19.4 W. E. B. Du Bois | Response to Washington, 1903

It has been claimed that the Negro can survive only through submission. Mr. Washington distinctly asks that black people give up, at least for the present, three things—
   First, political power,
   Second, insistence on civil rights,
   Third, higher education of Negro youth—
and concentrate all their energies on industrial education, the accumulation of wealth, and the conciliation of the South. This policy has been courageously and insistently advocated for over fifteen years, and has been triumphant for perhaps ten years. As a result of this tender of the palm-branch, what has been the return? In these years there have occurred:

1. The disfranchisement of the Negro.
2. The legal creation of a distinct status of civil inferiority for the Negro.
3. The steady withdrawal of aid from institutions for the higher training of the Negro.

These movements are not, to be sure, direct results of Mr. Washington's teachings; but his propaganda has, without a shadow of doubt, helped their speedier accomplishment. The question then comes: Is it possible, and probable, that nine millions of men can make effective progress in economic lines if they are deprived of political rights, made a servile caste, and allowed only the most meagre chance for developing their exceptional men? If history and reason give any distinct answer to these questions, it is an emphatic *No*. And Mr. Washington thus faces the triple paradox of his career:

1. He is striving nobly to make Negro artisans, business men, and property-owners; but it is utterly impossible, under modern competitive methods, for workingmen and property-owners to defend their rights and exist without the right of suffrage.
2. He insists on thrift and self-respect, but at the same time counsels a silent submission to civic inferiority such as is bound to sap the manhood of any race in the long run.
3. He advocates common-school and industrial training, and depreciates institutions of higher learning; but neither the Negro common-schools, nor Tuskegee itself, could remain open a day were it not for teachers trained in Negro colleges, or trained by their graduates.

Source: W. E. B. Du Bois, *The Souls of Black Folk: Essays and Sketches* (Chicago: A. C. McClurg, 1907), 51–52.

Interpret the Evidence

- Why does Washington believe that economic development is the key to racial progress?
- How does Du Bois challenge Washington's agenda? Why does he insist that political and social reforms are essential to black economic progress?

Put It in Context

How do Washington and Du Bois reflect in different ways the status of African Americans in the United States at the turn of the twentieth century?

Movement, a group that first met on the Canadian side of Niagara Falls because participants could not find accommodations open to blacks in Buffalo, New York. The all-black organization demanded the vote and equal access to public facilities for African Americans. By 1909 internal squabbling and a shortage of funds had crippled the group. That same year, however, Du Bois became involved in the creation of an organization that would shape the fight for racial equality throughout the twentieth century: the **National Association for the Advancement of Colored People (NAACP)**. In addition to Du Bois, Ida B. Wells, and veterans of the Niagara Movement, white activists played leading roles in forming the organization. They included Jane Addams; Mary White Ovington, a settlement house worker in Brooklyn; and William English Walling, a social worker, socialist, and cofounder of the Women's Trade Union League. The descendants of white abolitionists also contributed significantly to the birth of the group. Of the fifty-two white signers of the document calling for the creation of the NAACP, fifteen were former abolitionists or their descendants. Beginning in 1910, the NAACP initiated court cases challenging racially discriminatory voting practices and other forms of bias in housing and criminal justice. Its first victory came in 1915, when its lawyers convinced the Supreme Court to strike down the grandfather clause that discriminated against black voters (*Guinn v. United States*).

African Americans also pursued social justice initiatives outside the realm of politics. Southern blacks remained committed to securing a quality education for their children after whites failed to live up to their responsibilities under *Plessy v. Ferguson*. Governor James K. Vardaman of Mississippi, who served from 1904 to 1908, expressed the prevailing racist sentiment: "Education only spoils a good field hand and makes a shyster lawyer or a fourth-rate teacher. It is money thrown away." Black schools remained inferior to white schools, and African Americans did not receive a fair return from their tax dollars; in fact, a large portion of their payments helped subsidize white schools. To raise money for books, buildings, and teacher salaries, blacks voluntarily taxed themselves in addition to the property taxes they were required to pay the county to support schools. Du Bois calculated that black Mississippians paid 113 percent of the costs of their own schools through double taxation.

Black women played a prominent role in promoting education. For example, Charlotte Hawkins Brown, born in North Carolina and educated in Massachusetts, returned to her home state in 1901 and set up the Palmer Memorial Institute outside of Greensboro. In these endeavors, black educators received financial assistance from northern philanthropists, white club women interested in moral uplift of the black race, and religious missionaries seeking

converts in the South. By 1910 more than 1.5 million black children went to school in the South, most of them taught by the region's 28,560 black teachers. Thirty-four black colleges existed, and more than 2,000 African Americans held college degrees.

REVIEW & RELATE

⏐ What role did women play in the early-twentieth-century fight for social justice?

⏐ How did social reformers challenge discrimination against women and minorities?

 **LEARNINGCurve** bedfordstmartins.com/hewittlawson/LC

Morality and Social Control

In many cases, progressive initiatives crossed over from social reform into social control. Convinced that the "immorality" of the poor was the cause of social disorder, some reformers sought to impose middle-class standards of behavior and morality on the lower classes. As with other forms of progressivism, progressives interested in social control were driven by a variety of motives. However, regardless of their motives, efforts to prohibit alcohol, fight prostitution, and combat juvenile delinquency often involved attempts to repress and control the poor. Some social control progressives went even further in their effort to impose their own morality, calling for restrictions on immigration, particularly from southern and eastern Europe and Asia. Anti-immigration advocates viewed cultural and religious differences as a threat and sought to prevent such people from becoming part of American society in the first place.

Prohibition

Prohibition campaigns began long before the Civil War but scored few important successes until after 1865. In 1869 anti-alcohol forces established the Prohibition Party, and in 1881 Kansas became the first state whose constitution banned the consumption of alcohol. Women spearheaded the prohibition movement by forming the **Woman's Christian Temperance Union (WCTU)** in 1874. Frances Willard headed the group from 1879 until her death in 1898. Willard held a broad view of temperance reform that grew from religious, moral, and social justice convictions. Under her direction, the WCTU and its nationwide chapters supported women's suffrage, laws to end child labor, and labor unions. Willard built the temperance movement around the need to protect the home. Husbands and fathers who drank excessively were also likely to abuse their wives and children and to drain the family finances. Prohibiting the consumption of alcohol would, therefore, help combat these evils. At the same time, the quality of family and public life would be improved if women received the right to vote and young children completed their education without having to go to work. Although Willard died before progressive reform had gained momentum, she influenced activists such as Jane Addams. However, with her death, WCTU leaders withdrew from supporting broad social reforms and concentrated instead on the single issue of temperance.

At the turn of the twentieth century, the Anti-Saloon League (ASL) became the dominant force in the prohibition movement. Established in 1893, the league grew out of evangelical Protestantism, with Baptists and Methodists leading the way. The group had particular appeal in the rural South, where Protestant fundamentalism flourished. Between 1906 and 1917, twenty-one states, mostly in the South and West, banned liquor sales. However, concern over alcohol was not confined to the South. Middle-class progressives in northern cities, who identified much of urban decay with the influx of immigrants, saw the tavern as a breeding ground for immoral activities. In 1913 the ASL convinced Congress to pass the Webb-Kenyon Act, which banned the transportation of alcoholic beverages into dry states. After the United States entered World War I in 1917, reformers argued that prohibition would help win the war by conserving grain used to make liquor and by saving soldiers from intoxication. The Eighteenth Amendment, ratified in 1919, made prohibition the law of the land.

The Crusade against Vice

Alarmed by the expansion in the number of brothels and "streetwalkers" that accompanied the growth of cities, progressives sought to eliminate prostitution. Some framed the issue in terms of public health, linking prostitution to the spread of sexually transmitted diseases. Others presented the crusade as an effort to protect female virtue. In 1907 the muckraking *McClure's Magazine*, reporting on the spread of prostitution in Chicago, contended that many of the women were victims of "white slavery" and had been forced into prostitution against their will. Such reformers were generally interested only in white women, who, unlike African American and Asian women in similar circumstances, were considered sexual innocents coerced into prostitution. Still others claimed that prostitutes themselves were to blame, seeing women who sold their sexual favors as inherently immoral.

Reformers offered two different approaches to the problem. Taking the moralistic solution, Representative

James R. Mann of Chicago steered through Congress the White Slave Trade Act in 1910, banning the transportation of women across state lines for immoral purposes. This legislation became known as the Mann Act after its sponsor. By contrast, the American Social Hygiene Association, founded in 1914, subsidized scientific research into sexually transmitted diseases, funded investigations to gather more information, and drafted model ordinances for cities to curb prostitution. By 1915 every state had laws making sexual solicitation a crime. The United States' entry into World War I further helped curtail prostitution; brothels near military bases were closed because reformers argued that soldiers' health was at risk.

Prosecutors used the Mann Act to enforce codes of traditional racial as well as sexual behavior. In 1910 Jack Johnson, an African American boxer, defeated the white

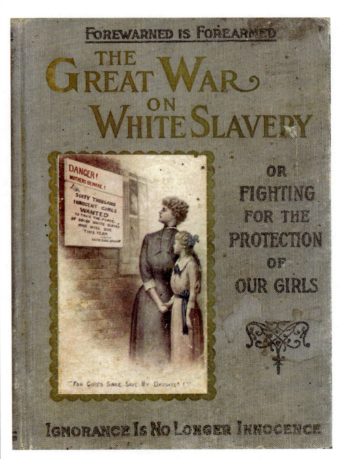

The Crusade against White Slavery

Published by Clifford B. Roe and B. S. Steadwell in 1911, *The Great War on White Slavery* campaigned against prostitution and the criminals who lured impoverished young women into what they called "the human stockyards . . . for girls." As an assistant state's attorney in Chicago, Roe prosecuted more than 150 cases against sex traffickers. He exemplified progressivism's moral reform impulse. © Mary Evans Picture Library/The Image Works heavyweight champion, Jim Jeffries. Black Americans took great pride in his triumph, while his victory upset some white men who were obsessed with preserving their racial dominance and masculine integrity. Johnson's relationships with white women further angered some whites, who eventually succeeded in bringing down the outspoken, black champion by prosecuting him on morals charges in 1913.

Moral crusaders also sought to eliminate the use and sale of narcotics. By 1900 approximately 250,000 people in the United States were addicted to opium, morphine, or cocaine—far fewer, however, than those who abused alcohol. Patent medicines, such as "Mrs. Winslow's Soothing Syrup," a remedy for crying babies, contained diluted amounts of opium, and cocaine was an ingredient in Coca-Cola until 1903. On the West Coast, immigration opponents associated opium smoking with the Chinese and tried to eliminate its use as part of their wider anti-Asian campaign. In alliance with the American Medical Association, which had a professional stake in the issue, reformers convinced Congress to pass the Harrison Narcotics Control Act of 1914, prohibiting the sale of narcotics except by a doctor's prescription.

Progressives also tried to combat juvenile delinquency. Led by women, these reformers lobbied for a juvenile court system that focused on rehabilitation rather than punishment for youthful offenders. Judge Ben Lindsay of Denver, Colorado, removed delinquents from dysfunctional homes and made them wards of the state. Despite progressives' sincerity, many youthful offenders doubted their intentions. Young women often appeared before a magistrate because their parents did not like their choice of friends, their sexual conduct, or their frequenting dance halls and saloons. These activities, which violated middle-class social norms, had now become criminalized, even if in a less coercive and punitive manner than that applied to adults.

Immigration Restriction

Moral reformers tended to perceive immigrants as innately predisposed to vice. As a result, some reformers sought to restrict immigration. Anti-immigrant sentiment often reflected racial and religious bigotry, as reformers concentrated on preventing Catholics, Jews, and all non-Europeans from entering the United States. Social scientists validated these prejudices by categorizing darker-skinned immigrants as inferior races. The harshest treatment was reserved for Asians. In 1882 Congress passed the Chinese Exclusion Act (see chapter 15), and in 1908 President Theodore Roosevelt entered into an executive agreement with Japan that reduced Japanese immigration to the United States. For many Californians, this agreement was not strict enough. In 1913

the state legislature passed a statute barring Japanese immigrants from buying land, a law that twelve other states subsequently enacted.

In 1917 reformers succeeded in further restricting immigration. Congress passed legislation to ban illiterates who could not read English or their native language from entering the country. The act also denied entry to other undesirables: "alcoholics," "feeble-minded persons," "epileptics," "people mentally or physically defective," "professional beggars," "anarchists," and "polygamists." In barring those considered unfit to enter the country, lawmakers intended to keep out those who could not support themselves and might become a public ward of the state and, in the case of anarchists and polygamists, people who threatened the nation's political and religious values. **See Document Project 19: Progressivism and Social Control, page 614.**

REVIEW & RELATE

What practices and behaviors of the poor did social control progressives find most alarming? Why?

What role did anti-immigrant sentiment play in motivating and shaping progressives' social control initiatives?

LEARNINGCurve bedfordstmartins.com/hewittlawson/LC

Good Government Progressivism

In an effort to diminish the power of corrupt urban political machines and unregulated corporations, progressives pushed for good government reforms, promoting initiatives they claimed would produce greater efficiency, openness, and accountability in government. Many of the progressives' proposed reforms appeared, at least on the surface, to give citizens more direct say in their government; however, a closer look reveals a more complicated picture.

Municipal and State Reform

Cities were at the forefront of government reform during the Progressive Era. Antiquated systems of municipal rule failed to keep up with the problems ushered in by immigration and accelerated urban growth. Political machines distributed city services to meet skyrocketing demands within a system bloated by corruption and graft (see chapter 18). Upper-middle-class businessmen and professionals fed up with wasteful and inefficient political machines sought to institute new forms of government that functioned more rationally and cost less.

The adoption of the commission form of government was a hallmark of urban reform. The idea originally came from the South in response to a hurricane in 1900 that destroyed the Texas Gulf coast city of Galveston and disabled its local government. Municipal leaders faced the crisis by establishing a commission composed of five men to operate the government. They replaced the old form of a mayor and city council with elected commissioners, each of whom ran a municipal department as if it were a business. By 1917 the commission form of government had spread to more than four hundred cities throughout the country. Governments with a mayor and city council also began to appoint city managers, who functioned as chief operating officers, to foster businesslike efficiency. The head of the National Cash Register Company, who helped bring the city manager system to Dayton, Ohio, praised it for resembling "a great business enterprise whose stockholders are the people."

To help overturn political machines, reformers adopted direct primaries so that voters could select candidates rather than allowing a handful of politicians to decide elections behind closed doors. Urban bosses had thrived on decentralized ward elections. To reverse the influence of immigrants clustered in ghettos who supported their own ethnic candidates and to topple the machines that catered to them, municipal reformers replaced district elections with citywide "at-large" elections. Ethnic enclaves lost not only their ward representatives but also a good deal of their influence because citywide election campaigns were expensive, shifting power to those who could afford to run. Good government progressives equated efficiency and honesty with democracy; however, rather than extending democracy to immigrant groups and racial minorities, these changes had the opposite effect. Working- and lower-class residents of cities still retained the right to vote, but their power was diluted.

In the South, where fewer immigrants lived, white supremacists employed these tactics to build on steps taken in the late nineteenth century to disfranchise African Americans. Southern lawmakers diminished whatever black political power remained by adopting at-large elections and commission governments. Throughout the South, direct primary contests (or "white primaries") were closed to blacks.

If urban progressivism fell short of putting democratic ideals into practice, it did produce a number of mayors who carried out genuine reforms. As Frederic C. Howe, a key adviser to Cleveland mayor Tom L. Johnson, observed, "The challenge of the city has become one of decent human existence." Elected in 1901, Johnson implemented measures to assess taxes more equitably, regulate utility companies, and reduce public transportation fares. Samuel "Golden Rule" Jones, who served as Toledo's mayor from 1897 to 1903, supported social justice measures by establishing an eight-hour workday for municipal employees, granting them paid vacations, and prohibiting child labor. Under Mayor Hazen Pingree, who served from 1889 to 1896, Detroit constructed additional schools and recreational facilities and put the unemployed to work on municipal projects during economic hard times.

Progressives also took action at the state level. Robert M. La Follette, Republican governor of Wisconsin from 1901 to 1906, led the way by initiating a range of reforms to improve the performance of state government and increase its accountability to constituents. During his tenure as governor, La Follette dismantled the statewide political machine by instituting direct party primaries, an expanded civil service, a law forbidding direct corporate contributions to political parties, a strengthened railroad regulatory commission, and a graduated income tax. In 1906 La Follette entered the U.S. Senate, where he battled for further reform.

Governors in other states picked up and expanded La Follette's progressive agenda. In New York, Governor Charles Evans Hughes implemented measures to regulate insurance companies and public utilities. In New Jersey, Governor Woodrow Wilson sought reforms similar to those in Wisconsin. On the West Coast, California's reform governor Hiram Johnson challenged the powerful Southern Pacific Railroad. In 1913 three-quarters of the states ratified the Seventeenth Amendment, which mandated that U.S. senators would be elected by popular vote, instead of being chosen by state legislatures. This constituted another effort to remove the influence of money from politics.

Conservation and Preservation of the Environment

The penchant for efficiency that characterized good government progressivism also shaped progressive efforts to conserve natural resources. As chief forester in the Department of Agriculture, Gifford Pinchot emphasized the efficient use of resources and sought ways to reconcile the public interest with private profit motives. His approach often won support from large lumber companies, which had a long-term interest in sustainable forests. Large companies also saw conservation as a way to drive their smaller competitors out of business, as large companies could better afford the additional costs associated with managing healthy forests.

Theodore Roosevelt and John Muir, 1903
Theodore Roosevelt (left) and John Muir, two leading conservationists of the Progressive Era, stand atop Glacier Point in Yosemite valley, California. Muir, who founded the Sierra Club, convinced Roosevelt to place Yosemite under federal control, which led to the establishment of a national park in 1906. Library of Congress

This gospel of efficiency faced a stiff test in California. After the devastating earthquake of 1906, San Francisco officials, coping with water and power shortages, asked the federal government to approve construction of a hydroelectric dam and reservoir in **Hetch Hetchy valley**, located in Yosemite National Park. The pragmatic Pinchot supported the project because he saw it as the best use of the land for the greatest number of people. The famed naturalist John Muir, who had spearheaded the establishment of Yosemite, strongly disagreed. He campaigned to save Hetch Hetchy from "ravaging commercialism" and warned against choosing economic gains over spiritual values. "Dam Hetch Hetchy!" Muir exclaimed. "As well dam for water-tanks the people's cathedrals and churches, for no holier temple has ever been consecrated by the heart of man." After a bruising seven-year battle, Pinchot (by this time a private citizen) triumphed. Still, this incursion into a national park, the first since the system was initiated in 1872 with Yellowstone National Park, helped spur the development of environmentalism as a political movement.

Besides the clash with preservationists, the Hetch Hetchy Dam project reveals another aspect of the progressive conservation movement. Like progressives who focused on urban and political issues, progressive conservationists had a racial bias. Conservationists such as Pinchot may have seen themselves as acting in the public interest, but their definition of "the public" did not include all Americans. In planning for the Hetch Hetchy Dam, progressives did not consult with the Mono Lake Paiutes who lived in Yosemite and who were most directly affected by the project. Conservation was meant to serve the interests of white San Franciscans and not those of the Indian inhabitants of Yosemite.

REVIEW & RELATE

- Who gained and who lost political influence as a result of progressive reforms?

- How did a commitment to greater efficiency shape progressives' political and environmental initiatives?

LEARNINGCurve bedfordstmartins.com/hewittlawson/LC

Presidential Progressivism

The problems created by industrialization and the growth of big business were national in scope. No municipal or state government had the authority, power, and finances to address issues that transcended political boundaries and affected people throughout the country. Recognizing this fact, prominent progressives sought national leadership positions. Two of the three early-twentieth-century presidents, Theodore Roosevelt and Woodrow Wilson, instituted progressive reforms during their terms. In the process, they reinvigorated the presidency, an office that had declined in power and importance during the late nineteenth century.

Theodore Roosevelt and the Square Deal

Born into a moderately wealthy New York family, Theodore Roosevelt graduated from Harvard in 1880 and entered government service. Appointed by William McKinley as assistant secretary of the navy in 1897, Roosevelt left his post the following year to form a regiment of soldiers—the "Rough Riders"—and fought in Cuba against Spanish forces. In 1898 voters in New York sent the popular war hero to Albany as the new Republican governor. Elected as William McKinley's vice president in 1900,

Roosevelt became president after McKinley's assassination a year later.

Roosevelt brought an activist style to the presidency. Rather than seeing himself as merely administering the nation's business, he considered his office a **bully pulpit**— a platform from which to promote his programs and from which he could rally public opinion. To this end, he used his energetic and extroverted personality to establish an unprecedented rapport with the American people, providing newspaper reporters with a limitless supply of colorful stories about his life and exploits.

For all his exuberance and energy, President Roosevelt pursued a moderate domestic course. Like his progressive colleagues, he opposed ideological extremism in any form. Rather than promoting any particular cause, Roosevelt believed that as head of state he could serve as an impartial arbiter among competing factions and determine what was best for the public. Reform was, in his view, the best defense against revolution.

As president, Roosevelt sought to provide economic and political stability, what he referred to as a "Square Deal." He insisted that "a republic such as ours can exist only by virtue of the orderly liberty which comes through the equal domination of the law over all men alike." The coal strike that began in Pennsylvania in 1902 gave Roosevelt an opportunity to play the role of impartial mediator and defender of the public good. Miners had gone on strike for an eight-hour workday, a pay increase of 20 percent, and recognition of their union. Roosevelt sympathized with the plight of the workers, but he was more concerned that a prolonged strike would choke the supply of heating fuel to consumers as winter approached. Union representatives agreed to have the president create a panel to settle the dispute, but George F. Baer, president of the Reading Railroad, which also owned the mines, pledged that he would never agree to the workers' demands. Disturbed by what he considered the owners' "arrogant stupidity," Roosevelt threatened to dispatch federal troops to take over and run the mines. When the owners backed down, the president established a commission that hammered out a compromise giving the strikers a 10 percent wage hike and a reduction of the workday to nine hours, but not union recognition.

At the same time, Roosevelt used his executive authority to tackle the problems caused by giant business trusts. In February 1902, the president instructed the Justice Department to sue the Northern Securities Company under the Sherman Antitrust Act (see chapter 16), a law that had rarely been used against big business since its passage in 1890. Northern Securities held monopoly control of the northernmost transcontinental railway lines. The powerful financier behind Northern Securities, J. P. Morgan, believed

that he could do business with Roosevelt as he had with previous presidents. "Send your man to my man and they can fix it up," Morgan informed Roosevelt. However, the president's man at the Justice Department responded: "We don't want to fix it up, we want to stop it." In 1904 the Supreme Court ordered that the Northern Securities Company be dissolved, ruling that the firm had restricted competition. With this victory, Roosevelt affirmed the federal government's power to regulate business trusts that violated the public interest. Overall, Roosevelt initiated twenty-five suits under the Sherman Antitrust Act, including litigation against the tobacco and beef trusts and the Standard Oil Company, actions that earned him the title of "trustbuster."

Roosevelt distinguished between "good" trusts, which acted responsibly, and "bad" trusts, which abused their power and hurt consumers. Railroads had earned an especially bad reputation with the public for charging higher rates to small shippers and those in remote regions while granting rebates to favored customers, such as Standard Oil. In 1903 Roosevelt helped persuade Congress to pass the Elkins Act, which outlawed railroad rebates. Three years later, the president increased the power of the Interstate Commerce Commission to set maximum railroad freight rates. In 1903 Roosevelt also secured passage of legislation that established the Department of Commerce and Labor. Within this cabinet agency, the Bureau of Corporations gathered information about large companies in an effort to promote fair business practices.

Soaring in popularity, Roosevelt ran for president in 1904 and easily defeated the Democratic nominee, Judge Alton B. Parker. During the next four years, the president applied antitrust laws even more vigorously than before. He steered through Congress various reforms concerning the railroads, such as the Hepburn Act (1906), which standardized shipping rates, and took a strong stand for conservation of public lands. Roosevelt charted a middle course between preservationists and conservationists. He reserved 150 million acres of timberland as part of the national forests, an action that delighted the preservationists. At the same time, he authorized the expenditure of more than $80 million in federal funds to construct dams, reservoirs, canals, and other conservation projects, largely in the West.

Not all reform came from Roosevelt's initiative. Congress passed two notable consumer laws in 1906 that reflected the multiple and sometimes contradictory forces that shaped progressivism. That year, Upton Sinclair published *The Jungle*, a muckraking novel that portrayed the impoverished lives of immigrant workers in Packingtown (Chicago) and the deplorable working conditions they endured. Outraged readers responded to the vivid description of the shoddy and filthy ways the meatpacking

"The Jungle"

Upton Sinclair's 1906 novel *The Jungle* exposed unsanitary conditions in the meat-packing industry and led to passage of the Meat Inspection Act and Pure Food and Drug Act that same year. In this photo from around 1905, workers at the Swift company process sausages as they roll off machines at ten feet per second.   Library of Congress

industry slaughtered animals and prepared beef for sale. The book revealed in grisly detail how the meat cut up for sausage "would be dosed with borax and glycerine, and dumped into hoppers, and made over again for home consumption." The largest and most efficient meatpacking firms had financial reasons to support reform as well. They were losing money because European importers refused to purchase tainted meat. Congress responded by passing the Meat Inspection Act, which benefited consumers and provided a way for large corporations to eliminate competition from smaller, marginal firms that could not afford to raise standards to meet the new federal meat-processing requirements.

In 1906 Congress also passed the Pure Food and Drug Act, which prohibited the sale of adulterated and fraudulently labeled food and drugs. The impetus for this law came from consumer groups, medical professionals, and government scientists. Dr. Harvey Wiley, a chemist in the Department of Agriculture, drove efforts for reform from within the government. He considered it part of his professional duty to eliminate harmful products (Table 19.1).

Roosevelt initially gave African Americans reason to believe that they, too, would get a square deal. In October 1901, at the outset of his first term, Roosevelt invited Booker T. Washington to a dinner at the White House. White supremacists in the South denounced the social gathering as a "damnable outrage." Though Roosevelt dismissed this criticism, he never invited another black guest. Also in his first term, Roosevelt supported the appointment of a few black Republicans to federal posts in the South. When segregationist whites chased Minnie Cox from her job as postmistress of Indianola, Mississippi, Roosevelt refused to accept her resignation and closed the post office.

Nevertheless, Roosevelt lacked a commitment to black equality and espoused the racist ideas of eugenics then in fashion (see chapter 18). He deplored the declining birthrate of native-born white Americans compared with that of eastern and southern European newcomers and African Americans, whom he considered inferior stock. He argued that unless Anglo-Saxon women produced more children, whites would end up committing "race suicide." "If the women flinch from breeding," Roosevelt worried, "the . . . death of the race takes place even quicker." Roosevelt never wavered in his belief in the superiority of the white race over people of color.

TABLE 19.1   National Progressive Legislation

Year	Legislation
1903	Department of Labor and Commerce established to promote fair business practices
1906	Pure Food and Drug Act
	Meat Inspection Act; Hepburn Act
1910	White Slave Trade Act
1913	Underwood Act reduces tariffs to benefit farmers
	Sixteenth Amendment (graduated income tax)
	Seventeenth Amendment (election of senators by popular vote)
	Federal Reserve System
1914	Harrison Narcotics Control Act
	Federal Trade Commission
	Clayton Antitrust Act
1916	Adamson Act provides eight-hour workday for railroad workers
	Keating-Owen Act outlaws child labor in firms engaged in interstate commerce
	Workmen's Compensation Act
1919	Eighteenth Amendment (prohibition)
1920	Nineteenth Amendment (women's suffrage)

Once he won reelection in 1904, Roosevelt had less political incentive to defy the white South. He stopped cooperating with southern black officeholders and maneuvered to build the Republican Party in the region with all-white support. However, his most reprehensible action involved an incident that occurred in Brownsville, Texas, in 1906. White residents of the town charged that black soldiers stationed at Fort Brown shot up the main street, killing one man and wounding another. Roosevelt ordered that unless the perpetrators stepped forward, the entire regiment would receive dishonorable discharges without a court-martial. Roosevelt never doubted the guilt of the black soldiers, and when no one admitted responsibility, he summarily dismissed 167 men from the military. Although the president spoke out against the brutality of lynching blacks in the South, he participated in this mass "legal lynching" of African American soldiers.

Taft Retreats from Progressivism

When Roosevelt decided not to seek another term as president in 1908, choosing instead to back William Howard Taft as his successor, he thought he was leaving his reform legacy in capable hands. A Roosevelt loyalist and an Ohio native, Taft had compiled a distinguished record as a federal judge, solicitor general of the United States, governor of the Philippines, and secretary of

war. Taft easily defeated the Democratic candidate, William Jennings Bryan, who was running for the presidency for the third and final time.

Taft's presidency did not proceed as Roosevelt and his progressive followers had hoped. Taft did not have the charisma or energy of his predecessor and appeared to move in slow motion compared with Roosevelt. More important, the new president, in contrast to Roosevelt, had a narrower view of the scope of his office and its power to shape public opinion. Taft proved a weak leader and frequently took stands opposite to those of progressives. After convening a special session of Congress in March 1909 to support lower tariffs, a progressive issue, the president retreated in the face of conservative Republican opposition in the Senate. That year, when lawmakers passed the Payne-Aldrich tariff, which raised duties on imports, Taft signed it into law, thereby alienating key progressive legislators such as Senator Robert M. La Follette. The president also remained aloof from the fight by House insurgents to curb the dictatorial powers of Speaker Joseph Cannon, a foe of reform.

The situation deteriorated even further in the field of conservation, which was close to Roosevelt's heart. When Pinchot criticized Taft's secretary of the interior, Richard Ballinger, for returning restricted Alaskan coal mines to private mining companies in 1910, Taft fired Pinchot. Taft did not oppose conservation—he transferred more land from private to public control than did Roosevelt—but his dismissal of Pinchot angered conservationists.

Even more harmful to Taft's political fortunes, Roosevelt turned against his handpicked successor. After returning from a hunting safari in Africa and a speaking tour of Europe in 1910, Roosevelt became increasingly troubled by Taft's missteps. The loss of the House of Representatives to the Democrats in the 1910 elections highlighted the split among Republicans that had developed under Taft. A year later, relations between the ex-president and the incumbent further deteriorated when Roosevelt attacked Taft for filing antitrust litigation against U.S. Steel for a deal that the Roosevelt administration had approved in 1907. Ironically, Roosevelt, known as a trustbuster, believed that filing more lawsuits under the Sherman Antitrust Act yielded diminishing returns, whereas Taft, the conservative, initiated more antitrust litigation than did Roosevelt.

The Election of 1912

Convinced that only he could heal the party breach, Roosevelt announced that he would run for the 1912 Republican presidential nomination. However, despite Roosevelt's widespread popularity among rank-and-file Republicans, Taft still controlled the party machinery and the majority of convention delegates. Losing to Taft on the first ballot, an embittered but optimistic Roosevelt formed a third party to sponsor his run for the presidency. Roosevelt excitedly told thousands of supporters gathered in Chicago, including Jane Addams and Gifford Pinchot, that he felt "as strong as a BULL MOOSE," which became the nickname for Roosevelt's new **Progressive Party**.

In accepting the nomination of his new party, Roosevelt articulated the philosophy of **New Nationalism**. He argued that the federal government should use its considerable power to fight against the forces of special privilege and for social justice for the majority of Americans. To this end, the Progressive Party platform advocated income and inheritance taxes, an eight-hour workday, the abolition of child labor, workers' compensation, fewer restrictions on labor unions, and women's suffrage. This last plank mobilized the efforts of women throughout the country who, like Jane Addams, supported the party that she said "pledged itself to the protection of children, to the care of the aged, to the relief of overworked girls, to the safeguarding of burdened men."

Roosevelt was not the only progressive candidate in the contest. The Democrats nominated Woodrow Wilson, the reform governor of New Jersey. The son of a Presbyterian minister, Wilson had the moral conviction of a pastor who knew what was best for his flock. As an alternative to Roosevelt's New Nationalism, Wilson offered his **New Freedom**. As a Democrat and a southerner (he was born in Virginia), Wilson had a more limited view of government than did the Republican Roosevelt. Wilson envisioned a society of small businesses, with the government's role confined to ensuring open competition among businesses and freedom for individuals to make the best use of their opportunities. Unlike Roosevelt's New Nationalism, Wilson's New Freedom did not embrace social reform and rejected federal action in support of women's suffrage and the elimination of child labor.

If voters considered either Roosevelt's or Wilson's brand of reform too mainstream, they could cast their ballots for Eugene V. Debs, the Socialist Party candidate who had been imprisoned for his leadership in the Pullman strike (see chapter 17). He favored overthrowing capitalism through peaceful, democratic methods and replacing it with government ownership of business and industry for the benefit of the working class.

The Republican Party split decided the outcome of the election. The final results gave Roosevelt 27 percent of the popular vote and Taft 23 percent. Together they had a majority, but because they were divided, Wilson became president, with 42 percent of the popular vote and 435 electoral votes. Finishing fourth, Debs did not win any electoral votes, but he garnered around a million popular votes (6 percent). Counting the votes for Wilson, Roosevelt, and Debs, the American electorate overwhelmingly cast their ballots for reform.

Woodrow Wilson and the New Freedom Agenda

Once in office, Wilson hurried to fulfill his New Freedom agenda. Even though he differed from Roosevelt about the scope of federal intervention, both men believed in a strong presidency. An admirer of the British parliamentary system, Wilson viewed the president as an active and strong leader whose job was to provide his party with a legislative program. The 1912 elections had given the Democrats control over Congress, and Wilson expected his party to support his New Freedom measures.

Tariff reduction came first. The Underwood Act of 1913 reduced import duties, a measure that appealed to southern and midwestern farmers who sought lower prices on the manufactured goods they bought that were subject to the tariff. The law also incorporated a reform that progressives had adopted from the Populists: the graduated income tax (tax rates that increase at higher levels of income). The ratification of the Sixteenth Amendment in 1913 provided the legal basis for the income tax after the Supreme Court had previously declared such a levy unconstitutional. The graduated income tax was meant to advance the cause of social justice by moderating income inequality. The need to recover revenues lost from lower tariffs provided an additional practical impetus for imposing the tax. Because the law exempted people earning less than $4,000 a year from paying the income tax, more than 90 percent of Americans owed no tax. Those with incomes exceeding this amount paid rates ranging from 1 percent to 6 percent on $500,000 or more.

Also in 1913, Wilson pressed Congress to consider banking reform. As chronic debtors who had to borrow against next year's crops, farmers favored a system supervised by the government that afforded them an ample supply of credit at low interest rates. Eastern bankers wanted reforms that would stabilize a system plagued by cyclical financial panics, the most recent in 1907, while keeping the banking system under the private control of bankers. The resulting compromise created the Federal Reserve System.

Woodrow Wilson and William Howard Taft

This photograph shows Woodrow Wilson (left) on inauguration day in 1913 with his predecessor, William Howard Taft. Taft, a Republican, had disappointed progressives, especially Theodore Roosevelt, during his one term in office. Wilson, a Democrat, would expand progressive reforms from 1913 to 1917. Not considered a jovial man, Wilson is seen here enjoying himself as he takes office.   Library of Congress

The act established twelve regional banks. These banks lent cash reserves to member banks in their districts at a "rediscount rate," a rate that could be adjusted according to the fluctuating demand for credit. Federal Reserve notes (paper money insured by the government) also became the medium of exchange and the foundation for a uniform currency. The Federal Reserve Board, appointed by the president and headquartered in Washington, D.C., supervised the system. Nevertheless, as with other progressive agencies, the experts selected to oversee the new banking system came from within the banking industry itself. Although farmers won a more rational and flexible credit supply, Wall Street bankers retained considerable power over the operation of the Federal Reserve System.

Next, President Wilson took two steps designed to help resolve the problem of economic concentration. First, in 1914 he persuaded Congress to create the Federal Trade Commission. Although the agency replaced Roosevelt's Bureau of Corporations, it pursued basically the same approach that Roosevelt had favored. The commission had the power to investigate corporate activities and prohibit "unfair" practices (which the law left undefined). Wilson's second measure directly attacked monopolies. Enacted in 1914, the Clayton Antitrust Law strengthened the Sherman Antitrust Act by banning certain corporate operations, such as price discrimination and overlapping membership on company boards, which undermined economic competition. The statute also exempted labor unions from

prosecution under antitrust legislation, reversing the policy initiated by the federal government in the wake of the Pullman strike (see chapter 17).

By the end of his second year in office, Wilson had achieved most of his New Freedom objectives. Political considerations, however, soon forced him to widen his progressive agenda and support measures he had previously rejected. With the Republican Party once again united after the electoral fiasco of 1912, Democrats lost a substantial number of seats in the 1914 congressional elections, though they still maintained a majority. Fearful for his prospects for reelection in 1916, Wilson resumed the campaign for progressive legislation. Wilson appealed to Roosevelt's constituency by supporting New Nationalism social justice measures. In 1916 he signed into law the Adamson Act, which provided an eight-hour workday and overtime pay for railroad workers; the Keating-Owen Act, outlawing child labor in firms that engaged in interstate commerce; and the Workmen's Compensation Act, which provided insurance for federal employees in case of injury. In supporting programs that required greater intervention by the federal government, Wilson had placed political expediency ahead of his professed principles. He would later show a similar flexibility when he lent his support to a women's suffrage amendment, a cause he had long opposed.

Despite facing a challenge from a united Republican Party led by progressive Charles Evans Hughes, a former governor of New York, Wilson won the 1916 election with slightly less than 50 percent of the vote. Wilson's reelection owed little to the support of African Americans. W. E. B. Du Bois, who backed Wilson in 1912 for pledging to "assist in advancing the interest of [the black] race," had become disillusioned with the president. Born in the South and with deep southern roots, Wilson surrounded himself with white appointees from the South, some of whom told racist jokes at cabinet meetings. Despite black protests, Wilson held a screening in the White House of the film *Birth of a Nation*, which glorified the Ku Klux Klan and denigrated African Americans. Making the situation worse, Wilson introduced racial segregation into government offices and dining facilities in the nation's capital, and blacks lost jobs in post offices and other federal agencies throughout the South. In Wilson's view, segregation and discrimination were in the "best interests" of African Americans.

Still, President Wilson achieved much of the progressive agenda—more, in fact, than he had intended to when he first came to office. By the beginning of his second term, the federal government had further extended regulation over the activities of corporations and banks. Big business and finance still wielded substantial power and maintained considerable leeway in conducting their own affairs, but Wilson had steered the government on a course that also benefited ordinary citizens, including passage of social justice measures he had originally opposed.

REVIEW & RELATE

- How did the progressive agenda shape presidential politics in the first two decades of the twentieth century?

- How and why did the role of the president in national politics change under Roosevelt, Taft, and Wilson?

LEARNINGCurve bedfordstmartins.com/hewittlawson/LC

Conclusion: The Progressive Legacy

By the end of the Progressive Era, Americans had come to expect more from their government. They were more confident that their food and medicine were safe, that children would not have to sacrifice their health and education by going to work, that women laborers would not be exploited, and that political officials would be more responsive to their wishes. As a result of the efforts of environmentalists as different as Gifford Pinchot and Gene Stratton-Porter, the nation expanded its efforts both to conserve and to preserve its natural resources. These and other reforms accomplished what Theodore Roosevelt,

Woodrow Wilson, and their fellow progressives wanted: to bring order out of chaos.

In challenging laissez-faire and championing governmental intervention, progressives did not intend to stamp out individualism or competition. These values were too embedded in the American political tradition, a system that held the allegiance of most reformers. Rather, progressives sought to balance individualism with social justice and social control. Despite cloaking many of their political reforms in democratic garb, middle- and upper-class progressives generally were more interested in augmenting their ability to advance their own agenda than in expanding opportunities for political participation for all Americans. Confident that they spoke for the "interests of the people," progressives had little doubt that increasing their own political power would be good for the nation as a whole.

Progressivism was not for whites only, but racial boundaries shaped the progressive movement. Blacks were active participants in progressivism, whether through extending educational opportunities, working in settlement houses, campaigning for women's suffrage, or establishing the NAACP. Nevertheless, racism was also a characteristic of progressivism. White southern reformers generally favored disfranchisement and segregation. Northern whites did not prove much more sympathetic, as Theodore Roosevelt's handling of the Brownsville incident shows. The southern-born Woodrow Wilson provided even more ample evidence of the racist dimensions of progressivism. Immigrants also found themselves unwelcome targets of moral outrage as progressives forced these newcomers to conform to middle-class standards of social behavior. Crusades for temperance, physical hygiene, and moral reform all shared a desire to mold people deemed inferior into proper citizens, uncontaminated by chronic vice and corruption.

Progressivism was not monolithic and included a range of disparate and overlapping efforts to reorder political, social, moral, and physical environments. Except for the brief existence of the Progressive Party in 1912, reformers did not have a tightly knit organization or a fixed agenda. Leaders were more likely to come from the middle class, but support came from the rich as well as the poor, depending on the issue. Of course, many Americans did not embrace progressive principles, as conservative opponents continued to hold power and to fight against reform. Nevertheless, by 1920 a combination of voluntary changes and government intervention had cleared the way to regulate corporations, increase governmental efficiency, and promote social justice. Progressives succeeded in ameliorating conditions that might have produced violent revolution and more disorder. In time, they would bring their ideas to reordering international affairs.

Chapter Review

Online Study Guide ▶ bedfordstmartins.com/hewittlawson

KEY TERMS

pragmatism (p. 593)

social gospel (p. 593)

muckrakers (p. 593)

Hull House (p. 594)

civic housekeeping (p. 594)

suffragists (p. 596)

Tuskegee Institute (p. 599)

National Association for the Advancement of Colored
   People (NAACP) (p. 602)

Woman's Christian Temperance Union (WCTU) (p. 602)

Hetch Hetchy valley (p. 606)

bully pulpit (p. 607)

Progressive Party (p. 610)

New Nationalism (p. 610)

New Freedom (p. 610)

REVIEW & RELATE

1. What late-nineteenth-century trends and developments influenced the progressives?

2. Why did the progressives focus on urban and industrial America?

3. What role did women play in the early-twentieth-century fight for social justice?

4. How did social reformers challenge discrimination against women and minorities?

5. What practices and behaviors of the poor did social control progressives find most alarming? Why?

6. What role did anti-immigrant sentiment play in motivating and shaping progressives' social control initiatives?

7. Who gained and who lost political influence as a result of progressive reforms?

8. How did a commitment to greater efficiency shape progressives' political and environmental initiatives?

9. How did the progressive agenda shape presidential politics in the first two decades of the twentieth century?

10. How and why did the role of the president in national politics change under Roosevelt, Taft, and Wilson?

TIMELINE OF EVENTS

1874	Woman's Christian Temperance Union (WCTU) founded
1889	Jane Addams and Ellen Starr establish Hull House
1890	National American Woman Suffrage Association formed
1895	Booker T. Washington delivers Atlanta address
1900	First commission form of government established in Galveston, Texas
1902	President Roosevelt settles coal strike
1903	National Women's Trade Union League founded
1906	Meat Inspection Act and Pure Food and Drug Act passed
1908	Race riot in Springfield, Illinois
1909	National Association for the Advancement of Colored People (NAACP) founded
1910	Gifford Pinchot is fired by President Taft
1912	Roosevelt forms Progressive Party
	Children's Bureau of the Department of Commerce and Labor established
1913	Sixteenth Amendment instituting a graduated income tax ratified
	Federal Reserve System created
1914	Harrison Narcotics Control Act passed
	Federal Trade Commission created
	Passage of Clayton Anti-Trust Act to benefit labor unions
1916	Keating-Owen Act outlaws child labor
	Workmen's Compensation Act provides disability insurance
1919	Eighteenth Amendment establishing prohibition ratified
1920	Nineteenth Amendment granting women the right to vote ratified

DOCUMENT 19.8

The Immigration Act of 1917

The wave of immigration from eastern and southern Europe between 1890 and 1914 prompted strenuous efforts to restrict immigration. Labor unions worried that an oversupply of cheap labor would drive down wages. Native-born whites, whose Protestant ancestors had arrived generations earlier, feared that the newer, primarily Jewish and Catholic immigrants endangered their moral and cultural values. In 1917 Congress enacted legislation to reduce the influx of foreigners. The new law included the following provisions outlining who should be denied entry.

SEC. 3. That the following classes of aliens shall be excluded from admission into the United States: All idiots, imbeciles, feeble-minded persons, epileptics, insane persons; persons who have had one or more attacks of insanity at any time previously; persons of constitutional psychopathic inferiority; persons with chronic alcoholism; paupers; professional beggars; vagrants; persons afflicted with tuberculosis in any form or with a loathsome or dangerous contagious disease; persons not comprehended within any of the foregoing excluded classes who are found to be and are certified by the examining surgeon as being mentally or physically defective, such physical defect being of a nature which may affect the ability of such alien to earn a living; persons who have been convicted of or admit having committed a felony or other crime or misdemeanor involving moral turpitude; polygamists, or persons who practice polygamy or believe in or advocate the practice of polygamy; anarchists, or persons who believe in or advocate the overthrow by force or violence of the Government of the United States, or of all forms of law, or who disbelieve in or are opposed to organized government, or who advocate the assassination of public officials, or who advocate or teach the unlawful destruction of property; persons who are members of or affiliated with any organization entertaining and teaching disbelief in or opposition to organized government, or who advocate or teach the duty, necessity, or propriety of the unlawful assaulting or killing of any officer or officers, either of specific individuals or of officers generally, of the Government of the United States or of any other organized government, because of his or their official character, or who advocate or teach the unlawful destruction of property; prostitutes, or persons coming into the United States for the purpose of prostitution or for any other immoral purpose; persons who directly or indirectly procure or attempt to procure or import prostitutes or persons for the purpose of prostitution or for any other immoral purpose; persons who are supported by or receive in whole or in part the proceeds of prostitution; persons hereinafter called contract laborers, who have been induced, assisted, encouraged, or solicited to migrate to this country by offers or promises of employment, whether such offers or promises are true or false, or in consequence of agreements, oral, written or printed, express or implied, to perform labor in this country of any kind, skilled or unskilled; persons who have come in consequence of advertisements for laborers printed, published, or distributed in a foreign country; persons likely to become a public charge; persons who have been deported under any of the provisions of this Act, and who may again seek admission within one year from the date of such deportation, unless prior to their reembarkation at a foreign port or their attempt to be admitted from foreign contiguous territory the Secretary of Labor shall have consented to their reapplying for admission; persons whose tickets or passage is paid for with the money of another, or who are assisted by others to come, unless it is affirmatively and satisfactorily shown that such persons do not belong to one of the foregoing excluded classes; persons whose ticket or passage is paid for by any corporation, association, society, municipality, or foreign Government, either directly or indirectly; stowaways, except that any such stowaway, if otherwise admissible, may be admitted in the discretion of the Secretary of Labor; all children under sixteen years of age, unaccompanied by or not coming to one or both of their parents, except that any such children may, in the discretion of the Secretary of Labor, be admitted if in his opinion they are not likely to become a public charge and are otherwise eligible.

Source: Immigration Act of 1917, 39 Stat. 875–76 (1917).

DOCUMENT 19.9
"Sanitary Precaution," c. 1914

Although progressives' interest in public health and sanitation was often motivated by a sincere desire to prevent the spread of disease, these concerns were often closely linked to racial and ethnic anxieties. Immigration opponents, for example, argued that certain immigrant groups, by virtue of an inherent disposition toward uncleanliness, posed a direct threat to public health. The cartoon here suggests a similar link between African American servants and the spread of disease.

Atlanta Journal-Constitution Historic Online Archives

Interpret the Evidence

1. What role does Frances Willard suggest women should play in controlling the behavior of men (Document 19.5)? What light does Willard's memoir shed on the role of motherhood in shaping progressive values?

2. What connection does the abstinence poster make between disease and vice (Document 19.6)? What do you make of the absence of a direct moral argument against promiscuity in the poster?

3. Why was eugenics so attractive to many progressive reformers (see Document 19.7)?

4. Who benefited and who lost from immigration restriction laws (Document 19.8), temperance laws, and antiprostitution laws?

5. What racial assumptions lie behind the cartoon on health threats (Document 19.9)?

Put It in Context

- How did the progressives' emphasis on disease reflect their larger vision of American society at the turn of the twentieth century?

- How did progressives' understanding of the sources of disease shape the kinds of "cures" they proposed for America's ills?

LEARNINGCurve
Check what you know.
bedfordstmartins.com/hewittlawson/LC

Library of Congress

The Granger Collection, New York

Puck magazine cover showing Theodore Roosevelt admiring "imperialism" crown on display, 1904.

Alabama troops of the 167th Infantry in a trench near Ancerviller, France, 1918.

20
Empire and Wars
1898–1918

Red Cross poster, 1917.

Library of Congress

AMERICAN HISTORIES

Alfred Thayer Mahan came from a military family. Born in 1840, he grew up in West Point, New York, where his father served as dean of the faculty at the U.S. Military Academy. Seeking to emerge from his father's shadow, Alfred attended the U.S. Naval Academy, from which he graduated and received his commission in 1861, just as the Civil War was getting under way. His wartime experience convinced him that the navy, with its plodding, antiquated wooden vessels, needed a dramatic overhaul.

After the war, Mahan continued his naval career. Rather than making his mark on the high seas, Captain Mahan built his reputation as a military historian and strategist at the U.S. Naval War College. In 1890 he published *The Influence of Sea Power upon History*, in which he argued that the great imperial powers in modern history—Spain, the Netherlands, Great Britain, and France—had succeeded because they possessed strong navies and merchant marines. In his view, sea power had allowed these nations to defeat their enemies, conquer territories, and establish colonies from which they extracted raw materials and opened markets for finished goods. Appearing at a time when European nations were embarking on a new round of empire building, this book and subsequent writings had an enormous influence on American imperialists, including Theodore Roosevelt. Mahan's work reinforced the belief of men like Roosevelt that the long-term prospects of the United States depended on the acquisition of strategic outposts in Asia and the Caribbean that could guarantee American access to overseas markets.

As the economic and strategic impor-tance of the Caribbean grew in the minds of imperial strategists such as Mahan and Roosevelt, the Cuban freedom fighter José Martí developed a very different vision of the region's future. Born in 1853 to Spanish immigrants who had migrated to Cuba for economic reasons, Martí got involved in the fight for Cuban independence from Spain as a teenager. In 1869, at age seventeen, he was arrested for protest activities during a revolutionary uprising against Spain. Sentenced to six years of hard labor, Martí was released after six months and was forced into exile. He returned to Cuba in 1878, only to be arrested and deported again the following year.

Martí settled in the United States, where, along with other Cuban exiles, he continued to promote Cuban independence and the establishment of a democratic republic. He conceived of the idea of *Cuba Libre* (Free Cuba) not just as a struggle for political independence but also as a social revolution that would erase unfair distinctions based on race and class. "Our goal," Martí declared in 1892, "is not so much a mere political change as a good, sound, and just and equitable system." Martí united disparate elements in expatriate communities in the United States and the Caribbean under the banner of a single Cuban Revolutionary Party.

When Cubans once again rebelled against Spain in 1895, Martí returned to Cuba to fight alongside his comrades. On May 19, 1895, only three months after he had returned to Cuba, Martí died in battle. Cuba ultimately won its independence from Spain, but Martí's vision of *Cuba Libre* was only partially realized. In 1898 the United States intervened on the side of the Cuban rebels, guaranteeing their victory, but not their freedom. America entered the war to gain control over Cuba, not to help Cubans take control of their own country. ●

both photos: Library of Congress

THE AMERICAN HISTORIES of Alfred Thayer Mahan and José Martí embodied disparate understandings of America's relationship with the rest of the world. Up until the late nineteenth century, most Americans associated colonialism with the European powers and saw overseas expansion as incompatible with American values of independence and self-determination. In this context, they shared Martí's point of view. The American imperialism espoused by Mahan and others, therefore, represented a reversal of traditional American attitudes. Supporters of American imperialism saw the acquisition and control of overseas territories, by force if necessary, as essential to the protection of American interests. This perspective would come to dominate American foreign policy in the early twentieth century. Theodore Roosevelt and Woodrow Wilson, progressive presidents who sanctioned increased federal regulation of economic and moral matters within the United States, also supported vigorous intervention in world affairs. Although Roosevelt and Wilson differed in style and approach, in foreign affairs they asserted America's right to use its power to secure order and thwart revolution wher-ever American interests were seen to be threatened. Having become a major power on the world stage in the early twentieth century, the United States chose to enter World War I, in which rival European alliances battled for imperial domination. The end of the war heightened America's critical role in world affairs but brought neither lasting peace nor the dissolution of empire.

The Awakening of Imperialism

The United States became a modern imperial power relatively late. In the decades following the Civil War, the U.S. government concentrated most of its energies on settling the western territories, pushing Native Americans aside, and extracting the region's resources. Unlike Europe, the United States possessed a sparsely inhabited frontier that would furnish land for its growing population, as well as raw materials and markets for its industries. By the end of the nineteenth century, however, sweeping economic, cultural, and social changes led many Americans to conclude that the time had come for the country to assert its power beyond its borders. Convinced of the argument for empire advanced by Mahan and other imperialists, American officials embraced an expansionist foreign policy. In a burst of overseas expansion from 1898 to 1904, the United States acquired Guam, Hawaii, the Philippines, and Puerto Rico; established a protectorate in Cuba; and exercised force to build a canal through Panama. These gains paved the way for subsequent U.S. intervention in Haiti, the Dominican Republic, and Nicaragua.

The Economics of Expansion

The industrialization of America and the growth of corporate capitalism stimulated imperialist desires in the late nineteenth century. Throughout its early history, the United States had sought overseas markets for exports, particularly its agricultural products. However, the importance of exports to the American economy increased dramatically in the second half of the nineteenth century, as industrialization gained momentum. In 1870 American exports totaled $500 million. By 1905 the value of American exports had increased sixfold to $1.5 billion (Figure 20.1). John D. Rockefeller's Standard Oil Company led the way in selling products to European and Asian markets, and firms such as Coca-Cola, Kodak, and McCormick earned profits by exporting soft drinks, cameras, and farm machinery, respectively.

The bulk of American exports went to the developed markets of Europe and Canada, which had the greatest purchasing power. Although the less economically advanced nations of Latin America and Asia did not have the same ability to buy American products, businessmen still considered these regions—especially China, with a population of millions of potential consumers—as future markets for American industries.

The desire to expand foreign markets remained a steady feature of American business interests. The fear that the domestic market for manufactured goods was shrinking gave this expansionist hunger greater urgency. The fluctuating business cycle of boom and bust that characterized the economy in the 1870s and 1880s reached its peak in the depression of the 1890s, the most severe economic downturn up to that point in American history. The social unrest that accompanied this depression, including protest marches and strikes (see chapter 17), worried business and political leaders about the stability of the country. The way to sustain prosperity and contain radicalism, many businessmen agreed, was to find foreign markets for goods that

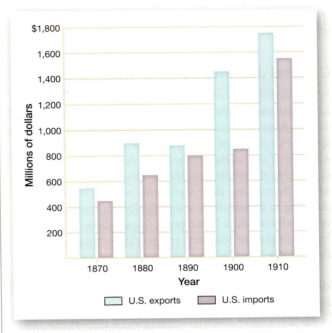

FIGURE 20.1   U.S. Exports and Imports, 1870–1910
As American industrial power increased at the end of the nineteenth century, exports increased dramatically. Between 1870 and 1910, U.S. exports more than tripled. Imports rose as well but were restrained by protective tariffs.

poured out of factories but could not be absorbed at home. Senator William Frye of Maine argued, "We must have the market [of China] or we shall have revolution."

Similar commercial ambitions led many Americans to see Hawaii as an imperial prize. Interest in the islands dated back to the early nineteenth century. American missionaries first visited the Hawaiian Islands in 1820. As missionaries tried to convert native islanders to Christianity, American businessmen sought to establish plantations on the islands, especially to grow sugarcane, as the market for sugar had grown rapidly during the 1870s and 1880s. In exchange for duty-free access to the U.S. sugar market, white Hawaiians signed an agreement in 1887 that granted the United States exclusive rights to a naval base at Pearl Harbor in Honolulu.

The growing influence of white sugar planters on the islands alarmed native Hawaiians. In 1891 Queen Liliuokalani, a strong nationalist leader who voiced the slogan "Hawaii for the Hawaiians," sought to increase the power of the indigenous peoples she governed, at the expense of the sugar growers. In 1893 white plantation owners, with the cooperation of the American ambassador to Hawaii and 150 U.S. marines, overthrew the queen's government. Once in command of the government, they entered into a treaty of annexation with the United States. However, President Grover Cleveland opposed annexation and withdrew the

Cuba Libre

The Cuban War for Independence began in 1895 around the concept of *Cubanidad*—pride of nation. José Martí envisioned that this war of national liberation from Spain would provide land to impoverished peasants and offer genuine racial equality for the large Afro-Cuban population that had been liberated from slavery less than a decade earlier, in 1886. Black Cubans, such as Antonio Maceo, flocked to the revolutionary cause and constituted a significant portion of the senior ranks in the rebel army.

The insurgents fought a brilliant guerrilla war. Facing some 200,000 Spanish troops, 50,000 rebels ground them down in a war of attrition. The Cuban insurgents burned crops, laid siege to land, and cut railroad lines to keep the Spaniards from using these vital resources. Within eighteen months, the rebellion had spread across the island and garnered the support of all segments of the Cuban population. The Spanish government's brutal attempts to crack down on the rebels only stiffened their resistance. By the end of 1897, the Spanish government recognized that the war was going poorly and offered the rebels a series of reforms that would give the island home rule within the empire but not independence. Sensing victory, the insurgents held out for total separation to realize their vision of **Cuba Libre**, an independent Cuba with greater social and racial equality.

The revolutionaries had every reason to feel confident as they wore down Spanish troops. First, they had help from the climate. One-quarter of Spanish soldiers had contracted yellow fever, malaria, and other tropical illnesses and remained confined to hospitals. The chief military commander of the rebel forces, General Maximo Gómez, bragged that his three best generals were "*Junio, Julio,* and *Agosto,*" referring to the months of June, July, and August, which ushered in the rainy season and increased the spread of disease. Second, mounting a successful counterinsurgency would have required far more troops than Spain

Cuban Revolutionary Soldiers

Under the command of General Maximo Gómez, these Cuban soldiers fought against Spanish forces in 1898. Gómez waged guerrilla warfare for Cuban independence from Spain before the United States entered the war. His army consisted of numerous Afro-Cubans, whose race troubled white American commanders when they occupied Cuba.   The Granger Collection, New York could spare. Its forces were spread too thin around the globe to keep the empire intact. In addition to Cuba, Spain stationed some 200,000 troops in Puerto Rico, the Philippines, and Africa. Finally, antiwar sentiment was mounting in Spain, and on January 12, 1898, Spanish troops mutinied in Havana. Speaking for many, a former president of Spain asserted: "Spain is exhausted. She must withdraw her troops and recognize Cuban independence before it is too late." U.S. Secretary of State John Sherman concurred: "Spain will lose Cuba. . . . She cannot continue the struggle."

The War of 1898

With the Cuban insurgents on the verge of victory, American policymakers, including President William McKinley, came to favor military intervention as a way to increase American control of postwar Cuba. By intervening before the Cubans won on their own, the United States staked its claim for determining the postwar relationship between the two countries and protecting its vital interests in the Caribbean, including the private property rights of American landowners in Cuba.

The American press, however, helped build support for American intervention not by focusing on economic interests and geopolitics but by framing the war as a matter of American honor. Most Americans followed the war through newspaper accounts. William Randolph Hearst's *New York Journal* competed with Joseph Pulitzer's *New York World* to see which could provide the most lurid coverage of Spanish atrocities. The two newspapers sent correspondents to Cuba to cover every grisly story they could find—and to make up stories, if necessary. Known disparagingly as **yellow journalism**, these sensationalist newspaper accounts aroused jingoistic outrage against Spain.

On February 9, 1898, the *Journal* printed a letter that had come into Hearst's possession. Under the headline "Worst Insult to the United States in History," the newspaper quoted a private letter from Enrique Depuy de Lôme, the Spanish minister in Washington, scorning President McKinley as a "weak" politician who pandered to "the crowd" to win public favor. Nearly a week later, on February 15, the battleship *Maine*, anchored in Havana harbor, exploded, killing 266 American sailors. American newspapers blamed Spain. The *World* shouted the rallying cry "Remember the *Maine*! To hell with Spain!" Assistant Secretary of the Navy Theodore Roosevelt seconded this sentiment by denouncing the explosion as a Spanish "act of treachery." Why the Spaniards would choose to blow up the *Maine* and provoke war with the United States while already losing to Cuba remained unanswered, but the incident was enough to turn American opinion toward war.

On April 11, 1898, McKinley asked Congress to declare war against Spain. The declaration included an amendment proposed by Senator Henry M. Teller of Colorado declaring that Cuba "ought to be free and independent." Yet the document left enough room for American maneuvering to satisfy the imperial ambitions of the McKinley administration. In endorsing independence, the war proclamation asserted the right of the United States to remain involved in Cuban affairs until it had achieved "pacification." On April 21, the United States officially went to war with Spain.

In going to war, McKinley embarked on an imperialistic course that had been building since the early 1890s. The president signaled the broader expansionist concerns behind the war when, shortly after it began, he successfully steered a Hawaiian annexation treaty through Congress. Businessmen joined imperialists in seizing the moment to create a commercial empire that would catch up to their European rivals.

It was fortunate for the United States that the Cuban insurgents had seriously weakened Spanish forces before the Americans arrived. The U.S. army, consisting of fewer than 30,000 men, lacked sufficient strength to conquer Cuba on its own, and McKinley had to mobilize some 200,000 National Guard troops and assorted volunteers. Theodore Roosevelt resigned from his post as assistant secretary of the navy and organized his own regiment, called "Rough Riders." American forces faced several problems: They lacked battle experience; supplies were inadequate; their uniforms were not suited for the hot, humid climate of a Cuban summer; and the soldiers did not have immunity from tropical diseases.

African American soldiers, who made up about one-quarter of the troops, encountered additional difficulties. As more and more black troops arrived in southern ports for deployment to Cuba, they faced increasingly hostile crowds, angered at the presence of armed African American men in uniform. In Tampa, Florida, where troops gathered from all over the country to be transported to Cuba, racial tensions exploded on the afternoon of June 8. Intoxicated white soldiers from Ohio grabbed a two-year-old black boy from his mother and used him for target practice, shooting a bullet through his shirtsleeve. In retaliation, African American soldiers stormed into the streets and exchanged gunfire with whites, leaving three whites and twenty-seven black soldiers wounded. Reporting the story of this "riot," the *Atlanta Constitution* denounced the "wild and demonic conduct of the [N]egro regulars," completely ignoring the behavior of the white troops that had prompted the fracas. Undaunted, black troops went on to distinguish themselves on Cuban battlefields.

Despite military inexperience, logistical problems, and racial tensions, the United States quickly defeated the

Filipino Prisoners of War
After the United States annexed the Philippines in 1899, Filipino rebels continued their struggle for independence. The United States had a more difficult time subduing the rebels led by Emilio Aguinaldo than they had defeating Spain, but after three years American forces triumphed. In this photograph, Filipino prisoners of war are held in Manila.   Library of Congress

and savagery such as the wild natives of the unconquered Philippine Islands could not approach." For many Americans, the "splendid little war" had turned into a sordid affair. Anti-imperialists claimed that the war had done nothing to affirm American manhood; rather, they charged, the United States acted as a bully, taking the position of "a strong man" fighting against "a weak and puny child."

Despite growing casualties on the battlefield and antiwar sentiment at home, the conflict ended with an American military victory. In March 1901, U.S. forces captured Aguinaldo and broke the back of the rebellion. Exhausted, the Filipino leader asked his comrades to lay down their arms. In July 1901, President McKinley appointed Judge William Howard Taft of Ohio as the first civilian governor to oversee the government of the Philippines. For the next forty-five years, except for a brief period of Japanese rule during World War II, the United States remained in control of the islands.

REVIEW & RELATE

Why did the United States go to war with Spain in 1898?

In what ways did the War of 1898 mark a turning point in the relationship between the United States and the rest of the world?

Extending U.S. Imperialism, 1899–1913

The War of 1898 turned the United States into an imperial nation. Once the war was over, and with its newly acquired empire in place, the United States sought to extend its influence, competing with its European rivals for even greater global power. President Theodore Roosevelt and his successors achieved Captain Mahan's dream of building a Central American canal and wielded American military and financial might in the Caribbean with little restraint. At the same time, the United States took a more active role in Asian affairs.

Theodore Roosevelt and "Big Stick" Diplomacy

After President McKinley was assassinated in 1901, Vice President Theodore Roosevelt succeeded him as president. As in domestic matters, Roosevelt believed in using power to protect American commercial and strategic interests as well as to preserve international order and stability. In his view, the United States required a strong military and the political will to use it. "It is contemptible for a nation, as for an individual," Roosevelt instructed Congress, "[to] proclaim its purposes, or to take positions which are ridiculous if unsupported by potential force, and then to refuse to provide this force." This Progressive Era interventionist, inspired by Captain Mahan's writings, welcomed his nation's new role as a major world power. From this point on, the United States would play the role of an international policeman, using force if necessary to keep the peace.

Explore

See Document 20.2 for Roosevelt's views on the virtue of exhibiting strength.

As the most important part of his international agenda, Roosevelt sought to demonstrate American might and preserve order in the Caribbean and Central and South America. The building of the Panama Canal provides a case in point. Mahan considered a canal across Central America as vital because it would provide faster access to Asian markets and improve the U.S. navy's ability to patrol two oceans effectively. The United States took a step toward realizing Mahan's goal in 1901, when it signed the Hay-Pauncefote Treaty with Britain, granting the United States the right to construct a canal connecting the Atlantic and Pacific Oceans. After first considering Nicaragua, Roosevelt settled on Panama as the prime location. A French company had already begun construction at this site and had completed two-fifths of the operation; however, when it ran out of money, it sold its holdings to the United States for the bargain price of $40 million.

Before the United States could resume building, it had to negotiate with the South American country of Colombia, which controlled Panama. Secretary of State Hay and Colombian representatives reached an agreement highly favorable to the Americans, which the Colombian government refused to ratify. When Colombia held out for a higher price, Roosevelt accused the Colombians of being "utterly incapable of keeping order" in Panama and declared that transit across Panama was vital to world commerce. In 1903 the president supported a pro-American uprising by sending warships into the harbor of Panama City, an action that prevented the Colombians from quashing the insurrection. Roosevelt quickly recognized the new government of Panama and signed a treaty with it granting the United States the right to build the canal and exercise "power and authority" over it. In 1914, under American control, the Panama Canal opened to sea traffic.

With the United States controlling Cuba, the Panama Canal, and Puerto Rico, President Roosevelt intended to deter any threats to America's power in the region. The economic instability of Central American and Caribbean nations provided Roosevelt with the opportunity to brandish what he called a "big stick" to keep these countries in check and prevent intervention by European powers also interested in the area. (The term comes from a proverb Roosevelt was fond of quoting: "Speak softly and carry a big stick.") Referring to neighboring countries to the south, the president grumbled: "These wretched republics cause me a great deal of trouble." In 1904, when the government of the Dominican Republic was teetering on the edge of bankruptcy and threatened to default on $22 million in European loans, Roosevelt sprang into action. He announced U.S. opposition to any foreign intervention to reclaim debts, a position that echoed the principles of the Monroe Doctrine, which in 1823 proclaimed that the United States would not tolerate outside intervention in the Western Hemisphere. However, the president went even further and added his own corollary to the Monroe Doctrine by affirming the right of the United States to intervene in the internal affairs of any country in Latin America or the Caribbean that displayed "chronic wrong-doing" and could not preserve order and manage its own affairs. The **Roosevelt Corollary** proclaimed what Cubans and Panamanians already knew: The United States considered the region south of its border to be within its sphere of influence. Retaining nominal independence, the countries of Central America and the Caribbean had to behave according to U.S. wishes or face American military invasion.

Opening the Door in China

Roosevelt displayed American power in other parts of the world. His major concern was protecting the **Open Door** policy in China that his predecessor McKinley had engineered to secure naval access to the China market. By 1900 European powers already dominated foreign access to Chinese markets, leaving scant room for newcomers. When the United States sent 2,500 troops to China in August 1900 to help quell a nationalist uprising against foreign involvement known as the Boxer uprising, European competitors in return were compelled to allow the United States free trade access to China.

In 1904 the Russian invasion of the southern Chinese province of Manchuria prompted the Japanese to attack the Russian fleet. Roosevelt held mixed emotions about the Japanese. The president admired Japanese military prowess, but he worried that if Japan succeeded in driving the Russians out of the area, it would cause "a real shifting of equilibrium as far as the white races are concerned." To prevent that from happening, Roosevelt convened a peace conference in Portsmouth, New Hampshire, in 1905. Under the agreement reached at the conference, Japan received stated commitment to the peaceful resolution of international issues, during his presidency the American military intervened repeatedly in Latin American affairs, and American troops fought on European soil in the bloody global conflict that contemporaries called the Great War.

Diplomacy and War

Despite his stated preference for moral diplomacy, Wilson preserved the U.S. sphere of influence in the Caribbean using much the same methods as had Roosevelt and Taft. To protect American investments from political disturbances and economic crises, the president sent marines to Haiti in 1915, to the Dominican Republic in 1916, and to Cuba in 1917.

The most serious challenge to Wilson's diplomacy came in Mexico, where he found his ideals tempered by reality. The **Mexican revolution** in 1911 spawned a civil war among various insurgent factions. The resulting instability threatened U.S. interests in Mexico, particularly oil. When Mexicans refused to accept Wilson's demands to install leaders he considered "good men," Wilson withdrew diplomatic recognition from Mexico. In a disastrous attempt to influence Mexican politics, Wilson sent the U.S. navy to the port of Veracruz on April 22, 1914, leading to a bloody clash that killed 19 Americans and 126 Mexicans. The situation worsened after Wilson first supported and then turned against one of the rebel competitors for power in Mexico, General Francisco "Pancho" Villa. In response to this betrayal, Villa and 1,500 troops rode across the border and attacked the town of Columbus, New Mexico. In July 1916, Wilson ordered General John Pershing to send 10,000 army troops three hundred miles into Mexico in an attempt to capture Villa. The operation was a complete failure that only further angered Mexican leaders and confirmed their sense that Wilson had no respect for Mexican national sovereignty. In January 1917, Wilson ordered Pershing to withdraw his troops.

The president had little choice. At the same time as the situation in Mexico was deteriorating, a much more serious problem was developing in Europe. On June 28, 1914, an ardent Serbian nationalist, intending to strike a blow against Austria-Hungary, assassinated the Austrian archduke Franz Ferdinand in Sarajevo, the capital of the province of Bosnia. This terrorist attack plunged Europe into what would become a world war, fracturing the unsteady peace that had been maintained for the previous forty years. On August 4, 1914, the Central Powers—Germany, the Ottoman empire, and Austria-Hungary—officially declared war against the Allies—Great Britain, France, and Russia (Italy joined them in 1915).

As the most powerful neutral nation, the United States looked on from afar. For the first three years of the Great War, Wilson kept the United States neutral, though privately he believed that a British defeat would be "fatal to our form of Government and American ideals."

Nevertheless, the president urged Americans to remain "in fact as well as in name impartial in thought as well as action." Peace activists sought to keep Wilson to his word. In 1915 women reformers and suffragists such as Jane Addams and Carrie Chapman Catt organized the Women's Peace Party to keep the United States out of war. One of its leaders, Lucia True Ames Mead, called replacing war with law "the most pressing reform before civilization to-day." Yet even Mead showed how difficult it was to keep a neutral mind. "There can be no peace," she exclaimed, "until the military domination of [Germany] is destroyed."

Wilson faced two key problems in keeping the country out of war. First, America had closer and more important economic ties with the Allies than with the Central Powers, a disparity that would only grow as the war went on. The Allies purchased more than $750 million in American goods in 1914, a figure that quadrupled over the next three years. By contrast, the Germans bought approximately $350 million worth of American products in 1914; by 1917 the figure had shrunk to $30 million. Moreover, when the Allies did not have the funds to pay for American goods, they sought loans from private bankers. Initially, the Wilson administration followed the wishes of Secretary of State William Jennings Bryan, who argued that providing these loans would violate "the true spirit of neutrality." In 1915, however, Wilson reversed course. Concerned that failure to keep up the prewar level of commerce with the Allies would hurt the country economically, the president authorized private loans. The gap in financial transactions with the rival war powers grew even wider; by 1917 American bankers had loaned the Allies $2.2 billion, compared with just $27 million to Germany.

The second problem facing Wilson arose from Great Britain's and Germany's differing war strategies. As the superior naval power, Britain established a blockade of the North Sea to quarantine Germany and starve it into submission. The British navy violated international law by mining the waters to bottle up the German fleet and keep foreign ships from supplying Germany with food and medicines. The blockade even ensnared U.S. ships, despite the fact that the United States, as a neutral nation, had the right to ship non-war items to Germany. However, Britain extended the list of prohibited items and hauled American vessels into British ports. Although Wilson protested this treatment, he did so weakly. He believed that the British could pay compensation for such violations of international law after the war.

Confronting a strangling blockade, Germany depended on the newly developed U-boat (*Unterseeboot*, or submarine) to counter the British navy. In February 1915, Germany declared a blockade of the British Isles and warned citizens of neutral nations to stay off British ships in the area. U-boats, which were lighter and sleeker than British battleships and merchant marine ships, relied on surprise. This strategy violated the rules of engagement under international maritime law, which required belligerent ships to allow civilians to leave passenger liners and cargo ships before firing. The British complicated the situation for the Germans by flying flags of neutral countries on merchant vessels and arming them with small "defensive" weapons. Therefore, if U-boats played by the rules and surfaced before inspecting merchant ships, they risked being blown out of the water by disguised enemy guns.

Under these circumstances, American neutrality could not last long. On May 15, 1915, catastrophe struck. Without surfacing and identifying itself, a German submarine off the Irish coast attacked the British luxury liner *Lusitania*, which had departed from New York City en route to England. Although the ship's stated objective was to provide passengers with relaxation, sumptuous dining, and dancing, its cargo contained a large supply of ammunition for British weapons. The U-boat's torpedoes rapidly sank the ship, killing 1,198 people, including 128 Americans.

Outraged Americans called on the president to respond; some, including Theodore Roosevelt, advocated the immediate use of military force. Despite his pro-British sentiments, Wilson resisted going to war. Instead, he held the Germans in "strict accountability" for their action. Appalled by the loss of human life, Wilson demanded that Germany refrain from further attacks against passenger liners and offer a financial settlement to the *Lusitania*'s survivors. Unwilling to risk war with the United States, the Germans consented.

Wilson had, however, only delayed America's entry into the war. By pursuing a policy of neutrality that treated the combatants unequally and by insisting that Americans had a right to travel on the ships of belligerent nations, the president diminished the chance that the United States would stay out of the war. Recognizing this situation, Secretary of State Bryan resigned following the *Lusitania* affair over what he considered the president's one-sided understanding of "strict accountability." Wilson quickly replaced him with a more pro-British secretary of state, Robert Lansing, who endorsed Wilson's expansion of the loan program to Britain.

Throughout 1916, Wilson pursued two separate but interrelated policies that embodied the ambivalence that he and the American people shared about the war. On the one hand, with Germany alternating between continued U-boat attacks and apologies, the president sought to build the country's military preparedness in the event of war. He signed into law the National Defense Act, which increased the size of the army, navy, and National Guard. On the other hand, Wilson stressed his desire to remain neutral and stay out of the war. With American public opinion divided on the Great War, Wilson chose to run for reelection as a peace candidate. The president sent his personal emissary, Colonel Edward House, to Europe to negotiate an armistice and end the fighting, without success. The Democrats adopted the slogan "He kept us out of war" and also emphasized the president's substantial record of progressive reform. Wilson won a narrow victory

against Charles Evans Hughes, the former governor of New York, who wavered between advocating peace and criticizing Wilson for not sufficiently supporting the Allies.

Making the World Safe for Democracy

As 1917 dawned, the Great War headed toward its third bloody year. Neither side wanted a negotiated peace because each counted on victory to gain sufficient territory and financial compensation to justify the great sacrifices in human lives and materiel caused by the conflict. Nevertheless, Wilson tried to persuade the belligerents to abandon the battlefield for the bargaining table. On January 22, 1917, he declared that the world needed a "peace without victory," one based on self-determination, freedom of the seas, respect for international law, and the end of hostile alliances. It was a generous vision from a nation that had made few sacrifices.

Germany quickly rejected Wilson's proposal. America had never been truly neutral, and Germany's increasingly desperate leaders saw no reason to believe that the situation would change. In 1915 and again in 1916, to prevent the United States from entering the war, Germany had pledged to refrain from using its most potent weapon, the U-boat, against passenger ships and merchant ships. However, the Germans now chose to change course and resume unrestricted submarine warfare, calculating that they could defeat the Allies before the United States declared war and its troops could make a substantial difference. On February 1, 1917, Germany announced that it would attack all ships, including unarmed American merchant vessels that penetrated its blockade of Great Britain. In response, Wilson used his executive power to arm merchant ships, bringing the United States one step closer to war.

The country moved even closer to war after the **Zimmermann telegram** became public. On February 24, the British turned over to Wilson an intercepted message from Arthur Zimmermann, the German foreign minister, to the Mexican government. The decoded note revealed that Germany had offered Mexico an alliance in the event that the United States joined the Allies. If the Central Powers won, Mexico would receive the territory it had lost to the United States in the mid-nineteenth century—Texas, New Mexico, and Arizona. When U.S. newspapers broke the story several days later, it inflamed public opinion and provided the Wilson administration another reason to fear a German victory.

In late February and March, German U-boats sank several armed American merchant ships, and on April 2, 1917, President Wilson asked Congress to declare war against Germany and the other Central Powers. After four days of vigorous debate led by opponents of the war—including the first female elected representative, Jeanette P. Rankin from Montana—Congress voted to approve the war resolution. However, the United States underscored its historic commitment against "entangling alliances" by gear up private enterprise to meet demand. However, the WIB was largely ineffective until March 1918, when the president found the right man to lead it. He chose Wall Street financier Bernard Baruch, who recruited staff from business enterprises that the board regulated. Baruch prodded businesses into compliance mainly by offering lucrative contracts rather than by coercion. Working for a token $1 a year (but still on their company payrolls), the members of this agency helped reduce the chaos of mobilization. Ultimately, these businessmen created a government partnership with the corporate sector that would last beyond the war.

Labor also experienced significant gains through government regulation. Shortages of workers and an outbreak of strikes—more than four thousand in 1917—hampered the war effort. In April 1918, Wilson created the **National War Labor Board (NWLB)** to settle labor disputes. The agency consisted of representatives from unions, corporations, and the public.

Recruitment Poster

Artist Howard Chandler Christy created this poster in 1917 to encourage enlistment in the U.S. navy. This illustration appealed to masculinity not just by showing an attractive woman but also by challenging potential recruits to "Be a Man and Do It."   Library of Congress

In exchange for obtaining a "no strike pledge" from organized labor, the NWLB supported an eight-hour workday with time-and-a-half pay for overtime, labor's right to collective bargaining, and equal pay for equal work by women.

The NWLB fell short of reaching this last goal, but the war employed more than a million women who had not held jobs before. As military and government services expanded, women found greater opportunities as telephone operators, nurses, and clerical workers. At the same time, the number of women employed as domestic servants declined. Women took over formerly male jobs driving streetcars, delivering ice, assembling airplane motors, operating drill presses, oiling railroad engines, and welding parts. Yet women's incomes continued to lag significantly behind those of men performing the same tasks.

Americans probably experienced the expanding scope of government intervention most directly through the efforts of three new agencies that regulated consumption and travel. Wilson appointed Herbert Hoover, a progressive mining engineer, to head the Food Administration. Hoover sought to increase the military and civilian food supply mainly through voluntary conservation measures. He generated a massive publicity campaign urging Americans to adopt "wheatless Mondays," "meatless Tuesdays," and "porkless Thursdays and Saturdays." Chicago housewives demonstrated their ingenuity in cooking leftovers, as evidenced by a sharp decline in the volume of raw garbage in the city. The government also mobilized schoolchildren to plant vegetable gardens to increase food production for the home front. Wilson considered children's work in the School Garden Army "just as real and patriotic an effort as the building of ships or the firing of cannon."

Consumers saved gas and oil under the prodding of the Fuel Administration. The agency encouraged fuel "holidays" along the line of Hoover's voluntary restrictions and created daylight saving time to conserve fuel by adding an extra hour of sunlight to the end of the workday. The Fuel Administration also offered higher prices to coal companies in order to increase productivity. Patterns of consumer travel changed under government regulation. The Railroad Administration acted more forcefully than most other agencies. Troop and supply shipments depended on the efficient operation of the railways. The administration controlled the railroads during the war, coordinating train schedules, overseeing terminals and regulating ticket prices, upgrading tracks, and raising workers' wages.

Winning Hearts and Minds

America's entry into the Great War did not immediately end the significant antiwar sentiment. Consequently, Wilson waged a campaign to rally support for his aims and to stimulate patriotic fervor. To generate enthusiasm and ensure loyalty, the president appointed Denver journalist George Creel to head the **Committee on Public Information (CPI)**, which focused on generating propaganda. Creel recruited a vast network of lecturers to speak throughout the country and spread patriotic messages. The committee coordinated rallies to sell bonds and raise money to fund the war. The CPI persuaded reporters to censor their war coverage, and most agreed in order to avoid government intervention. The agency helped produce films depicting the Allies as heroic saviors of humanity and the Central Powers as savage beasts. The CPI also distributed colorful and sometimes lurid posters emphasizing the depravity of the enemy and the nation's moral responsibility to defeat the Central Powers. All the talk of fighting for democracy encouraged groups with long-standing grievances because of their treatment at home to rally around the flag. W. E. B. Du Bois, one of the founders of the NAACP, backed Wilson's democratic aims in the hope that the war would lead to racial equality in the United States.

Explore

See Documents 20.4 and 20.5 for Du Bois's thoughts on supporting the war.

Propaganda did not, however, prove sufficient, and many Americans remained deeply divided about the war. To suppress dissent, Congress passed the Espionage Act in 1917 and the Sedition Act a year later. Both limited freedom of speech by criminalizing certain forms of expression. The **Espionage Act** prohibited antiwar activities, including interfering with the draft. It also banned the mailing of publications advocating forcible interference with any laws. The **Sedition Act** punished individuals who expressed beliefs disloyal or abusive to the American government, flag, or military uniform. Of the slightly more than two thousand prosecutions under these laws, only a handful concerned charges of actual sabotage or espionage. Most defendants brought to trial were critics who merely spoke out against the war. In 1918, for telling a crowd that the military draft was a form of slavery that turned inductees into "cannon fodder," the Socialist Party's Eugene V. Debs was tried, convicted, and sentenced to ten years under the Espionage Act. (President Warren G. Harding pardoned Debs in 1921.) The Justice Department also went after the Industrial Workers of the World (IWW), which continued to initiate labor strikes during the war. The government broke into the offices of the IWW, ransacked the Wobblies' files for evidence of disloyalty, and arrested more than 130 members, including their dynamic leader Big Bill Haywood, who subsequently fled to the Soviet Union to avoid jail.

Government efforts to promote national unity and punish those who did not conform prompted local communities to enforce "one hundred percent Americanism." Civic groups banned the playing of German music and operas from concert halls, and schools prohibited teaching the German language. Arbiters of culinary taste, prompted by patriotic enthusiasm, renamed foods with German origins—sauerkraut became "liberty cabbage," and hamburgers became "liberty sandwiches." Such sentiments were expressed in a more sinister fashion when mobs assaulted German Americans.

Prejudice toward German Americans was further inflamed by the formation of the **American Protective League (APL)**, a quasi-official association endorsed by the Justice Department. Consisting of 200,000 chapters throughout the country, the APL employed individuals to spy on German residents suspected of disloyal behavior. In cooperation with the Bureau of Investigation (later the FBI), APL members tried to uncover German spies, but most often they found little more than German immigrants who merely retained attachments to family and friends in their homeland. Gossip and rumor fueled many of the league's loyalty probes. In May 1918, the APL sent one of its agents to investigate the cook of a family living in Manhattan, because she allegedly had "a picture of the Kaiser in her room" and was "very pro-German and talks in favor of the Germans." The investigator found no photograph of the kaiser or any other evidence of suspicious behavior.

The repressive side of progressivism came to the fore in other ways as well. Anti-immigrant bias, shared by many reformers, flourished. The effort to conserve manpower and grain supplies bolstered the impulse to control standards of moral behavior, particularly those associated with immigrants, such as drinking. This anti-immigrant prejudice in part explains the ratification of the Eighteenth Amendment in 1919, prohibiting the sale of all alcoholic beverages. Yet not all the moral indignation unleashed by the war resulted in restriction of freedom. After considerable wartime protest and lobbying, women suffragists succeeded in securing the right to vote (see chapter 19).

Waging Peace

In January 1918, ten months before the war ended, President Wilson presented Congress with his plan for peace without rancor. Wilson centered his ideas around **Fourteen Points**, principles that he hoped would prevent future wars. Based on his assessment of the causes of the Great War, Wilson envisioned a generous peace treaty that included freedom of the seas, open diplomacy and the abolition of secret treaties, free trade, self-determination for colonial subjects, and a

DOCUMENTS 20.4 AND 20.5

African Americans and the War: Two Views

African Americans played an active role in the war effort; however, given their poor treatment by much of white America, it is not surprising that many blacks were ambivalent about their service. In a controversial editorial in the *Crisis*, the journal of the NAACP, W. E. B. Du Bois urged the black community to "close ranks" with the rest of American society to fight Germany. Du Bois hoped that their service would lead to greater acceptance for African Americans by white society. Less than a year later, Du Bois published a bitter attack against the treatment of African American soldiers and enduring American racism.

Explore

20.4   W. E. B. Du Bois | "Close Ranks," 1918

This is the crisis of the world. For all the long years to come men will point to the year 1918 as the great Day of Decision, the day when the world decided whether it would submit to military despotism and an endless armed peace—if peace it could be called—or whether they would put down the menace of German militarism and inaugurate the United States of the World.

We of the colored race have no ordinary interest in the outcome. That which the German power represents today spells death to the aspirations of Negroes and all darker races for equality, freedom, and democracy. Let us not hesitate. Let us, while this war lasts, forget our special grievances and close our ranks shoulder to shoulder with our own white fellow citizens and the allied nations that are fighting for democracy. We make no ordinary sacrifice, but we make it gladly and willingly with our eyes lifted to the hills.

Source: W. E. B. Du Bois, "Close Ranks," *The Crisis*, July 1918, 111.

---

reduction in military spending. More important than any specific measure, Wilson's proposal hinged on the creation of the **League of Nations**, a body of large and small nations that would guarantee peaceful resolution of disputes and back up decisions through collective action, including the use of military force as a last resort.

Following the armistice that ended the war on November 11, 1918, Wilson personally took his message to the Paris Peace Conference, the postwar meeting of the victorious Allied nations that would set the terms of the peace. The first sitting president to travel overseas, Wilson was greeted in Paris by joyous crowds when he arrived leading the American delegation.

For nearly six months, Wilson tried to convince reluctant Allied leaders to accept the central components of his plan. Having exhausted themselves financially and having suffered the loss of a generation of young men, the Allies intended to scoop up the spoils of victory and make the Central Powers pay dearly. The European Allies intended to hold on to their respective colonies regardless of Wilson's call for self-determination, and as a nation that depended on a strong navy, Britain refused to limit its options by discussing freedom of the seas. Perhaps Georges Clemenceau, France's president, best expressed his colleagues' skepticism about Wilson's idealistic vision: "President Wilson and his Fourteen Points bore me. Even God Almighty has only ten!"

During the conference, Wilson was forced to compromise on a number of his principles in order to retain the cornerstone of his diplomacy—the establishment of the League of Nations. He abandoned his hope for peace without bitterness by agreeing to a "war guilt" clause that levied huge economic reparations on Germany for starting the war. He was willing to sacrifice some of his ideals because the league took on even greater importance in the wake of the Communist revolution in Russia. The president believed that capitalism, as regulated and reformed during the Progressive Era, would raise living conditions throughout the world as it had done in the United States, would prevent the spread of communism, and would benefit U.S. commerce by paving the way to free trade. Wilson needed the league to keep the peace so that war-ravaged and

Explore

20.5 W. E. B. Du Bois | "Returning Soldiers," 1919

We are returning from war! . . .

. . . We return from the slavery of uniform which the world's madness demanded us to don to the freedom of civil garb. We stand again to look America squarely in the face and call a spade a spade. We sing: This country of ours, despite all its better souls have done and dreamed, is yet a shameful land.

It *lynches*. . . .

It *disfranchises* its own *citizens*. . . .

It encourages *ignorance*. . . .

It *steals* from us. . . .

It *insults* us. . . .

This is the country to which we Soldiers of Democracy return. This is the fatherland for which we fought! But it is *our* fatherland. It was right for us to fight. The faults of *our* country are *our* faults. Under similar circumstances, we would fight again. But by the God of Heaven, we are cowards and jackasses if now that that war is over, we do not marshal every ounce of our brain and brawn to fight a sterner, longer, more unbending battle against the forces of hell in our own land.

We *return*.

We *return from fighting*.

We *return fighting*.

Make way for Democracy! We saved it in France, and by the Great Jehovah, we will save it in the United States of America, or know the reason why.

Source: W. E. B. Du Bois, "Returning Soldiers," *The Crisis*, May 1919, 13–14.

Interpret the Evidence

- In both articles, how does Du Bois explain why African Americans fought in World War I?
- What did Du Bois see as the greatest threat to the black community in 1918? What about in 1919? Why do you think Du Bois reversed his position?

Put It in Context

What do both these editorials reveal about the treatment of black Americans during World War I?

recovering nations had the opportunity to practice economic freedom and political democracy. In the end, the president won agreement for the establishment of his cherished League of Nations. The final treaty signed at the palace of Versailles, just outside Paris, authorized the league to combat aggression against any member nation through collective military action.

The Failure of Ratification

In July 1919, after enduring bruising battles in Paris, Wilson returned to Washington, D.C., only to face another wrenching struggle in the Senate over ratification of the Versailles treaty. The odds were stacked against Wilson from the start. The Republicans held a majority in the Senate, and Wilson needed the support of two-thirds of the Senate to secure ratification. Moreover, Henry Cabot Lodge, the Republican chairman of the Senate Foreign Relations Committee, opposed Article X of the League of Nations covenant, which sanctioned collective security arrangements against military aggression. Lodge argued that such an alliance compromised the United States' independence in conducting its own foreign relations. The Massachusetts senator wanted the United States to preserve the possibility of unilateral action without being restrained by the league's policies. Lodge had at least thirty-nine senators behind him, more than enough to block ratification. Conceding the need to protect the country's national self-interest, the president agreed to modifications to the treaty so that the Monroe Doctrine and America's obligations in the Caribbean and Central America were kept intact. Lodge, who loathed Wilson, was not satisfied and insisted on adding fourteen "reservations" limiting compliance with the treaty, including strong language affirming Congress's right to declare war before agreeing to a League of Nations military action.

Wilson's stubbornness more than equaled Lodge's, and the president refused to compromise further over the league. Insisting that he was morally bound to honor the treaty he had negotiated in good faith, Wilson rejected additional changes demanded by Lodge and his supporters. Making matters worse, Wilson faced resistance from sixteen lawmakers dubbed "irreconcilables," who opposed the league under any circumstances. Mainly Republicans from the Midwest and West, they voiced the traditional American rejection of entangling alliances.

To break the logjam, the president attempted to rally public opinion behind him. In September 1919, he embarked on a nationwide speaking tour to carry his message directly to the American people. Over a three-week period, he traveled eight thousand miles by train, keeping a grueling schedule that exhausted him. After a stop in Pueblo, Colorado, on September 25, Wilson collapsed and canceled the rest of his trip. On October 2, Wilson suffered a massive stroke that nearly killed him. The effects of the stroke, which left him partially paralyzed, emotionally unstable, and mentally impaired, dimmed any remaining hopes of compromise. The full extent of his illness was kept from the public, and his wife, Edith, ran the White House for the next eighteen months.

On November 19, 1919, the Senate rejected the amended treaty. The following year, Wilson had one final chance to obtain ratification, but still he refused to accept reservations. He ignored leaders of his own party who were willing to vote for the Republican-sponsored amendments. "Let Lodge compromise," the president responded defiantly. In March 1920, treaty ratification failed one last time, falling just seven votes short of the required two-thirds majority. Had Wilson shown the same willingness to compromise that he had in Paris, the outcome might have been different. In the end, however, the United States never signed the Treaty of Versailles or joined the League of Nations, weakening the league and diminishing the prospects for long-term peace.

REVIEW & RELATE

- What steps did the U.S. government take to control the economy and public opinion during World War I?

- How did President Wilson's wartime policies and his efforts to shape the peace that followed reflect his progressive roots?

 **LEARNINGCurve** bedfordstmartins.com/hewittlawson/LC

Conclusion: An American Empire

In the final decade of the nineteenth century, the United States transformed itself into an imperial power. Presidents McKinley and Roosevelt carried out the strategy outlined by Captain Alfred Thayer Mahan to enlarge the navy, construct a canal linking the Atlantic and Pacific Oceans, and acquire coaling stations and bases in the Pacific to service the fleet. U.S. officials disregarded the nationalistic aspirations of freedom fighters such as José Martí in Cuba and Emilio Aguinaldo in the Philippines in favor of the imperial spoils gained from winning the War of 1898. The United States justified intervention on moral grounds predicated on racist beliefs: As a fit and manly nation, the United States had the responsibility to uplift inferior peoples to "civilized" standards and make them capable of self-government. This justification quickly wore thin. To crush the rebellion in the Philippines, the military engaged in atrocities that called into question the honor and virtue of the United States. Once it achieved victory in the Philippines, the nation concentrated its efforts on maintaining territories primarily for commercial purposes. Within the few short years from 1898 to 1904, this commercial empire had fallen into place.

The progressive presidents, Roosevelt and Wilson, created and sustained an American empire. They disagreed significantly in approach—Roosevelt favoring force, Wilson preferring negotiations; Roosevelt a realist, Wilson a moralist—but in practice they shared a willingness to use military power to protect national interests. These two presidents helped construct the modern American state, an expanded federal government that officially sanctioned cooperation with responsible corporate leaders. This relationship reached its peak during World War I. In mobilizing the home front, the Wilson administration blurred the line between public and private business by expanding the reach of government over the economy and curtailed personal liberty.

In 1917, because of its heavy reliance on trade with foreign countries, especially in Europe, the United States confronted its first major international crisis of the twentieth century. Wilson reluctantly led the country into war to guarantee a world order in which reasonable nations attempted to resolve controversies through negotiation, not violence. The failure of the United States to join the League of Nations, for which the president was largely responsible, shattered that idealistic dream.

The United States retreated from joining an international body offering collective security, but it did not isolate itself from participation in the world. The country emerged from the war in excellent financial shape; it had become the leading foreign creditor, and its industrial capacity had greatly expanded. Tending its commercial empire in the Caribbean and Central America, the United States probed for new markets in Asia and the Middle East. It would take another two decades for policymakers to realize that the country's refusal to support a strong collective response to expansionist aggression posed serious dangers for American commerce and values.

Chapter Review

Online Study Guide ▶ bedfordstmartins.com/hewittlawson

KEY TERMS

jingoists (p. 624)
Cuba Libre (p. 626)
yellow journalism (p. 627)
Teller Amendment (p. 628)
Platt Amendment (p. 628)
Anti-Imperialist League (p. 628)
Roosevelt Corollary (p. 631)
Open Door (p. 631)
dollar diplomacy (p. 633)
Mexican revolution (p. 634)
Zimmermann telegram (p. 635)
War Industries Board (WIB) (p. 637)
National War Labor Board (NWLB) (p. 638)
Committee on Public Information (CPI) (p. 639)
Espionage Act (p. 639)
Sedition Act (p. 639)
American Protective League (APL) (p. 639)
Fourteen Points (p. 639)
League of Nations (p. 640)

REVIEW & RELATE

1. What role did economic developments play in prompting calls for an American empire? What role did social and cultural developments play?

2. Why did the United States embark on building an empire in the 1890s and not decades earlier?

3. Why did the United States go to war with Spain in 1898?

4. In what ways did the War of 1898 mark a turning point in the relationship between the United States and the rest of the world?

5. How did the United States assert its influence and control over Latin America in the early twentieth century?

6. How did U.S. policies in Latin America mirror U.S. policies in Asia?

7. In what ways, if any, did President Wilson's approach to Latin American affairs differ from that of his predecessors?

8. Why did President Wilson find it so difficult to keep the United States out of World War I?

9. What steps did the U.S. government take to control the economy and public opinion during World War I?

10. How did President Wilson's wartime policies and his efforts to shape the peace that followed reflect his progressive roots?

TIMELINE OF EVENTS

1880–1900	U.S. creates third most powerful navy in the world
1890	Alfred Mahan publishes *The Influence of Sea Power upon History*
1893	American plantation owners overthrow Queen Liliuokalani of Hawaii
1895	Cuban War for Independence begins
1898	U.S. battleship *Maine* explodes
	The War of 1898 begins
	Anti-Imperialist League founded
1899–1902	Philippine-American War
1901	Platt Amendment passed
1904	Roosevelt Corollary announced
1909	U.S. intervenes in Nicaragua on behalf of American fruit and mining companies
1914	Panama Canal opens under American control
	World War I begins
1915	German submarine sinks the *Lusitania*
1916	Wilson sends U.S. troops into Mexico to capture Pancho Villa
1917	Zimmermann telegram becomes public
	United States enters World War I
	Espionage Act passed
	War Industries Board established
	Committee on Public Information established
1918	Sedition Act passed
	National War Labor Board established
	Germany surrenders, ending World War I
1919	Wilson loses battle for ratification of Treaty of Versailles

Imperialism versus Anti-Imperialism

On January 16, 1893, the USS *Boston* sailed into Honolulu harbor, in a show of support for American businessmen who were aligned against Queen Liliuokalani, Hawaii's ruling monarch. Liliuokalani sought to overturn the 1887 constitution that had been forced on King Kalākaua. This "Bayonet Constitution," as it came to be known, favored American and other foreign interests and limited the political power of native islanders, the poor, and the monarchy. The day after American forces landed, Liliuokalani abdicated and a provisional government, the Republic of Hawaii, was set up under the control of American sugar growers. Native Hawaiians continued to rebel against their American-dominated government, and in 1897 representatives from several political groups issued the Hawaiian Memorial (Document 20.6). This petition for self-rule failed, and Hawaii was formally annexed in 1898. In that same year, U.S. territorial acquisitions from the War of 1898 intensified the heated debate over American imperialism and the principles of self-governance and democracy.

The following documents reveal the viewpoints of imperialists, anti-imperialists, and colonized people. Those supporting imperialism could find no greater advocate than Senator Albert Beveridge of Indiana, who served from 1899 to 1911. His speech entitled "The March of the Flag," compared Philippine colonization to U.S. westward expansion across North America and argued that Filipinos were a childlike and savage race incapable of self-governance (Document 20.7). A different view of the Philippine conflict came from a New Hampshire woman who in 1899 wrote to her local newspaper to scold American women for failing to speak out against the "murderous, cowardly, dastardly war" in the Philippines (Document 20.9). Throughout this period—on the Senate floor and in town meeting halls, schoolrooms, national magazines, and local newspapers—Americans deliberated the significance and implications of international expansion.

DOCUMENT 20.6

The Hawaiian Memorial, 1897

Hawaiian political groups sent the following petition (also called a memorial) to the U.S. government as a formal request to remove the provisional government of the Hawaiian Islands, which they viewed as illegitimate. Although the U.S. Senate initially refused to ratify President McKinley's effort to annex Hawaii in 1897, the following year Congress adopted a joint resolution annexing Hawaii as a territory.

To the President, the Congress, and the People of the United States of America:

This Memorial respectfully represents as follows:

1. That your memorialists are residents of the Hawaiian Islands; that the majority of them are aboriginal Hawaiians; and that all of them possess the qualifications provided for electors of representatives in the Hawaiian Legislature by the Constitution and laws prevailing in the Hawaiian Islands at the date of the overthrow of the Hawaiian Constitutional Government, January 17, 1893.

2. That the supporters of the Hawaiian Constitution of 1887 have been, thence to the present time, in the year 1897, held in subjection by the armed forces of the Provisional Government of the Hawaiian Islands, and of its successor, the Republic of Hawaii, and have never yielded and do not acknowledge a spontaneous or willing allegiance or support to said Provisional Government, or to said Republic of Hawaii.

3. That the Government of the Republic of Hawaii has no warrant for its existence in the support of the people of these islands; that it was proclaimed and instituted and has hitherto existed and now exists without considering the rights and wishes of a great majority of the residents, native and foreign-born, of the Hawaiian Islands; and especially that said Government exists and maintains itself solely by force of arms, against the rights and wishes of almost the entire aboriginal population of these islands.

4. That said Republic is not and never has been founded or conducted upon a basis of popular government or republican principles; that its Constitution was adopted by a convention, a majority of whose members were self-appointed, and the balance of whose members were elected by a numerically insignificant minority of the white and aboriginal male citizens and residents of these islands. . . .

5. That the Constitution so adopted by said convention has never been submitted to a vote of the people of these islands, but was promulgated and established over the said islands, and has ever since been maintained only by force of arms, and with indifference to the will of practically the entire aboriginal population, and a vast majority of the whole population of these islands.

6. That the said Government, so existing under the title of the Republic of Hawaii, assumes and asserts the right to extinguish the Hawaiian nationality, heretofore existing, and to cede and convey all rights of sovereignty in and over the Hawaiian Islands and their dependencies to a foreign power, namely, to the United States of America.

7. That your memorialists have learned with grief and dismay that the President of the United States has entered into, and submitted for ratification by the United States Senate, a treaty with the Government of the Republic of Hawaii, whereby it is proposed to extinguish our existence as a nation, and to annex our territory to the United States. . . .

9. That your memorialists humbly but fervently protest against the consummation of this invasion of their political rights; and they earnestly appeal to the President, the Congress, and the people of the United States to refrain from further participating in the wrong so proposed; and they invoke in support of

(continued on page 646)

this memorial the spirit of that immortal instrument, the Declaration of American Independence; and especially the truth therein expressed, that governments derive their just powers from the consent of the governed—and here repeat that the consent of the people of the Hawaiian Islands to the forms of government imposed by the so-called Republic of Hawaii, and to said proposed treaty of annexation, has never been asked by and is not accorded, either to said government or to said project of annexation.

10. That the consummation of the project of annexation dealt with in said treaty would be subversive of the personal and political rights of these memorialists and of the Hawaiian people and nation. . . .

11. Wherefore your memorialists respectfully submit that they, no less than the citizens of any American Commonwealth, are entitled to select, ordain, and establish for themselves such forms of government as to them shall seem most likely to effect their safety and happiness. . . .

12. And your memorialists humbly pray the President, Congress, and the people of the United States that no further steps be taken toward the ratification of said treaty, or toward the extinguishment of the Hawaiian nationality, or toward the absorption of the Hawaiian people and territory into the body politic and territory of the United States of America, at least until the Hawaiian people, as represented by those citizens and residents of the Hawaiian Islands who, under the provisions of the Hawaiian Constitution, promulgated July 7, 1887, would be qualified to vote for representatives in the Legislature, shall have had the opportunity to express, at the ballot-box, their wishes as to whether such project of annexation shall be accepted or rejected.

13. And your memorialists, for themselves, and in behalf of the Hawaiian people and of the residents of the Hawaiian Islands, pledge their faith that if they shall be accorded the privilege of voting upon said questions, at a free and fair election to be held for that purpose, and if a fair count of the votes that shall be cast at such election shall show a majority in favor of such annexation, these memorialists and the Hawaiian people will yield a ready and cheerful acquiescence in said project.

Signed

J. Kalua Kahookano, Samuel K. Pua, F. J. Testa, C. B. Maile, Samuel K. Kamakaia, Citizens' Committee

James Keauiluna Kaulia, President of the Hawaiian Patriotic League

David Kalauokalani, President of the Hawaiian Political Association

Source: "The Hawaiian Memorial," *City and State*, December 2, 1897, 143.

DOCUMENT 20.7

Albert Beveridge | The March of the Flag, 1898

In September 1898, Albert Beveridge, who was campaigning to become U.S. senator from Indiana, gave a rousing speech supporting the annexation of Spain's former colonies. At the time of this address, the war with Spain had ended, but American troops still occupied the Philippines. Once in office, Beveridge was an ardent supporter of American imperial policies.

HAWAII IS OURS; Porto Rico is to be ours; at the prayer of her people Cuba finally will be ours; in the islands of the East, even to the gates of Asia, coaling stations are to be ours at the very least; the flag of a liberal government is to float over the Philippines, and may it be the banner that [Zachary] Taylor unfurled in Texas and [John] Fremont carried to the coast.

The Opposition tells us that we ought not to govern a people without their consent. I answer, the rule of liberty that all just government derives its authority from the consent of the governed, applies only to those who are capable of self-government. We govern the Indians without their consent, we govern our territories without their consent, we govern our children without their consent. How do they know [what] our government would be without their consent? Would not the people of the Philippines prefer the just, humane, civilizing government of this Republic to the savage, bloody rule of pillage and extortion from which we have rescued them?

And, regardless of this formula of words made only for enlightened, self-governing people, do we owe no duty to the world? Shall we turn these peoples back to the reeking hands from which we have taken them? Shall we abandon them, with Germany, England, Japan, hungering for them? Shall we save them from those nations, to give them a self-rule of tragedy?

They ask us how we shall govern these new possessions. I answer: Out of local conditions and the necessities of the case, methods of government will grow. If England can govern foreign lands, so can America. If Germany can govern foreign lands, so can America. If they can supervise protectorates, so can America. Why is it more difficult to administer Hawaii than New Mexico or California? Both had a savage and an alien population; both were more remote from the seat of government when they came under our dominion than the Philippines are today.

Will you say by your vote that American ability to govern has decayed; that a century's experience in self-rule has failed of a result? Will you affirm by your vote that you are an infidel to American power and practical sense? Or will you say that ours is the blood of government; ours the heart of dominion; ours the brain and genius of administration? Will you remember that we do but what our fathers did—we but pitch the tents of liberty farther westward, farther southward—we only continue the march of the flag?

The march of the flag! In 1789 the flag of the Republic waved over 4,000,000 souls in thirteen states, and their savage territory which stretched to the Mississippi, to Canada, to the Floridas. The timid minds of that day said that no new territory was needed, and, for the hour, they were right. But Jefferson, through whose intellect the centuries marched; Jefferson, who dreamed of Cuba as an American state; Jefferson, the first Imperialist of the Republic—Jefferson acquired that imperial territory which swept from the Mississippi to the mountains, from Texas to the British possessions, and the march of the flag began!

The infidels to the gospel of liberty raved, but the flag swept on! The title to that noble land out of which Oregon, Washington, Idaho, and Montana have been carved was uncertain; Jefferson, strict constructionist of constitutional power though he was, obeyed the Anglo-Saxon impulse within him, whose watchword then and whose watchword throughout the world today is, "Forward!": another empire was added to the Republic, and the march of the flag went on! . . .

(continued on page 648)

The ocean does not separate us from lands of our duty and desire—the oceans join us, rivers never to be dredged, canals never to be repaired. Steam joins us; electricity joins us—the very elements are in league with our destiny. Cuba not contiguous! Porto Rico not contiguous! Hawaii and the Philippines not contiguous! The oceans make them contiguous. And our navy will make them contiguous.

But the Opposition is right—there is a difference. We did not need the western Mississippi Valley when we acquired it, nor Florida, nor Texas, nor California, nor the royal provinces of the far northwest. We had no emigrants to people this imperial wilderness, no money to develop it, even no highways to cover it. No trade awaited us in its savage fastnesses [remote places]. Our productions were not greater than our trade. There was not one reason for the land-lust of our statesmen from Jefferson to Grant, other than the prophet and the Saxon within them. But, today, we are raising more than we can consume, making more than we can use. Therefore we must find new markets for our produce.

And so, while we did not need the territory taken during the past century at the time it was acquired, we do need what we have taken in 1898, and we need it now. The resources and the commerce of these immensely rich dominions will be increased as much as American energy is greater than Spanish sloth. In Cuba, alone, there are 15,000,000 acres of forest unacquainted with the ax, exhaustless mines of iron, priceless deposits of manganese, millions of dollars' worth of which we must buy, today, from the Black Sea districts. There are millions of acres yet unexplored.

The resources of Porto Rico have only been trifled with. The riches of the Philippines have hardly been touched by the fingertips of modern methods. And they produce what we consume, and consume what we produce—the very predestination of reciprocity—a reciprocity "not made with hands, eternal in the heavens." They sell hemp, sugar, cocoanuts, fruits of the tropics, timber of price like mahogany; they buy flour, clothing, tools, implements, machinery, and all that we can raise and make. Their trade will be ours in time. Do you indorse that policy with your vote?

Source: Albert J. Beveridge, *The Meaning of the Times and Other Speeches* (Indianapolis: Bobbs-Merrill, 1908), 48–50, 52–53.

DOCUMENT 20.8

"There's Plenty of Room at the Table," 1906

The satirical weekly magazine *Judge* was a strong supporter of President McKinley and the Republican Party. Its illustrations often depicted imperial expansion as good for the American public as well as for colonized nations.

THERE'S PLENTY OF ROOM AT THE TABLE. WHY NOT ASK THE HUNGRY LITTLE FELLOW TO SIT DOWN?

DOCUMENT 20.9

Anti-Imperialism Letter, 1899

What began in 1898 as a conflict to free the Philippines from Spanish control quickly became a struggle to subdue Filipino rebels intent on establishing their own government. The following letter was written to the *Springfield (Massachusetts) Republican* just one month after the new Philippine Republic declared war on the United States. The brutality of the fighting caused many Americans to question the motives and methods of American imperial aspirations.

To The Editor of the Republican:

I cannot longer hold my peace, though only a woman. I am thankful to see today that the business men (some of them, I should say) have started a plan for the cessation of this murderous, cowardly, dastardly war. Also I saw yesterday that Gamaliel Bradford [an American writer and poet] has volunteered to speak in the same just and holy cause wheresoever needed. This is the thing I have longed to see done weeks and weeks ago. The "peace" treaty never would have been ratified if the nation had been waked up to the meaning of its iniquity. Speaking everywhere is needed, such as we had at the beginning of the civil war, giving light to the thousands that now do not care. "It is no business of theirs." "Congress will take care," they say, reading the papers that hurrah for McKinley. What do they know about it? They don't feel the burden much yet. Taxes are bad enough, but those that must come with the McKinley policy long continued, they don't feel yet. It is healthy for all they see out there, none of theirs have died, and it's only the Filipinos mostly that are killed: and we are to be a "bigger country." What the whole country needs is to rouse the people, that they demand that this sin shall cease, that America's shame may be wiped out ere it is too late!

I blush for my sisters who call themselves "Colonial Dames," "Daughters of the Revolution," "Abraham Lincoln circle of the Ladies of the Grand Army," and such patriotic sounding titles, where is their claim to such? In all these months of anxiety and anguish never one word of protest have I heard of their breathing! They have gathered for various social reasons and held good times, but the solemn duties and responsibilities that should be their first concern seem to have been utterly ignored. Cannot they be induced to begin likewise an appeal in every place where their orders exist, signed by every woman who has at heart the love of her country and its true honor. Only that something should be done! While we wait the islanders are being murdered by hundreds and a price put on the head of their brave leader!

J. W. P.

Source: Letter to the editor, *Springfield Republican*, March 16, 1899.

DOCUMENT 20.10

"Civilization Begins at Home," 1898

Newspapers and magazines waged their own battles for and against U.S. expansion overseas. The *New York World* built its circulation through sensationalism and the extensive use of illustrations. This cartoon from the *World* questions the imperialist mission to spread the benefits of civilization to "uncivilized" parts of the world. While President McKinley contemplates a map of the Philippines, Lady Justice reveals racial problems at home.

"CIVILIZATION BEGINS AT HOME."   *THE WORLD — NEW YORK*

General Research Division, The New York Public Library, Astor, Lenox and Tilden Foundations

Interpret the Evidence

1. Why do the petitioners of the Hawaiian Memorial (Document 20.6) claim that the provisional government is illegitimate? How do they describe their government and people before annexation, and how do they characterize the United States?

2. Why does Albert Beveridge claim that it is the United States' duty to colonize the Philippines, and what does he think are the benefits to Americans and Filipinos (Document 20.7)? How does he respond to the anti-imperialist argument that America shouldn't govern a people without their consent?

3. What common arguments against American colonization connect the Hawaiian Memorial (Document 20.6), the letter from J. W. P. (Document 20.9), and the cartoon "Civilization Begins at Home" (Document 20.10)?

4. How do imperialists and anti-imperialists portray each other in these documents?

5. How are the sentiments of Rudyard Kipling (Document 20.1) and Theodore Roosevelt (Document 20.2) echoed in these imperialist arguments?

6. How did imperialists and anti-imperialists shape their arguments to appeal to either men or women?

Put It in Context

- Why did the arguments of the imperialists prevail over those of anti-imperialists from 1898 to 1904? In what ways do you think the anti-imperialist arguments might have contributed to reshaping the imperialist cause after that time?

background photo: page 648, Library of Congress

The Granger Collection, New York

The Granger Collection, New York

Three women strolling on Seventh Avenue in Harlem, 1927.

Cover of *Vanity Fair* magazine, December 1927.

21

An Anxious Affluence

1919–1929

Library of Congress

Prohibition agents pouring out liquor in New York City, c. 1921.

AMERICAN HISTORIES

David Curtis (D. C.) Stephenson's relentless pursuit of the American dream kept him constantly on the move. Born in 1891 to Texas sharecroppers, Stephenson moved with his family to the Oklahoma Territory in 1901. After quitting school at age sixteen, he drifted around the state for more than a decade, working for a string of newspapers and gaining a reputation as a heavy drinker and a ladies' man. In 1915 he married and appeared to settle down; however, he soon lost his newspaper job, abandoned his pregnant wife, and hit the road working for one newspaper after another in between binges of drunkenness. His wife divorced him, and in 1917 Stephenson joined the army to fight in World War I. He was stationed stateside, but his service was marked by a series of drunken brawls and sexual misadventures. Nevertheless, he rose to the rank of second lieutenant and received an honorable discharge in 1919.

Stephenson remarried and settled in Indiana, where he finally found financial and political success. In 1920 he joined the Ku Klux Klan (KKK), the Reconstruction-era organization that had reemerged in 1915 in Georgia. The newly revived Klan spread beyond the South, targeting African Americans, recent immigrants, Jews, and Catholics as enemies of traditional Protestant family values. Stephenson directed Klan operations in twenty-three states, building a profitable empire on fear and prejudice as well as get-rich-quick schemes that appealed to the spirit of American adventure. A few years later, however, his old pattern of self-destruction led to his arrest and conviction on rape and

653

second-degree murder charges and the end of his Klan career.

Ossian Sweet also pursued the American dream. Like Stephenson, he rose from humble beginnings, but he had far more to overcome. The descendant of slaves, Sweet was born in 1895 and grew up in the central Florida town of Bartow. Hoping to shield him from the violence that whites used to keep Bartow's blacks in their place, Sweet's parents sent him north when he was thirteen years old to get an education.

After attending Wilberforce University in Ohio and Howard Medical School in Washington, D.C., Sweet moved to Detroit in 1921 to open a medical practice in the city's ghetto known as "Black Bottom." He married, and in 1924 the Sweets decided to buy a house for their growing family, which now included an infant daughter, in a working-class neighborhood occupied exclusively by whites. Before the Sweets moved in, their white neighbors, with Klan backing, began organizing to keep them out.

D. C. Stephenson and Ossian Sweet

When the Sweet family finally moved into their house on September 8, 1925, they encountered a hostile crowd in the street. Dr. Sweet had brought some backup with him, including two of his younger brothers and several friends. Armed in case the mob got out of hand, the Sweets and their defenders fired their weapons at the crowd after rocks smashed through the upstairs windows of the house. When the shooting stopped and the police restored calm, one white man lay dead and another wounded. Dr. Sweet, his wife Gladys, and the other nine occupants of his house went on trial on first-degree murder charges. The NAACP represented the eleven defendants and hired the famous criminal defense attorney Clarence Darrow. After two trials—the first ended in a hung jury—Darrow won an acquittal for his clients in 1926. •

photos: © Bettmann/CORBIS; Courtesy of the Burton Historical Collection, Detroit Public Library

THE AMERICAN HISTORIES of Ossian Sweet and D. C. Stephenson illustrate the competing forces that shaped the 1920s. Both achieved a measure of financial success, but they did so in the post–World War I atmosphere of growing social friction and intense racial resentments. After serving in the war, many blacks and ethnic minorities had a greater sense of pride in themselves. When Sweet's parents decided to send him north to get an education, they were responding to the racial violence that plagued the South, but they were also demonstrating their belief that a better life was possible for their son. By contrast, Stephenson grew wealthy by tapping into the same racial tensions that shaped the Sweets' lives. Just as the census of 1890 had announced the end of the frontier, the census of 1920 indicated that the population of rural America had dwindled and that the majority of Americans now lived in cities with more than 2,500 people. Many who considered themselves "100 percent Americans," born and bred in small towns or living in

sections of cities with homogeneous populations, believed that racial and ethnic minorities threatened their power. Although the general prosperity of the period masked the tensions lying beneath the surface, it did not eliminate them. As the experiences of D. C. Stephenson and Ossian Sweet show, the decade following the end of World War I opened up fresh avenues for economic prosperity as well as new sites for cultural clashes exacerbated by the tensions of modern America.

Postwar Turmoil

The return of peace in 1918 brought with it problems that would persist into the 1920s. Government efforts to suppress opposition to U.S. involvement in World War I fostered an atmosphere of repression that continued after the war ended, culminating in a wave of anti-Communist actions known as the Red scare. An influenza epidemic that killed hundreds of thousands of Americans and millions of people around the world heightened the climate of fear. Finally, the abrupt and painful transition away from a wartime economy produced inflation, labor unrest, and escalating racial tensions. The 1920s would come to be known as a decade of prosperity, but in the years immediately following the war the prospects for growth and stability seemed bleak.

The Supreme Court and Civil Liberties

On March 3, 1919, the Supreme Court invoked the Espionage Act to uphold the conviction of Charles Schenck, the general secretary of the Socialist Party, for mailing thousands of leaflets opposing the military draft. Delivering the Court's unanimous opinion, Justice Oliver Wendell Holmes argued that during wartime Congress has the authority to prohibit individuals from using words that create "a clear and present danger" to the safety of the country. Although the trial record failed to show that Schenck's leaflets had convinced any young men to resist conscription, the Court upheld his conviction under Holmes's doctrine.

Later in 1919, the Supreme Court demonstrated what a slippery slope the "clear and present danger" test presented for freedom of speech in a case that concerned what many American leaders believed posed a great threat to the nation: the spread of worldwide communism, the system of government that challenged capitalism. The success of the Bolshevik Revolution in Russia in 1917 and the subsequent creation of the Union of Soviet Socialist Republics terrified officials of capitalist countries in western Europe and the United States. Their concerns escalated in 1918, when Russia, until then an Allied power, signed a separate treaty with Germany and pulled out of the war (see chapter 20). In response, President Woodrow Wilson ordered U.S. troops to assist anti-Communist Russian forces fighting against the Bolshevik regime.

Wilson's actions generated vocal opposition from American supporters of the Russian Revolution. In New York City, a small group of anarchists and socialists welcomed the fall of capitalism in Russia and the prospects of a worker-controlled state that would promote economic democracy. Many of these activists were immigrants who had fled from Russia to avoid czarist repression against political dissidents and Jews. In August 1918, a handful of anarchists, including Jacob Abrams, dropped leaflets off a building on the Lower East Side urging workers to protest "barbaric [American] intervention" and calling on them to engage in "a general strike" until the United States removed its troops from Russia. The government prosecuted six defendants, five men and one woman, for violating the Espionage and Sedition Acts; the jury found all of them

guilty. On November 10, 1919, in *Abrams v. United States*, the Supreme Court affirmed the trial verdict, finding the distribution of the incendiary leaflets in wartime illegal.

See Document Project 21: The *Abrams* Case and the Red Scare, page 677.

The Red Scare, 1919–1920

The conviction in the *Abrams* case reflected broader concern over the **Red scare**—the fear of Communist-inspired radicalism in the wake of the Russian Revolution. Though communism failed to gain a foothold in the United States, the actions of a tiny contingent of radicals kept the threat alive and played into the hands of ambitious politicians and business leaders who wanted to crush labor agitation, which they perceived as anti-American.

Immediate postwar economic problems further increased the anxiety of American citizens, reinforcing the position of officials who sought to restore order by suppressing radicals. Industries were slow to convert their plants from military to civilian production, and consumer goods therefore remained in short supply. The war had brought jobs and higher wages on the home front, and consumers who had been restrained by wartime rationing were eager to spend their savings. With demand greatly exceeding supply, however, prices soared by 77 percent, frustrating consumers. At the same time, farmers, who had benefited from wartime conditions, faced falling crop prices as European nations resumed agricultural production and the federal government ended price supports.

A series of widespread strikes launched by labor unions in 1919 contributed to the fear that the United States was under assault by sinister, radical forces. As skyrocketing inflation undercut wages and employers launched a new round of union-busting efforts, labor went on the offensive. In 1919 more than four million workers went on strike nationwide, including those in key industries such as steel, transportation, and shipbuilding. In September, striking Boston policemen left the city unguarded, resulting in widespread looting and violence. Massachusetts governor Calvin Coolidge sent in the National Guard to break the strike and restore order.

Public officials and newspapers decried the violence, but they also greatly exaggerated the peril. Communists and socialists did support some union activities; however, few of the millions of workers who struck for higher wages and better working conditions had ties to extremists or sought to overthrow capitalism. The major prewar radical organization, the Industrial Workers of the World, never recovered from the government harassment that had crippled it during World War I. Postwar Communist parties in the United States claimed fewer than seventy thousand followers. However, scattered acts of real violence allowed government and business leaders to stir up anxieties about the Communist threat. On May 1, 1919, radicals sent more than thirty incendiary devices through the mail to prominent Americans, though authorities defused them before the mail bombs reached their intended targets. The following month, bombs exploded in eight cities, including one at the doorstep of the home of A. Mitchell Palmer, the attorney general of the United States, who emerged shocked but uninjured.

After the attack on his home, Palmer launched a government crusade to root out and prosecute Communist extremists. Like many American officials, Palmer traced the source of radicalism to recent immigrants, mainly those from Russia and eastern and southern Europe. To track down what he called the "moral perverts and hysterical neurasthenic [neurotic] women who abound in communism," Palmer selected J. Edgar Hoover,

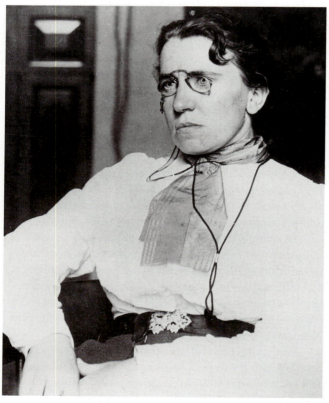

Emma Goldman

Emma Goldman was a Russian anarchist who immigrated to the United States in 1885. She challenged capitalism and led campaigns in support of industrial workers and women's sexual and political freedom. An outspoken critic of World War I and the military draft, "Red Emma" was deported to Russia in 1919 after a roundup of alien radicals by the Justice Department.   The Granger Collection, New York

a young Washington, D.C., lawyer, to head the General Intelligence Division in the Department of Justice. In November 1919, based on Hoover's research and undercover activities, government agents in twelve cities rounded up and arrested hundreds of foreigners, including the anarchist and feminist Emma Goldman. Goldman, along with some 250 people caught in the government dragnet, were soon deported to Russia. Over the next few months, the **Palmer raids** continued in more than thirty cities. Authorities seized approximately six thousand suspected radicals from their homes and community centers, took them to police stations, interrogated them without the benefit of legal counsel, and held them incommunicado without stipulating the charges against them. Of the thousands arrested, the government found reason to deport 556. The raids failed to uncover extensive plots to overthrow the U.S. government, nor did they lead to the arrest of the bombers.

Initially, most American citizens supported the Palmer raids, but their enthusiasm quickly waned. Many came to see the violations of civil liberties that accompanied the raids as a greater threat to the nation's traditions than the existence of a handful of American Communists. In 1920 a group of pacifists, progressives, and constitutional lawyers formed the American Civil Liberties Union (ACLU) to monitor government abridgments of the Bill of Rights. Although the Palmer raids ended, the Red scare manifested itself in different forms throughout the 1920s. After J. Edgar Hoover became director of the Bureau of Investigation (later renamed the Federal Bureau of Investigation) in 1921, he continued spying on suspected radicals, collecting information on a variety of Americans, and increasing his power over the next several decades.

Compounding the anxieties fueled by the Red scare, a medical crisis plunged Americans into panic. In late 1918, just as World War I was ending, an influenza epidemic struck the United States. Part of a worldwide contagion, the disease infected nearly 20 percent of the U.S. population and killed more than 675,000 people. Soldiers returning home from the war brought the flu virus with them. Infants and the elderly succumbed, as well as able-bodied young men and women. As the death toll mounted over the course of 1919, terror gripped the nation. Susanna Turner, a volunteer at an emergency hospital in Philadelphia, recalled: "The fear in the hearts of people just withered them. They were afraid to go out, afraid to do anything. If you asked a neighbor for help, they wouldn't do so because they weren't taking any chances. It was a horror-stricken time." A staggering 50 to 100 million people worldwide are estimated to have died from the flu before it subsided in 1920.

Racial Violence in the Postwar Era

Racial strife also heightened postwar anxieties. Drawn by the promise of wartime industrial jobs, more than 400,000 African Americans left the South beginning in 1917 and 1918 and headed north hoping to escape poverty and racial discrimination. (By 1930 another 800,000 blacks had left the South.) This exodus became known as the **great migration**. Black newspapers such as the *Chicago Defender* circulated throughout the South, offering glowing stories of the opportunities that adventurous blacks would find if they moved. Some 75,000 southern blacks heeded the call and relocated to Chicago. During World War I, many found work in steel mills, meatpacking, shipbuilding, and other heavy industries, but most were relegated to low-paying jobs. Still, as a carpenter earning $95 a month wrote from Chicago to a friend back in Hattiesburg, Mississippi: "I should have been here 20 years ago. I just begin to feel like a man." Most African American women remained employed as domestic workers, but more than 100,000 obtained manufacturing jobs.

For many blacks, however, the North was not the "promised land" they expected. Instead, they encountered bitter opposition from white migrants from the South competing for employment and scarce housing. As black and white veterans returned from the war, racial hostilities exploded. In 1919 race riots erupted in twenty-five cities throughout the country, including one in Washington, D.C., that left a deep impression on Ossian Sweet, who witnessed it firsthand.

The worst of these disturbances occurred in Chicago during what James Weldon Johnson, a poet and an NAACP official, called "Red Summer." On a hot July day, a black youth swimming at a Lake Michigan beach inadvertently crossed over into an area of water customarily reserved for whites. In response, white bathers shouted at the swimmer to return to the black section of the beach. To make their

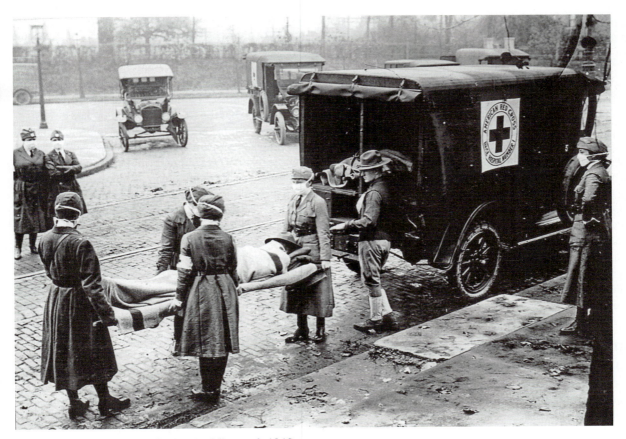

The Influenza Epidemic, St. Louis, Missouri, 1918

When the influenza epidemic hit Missouri in October 1918, the mayor of St. Louis closed "all theaters, moving picture shows, schools, pool and billiard halls, Sunday schools, cabarets, lodges, societies [churches], public funerals, open air meetings, dance halls and conventions." Despite these precautions and efforts by the Red Cross, within a month more than 21,000 people in Missouri became ill, and 500 perished. © akg-images/The Image Works point more forcefully, they hurled stones at him. The black swimmer drowned, and word of the incident quickly spread through white and black neighborhoods in Chicago. For thirteen days, mobs of blacks and whites attacked each other, ransacked businesses, and torched homes. Over the course of the riots, at least 15 whites and 23 blacks died, 178 whites and 342 blacks were injured, and more than a thousand black families were left homeless. Against this background, D. C. Stephenson's Ku Klux Klan began to flourish in the North.

REVIEW & RELATE

What factors combined to produce the turmoil of the immediate postwar period?

What factors contributed to the rise in racial tensions that accompanied the transition from wartime to peacetime?

 LEARNINGCurve bedfordstmartins.com/hewittlawson/LC

People of Plenty

Despite the turbulence of the immediate postwar period and the persistence of underlying social and racial tensions, the 1920s were a time of vigorous economic growth. Between 1922 and 1927, the economy grew by 7 percent a year, the largest peacetime rate up to that point. Over the decade, the gross domestic product (then called the gross national product), per capita income, and the average purchasing power of wage earners all soared. At the same time, unemployment rates remained low, as producers added new workers in an effort to keep up with increasing consumer demand. Aligning themselves with big business, government officials took an active role in stimulating economic growth. Their efforts shaped and accelerated economic developments that amounted to a second industrial revolution.

Government Promotion of the Economy

The general prosperity of the 1920s owed a great deal to backing by the federal government. Republicans controlled the presidency and Congress, and though they claimed to stand for principles of laissez-faire and opposed various economic and social reforms, they were willing to use governmental power to support large corporations and the wealthy.

Senator Warren G. Harding of Ohio, who was elected president in 1920, pledged to restore "normalcy" after World War I and the tumult of the Red scare. Summing up

the Republican philosophy, Harding declared that he and his party wanted "less government in business and more business in government." Harding's cabinet appointments reflected this goal. Treasury Secretary Andrew Mellon, a banker and an aluminum company titan, believed that the government should stimulate economic growth by reducing taxes on the rich, raising tariffs to protect manufacturers from foreign competition, and trimming the budget. The Republican Congress enacted much of this agenda, reducing spending and lowering inheritance and corporate taxes. During the Harding administration, tax rates for the wealthy, which had skyrocketed during World War I, plummeted from 66 percent to 20 percent. Mellon believed that those on the lower rungs of the economic ladder would prosper once business people invested the extra money they received from tax breaks into expanding production. Supposedly, the wealth would trickle down through increased jobs and purchasing power. At the same time, Republicans turned Progressive Era regulatory agencies such as the Federal Trade Commission and the Federal Reserve Board into boosters for major corporations and financial institutions by weakening regulatory enforcement.

Secretary of Commerce Herbert Hoover had an even greater impact than Mellon in cementing the government-business partnership during the 1920s. A progressive who ably headed the Food Administration during World War I, Hoover believed that the federal government had a role to play in the economy and in lessening economic suffering. Rejecting government control of business activities, however, he insisted on voluntary cooperation between the public and private sectors. The secretary of commerce favored the creation of trade associations in which businesses would collaborate to stabilize production levels, prices, and wages. In turn, the Commerce Department would provide helpful data and information to improve productivity and trade.

Hoover's vision fit into a larger Republican effort to weaken unions by promoting voluntary business-sponsored worker welfare initiatives. For example, under the **American Plan** (the name itself implied that unions were "un-American"), some firms established health insurance and pension plans for their workers. As early as 1914, Henry Ford provided his autoworkers over twenty-two years old "a share in the profits of the house" equal to a minimum wage of $5 a day, and he cut the workday from nine hours to eight hours. Already under pressure from such tactics, unions were further damaged by a series of Supreme Court rulings that restricted strikes and overturned hard-won union victories such as child labor legislation and minimum wage laws. By 1929 union membership had dropped from approximately five million to three million, or about 10 percent of the industrial labor market.

Modern Technology and the Pioneer Spirit

From left to right sit Henry Ford, Thomas Edison, President Warren G. Harding, and Harvey Firestone on a camping trip in Maryland in 1921. Through their inventions and technological innovations, Ford, Edison, and Firestone changed the way Americans lived at the beginning of the twentieth century.   Ohio Historical Society

Scandals during the presidency of Warren G. Harding diminished its luster but did not tarnish the shine of Republican economic policy. The **Teapot Dome scandal** grabbed the most headlines. In 1921 Interior Secretary Albert Fall collaborated with Navy Secretary Edwin Denby to transfer naval oil reserves to the Interior Department. Fall then parceled out these properties to private companies. As a result, Harry F. Sinclair's Mammoth Oil Company received a lease to develop the Teapot Dome section in Wyoming. In return for this handout, Sinclair delivered more than $300,000, much of it in cash, to Fall. In the wake of congressional hearings launched by Senator Thomas J. Walsh of Montana, one of the few progressives remaining in Congress, Fall and Sinclair were convicted on a number of criminal charges and sent to jail.

Harding's sudden death from a heart attack in August 1923 brought Vice President Calvin Coolidge to the presidency. The former Massachusetts governor, who had sent state troops to quell the Boston police strike in 1919, distanced himself from the scandals of his predecessor's administration but reaffirmed Harding's economic policies. "The chief business of the American people is business," President Coolidge remarked succinctly.

Americans Become Consumers

The 1920s marked a period of economic expansion and general prosperity. National income rose from approximately $63 billion to $88 billion and per capita income jumped from $641 to $847, an increase of 32 percent. The purchasing power of wage earners climbed approximately 20 percent.

This great spurt of economic growth in the 1920s resulted from the application of technological innovation and scientific management techniques to industrial production (Figure 21.1). Perhaps the greatest innovation came with the introduction of the assembly line. First used in the automobile industry before World War I, the assembly line moved the product to a worker who performed a specific task before sending it along to the

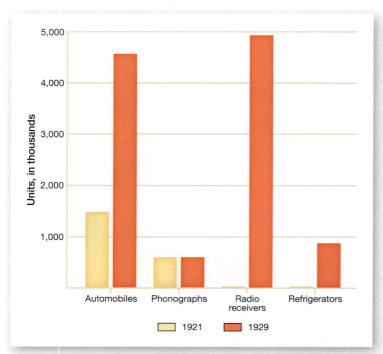

FIGURE 21.1   Production of Consumer Goods, 1921 and 1929
Rising per capita income, lower manufacturing costs, urban electrification, and advertising spurred the production of consumer goods in the 1920s. The most popular new items—automobiles and radios—brought Americans together through better transportation and communication.

Although such household items changed the lives of many Americans, no single product had as profound an effect on American life in the 1920s as the automobile. Auto sales soared in the 1920s from 1.5 million to 5 million, making Henry Ford a multimillionaire and fueling the growth of related industries such as steel, rubber, petroleum, and glass. In 1929 Ford and his competitors at General Motors, Chevrolet, and Oldsmobile employed nearly 4 million workers, and around one in eight American workers toiled in factories connected to automobile production.

The automobile also changed day-to-day living patterns. Although most roads and highways consisted of dirt and contained rocks and ruts, enough were paved to extend the boundaries of suburbs farther from the city. By the end of the 1920s, around 17 percent of Americans lived in suburbia. Cars allowed families to travel to vacation destinations at greater distances from their homes. Even the roadside landscape changed to accommodate weary travelers, as gas stations, diners, and motels sprang up to serve them, and advertisers constructed billboards along the roads to remind them of what they needed. Each year, vacation resorts on the east and west coasts of Florida attracted thousands of tourists who drove south to enjoy the state's balmy climate and beautiful beaches. The use of automobile technology blended the conveniences of modern America with the primitiveness of the environment. Outdoor camping became the craze.

The automobile also provided new dating opportunities for young men and women. At the turn of the twentieth century, a young man courted a woman by going to her home and sitting with her on the sofa or out on the porch under the watchful eyes of her parents and family members. When the couple left the house, they might walk to a park and listen to a bandstand concert, again in the company of others. With the arrival of the automobile, couples could move from the couch in the parlor to the backseat of a car, away from adult supervision. Driving to a "lover's lane" in a Model T and drinking from a flask of prohibited alcohol, the young couple could explore new sexual terrain that had been denied them in the past (most likely "petting"—kissing and rubbing rather than intercourse).

Although Ford and his fellow manufacturers had succeeded in lowering prices for consumers, they still had to convince Americans to spend their hard-earned money to purchase their products. Turning for help to New York City's Madison Avenue, the location of the fledgling advertising industry, manufacturers nearly tripled their spending on advertising over the course of the 1920s. Firms

next worker. This deceptively simple system, perfected by Henry Ford, saved enormous time and energy by emphasizing repetition, accuracy, and standardization. As a result, a new car rolled out of one of Ford's auto plants in less than a minute—earlier it had taken twelve and a half hours. Streamlined production lowered costs, which, in turn, allowed Ford to lower prices. The price of a new Model T dropped from $725 in 1910 to $290 in the early 1920s.

Besides the automobile, the **second industrial revolution** focused on the production of consumer-oriented goods previously considered luxuries. The electrification of urban homes created demand for a wealth of new laborsaving appliances; rural areas, most of which lacked electricity, did not benefit. Refrigerators, washing machines, toasters, and vacuum cleaners appealed to middle-class housewives whose husbands could afford to purchase them. Wristwatches replaced bulkier pocket watches. Radios became the chief source of home entertainment, and families gathered around the radio console to listen to music, news, and sports. Religious and political radio programs helped spread their particular faiths and ideologies, and those farmers equipped with electricity depended on the radio for weather reports and agricultural prices.

pitched their products around price and quality, but they directed their efforts more than ever to the personal psychology of the consumer. Advertisers played on consumers' unexpressed fears, unfulfilled desires, hopes for success, and sexual fantasies. The producers of Listerine mouthwash transformed a product previously used to disinfect hospitals into one that fought the dreaded but made-up disease of halitosis (bad breath). Advertisers told people that they could measure success through consumption. Purchasing a General Electric (GE) all-steel refrigerator not only would preserve food longer but also would enhance the owners' reputation among their neighbors. "Happy to own it . . . proud to show it" headlined one ad explaining the virtues of GE's new product.

Explore

See Document 21.1 for a typical GE advertisement from 1928.

Although average wages and incomes rose during the 1920s, the majority of Americans did not have the disposable income to afford the bounty of new consumer goods. To resolve this problem, companies extended credit in dizzying amounts. By 1929 consumers purchased 60 percent of their cars and 80 percent of their radios and furniture on credit in the form of installment plans and owed a total of $3 billion. "Buy now and pay later" became the motto of corporate America. By putting a small amount down and making monthly payments with interest, people could obtain an assortment of consumer items they otherwise could not afford.

Perilous Prosperity

Prosperity in the 1920s was real enough, but behind the impressive financial indicators flashed warnings that profound danger loomed ahead. Perhaps most important, the boom was accompanied by growing income inequality. A majority of workers lived below the poverty line, and farmers plunged deeper into hard times. Corporate profits increased much faster than wages, resulting in a disproportionate share of the wealth going to the rich. The combined income of the top 1 percent of families was greater than that of the 42 percent at the bottom (Figure 21.2); 66 percent lived below the income level ($1,800 to $2,000 annually) necessary to maintain an adequate standard of living. In addition, less than 1 percent of families accumulated 34 percent of the nation's savings, while around 78 percent of families had no savings at all.

Income inequality was a critical problem because America's new mass-production economy depended on ever-increasing consumption, and higher income groups

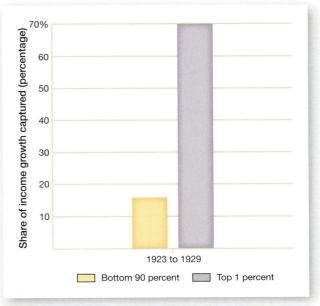

FIGURE 21.2   Income Inequality, 1923–1929

Although the U.S. economy expanded rapidly in the early 1920s, the accumulation of vast wealth among a small percentage of Americans created growing inequality. Although most Americans could purchase new consumer goods only by buying on credit, the richest 1 percent engaged in risky stock and real estate ventures to further enhance their wealth.

could consume only so much, no matter how much of the nation's wealth they controlled. While the expansion of consumer credit helped hide this fundamental weakness, the low wages earned by most Americans drove down demand over time. Cutbacks in demand forced manufacturers to reduce production, thereby reducing jobs and increasing unemployment. In the days before unemployment insurance, this placed an increased burden on families to make ends meet and dragged down the demand for consumer goods even further. By 1926, as a result of lagging purchasing power, the growth of automobile sales had begun to slow, as did new housing construction—signs of an economy heading for trouble.

At the same time, the wealthy few used their disproportionate savings to speculate in the stock market and risky real estate ventures. To encourage investments, brokers promoted buying stocks on margin (credit) and required down payments of only a fraction of the market price. Without vigilant governmental oversight, banks and lending agencies extended credit without taking into account what would happen if a financial panic occurred and they were suddenly required to call in all of their loans. To make matters worse, the banking system operated on shaky financial grounds, combining savings facilities with speculative lending operations. With minimal interference from the

General Electric Refrigerator Advertisement, 1928

The 1920s boom in the production of household goods posed a challenge for business marketers and advertisers. They had to convince consumers that items once regarded as luxuries were now necessities that would improve their lives. Many of these advertisements were directed at women who, as housewives, managed the family budget and made the purchases. The General Electric Company played a leading role in winning women over to buying their products.

Explore

Why do women need "first aid" in the kitchen?

What do the items in the refrigerator reveal about food and consumer expectations in the 1920s?

How does this ad use the authority of science to persuade consumers?

First aid in entertaining

FIRST aid in entertaining, nowadays, is a General Electric Refrigerator. If you have one, you can make those delicious, *different* salads and aspics and desserts. You can make them at your leisure—the same morning, or the day before, or whenever you wish. There's plenty of room to store them. There's the scientific cold to keep them fresh.

You will like the simplicity of the General Electric Refrigerator. It never needs oiling. It hasn't a drain-pipe or a belt or a fan. All its machinery is enclosed in the hermetically sealed casing mounted on top of the cabinet. And there is a remarkably large shelf area because the chilling chamber is so compact. All the models are up on legs, so the floor under them can easily be cleaned.

General Electric's world-famed engineers and scientists worked for fifteen years to develop this supremely practical and efficient refrigerator—to make it quiet, portable and economical to run.

Already it is giving flawless service in more than fifty thousand homes. Ask these users about the General Electric and make comparisons before you buy. There is a wide range of models and prices. Write us today for Booklet S-6B, which is completely descriptive.

GENERAL ELECTRIC Refrigerator

ELECTRIC REFRIGERATION DEPARTMENT · OF GENERAL ELECTRIC COMPANY · HANNA BUILDING · CLEVELAND, OHIO

Private Collection/© The Advertising Archives/Bridgeman Images

Put It in Context

What does this ad convey about the role of women in the 1920s?

Federal Trade Commission, business people frequently managed firms in a reckless way that created a high level of interdependence among them. For example, Samuel Insull, who owned a gas and electric utilities empire, was the chairman of the board of sixty-five companies, a director of eighty-five others, and the president of an additional seven corporations. This interlocking system of corporate ownership and control meant that the collapse of one company could bring down many others, while also imperiling the banking houses that had generously financed them.

Rampant real estate speculation in Florida foreshadowed these dangers, as private developers and the state government promoted tourism and land purchases. In many cases, investors bought properties sight unseen, as speculators and unscrupulous agents worked under the assumption that land values would continue to increase forever. However, severe storms in 1926 and 1928 abruptly halted the increase in land values. Land prices spiraled downward, speculators defaulted on bank loans, and financial institutions tottered.

Throughout the 1920s, fortunes plummeted for farmers as well. Despite the growing urbanization of the nation, farmers still made up one-third of the population. Declining world demand following the end of World War I, together with increased productivity because of the mechanization of agriculture, drove down farm prices and income. Between 1925 and 1929, falling wheat and cotton prices cut farm income in half. The collapse of farm prices had the most devastating effects on tenants and sharecroppers who were forced off their lands through mortgage foreclosures. Around three million displaced farmers migrated to cities, where they had to compete with unskilled laborers for factory jobs and often found themselves among the ranks of the unemployed.

Internationally, the United States encountered serious economic obstacles. World War I had destroyed European economies, leaving them ill equipped to repay the $11 billion they had borrowed from the United States. Much of the Allied recovery, and hence the ability to repay debts, depended on obtaining the reparations imposed on Germany at the conclusion of World War I (see chapter 20). Germany, however, was in even worse shape than France and Britain and could not meet its obligations. Without a prosperous Europe, the American economy suffered. In 1924 the U.S. government sent Charles G. Dawes, a banker and soon to become Coolidge's vice president, to negotiate with Britain, France, and Germany to find a solution to their mutual problem. Under the terms of the eventual agreement, the United States provided loans to Germany to pay its reparations. In turn, Britain and France reduced the size of Germany's payments. The result was a series of circular payments. American banks loaned money to Germany, which used the money to pay reparations to Britain and France, which, in turn, used Germany's reparations payments to repay debts owed to American banks. What appeared a satisfactory resolution at the time ultimately proved a calamity. In undertaking this revolving-door solution, American bankers added to the cycle of spiraling credit and placed themselves at the mercy of unstable European economies. Compounding the problem, Republican administrations in the 1920s supported high tariffs on imports, reducing foreign manufacturers' revenues and therefore their nations' tax receipts, making it more difficult for these countries to pay off their debts.

REVIEW & RELATE

Describe the relationship between business and government in the 1920s.

Why was a high level of consumer spending so critical to 1920s prosperity, and why was the economic expansion of the 1920s ultimately unsustainable?

LEARNINGCurve bedfordstmartins.com/hewittlawson/LC

Challenges to Social Conventions

While most of the nation ignored growing evidence of the fragility of American prosperity, the social and cultural consequences of the second industrial revolution received considerable attention, as new, distinctly modern cultural patterns emerged. Advertising and credit, two of the mainstays of modern capitalism, sought to bypass the time-honored virtues of saving and living within one's means. Conventional sexual standards came under assault from the growth of the film and automobile industries, which influenced fashion styles and dating practices. In addition to moral and social behavior, traditional racial assumptions came under attack. African American writers and artists condemned the kind of racism Ossian Sweet experienced, drew on their rich racial legacies, and produced a cultural renaissance. Other blacks, led by the Jamaican immigrant Marcus Garvey, rejected the integrationist strategy of the NAACP in favor of black nationalism.

Breaking with the Old Morality

Challenges to the virtues of thrift and sacrifice were accompanied by a transformation of the moral codes of late-nineteenth-century America, especially those relating to sex. The entertainment industry played a large role in promoting

Augusta Savage

Born in Florida, Augusta Savage joined other artists in moving to New York City in the 1920s as part of the Harlem Renaissance. She took formal art classes at the Cooper Union, working mainly in clay. In addition to the sculpture of the young boy here, Savage produced busts of W. E. B. Du Bois and Marcus Garvey.   Hansel Mieth/Time & Life Pictures/Getty Images

Black music became a vibrant part of mainstream American popular culture in the 1920s. Traveling musicians such as Ferdinand "Jelly Roll" Morton, Louis Armstrong, Edward "Duke" Ellington, and singer Bessie Smith developed and popularized two of America's most original forms of music—jazz and the blues. Emerging from brothels and bars in the South, these unique compositions grew out of the everyday experiences of black life and expressed the thumping rhythms of work, pleasure, and pain. Such music did not remain confined to dance halls and clubs in black communities; it soon spread to white musicians and audiences for whom the hot beat of jazz rhythms meant emotional freedom and the expression of sexuality.

Marcus Garvey and Black Nationalism

In addition to providing a fertile ground for African American intellectuals, Harlem became the headquarters of the most significant alternative black political vision of the 1920s. In 1916 the Jamaican-born Marcus Mosiah Garvey settled in Harlem and became the leading exponent of black nationalism. In 1914 Garvey had set up the **Universal Negro Improvement Association (UNIA)** in Jamaica, an organization through which he promoted racial separation and pride. Unlike the leaders of the NAACP, who sought equal access to American institutions and cooperation with whites, Garvey favored a "Back to Africa" movement that would ultimately repatriate

Du Bois had spoken of in *The Souls of Black Folk* (1903). James Weldon Johnson, a writer and the chief executive of the NAACP, commented: "The final measure of the greatness of all peoples is the amount and standard of the literature and art they have produced." The poets, novelists, and artists of the Harlem Renaissance captured the imagination of blacks and whites alike. Many of these artists increasingly rejected white standards of taste as well as staid middle-class, black values. Writers Langston Hughes and Zora Neale Hurston in particular drew inspiration from the vernacular of African American folk life. In 1926 Hughes defiantly asserted: "We younger Negro artists who create now intend to express our dark-skinned selves without fear or shame. If white people are pleased, we are glad. If they are not, it doesn't matter."

many black Americans to their ancestral homelands on the African continent. Together with the indigenous black African majority, transplanted African Americans would help overthrow colonial rule and use their power to assist black people throughout the world.

Garvey's appeal did not rely primarily on this utopian project. Instead, the UNIA concentrated on building the economic strength of black communities in the United States through self-help. In the pages of his newspaper, *Negro World*, Garvey promoted ventures such as his Black Star Line steamship company, established in 1919. After raising more than $200,000 in less than four months, the company acquired a fleet of three less-than-seaworthy ships on which it planned to transport passengers between the United States, the West Indies, and Africa. The UNIA's companies opened up

Marcus Garvey
Dressed in military regalia topped off with a plumed hat, the Jamaican immigrant Marcus Garvey embodied the spirit of black nationalism after World War I. His Universal Negro Improvement Association, headquartered in Harlem, attracted a sizable following in the United States, the Caribbean, Central America, Canada, and Africa. Garvey advocated black political and economic independence.   NY Daily News via Getty Images

blue-collar and white-collar jobs to black men and women that were generally unavailable to them in white-owned firms.

In addition to offering an outlet for dreams of economic advancement, Garvey tapped into the racial discontent of African Americans for whom living in the United States had proven so difficult. He denounced what he saw as the accommodationist efforts of the NAACP and declared, "To be a Negro is no disgrace, but an honor, and we of the UNIA do not want to become white." Indeed, he proclaimed "Black is Beautiful" and asserted that both God and Jesus were black. Ironically, the UNIA and D. C. Stephenson's Klan agreed on the necessity of racial segregation, though Garvey never accepted the premise that blacks were inferior. Garvey dressed in a military uniform with a saber dangling from his belt and a plumed hat atop his

head. His appeals to black manhood were also accompanied by a celebration of black womanhood. He set up the Black Cross Nurses, and his wife, Amy Jacques Garvey, went beyond her husband's traditional notions of femininity to extol the accomplishments of black women in politics and culture. Garveyism became the first mass African American movement in U.S. history and was especially effective in recruiting working-class blacks. UNIA branches were established in thirty-eight states throughout the North and South and attracted some 500,000 members.

Given his ideas and outspokenness, Garvey soon made powerful enemies. Du Bois and fellow members of the NAACP despised him. The black socialist labor leader A. Philip Randolph, who saw the UNIA program as just another form of exploitative capitalism, labeled Garvey an "unquestioned fool and ignoramus." Yet Garvey's downfall came from his own business practices. Convicted in 1925 of mail fraud related to his Black Star Line, Garvey served two years in federal prison until President Coolidge commuted his term and had the Jamaican citizen deported. Garvey continued to carry on his activities from England, but without his presence the UNIA lost most of its following in the United States.

REVIEW & RELATE

- How did new forms of entertainment challenge traditional morality and traditional gender roles?

- Describe the black cultural and intellectual renaissance that flourished in the 1920s.

 LEARNINGCurve bedfordstmartins.com/hewittlawson/LC

Culture Wars

Attacks on traditional cultural and racial values did not go uncontested. During this era when technological innovations overturned traditional economic values, when modes of social behavior were in a state of flux, and when white supremacy came under assault, it is not surprising that many segments of the population resisted these changes. Rallying around ethnic and racial purity, Protestant fundamentalism, and family values, defenders of an older America attempted to roll back the tide of modernity.

Nativists versus Immigrants

The 1920s experienced a surge in nativist (anti-immigrant) and racist thinking that in many ways reflected long-standing fears. The end of World War I brought a new wave of Catholic and Jewish emigration from eastern and southern Europe, triggering religious prejudice among Protestants. Just as immigrants had been linked to socialism and anarchism in the 1880s and 1890s, old-stock Americans associated these immigrants with immoral behavior and political radicalism and saw them as a threat to their traditional culture and values. Moreover, as in the late nineteenth century, native-born workers saw immigrants as a source of cheap labor that threatened their jobs and wages.

The **Sacco and Vanzetti case** provides the most dramatic evidence of this nativism. In 1920 a botched robbery at a shoe company in South Braintree, Massachusetts, resulted in the murder of the bookkeeper and guard. Police arrested Nicola Sacco, a shoemaker, and Bartolomeo Vanzetti, a fish peddler, and charged them with the crime. These two Italian immigrants shared radical political views as anarchists and World War I draft evaders. The subsequent trial revolved around their foreign birth and ideology more than the facts pertaining to their guilt or innocence. The presiding judge at the trial referred to the accused as "anarchistic bastards" and "damned dagos" (a derogatory term for "Italians"). Convicted and sentenced to death, Sacco and Vanzetti lost their appeals for a new trial. Criticism of the verdict came from all over the world. Workers in Mexico, Argentina, Uruguay, France, and Morocco organized vigils and held rallies in solidarity with the condemned men. The American minister to Venezuela reported that "practically all the lower classes regarded them as martyrs." Despite support from influential lawyers such as Harvard's Felix Frankfurter, the two men were executed in the electric chair in 1927.

The Sacco and Vanzetti case provides an extreme example of 1920s nativism, but the anti-immigrant views that contributed to the two men's conviction and execution were commonplace during the period and shared by Americans across the social spectrum. Many Americans, including Henry Ford, saw immigrants as a threat to cherished traditions. In his commitment to "One-Hundred Percent Americanism," Ford tried to preserve traditional values. He strongly supported prohibition and denounced the frenetic sounds and sexual overtones of Jazz Age music and dancing. Ford felt that immigrants were the cause of a decline in American morality. He contended that aliens did not understand "the principles which have made our [native] civilization," and he blamed the influx of foreigners for society's "marked deterioration" during the 1920s. He stirred up anti-immigrant prejudices mainly by targeting Jews. Believing that an international Jewish conspiracy was attempting to subvert non-Jewish societies, Ford serialized in his company newspaper the so-called

Protocols of the Elders of Zion, an anti-Semitic tract concocted in czarist Russia to justify pogroms against Jews. Ford continued to publish it even after the document was proven a fake in 1921.

Ford joined other nativists in supporting legislation to restrict immigration. In 1924 Congress passed the **National Origins Act**, a quota system on future immigration. The measure limited entry by any foreign group to 2 percent of the number of people of that nationality who resided in the United States in 1890. The statute's authors were interested primarily in curbing immigration from eastern and southern Europe. They chose 1890 as the benchmark for immigration because most newcomers from those two regions entered the United States after that year. Quotas established for northern Europe, about 70 percent of the total, went unfilled, while those for southern and eastern Europe could not accommodate the vast number of people who sought admission. The law continued to bar East Asian immigration altogether.

With immigration of those considered "undesirable" severely if not completely curtailed, some nativist reformers shifted their attention to Americanization, which developed into one of the largest social and political movements in American history. Speaking about immigrants, educator E. P. Cubberly said, "Our task is to break up their groups and settlements, to assimilate and amalgamate these people as a part of our American race, to implant in their children the northern-European conception of righteousness, law and order, and popular government." Business corporations conducted Americanization and naturalization classes on factory floors. Schools, patriotic societies, fraternal organizations, women's groups, and labor unions launched citizenship classes. Even the U.S. Catholic hierarchy joined the effort by prohibiting the creation of new parishes based on nationality and increasingly requiring the use of English for confessions and sermons.

In the Southwest and on the West Coast, whites aimed their Americanization efforts at the growing population of Mexican Americans. Subject to segregated education, Mexican Americans were expected to speak English in their classes. "The opening of school," an Arizona teacher's journal noted, "will provide an opportunity for all the Mexican children . . . to study under separate tutelage until they have acquired a thorough mastery of the English language." Anglo school administrators and teachers generally believed that Mexican Americans were suited for farmwork and manual trades. For Mexican Americans, therefore, Americanization meant vocational training and preparation for low-status, low-wage jobs.

Despite attempts at Americanization, ethnic groups did not dissolve into a melting pot and lose their cultural identities. First-generation Americans—the children of immigrants—learned English, enjoyed American popular culture, and dressed in fashions of the day. Yet in cities around the country where immigrants had settled, ethnic enclaves remained intact and preserved the religious practices and social customs of their residents. Americanization may have watered down the "vegetable soup" of American diversity, but it did not completely eliminate the variety and distinctiveness of its flavors.

Resurrection of the Ku Klux Klan

Nativism received its most spectacular boost from the reemergence of the Ku Klux Klan in 1915. Originally an organization dedicated to terrorizing emancipated African Americans and their white Republican allies in the South during Reconstruction, the KKK branched out during the 1920s to the North and West. In addition to blacks, the new Klan targeted Catholics and Jews, as well as anyone who was alleged to have violated community moral values. The organization consisted of a cross section of native-born Protestants primarily from the middle and working classes who sought to reverse a perceived decline in their social and economic power. Revived by W. J. Simmons, a former Methodist minister, the new Klan celebrated its founding at Stone Mountain, Georgia, near Atlanta. There, Klansmen bowed to the twin symbols of their cause, the American flag and a burning cross that represented their fiery determination to stand up for Christian morality and against all those considered "un-American." People flocked to the new KKK. By the mid-1920s, Klan membership totaled more than three million men and women. Tens of thousands of members outfitted in white sheets and pointed hoods openly paraded down Pennsylvania Avenue in Washington, D.C., the route of presidential inaugurations. Not confined to rural areas, the revived Klan counted a significant following in D. C. Stephenson's Indianapolis and Ossian Sweet's Detroit, as well as in Chicago, Denver, Portland, and Seattle. Rural dwellers who had moved into cities with large numbers of black migrants and recent immigrants found solace in Klan vows to preserve "Native, white, Protestant supremacy."

The phenomenal growth of the KKK in the 1920s probably resulted more from the desire to reestablish traditional values than from sheer hostility toward blacks. In the face of challenges to traditional values, a changing sexual morality, and the flaunting of prohibition, wives joined their husbands as devoted followers. Protestant women appreciated the Klan's message condemning abusive husbands and fathers and the group's affirmation of the status of white Protestant women as the embodiment of virtue. In the post-suffrage era, the Klan also provided its female members with an incentive to vote by encouraging them to counteract the influence of newly enfranchised Catholic, Jewish, Latina, and African American women.

Explore

See Documents 21.3 and 21.4 for two perspectives on the KKK.

Like the original Klan, its successor resorted to terror tactics. Acting under cover of darkness and concealed in robes and hoods, Klansmen burned crosses to scare their victims, many of whom they beat, kidnapped, tortured, and murdered. To gain greater legitimacy and to appeal to a wider audience, the Klan also participated in electoral politics. The KKK succeeded in electing governors in Georgia and Oregon, a U.S. senator from Texas, numerous state legislators, and other officials in California, Indiana, Michigan, Ohio, and Oklahoma. Politicians routinely joined the Klan to advance their careers, whether they shared its views or not. For example, Hugo Black, a Klansman from Alabama, won election as U.S. senator and was appointed to the Supreme Court, where he accumulated a distinguished record as a progressive jurist.

Fundamentalism versus Modernism

Protestant fundamentalists also fought to uphold traditional values against modern-day incursions. Around 1910, two wealthy Los Angeles churchgoers had subsidized and distributed a series of booklets called *The Fundamentals*, incorporating many statements about the literal truth of the Bible. With three million copies in circulation nationwide, the booklets informed readers that the Bible offered a true account of the genesis and development of humankind and the world and that its words had to be taken literally. After 1920, believers of this approach to interpreting the Bible became known as "fundamentalists." Their preachers spread the message of old-time religion through carnival-like revivals, and preachers used the new medium of radio to broadcast their sermons. Fundamentalism divided many Protestant denominations, but its appeal was strongest in the Midwest and the South—the so-called Bible belt—where residents felt deeply threatened by the secular aspects of modern life that left their conventional religious teachings open to skepticism and scorn.

Nothing bothered fundamentalist Protestants as much as Charles Darwin's theory of evolution. In *On the Origin of*

DOCUMENTS 21.3 AND 21.4

Men and Women of the KKK: Two Views

While the new Ku Klux Klan grew in power and visibility, many Americans also resisted and ridiculed the organization. In the first selection, journalist Gerald Johnson describes the typical KKK member. The second selection, an excerpt from the bylaws of a Maryland chapter of the Women of the Ku Klux Klan, indicates the group's devotion to the responsibilities of traditional womanhood. Nearly half a million women joined the women's auxiliaries of the KKK.

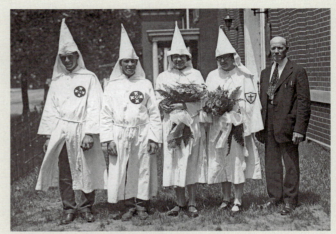

Ku Klux Klan Wedding, 1925 Getty Images

Explore

21.3 Gerald W. Johnson | The Ku Kluxer, 1924

The Ku Klux Klan was swept beyond the racial boundaries of the Negro and flourishes now in the Middle West because it is a perfect expression of the American idea that the voice of the people is the voice of God. The belief that the average klansman is consciously affected by an appeal to his baser self is altogether erroneous. In the voice of the organizer he hears a clarion call to knightly and selfless service. It strikes him as in no wise strange that he should be so summoned; is he not, as an American citizen, of the nobility? Politics has been democratized. Social usage has been democratized. Religion has been most astoundingly democratized. Why, then, not democratize chivalry?

The klansman has already been made, in his own estimation, politically a monarch, socially a peer of the realm, spiritually a high priest. Now the Ku Klux Klan calls him to step up and for the trifling consideration of ten dollars he is made a Roland, a Lancelot, a knight-errant vowed to the succor of the oppressed, the destruction of ogres and magicians, the defense of the faith. Bursting with noble ideals and lofty aspirations, he accepts the nomination. The trouble is that this incantation doesn't work, as none of the others has worked, except in his imagination. King, aristocrat, high priest as he believes himself to be, he is neither royal, noble, nor holy. So, under his white robe and pointed hood he becomes not a Chevalier Bayard [French knight] but a thug.

Source: Gerald W. Johnson, "The Ku Kluxer," *The American Mercury*, February 1924, 209–10.

Species (1859), Darwin replaced the biblical story of creation with a scientific theory of the emergence and development of life that centered on evolution and natural selection. Fundamentalists rejected this explanation and repudiated the views of fellow Protestants who attempted to reconcile Darwinian evolution with God's Word by reading the Bible as a symbolic representation of what might have

happened. Few people had actually read Darwin, and fundamentalists derided him by emphasizing the popular misconception that he had written that human beings had descended directly from apes (in fact, he maintained that simians and humans had a common ancestor). To combat any other interpretation but the biblical one, in 1925 lawmakers in Arkansas, Florida, Mississippi, Oklahoma,

Explore

21.4 Women of the Ku Klux Klan, 1927

Objects and Purposes

SECTION 1. The objects of this Order shall be to unite white female persons, native-born Gentile citizens of the United States of America, who owe no allegiance of any nature or degree to any foreign government, nation, institution, sect, ruler, person, or people; whose morals are good; whose reputations and vocations are respectable; whose habits are exemplary; who are of sound minds and 18 years or more of age, under a common oath into a Sisterhood of strict regulation, to cultivate and promote patriotism toward our Civil Government; to practice an honorable clannishness toward each other; to exemplify a practical benevolence; to shield the sanctity of the home and the chastity of womanhood; to maintain forever white supremacy; to teach and faithfully inculcate a high spiritual philosophy through an exalted ritualism, and by a practical devotion to conserve, protect, and maintain the distinctive institutions, rights, privileges, principles, traditions, and ideals of a pure Americanism.

SEC. 2. To create and maintain an institution by which the present and succeeding generations shall commemorate the great sacrifice, chivalric service, and imperishable achievements of the Ku Klux Klan and the Women of the Reconstruction period of American History, to the end that justice and honor be done the sacred memory of those who wrought through our mystic society during that period, and that their valiant accomplishments be not lost to posterity; to perpetuate their faithful courage, noble spirit, peerless principles, and faultless ideals; to hold sacred and make effective their spiritual purpose in this and future generations, that they be rightly vindicated before the world by a revelation of the whole truth.

Source: Women of the KKK (Maryland) Records, Schlesinger Library, Radcliffe Institute, Harvard University, reprinted in *Modern American Women*, ed. Susan Ware (Boston: McGraw-Hill, 2002), 136–37.

Interpret the Evidence

- How does Johnson describe the typical KKK member?
- How do each of these statements identify the central purpose of the KKK?

Put It in Context

Why did the KKK and other nativist groups appeal to so many people during the 1920s?

and Tennessee made it illegal to teach in public schools and colleges "any theory that denies the story of the Divine Creation of man as taught in the Bible."

Shortly after the anti-evolution law passed, the town of Dayton, Tennessee, decided to take advantage of it. Local business people and town boosters wanted to put their town on the map and attract new investment to the area.

They recruited John Scopes, a general science high school teacher and part-time football coach. Scopes defied the law by lecturing from a biology textbook that presented Darwin's theory. At the same time, the interests of the town boosters converged with those of the ACLU, which wanted to challenge the restrictive state statute on the grounds of free speech and academic freedom and attract new members to the organization. Together, these two very different groups succeeded in turning an ordinary judicial hearing into the "trial of the century."

The resulting trial brought Dayton more fame, much of it negative, than the planners had bargained for. When court convened in July 1925, millions of people listened over the radio to the first trial ever broadcast. Reporters from all over the country descended on Dayton to keep their readers informed of the proceedings, while cynical journalists such as H. L. Mencken ridiculed Dayton and its residents.

Inside the courtroom, a monumental confrontation took place. Clarence Darrow headed the defense team. A controversial and colorful criminal lawyer from Chicago, who in a few months would defend Ossian Sweet, Darrow doubted the existence of God. On the other side, William Jennings Bryan, three-time Democratic candidate for president and secretary of state under Woodrow Wilson, assisted the prosecution. As a Protestant fundamentalist, Bryan believed that accepting scientific evolution would undermine the moral basis of politics and that communities should have the right to determine their children's school curriculum. A Seventh-Day Adventist minister summed up what the fundamentalists considered to be at stake: "[Darwin's theory] breeds corruption, lust, immorality, greed, and such acts of criminal depravity as drug addiction, war, and atrocious acts of genocide."

The presiding judge, John T. Raulston, set the tone for the trial by beginning each session with a prayer. He ruled that scientists could not take the stand to defend evolution because he considered their testimony "hearsay," given that they had not been present at the creation. The defense nearly collapsed until Darrow called the willing Bryan to the stand as "an expert on the Bible." The clash of these two titans provided excellent theater but changed few minds. The jury took only eight minutes to declare Scopes guilty. Two weeks after the trial, Bryan died in his sleep, still convinced that his views had prevailed. Scopes's conviction was overturned by an appeals court on a technicality. Yet fundamentalists remained as certain as ever in their beliefs, and anti-evolution laws stayed in force until the 1970s. The trial had not "settled" anything. Rather, it served to highlight a cultural division over the place of religion in American society that persists to the present day.

REVIEW & RELATE

- What was the connection between anti-immigrant sentiment and the defense of tradition during the 1920s?
- Who challenged the new morality associated with modernization? Why?

Politics and the Fading of Prosperity

These cultural clashes tore the Democratic Party apart, leaving Republicans in command of national politics. As it attracted a growing number of urban immigrants to its ranks alongside its customary base of white southerners, the Democratic Party tried to reconcile the tensions between traditional and modern America. Its failure to do so kept Republicans in power despite growing evidence of their inability to resolve serious economic problems. Although many progressives continued to press for reform, they were all but powerless to prevent the coming economic crisis.

The Battle for the Soul of the Democratic Party

The 1924 presidential election exposed the social and cultural fault lines within the Democratic Party. Since the end of Reconstruction and the "redemption" of the South by southern Democrats, the Republican Party had ceased to compete for office in the region. Southern Democrats, along with party supporters from the rural Midwest, shared strong fundamentalist religious beliefs and an enthusiasm for prohibition that usually placed them at odds with big-city northern Democrats. The urban wing of the party increasingly represented immigrant populations that rejected prohibition as contrary to their social practices and supported political machines, which many rural Democrats found odious and an indicator of cultural degradation. These distinctions, however, were not absolute—some rural dwellers opposed prohibition, and some urbanites supported temperance.

Delegates to the 1924 Democratic convention in New York City had trouble deciding on a party platform and a presidential candidate. When urban delegates from the Northeast attempted to insert a plank condemning D. C. Stephenson's Ku Klux Klan for its intolerance, they lost by a thin margin. Proponents of this measure owed their defeat to the sizable number of convention delegates who either belonged to the Klan or had been backed by it.

The selection of the presidential ticket proved even more divisive. Urban Democrats favored the nomination of New York governor Alfred E. Smith. Smith came from an Irish Catholic immigrant family, had grown up on New York City's Lower East Side, and was sponsored by the Tammany Hall machine. The epitome of everything that rural Democrats despised, Smith further angered opponents with his outspoken denunciation of prohibition. Prohibitionists fiercely opposed Smith, and he lost the

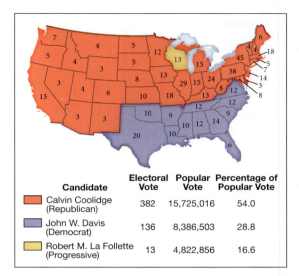

Candidate	Electoral Vote	Popular Vote	Percentage of Popular Vote
Calvin Coolidge (Republican)	382	15,725,016	54.0
John W. Davis (Democrat)	136	8,386,503	28.8
Robert M. La Follette (Progressive)	13	4,822,856	16.6

MAP 21.1   The Election of 1924
Republican Calvin Coolidge, who became president in August 1923 on the death of Warren Harding, continued Harding's policies of limited government regulation and corporate tax cuts. Coolidge easily defeated Democrat John Davis, whose strength was confined to the South. Running as the Progressive Party candidate, Senator Robert La Follette won 16 percent of the popular vote but carried only his home state of Wisconsin, with 13 electoral votes.

nomination to John W. Davis, a West Virginia Protestant and a supporter of prohibition. The intense intraparty fighting left the Democrats deeply divided going into the general election. To no one's surprise, Davis lost to Calvin Coolidge in a landslide (Map 21.1).

In 1928, however, when the Democrats met in Houston, Texas, the delicate cultural equilibrium within the Democratic Party had shifted in favor of the urban forces. With Stephenson and the Klan discredited and no longer a force in Democratic politics, the delegates nominated Al Smith as their presidential candidate. To balance the ticket, they tapped for vice president Joseph G. Robinson, a senator from Arkansas, a Protestant, and a supporter of prohibition.

The Republicans selected Herbert Hoover, one of the most popular men in the United States. His biography read like a script of the American dream. Born in Iowa to a Quaker family, he became an orphan at the age of nine and moved to Oregon to live with relatives. After graduating from Stanford University in 1895, he began a career as a prosperous mining engineer and a successful businessman. Affectionately called "the Great Humanitarian" for his European relief efforts after World War I, Hoover served as secretary of commerce during the Harding and Coolidge administrations. His name became synonymous with the Republican prosperity of the 1920s. In accepting his party's nomination for president in 1928, Hoover optimistically

declared: "We in America today are nearer to the final triumph over poverty than ever before in the history of the land." A Protestant supporter of prohibition from a small town, Hoover was everything Smith was not.

The outcome of the election proved predictable. Running on prosperity and pledging a "chicken in every pot and two cars in every garage," Hoover trounced Smith with 58 percent of the popular vote and more than 80 percent of the electoral vote. Despite the weakening economy, Smith lost usually reliable Democratic votes to religious and ethnic prejudices. The New Yorker prevailed only in Massachusetts, Rhode Island, and six southern states but failed to win his home state. A closer look at the election returns showed a significant party realignment under way. Smith succeeded in identifying the Democratic Party with urban, ethnic-minority voters and attracting them to the polls. Despite the landslide loss, he captured the twelve largest cities in the nation, all of which had gone Republican four years earlier. In another fifteen big cities, Smith did better than the Democrat ticket had done in the 1924 election, thereby encouraging the country's ethnic minorities to support the party of Thomas Jefferson and Woodrow Wilson. To break the Republicans' national dominance, the Democrats would need a candidate who appealed to both traditional and modern Americans. Smith's defeat, however, laid the foundation for future Democratic political success.

Where Have All the Progressives Gone?

The Democrats and Republicans were not the only parties that attracted voters in the 1920s. Some voters continued to cast their ballot for the Socialist Party. Others took the opportunity to voice their disapproval of Republican policies by voting for the remaining progressive candidates. Progressives did manage to hold on to seats in Congress, and in 1921 they helped pass the Shepherd-Towner Act, which appropriated federal funds to establish maternal and child centers (see chapter 19). But their efforts to restrict the power of the Supreme Court, reduce tax cuts for the wealthy, nationalize railroads, and extend agricultural relief to farmers were rebuffed by conservative legislative majorities. In 1924 reformers nominated Senator Robert M. La Follette of Wisconsin to run for president on a revived Progressive Party ticket, but he came in a distant third and won only five million popular votes and the electoral votes of his home state. The Progressive Party collapsed soon after La Follette died in 1925.

Still, progressivism managed to stay alive on the local and state levels. Gifford Pinchot, a Roosevelt ally and a champion of conservation (see chapter 19), twice

Robert M. La Follette, 1924
Wisconsin senator Robert M. La Follette, running for president on the Progressive Party ticket in 1924, speaks to party women during his campaign. La Follette and his running mate, Senator Burton K. Wheeler of Montana, favored higher taxes for the wealthy, collective bargaining rights for factory workers, and limits on Supreme Court power. FPG/Getty Images

won election as governor of Pennsylvania starting in 1922. Social workers continued their efforts to alleviate urban poverty and lobby for government assistance to the poor. Even at the national level, women in the Children's Bureau maintained the progressive legacy by supporting assistance to families and devising social welfare proposals. Progressivism did not disappear during the 1920s, but it did fight an uphill and often losing battle during an age of conservative political ascendancy. Its weakness contributed to the government's failure to check the worst corporate and financial practices, a failure that would play a role in the nation's economic collapse.

Financial Crash

On October 29, 1929, a day that became known as **Black Tuesday**, stock market prices tumbled. Over the previous five years, the rising market, bolstered by optimistic buyers, earned huge profits for investors, and the value of stocks

nearly doubled. In late October, panicked sellers sent stock prices into free fall, culminating in the selling of more than 16 million shares valued at $32 billion on October 29. Although only 2.5 percent of Americans owned stock, the stock market crash had an enormous impact on the economy and the rest of the world. Because so much of the stock boom depended on generous margin requirements (a down payment of only 5 to 10 percent), when investor-borrowers got caught short by falling prices, they could not repay the financial institutions that had extended them credit. Banks and lending agencies, with their interlocking management and overextension of credit, had difficulty withstanding the turmoil unleashed by the stock market crash.

The 1929 crash did not cause the decade-long Great Depression that followed. The seeds for the greatest economic catastrophe in American history had been planted earlier. The economy had endured a series of panics and depressions in the past, but nothing like what happened between 1929 and 1940. The causes stemmed from flaws in an economic system that produced a great disparity of wealth, inadequate consumption, overextension of credit both at home and abroad, and the government's unwillingness to relieve the plight of farmers. Republican administrations made matters worse by lowering taxes on the rich and raising tariffs to benefit manufacturers. The Federal Reserve Board exacerbated the situation by keeping interest rates high, thereby making it difficult for people to get loans and repay debts. The failure was not that of the United States alone; the depression affected capitalist nations throughout the world. The stock market collapse crushed whatever confidence the American public had that the unfettered law of supply and demand and laissez-faire economics could ensure prosperity.

REVIEW & RELATE

How did divisions within the Democratic Party contribute to Republican political dominance in the 1920s?

What underlying economic weaknesses led to the Great Depression?

 LEARNINGCurve bedfordstmartins.com/hewittlawson/LC

Conclusion: The Roaring Twenties

While the second industrial revolution spurred extraordinary prosperity, the 1920s ended in an unprecedented economic collapse. During the decade, industrialists produced and marketed wares in a manner that drew the mass of Americans into the economy as laborers and consumers. Automobiles, fueled by gasoline, traveled up and down streets and highways. Electricity powered household appliances and ran movie projectors in theaters throughout the nation. People living in California, Michigan, Florida, or New Jersey had similar opportunities to buy consumer products and partake in a mass culture made possible by movies and radio. Producing for a mass market, industrial giants like Henry Ford transformed the nature of work and pleasure. The assembly line revolutionized the pace of labor and turned it into a standardized routine. The automobile transformed dating patterns and opened up new opportunities for the exploration of romance and sex.

For most Americans earning very modest incomes, the fruits of the consumer revolution were beyond their reach. The image of the 1920s as an era of widespread prosperity is exaggerated. Most Americans lived at or below the poverty line and earned just enough money to acquire the bare necessities. They could live beyond their means through an ample supply of credit, but their poverty contrasted with the increasing concentration of wealth in the hands of the richest Americans. Businessmen like Henry Ford attempted to take care of their workers through higher wages and assorted benefits, but their paternalism depended on the continuation of good economic times. The stock market crash of 1929 and the ensuing Great Depression exposed the shortcomings of the corporate business world, inadequate oversight by the federal government, and an overreliance on the private sector to look after the nation's economic health.

The weaknesses of the economy, which appear clear in retrospect, were often hidden behind the clash over cultural differences. Guardians of traditional morality and values worried about the effects of more than fifty years of industrialization, immigration, and urbanization. Issues such as the enforcement of prohibition, the teaching of evolution in the schools, and whether a Catholic should be elected president dominated political discussion, while efforts to assist farmers and workers were unsuccessful. These battles marked a turning point in American history— the transition from a traditional, rural, Protestant society to an urban, ethnically and religiously diverse one. The widespread popularity of D. C. Stephenson's Ku Klux Klan throughout the South and the North demonstrated that the older America of white, northern European Protestants did not intend to relinquish political or cultural power without a struggle. At the same time, ethnic minorities represented by Al Smith had no intention of backing down. Neither did millions of African Americans, whether they joined the NAACP, as did Ossian Sweet, or supported Marcus Garvey's UNIA. During the next decade, Americans from all backgrounds would battle more than cultural threats; they would fight for their economic survival.

Chapter Review

Online Study Guide ▶ bedfordstmartins.com/hewittlawson

KEY TERMS

Red scare (p. 655)
Palmer raids (p. 656)
great migration (p. 657)
American Plan (p. 658)
Teapot Dome scandal (p. 659)
second industrial revolution (p. 660)
new woman (p. 664)
Lost Generation (p. 664)
New Negro (p. 665)
Universal Negro Improvement Association (UNIA) (p. 666)
Sacco and Vanzetti case (p. 668)
National Origins Act (p. 668)
Black Tuesday (p. 674)

REVIEW & RELATE

1. What factors combined to produce the turmoil of the immediate postwar period?

2. What factors contributed to the rise in racial tensions that accompanied the transition from wartime to peacetime?

3. Describe the relationship between business and government in the 1920s.

4. Why was a high level of consumer spending so critical to 1920s prosperity, and why was the economic expansion of the 1920s ultimately unsustainable?

5. How did new forms of entertainment challenge traditional morality and traditional gender roles?

6. Describe the black cultural and intellectual renaissance that flourished in the 1920s.

7. What was the connection between anti-immigrant sentiment and the defense of tradition during the 1920s?

8. Who challenged the new morality associated with modernization? Why?

9. How did divisions within the Democratic Party contribute to Republican political dominance in the 1920s?

10. What underlying economic weaknesses led to the Great Depression?

TIMELINE OF EVENTS

1914	Universal Negro Improvement Association (UNIA) formed
1915	Ku Klux Klan revived
1917–1918	400,000 African Americans leave South as part of great migration
1917	Russian Revolution begins
1918–1920	Worldwide influenza epidemic
1919	4 million workers go on strike nationwide
	Race riots erupt in twenty-five U.S. cities
	Radicals mail incendiary devices to prominent Americans
	Palmer raids begin
1920	American Civil Liberties Union (ACLU) formed
	David Curtis Stephenson joins the Ku Klux Klan
1920s	Harlem Renaissance
1921	J. Edgar Hoover becomes director of the Bureau of Investigation (later the FBI)
	Teapot Dome scandal
1924	National Origins Act passed
	Charles Dawes negotiates with the Allies to reduce Germany's reparations payments
1925–1929	U.S. farm income drops by 50 percent
1925	Scopes trial
1926	Ossian Sweet and family acquitted of first-degree murder charges
1927	Sacco and Vanzetti executed
1928	Democrat Al Smith loses presidential election but wins ten largest cities
1929	Stock market crash sparks Great Depression

The *Abrams* Case and the Red Scare

In August 1918, New York City police arrested five Russian immigrants and charged them with violating the Espionage and Sedition Acts passed during World War I. The defendants were part of an anarchist group called Frayhayt (Freedom). Late in the summer of 1918, the group distributed two leaflets—one in Yiddish and one in English—that criticized President Wilson and the U.S. military intervention against Russia's Bolshevik government. It also called for a general workers' strike to protest Wilson's policy. During police interrogations, Jacob Schwartz was beaten so badly that he died from his injuries. The other four defendants were tried and convicted in October 1918 and sentenced to between fifteen and twenty years in prison. When they appealed their convictions, the U.S. Supreme Court upheld the verdict. In 1921 the defendants were deported to the Soviet Union.

Abrams v. United States upheld the "clear and present danger" principle first established in *Schenck v. United States* (1919). In the *Schenck* case, Justice Oliver Wendell Holmes wrote the unanimous decision establishing that free speech could be legally restricted only if it posed a clear threat to public safety. Eight months later, Holmes changed his mind and broke with the majority of his fellow justices in their application of his "clear and present danger" test to the *Abrams* case. In his famous dissent (Document 21.7), Holmes insisted that the prosecution had failed to prove intent on the part of the anarchists to harm the United States and further argued that a threat must be "clear and *imminent* [emphasis added]" before free speech could be limited, even during wartime.

Like thousands of other anarchists, socialists, and Communists, the *Abrams* defendants were victims of the "Red scare" that suppressed radical activities during and immediately after World War I. The following documents explore different aspects of the Red scare and the *Abrams* case. As you examine these sources, consider to what extent national security concerns should allow the government to curtail free speech rights.

677

LEARNINGCurve
Check what you know.
bedfordstmartins.com/hewittlawson/LC

Library of Congress

Carol M. Highsmith Archive, Library of Congress

Children of Mexican cotton laborers, Casa Grande, Arizona, 1937.

WPA mural, Cohen Building, Washington, D.C.

22
Depression, Dissent, and the New Deal
1929–1940

Library of Congress

Line of men inside the State Employment Service in San Francisco, California, waiting to register for benefits, 1938.

Anna Eleanor Roosevelt came from an old Dutch American family of wealthy merchants and bankers. In 1901, at the age of fifteen, she saw her uncle Theodore succeed William McKinley as president. Like other girls of her generation, Eleanor was expected to marry and become a "charming wife." Eleanor appeared well on her way toward doing so when she struck up a relationship with her distant cousin Franklin Delano Roosevelt, whom she married in 1905. Over a ten-year period, Eleanor gave birth to six children, further reinforcing her status as a traditional woman of her class.

Two events, however, set her life on a very different path than the one she had embarked on when she married Franklin. First, thirteen years into her marriage Eleanor discovered that her husband was having an affair with her social secretary, Lucy Mercer. She did not divorce him but made it clear that she would stay with him primarily as a mother to their children and a political partner. Second, in 1921 the thirty-nine-year-old Franklin contracted polio. Although he recovered, Franklin would never walk again or stand without the aid of braces. From this point on, Eleanor threw herself into public life, taking a more active role in her husband's political career and writing about personal and political issues for a range of publications.

After her husband won the presidency in 1932, Eleanor did not function as a typical First Lady. She played a very public role promoting her husband's agenda, and she also took advantage of her own extensive network of friends and acquaintances in labor

687

agricultural and industrial imports. However, other countries retaliated by lifting their import duties, which hurt American companies because it diminished demand for American exports.

In an exception to his aversion to spending, Hoover lobbied Congress to create the Reconstruction Finance Corporation (RFC) to supply loans to banks in danger of collapsing, financially strapped railroads, and troubled insurance companies. By injecting federal dollars into these critical enterprises, the president and lawmakers expected to produce dividends that would trickle down from the top of the economic structure to the bottom. Renewed investment supposedly would increase production, create jobs, raise the income of workers, and generate consumption and economic recovery. In 1932 Congress gave the RFC a budget of $1.5 billion to employ people in public works projects, a significant allocation for those individuals hardest hit by the depression.

This notable departure from Republican economic philosophy fell short of its goal. The RFC spent its budget too cautiously, and its funds reached primarily those institutions that could best afford to repay the loans, ignoring the companies in the greatest difficulty. Whatever the president's intentions, wealth never trickled down. Hoover was not indifferent to the plight of others so much as he was incapable of breaking away from his ideological preconceptions. He refused to support expenditures for direct relief (what today we call welfare) and hesitated to extend assistance for work relief because he believed that it would ruin individual initiative and character.

Hoover and the United States did not face the Great Depression alone; it was a worldwide calamity. By 1933 Germany, France, and Great Britain all faced mass unemployment. In Britain, one survey showed that around 20 percent of the population lacked sufficient food, clothing, and housing. As with American agriculture, European farmers had been suffering since the 1920s from falling prices and increased debt, and the depression further exacerbated this problem. In this climate of extreme social and economic unrest, authoritarian dictators came to power in a number of European countries, including Germany, Italy, Spain, and Portugal. Each claimed that his country's social and economic problems could be solved only by placing power in the hands of a single, all-powerful leader.

Hoovervilles and Dust Storms

The depression hit all areas of the United States hard. In large cities, families crowded into apartments with no gas or electricity and little food to put on the table. In Los Angeles, people cooked their meals over wood fires in backyards. An observer in Philadelphia reported a house containing a family of eleven. "They've got no shoes, no pants," he lamented. "In the house, no chairs. My God, you go in there, you cry, that's all." In many cities, the homeless constructed makeshift housing consisting of cartons, old newspapers, and cloth—shanties that journalists derisively dubbed **Hoovervilles**. Thousands of hungry citizens wound up living under bridges in Portland, Oregon; in wrecked autos in city dumps in Brooklyn, New York, and Stockton, California; and in abandoned coal furnaces in Pittsburgh. In Chicago, a fight broke out among fifty men over scraps of food placed in the garbage outside of a restaurant.

Rural workers fared no better. Landlords in West Virginia and Kentucky evicted coal miners and their families from their homes in the dead of winter, forcing them to live in tents. Farmers in the Great Plains, who were already experiencing foreclosures, were little prepared for the even greater natural disaster that lay waste to their farms. In the early 1930s, dust storms swept through western Kansas, eastern Colorado, western Oklahoma, the Texas Panhandle, and eastern New Mexico, destroying crops and plant and animal life. The storms resulted from both climatological and human causes. A series of droughts had destroyed crops and turned the earth into sand, which gusts of wind deposited on everything that lay in their path. Though they did not realize it at the time, plains farmers, by focusing on growing wheat for income, had neglected planting trees and grasses that would have kept the earth from eroding and turning into dust. Instead, dust storms brought life to a grinding halt, blocking out the midday sun. **See Document Project 22: The Depression in Rural America, page 712.**

As the storms continued through the 1930s, most residents—approximately 75 percent—remained on the plains and rode out the blizzards of dust. Millions, however, headed for California by train, automobiles, and trucks looking for relief from the plague of swirling dirt and hoping to find jobs in the state's fruit and vegetable fields. Although they came from several states besides Oklahoma, these migrants came to be known as "Okies," a derogatory term used by those who resented and looked down on the poverty-stricken newcomers to their communities. John Steinbeck's novel *The Grapes of Wrath* (1939) portrayed the plight of the fictional Joad family, as storms and a bank foreclosure destroyed their Oklahoma farm and sent them on the road to California. "[Route] 66 is the path of a people in flight," Steinbeck wrote, "refugees from dust and shrinking land, from the thunder of tractors and shrinking ownership, from the

Hooverville, 1932

By the third year of the Great Depression, impoverished Americans were still living in makeshift accommodations called Hoovervilles, which popped up around the nation. These children are staying with their family in a camp in Washington, D.C. The signs target President Herbert Hoover as the source of their misery and condemn him for not taking action to relieve their economic distress.   MPI/Getty Images

desert's slow northward invasion, from the twisting winds that howl up out of Texas, from the floods that bring no richness to the land and steal what little richness is there." By no means did all the migrants suffer the misfortunes of the Joads, and many of them succeeded in establishing new lives in the West.

Challenges for Minorities

Given the demographics of the workforce, the overwhelming majority of Americans who lost their jobs were white men; yet racial and ethnic minorities, including African Americans, Latinos, and Asian Americans, suffered disproportionate hardship. Racial discrimination had kept these groups from achieving economic and political equality, and the Great Depression added to their woes.

Traditionally the last hired and the first fired, blacks occupied the lowest rungs on the industrial and agricultural ladders. "The depression brought everybody down a peg or two," the African American poet Langston Hughes wryly commented. "And the Negroes had but

few pegs to fall." Despite the great migration to the North during and after World War I, three-quarters of the black population still lived in the South. They worked mostly as farmers, but 80 percent did not own their own land. Mainly sharecroppers and tenant farmers, black southerners were mired in debt that they could not repay as crop prices plunged to record lows during the 1920s. As white landowners struggled to save their farms by introducing machinery to cut labor costs, they forced black sharecroppers off the land and into even greater poverty. Nor was the situation better for black workers employed at the lowest-paying jobs as janitors, menial laborers, maids, and laundresses. On average, African Americans earned $200 a year, less than one-quarter of the average wage of white factory workers.

The economic misfortune that African Americans experienced was compounded by the fact that they lived in a society rigidly constructed to preserve white supremacy. The 25 percent of blacks living in the North faced racial discrimination in employment, housing, and the criminal justice system, but at least they could express their opinions and desires by voting. In Chicago, the growing African American community elected a black congressman, the Republican Oscar DePriest. By contrast, black southerners remained segregated and disfranchised by law. The depression also exacerbated racial tensions, as whites and blacks competed for the shrinking number of jobs. Lynching, which had declined from fifty-nine murders of blacks in 1921 to seven in 1929, surged upward—in 1933 twenty-four blacks lost their lives to this form of terrorism.

Events in Scottsboro, Alabama, reflected the special misery African Americans faced during the Great Depression. Trouble erupted in 1931. Two young, unemployed white women, Ruby Bates and Victoria Price, snuck onto a freight train heading to Huntsville, Alabama. Before the train reached the Scottsboro depot, a fight broke out between black and white men on top of the freight car occupied by the two women. After the train pulled in to

Scottsboro, the local sheriff arrested nine black youths between the ages of twelve and twenty. Charges of assault quickly escalated into rape, when the women told authorities that the black men in custody had molested them on board the train. The accused narrowly escaped a mob lynching when the governor sent in the National Guard to ensure that they stood trial.

Going to court, however, did not guarantee a fair trial. The court-appointed attorney was less than competent and had little time to prepare his clients' cases. It probably made little difference, as the all-white male jury swiftly convicted the accused; only the youngest defendant was not sentenced to death. The Communist Party, whose membership had increased as despair over the depression mounted, rushed to defend the youths, providing legal and financial assistance for them and their families. The Supreme Court spared the lives of the **Scottsboro Nine** by overturning their guilty verdicts in 1932 on the grounds that the defendants did not have adequate legal representation and again in 1935 because blacks had been systematically excluded from the jury pool. Although Ruby Bates had recanted her testimony and there was no physical evidence of rape, retrials in 1936 and 1937 produced the same guilty verdicts, but this time the defendants did not receive the death penalty—a minor victory considering the charges. State prosecutors dismissed charges against four of the accused, all of whom had already spent six years in jail. Despite international protests against this racist injustice, the last of the remaining five did not leave jail until 1950.

> **Explore**
>
> See Document 22.1 for a letter from one of the Scottsboro Nine.

Racism also worsened the impact of the Great Depression on Spanish-speaking Americans. Mexicans and Mexican Americans made up the largest segment of the Latino population living in the United States at the outset of the depression. Concentrated in the Southwest and California, they worked in a variety of low-wage factory jobs and as migrant laborers in fruit and vegetable fields. The depression reduced the Mexican-born population living in the United States in two ways. The federal government began deporting unemployed workers back to Mexico, as many as 500,000, some of whom may have been American citizens. Many more returned to Mexico voluntarily when demand for labor in the United States dried up.

Those who remained endured growing hardships. Relief agencies refused to provide them with the same benefits as whites. Like African Americans, they encountered discrimination in public schools, in public accommodations, and at the ballot box. Conditions remained harshest for migrant workers toiling long hours for little pay and living in overcrowded and poorly constructed housing. Employers had little incentive to improve the situation because there were plenty of white migrant workers to fill their positions. The same held true in factories. Employers justified keeping pay low by claiming that Mexican workers would only spend pay raises on "tequila and worthless trinkets in the dime stores."

The transient nature of agricultural work and the legal vulnerability of Mexican laborers who were not citizens made it difficult for workers to organize, but Mexican American laborers engaged in dozens of strikes in California and Texas in the early 1930s. Most ended in defeat, but a few, such as a five-week strike of pecan shellers in San Antonio, Texas, led by Luisa Moreno, won better working conditions and higher wages. Despite these hard-fought victories, the condition of Latinos remained precarious.

On the West Coast, Asian Americans also remained economically and politically marginalized. Barred from entry into the United States after passage of the 1924 National Origins Act, the Japanese population remained steady. Japanese immigrants (*issei*) eked out a living as small farmers, grocers, and gardeners, despite California laws preventing them from owning land. Many college-educated *Nisei* (U.S.-born children) found few professional opportunities available to them, and they often returned to work in family businesses. The depression magnified the problem. Like other racial and ethnic minorities, the Japanese found it harder to find even the lowest-wage jobs now that unemployed whites were willing to take them. As a result, about one-fifth of Japanese immigrants returned to Japan during the 1930s.

The Chinese suffered a similar fate. They remained isolated in ethnic communities along the West Coast. Discriminated against in schools and most occupations, many operated restaurants and laundries. Chinese immigrants had been barred from entering the United States since the Chinese Exclusion Act of 1882. Yet approximately 45 percent of people of Chinese ancestry had been born in the United States and thus were citizens. During the depression, those Chinese who did not obtain assistance through governmental relief turned instead to their own community organizations and to extended families to help them through the hard times.

Filipinos, who lived mainly on the Pacific coast and worked as low-wage agricultural workers, were subject to the same kind of racial animosity as other darker-skinned minorities, despite their colonial relationship with the United States. In 1934 anti-Filipino hostility reached its height when Congress passed the

DOCUMENT 22.1

Andy Wright | Plea from One of the Scottsboro Nine, 1937

Andy Wright was nineteen when he was arrested along with eight other black youths and charged with raping two white women. Wright was twice convicted of the charges and was not paroled until 1944. In this letter to the editor of the *Nation* magazine, Wright pleads his case after his second conviction. He contends that he was framed and tries to bring the misconduct of both the police investigators and the trial judge to the attention of the public.

Explore

Dear Sirs:

I am quite sure you all have read the outcome of my trial, and seen that I was given a miscarriage of justice. I feel it is my duty to write you all the facts of my case, which you perhaps overlooked, or perhaps it was not published in the papers. I was framed, cheated, and robbed of my freedom. First, beginning March 25, 26, and 27, 1931, I wasn't charged with criminal assault on either girl, and was carried through the first, second, and third degree, and even on the basis I would gain my freedom by turning state evidence against the other eight boys. Just because I didn't know nothing, nor neither would I lie on the other boys the charge of rape was framed and placed against me on the 28th day of March, 1931.

I was tried, convicted, and given the death sentence, and in November, 1932, the Supreme Court of the United States reversed the sentence and a retrial ordered. The 19th day of July, 1937, I was retried and sentenced to 99 years' imprisonment.

Now I wish to call your attention to how the judge charged the jury. He charged them in a perjury way. Out of his one hour and twenty-five minutes summation he only mentioned acquittal three times and each time he contradicted it by saying if you juries find a doubt which goes to me reconsider it. Never did he mention a single defense witness in his hour and twenty-five minutes summation to the jury.

How can I receive justice in the state of Alabama, especially of Morgan County, when perjury is used against me and my attorneys too? And I beg you, dear friends, readers, all stick together and work and struggle together and see that justice be brought to light. Let us all pull and struggle together and see that justice be done. It is not that I hate to go to prison, but I am innocent, and the slander is being thrown on our race of people and my family, is my reason of wanting to fight harder than ever.

ANDY WRIGHT
Montgomery, Ala., July 24

Source: Andy Wright, letter to the editors, *The Nation*, August 7, 1937, 159–60.

Interpret the Evidence

- According to Wright, why did the police decide to frame him?
- Why did Wright send his letter to the *Nation*, a magazine whose readers are mostly in the North?

Put It in Context

Why was it unlikely that a black man in Alabama could receive a fair trial on the charge of raping a white woman?

Mexican Migrant Farmworkers
This photograph by Dorothea Lange shows a Mexican migrant and his child harvesting carrots in the Imperial Valley of California in 1935. Demand for Mexican labor declined during the Great Depression as displaced farmers from the Dust Bowl moved west to take jobs formerly held by Mexicans. Government deportations further decreased the number of undocumented Mexican laborers in the United States.   Copyright the Dorothea Lange Collection, the Oakland Museum of California, City of Oakland. Gift of Paul S. Taylor.

Tydings-McDuffie Act. The measure accomplished two aims at once: The act granted independence to the Philippines, and it restricted Filipino immigration into the United States.

Families under Strain

With millions of men unemployed, women faced increased family responsibilities. Stay-at-home wives had to care for their children and provide emotional support for out-of-work husbands who had lost their role as the family breadwinner. Despite the loss of income, homemakers continued their daily routines of shopping, cooking, cleaning, and child rearing.

Disproportionate male unemployment led to an increase in the importance of women's income. The depression hit male-dominated industries like steel mills and automakers the hardest. As a result, men were more likely to lose their jobs than women, who were concentrated in low-paying jobs like domestic service, nursing, and secretarial work. Although more women held on to their jobs, their often meager wages had to go further, since many now had to support unemployed fathers and husbands. During the 1930s, federal and local governments sought to increase male employment by passing laws to keep married women from holding civil service and teaching positions. Nonetheless, more and more married women entered the workplace, and by 1940 the

proportion of women in the job force had grown by about 25 percent.

As had been the case in previous decades, a higher proportion of African American women than white women worked outside the home in the 1930s. By 1940 less than 40 percent of African American women held jobs, compared to about 25 percent of white women. Racial discrimination played a key role in establishing this pattern. Black men faced higher unemployment rates than did their white counterparts, and what work was available was often limited to the lowest-paying jobs. As a result, black women faced greater pressure to supplement family incomes. Still, unemployment rates for black women reached as high as 50 percent during the 1930s. During more prosperous times, they had worked in white homes as domestic servants, but the depression forced white families to cut back on household expenses. Many African American women lost some of their domestic jobs to white working-class women who could find work nowhere else.

Despite increased burdens, most American families remained intact and discovered ways to survive the economic crisis. They pared down household budgets, made do without telephones and new clothes, and held on to their automobiles for longer periods of time. What money they managed to save they often spent on movies. Comedies, gangster movies, fantasy tales, and uplifting films helped viewers forget their troubles, if only for a few hours. Radio remained the chief source of entertainment, and radio sales doubled in the 1930s as listeners tuned in to soap operas, comedy and adventure shows, news reports, and musical programs.

The Season of Discontent

As the depression deepened, angry citizens found a variety of ways to express their discontent. Farmers had suffered economic hardship longer than any other group. Even before 1929, they had seen prices spiral downward, but in the early 1930s agricultural income plummeted 60 percent, and one-third of farmers lost their land (Figure 22.2). Some farmers decided that the time had come for drastic action. In the summer of 1932, Milo Reno, an Iowa farmer, created the Farm Holiday Association to organize farmers in order to keep their produce from going to market and thereby raise prices. Strikers blocked roads and kept reluctant farmers in line by smashing their truck windshields and headlights and slashing their tires. When law enforcement officials arrested fifty-five demonstrators in Council Bluffs, thousands of farmers marched on the jail and forced their release. The boycott spread to Nebraska and Wisconsin, and the violence increased. Despite armed attempts to prevent foreclosures and the intentional destruction of vast quantities of farm produce, the Farm Holiday Association failed to achieve its goal of raising prices.

Disgruntled urban residents also resorted to protest. Although the Communist Party remained a tiny group of just over 10,000 members in 1932, it played a large role in organizing the dispossessed. In major cities such as New York, Communists set up unemployment councils and led marches and rallies demanding jobs and food. In Harlem, the party endorsed rent strikes by African American apartment residents against their landlords. Party members did not confine their activities to the urban Northeast. They also went south to defend the Scottsboro Nine and to organize industrial workers in the steel mills of Birmingham and sharecroppers in the surrounding rural areas of Alabama. On the West Coast, Communists played an active role in the motion picture business, unionized seamen and waterfront workers, and led strikes.

One of the most visible protests of the early 1930s centered on events at the Ford factory in Dearborn, Michigan. As the depression worsened after 1930, Henry Ford, who had initially pledged to keep employee wages steady, changed his mind and reduced wages. The paternalistic Ford declared that it was "a good thing the recovery is prolonged. Otherwise people wouldn't profit by the illness." His laborers thought otherwise. On March 7, 1932, spearheaded by Communists, three thousand autoworkers marched from Detroit to Ford's River Rouge plant in nearby Dearborn. When they reached the factory town, they faced policemen

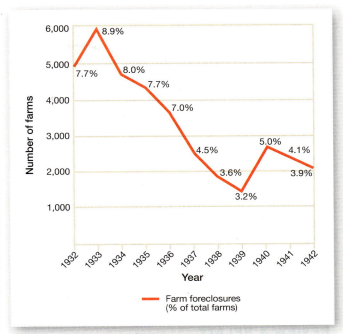

FIGURE 22.2 Farm Foreclosures, 1932–1942

A drop of 60 percent in prices led to a wave of farm foreclosures and rural protests in the early 1930s. From 1934 on, federal programs that promoted rural electrification, crop allotments, commodity loans, and mortgage credits allowed many farmers to retain their land. But tenant farmers and sharecroppers, particularly in the South, rarely benefited from these programs.

indiscriminately firing bullets and tear gas, which killed four demonstrators. The attack provoked great outrage. Around forty thousand mourners attended the funeral of the four protesters; sang the Communist anthem, the "Internationale"; and surrounded the caskets, which were draped in a red banner emblazoned with a picture of Bolshevik hero Vladimir Lenin.

Protests spread beyond Communist agitators. The federal government faced an uprising by some of the nation's most patriotic and loyal citizens—World War I veterans. Scheduled to receive a $1,000 bonus for their service, unemployed veterans could not wait until the payment date arrived in 1945. Instead, in the spring of 1932 a group of ex-soldiers from Portland, Oregon, set off on a march on Washington, D.C., to demand immediate payment of the bonus by the federal government. By the time they reached the nation's capital, the ranks of this **Bonus Army** had swelled to around twenty thousand veterans. They camped in the Anacostia Flats section of the city, constructed ramshackle shelters, and in many cases moved their families in with them. After intensive lobbying efforts, the House approved a bonus bill, but the Senate rejected it. Discouraged, many veterans abandoned the makeshift camps and returned home.

National Recovery Administration Eagles

President Roosevelt initiated the National Recovery Administration in 1933 as the centerpiece of his New Deal to stimulate economic growth. The city of Miami Beach employed these bathing beauties to attract conventioneers and vacationers to its hotels. Under the NRA code, they worked a forty-hour week and showed their satisfaction by sporting the NRA blue eagle insignia on their backs. © Bettmann/CORBIS

the landowners, who did not always distribute the designated funds owed to the sharecroppers. Though poor white farmers felt the sting of this injustice, the system of white supremacy existing in the South guaranteed that blacks suffered most.

After the Supreme Court voided the AAA in 1936 for imposing an unlawful tax on food processors in order to fund the subsidies, Congress enacted several pieces of legislation designed to limit production and provide aid to small farmers. The second AAA, passed in 1938, offered agricultural subsidies to reduce cultivation on the basis of conservation and soil erosion prevention, which overcame judicial objections. To deal with continuing rural poverty among sharecroppers and tenant farmers, Congress provided loans for displaced farmers.

The Roosevelt administration exhibited its boldest initiative in creating the **Tennessee Valley Authority (TVA)** in 1933 to bring low-cost electric power to rural areas and help redevelop the entire Tennessee River valley region through flood-control projects. In contrast to the AAA and other farm programs in which control stayed in private hands, the TVA owned and supervised the building and operation of public power plants, starting with the Muscle Shoals Dam in Alabama, which progressives had lobbied for since the 1920s. For farmers outside the Tennessee River valley, the Rural Electrification Administration helped them obtain cheap electric power starting in

1935, and for the first time tens of thousands of farmers experienced the modern conveniences that electricity brought (though most farmers would not get electric power until after World War II).

Roosevelt and Congress also acted to deal with the soil erosion problem behind the dust storms. In 1933, the Department of Interior established a Soil Erosion Service, and two years later Congress created a permanent Soil Conservation Service in the Department of Agriculture. Although these measures would prove beneficial in the long run, they did nothing to prevent even more severe storms from rolling through the Dust Bowl, as it was now known, in 1935 and 1936.

At the same time, Roosevelt concentrated on industrial recovery. He kept Hoover's RFC intact, but he went far beyond his predecessor in sanctioning government participation in the economy. In 1933 Congress passed the National Industrial Recovery Act, which established the **National Recovery Administration (NRA)**. This agency allowed business, labor, and the public (represented by government officials) to create codes to regulate production, prices, wages, hours, and collective bargaining. Designers of the NRA expected that if wages rose and prices remained stable, consumer purchasing power would climb, demand would grow, and businesses would put people back to work. For this plan to work, business people needed to keep prices steady by absorbing some of the costs of higher wages. The head of the

NRA, Hugh S. Johnson, a veteran of the War Industries Board during World War I, engaged in a highly visible public relations campaign. Johnson argued that regulatory codes were good for everyone. Like rules for a fair fight, they would "eliminate eye-gouging and knee-groining and ear-chewing in business," Johnson proclaimed. Businesses and industries that joined the NRA displayed the symbol of a blue eagle to signal their participation, and officials whipped up patriotic fervor on its behalf.

However, the NRA did not function as planned, nor did it bring the desired recovery. Businesses did not exercise the necessary restraint to keep prices steady. Large manufacturers dominated the code-making committees, and because Roosevelt had suspended enforcement of the antitrust law, they could not resist taking collective action to force smaller firms out of business. The NRA legislation guaranteed labor the right to unionize, but the agency did not vigorously enforce collective bargaining. The government failed to intervene to redress the imbalance of power between labor and management because Roosevelt depended primarily on big business to generate economic improvement. Moreover, the NRA had created codes for too many businesses, and government officials could not properly oversee them all. In 1935 the Supreme Court delivered the final blow to the NRA by declaring it an unconstitutional delegation of legislative power to the president.

Direct Assistance and Relief

Economic recovery programs were important, but they took time to take effect, and many Americans needed immediate help. Thus relief efforts and direct job creation were critical parts of the New Deal. Created in the early months of Roosevelt's term, the Federal Emergency Relief Administration (FERA) provided cash grants to states to revive their bankrupt relief efforts. Unlike Hoover's RFC, the FERA did not expect states to repay the loans, but it left administration of the programs to state and local agencies. Roosevelt chose Harry Hopkins, the chief of New York's relief agency, to head the FERA and distribute its initial $500 million appropriation. On the job for two hours, Hopkins had already spent $5 million. He did not calculate whether a particular plan "would work out in the long run," because, as he remarked, "people don't eat in the long run—they eat every day."

Harold Ickes, secretary of the interior and director of the Public Works Administration (PWA), oversaw efforts to rebuild the nation's infrastructure. Funding architects, engineers, and skilled workers, the PWA built the Grand Coulee, Boulder, and Bonneville dams in the West; the Triborough Bridge in New York City; 70 percent of all new schools constructed between 1933 and 1939; and a variety of municipal buildings, sewage plants, port facilities, and hospitals.

Yet neither the FERA nor the PWA provided enough emergency relief to the millions who faced the winter of 1933–1934 without jobs or the money to heat their homes. In response, Hopkins persuaded Roosevelt to launch a temporary program to help needy Americans get through this difficult period. Both men favored "work relief"— giving people jobs rather than direct welfare payments whenever practical. The Civil Works Administration (CWA) lasted four months, but in that brief time it employed more than 4 million people on about 400,000 projects that built 500,000 miles of roads, 40,000 schools, 3,500 playgrounds, and 1,000 airports. Montana got its state capitol building renovated, Pittsburgh erected its Cathedral of Learning, Boston's unemployed teachers went back to their classes, writers and artists remained at their desks and canvases, singers toured the nation, and ninety-four Indians restocked the Kodiak Islands off the coast of Alaska with rabbits.

Explore

See Document 22.2 for a criticism of direct relief assistance.

One of Roosevelt's most successful relief programs was the **Civilian Conservation Corps (CCC)**, created shortly after he entered the White House. The CCC recruited unmarried men between the ages of eighteen and twenty-five for a two-year stint. It removed them from relief rolls and the glut of the job market and put them to work planting forests; cleaning up beaches, rivers, and parks; and building bridges and dams. To build discipline, the U.S. army ran the CCC, furnished uniforms, and set up military-style camps. Participants received $1 per day, and the government sent $25 of the $30 in monthly wages directly to their families, helping make this the most popular of all New Deal programs. The CCC employed around 2.5 million men and lasted until 1942.

New Deal Critics

Despite the unprecedented efforts of the Roosevelt administration to spark recovery, provide relief, and encourage reform between 1933 and 1935, the country remained in depression, and unemployment still hovered around 20 percent. A liberal but not a radical, Roosevelt found himself under attack from both the left and the right. On the right, conservatives questioned New Deal spending and the growth of big government. On the left, the president's critics argued that he had not done enough to topple

DOCUMENT 22.2

Minnie Hardin | Letter to Eleanor Roosevelt, 1937

During the 1930s, Americans wrote to President Roosevelt and the First Lady in unprecedented numbers, revealing their personal desperation and their belief that the Roosevelts would respond to their individual pleas. Though most requested government assistance, not all letter writers favored the New Deal. In the following letter written to Eleanor Roosevelt in 1937, Minnie Hardin of Columbus, Indiana, expresses her frustration with direct relief programs.

Explore

How might Hardin explain the existence of poverty in America?

How does Hardin's "square deal" differ from Roosevelt's New Deal?

What impact did New Deal policies have on Hardin's life?

Mrs. Roosevelt:

I suppose from your point of view the work relief, old age pensions, slum clearance, and all the rest seems like a perfect remedy for all the ills of this country, but I would like for you to see the results, as the other half see them.

We have always had a shiftless, never-do-well class of people whose one and only aim in life is to live without work. I have been rubbing elbows with this class for nearly sixty years and have tried to help some of the most promising and have seen others try to help them, but it can't be done. We cannot help those who will not try to help themselves and if they do try, a square deal is all they need, and by the way that is all this country needs or ever has needed: a square deal for all and then, let each paddle their own canoe, or sink.

There has never been any necessity for any one who is able to work, being on relief in this locality, but there have been many eating the bread of charity and they have lived better than ever before. I have had taxpayers tell me that their children came from school and asked why they couldn't have nice lunches like the children on relief. The women and children around here have had to work at the fields to help save the crops and several women fainted while at work and at the same time we couldn't go up or down the road without stumbling over some of the reliefers, moping around carrying dirt from one side of the road to the other and back again, or else asleep. I live alone on a farm and have not raised any crops for the last two years as there was no help to be had. I am feeding the stock and have been cutting the wood to keep my home fires burning. There are several reliefers around here now who have been kicked off relief but they refuse to work unless they can get relief hours and wages, but they are so worthless no one can afford to hire them.

Source: Minnie Hardin, letter to Eleanor Roosevelt, December 14, 1937, Eleanor Roosevelt Papers, Series 190, Miscellaneous, 1937, Franklin D. Roosevelt Library.

Put It in Context

How did Hardin's beliefs about the causes of poverty shape her view of the New Deal?

wealthy corporate leaders from power and relieve the plight of the downtrodden.

The Great Depression and Hoover's inability to ameliorate its most damaging effects dealt a serious blow to the Republican Party and to the conservative opposition to federal government intervention with which it was identified. In 1934 officials of the Du Pont Corporation and General Motors formed the American Liberty League. The group, according to one of its founders, set out to educate the nation about "the value of encouraging people to work; encouraging people to get rich." From the point of view of the league's founders, the New Deal was little more than a vehicle for the spread of socialism and communism. The organization spent $1 million attacking what it considered to be Roosevelt's "dictatorial" policies and his assaults on free enterprise. The league, however, failed to attract support beyond a small group of northern industrialists, Wall Street bankers, and a few disaffected Democrats.

Roosevelt also faced criticism from the left. Communist Party membership reached its peak of around 75,000 in 1938, and though the party remained relatively small in numbers, it attracted intellectuals and artists whose voices could reach the larger public. The party's efforts to save the Scottsboro Nine boosted its appeal among African Americans. Party members also led unionizing drives in both the North and the South and displayed great talent and energy in organizing workers where resistance to unions was greatest. In the mid-1930s, the party followed the Soviet Union's antifascist foreign policy and joined with left-leaning, non-Communist groups, such as unions and civil rights organizations, to oppose the growing menace of fascism in Europe, particularly in Germany and Italy. By the end of the decade, however, the party had lost many members, as revelations about the tyrannical behavior of the Soviet dictator Joseph Stalin emerged and after the Soviet Union reversed its anti-Nazi foreign policy.

The greatest challenge to Roosevelt came from a trio of talented men who reflected diverse beliefs. Through charisma, organizational skills, or a combination of both, each of them created his own national campaign criticizing the New Deal. Francis Townsend, a retired California physician, proposed a "Cure for Depressions." In 1934 he formed the Old-Age Revolving Pensions Corporation, whose title summed up the doctor's idea. Townsend would have the government give all Americans over the age of sixty a monthly pension of $200 if they retired and spent the entire stipend each month. He promoted this scheme as a simple panacea for the ailing economy. Retirements would open up jobs for younger workers, and the income these workers received, along with the pension for the elderly, would pump ample funds into the economy to promote recovery. The government would fund the Townsend plan with a 2 percent "transaction" or sales tax. By 1936 Townsend Clubs had attracted about 3.5 million members throughout the country, and one-fifth of all adults in the United States signed a petition endorsing the Townsend plan.

While Townsend appealed mainly to the elderly, Charles E. Coughlin attracted Catholics and a lower-middle-class following. An outspoken priest from the Detroit suburb of Royal Oak, Michigan, Father Coughlin used his popular national radio broadcasts to talk about economic and political issues. Originally a Roosevelt supporter, by 1934 Coughlin had begun criticizing the New Deal for catering to greedy bankers. He spoke to millions of radio listeners about the evils of the Roosevelt administration, the godless Communists who had allegedly infested it, and international bankers—coded language referring to Jews—who supposedly manipulated it. In 1935 Coughlin's popularity reached its peak as he organized the National Union for Social Justice, which supported monetary inflation to help debt-ridden farmers and the nationalization of banks to control lending practices. As the decade wore on, his strident anti-Semitism and his growing fondness for fascist dictatorships abroad overshadowed his economic justice message, and Catholic officials ordered him to stop broadcasting.

Father Charles E. Coughlin

Father Charles E. Coughlin spoke at Cleveland Stadium in 1936 on behalf of Ohio congressional candidates who had been endorsed by his National Union for Social Justice. Coughlin, a Catholic priest and a stern critic of President Roosevelt, advocated the nationalization of banks and other industries, protection of worker rights, and monetary reform. Despite Coughlin's outspoken opposition, Roosevelt easily won reelection in 1936. Library of Congress

Huey Pierce Long of Louisiana, known as "the Kingfish," posed the greatest political threat to Roosevelt. Unlike Townsend and Coughlin, Long had built and operated a successful political machine, first as governor and then as U.S. senator, taking on the special interests of oil and railroad corporations in his home state. Early on he had backed Roosevelt, but Long found the New Deal wanting. "Not a single thin dime of concentrated, bloated, pompous wealth, massed in the hands of a few people," Long claimed, "has been raked down to relieve the masses." In 1934 Long established the **Share Our Wealth** society, promising to make "every man a king" by presenting families with a $5,000 homestead and a guaranteed annual income of $2,000. To accomplish this, Long proposed levying heavy income and inheritance taxes on the wealthy. Although the financial calculations behind his bold plan did not add up, Share Our Wealth clubs counted some seven million members. The swaggering senator departed from most of his segregationist southern colleagues by appealing to a coalition of disgruntled farmers, industrial workers, and African Americans (as governor of Louisiana, he supported repeal of the poll tax). Before Long could help lead a third-party campaign for president, he was shot and killed in 1935.

REVIEW & RELATE

What steps did Roosevelt take to stimulate economic recovery and provide relief to impoverished Americans during his first term in office?

What criticisms did Roosevelt's opponents level against the New Deal?

LEARNINGCurve bedfordstmartins.com/hewittlawson/LC

The New Deal Moves to the Left

Facing criticism from within his own party about the pace and effectiveness of the New Deal, and with the 1936 election looming, Roosevelt moved to the left. He adopted harsher rhetoric against recalcitrant corporate leaders; beefed up economic and social programs for the unemployed, the elderly, and the infirm; and revived measures to redress the power imbalance between management and labor. In doing so, he fashioned a political coalition that would deliver a landslide victory in 1936 and allow the Democratic Party to dominate electoral politics for the next three decades.

Expanding Relief Measures

Even though the New Deal had helped millions of people, millions of others still felt left out, as the popularity of Townsend, Coughlin, and Long indicated. "We the people voted for you," a Columbus, Ohio, worker wrote the president in disgust, "but it is a different story now. You have faded out on the masses of hungry, idle people. . . . The very rich is the only one who has benefited from your new deal."

In 1935 the president seized the opportunity to win his way back into the hearts of the "forgotten Americans"—poor farmers, industrial workers, and marginalized minority groups. Although Roosevelt favored a balanced budget, political necessity forced him to embark on deficit spending to expand the New Deal. Federal government expenditures would now exceed tax revenues, but New Dealers argued that these outlays would stimulate job creation and economic growth, which ultimately would replenish government coffers. Based on the highly successful but short-lived Civil Works Administration, the **Works Progress Administration (WPA)** provided jobs for the unemployed with a far larger budget, starting out with $5 billion. To ensure that the money would be spent, Roosevelt appointed Harry Hopkins to head the agency. Although critics condemned the WPA for employing people on unproductive "make-work" jobs and jibed that its initials stood for "We Poke Around"—a criticism not entirely unfounded—overall the WPA did a great deal of good. The agency constructed or repaired more than 100,000 public buildings, 600 airports, 500,000 miles of roads, and 100,000 bridges. The WPA employed about 8.5 million workers during its eight years of operation.

The WPA also helped artists, writers, and musicians. Under its auspices, the Federal Writers Project, the Federal Art Project, the Federal Music Project, and the Federal Theater Project encouraged the production of cultural works and helped bring them to communities and audiences throughout the country. Actors staged plays, dancers performed ballets, and musicians held recitals outside the usual centers of high culture in New York, Boston, and Chicago. Writers Richard Wright, Ralph Ellison, Clifford Odets, Saul Bellow, John Cheever, Margaret Walker, and many others nourished both their works and their stomachs while employed by the WPA. Painters created elaborate murals on the walls of post offices and other government buildings. Historians and folklorists researched and prepared city and state guides and interviewed black ex-slaves whose narratives of the system of bondage would otherwise have been lost.

New Deal Art

The Works Progress Administration, established by the Roosevelt administration in 1935, put Americans to work amid the ongoing depression. The WPA's Federal Art Project employed artists such as Ingrid E. Edwards of Minnesota, whose painting *Communications* features a newspaper boy, a telephone operator, a radio announcer, and a railroad train. Many of these works adorned public buildings.
Collection of Minnesota Historical Society. Lent by Fine Arts Collection, Public Buildings Service, U.S. General Services. Gift of Ah-Gwah Ching Archive

In addition to the WPA, the National Youth Administration (NYA) employed millions of young people. The NYA provided part-time work to 600,000 college undergraduates, 1.5 million high school students, and 2.6 million jobless youth who no longer attended school. Their work ranged from clerical assignments and repairing automobiles to building tuberculosis isolation units and renovating schools. Heading the NYA in Texas, the young Lyndon B. Johnson worked hard to expand educational and construction projects to unemployed whites and blacks. The Division of Negro Affairs, headed by the Florida educator Mary McLeod Bethune and the only minority group subsection in the NYA, ensured that African American youths would benefit from the programs sponsored by the agency.

Despite their many successes, these relief programs had a number of flaws. The WPA paid participants relatively low wages. The $660 in annual income earned by the average worker fell short of the $1,200 that a family needed to survive. In addition, the WPA limited participation to one family member. In most cases, this meant the male head of the household. As a result, women made up only about 14 percent of WPA workers, and even in the peak year of 1938, the WPA hired only 60 percent of eligible women. With the exception of the program for artists, most women hired by the WPA worked in lower-paying jobs than men.

Establishing Social Security

The elderly also required immediate relief and insurance in a country that lagged behind the rest of the industrialized world in helping its aged workforce. In August 1935, the president rectified this shortcoming and signed into law the **Social Security Act**. The measure provided that at age sixty-five, eligible workers would receive retirement payments funded by payroll taxes on employees and employers. The law also extended beyond the elderly by providing unemployment insurance for those temporarily laid off from work and welfare payments for the disabled who were permanently out of a job as well as for destitute, dependent children of single parents.

The Social Security program had significant limitations. The act excluded farm, domestic, and laundry workers, who were among the neediest Americans and were disproportionately African American. The reasons for these exclusions were largely political. The president needed southern Democrats to support this measure, and as a Mississippi newspaper observed: "The average Mississippian can't imagine himself chipping in to pay pensions for able bodied Negroes to sit around in idleness." The system of financing pensions also proved unfair. The payroll tax, which imposes the same fixed percentage on all incomes, is a regressive tax, one that falls hardest on those with lower incomes. The regressiveness of the tax proved to be an additional handicap for immediate economic recovery because the tax payments took purchasing power out of the hands of workers, whereas pension payments would not begin for several years. Social Security also disadvantaged working women, who on average earned less than men; nor did it take into account the unpaid labor of women who remained in the home to take care of their children.

Even with its flaws, Social Security revolutionized the expectations of American workers. It created a compact between the federal government and its citizens, and workers insisted that their political leaders fulfill their moral responsibilities to keep the system going. President Roosevelt recognized that the tax formula might not be economically sound, but he had a higher political objective in mind. He believed that payroll taxes would give contributors the right to collect their benefits and that "with those taxes in there, no damn politician can ever scrap my social security program." Social Security also helped create a larger middle-class constituency for Roosevelt and the Democratic Party.

Organized Labor Strikes Back

In 1935 Congress passed the **National Labor Relations Act**, also known as the Wagner Act for its leading sponsor, Senator Robert F. Wagner Sr. of New York. The law created the National Labor Relations Board (NLRB), which protected workers' right to organize labor unions without owner interference. During the 1930s, union membership rolls soared from fewer than 4 million workers to more than 10 million, including more than

800,000 women. At the outset of the depression, barely 6 percent of the labor force belonged to unions, compared with 33 percent in 1940.

Government efforts boosted this growth, but these spectacular gains were due primarily to workers' grassroots efforts set in motion by economic hard times. Workers in key industries—automobiles, steel, rubber, and textiles—took the lead. The number of striking workers during the first year of the Roosevelt administration soared from nearly 325,000 to more than 1.5 million. Organizers such as Luisa Moreno traveled the country to bring as many people as possible into the union movement. The most important development within the labor movement occurred in 1935, with the creation of the Congress of Industrial Organizations (CIO). After the American Federation of Labor (AFL), which consisted mainly of craft unions, rejected a proposal by John L. Lewis of the United Mine Workers to incorporate industrial workers under its umbrella, Lewis and representatives of seven other AFL unions defected and formed the CIO. Unlike the AFL, the new union sought to recruit a wide variety of workers without respect to race, gender, or region.

In 1937, two years after its founding, the CIO mounted a full-scale organizing campaign. More than 4.5 million workers participated in some 4,700 strikes, strangling mass-production industries. Unions found new ways to protest poor working conditions and arbitrary layoffs. Members of the United Auto Workers (UAW), a CIO affiliate, launched a **sit-down strike** against General Motors (GM) in Flint, Michigan, to win union recognition, higher wages, and better working conditions. Strikers refused to work but remained in the plants, shutting them down from the inside. Workers felt a new sense of power and confidence, a belief that they were more important than machines. "We learned we can take the plant," one striker gloated. "We already knew how to run them." When the company sent in local police forces to evict the strikers on January 11, 1937, the barricaded workers bombarded the police with spare machine parts and anything that was not bolted down. The community rallied around the strikers, and wives and daughters called "union maids" formed the Women's Emergency Brigade, which supplied sit-downers with food and water and kept up their morale. Neither the state nor the federal government interfered with the work stoppage, and after six weeks GM acknowledged defeat and recognized the UAW. Most of the other auto companies soon followed, though Henry Ford's was one of the last.

Despite some setbacks in 1937, especially in the steel industry, most strikes were settled in the union's

Women's Emergency Brigade

In December 1936, the United Auto Workers initiated a sit-down strike against General Motors in Flint, Michigan, for union recognition, better working conditions, and higher wages. The following month, a group of their women relatives, friends, and coworkers organized the Women's Emergency Brigade and held demonstrations and successfully rallied public support for the strikers. © Bettmann/CORBIS

favor, and by the end of the decade "big labor," as the AFL and CIO unions were known, had become a significant force in American politics and a leading backer of the New Deal. However, this big labor/big government alliance left out non-unionized industrial and agricultural workers, many of whom were African American or other minorities and lacked adequate bargaining power. Employers often passed on the burden of higher industrial wages to consumers in the form of higher prices.

A Half Deal for Minorities

President Roosevelt made significant gestures on behalf of African Americans. He appointed Mary McLeod Bethune and Robert Weaver to staff New Deal agencies and gathered an informal "Black Cabinet" in the nation's capital to advise him on matters pertaining to race. He also reversed the racial segregation policy his Democratic predecessor Woodrow Wilson had initiated in federal offices and facilities. The Roosevelt administration established the Civil Liberties Unit (later renamed Civil Rights Section) in the Department of Justice, which investigated racial discrimination. Eleanor Roosevelt acted as a visible symbol of the White House's concern with the plight of blacks, a role that culminated in her public support for the black singer Marian Anderson. In 1939 Eleanor Roosevelt quit the Daughters of the American Revolution, a women's organization, when it refused

to allow Anderson to hold a concert in Constitution Hall in Washington, D.C. Instead, the First Lady brought Anderson to sing on the steps of the Lincoln Memorial before an integrated audience of 75,000 and to millions more on the radio.

Perhaps the greatest measure of Franklin Roosevelt's impact on African Americans came when large numbers of black voters switched from the Republican to the Democratic Party in 1936, a pattern that has lasted to the present day. "Go turn Lincoln's picture to the wall," a black observer wryly commented after the election. "That debt has been paid in full."

Yet overall the New Deal did little to break down racial inequality. President Roosevelt believed that the plight of African Americans would improve, along with all downtrodden Americans, as New Deal measures restored economic health. Black leaders disagreed. They argued that the NRA's initials stood for "Negroes Ruined Again" because the agency displaced black workers and approved lower wages for blacks than for whites. The AAA dislodged black sharecroppers, a problem later ameliorated somewhat by New Deal programs such as the Farm Security Administration. New Deal programs such as the CCC and those for building public housing maintained existing patterns of segregation. Both the Social Security Act and the Fair Labor Standards Act omitted from coverage jobs that black Americans were most likely to hold. When members of Congress did propose legislation to combat

The Indian New Deal

John Collier, commissioner of Indian affairs under President Roosevelt, favored a New Deal for Native Americans. An advocate for Indian culture, Collier implemented reform legislation that replaced the policy of Indian assimilation with that of self-determination. In this 1935 photograph, Collier watches his boss, Secretary of the Interior Harold Ickes, sign the Flathead [Montana] Indian Constitution as tribal leaders look on.
© Bettmann/CORBIS

lynching and eliminate the poll tax on voting, Roosevelt offered only lukewarm support for fear of alienating his southern Democratic allies; consequently, these bills went down to defeat.

This pattern of halfway reform persisted for other minorities. Since the end of the Indian wars in 1890 (see chapter 15), Native Americans had lived in poverty, forced onto reservations that offered few economic opportunities and where whites carried out a relentless assault on their culture. By the early 1930s, American Indians earned an average income of less than $50 a year—compared with $800 for whites—and their unemployment rate was three times higher than that of white Americans. For the most part, they lived on lands that whites had given up on as unsuitable for farming or mining. The policy of assimilation established by the Dawes Act of 1887 had exacerbated the problem by depriving Indians of their cultural identities as well as their economic livelihoods. In 1934 the federal government reversed its course. Spurred on by John Collier, the commissioner of Indian affairs, Congress passed the **Indian Reorganization Act (IRA)**, which terminated the Dawes Act, authorized self-government for those living on reservations, extended tribal landholdings, and pledged to uphold native customs and language.

Although the IRA brought economic and social improvements for Native Americans, many problems remained. Despite his considerable efforts, Collier approached Indian affairs from the top down. One historian remarked that Collier had "the zeal of a crusader who knew better than the Indians what was good for them." The Indian commissioner failed to appreciate the diversity of native tribes and administered laws that contradicted Native American political and economic practices. For example, the IRA required the tribes to operate by majority rule, whereas many of them reached decisions through consensus, which respected the views of the minority. Although 174 tribes accepted the IRA, 78 tribes, including the Seneca, Crow, and Navajo, rejected it.

Twilight of the New Deal

Roosevelt's shift to the left paid political dividends, and in 1936 the president won reelection by a landslide. His sweeping victory proved to be one of the rare critical elections that signified a fundamental political realignment. Democrats replaced Republicans as the majority party in the United States, overturning thirty-six years of Republican rule. While Roosevelt had won convincingly in 1932, not until 1936 did the president put together a stable coalition that could sustain Democratic dominance for many years to come.

In 1936 Roosevelt trounced Alfred M. Landon, the Republican governor of Kansas, and Democrats increased their congressional majorities by staggering margins. The vote broke down along class lines. Roosevelt won the votes of 80 percent of union members, 81 percent of unskilled workers, and 84 percent of people on relief, compared with only 42 percent of high-income voters. Millions of new voters came out to the polls, and most of them supported Roosevelt's New Deal coalition of the poor, farmers, urban ethnic minorities, unionists, white southerners, and African Americans.

The euphoria of his triumph, however, proved short-lived. An overconfident Roosevelt soon reached beyond his electoral mandate and within two years found himself unable to extend the New Deal. In 1937 Roosevelt asked Congress to increase the size of the Supreme Court through a **court-packing plan**. He justified this as a matter of reform, claiming that the present nine-member Court could not handle its workload, much of it generated by the avalanche of New Deal legislation. Roosevelt attributed a good deal of the problem to the advanced age of six of the nine justices, who were over seventy years old. Under his proposal, the president would make one new appointment for each judge over the age of seventy who did not retire so long as the bench did not exceed fifteen members. In reality, Roosevelt schemed to "pack" the Court with supporters to prevent it from declaring New Deal legislation such as Social Security and the Wagner Act unconstitutional.

The plan backfired. Conservatives charged Roosevelt with seeking to destroy the separation of powers enshrined in the Constitution among the executive, legislative, and judicial branches. They portrayed the president as a "dictator," which, although a distorted characterization, touched a nerve in those concerned with the rise of tyrants in Germany and Italy. In the end, the president failed to expand the Supreme Court, but he preserved his legislative accomplishments. In a series of rulings, the chastened Supreme Court approved Social Security, the Wagner Act, and other New Deal legislation. Nevertheless, the political fallout from the court-packing fight damaged the president and his plans for further legislative reform.

Explore

See Documents 22.3 and 22.4 for two views on Roosevelt's court-packing plan.

Roosevelt's court-packing plan alienated many southern Democratic members of Congress who previously had sided with the president. Traditionally suspicious of the power of the federal government, southern lawmakers worried that Roosevelt was going too far toward centralizing power in Washington at the expense of states' rights. Southern Democrats formed a coalition with conservative northern Republicans who shared their concerns about the expansion of federal power and excessive spending on social welfare programs. Their antipathy toward labor unions, especially in the wake of the sit-down strikes, further bound them together. Although they held a minority of seats in Congress, this **conservative coalition** could block unwanted legislation by using the filibuster in the Senate (unlimited debate that could be shut down only with a two-thirds vote). The coalition could not defeat Roosevelt's **Fair Labor Standards Act** (1938), which established minimum wages at 40 cents an hour and maximum working hours at forty per week, but after 1938 these conservatives made sure that no other New Deal legislation passed.

Roosevelt also lost support because the recession of 1937 overlapped with the Supreme Court fight. When federal spending soared after passage of the WPA and other relief measures adopted in 1935, the president lost his economic nerve for deficit spending. He called for reduced spending, which increased unemployment and slowed economic recovery. At the same time, as the Social Security payroll tax took effect, it reduced the purchasing power of workers, thereby exacerbating the impact of reduced government spending. This "recession within the depression" further eroded congressional support for the New Deal.

The country was still deep in depression in 1939. Unemployment was at 17 percent, with more than 11 million people out of work. Most of those who were poor at the start of the Great Depression remained poor. Recovery came mainly to those who were temporarily impoverished as a result of the economic crisis. The distribution of wealth remained skewed toward the top. In 1933 the richest 5 percent of the population controlled 31 percent of disposable income; in 1939 the figure stood at 26 percent.

Against this backdrop of persistent difficult economic times, the president's popularity began to fade. In the midterm elections of 1938, Roosevelt campaigned against Democratic conservatives in an attempt to reinvigorate his New Deal coalition. His efforts failed to purge the conservatives he hoped to unseat and upset many ordinary citizens who associated the tactic with that used by European dictators who had recently risen to power. As the decade came to a close, Roosevelt turned his attention away from the New Deal and increasingly toward a new war in Europe that, like

DOCUMENTS 22.3 AND 22.4

Packing the Supreme Court: Two Views

In his first term, President Roosevelt secured legislation to implement his New Deal; however, by 1937 the Supreme Court had overturned several key pieces of New Deal legislation, arguing that Congress had exceeded its constitutional authority. As the Social Security Act and the National Labor Relations Act came up for review before the Court, Roosevelt tried to dilute the influence of the Court's conservative majority. Following his landslide reelection in 1936, he asked Congress to enlarge the Court so that he could appoint justices more favorable to his liberal agenda. The following cartoons take opposing positions on Roosevelt's court-packing plan.

Explore

22.3 The Great Emancipator, 1937

THE GREAT EMANCIPATOR—1937

Franklin D. Roosevelt Library

Explore

22.4 Retire or Move Over, 1937

Interpret the Evidence

- Why does the first cartoonist compare Roosevelt to Abraham Lincoln?
- How does the second cartoonist's idea of freedom differ from that of the first?

Put It in Context

How do both cartoons appeal to the hopes and fears of the American public during the late 1930s?

World War I twenty-five years earlier, threatened to engulf the entire world.

REVIEW & RELATE

Why and how did the New Deal shift to the left in 1934 and 1935?

Despite the president's landslide victory in 1936, why did the New Deal stall during Roosevelt's second term in office?

LEARNINGCurve bedfordstmartins.com/hewittlawson/LC

Conclusion: New Deal Liberalism

Franklin Roosevelt succeeded in expanding the scope of public authority. The New Deal brought unprecedented government involvement in the lives of people, whether rich or poor. Businesses were subject to increased regulation even as they retained control over hiring and firing, production, and pricing. The federal government grew considerably during the 1930s, jumping from 605,000 employees to more than 1 million, and turned citizens' attention from local and state authorities to officials in Washington, D.C. Yet the New Deal rescued the capitalist system, doing little to alter the fundamental structure of the American economy. It left corporations, the stock market, farms, and banks in the hands of private enterprise. Indeed, by the end of the 1930s large corporations had more power over markets than ever before. Income and wealth remained unequally distributed, nearly to the same extent as it had been before Roosevelt took office in 1933.

Roosevelt forged a middle path between reactionaries and revolutionaries at a time when the fascist tyrants Adolf Hitler and Benito Mussolini gained power in Germany and Italy respectively and Joseph Stalin ruthlessly consolidated his rule in the Communist Soviet

Union. By contrast, the American president expanded democratic capitalism, bringing a broader cross section of society to the decision-making table. Big business no longer held unilateral authority but instead found its power balanced by big labor, big agriculture, and big government. Roosevelt's "broker state" of multiple competing interests provided for greater democracy than a government dominated exclusively by business elites. This system did not benefit those who remained unorganized and wielded little power, but marginalized groups—African Americans, Latinos, and Native Americans—did receive greater recognition and self-determination from the federal government. Moreover, in the coming decades these groups, too, would find ways to take advantage of the power of collective action and claim a place at the bargaining table.

President Roosevelt also solidified the institution of the presidency as the focal point for public leadership. His cheerfulness, hopefulness, and pragmatism rallied millions of individuals behind him. Even after Roosevelt died in 1945, the public retained its expectation that leadership came from the White House.

Through his programs and force of personality, Franklin Roosevelt convinced Americans that he cared about their welfare and that the federal government would not ignore their suffering. With his chin cocked upward, a fedora hat on his head, and a cigarette holder protruding from his smiling mouth, Roosevelt assured the depression-weary public that it had somewhere to turn for relief. He was not universally beloved: Millions of Americans despised him because they thought he was leading the country toward socialism, and he did not solve all the problems the country faced—it would take government spending for World War II to end the depression. Still, together with his wife Eleanor, Franklin Roosevelt conveyed a sense that the American people belonged to a single community, capable of banding together to solve the country's problems, no matter how serious they were or how intractable they might seem.

Chapter Review

Online Study Guide ▶ bedfordstmartins.com/hewittlawson

KEY TERMS

REVIEW & RELATE

1. How did President Hoover respond to the problems and challenges created by the Great Depression?

2. How did different segments of the American population experience the depression?

3. What steps did Roosevelt take to stimulate economic recovery and provide relief to impoverished Americans during his first term in office?

4. What criticisms did Roosevelt's opponents level against the New Deal?

5. Why and how did the New Deal shift to the left in 1934 and 1935?

6. Despite the president's landslide victory in 1936, why did the New Deal stall during Roosevelt's second term in office?

TIMELINE OF EVENTS

1931	Scottsboro Nine tried for rape
1932–1939	Dust storms sweep through Great Plains
1932	Creation of Reconstruction Finance Corporation
	River Rouge autoworkers' strike
	Milo Reno creates the Farm Holiday Association
	Bonus Army marches on Washington, D.C.
1933	Roosevelt takes steps to stabilize banking and financial systems
	Agricultural Adjustment Act passed
	Federal Emergency Relief Administration (FERA) created
	Tennessee Valley Authority (TVA) created
	National Recovery Administration (NRA) created
	Civilian Conservation Corps (CCC) created
1934	Indian Reorganization Act (IRA) passed
	Francis Townsend forms Old-Age Revolving Pensions Corporation
	Huey Long establishes Share Our Wealth movement
	Securities and Exchange Commission (SEC) established
1935	Charles E. Coughlin organizes National Union for Social Justice
	Works Progress Administration (WPA) established
	Social Security Act passed
	National Labor Relations Act passed
	Congress of Industrial Organizations (CIO) founded
	Creation of the Soil Conservation Service
1937	United Auto Workers conduct sit-down strikes against General Motors in Flint, Michigan
	Roosevelt proposes to increase the size of the Supreme Court
1938	Fair Labor Standards Act passed

The Depression in Rural America

During the 1930s, rural Americans' lives were devastated by the twin disasters of the Great Depression and, in the Great Plains, the most sustained drought in American history. But both problems only deepened the already difficult lives of many farmers. Agriculture in the South had long been dominated by sharecropping, a system that hampered crop diversification and left many African American tenant farmers vulnerable to exploitation by white landowners. In the Midwest, farmers had spent decades overgrazing pastures and exhausting the soil through overproduction. Prices dropped dramatically throughout the 1920s, and farmers were the only group whose incomes fell during that decade.

When the depression hit, many farmers did not have the resources to stay on their land, and farm foreclosures tripled in the early 1930s. Sharecroppers, tenant farmers, and former farm owners left their homes to find better opportunities, and a million people left the Great Plains alone. Most ended up as migrant agricultural laborers in farms and orchards on the West Coast. Feeling overrun by refugees, California passed a law in 1937 making it a misdemeanor to bring into California any indigent person who was not a state resident. This law remained in effect until 1941.

Under the New Deal, the federal government acted in a number of ways to relieve the plight of farmers around the country. The Agricultural Adjustment Act attempted to raise crop prices and stabilize agricultural incomes by encouraging farmers to cut production. The Farm Credit Act helped some farmers refinance mortgages at a lower rate, the Rural Electrification Administration brought electricity to farm areas previously without it, and the Soil Conservation Service advised farmers on how to properly cultivate their hillsides. The report of the Great Plains Committee (Document 22.10), another Roosevelt creation, details additional recommendations for helping the agricultural economy in the Midwest.

The following documents on the lives of farmers, sharecroppers, migrants, and labor organizers during the 1930s shed light on many aspects of the Great Depression. Consider what they reveal about the challenges faced by rural Americans and how different individuals and groups responded to those problems.

DOCUMENT 22.5

Ann Marie Low | Dust Bowl Diary, 1934

When massive dust storms swept through the Midwest beginning in the early 1930s, they blew away the topsoil of a once productive farm region and created hazardous living conditions. Residents needed to clean and wash repetitively to perform even simple daily tasks. Ann Marie Low, a young woman living with her family in southeastern North Dakota, describes in her diary the monotony and difficulty of life in the Dust Bowl.

May 21, 1934, Monday . . .

Saturday Dad, Bud, and I planted an acre of potatoes. There was so much dirt in the air I couldn't see Bud only a few feet in front of me. Even the air in the house was just a haze. In the evening the wind died down, and Cap came to take me to the movie. We joked about how hard it is to get cleaned up enough to go anywhere.

The newspapers report that on May 10 there was such a strong wind the experts in Chicago estimated 12,000,000 tons of Plains soil was dumped on that city. By the next day the sun was obscured in Washington, D.C., and ships 300 miles out at sea reported dust settling on their decks.

Sunday the dust wasn't so bad. Dad and I drove cattle to the Big Pasture. Then I churned butter and baked a ham, bread, and cookies for the men, as no telling when Mama will be back.

May 30, 1934, Wednesday

Ethel got along fine, so Mama left her at the hospital and came to Jamestown by train Friday. Dad took us both home.

The mess was incredible! Dirt had blown into the house all week and lay inches deep on everything. Every towel and curtain was just black. There wasn't a clean dish or cooking utensil. There was no food. Oh, there were eggs and milk and one loaf left of the bread I baked the weekend before. I looked in the cooler box down the well (our refrigerator) and found a little ham and butter. It was late, so Mama and I cooked some ham and eggs for the men's supper because that was all we could fix in a hurry. It turned out they had been living on ham and eggs for two days.

Mama was very tired. After she had fixed starter for bread, I insisted she go to bed and I'd do all the dishes.

It took until 10 o'clock to wash all the dirty dishes. That's not wiping them—just washing them. The cupboards had to be washed out to have a clean place to put them.

Saturday was a busy day. Before starting breakfast I had to sweep and wash all the dirt off the kitchen and dining room floors, wash the stove, pancake griddle, and dining room table and chairs. There was cooking, baking, and churning to be done for those hungry men. Dad is 6 feet 4 inches tall, with a big frame. Bud is 6 feet 3 inches and almost as big-boned as Dad. We say feeding them is like filling a silo.

Mama couldn't make bread until I carried water to wash the bread mixer. I couldn't churn until the churn was washed and scalded. We just couldn't do anything until something was washed first. Every room had to have dirt almost shoveled out of it before we could wash floors and furniture.

We had no time to wash clothes, but it was necessary. I had to wash out the boiler, wash tubs, and the washing machine before we could use them. Then every towel, curtain, piece of bedding, and garment had to be taken outdoors to have as much dust as possible shaken out before washing. The cistern is dry, so I had to carry all the water we needed from the well.

Source: Ann Marie Low, *Dust Bowl Diary* (Lincoln: University of Nebraska Press, 1984), 96–97.

The Life of a White Sharecropper, 1938

In 1936 workers in the WPA's Federal Writers Project began the Folklore Project. Interviewers spoke with thousands of ordinary individuals to document their home lives, education, occupations, political and religious views, and the impact of the Great Depression on their families. Folklore Project worker Claude Dunnagan collected the following story from a white sharecropping family in Longtown, North Carolina.

I guess we been hard luck renters all our lives—me and Morrison both. They was ten young'uns in my family, and I was next to the youngest. We had it awful hard. . . . We went to Yadkin County and rented an old rundown farm for a share of what we could raise. The crops wasn't any good that year, the landlord came and got what we had raised and had the auctioneers come and sell our tools and furniture. They was a bunch of people at the sale that day from all around. I was standin' there watchin' the man sell the things when I saw a good lookin' man in overalls lookin' toward me. He watched me all durin' the sale and I knew what he was thinkin'. That was the first time I ever saw Allison. I reckon he fell in love with me right off, for we was married a few days later. Allison didn't have no true father. His mother wasn't married, and he was raised up by his kin folks. Then we moved to a little farm near Longtown, about ten miles away. The owner said we could have three-fourths of what we raised. The first two years the crops turned out pretty good so we could pay off the landlord and buy a little furniture . . . a bed and table and some chairs. Then the first baby came on. That was Hildreth. He's out in the field workin' now, suckerin' [removing sprouts] tobacco. . . . By that time, we was able to get a cow, and that came in good, for the baby was awful thin and weak. . . .

Hildreth was only six, but he could help a lot, pullin' and tyin' the tobacco, and helpin' hang it in the barn. We got out more tobacco that year than any other, but when we took it to market in Winston, they wasn't payin' but about twelve cents a pound for the best grade, so when we give the landlord his share and paid the fertilizer bill, we didn't have enough left to pay the doctor and store bill. We didn't know what we was goin' to do durin' the winter. Allison had raised a few vegetables and apples, so we canned what we could and traded the rest for some cotton cloth up at the store so the children would have something to wear that winter. Allison got a job helpin' build a barn for a neighbor, but it didn't last but two days. The neighbor gave him two second hand pairs of overalls for the work. . . .

Things are a lot better for the renter today than in the past. It used to be we couldn't get enough to eat and wear. Now we got a cow, a hog, and some chickens. Allison bought a second-hand car and every Sunday afternoon we ride somewhere. It's the only time we ever get away from home.

The landlord gives us five-sixths of what we raise, so we get along pretty good when the crops are fair. Of course we have to furnish the fertilizer and livestock. This year we had seven barns of tobacco and four acres of corn. Wheat turned out pretty good, too. We raised forty-three bushels, and I hear the price is going to be fair at the roller mill. I canned about all our extra fruits and vegetables. I reckon we still got about a hundred cans in the pantry.

Source: Library of Congress, Manuscript Division, WPA Federal Writers Project Collection.

DOCUMENT 22.7

Sharecropping Family in Washington County, Arkansas, 1935

The Resettlement Administration (later the Farm Security Administration) documented the plight of migrant farmworkers and sharecroppers in numerous photographs. The following photo, taken by the noted photojournalist Arthur Rothstein, depicts a sharecropper's wife and daughters in Washington County, Arkansas, in 1935.

Franklin D. Roosevelt Library

DOCUMENT 22.8

John Steinbeck | The Harvest Gypsies, 1936

In 1936 the *San Francisco News* hired John Steinbeck to write a series of articles on Dust Bowl migrants in California. Steinbeck toured farm sites and shantytowns, and his work on these articles formed the basis of his Pulitzer Prize–winning novel *The Grapes of Wrath*. The following selection is from the second installment of his newspaper series.

This is a family of six; a man, his wife, and four children. They live in a tent the color of the ground. Rot has set in on the canvas so that the flaps and the sides hang in tatters and are held together with bits of rusty baling wire. There is one bed in the family and that is a big tick [sack mattress] lying on the ground inside the tent.

They have one quilt and a piece of canvas for bedding. The sleeping arrangement is clever. Mother and father lie down together and two children lie between them. Then, heading the other way, the other two children lie, the littler ones. If the mother and father sleep with their legs spread wide, there is room for the legs of the children.

There is more filth here. The tent is full of flies clinging to the apple box that is the dinner table, buzzing about the foul clothes of the children, particularly the baby, who has not been bathed nor cleaned for several days. This family has been on the road longer than the builder of the paper house. There is no toilet here, but there is a clump of willows nearby where human feces lie exposed to the flies—the same flies that are in the tent.

Two weeks ago there was another child, a four year old boy. For a few weeks they had noticed that he was kind of lackadaisical, that his eyes had been feverish. They had given him the best place in the bed, between father and mother. But one night he went into convulsions and died, and the next morning the coroner's wagon took him away. It was one step down.

They know pretty well that it was a diet of fresh fruit, beans, and little else that caused his death. He had no milk for months. With this death there came a change of mind in his family. The father and mother now feel that paralyzed dullness with which the mind protects itself against too much sorrow and too much pain.

And this father will not be able to make a maximum of four hundred dollars a year any more because he is no longer alert; he isn't quick at piecework, and he is not able to fight clear of the dullness that has settled on him. His spirit is losing caste rapidly.

The dullness shows in the faces of this family, and in addition there is a sullenness that makes them taciturn. Sometimes they still start the older children off to school, but the ragged little things will not go; they hide in ditches or wander off by themselves until it is time to go back to the tent, because they are scorned in the school.

The better-dressed children shout and jeer, the teachers are quite often impatient with these additions to their duties, and the parents of the "nice" children do not want to have disease carriers in the schools.

The father of this family once had a little grocery store and his family lived in back of it so that even the children could wait on the counter. When the drought set in there was no trade for the store any more.

This is the middle class of the squatters' camp. In a few months this family will slip down to the lower class. Dignity is all gone, and spirit has turned to sullen anger before it dies.

Source: John Steinbeck, "The Harvest Gypsies," *San Francisco News*, October 7, 1936.

DOCUMENT 22.9

Frank Stokes | Let the Mexicans Organize, 1936

While union organizers made some gains in the industrial sector, they made little headway in the agricultural fields of California. Frank Stokes was a citrus grower who broke with his fellow farmers to support migrant labor organizing. In the following selection, Stokes argues in favor of unionization among migrant Mexican farmworkers.

The Mexican is to agricultural California what the Negro is to the medieval South. His treatment by the vegetable growers of the Imperial Valley is well known. What has happened to him in the San Joaquin has likewise been told. But for a time at least it appeared that the "citrus belt" was different. Then came the strike of the Mexican fruit pickers in Orange County. In its wake came the vigilantes, the night riders, the strike-breakers, the reporters whose job it was to "slant" all the stories in favor of the packers and grove owners. There followed the State Motor Patrol, which for the first time in the history of strike disorders in California set up a portable radio broadcasting station "in a secret place" in the strike area "to direct law-and-order activities." And special deputy badges blossomed as thick as Roosevelt buttons in the recent campaign.

Sheriff Jackson declared bravely: "It was the strikers themselves who drew first blood so from now on we will meet them on that basis." "This is no fight," said he, "between orchardists and pickers. It is a fight between the entire population of Orange County and a bunch of Communists." However, dozens and dozens of non-Communist Mexican fruit pickers were jailed; 116 were arrested en masse while traveling in automobiles along the highway. They were charged with riot and placed under bail of $500 each. . . . After fifteen days in jail the hearing was finally held—and the state's witnesses were able to identify only one person as having taken part in the trouble. . . . Judge Ames of the Superior Court ordered the release of all but one identified prisoner and severely criticized the authorities for holding the Mexicans in jail for so long a time when they must have known it would not be possible to identify even a small portion of the prisoners.

For weeks during the strike newspaper stories described the brave stand taken by "law-abiding citizens." These stories were adorned with such headlines as "Vigilantes Battle Citrus Strikers in War on Reds." During all this time, so far as I know, only one paper—the Los Angeles *Evening News*—defended the fruit pickers. . . .

These Mexicans were asking for a well-deserved wage increase and free transportation to and from the widely scattered groves; they also asked that tools be furnished by the employers. Finally they asked recognition of their newly formed union. Recognition of the Mexican laboring man's union, his cooperative organization formed in order that he might obtain a little more for his commodity, which is labor—here was the crucial point. The growers and packers agreed to furnish tools; they agreed to furnish transportation to and from the groves. They even agreed to a slight wage increase, which still left the workers underpaid. But recognition of the Mexican workers' union? Never! . . .

Not only in the fields are the Mexican people exploited. Not only as earners but as buyers they are looked upon as legitimate prey—for old washing machines that will not clean clothes, for old automobiles that wheeze and let down, for woolen blankets made of cotton, for last season's shop-worn wearing apparel. Gathered in villages composed of rough board shanties or drifting with the seasons from vegetable fields of the Imperial Valley to the grape vineyards of the San Joaquin, wherever they go it is the same old, pathetic story. Cheap labor!

Source: Frank Stokes, "Let the Mexicans Organize," *The Nation*, December 19, 1936, 731–32.

DOCUMENT 22.10

Report of the Great Plains Committee, 1937

In 1936 President Roosevelt established the Great Plains Committee to investigate the causes of the Dust Bowl and possible solutions for the region. The committee's report, submitted the following year, outlined how federal, state, and local government agencies could work together to restore the Great Plains to economic health. One of the witnesses the committee called to testify was Otis Nation, an organizer for the Oklahoma Tenant Farmers' Union, whose testimony follows.

Much has been written of our droughts here in Oklahoma, and how they have driven the farmers from the land. But little has been said of the other tentacles that choke off the livelihood of the small owner and the tenant. We do not wish to minimize the seriousness of these droughts and their effects on the farming population. But droughts alone would not have permanently displaced these farmers. The great majority of migrants had already become share-tenants and sharecroppers. The droughts hastened a process that had already begun. We submit the following as the cases for migratory agricultural workers:

1. *High interest rates.* Often a farmer borrows money for periods of 10 months and is charged an interest rate of 10 percent. These rates are charged when crops are good and when they fail. Through such practices the farmer loses his ownership; he becomes a tenant, then a sharecropper, then a migrant.

2. *The tenant and sharecropping system.* When share tenants are charged $33\frac{1}{3}$ percent of all corn or feed crops and 25 percent or more on cotton, plus 10 percent on all money borrowed at the bank, when sharecroppers are charged 50 to 75 percent of all he produces to the landlords, plus 10 percent for the bank's share on money invested; when these robbing practices are carried on in a community or a State, is it surprising that 33,241 farm families have left Oklahoma in the past 5 years?

3. *Land exhaustion, droughts, soil erosion, and the one-crop system of farming.* Lacking capital and equipment, small farmers have been unable to terrace their land conduct other soil-conservation practices. The tenant and sharecropping system is chiefly responsible for the one-crop system. The landlord dictates what crops are to be planted—invariably cotton—and the tenant either plants it or gets off.

4. *Unstable markets.* Approximately a month and a half before the wheat harvest this year the price for this product was 93 cents here in Oklahoma City. But at harvest time the farmer sold his wheat for 46 cents to 60 cents per bushel, depending on the grade. . . . Kaffir [a grain sorghum] was selling

for $1.30 one month ago, and yesterday we sold some for 85 cents per hundred. . . .

It is obvious to all of us that farm prices are set by speculators. The farmer's losses at the market have contributed in no small part to the farmer losing his place on the land. Higher prices for farm products are quoted when the farmer has nothing to sell.

5. *Tractor farming.* In Creek County, Okla., we have the record of one land-owner purchasing 3 tractors and forcing 31 of his 34 tenants and croppers from the land. Most of these families left the State when neither jobs nor relief could be secured. This is over 10 families per machine, 10 families who must quit their profession and seek employment in an unfriendly, industrialized farming section of Arizona or California. Many of these families were even unable to become "Joads" [the fictional family in *The Grapes of Wrath*] in these other States, and had to seek relief from an unfriendly national administration and a more unfriendly State administration. . . .

At this hearing we will have all kinds of statistical material presented and arguments based on this material. But I am one of those who is more interested in the people, my people, than in mere figures. I do not agree with those who say "the no-good must always be weeded out." I say that all of these people, casually referred to in statistical ms, are 100-percent Americans. There are no more important problems facing us an the problem of stopping this human erosion and rehabilitating those unfortunates who have already been thrown off the land. Certainly it is un-American for Americans to be starved and dispossessed of their homes in our land of plenty. Those who seek to exploit and harass these American refugees, the migratory workers, are against our principles of democracy.

Source: U.S. Congress, House Select Committee to Investigate the Interstate Migration of Destitute Citizens (Washington: Government Printing Office, 1940–1941), 2102.

Interpret the Evidence

1. What does Ann Marie Low's description of a typical day suggest about the particular challenges women faced during the Dust Bowl era (Document 22.5)?

2. Compare the living conditions described by a white southern sharecropper (Document 22.6) to those of the migrant family described by John Steinbeck (Document 22.8). How does the poverty of the two families differ? How would you explain the differences you note?

3. Compare the sharecropper's story (Document 22.6) with the photograph of the Arkansas family (Document 22.7). Do the subjects seem to react to the Great Depression in the same way? Do they seem hopeful or hopeless?

4. According to Frank Stokes, how did the fruit packers and grove owners characterize their conflict with the Mexican farmworkers (Document 22.9)? In what ways did their characterization draw on more general conservative criticisms of the New Deal?

5. According to the Great Plains Committee testimony (Document 22.10), what role did human-caused factors play in producing the misery that accompanied the dust storms of the early 1930s?

Put It in Context

- What do these documents tell us about expectations regarding government help during the Great Depression?

background photos: pages 714 and 718, Library of Congress

LEARNINGCurve
Check what you know.
bedfordstmartins.com/hewittlawson/LC

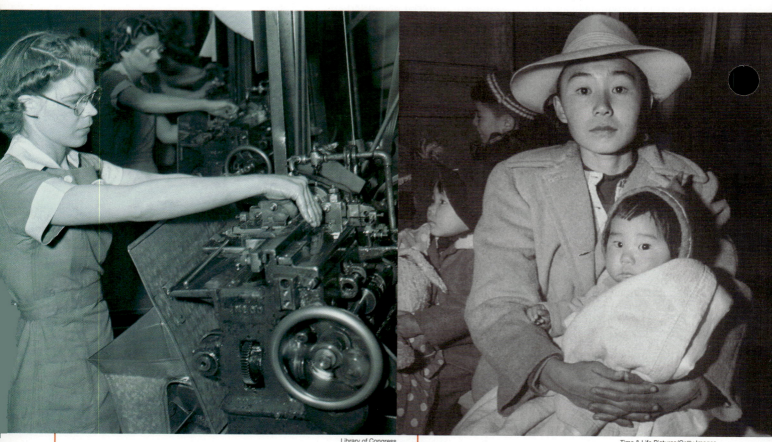

Library of Congress

Time & Life Pictures/Getty Images

Woman working at the Republic Drill and Tool Company in Chicago, Illinois, 1942.

Japanese American woman and child at internment camp, Tule Lake, California.

23

World War II

1933–1945

Library of Congress

Tuskegee airman Edward C. Gleed, March 1945.

AMERICAN HISTORIES

One month after Japan attacked the U.S. naval base at Pearl Harbor on December 7, 1941, and the United States entered World War II, President Franklin Roosevelt approved a full-scale effort to develop an atomic bomb. As scientific director of this top-secret program, called the Manhattan Engineering District Project, physicist J. Robert Oppenheimer orchestrated the work of more than 3,000 scientists, technicians, and military personnel at the Los Alamos Laboratories near Santa Fe, New Mexico. The thirty-seven-year-old Oppenheimer, the son of German American Jews, had studied theoretical physics in England and Germany and then returned to the United States to teach physics. He was also interested and engaged in world events. When the Nazis began persecuting German Jews in the early 1930s, Oppenheimer helped Jews gain asylum in the United States.

On July 16, 1945, Oppenheimer and his team successfully tested their new weapon. The explosion, which had a force equal to more than 18,000 tons of TNT, lit up the predawn sky with a blast so powerful that it broke a window 125 miles away and so bright that a blind woman claimed she saw a flash of light. A mushroom cloud shot up 41,000 feet into the sky over ground zero, where a 1,200-foot-wide crater had formed. Oppenheimer understood that the world had been permanently transformed. Quoting from Hindu scriptures, he remembered thinking at the moment of the explosion, "I am become death, destroyer of worlds."

On August 6, 1945, Army Air Corps planes dropped an atomic bomb on the Japanese city of Hiroshima and three days later another one on Nagasaki, resulting in the deaths of more than 200,000 civilians. Profoundly shaken by the death and destruction his efforts had produced, Oppenheimer observed: "If atomic bombs are to be added to the arsenals of a warring world, or to the arsenals of nations preparing for war, then the time will come when mankind will curse the names of Los Alamos and Hiroshima."

While Oppenheimer and his team remained cloistered at Los Alamos, Fred Korematsu and some 112,000 Japanese Americans lived in internment camps, imprisoned for no other reason than their Japanese ancestry. Born in Oakland, California, in 1919 to Japanese immigrants, Fred and his three brothers grew up like many first-generation Americans. Fred's parents spoke Japanese at home and maintained the cultural traditions of their native land, while their sons learned English in public school, ate hamburgers, and played football and basketball like other children their age. After graduating from high school in 1938, Korematsu worked on the Oakland docks as a welder.

After the 1941 bombing of Pearl Harbor, residents on the West Coast turned their anger on the Japanese and Japanese Americans living among them. As assimilated as Fred Korematsu and many other Nisei (the U.S.-born children of Japanese immigrants) had become, white Americans doubted their loyalty and viewed them as a threat to national security. Korematsu could no longer get a haircut in a white-owned barbershop; the

Boilermakers Union expelled him, and he lost his job as a welder; and he was not allowed to join the U.S. coast guard because of his race.

These indignities foreshadowed events to come. On March 21, 1942, President Roosevelt issued Executive Order 9066 authorizing military commanders on the West Coast to take any measures necessary to promote national security. Consequently, officials imposed a curfew on Japanese Americans, excluded them from designated areas, and prohibited them from traveling more than twenty-five miles from their homes. On May 9, the military ordered Korematsu's family to report to Tanforan Racetrack in San Mateo, from which they would be transported to internment camps throughout the West. Although the rest of his family complied with the order, Fred refused. He adopted the name "Clyde Sarah" and claimed to be of Spanish-Hawaiian ancestry. However, Korematsu's efforts to resist internment failed. Three weeks later, he was arrested and later transferred to the Topaz internment camp in south-central Utah. Found guilty of violating the original evacuation order, Korematsu received a sentence of five years of probation. When he appealed his conviction to the U.S. Supreme Court in 1944, the high court upheld the verdict. By the time the first atomic bomb exploded over Hiroshima, the government had closed down the internment camp where Fred Korematsu lived, and he had regained his freedom. ●

THE AMERICAN HISTORIES of both Fred Korematsu and J. Robert Oppenheimer were shaped by the profound changes brought about by war. Korematsu was subjected to the full force of anti-Japanese sentiment that followed the attack on Pearl Harbor, while Oppenheimer played a key role in developing a weapon that he feared would lead to the destruction of mankind. Both men experienced a mixture of hope and uneasiness as they looked ahead to the postwar world.

The war that these two men experienced in such different ways marked a critical point for the United States in the twentieth century. World War II finally ended the Great Depression, cementing the trend toward government intervention in the economy that had begun with the

New Deal. With the war fought almost entirely on foreign soil, the United States converted its factories to wartime production and became the "arsenal of democracy," putting millions of Americans to work in the process, including African Americans, other minorities, and women. All Americans contributed to the war effort, whether they wanted to or not, through rationing and higher taxes. Overseas, soldiers fought fierce battles in Europe, Africa, and Asia. The combined military power of the Allies, led by the United States, Great Britain, and the Soviet Union, finally defeated the Axis nations of Germany, Italy, and Japan, but not until the fighting had killed 60 to 70 million people, more than half of whom were civilians, and ushered in the Atomic Age.

The Road toward War

The end of World War I did not bring peace and prosperity to Europe. The harsh peace terms imposed on the Central Powers in 1919 left the losers, especially Germany, deeply resentful. The war saddled both sides with a huge financial debt and produced economic instability, which contributed to the Great Depression. In the Far East, Japanese invasions of China and Southeast Asia threatened America's Open Door policy (see chapter 20). The failure of the United States to join the League of Nations dramatically reduced the organization's ability to maintain peace and stability. German expansionism in Europe in the late 1930s moved President Roosevelt and the nation toward war, but it took the Japanese attack on Pearl Harbor to bring the United States into the global conflict.

The Growing Crisis in Europe

Despite its failure to join the League of Nations, the United States did not withdraw from international affairs behind a wall of total isolationism in the 1920s. It participated in arms control negotiations; signed the Kellogg-Briand Pact, which outlawed war as an instrument of national policy but proved unenforceable; and expanded its foreign investments in Central and Latin America, Asia, the Middle East, and western Europe. In 1933 a new possibility for trade emerged when the Roosevelt administration extended diplomatic recognition to the Soviet Union (USSR).

Overall, the country did not retreat from foreign affairs so much as it refused to enter into collective security agreements that would restrain its freedom of action. To the extent that American leaders practiced isolationism, they did so mainly in the political sense of rejecting internationalist organizations such as the League of Nations and the World Court, institutions that might require military cooperation to implement their decisions.

The experience of World War I had reinforced this brand of political isolationism, which was reflected in an outpouring of antiwar sentiments in the late 1920s and early 1930s. Best-selling novels like Ernest Hemingway's *Farewell to Arms* (1929), Erich Maria Remarque's *All Quiet on the Western Front* (1929), and Dalton Trumbo's *Johnny Got His Gun* (1939) presented graphic depictions of the horror and futility of war. Beginning in 1934, Senate investigations chaired by Gerald Nye of North Dakota concluded that bankers and munitions makers— "merchants of death" as one contemporary writer labeled them—had conspired to push the United States into war in 1917. Nye's hearings appealed to popular antibusiness sentiment in Depression-era America.

Following the Nye committee hearings, Congress passed a series of **Neutrality Acts**, each designed to make it more difficult for the United States to become entangled in European armed hostilities. In 1935 Congress prohibited the sale of munitions to either warring side and authorized the president to warn Americans against traveling on passenger liners of belligerent nations. The following year, lawmakers added private loans to the ban, and in 1937 they required belligerents to pay cash for nonmilitary purchases and ship them on their own vessels—so-called cash-and-carry provisions.

Events in Europe, however, made U.S. neutrality ever more difficult to maintain. After rising to power as chancellor of Germany in 1933, Adolf Hitler revived Germany's economic and military strength despite the Great Depression. Hitler installed National Socialism (Nazism) at home and established the empire of the Third Reich abroad. The *Führer* (Leader) whipped up patriotic fervor by scapegoating and persecuting Communists and Jews. To garner support for his actions, Hitler manipulated German feelings of humiliation for losing World War I and having been forced to sign the "war guilt" clause (see chapter 20) and pointed to the disastrous effects of the country's inflation-ridden economy. In 1936 Hitler sent troops to occupy the Rhineland between Germany and France in blatant violation of the Treaty of Versailles.

Hitler did not stop there. Citing the need for more *lebensraum* (space for living) for the Germanic people, he pushed for German expansion into eastern Europe. In March 1938, he forced Austria to unite with Germany. In September of that year, Hitler signed the Munich Accord with Great Britain and France, allowing Germany to annex the Sudetenland, the mainly German-speaking, western region of Czechoslovakia. Hitler still wanted more land and was convinced that his western European rivals would not stop him, so in March 1939 he sent German troops to invade and occupy the rest of Czechoslovakia. Hitler proved correct; Britain and France did nothing in response, in hopes that he would stop with Czechoslovakia—what critics of inaction called "appeasement."

Hitler's Italian ally, Benito Mussolini, joined him in war and conquest. In 1935 Italian troops invaded Ethiopia; deposed its leader, Emperor Haile Selassie; and occupied the small African nation. The following year, both Germany and Italy intervened in the Spanish civil war, providing military support for General Francisco Franco in his effort to overthrow the democratically elected, socialist republic of Spain. While the United States and Great Britain remained on the sidelines, only the Soviet Union officially assisted the Loyalist defenders of the Spanish republic. In violation of American law, private citizens, many of whom were Communists, volunteered to serve on the side of the Spanish Loyalists and fought on the battlefield as the Abraham Lincoln Brigade. Other sympathetic Americans, such as J. Robert Oppenheimer, feared the spread of dictatorships and provided financial assistance for the anti-Franco government. Despite these efforts, Franco's forces seized control of Spain in early 1939, another victory for Hitler and Mussolini.

The Challenge to Isolationism

As Europe drifted toward war, public opinion polls revealed that most Americans wanted to stay out of any European conflict. The president, however, thought it likely that the United States would eventually need to assist the Western democracies. Given the United States' economic dominance in the world and its dependence on international commerce, Roosevelt feared that Germany and Italy threatened a stable world order. Still, Roosevelt had to tread lightly in the face of the Neutrality Acts that Congress had passed between 1935 and 1937 and overwhelming public opposition to American involvement in Europe.

Germany's aggression in Europe eventually led to full-scale war. When Germany invaded Poland in September 1939, Britain and France declared war on Germany and Italy. Just before the invasion, the Soviet Union had signed a nonaggression agreement with Germany, which carved up Poland between the two nations and permitted the USSR to occupy the neighboring Baltic states of Latvia, Lithuania, and Estonia. Soviet leader Joseph Stalin had few illusions about Hitler's ultimate design on his own nation, but he concluded that by signing this pact he could secure his country's western borders and buy additional time. (In June 1941, the Germans broke the pact and invaded the Soviet Union.)

Roosevelt responded to the outbreak of war by reaffirming U.S. neutrality. Unlike Woodrow Wilson, however, he recognized that this position would be hard to maintain, asserting, "This nation will remain a neutral nation, but I cannot ask that every American remain neutral in thought as well," and "Even a neutral cannot be asked to close his mind or close his conscience." Despite his sympathy for the Allies, which most Americans had come to share, the president stated his hope that the United States could stay out of the war: "Let no man or woman thoughtlessly or falsely talk of Americans sending its armies to European fields."

With the United States on the sidelines, German forces marched toward victory. By the spring of 1940, German armies had launched a *blitzkrieg* (lightning war) across Europe, defeating and occupying Denmark, Norway, the Netherlands, Belgium, and Luxembourg. The greatest shock occurred in June 1940 when France fell to the German onslaught and Nazi troops marched into Paris. Britain now stood virtually alone, and its position seemed tenuous. The British had barely succeeded in evacuating their forces from France by sea when the German Luftwaffe (air force) began a relentless bombing campaign on London and other targets in the Battle of Britain.

With German victories mounting, committed opponents of American involvement in foreign wars organized the **America First Committee**. Gerald Nye helped found the organization, which attracted New Deal critics such as Father Charles Coughlin and William Lemke; business leaders who opposed Roosevelt, such as Sears, Roebuck head Robert Wood; and aviation hero Charles A. Lindbergh, who admired what Hitler had accomplished in building up the Luftwaffe. America First tapped into the feeling of isolationism and concern among a diverse group of Americans who did not want to get dragged into another foreign war.

The surrender of France and the Battle of Britain drastically changed Americans' attitude toward entering the war. Before Germany invaded France, 82 percent of Americans thought that the United States should not aid the Allies. After France's defeat, in a complete turnaround, some 80 percent of Americans favored assisting Great Britain in some way, though most expected that this aid would lead to further U.S. involvement. However, four out of five Americans polled opposed immediate entry into the war. As a result, the politically astute Roosevelt portrayed all U.S. assistance to Britain as a way to prevent American military intervention by allowing Great Britain to defeat the Germans on its own.

From September 1940 to November 1941, the Roosevelt administration helped Britain in any way it could, short of going to war against Germany. On September 2, 1940, the

America First Committee Rally, 1941

Organized in 1940, the America First Committee campaigned against U.S. entry into World War II. Led by isolationists such as North Dakota senator Gerald Nye and the popular aviator Charles Lindbergh, the group blamed eastern bankers, British sympathizers, and Jewish leaders for promoting war fever. The committee dissolved soon after this 1941 rally and the Japanese attack on Pearl Harbor.　Scherl-Suddeutsche/Granger, NYC

president sent fifty obsolete destroyers to the British in return for leases on British naval bases in Newfoundland, Bermuda, and the British West Indies. These aging warships did not have much military value, but they provided a great morale boost to the British, who were being pounded by German air attacks. Two weeks later, on September 16, Roosevelt persuaded Congress to pass the Selective Service Act, the first peacetime military draft in U.S. history, which quickly registered more than 16 million men.

This political maneuvering came as Roosevelt campaigned for an unprecedented third term in 1940. He defeated the Republican Wendell Willkie, a Wall Street lawyer who shared Roosevelt's anti-isolationist views. However, both candidates accommodated voters' desire to stay out of the European war, and Roosevelt went so far as to promise American parents: "Your boys are not going to be sent into any foreign war."

Roosevelt's campaign promises did not halt the march toward war. Roosevelt succeeded in pushing Congress to pass the **Lend-Lease Act** in March 1941. With Britain running out of money and its shipping devastated by German submarines, this measure circumvented the cash-and-carry provisions of the Neutrality Acts. The United States would lend or lease equipment, but no one expected the recipients to return the used weapons and other commodities. As one critic of the act declared, "Lending war equipment is a good deal like chewing gum, you don't really want it back!" To protect British ships

carrying American supplies, the president extended naval and air patrols in the North Atlantic. In response, German submarines began sinking U.S. ships. By May 1941, Germany and the United States were engaged in an undeclared naval war.

The United States Enters the War

Financially, militarily, and ideologically, the United States had aligned itself with Britain, and Roosevelt expected that the nation would soon be formally at war. After passage of the Lend-Lease Act, American and British military planners agreed that defeating Germany would become the top priority if the United States entered the war. In August 1941, Roosevelt and British prime minister Winston Churchill met in Newfoundland, where they signed the **Atlantic Charter**, a lofty statement of war aims that included principles of freedom of the seas, self-determination, free trade, and "freedom from fear and want"—ideals that laid the groundwork for the establishment of a postwar United Nations. At the same meeting, Roosevelt promised Churchill that the United States would protect British convoys in the North Atlantic as far as Iceland while the nation waited for a confrontation with Germany that would rally the American public in support of war. The president got what he wanted. After several attacks on American ships by German submarines in September and October, the president persuaded Congress to repeal the neutrality legislation of the 1930s and allow American ships to sail across the Atlantic to supply Great Britain. By December, the nation was close to open war with Germany.

The event that finally prompted the United States to enter the war, however, occurred not in the Atlantic but in the Pacific Ocean. For nearly a decade, U.S. relations with Japan had deteriorated over the issue of China's independence. American Christian missionaries had established their presence in China, and since the turn of the twentieth century the U.S. government had promoted the Open Door policy to protect its access to Chinese markets. The United States did little to challenge the Japanese invasion and occupation of Manchuria in 1931, but after Japanese armed forces moved farther into China in 1937, Roosevelt took action. The president skirted the Neutrality Acts by refusing to declare war, but he did supply arms to China. When a bombing raid by Japanese planes inadvertently sank the U.S. gunboat *Panay* in the Yangtze River and killed two sailors, Japan apologized, thereby temporarily reducing tensions between the two countries.

Yet relations between Japan and the United States did not substantially improve. In 1940 the Japanese government signed the Tripartite Pact with Germany and Italy, which created a mutual defense agreement among the Axis powers. That same year, Japanese troops invaded northern Indochina, and Roosevelt responded by embargoing sales

---

DOCUMENTS 23.1 AND 23.2

American Reactions to Pearl Harbor: Two Views

Few Americans would forget where they were or how they felt when they first learned of the Japanese attack on Pearl Harbor. The following documents describe the experiences of two women: Monica Conter, a U.S. army nurse on duty at Pearl Harbor during the Japanese attack, and Monica Sone, a Nisei who was a student at the University of Washington in December 1941. Sone and her family were eventually placed in an internment camp in Idaho.

Explore

23.1 Monica Conter | Letter to Her Parents, December 22, 1941

The wounded started coming in 10 minutes after the 1st attack. We called Tripler [Hospital] for more ambulances—they wanted to know if we were having "Maneuvers." Imagine! Well, the sight in our hospital I'll never forget. No arms, no legs, intestines hanging out etc. . . . In the meantime, the hangars all around us were burning—and that awful "noise." Then comes the second attack—We all fell face down on the wounded in the halls, O.R., and everywhere and heard the bombers directly over us. We (the nurses and the doctors) had no helmets nor gas masks—and it really was a "helpless" feeling. One of the soldiers who works for my ward saw me and so we shared helmets together. In the meantime, the bombs were dropping all around us and when a 500 lb. bomb dropped about CENSORED from the CENSORED, we waited for the plane to come in as it felt like it had hit us—then they were gone. CENSORED.

All our electric clocks stopped on the dot. The dead were placed in back of the hospital, the walking wounded went in trucks to Tripler, and the seriously injured in the ambulances. We used our place as an "Evacuation Hospital." . . . The mayor sent out 20 cases of whiskey so that helped some—that is, the uninjured who were going around in a daze. Of course, it was used medicinally too. We worked, and worked, and worked—and when night came on "Blackout" (I'm used to it now). . . . For a week the nurses slept in uniform on the ward in one of the officer's rooms.

Source: Lisa Grunwald and Stephen J. Adler, eds., *Women's Letters: America from the Revolutionary War to the Present* (New York: Dial Press, 2005), 548.

of aviation fuel and scrap metal, products that Japan needed for war. This embargo did not deter the Japanese; in July, they occupied the remainder of Indochina to gain access to the region's natural resources. The Roosevelt administration retaliated by freezing Japanese assets and cutting off all trade with Japan. The two countries maneuvered to the edge of war.

On the quiet Sunday morning of December 7, 1941, Japan attacked the U.S. Pacific Fleet stationed at Pearl Harbor in Honolulu, Hawaii. This surprise air and naval assault killed more than 2,400 Americans and damaged eight battleships, three cruisers, three destroyers, and nearly two hundred airplanes. The bombing raid abruptly ended isolationism and rallied the American public behind President Roosevelt, who pronounced December 7 "a date which will live in infamy." The next day, Congress overwhelmingly voted to go to war with Japan, and on December 11 Germany and Italy declared war on the United States in response. In little more than a year after his reelection pledge to keep the country out of war, Roosevelt sent American men to fight overseas.

Explore

See Documents 23.1 and 23.2 for two perspectives on the bombing of Pearl Harbor.

Explore

23.2 Monica Sone | Memories of Pearl Harbor

On a peaceful Sunday morning, December 7, 1941, Henry, Sumi, and I were at choir rehearsal singing ourselves hoarse in preparation for the annual Christmas recital of Handel's "Messiah." Suddenly Chuck Mizuno, a young University of Washington student, burst into the chapel, gasping as if he had sprinted all the way up the stairs.

"Listen, everybody!" he shouted. "Japan just bombed Pearl Harbor . . . in Hawaii. It's war!"

The terrible words hit like a blockbuster, paralyzing us. Then we smiled feebly at each other, hoping this was one of Chuck's practical jokes. Miss Hara, our music director, rapped her baton impatiently on the music stand and chided him, "Now Chuck, fun's fun, but we have work to do. Please take your place. You're already half an hour late."

But Chuck strode vehemently back to the door. "I mean it, folks, honest! I just heard the news over my car radio. Reporters are talking a blue streak. Come on down and hear it for yourselves."

. . . I felt as if a fist had smashed my pleasant little existence, breaking it into jigsaw puzzle pieces. An old wound opened up again, and I found myself shrinking inwardly from my Japanese blood, the blood of an enemy. I knew instinctively that the fact that I was an American by birthright was not going to help me escape the consequences of this unhappy war.

One girl mumbled over and over again, "It can't be, God, it can't be!" Someone else was saying, "What a spot to be in! Do you think we'll be considered Japanese or Americans?"

A boy replied quietly, "We'll be Japs, same as always. But our parents are enemy aliens now, you know."

A shocked silence followed.

Source: Monica Sone, *Nisei Daughter* (Boston: Little Brown, 1953), 145–46.

Interpret the Evidence

- How did the attack on Pearl Harbor directly affect both women's lives?
- How did each woman feel about Japan and America?

Put It in Context

What does the experience of Japanese Americans during World War II indicate about constitutional guarantees of civil liberties during wartime?

REVIEW & RELATE

How did American public opinion shape Roosevelt's foreign policy in the years preceding U.S. entry into World War II?

What events in Europe and the Pacific ultimately brought the United States into World War II?

 LEARNINGCurve bedfordstmartins.com/hewittlawson/LC

Global War

World War II pitted the "Grand Alliance" of Great Britain, the Soviet Union, the French government in exile, and the United States against the Axis powers of Germany, Japan, and Italy. The Allies consisted of the world's leading colonial power, Great Britain; the world's lone Communist nation, the Soviet Union; and the world's strongest capitalist country, the United States—ingredients for an uncomfortable alliance. From the outset, the United States deployed military forces to contain Japanese aggression, but its most immediate concern was to defeat Germany. Before battles in Europe, Asia, and four other continents concluded, more than 60 million people perished, including 405,000 Americans. Six million Jewish civilians died in the Holocaust, the Nazi regime's genocidal effort to eradicate Europe's Jewish population. The Soviet Union experienced the greatest losses—nearly 27 million soldiers and civilians, more than two-fifths of all those killed.

War in Europe

United against Hitler, the Grand Alliance divided over how quickly to mount a counterattack directly on Germany. The Soviet Union, which bore the brunt of the fighting in trying to repel the German army's invasion, demanded the speedy opening of a **second front** through France and into Germany to take the pressure off its forces. The British wanted to fight first in northern Africa and southern Europe, in part to remove Axis forces from territory that endangered their economic interests in the Mediterranean and the oil-rich Middle East and in part to buy time to rebuild their depleted fighting strength. President Roosevelt understood Soviet demands for immediately establishing a second front, but such a plan would involve fierce and bloody battles to attack the center of Axis strength. The president did not want to risk losing public support early in the war if the United States experienced heavy casualties. He approved his military advisers' plans for an invasion of France from England in 1943, but in the meantime he

agreed with Churchill to fight the Germans and Italians on the periphery of Europe.

From a military standpoint, this circuitous approach proved successful. In October 1942, British forces in North Africa overpowered the Germans at El Alamein, pushing them out of Egypt and removing their threat to the Suez Canal. The following month, British and American troops landed in Algeria and Morocco, controlled by the pro-Nazi French government, and under the British general Bernard Montgomery and the American general George S. Patton they engaged the desert forces of the German general Erwin Rommel. After some early defeats, the combined strength of British and American ground, air, and naval forces drove the Germans out of Africa in May 1943.

These military victories failed to relieve political tensions among the Allies. Although the Soviets had managed to stop the German offensive against Stalingrad, the deepest penetration of enemy troops into their country, Stalin expected the second front to begin as promised in the spring of 1943. He was bitterly disappointed when Roosevelt, hoping to replenish military resources that had been lost in North Africa, postponed the cross–English Channel invasion of France until 1944. To Stalin, it appeared as if his allies were looking to gain a double triumph by letting the Communists and Nazis beat each other into submission. Churchill's strong anti-Communist beliefs fueled Stalin's suspicions.

Instead of opening a second front in France, British, American, and Canadian troops invaded Italy from its southern tip in July 1943. Their initial victories quickly led to the removal of Mussolini and his retreat to northern Italy, where he lived under German protection (Map 23.1). Not until June 4, 1944, did the Allies occupy Rome in central Italy and force the Germans to retreat.

To overcome Stalin's dissatisfaction with the postponement of opening the second front, President Roosevelt issued orders to give the Soviets unlimited access to Lend-Lease supplies to sustain their war efforts and to care for their citizens. In November 1943, the American president and the British prime minister met with the Soviet leader in Tehran, Iran. Roosevelt and Stalin seemed to get along well. Stalin agreed to deploy troops against Japan after the war in Europe ended, and Roosevelt agreed to open the second front within six months. Churchill joined Roosevelt and Stalin in supporting the creation of an international organization to ensure postwar peace.

This time the Americans and British kept their word, and the Allies finally embarked on the second-front invasion. Under the command of General Dwight D. Eisenhower, on June 6, 1944—called **D Day**—more than 1.5 million American, British, and Canadian troops crossed the English Channel in 4,000 boats and landed on the

MAP 23.1   World War II in Europe, 1941–1945

By late 1941, the Axis powers had brought most of Europe and the Mediterranean region under their control. But between 1942 and 1945, the Allied powers drove them back. Critical victories at Leningrad and Stalingrad, in North Africa, and on the beaches of Normandy forced the retreat, and then the defeat, of the Axis powers.

beaches of Normandy, France. Paratrooper landings behind German lines and naval bombardments supported this astonishing amphibious assault. Despite deadly machine-gun fire from German troops placed on higher ground, the Allied forces managed to establish a beachhead. The bravery and discipline of the troops, along with their superior numbers, overcame the Germans and opened the way for the Allies to liberate Paris in August 1944. By the end of the year, the Allies had regained control of the rest of France and most of Belgium.

Amid these Allied victories, Roosevelt won a fourth term against Republican challenger Thomas E. Dewey, governor of New York. He dumped from the campaign ticket his vice president, Henry A. Wallace, a liberal on economic and racial issues, and replaced him with Senator Harry S. Truman of Missouri, who was more acceptable to southern voters. Despite his declining health, Roosevelt won easily with 432 electoral votes and a margin of more than 3.5 million popular votes.

War in the Pacific

With the Soviet Union bearing the brunt of the fighting in eastern Europe, the United States shouldered the burden of fighting Japan. U.S. military commanders began a two-pronged counterattack in the Pacific in 1942. General

Douglas MacArthur, whose troops had escaped from the Philippines as Japanese forces overran the islands in May 1942, planned to regroup in Australia, head north through New Guinea, and return to the Philippines. At the same time, Admiral Chester Nimitz directed the U.S. Pacific Fleet from Hawaii toward Japanese-occupied islands in the western Pacific. If all went well, MacArthur's ground troops and Nimitz's naval forces would combine with General Curtis LeMay's air forces to overwhelm Japan.

All went according to plan in 1942. Shortly after the Philippines fell to the Japanese, the Allies won a major victory in May in the Battle of the Coral Sea, off the northwest coast of Australia. The following month, the U.S. navy achieved an even greater victory when it defeated the Japanese in the Battle of Midway Island, northwest of Hawaii. In August, the fighting moved to the Solomon Islands, east of New Guinea, where U.S. forces waged fierce battles at Guadalcanal Island. After six months of heavy casualties on both sides, the Americans finally dislodged the Japanese. By late 1944, American, Australian, and New Zealand troops had put the Japanese on the defensive with further victories in the Mariana Islands, north of Guam, and the Marshall Islands, east of the Philippines, allowing General MacArthur to return to the island that the Japanese had forced him to abandon three years earlier.

In 1945 the United States mounted its final offensive against Japan. In preparation for an invasion of the Japanese home islands, American marines won important battles on Iwo Jima and Okinawa, two strategic islands off the coast of Japan. The fighting proved costly—on Iwo Jima alone, the Japanese fought and died nearly to the last man while killing 6,000 Americans and wounding 20,000 others, demonstrating that the Japanese would ferociously defend their homeland against the American invasion planned for November. At the same time, the U.S. Army Air Corps conducted firebomb raids over Tokyo and other major cities, killing some 330,000 Japanese civilians. These attacks were conducted by newly developed B-29 bombers, which could fly more than 3,000 miles and could be dispatched from Pacific island bases captured by the U.S. military. The purpose of this strategic bombing was to destroy Japan's economic capability to sustain the war rather than to destroy their military forces. B-29s dropped bombs that set fire to Japanese buildings, which were constructed mainly of wood, and ignited firestorms that caused widespread destruction. At the same time, the navy blockaded Japan, further crippling its economy and reducing its supplies of food, medicine, and raw materials (Map 23.2). Still, the Japanese government refused to surrender and indicated its determination to resist by launching *kamikaze* attacks (suicidal airplane crashes) on American warships and airplanes.

Ending the War

With victory in sight in both Europe and the Pacific, the Allies addressed problems of postwar relations. In February 1945, Roosevelt and Churchill met with Stalin in the resort city of Yalta in the Ukraine. There they clashed over the question of the postwar government of Poland and whether to recognize the claim of the Polish government in exile in London, which the United States and Great Britain supported, or that of the pro-Soviet government, which had spent the war in the USSR. The loosely worded **Yalta Agreement** that resulted from the conference called for the establishment of permanent governments in Poland and the rest of eastern Europe through free elections. Because the USSR considered Poland vital to its national security—it had been invaded from Europe through Poland twice in the past thirty years—the Soviets interpreted the Yalta accord differently than did the Americans and the British, a difference of opinion that soon degenerated into a serious rupture in relations among the parties known as the "Big Three."

Despite this controversy, the Allies left Yalta united over other issues. They renewed their commitment to establishing the United Nations, and the Soviets reaffirmed their intention to join the war against Japan three months after Germany's surrender. The Allies also reached a tentative agreement on postwar Germany. The United States, Great Britain, the Soviet Union, and France would parcel out the defeated country into four zones, each occupied by one of the powers. They would further subdivide Berlin into four sectors because the capital city fell within the Soviet occupation area. As with the accord over Poland, the agreement concerning Germany created tension after the war.

The Yalta Conference concluded just as the final assault against Germany was under way. The Germans had launched one last offensive in mid-December 1944. Mobilizing troops from remaining outposts in Belgium, they attacked Allied forces in what became known as the Battle of the Bulge because of the way that their assault looked when sketched on Allied maps. After an initial German drive into enemy lines, American and British fighting men recovered and sent the Germans retreating across the Rhine River and back into Germany. Pushing from the west, General Eisenhower stopped at the Elbe River, where he had agreed to meet up with Red Army troops who were charging from the east to Berlin. After an intense assault by the Soviets, the German capital of Berlin fell, and on April 25 Russian and American forces linked up in Torgau on the Elbe River. They achieved this triumph two weeks after Franklin Roosevelt died at the age of sixty-three from a cerebral hemorrhage. On April 30, 1945, with Berlin shattered, Hitler committed suicide in his bunker. A few days earlier, Italian antifascist partisans had

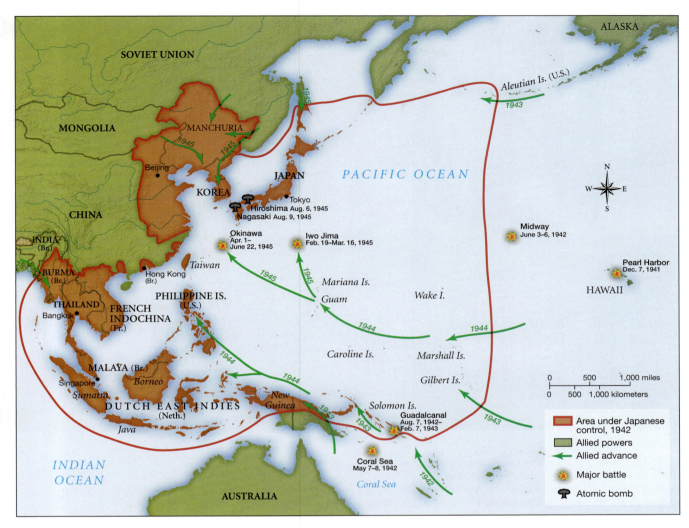

MAP 23.2   World War II in the Pacific, 1941–1945

After bombing Pearl Harbor on December 7, 1941, Japan captured the Philippines and wrenched control of Asian colonies from the British, French, and Dutch and then occupied eastern China. The Allied powers, led by U.S. forces, eventually defeated Japan by winning a series of hard-fought victories on Central Pacific islands and by bombing Hiroshima and Nagasaki.

captured and executed Mussolini in northern Italy. On May 2, German troops surrendered in Italy, and on May 7 the remnants of the German government formally surrendered. The war in Europe ended the next day.

With the war over in Europe, the United States made its final push against Japan. Since 1942, J. Robert Oppenheimer and his team of scientists and engineers had labored feverishly to construct an atomic bomb. Few people knew about this top-secret project, and Congress appropriated $2 billion without knowing its true purpose. Under Colonel Leslie Groves of the Army Corps of Engineers, the military supervised the **Manhattan Project**, which operated at five sites around the country. The need for tight security hampered the project because the military did not want scientists in different locations to confer with one another.

Vice President Harry S. Truman did not learn about the details of the Manhattan Project until Roosevelt's death in April 1945, and in July he found out about the first atomic test while en route to a conference in Potsdam, Germany, with Stalin and Churchill. He ordered the State Department to issue a vaguely worded ultimatum to the Japanese demanding their immediate surrender or else face annihilation, though the message did not state specifically by what means. When Japan indicated that it would surrender if the United States allowed the country to retain its emperor, Hirohito, the Truman administration refused and demanded unconditional surrender. As a further blow

The Big Three at Yalta

In February 1945, with the war in Europe coming to a close, the three main Allied leaders—Winston Churchill, Franklin Roosevelt, and Joseph Stalin—met at Yalta, a Crimean city on the Black Sea. They reached agreements on the postwar status of Germany and eastern Europe and Soviet entry into the war against Japan. Roosevelt died two months later.   Franklin D. Roosevelt Library

to Japan, Stalin was preparing to send the Soviet military to attack Japanese troops in Manchuria on August 8, which would seriously weaken Japan's ability to hold out.

On August 6, before the Soviets' planned invasion, the *Enola Gay*, an American B-29 Super Fortress bomber, dropped an atomic bomb on Hiroshima. The weapon immediately killed 80,000 civilians, and tens of thousands later died slowly from radiation poisoning. Three days later, on August 9, Japan still had not surrendered, and the Army Air Corps dropped another atomic bomb on Nagasaki, killing more than 100,000 civilians. Following these bombings and the advance of the Soviet army into Manchuria, Japan announced on August 14 that it would surrender; the formal surrender ceremony took place on September 2, 1945.

At the time, very few Americans questioned the decision to drop atomic bombs on Japan. Truman believed, probably correctly, that had Roosevelt been alive, he would have authorized use of the bombs. Newly on the job, Truman hesitated to reverse a decision already reached by

his predecessor. He reasoned that his action would save American lives because the U.S. military would not have to launch a costly invasion of Japan's home islands. He also felt justified in giving the order because he sought retaliation for the surprise attack on Pearl Harbor and for Japanese atrocities against American soldiers, especially in the Philippines. With an invasion of Japan planned for November and projections for the loss of American lives ranging from hundreds of thousands to 2 million, the servicemen slated to fight there, as well as their relatives, friends, and neighbors, welcomed Truman's decision. **See Document Project 23: The Decision to Drop the Atomic Bomb, page 747.**

Evidence of the Holocaust

The end of the war revealed the full extent and horror of Germany's calculated and methodical slaughter of certain religious, ethnic, and political groups. As Allied troops liberated Germany and Poland, they saw for themselves the

Holocaust Survivors at Mauthausen

Constructed by the Nazis in Austria, the Mauthausen-Gusen concentration camp housed Jews, Communists, homosexuals, Soviet prisoners of war, and opponents of Franco's fascist regime in Spain. Tens of thousands of prisoners died at this forced labor camp. This photograph shows surviving Spanish inmates tearing down the Nazi eagle from atop the entrance after they were liberated in May 1945.   United States Holocaust Memorial Museum

brutality of the Nazi concentration camps that Hitler had set up to execute or work to death 6 million Jews and another 5 million "undesirables"—Slavs, Poles, Gypsies, homosexuals, the physically and mentally disabled, and Communists. At Buchenwald and Dachau in Germany and at Auschwitz in Poland, the Allies encountered the skeletal remains of inmates tossed into mass graves, dead from starvation, illness, and executions. Crematoria on the premises contained the ashes of inmates first poisoned and then incinerated. Troops also freed the "living dead," those still alive but seriously ill and undernourished. One U.S. soldier reported his initial impression of the inmates: "They were . . . all skin and bones. They were sick, starving, and dying."

These horrific discoveries shocked the public, but evidence of what was happening had appeared early in the war. Journalists like Varian Fry had outlined the Nazi atrocities against the Jews several years before. "Letters, reports, tables all fit together. They add up to the most

appalling picture of mass murder in all human history," Fry wrote in the *New Republic* magazine in 1942. He called on Roosevelt and Churchill to speak out forcefully, urged the pope to excommunicate Catholics who participated in Nazi crimes, and proposed sending food to occupied countries to counter the Nazi claim that they were killing Jews and Poles because there was not enough food to go around.

The Roosevelt administration did little in response, despite receiving evidence of the Nazi death camps beginning in 1942. It chose not to send planes to bomb the concentration camps or the railroad lines leading to them, deeming it too risky militarily and too dangerous for the inmates. In a less defensible decision, the Roosevelt administration refused to relax immigration laws to allow Jews and other persecuted minorities to take refuge in the United States, and only 21,000 managed to find asylum. The State Department, which could have modified these policies, was staffed with anti-Semitic officials, and though

President Roosevelt expressed sympathy for the plight of Hitler's victims, he believed that winning the war as quickly as possible was the best way to help them.

REVIEW & RELATE

How did the Allies win the war in Europe and in the Pacific?

How did tensions among the Allies shape both their military strategy and their postwar plans?

LEARNINGCurve bedfordstmartins.com/hewittlawson/LC

The Home-Front Economy

The global conflict had profound effects on the American home front. World War II ended the Great Depression, restored economic prosperity, and increased labor union membership. At the same time, it smoothed the way for a closer relationship between government and private defense contractors, later referred to as the **military-industrial complex**. The war extended U.S. influence in the world and offered new economic opportunities at home. Despite fierce and bloody military battles throughout the world, Americans kept up morale by rallying around family and community.

Managing the Wartime Economy

To mobilize for war, President Roosevelt increased federal spending to unprecedented levels. Federal government employment during the war expanded to an all-time high of 3.8 million workers, four times as many as during the New Deal, setting the foundation for a large, permanent Washington bureaucracy. War orders fueled economic growth, productivity, and employment. In 1939 the federal budget stood at $9 billion; by the end of the war, it had grown to more than $100 billion. The gross national product increased from $91 billion to $166 billion during the war (Figure 23.1), union membership rose from around 9 million to nearly 15 million, and unemployment dropped from 8 million to less than 1 million. The armed forces helped reduce unemployment significantly by enlisting 12 million men and women, 7 million of whom had been unemployed. Workers earned extra income for overtime work, but because of the rationing of consumer goods, Americans had to defer personal spending.

Prosperity was not limited to any one region. The industrial areas of the Northeast and Midwest once again boomed, as automobile factories converted to building tanks

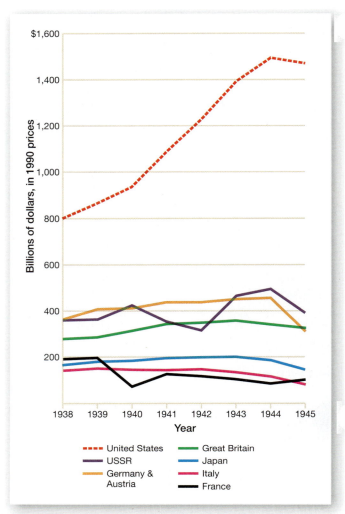

FIGURE 23.1   Real Gross Domestic Product of the Great Powers, 1938–1945

Although World War II stalled or damaged the economic productivity of most of the warring nations, the U.S. economy grew dramatically between 1938 and 1944. With all the battles taking place outside the continental United States, the demand for food, weapons, ships, airplanes, gasoline, and other items by Great Britain and other Allied powers ensured increased employment, productivity, and profits for American workers.   Data from Mark Harrison, ed., *The Economics of World War II: Six Great Powers in International Comparison* (Cambridge: Cambridge University Press, 1998), 11.

and other military vehicles, oil refineries processed gasoline to fuel them, steel and rubber companies manufactured parts to construct these vehicles and the weapons they carried, and textile and shoe plants furnished uniforms and boots for soldiers to wear. As farmers provided food for the nation and its allies, the index of farm production (which was 100 in 1939) jumped from 108 in 1940 to 126 in 1946. The economy diversified geographically. Fifteen million Americans—11 percent of the entire population—migrated between 1941 and 1945, and another 12 million left their homes and joined the armed forces. The war transformed the agricultural South into a budding industrial region. The federal government poured more than $4 billion in contracts into the South to operate military camps, contract with textile factories to clothe the military, and use its ports to build and launch warships. The availability of jobs in southern cities attracted sharecroppers and tenant farmers, black and white, away from the countryside and promoted urbanization while reducing the region's dependency on the plantation economy. In similar fashion, the West Coast prospered because it was the gateway to the Pacific war. The federal government established aircraft plants and ship-building yards in California, Oregon, and Washington, resulting in extraordinary population growth in Los Angeles, San Diego, San Francisco, Portland, and Seattle. Black and white migrants from Texas, Mississippi, and Louisiana headed west to take advantage of these opportunities.

Following the attack on Pearl Harbor, Congress passed the War Powers Act, which authorized the president to reorganize federal agencies any way he thought necessary to win the war. Roosevelt replaced the agencies he had created to combat the Great Depression with another outpouring of organizations to fight the Axis powers. In 1942 the president established the **War Production Board** to oversee the economy. The agency enticed business corporations to meet ever-increasing government orders by negotiating lucrative contracts that helped underwrite their costs, lower their taxes, and guarantee large profits. During the course of the war, corporate net profits nearly doubled. The government also suspended antitrust enforcement, giving private companies great leeway in running their enterprises. Much of the antibusiness hostility generated by the Great Depression evaporated as the Roosevelt administration recruited business executives to supervise government agencies for the token pay of $1 a year. Indeed, the close relationship between the federal government and business that emerged during the war produced the military-industrial complex—the government-business alliance that would have a vast influence on the future development of the economy.

In the first three years of the war, the United States increased military production by some 800 percent. American factories accounted for more than half of worldwide manufacturing output. On their best days, U.S. plants built a ship a day and an airplane every five minutes. By 1945 the United States had produced 86,000 tanks, nearly 300,000 airplanes, 15 million rifles and machine guns, and 6,500 ships.

Financing this enormous enterprise took considerable effort. The federal government spent more than $320 billion, ten times the cost of World War I. To pay for the war, the federal government sold $100 billion in bonds, only about half of what was needed. The rest came from increased income tax rates, which for the first time affected low- and middle-income workers who had paid little or no tax before. At the same time, the tax rate for the wealthy was boosted to 94 percent. In addition to paying higher taxes, American consumers shouldered the burden of inflation. Shortages in household and personal goods produced higher prices, which meant lower purchasing power. During the war, consumer prices jumped by 28 percent, despite the efforts of another federal agency, the Office of Price Administration, to stabilize them.

Building up the armed forces was the final ingredient in the mobilization for war. In 1940 about 250,000 soldiers were serving in the U.S. military, compared with Germany's 6 to 8 million troops. By 1945 American forces had grown to more than 12 million men and women through voluntary enlistments and a draft of men between the ages of eighteen and forty-five. The military reflected the diversity of the U.S. population. The sons of immigrants fought alongside the sons of older-stock Americans. Although the military tried to exclude homosexuals, they managed to join the fighting forces. Some 700,000 African Americans served in the armed forces, but civilian and military officials confined them to segregated units in the army, assigned them to menial work in the navy, and excluded them from the U.S. Marine Corps. The Army Air Corps created a segregated fighting unit trained at Tuskegee Institute in Alabama, and these Tuskegee airmen, like their counterparts among the ground forces, distinguished themselves in battle. Women could not fight in combat, but 140,000 joined the Women's Army Corps, and 100,000 joined the navy's WAVES (Women Accepted for Voluntary Emergency Service). In these and other service branches, women contributed mainly as nurses and performed transportation and clerical duties.

The concentration of power in the executive branch that accompanied the war effort, together with the president's expanded role in international diplomacy, fostered what historian Arthur Schlesinger Jr. termed "the imperial presidency." As commanders in chief, Roosevelt and his successors waged war and negotiated peace by controlling and manipulating the flow of information that reached Congress and the American public. Together with the burgeoning military-industrial complex, the imperial presidency redistributed power both within Washington and throughout the country at large.

The government relied on corporate executives to manage wartime economic conversion, but without the sacrifice and dedication of American workers, their efforts would have failed. The demands for wartime production combined with the departure of millions of American workers to the military created a labor shortage that gave unions increased leverage. By 1945 the membership rolls of organized

Tuskegee Airmen
Twenty black pilots, among those known as the Tuskegee airmen, line up for a photograph, which they signed. The Army Air Corps created two segregated units of African American airmen, the 442nd Bombardment Group and the 99th Pursuit Squadron. The latter flew combat missions in Europe. The success of the Tuskegee airmen contributed to the postwar desegregation of the armed forces.   Courtesy National Park Service, Museum Management Program and Tuskegee Institute National Historic Site, TUAI 31, http://www.cr.nps .gov/museum/exhibits/tuskegee/lgimage/air28.htm

labor had grown from 9 million to nearly 14 million. In 1942 the Roosevelt administration established the **National War Labor Board,** which regulated wages, hours, and working conditions and authorized the government to take over plants that refused to abide by its decisions. Unions at first refrained from striking but later in the war organized strikes to protest the disparity between workers' wages and corporate profits. In 1943 Congress responded by passing the Smith-Connally Act, which prohibited walkouts in defense industries and set a thirty-day "cooling-off" period before unions could go out on strike.

New Opportunities for Women

World War II opened up new opportunities for women in the paid workforce. Between 1940 and the peak of wartime employment in 1944, the number of employed women rose more than 50 percent to 6 million. Given severe labor

shortages caused by increased production and the exodus of male workers into the armed forces, for the first time in U.S. history married working women outnumbered single working women. At the start of the war, about half of women employees held poorly paid clerical, sales, and service jobs. Women in manufacturing labored mainly in low-wage textile and clothing factories. During the war, however, the overall number of women in manufacturing grew 141 percent; in industries producing directly for war purposes, the figure jumped by 463 percent. By contrast, the number of women in domestic service dropped by 20 percent. As women moved into defense-related jobs, their incomes also improved.

As impressive as these figures are, they do not tell the whole story. First, although married women entered the job market in record numbers, most of these workers were older and without young children. Women over the age of thirty-five accounted for 60 percent of those entering the workforce. The government did little to encourage young mothers to work, and few efforts were made to provide assistance for child care for those who did. One notable exception was the Kaiser Corporation shipyards, which operated child care facilities twenty-four hours a day. In contrast to this situation, in Great Britain child care programs were widely available. Second, openings for women in manufacturing jobs did not guarantee equality. Women received lower wages for work comparable to the work that men performed, and women did not have the same chances for advancement. Typical union benefits, such as seniority, hurt women, who were generally the most recent hires. In fact, some contracts stipulated that women's tenure in jobs previously held by men would last only for the duration of the war.

Gender stereotypes continued to dominate the workforce and society in general. Magazine covers with the image of "Rosie the Riveter," a woman with her sleeves rolled up and her biceps bulging, became a symbol for the recruitment of women, but reality proved different. The government, private employers, and mass media advertised for women workers by adapting traditional views of women to their new roles. One piece of literature suggested that an overhead crane operated "just like a gigantic clothes wringer" and that winding wire spools was very much like crocheting. Women who took war jobs were viewed not so much as war workers but as women temporarily occupying "men's jobs" during the emergency. As the war drew to a close, public relations campaigns shifted gears and encouraged the same women they had recently recruited to prepare to return home.

Explore

See Documents 23.3 and 23.4 on women's roles during World War II.

Everyday Life on the Home Front

Morale on the home front remained generally high during the war, as prosperity returned and American casualties proved relatively light compared with those of other allied nations. As in World War I, the government set up an agency, the Office of War Information, to promote patriotism and urge Americans to contribute to the war effort any way they could. Schoolchildren collected scrap metal and rubber to donate to the production of military vehicles and weapons, and families planted "victory gardens" to grow

Ration Card

Gasoline rationing, administered by the Office of Price Administration, began in May 1942. Drivers holding this "B" card, such as industrial workers, were considered essential to the war effort and could purchase eight gallons a week. Nonessential drivers were allocated half that amount. By the end of July 1942, the government had issued more than 850,000 of these cards.   Home Front Coupons, Rare Book, Manuscript, and Special Collections Library, Duke University

vegetables for domestic consumption. Mothers and daughters helped staff USO (United Service Organizations) dances and recreational activities for soldiers headquartered in the United States. Americans also contributed to the war effort by adhering to restrictions on the consumption of consumer goods. Rationing cards restricted purchases of gasoline for cars and for food such as meat, butter, and sugar.

Hollywood kept the American public entertained, and movie attendance reached a record high of more than 100 million viewers. Films portrayed the heroism of soldiers on battlefields in Guadalcanal and Bataan. They celebrated the courage of Russian allies in propaganda epics such as *Mission to Moscow* (1943) and explored the depth of personal and political loyalties in classics such as *Casablanca* (1943). Hollywood stars signed up for the military, and some fought overseas; others, such as Ronald Reagan, made informational films and entertained the troops. A number of Hollywood celebrities, including the comedic actor Carole Lombard, helped raise funds in war bond drives. Others such as Betty Grable kept up servicemen's spirits by posing for photos that GI's pinned up in their lockers, tents, and equipment.

For many, life went on, but not quite in the same way. Around 15 million Americans moved during the war, with more than half of them relocating out of state. With husbands at war and wives at work, many children became "latchkey kids" who stayed home alone after school until their mothers or fathers returned from their jobs. With less

Women Workers during Wartime: Two Views

During the war, women worked in industrial jobs in unprecedented numbers. Corporations and the federal government actively recruited women through posters and advertisements and promised women that factory work was something that would benefit themselves, their families, and their nation. As the Allies neared victory, however, the message changed, and women were urged to prepare to return to the home to open up jobs for returning soldiers.

Explore

23.3 Recruitment Poster, 1942

Library of Congress

Explore

23.4 ADEL Advertisement, 1944

Interpret the Evidence

- How do the messages and images of the women in the poster and the advertisement differ? Do you find any similarities?
- How does the 1942 poster portray women's transition from home to work?
- How does the 1944 advertisement emphasize the coming transition from work to home?

Put It in Context

Why were women so important in winning the war?

parental supervision, juvenile delinquency rose, resulting in increased teenage arrests for robbery, vandalism, and loitering. Prostitution flourished around military installations, and with it came more cases of sexually transmitted diseases. High school graduation rates, especially for boys, fell sharply, but many of the dropouts found jobs to add to the family income and relieve the labor shortage. With the end of the Great Depression and with more young people working, marriage rates increased, and couples wed at a younger age. By 1945 the winding down of the war and the rapidly increasing number of marriages produced the first signs of a "baby boom." At the same time, the stresses of life during wartime, including long separations of husbands and wives, also resulted in higher divorce rates.

REVIEW & RELATE

How did the war accelerate the trend that began during the New Deal toward increased government participation in the economy?

How did the war affect life on the home front for the average American?

 LEARNINGCurve bedfordstmartins.com/hewittlawson/LC

Fighting for Equality at Home

The war also had a significant impact on race relations. The fight to defeat Nazism, a doctrine based on racial prejudice and white supremacy, offered African Americans a chance to press for equal opportunity at home. By contrast, Japanese Americans experienced intensified discrimination and oppression as wartime anti-Japanese hysteria led to the internment of Japanese Americans, an erosion of their civil rights. They were freed toward the end of the war, but their incarceration left scars. Finally, Mexican Americans benefited from wartime jobs but continued to experience ethnic prejudice.

The Origins of the Civil Rights Movement

In 1941 A. Philip Randolph, the head of the Brotherhood of Sleeping Car Porters, applied his labor union experience to the struggle for civil rights. He announced that he planned to lead a 100,000-person march on Washington, D.C., in June 1941 to protest racial discrimination in government and war-related employment as well as segregation in the military. Although Randolph believed in an interracial alliance of working people, he insisted that participation in the march be open only to African Americans. He took this position because he wanted

to show that blacks could lead their own movement and to prevent the presence of white Communists from diverting attention from the message. Inching the country toward war, but not yet engaged militarily, President Roosevelt wanted to avoid any embarrassment the proposed march would bring to the forces supporting democracy and freedom. With his wife Eleanor serving as go-between, Roosevelt agreed to meet with Randolph and worked out a compromise. Randolph called off the march, and in return, on June 25, 1941, the president issued Executive Order 8802, creating the **Fair Employment Practice Committee (FEPC)**. Roosevelt refused to order the desegregation of the military, but he set up a committee to investigate inequality in the armed forces. Although the FEPC helped African Americans gain a greater share of jobs in key industries than they had before, the effect was limited because the agency did not have enforcement power.

The march on Washington movement was emblematic of rising civil rights activity. Black leaders proclaimed their own "two-front war" with the symbol of the "Double V" to represent victory against racist enemies both abroad and at home. The National Association for the Advancement of Colored People continued its policy of fighting racial discrimination in the courts. In 1944 the organization won a significant victory in a case from Texas, *Smith v. Allwright*, which outlawed all-white Democratic primary elections in the traditionally one-party South. As a result of the decision, the percentage of African Americans registered to vote in the South doubled between 1944 and 1948. In 1942 early civil rights activists also founded the interracial Congress of Racial Equality (CORE) in Chicago. CORE protested directly against racial inequality in public accommodations. Its members, including the black pacifists Bayard Rustin and James Farmer, organized "sit-ins" at restaurants and bowling alleys that refused to serve African Americans. Students at Howard University in Washington, D.C., used the same tactics, with some success, to protest racial exclusion from restaurants and cafeterias in the nation's capital. Although these demonstrations did not get the national attention that postwar protests would, they constituted the prelude to the civil rights movement.

Explore

See Document 23.5 for a letter from black soldiers on discrimination in the army.

Population shifts on the home front during World War II exacerbated racial tensions, resulting in violence. As jobs opened up throughout the country at military installations and defense plants, hundreds of thousands of African Americans moved from the rural South to the urban South, the North, and the West. Cities could not handle this rapid influx of people and failed to provide sufficient housing to

DOCUMENT 23.5

Letter from Black Soldiers, 1943

During World War II, many black soldiers and their families wrote to popular African American newspapers such as the *Pittsburgh Courier* to publicize discrimination in the armed forces. In the following letter to the editor, a group of black soldiers describes their mistreatment at an army base in Colorado, showing that racial discrimination was not confined to the South.

Explore

The Pittsburgh Courier
April 26, 1943
Dear Sirs:

We are soldiers who are stationed at Fort Logan, Colorado. We would appreciate it to the highest if our little article was printed in your paper against discrimination.

How does the treatment of these soldiers contradict the goals of the war?

We are colored soldiers who have been discriminated against terribly to the extent where we just can't possibl[y] stand any more. We're supposed to be representing part of the Army in which we're fighting for equality, justice, and humanity so as all men, no matter of race, color, or creed, can be free to worship any way that they please.

Here on the Post we're treated like dogs. We work on different positions, sometimes for 9 or 10 hours daily. In the mornings we report to one particular job and at noon we are taken from the former one into a complete[ly] new one by orders of the white N.C.O.s (meaning Non-commissioned Officers) and at these jobs we

How do the soldiers characterize their experience at the base?

work at a very tiresome task, one that is unfit even for a dog. And yet the whites which are supposed to be a labor battalion just sit down and watch us do their work.

Even in eating time we were told to remain at attention outside the messhall until the whites have finished eating, then we go and eat what's left over—food which is cold, tasteless, and even sometimes dirty from sitting on tables from left overs. . . .

Why can't we eat, live, and be respected as the whites? We're constantly being cursed at, and mocked. But yet we too have to die as well as them, and even perhaps beside them. . . .

People on the outside don't know how we boys, their boys, are being treated here and perhaps on some of the other bad camps near or far. That's the reason

What do the letter writers hope to gain?

we're writing to you to please print this article to let everyone hear our story and give us a chance. Yes, that is all we ask—a chance to prove to the whole world that we colored people are no one's fools. Just give us a chance to show our color.

Source: Philip McGuire, ed., *Taps for a Jim Crow Army: Letters from Black Soldiers in World War II* (Lexington: University Press of Kentucky, 1983), 64–65.

Put It in Context

What is the connection between the experiences described in this letter and the start of the civil rights movement?

accommodate those who migrated in search of employment. Competition between white and black workers for scarce housing spilled over into tensions in crowded transportation and recreational facilities. In 1943 the stress caused by close wartime contact between the races exploded in more than 240 riots. The most serious one occurred in Detroit, where federal troops had to restore order after whites and blacks fought with each other following a dispute at a popular amusement park that killed thirty-four people.

Struggles for Mexican Americans

Immigration from Mexico increased significantly during the war. To address labor shortages in the Southwest and on the Pacific coast, in 1942 the United States negotiated an agreement with Mexico for contract laborers (*braceros*) to enter the country for a limited time to work as farm laborers and in factories. From the Southwest, Mexican migrants found their way to industrial cities of the Midwest and California. Most U.S. residents of Mexican ancestry were, however, American citizens. Like other Americans, they settled into jobs to help fight the war, while more than 300,000 Mexican Americans served in the armed forces.

The war heightened Mexican Americans' consciousness of their civil rights. As one Mexican American World War II veteran recalled: "We were Americans, not 'spics' or 'greasers.' Because when you fight for your country in a World War, against an alien philosophy, fascism, you are an American and proud to be in America." In southern California, Ignacio Lutero Lopez, the publisher of the newspaper *El Espectador* (The Spectator), campaigned against segregation in movie theaters, swimming pools, and other public accommodations. He organized boycotts against businesses that discriminated against or excluded Mexican Americans. Wartime organizing led to the creation of the Unity Leagues, a coalition of Mexican American business owners, college students, civic leaders, and GIs that pressed for racial equality. In Texas, Mexican Americans joined the League of United Latin American Citizens (LULAC), a largely middle-class group that challenged racial discrimination and segregation in public accommodations. Members of the organization emphasized the use of negotiations to redress their grievances, but when they ran into opposition, they resorted to economic boycotts and litigation. The war encouraged LULAC to expand its operations in Arizona and throughout the Southwest.

Mexican American citizens encountered hostility from recently transplanted whites and longtime residents. Tensions were greatest in Los Angeles. A small

Zoot Suit Riots, 1943

This photograph shows two Latino youths after they were attacked by a group of sailors who slashed their clothing during the zoot suit riots in Los Angeles in June 1943. They are wearing the popular zoot suit style of wide shirt collars and baggy pants tapered at the bottom.   Hulton Archive/Getty Images

group of Mexican American teenagers joined gangs and identified themselves by wearing zoot suits—colorful, long, loose-fitting jackets with padded shoulders and baggy pants tapered at the bottom. Not all zoot-suiters were gang members, but many outside their communities failed to make this distinction. Dressed in wide-brimmed hats worn atop slicked-back hair, with pocket watches and chains dangling from their trousers, these young men offended white sensibilities of fashion and proper decorum. Sailors stationed at naval bases in southern California found their dress and swagger provocative. On the night of June 4, 1943, squads of seamen stationed in Long Beach invaded Mexican American neighborhoods in East Los Angeles, indiscriminately attacked both zoot-suiters and those not dressed in this garb on the streets, and beat them up. The police sided with the sailors and arrested Mexican American youths who tried to fight back. After four days, the **zoot suit riots** ended as civilian and military authorities restored order. In response, the Los Angeles city council banned the wearing of zoot suits in public and made it a criminal offense.

The Ordeal of Japanese Americans

World War II marked a significant crossroads for the protection of civil liberties, the freedoms people have from government interference as enshrined in the Bill of Rights. In general, the federal government did not repress civil liberties as harshly as it had during World War I, primarily because opposition to World War II was not nearly as great. The chief potential for radical dissent came from the Communist Party, but after the Germans attacked the Soviet Union in June 1941, Communists and their sympathizers rallied behind the war effort and did whatever they could to stifle any protest that threatened the goal of defeating Germany. On the other side of the political spectrum, after the attack on Pearl Harbor conservative isolationists in the America First Movement quickly threw their support behind the war.

Of the three ethnic groups associated with the Axis enemy—Japanese, Germans, and Italians—Japanese Americans received by far the worst treatment from the civilian population and state and federal officials. Germans had experienced animosity and repression on the home front during World War I (see chapter 20), but like Italian immigrants they had generally assimilated into the wider population. When baseball was the national pastime during the 1930s and 1940s, Lou Gehrig, of German ancestry, and his Italian American teammate Joe DiMaggio of the New York Yankees reigned as popular heroes. At the same time, Fiorello La Guardia, an Italian American, had a large following as mayor of New York City. In addition, German Americans and Italian Americans had spread out across the country, while Japanese Americans remained concentrated in distinct geographical pockets along the West Coast. Although German Americans and Italian Americans experienced prejudice, they had come to be considered racially white, unlike Japanese Americans. Nevertheless, the government arrested about 1,500 Italians considered "enemy aliens" and placed around 250 of them in internment camps. It also arrested more than 11,000 Germans, some of them American citizens who were considered a danger.

The **internment**, or forced relocation and detainment, of Italians and Germans in the United States paled in comparison with that of the Japanese. Nearly all people of Japanese descent lived along the West Coast. Government officials relocated all of those living there—citizens and noncitizens alike—to camps in Arizona, Arkansas, California, Colorado, Idaho, Texas, Utah, and Wyoming. In Hawaii, the site of the Japanese attack on Pearl Harbor,

the Japanese population, nearly one-third of the territory's population, was too large to transfer and instead lived under martial law. Only a thousand or so were interned. The few thousand Japanese Americans living elsewhere in the continental United States remained in their homes.

It did not matter that Fred Korematsu had been born in the United States, had a white girlfriend of Italian heritage, and counted whites among his best friends. His parents had come from Japan, and for much of the American public, his racial heritage meant that he was not a true American. As one American general put it early in the war, "A Jap's a Jap. It makes no difference whether he is an American citizen or not." Along with more than 100,000 people of Japanese descent, two-thirds of whom were American citizens, Korematsu spent most of the war in an internment camp. Unlike Nazi concentration camps, these facilities did not work inmates to death or execute them. Yet Japanese Americans lost their freedom and protection under the Bill of Rights and the Fourteenth Amendment. Distinguished American leaders—including President Roosevelt, California attorney general Earl Warren, and Supreme Court justice Hugo Black—convinced themselves that depriving Japanese Americans of their civil liberties did not result from racism. Despite scant evidence that Japanese Americans were disloyal or harbored spies or saboteurs, U.S. officials chose to believe that as a group they threatened national security. The government established a system that questioned German Americans and Italian Americans on an individual basis if their loyalty came under suspicion. By contrast, U.S. officials identified all Japanese Americans and Japanese resident aliens with the nation that had attacked Pearl Harbor, and incarcerated them. In this respect, the United States was not unique. Following the United States' lead, Canada interned its Japanese population, more than 75 percent of whom held Canadian citizenship.

For their part, Japanese Americans made the best they could out of this situation. They had been forced to dispose of their homes and sell their possessions and businesses quickly, either selling or renting them at very low prices or simply abandoning them. They left their neighborhoods with only the possessions they could carry. They lived in wooden barracks divided into one-room apartments and shared communal toilets, showers, laundry, and dining facilities. The camps provided schools, recreational activities, and opportunities for religious worship, except for Shintoism, the official religion of Japan. Some internees attempted to farm, but the arid land on which the camps were located made this nearly impossible. Inmates who worked at jobs within the camp earned monthly wages of

HEART MT.WYO 1943   J. MIYAUCHI

Japanese American Internment

This painting was made by one of the more than 10,000 Japanese American inmates at the Heart Mountain Relocation Camp in Wyoming who were interned during World War II. Most of the internees were American citizens of Japanese descent from the West Coast. The scene depicts the camp's isolation yet conveys the enduring spirit of the artist.   "Heart Mt. Wyo 1943" (detail), by J. Miyauchi. Reprinted by permission of the Heart Mountain Wyoming Foundation, 2009. 026

$12 to $19, far less than they would have received outside the camps.

Japanese Americans responded to their internment in a variety of ways. Many formed community groups, and some expressed their reactions to the emotional upheaval by writing of their experiences or displaying their feelings through artwork. Contradicting beliefs that their ancestry made them disloyal or not real Americans, some 18,000 men joined the army, and many fought gallantly in some of the war's fiercest battles on the European front with the 442nd Regiment, one of the most heavily decorated units in the military. Nisei soldiers were among the first, along with African American troops, to liberate Jews from German concentration camps. Others, like Korematsu, remained in the camps and challenged the legality of President Roosevelt's executive order, which had allowed military officials to exclude Japanese Americans from certain areas and evacuate them from their homes. Gordon Hirabayashi, a student at the University of Washington, had filed suit against the establishment of a curfew specifically targeted at Japanese Americans. In 1942 the Supreme Court rejected his appeal, as it did Korematsu's two years later. Finally, in December 1944, shortly after he won election to his fourth term as president, Roosevelt rescinded Executive Order 9066.

In contrast to the treatment of Japanese Americans, the status of Chinese Americans improved markedly during the war. With China under Japanese occupation, Congress repealed the Chinese Exclusion Act in 1943, making the Chinese the first Asians who could become naturalized citizens. Chinese American men also fought in integrated military units like their Filipino peers. For the first time, the war opened up jobs to Chinese American men and women outside their ethnic economy.

Despite the violation of the civil liberties of Japanese American citizens, the majority did not become embittered against the United States. Rather, most of the internees returned to their communities after the war and resumed their lives, still intent on pursuing the American dream from which they had been so harshly excluded; however, some 8,000 Japanese Americans renounced their U.S. citizenship and repatriated to Japan in 1945. After briefly moving to Detroit, Korematsu returned to San Leandro, California, with his wife and two children. Still, Korematsu had trouble finding regular employment because he had a criminal record for violating the exclusion order. Unlike most inmates of German concentration camps, Korematsu survived, but in the name of national security the government had established the precedent of incarcerating groups deemed "suspect." It took four decades for the U.S. government to admit its mistake and apologize, and in 1988 Congress awarded reparations of $20,000 to each of the 60,000 living internees. In 1998 President Bill Clinton awarded Korematsu the Presidential Medal of Freedom—the highest decoration a civilian can receive.

REVIEW & RELATE

- What new challenges and opportunities did the war present to minority groups?
- Why were Japanese Americans singled out as a particular threat to national security?

 LEARNINGCurve bedfordstmartins.com/hewittlawson/LC

Conclusion: The Impact of World War II

Like Woodrow Wilson before World War I, Franklin Roosevelt initially charted a course of neutrality before the United States entered World War II. Yet Roosevelt believed that the rise of European dictatorships and their expansionist pursuits throughout the world threatened American national security. He saw signs of trouble early, but responding to antiwar sentiment from lawmakers and the American public, he maneuvered carefully to keep the nation from going to war. Like President Lincoln preceding the Confederate bombardment of Fort Sumter, Roosevelt waited for a blatant enemy attack before declaring war. The Japanese attack on Pearl Harbor in 1941 provided that justification.

On the domestic front, World War II accomplished what Franklin Roosevelt's New Deal could not. Prosperity and nearly full employment returned only after the nation's factories began supplying the Allies and the United States joined in the fight against the Axis powers. Mobilization for war also completed what the New Deal had begun: the tremendous growth and centralization of power in the federal government. Washington, D.C., became the chief source of authority to which Americans looked for solutions to problems concerning economic security and financial development. Most people looked to the future with optimism following sixteen years of depression and war.

The federal government showed that it would use its authority to expand equal rights for African Americans. The war swung national power against racial discrimination, and various civil rights victories during the war served as precursors to the civil rights movement of subsequent decades. The war also heightened Mexican Americans' consciousness of oppression and led them to organize for civil rights. In neither case, however, did the war erase white prejudice.

At the same time, the federal government did not hesitate to trample on the civil liberties of Japanese Americans. The president succumbed to wartime antagonism against Japanese immigrants and their children. However, the same did not happen to the white descendants of the other Axis nations. Yet like white and black Americans, the Nisei displayed their patriotism by distinguishing themselves as soldiers on the battlefields of Europe.

The war brought women into the workforce as never before, providing a measure of independence and distancing them from their traditional roles as wives and mothers. Nevertheless, the government and private employers made it clear that they expected most female workers to give up their jobs to returning servicemen and to become homemakers once the war ended.

Finally, the war thrust the United States onto the world stage as one of the world's two major superpowers alongside the Soviet Union. This position posed new challenges. In sole possession of the atomic bomb, the most powerful weapon on the planet, and fortified by a robust economy, the United States filled the international power vacuum created by the weakening and eventual collapse of the European colonial empires. The fragile alliance that had held together the United States and the Soviet Union shattered soon after the end of World War II. The Atomic Age, which J. Robert Oppenheimer helped usher in with a powerful weapon of mass destruction, and the government oppression that Korematsu endured in the name of national security did not disappear. Rather, they expanded in new directions and shaped the lives of all Americans for decades to come.

DOCUMENT 23.6

Recommendations on the Immediate Use of Nuclear Weapons, June 16, 1945

Secretary of War Henry Stimson received the following memorandum from the scientific advisory panel of the Manhattan Project, a group that included J. Robert Oppenheimer. The memorandum was written one month before the successful "Trinity" test on July 16, and in it the panel recommends the use of atomic weapons against Japan.

You have asked us to comment on the initial use of the new weapon. This use, in our opinion, should be such as to promote a satisfactory adjustment of our international relations. At the same time, we recognize our obligation to our nation to use the weapons to help save American lives in the Japanese war.

(1) To accomplish these ends we recommend that before the weapons are used not only Britain, but also Russia, France, and China be advised that we have made considerable progress in our work on atomic weapons, that these may be ready to use during the present war, and that we would welcome suggestions as to how we can cooperate in making this development contribute to improved international relations.

(2) The opinions of our scientific colleagues on the initial use of these weapons are not unanimous: they range from the proposal of a purely technical demonstration to that of the military application best designed to induce surrender. Those who advocate a purely technical demonstration would wish to outlaw the use of atomic weapons, and have feared that if we use the weapons now our position in future negotiations will be prejudiced. Others emphasize the opportunity of saving American lives by immediate military use, and believe that such use will improve the international prospects, in that they are more concerned with the prevention of war than with the elimination of this specific weapon. We find ourselves closer to these latter views; we can propose no technical demonstration likely to bring an end to the war; we see no acceptable alternative to direct military use.

(3) With regard to these general aspects of the use of atomic energy, it is clear that we, as scientific men, have no proprietary rights. It is true that we are among the few citizens who have had occasion to give thoughtful consideration to these problems during the past few years. We have, however, no claim to special competence in solving the political, social, and military problems which are presented by the advent of atomic power.

Source: U.S. National Archives, Record Group 77, Records of the Chief of Engineers, Manhattan Engineer District, Harrison-Bundy file, folder #76.

DOCUMENT 23.7

Petition to the President of the United States, July 17, 1945

Some advisers urged President Truman to seek an alternative to dropping atomic bombs on Japan, such as demonstrating the weapon on an uninhabited island for Japanese and international observers or giving Japan the results of the test in New Mexico. One day after the Trinity test, seventy scientists involved in the Manhattan Project wrote to President Truman arguing against the bomb's use.

Discoveries of which the people of the United States are not aware may affect the welfare of this nation in the near future. The liberation of atomic power which has been achieved places atomic bombs in the hands of the Army. It places in your hands, as Commander-in-Chief, the fateful decision whether or not to sanction the use of such bombs in the present phase of the war against Japan.

We, the undersigned scientists, have been working in the field of atomic power. Until recently we have had to fear that the United States might be attacked by atomic bombs during this war and that her only defense might lie in a counterattack by the same means. Today, with the defeat of Germany, this danger is averted and we feel impelled to say what follows:

The war has to be brought speedily to a successful conclusion and attacks by atomic bombs may very well be an effective method of warfare. We feel, however, that such attacks on Japan could not be justified, at least not unless the terms which will be imposed after the war on Japan were made public in detail and Japan were given an opportunity to surrender.

If such public announcement gave assurance to the Japanese that they could look forward to a life devoted to peaceful pursuits in their homeland and if Japan still refused to surrender our nation might then, in certain circumstances, find itself forced to resort to the use of atomic bombs. Such a step, however, ought not to be made at any time without seriously considering the moral responsibilities which are involved.

The development of atomic power will provide the nations with new means of destruction. The atomic bombs at our disposal represent only the first step in this direction, and there is almost no limit to the destructive power which will become available in the course of their future development. Thus a nation which sets the precedent of using these newly liberated forces of nature for purposes of destruction may have to bear the responsibility of opening the door to an era of devastation on an unimaginable scale.

If after this war a situation is allowed to develop in the world which permits rival powers to be in uncontrolled possession of these new means of destruction, the cities of the United States as well as the cities of other nations will be in continuous danger of sudden annihilation. All the resources of the United States, moral and material, may have to be mobilized to prevent the advent of such a world situation. Its prevention is at present the solemn responsibility of the United States—singled out by virtue of her lead in the field of atomic power.

The added material strength which this lead gives to the United States brings with it the obligation of restraint and if we were to violate this obligation our moral position would be weakened in the eyes of the world and in our own eyes. It would then be more difficult for us to live up to our responsibility of bringing the unloosened forces of destruction under control.

In view of the foregoing, we, the undersigned, respectfully petition: first, that you exercise your power as Commander-in-Chief, to rule that the United States shall not resort to the use of atomic bombs in this war unless the terms which will be imposed upon Japan have been made public in detail and Japan knowing these terms has refused to surrender; second, that in such an event the question whether or not to use atomic bombs be decided by you in the light of the considerations presented in this petition as well as all the other moral responsibilities which are involved.

Source: U.S. National Archives, Record Group 77, Records of the Chief of Engineers, Manhattan Engineer District, Harrison-Bundy file, folder #76.

DOCUMENT 23.8

President Harry S. Truman | Press Release on the Atomic Bomb, August 6, 1945

After the first atomic bomb, nicknamed "Little Boy," was dropped on Hiroshima, President Truman released the following statement to the public. In it, Truman explains the development of the bomb, its destructive power, and why it was used against Japan. This statement was made before the second bomb was dropped on Nagasaki and before Japan's surrender.

SIXTEEN HOURS AGO an American airplane dropped one bomb on [Hiroshima] and destroyed its usefulness to the enemy. That bomb had more power than 20,000 tons of T.N.T. It had more than two thousand times the blast power of the British "Grand Slam" which is the largest bomb ever yet used in the history of warfare.

The Japanese began the war from the air at Pearl Harbor. They have been repaid many fold. And the end is not yet. With this bomb we have now added a new and revolutionary increase in destruction to supplement the growing power of our armed forces. In their present form these bombs are now in production and even more powerful forms are in development.

It is an atomic bomb. It is a harnessing of the basic power of the universe. The force from which the sun draws its power has been loosed against those who brought war to the Far East. . . .

We are now prepared to obliterate more rapidly and completely every productive enterprise the Japanese have above ground in any city. We shall destroy their docks, their factories, and their communications. Let there be no mistake; we shall completely destroy Japan's power to make war.

It was to spare the Japanese people from utter destruction that the ultimatum of July 26 was issued at Potsdam. Their leaders promptly rejected that ultimatum. If they do not now accept our terms they may expect a rain of ruin from the air, the like of which has never been seen on this earth. Behind this air attack will follow sea and land forces in such numbers and power as they have not yet seen and with the fighting skill of which they are already well aware. . . .

The fact that we can release atomic energy ushers in a new era in man's understanding of nature's forces. Atomic energy may in the future supplement the power that now comes from coal, oil, and falling water, but at present it cannot be produced on a basis to compete with them commercially. Before that comes there must be a long period of intensive research.

It has never been the habit of the scientists of this country or the policy of this Government to withhold from the world scientific knowledge. Normally, therefore, everything about the work with atomic energy would be made public.

But under present circumstances it is not intended to divulge the technical processes of production or all the military applications, pending further examination of possible methods of protecting us and the rest of the world from the danger of sudden destruction.

I shall recommend that the Congress of the United States consider promptly the establishment of an appropriate commission to control the production and use of atomic power within the United States. I shall give further consideration and make further recommendations to the Congress as to how atomic power can become a powerful and forceful influence towards the maintenance of world peace.

Source: Press Release by the White House, August 6, 1945, Ayers Papers, Truman Library.

DOCUMENT 23.9

Hiroshima, August 6, 1945

In this photograph, a survivor stands among the ruins of Hiroshima. The bomb that was dropped on the city destroyed 5 square miles and killed 70,000 to 80,000 people. Three days later, the United States dropped a second atomic bomb on Nagasaki.

AP Photo/Stanley Troutman

DOCUMENT 23.10

U.S. Strategic Bombing Survey, 1946

After the war, President Truman called for a series of surveys on the effectiveness of strategic bombing campaigns in Europe and Asia and on the effects of the atomic bombs on Hiroshima and Nagasaki. The survey on the Pacific war included interviews with Japanese military and government leaders as well as information from Japanese wartime documents. It concluded that the use of the atomic bombs was unnecessary because even without them Japan would have surrendered in the fall of 1945.

4. When Japan was defeated without invasion, a recurrent question arose as to what effect the threat of a home island invasion had had upon the surrender decision. It was contended that the threat of invasion, if not the actual operation, was a requirement to induce acceptance of the surrender terms. On this tangled issue the evidence and hindsight are clear. The fact is, of course, that Japan did surrender without invasion, and with its principal armies intact. Testimony before the Survey shows that the expected "violation of the sacred homeland" raised few fears which expedited the decision to surrender beforehand. Government and Imperial household leaders felt some concern for the "destruction of the Japanese people," but the people were already being shattered by direct air attacks. Anticipated landings were even viewed by the military with hope that they would afford a means of inflicting casualties sufficiently high to improve their chances of a negotiated peace. Preparation of defenses against landings diverted certain resources from dispersal and cushioning moves which might have partially mitigated our air blows. But in Japan's then depleted state, the diversion was not significant. The responsible leaders in power read correctly the true situation and embraced surrender well before invasion was expected.

5. So long as Germany remained in the war that fact contributed to the core of Japanese resistance. Slight evidence exists that some hope was held for a long-promised German miracle weapon. A telegram received on 6 May in the German embassy at Tokyo revealed that Hitler was dead, the promised new weapon had failed to materialize, and that Germany would surrender within a matter of hours. [Adviser Marquis Koichi] Kido believed, presumably on Japanese Army representations, that the Army would not countenance peace moves so long as Germany continued to fight. It is not clear whether this was a face-saving position, designed to avoid a prior Japanese surrender. In any case on 9 May 1945, immediately after the Nazi capitulation, General Anami, the War Minister, asked the cabinet for an Imperial conference to reconsider the war situation. The significant fact, however, is that Japan was pursuing peace before the Nazis collapsed, and the impoverishment and fragmentation of the German people had already afforded a portent of similar consequences for an intransigent Japan.

6. The Hiroshima and Nagasaki atomic bombs did not defeat Japan, nor by the testimony of the enemy leaders who ended the war did they persuade Japan to accept unconditional surrender. The Emperor [Hirohito], the lord privy seal, the prime minister, the foreign minister, and the navy minister had decided as early as May of 1945 that the war should be ended even if it meant acceptance of defeat on allied terms. The war minister and the two chiefs of staff opposed unconditional surrender. The impact of the Hiroshima attack was to bring further urgency and lubrication to the machinery of achieving peace, primarily by contributing to a situation which permitted the prime minister to bring the Emperor overtly and directly into a position where his decision for immediate acceptance of the Potsdam declaration could be used to override the remaining objectors. Thus, although the atomic bombs changed no votes of the Supreme War Direction Council concerning the Potsdam terms, they did foreshorten the war and expedite the peace. . . .

There is little point in attempting more precisely to impute Japan's unconditional surrender to any one of the numerous causes which jointly and cumulatively were responsible for Japan's disaster. Concerning the absoluteness of her defeat there can be no doubt. The time lapse between military impotence and political acceptance of the inevitable might have been shorter had the political structure of Japan permitted a more rapid and decisive determination of national policies. It seems clear, however, that air supremacy and its exploitation over Japan proper was the major factor which determined the timing of Japan's surrender and obviated any need for invasion.

Based on a detailed investigation of all the facts and supported by the testimony of the surviving Japanese leaders involved, it is the Survey's opinion that certainly prior to 31 December 1945, and in all probability prior to 1 November 1945, Japan would have surrendered even if the atomic bombs had not been dropped, even if Russia had not entered the war, and even if no invasion had been planned or contemplated.

Source: United States Strategic Bombing Survey: Japan's Struggle to End the War, July 1, 1946, Elsey Papers, Truman Library.

DOCUMENT 23.11

Father Johannes Siemes | Eyewitness Account of the Hiroshima Bombing, 1945

Father Johannes Siemes, a German priest living in Japan, wrote the following eyewitness account of the Hiroshima bombing. Siemes lived less than a mile outside the city, and after the attack he went into Hiroshima to look for other priests from his order. He gave this account to Bishop Franklin Corley, an American soldier and one of the first Americans to enter the city.

After we have had a few swallows and a little food, Fathers Stolte, Luhmer, Erlinghagen, and [I] take off once again to bring in the family. Father Kleinsorge requests that we also rescue two children who had lost their mother and who had lain near him in the park. On the way, we were greeted by strangers who had noted that we were on a mission of mercy and who praised our efforts. We now met groups of individuals who were carrying the wounded about on litters. As we arrived at the Misasa Bridge, the family that had been there were gone. They might well have been borne away in the meantime. There was a group of soldiers at work taking away those that had been sacrificed yesterday.

More than thirty hours had gone by until the first official rescue party had appeared on the scene. We find both children and take them out of the park: six-year old girl who was uninjured, and a twelve-year old girl who had been burned about the head, hands, and legs, and who had lain for thirty hours without care in the park. The left side of her face and the left eye were completely covered with blood and pus, so that we thought that she had lost the eye. When the wound was later washed, we noted that the eye was intact and that the lids had just become stuck together. On the way home, we took another group of three refugees with us. The first wanted to know, however, of what nationality we were. They, too, feared that we might be Americans who had parachuted in. When we arrived in Nagatsuka, it had just become dark.

We took under our care fifty refugees who had lost everything. The majority of them were wounded and not a few had dangerous burns. Father Rektor treated the wounds as well as he could with the few medicaments that we could, with effort, gather up. He had to confine himself in general to cleansing the wounds of purulent [consisting of pus] material. Even those with the smaller burns are very weak and all suffered from diarrhea. . . .

Thousands of wounded who died later could doubtless have been rescued had they received proper treatment and care, but rescue work in a catastrophe of this magnitude had not been envisioned; since the whole city had been knocked out at a blow, everything which had been prepared for emergency work was lost, and no preparation had been made for rescue work in the outlying districts. Many of the wounded also died because they had been weakened by under-nourishment and consequently lacked in strength to recover. Those who had their normal strength and who received good care slowly healed the burns which had been occasioned by the bomb. There were also cases, however, whose prognosis seemed good who died suddenly. There were also some who had only small external wounds who died within a week or later, after an inflammation of the pharynx and oral cavity had taken place. . . .

Only several cases are known to me personally where individuals who did not have external burns later died. Father Kleinsorge and Father Cieslik, who were near the center of the explosion, but who did not suffer burns, became quite weak some fourteen days after the explosion. Up to this time small incised wounds had healed normally, but thereafter the wounds which were still unhealed became worse and are to date (in September) still incompletely healed. The attending physician diagnosed it as leucopenia [a decrease in white blood cells]. There thus seems to be some truth in the statement that the radiation had some effect on the blood. I am of the opinion, however, that their generally undernourished and weakened condition was partly responsible for these findings. It was noised about that the ruins of the city emitted deadly rays and that workers who went there to aid in the clearing died, and that the central district would be uninhabitable for some time to come.

Source: Father Johannes Siemes, "Hiroshima, August 6, 1945," *Bulletin of the Atomic Scientists* 1, no. 11 (1946): 5–6.

Interpret the Evidence

1. Why do the scientists in favor of using the bomb believe it should be used against Japan (Document 23.6)?

2. What arguments do the scientists who oppose dropping the atomic bomb on Japan put forward (Document 23.7)? Under what conditions do they believe the use of the bomb would be justified?

3. How do both groups of scientists place the use of the bomb within the context of postwar international relations?

4. What reasons does Truman give for dropping the bomb (Document 23.8)?

5. According to the strategic bombing survey, what factors delayed Japan's acceptance of unconditional surrender (Document 23.10)?

6. How does what you see in the photograph of the day after the bombing of Hiroshima (Document 23.9) compare with the eyewitness account in Document 23.11? Which do you find more powerful and why?

Put It in Context

- What do you think was the primary reason the United States dropped the atomic bomb on Japan?

- After reading these documents, do you think the United States should have sought a different way to end the war? Why or why not?

background photos: pages 753 and 754, Library of Congress

Time & Life Pictures/Getty Images

© SuperStock

War veterans and other students taking notes at the University of Iowa, 1947.

Schoolchildren reciting the pledge of allegiance, 1950s.

24
The Opening of the Cold War
1945–1954

Time & Life Pictures/Getty Images

U.S. soldier in Korea, 1951.

AMERICAN HISTORIES

Did one American's fears about Soviet intentions spark a decades-long conflict that threatened the world with nuclear destruction? Certainly no one person can be held responsible for the Cold War between the United States and the Soviet Union, but George Frost Kennan played a critical role in shaping the confrontation between these two superpowers. Kennan's views were based on extensive experience with the Soviets. A graduate of Princeton University, where he majored in history, and a career diplomat, Kennan served two tours of duty at the U.S. Embassy in Moscow. During the first, from 1933 to 1937, he witnessed the brutality of the Stalin regime, as countless "enemies of the state" were arrested, exiled, or executed in Stalin's purges. His experiences convinced him that there was little basis for a positive relationship between the United States and the Soviet Union.

Kennan's second tour of duty in Moscow, from 1944 to 1946, came at a critical juncture in U.S.-Soviet relations. As the war came to a close, tensions over the nature of the postwar world escalated, and by 1946 the wartime alliance had collapsed. Against this backdrop, Kennan sent an 8,000-word telegram to Secretary of State James F. Byrnes outlining a proposal for future U.S. strategy. Convinced that Stalin was committed to expanding communism throughout the world, Kennan advised President Harry S. Truman to adopt a policy of *containment*. In Kennan's view, all Soviet efforts at expansion should be met with firm resistance. At the same time, the United States should take an active role in rebuilding the economies of war-torn Western

757

European countries, thereby reducing the appeal of communism to their populations. Kennan's concept of containment would become the basis for President Truman's foreign policy and would establish the initial strategic parameters of the Cold War.

Kennan, however, was not a rigid cold warrior. He soon insisted that his containment strategy had been misunderstood. As the Cold War intensified and expanded, Kennan argued that containment would work best through political and economic rather than military means. Increasingly, his views fell out of favor at the State Department, and Kennan left in 1950 in a disagreement with the Truman administration's growing militarization of the conflict with the Soviet Union.

Julius and Ethel Rosenberg were casualties of the Cold War that Kennan helped shape. Accused of passing military secrets to the Soviet Union, they were tried for espionage in an atmosphere of growing anti-Communist fervor. Ethel Greenglass and her future husband, Julius Rosenberg, both grew up in families that suffered economically during the Great Depression. During the 1930s, Ethel worked as a secretary in New York City and took part in labor union organizing. Like other young idealists of the period, she became disillusioned with capitalism and joined the Young Communist League. Julius attended the City College of New York, where he, too,

joined the Young Communist League. Three years after they met in 1936, Julius and Ethel married and started a family.

During World War II, Julius worked for the Army Signal Corps as an engineer, but his political past came back to haunt him. In 1945 he lost his job after a security investigation revealed his Communist Party membership. Five years later, the federal government charged that during World War II the Rosenbergs had provided classified information about the construction of the atomic bomb to the Soviet Union, charges that the Rosenbergs denied.

A jury found them guilty on April 5, 1951, and the presiding judge sentenced them to death under the 1917 Espionage Act, which prohibited the transmission of information "relating to the national defense" to a foreign government. Despite an international campaign for clemency and after unsuccessful appeals to the Supreme Court, on June 19, 1953, the Rosenbergs became the only two American civilians executed for espionage during the Cold War. Though recent evidence has confirmed Julius Rosenberg's role as a spy, the case against Ethel remains inconclusive. Without the heightened Cold War climate that then existed in the country, it is likely that neither would have gone to the electric chair. •

photos: Library of Congress; AFP/Getty Images

THE AMERICAN HISTORIES of both George Kennan and Julius and Ethel Rosenberg revolved around their views of communism and the Soviet Union. Kennan designed an approach to containing Soviet aggression based on his close dealings with Stalin—one that he believed would check Soviet expansion without precipitating another world war. The Rosenbergs believed in communism's promise of social and economic equality and saw the Soviet Union as a defense against Nazi aggression—views that led Julius into spying for the Soviets, a U.S. ally, during World War II. Kennan and the Rosenbergs were famous in their time and played prominent roles in the Cold War, but in at least one respect they were unexceptional. As the Cold

War deepened over the course of the 1950s, the lives of all Americans would be profoundly shaped by the epic military and ideological battle between the superpowers.

The Origins of the Cold War, 1945–1947

The wartime partnership between the United States and the Soviet Union (USSR) was an alliance of necessity. Putting aside ideological differences and a history of mutual distrust, the two nations joined forces to combat Nazi aggression. As long as the Nazi threat existed, the alliance held, but as the war ended and attention turned to the postwar world, the allies became adversaries. The two nations did not engage directly in war, but they entered into a struggle for political, economic, and military superiority known as the Cold War. In general, most Cold War maneuvers did not take place on battlefields; rather they consisted of building military and economic alliances to establish spheres of influence, stopping short of "hot wars" (actual fighting) between the United States and the Soviet Union.

Mutual Misunderstandings

Guided by competing ideological and economic values, the United States and the Soviet Union pursued their national interests on the world stage in a manner that led to dangerous confrontations. After World War II, the United States came to believe that the Soviet Union desired world revolution to spread communism, a doctrine hostile to free market individualism. At the same time, the Soviet Union viewed the United States as seeking to make the world safe for capitalism, thereby reducing Soviet chances to obtain economic resources and rebuild its war-shattered economy. Thus each nation tended to see the other's actions in the most negative light possible and to see global developments as a zero-sum game, one in which every victory for one side was necessarily a defeat for the other.

Problems had already surfaced during World War II, but President Franklin D. Roosevelt and Joseph Stalin were able to keep tensions in check (see chapter 23). The president went a long way toward defusing Stalin's concerns at the Yalta Conference in 1945. Stalin viewed the Eastern European countries that the Soviets had liberated from the Germans, especially Poland, as a buffer to protect his nation from future attacks by Germany. He refused to allow hostile, anti-Communist governments to rule these countries and wanted to maintain a regional sphere of influence favorable to Soviet foreign policy objectives. Roosevelt understood Stalin's reasoning, and he recognized political realities: The Soviet military already occupied Eastern Europe, a state of affairs that increased Stalin's bargaining position. Still, while accepting Stalin's basic position, the president insisted that the Yalta Agreement include a guarantee of free elections in Eastern Europe. Roosevelt believed in spreading democracy and freedom, but he was also a realist, and the Yalta Agreement reflected his effort to strike a delicate balance.

By contrast, his successor, Harry S. Truman, took a much less nuanced approach to U.S.-Soviet relations. He believed that the Soviets threatened "a barbarian invasion of Europe," and he intended to deter it. Stalin's ruthless purges within the Soviet Union in the 1930s and 1940s, which led to the deaths of millions of his opponents, convinced Truman that the Soviet dictator was paranoid and extremely dangerous. President Truman did not expect the United States to achieve "100 percent of what we propose" in negotiations with the Russians, but "we should be able to get eighty-five percent." In his first meeting with Soviet foreign minister Vyacheslav Molotov in April 1945, Truman rebuked the Russians for failing to support free elections in Poland. Molotov, recoiling from the sharp tone of Truman's remarks, replied: "I have never been talked to like that in my life."

Despite this rough start, Truman did not immediately abandon the idea of cooperation with the Soviet Union. At the Potsdam Conference in Germany in July 1945, Truman and Stalin agreed on several issues (see chapter 23). The two leaders reaffirmed the concept of free elections in Eastern Europe; Soviet troop withdrawal from the oil fields of northern Iran, which bordered the USSR; and the partition of Germany into four Allied occupation zones. (Berlin was also divided into four occupation zones.) After Stalin assured Truman that he did not support the Communist revolution in China against the Western-backed government of Jiang Jieshi (Chiang Kai-shek), Truman wrote, "I can deal with Stalin. He is honest—but smart as hell."

Within six months of the war's end, the president had changed his mind, and relations between the two countries quickly soured. The United States was the only nation in the world with the atomic bomb, which it had used on Japan, and boasted the only economy reinvigorated by the war. As a result, the Truman administration believed that it held the upper hand against the Soviets and could gain most of what it wanted. With this in mind, the State Department offered the Soviets a $6 billion loan, which they needed to help rebuild their war-ravaged economy. But when the Soviets undermined free elections in Poland in 1946 and established a compliant government, the United States withdrew the offer. Soviet troops also remained in northern Iran, closing off the oil fields to potential capitalist enterprises. The failure to reach agreement over international control of atomic energy proved the last straw. Before reaching an accord, the United States wanted to make sure it would keep its atomic weapons, while the Soviets first wanted the United States to destroy its nuclear arsenal. Clearly, the former World War II allies did not trust each other, and each suspected the other of trying to gain an atomic advantage.

Truman had significantly underestimated the strength of the Soviet position. The Soviets were well on their way toward building their own atomic weapons, negating the Americans' nuclear advantage. In the meantime, until the Russians obtained the bomb, they could rely on the power of their huge army—the largest in the world—poised in Eastern Europe. The Soviets could also ignore the enticement of U.S. economic aid by taking resources from East Germany and mobilizing the Russian people to rebuild their country's industry and military. Indeed, on February 9, 1946, Stalin delivered a tough speech to rally Russians to make sacrifices to enhance national security. By asserting that communism was "a better form of organization than any non-Soviet social system," he implied, according to George Kennan, that capitalist nations could not coexist with communism and that future wars were unavoidable unless communism triumphed over capitalism.

Whether Stalin meant this speech as an unofficial declaration of a third world war was not clear, but U.S. leaders interpreted it this way. A few days after Stalin spoke, Kennan sent his 8,000-word telegram from the U.S. Embassy in Moscow to Washington, blaming the Soviets for stirring up international tensions and confirming that Stalin could not be trusted. "Driven by a neurotic view of world affairs," Kennan maintained, "[the Soviet Union] would respond only to force." The following month, on March 15, former British prime minister Winston Churchill gave a speech in Truman's home state of Missouri, which the president read in advance and presumably approved. Declaring that "an iron curtain has descended across the Continent" of Europe, Churchill observed that "there is nothing [the Russians] admire so much as strength, and there is nothing for which they have less respect than for military weakness." This comment reaffirmed Truman's sentiments expressed the previous year: "Unless Russia is faced with an iron fist and strong language another war is in the making." The message was clear: Unyielding resistance to the Soviet Union was the only way to avoid another world war.

DOCUMENTS 24.1 AND 24.2

Reactions to Soviet Policy in Europe: Two Views

By the late 1940s, tensions between the two superpowers threatened to erupt into armed conflict. Opinion within the U.S. government about how to respond to this challenge ranged widely: Some urged cooperation, while others argued for aggressive confrontation with the Soviet Union. The following selections illustrate the nature of this important postwar debate. In his famous "iron curtain" speech, Winston Churchill condemned Soviet policies in Europe. The same year, Secretary of Commerce Henry Wallace criticized aggressive responses to the Soviet Union.

Explore

24.1 Winston Churchill | The Iron Curtain, 1946

A shadow has fallen upon the scenes so lately lighted by the Allied victory. Nobody knows what Soviet Russia and its Communist international organization intends to do in the immediate future, or what are the limits, if any, to their expansive and proselytizing tendencies. I have a strong admiration and regard for the valiant Russian people and for my wartime comrade, Marshal Stalin. There is deep sympathy and goodwill in Britain—and I doubt not here also—towards the peoples of all the Russias and a resolve to persevere through many differences and rebuffs in establishing lasting friendships. We understand the Russian need to be secure on her western frontiers by the removal of all possibility of German aggression. We welcome Russia to her rightful place among the leading nations of the world. We welcome her flag upon the seas. Above all, we welcome constant, frequent, and growing contacts between the Russian people and our own people on both sides of the Atlantic. It is my duty however, for I am sure you would wish me to state the facts as I see them to you, to place before you certain facts about the present position in Europe.

From Stettin in the Baltic to Trieste in the Adriatic, an iron curtain has descended across the Continent. Behind that line lie all the capitals of the ancient states of Central and Eastern Europe. Warsaw, Berlin, Prague, Vienna, Budapest, Belgrade, Bucharest, and Sofia, all these famous cities and the populations around them lie in what I must call the Soviet sphere, and all are subject in one form or another, not only to Soviet influence but to a very high and, in many cases, increasing measure of control from Moscow.

Source: Robert Rhodes James, ed., *Winston S. Churchill: His Complete Speeches, 1897–1963*, vol. 7, *1943–1949* (New York: Chelsea House Publishers, 1974), 7290.

Not all Americans agreed with this view. Although some 60 percent of the public believed that cooperation with the Soviets was unlikely, a minority argued that a more amicable relationship was possible. Led by Roosevelt's former vice president Henry Wallace, who served as Truman's secretary of commerce, critics voiced concern about taking a "hard line" against the Soviet Union. Stalin was pursuing a policy of expansion, they agreed, but for limited reasons. Wallace claimed that the Soviets merely wanted to protect their borders by surrounding themselves with friendly countries, just as the United States had done by establishing spheres of influence in the Caribbean. Except for Poland and Romania, Stalin initially accepted an array of governments in Eastern Europe, allowing free elections in Czechoslovakia, Hungary, and, to a lesser extent, Bulgaria. Only as Cold War tensions

escalated did the Soviets tighten control over all of Eastern Europe, snuffing out any semblance of democracy. Critics such as Wallace considered this outcome the result of a self-fulfilling prophecy; by misinterpreting Soviet motives, the Truman administration pushed Stalin to counter the American hard line with a hard line of his own.

Explore

See Documents 24.1 and 24.2 for comments from Winston Churchill and Henry Wallace.

The Truman Doctrine

By 1947 U.S.-Soviet relations had reached a new low. International arms control had proven futile, the United States had gone to the United Nations to pressure the Soviets

Explore

24.2 Henry Wallace | The Way to Peace, 1946

"Getting tough" never bought anything real and lasting—whether for schoolyard bullies or businessmen or world powers. The tougher we get, the tougher the Russians will get.

Throughout the world there are numerous reactionary elements which had hoped for Axis victory—and now profess great friendship for the United States. Yet, these enemies of yesterday and false friends of today continually try to provoke war between the United States and Russia. They have no real love of the United States. They only long for the day when the United States and Russia will destroy each other. We must not let our Russian policy be guided or influenced by those inside or outside the United States who want war with Russia. This does not mean appeasement. . . .

The real peace treaty we now need is between the United States and Russia. On our part, we should recognize that we have no more business in the political affairs of Eastern Europe than Russia has in the political affairs of Latin America, Western Europe, and the United States. We may not like what Russia does in Eastern Europe. Her type of land reform, industrial expropriation, and suppression of basic liberties offends the great majority of the people of the United States. But whether we like it or not the Russians will try to socialize their sphere of influence just as we try to democratize our sphere of influence. . . .

Russia must be convinced that we are not planning for war against her and we must be certain that Russia is not carrying on territorial expansion or world domination through native communists faithfully following every twist and turn in the Moscow party line. But in this competition, we must insist on an open door for trade throughout the world. There will always be an ideological conflict—but that is no reason why diplomats cannot work out a basis for both systems to live safely in the world side by side.

Source: Henry Wallace, "The Way to Peace," in *The Annals of America* (Chicago: Encyclopedia Britannica, 1968), 16:372–73.

Interpret the Evidence

- How does each man view the prospect of "toughness" toward the Soviet Union?
- What legitimate Soviet interests do both Wallace and Churchill acknowledge? On what policies toward the Soviets do they differ, and why?

Put It in Context

Why do you think American foreign policy conformed to Churchill's perspective in the postwar period?

to withdraw from Iran, and the rhetoric from both sides had become warlike. From the American vantage point, Soviet actions to expand communism in Eastern Europe appeared to threaten democracies in Western Europe. By contrast, the Soviets viewed the United States as seeking to extend economic control over nations close to their borders and to weaken communism in the Soviet Union.

Events in Greece allowed Truman to take the offensive and apply Kennan's policy of containment. The Mediterranean Sea linked the United Kingdom (formerly Great Britain) to the Middle East, the Suez Canal, and its Asian colonies, and the British therefore considered it vitally important to keep Greece within its sphere of influence. During the war, Churchill and Stalin had agreed that after the war the United Kingdom (UK) would resume its oversight of Greece, while the Soviets would predominate in Eastern Europe. All did not go according to plan. In 1946 a civil war broke out in Greece between the right-wing monarchy, which the UK supported, and a coalition of insurgents consisting of members of the wartime anti-Nazi resistance, Communists, and non-Communist opponents of the repressive government. Under normal conditions, the British would have provided the necessary resources to prop up the Greek government. The United Kingdom, however, was exhausted by the war and in desperate financial shape, so it had no choice but to turn to the United States for help.

The Truman administration agreed to help the UK. Although the Greeks were fighting a civil war, the president and his advisers viewed the situation differently. They believed that the presence of Communists among the Greek rebels meant that Moscow was behind the insurgency. In fact, Stalin was not aiding the revolutionaries; the assistance came from the Communist leader of Yugoslavia, Josip Broz Tito, who acted independently of the Soviets and would soon break with them. Following Kennan's lead in advocating containment, Truman incorrectly believed that all Communists around the world were ultimately controlled by the Kremlin.

While Truman was convinced that the United States had to intervene in Greece to contain the spread of communism, he still had to convince the Republican-controlled Congress and the American people to go along. In 1946 the Republicans had run on a platform of lowering taxes and cutting government spending—positions that enjoyed considerable public support and were incompatible with appropriating huge sums to support the Greek government. In order to overcome potential opposition to its plans, the Truman administration exaggerated the danger of Communist control of Greece. Truman sent Undersecretary of State Dean Acheson to testify before a congressional committee that "like apples in a barrel infected by one rotten one, the corruption of Greece would infect Iran and all to the east." The administration's presentation of the issues to the American public was even more dramatic. On March 12, 1947, Truman gave a speech to a joint session of

Congress that was broadcast over national radio to millions of listeners. He interpreted the civil war in Greece as a titanic struggle between freedom and totalitarianism that threatened the free world. "I believe," the president declared, "that it must be the policy of the United States to support free peoples who are resisting attempted subjugation by armed minorities or by outside pressures." Truman's rhetoric stretched the truth on many counts—the armed minorities to which the president referred had fought the Nazis; the Soviets did not supply the insurgents; the right-wing monarchy, propped up by the military, was hardly democratic; and the United Kingdom had long exerted "outside pressure." Truman achieved his goal of frightening both lawmakers and the public, and Congress appropriated $400 million in military aid to fortify the existing governments of Greece and neighboring Turkey.

The **Truman Doctrine**, which pledged to contain the expansion of communism, was the cornerstone of American foreign policy throughout the Cold War. The United States committed itself to shoring up governments, whether democratic or dictatorial, as long as they were avowedly anti-Communist. Americans believed that the rest of the world's nations wanted to be like the United States and therefore would not willingly accept communism, which they thought could be imposed only from the outside by the Soviet Union and never reasonably chosen from within.

Although Truman misread Soviet intentions with respect to Greece, Stalin's regime had given him cause for worry. Soviet actions that imposed communism in Poland, along with the USSR's refusal to withdraw troops from the Baltic states of Latvia, Lithuania, and Estonia, reinforced the president's concerns about Soviet expansionism and convinced many in the U.S. government that Stalin had no intention of abiding by his wartime agreements. Difficulties in negotiating with the Soviets about international control of atomic energy further worried American foreign-policy makers about Russian designs for obtaining the atomic bomb.

The Marshall Plan and Economic Containment

George Kennan's version of containment called for economic and political aid to check Communist expansion. In this context, to forestall Communist inroads and offer humanitarian assistance to Europeans facing homelessness and starvation, the Truman administration offered economic assistance to the war-torn continent. Secretary of State George Marshall recognized that if the United States did not offer help, European nations would face "economic, social, and political deterioration of a very grave character," which in turn might plunge the world and the United States, which depended heavily on European markets, into another Great Depression. In a June 1947 speech that drew heavily on Kennan's ideas, Marshall sketched out a plan to provide financial assistance to Europe. Although he invited any country, including the Soviet Union, that experienced "hunger, poverty, desperation, and chaos" to apply for aid, Marshall did not expect Stalin to ask for assistance. To do so would require the Soviets to supply information to the United States concerning the internal operations of their economy and to admit to the failure of communism.

Following up Marshall's speech, Truman asked Congress in December 1947 to authorize $17 billion for European recovery. With conservative-minded Republicans still in control of Congress, the president's spending request faced steep opposition. The Soviet Union inadvertently came to Truman's political rescue. Stalin interpreted the proposed **Marshall Plan** of economic assistance as a hostile attempt by the United States to gain influence in Eastern Europe. To forestall this possibility, in late February 1948 the Soviets extinguished the remaining democracy in Eastern Europe by engineering a Communist coup in Czechoslovakia. Congressional lawmakers viewed this action as further proof of Soviet aggression. In April 1948, they approved the Marshall Plan, providing $13 billion in economic assistance to sixteen European countries over the next five years.

Explore

See Document 24.3 for the Soviet Union's reaction to the Marshall Plan.

DOCUMENT 24.3

Vyacheslav Molotov | Soviet Objections to the Marshall Plan, 1947

Shortly after Secretary of State George Marshall proposed the Marshall Plan to grant economic assistance to Europe, France and the United Kingdom invited Soviet leaders to a conference in Paris to discuss their response to General Marshall's offer. In the following selection, Soviet foreign minister Vyacheslav Molotov lays out an alternative vision of economic assistance, which implicitly rejects the Marshall Plan.

Explore

When efforts are directed toward Europe helping herself in the first place and developing her economic potentialities as well as the exchange of goods between countries, such efforts are in conformity with the interests of the countries of Europe. When, however, it is stated . . . that the decisive hold on the rehabilitation of the economic life of European countries should belong to the United States and not to the European countries themselves, such a position stands in contradiction to the interests of European countries since it might lead to a denial of their economic independence, which denial is incompatible with national sovereignty.

The Soviet delegation believes that internal measures and the national efforts of each country should have a decisive importance for the countries of Europe and not make calculations for foreign support which should be of secondary importance. The Soviet Union has always counted above all on its own powers and is known to be on a steady way of progress of its economic life.

The first form of cooperation is based on the development of political and economic relations between states possessing equal rights and in that case their national sovereignty does not suffer from foreign interference.

Such is the democratic basis for international cooperation which brings nations closer together and facilitates the task of their mutual aid.

Source: U.S. Department of State, *A Decade of American Foreign Policy: Basic Documents, 1941–1949* (Washington, D.C.: Department of State Printing Office, 1985), 969.

Interpret the Evidence

- Why does Molotov think that accepting U.S. assistance would be against the interests of European countries?
- What does Molotov claim should be the basis for international cooperation?

Put It in Context

How did the U.S. government interpret Soviet rejection of the Marshall Plan?

REVIEW & RELATE

Why did American policymakers believe that containing Communist expansion should be the foundation of American foreign policy?

What role did mutual misunderstandings and mistrust play in the emergence of the Cold War?

✔ *LEARNINGCurve* bedfordstmartins.com/hewittlawson/LC

The Cold War Hardens, 1948–1952

After 1947, the Cold War intensified. Both sides increased military spending and took measures to enhance their military presence around the world. Fueled by growing distrust, the Soviet Union and the United States engaged in inflammatory rhetoric that added to the danger that the conflict posed to world peace. In 1950 the United States, in cooperation with the United Nations, sent troops to South Korea to turn back an invasion from the Communist North. During the late 1940s and early 1950s, the president gained expanded power to initiate wars and increase spending for military and national security agencies.

Military Containment

The New Deal and World War II had increased the power of the president and his ability to manage economic and military crises. The Cold War further strengthened the presidency and shifted the balance of governmental power to the executive branch, creating what has been called the **imperial presidency**.

As the Cold War heated up, Congress granted the president enormous authority over foreign affairs and internal security. The National Security Act, passed in 1947, created the Department of Defense as a cabinet agency (replacing the Department of War), consolidated control of the various military services under its authority, and established the Joint Chiefs of Staff, composed of the heads of the army, navy, air force, and marines. To advise the president on military and foreign affairs, the act set up the **National Security Council (NSC)**, a group presided over by the national security adviser. The NSC also consisted of the secretaries of state, defense, the army, the navy, and the air force and any others the president might choose to designate.

In addition to this panel, the National Security Act established the Central Intelligence Agency (CIA) as part of the executive branch. Because of the nation's poor experience analyzing intelligence prior to World War II, the CIA was given the responsibility of coordinating intelligence gathering and conducting espionage abroad to counter Soviet spying operations. Another new intelligence agency, the National Security Agency, created in 1949, monitored overseas communications through the latest technological devices. Together, these agencies enhanced the president's ability to conduct foreign affairs with little congressional oversight and out of public view.

By 1948 the Truman administration had decided that an economically healthy Germany, with its great industrial potential, provided the key to a prosperous Europe

The Berlin Airlift

This group of West Berliners waits anxiously as an American C-47 cargo plane prepares to land at Tempelhof Airfield to deliver food in July 1948. The Soviets had blockaded ground transportation to the Allied sector of West Berlin, prompting President Truman to airlift supplies. Three years after the war ended, the photograph shows Germany still in ruins.   Time & Life Pictures/Getty Images and consequently a depression-proof United States. Rebuilding postwar Germany would also fortify the eastern boundary of Europe against Soviet expansion. In mid-1948, the United States, United Kingdom, and France consolidated their occupation zones, created the Federal Republic of Germany (West Germany), and initiated economic reforms to stimulate a speedy recovery. This prompted the Soviet Union, which saw a strong Germany as a threat to its national security, to respond in a belligerent manner. Stalin closed the access roads from the border of West Germany to Berlin, located in the Soviet zone of East Germany, effectively cutting off the city from the West.

The Soviet blockade of West Berlin turned the Cold War even colder. Without provisions from the United States and its allies in West Germany, West Berliners could not survive.

In an effort to break the blockade, Truman ordered a massive airlift known as "Operation Vittles," during which American and British planes transported more than 2.5 million tons of supplies to West Berlin. After nearly a year of these flights, the **Berlin airlift** ended in the spring of 1949 when the Russians backed off and once again allowed their adversaries to supply West Berlin on the ground.

Although the two superpowers narrowly avoided war over Berlin, their subsequent actions kept the conflict alive. Both nations fashioned military alliances to keep the other at bay. In April 1949, the United States joined eleven European countries in the **North Atlantic Treaty Organization (NATO)**. A peacetime military alliance, NATO established a collective security pact in which an attack on one member was viewed as an attack on all (Map 24.1). Pledging to defend Europe,

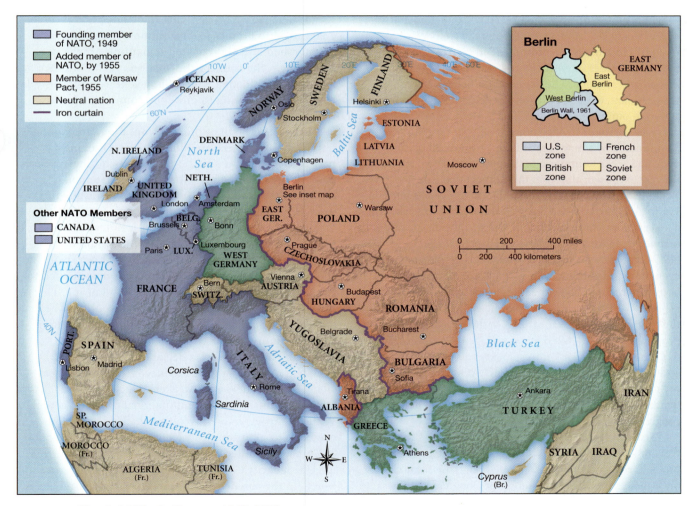

MAP 24.1   The Cold War in Europe, 1945–1955

In 1946, the four major victorious wartime allies divided Germany and Berlin into distinct sectors, leading to increasing conflict. Between 1949 and 1955, the descent of what Winston Churchill called the "iron curtain" of communism and the creation of rival security pacts headed by the United States and the Soviet Union hardened these postwar divisions into a prolonged Cold War.

Truman dispatched four army divisions to Western Europe to show his resolve against Soviet aggression. In 1949 the Russians followed suit by organizing the Council for Mutual Economic Assistance to help their satellite nations rebuild and six years later by creating the Warsaw Pact military alliance, the respective counterparts in Eastern Europe to the Marshall Plan and NATO.

Amid the growing militarization of the Cold War, 1949 brought two new shocks to the United States and its allies. First, in September the Russians successfully tested an atomic bomb. Second, Communist forces within China led by Mao Zedong and Zhou Enlai succeeded in overthrowing the U.S.-backed government of Jiang Jieshi and creating the People's Republic of China. These two events convinced many in the United States that the threat posed by communism was escalating rapidly.

In response, the National Security Council met to reevaluate U.S. strategy in fighting the Cold War. In April 1950, the NSC recommended to Truman that the United States intensify its containment policy both abroad and at home. The document it handed over to the president, entitled **NSC-68**, spelled out the need for action in ominous language. "The Soviet Union, unlike previous aspirants to hegemony," NSC-68 warned, "is animated by a new fanatic faith, antithetical to our own, and seeks to impose its absolute authority over the rest of the world. It is in this context that this Republic and its citizens . . . stand in their deepest peril." Having sketched out the dire threat posed by Russia's acquisition of the atomic bomb, the NSC made specific recommendations to combat this new challenge. NSC-68 proposed that the United States develop an even more powerful nuclear weapon, the hydrogen bomb; increase military spending; and continue to negotiate NATO-style alliances around the globe. Departing from the original guidelines for the CIA, the president's advisers proposed that the United States engage in "covert means" to foment and support "unrest and revolt in selected strategic [Soviet] satellite countries." At home, the government should prepare Americans for the Communist danger by enhancing internal security and civil defense programs.

Truman agreed with many of the principles behind NSC-68 but worried about the cost of funding it. The problem remained a political one. Though the Democrats once again controlled both houses of Congress, there was little sentiment to raise taxes and slash the economic programs established during the New Deal. However, circumstances abruptly changed when, in June 1950, shortly after the president received the NSC report, Com-munist North Korea invaded U.S.-backed South Korea. In response to this attack, Truman took the opportunity to put into practice key recommendations of NSC-68.

The Korean War

Like Germany, Korea emerged from World War II divided between U.S. and Soviet spheres of influence. Above the 38th parallel, which divided the Korean peninsula, the Communist leader Kim Il Sung ruled North Korea with support from the Soviet Union. Below that latitude, the anti-Communist leader Syngman Rhee governed South Korea. The United States supported Rhee, but with American forces occupying Japan and the Philippines, in January 1950 Secretary of State Dean Acheson did not regard South Korea as part of the vital Asian "defense perimeter" that the United States guaranteed to protect from Communist aggression. Truman had already removed remaining American troops from the country the previous year. On June 25, 1950, an emboldened Kim Il Sung sent troops to invade South Korea, seeking to unite the country under his leadership.

In the aftermath of the invasion, Korea took on new importance to American policymakers. Drawing a parallel between the situation in Korea and the appeasement of the Nazis before World War II, Truman remarked that he had seen strong nations invade the weak before and that the failure of democracies to act only encouraged aggressors. If South Korea fell, the president believed, Communist leaders would be "emboldened to override nations closer to our own shores." Thus the Truman Doctrine was now applied to Asia as it had previously been applied to Europe. This time, however, American financial aid would not be enough. It would be up to the U.S. military to contain the Communist threat.

Truman did not seek a declaration of war from Congress. According to Acheson, consulting Congress would delay matters and "weaken and confuse [our] will." Instead, Truman chose a multinational course of action. With the Soviet Union boycotting the United Nations over its refusal to admit the Communist People's Republic of China, the United States obtained authorization from the UN Security Council to send a peacekeeping force to Korea. In the absence of a declaration of war, Truman, as commander in chief, sent American troops to enforce what he called a "police action." Fifteen other countries joined UN forces, but the United States supplied the bulk of the troops, as well as their commanding officer,

General Douglas MacArthur. In reality, MacArthur reported to the president, not the United Nations.

Before MacArthur could mobilize his forces, the North Koreans had penetrated most of South Korea, except for the port of Pusan on the southwest coast of the peninsula. In a daring counterattack, on September 15, 1950, MacArthur dispatched land and sea forces to capture Inchon, northwest of Pusan on the opposite coast, to cut off North Korean supply lines. Joined by UN forces pushing out of Pusan, MacArthur's Eighth Army troops chased the enemy northward in retreat back over the 38th parallel.

> **Explore**
>
> See Document 24.4 for a letter from an American Red Cross worker in Korea.

Now Truman had to make a key decision. MacArthur wanted to invade North Korea, defeat the Communists, and unify the country under Syngman Rhee. Instead of sticking to his original goal of containing Communist aggression against South Korea, Truman succumbed to the lure of liberating all of Korea from the Communists. MacArthur received permission to proceed, and on October 9 his forces crossed

---

DOCUMENT 24.4

Helen Stevenson | Letter from Korea, 1951

American Red Cross worker Helen Stevenson wrote the following letter to her parents just weeks after she arrived in Korea. In her correspondence, Stevenson described her work for the Red Cross's Clubmobile unit in war-torn Pusan. Stevenson later married a New Jersey governor and served in the U.S. House of Representatives in the 1970s.

Explore

We do not let South Korean soldiers come into the club. It seems that the higher-ups feel that we would be completely taken over by them. (Of this I am not convinced.) I am glad you can't see the way that we as Americans treat the S. Koreans who work for us. It nearly kills me when I see some of the things they do to the S. K's who work for the army, and there are a great many of them. In the first place we treat these people as if we were occupying them, as if we were or had been at war with them. That is not the case at all, as you know. One day an American Major friend of mine took me out of town to see the S. Korean Officers training school. Some American officers work out there with the S. K. officers teaching them American ways, tactics, etc. The Major told me that he had talked to these S. K. officers and the general opinion among them was that they resented very much the Americans being here. And that they wanted to see their country united and as long as it was UNITED they did not care under what kind or type of government. They also told this major that they knew full well that the Americans were here for their own interests and not in any way for the interests of Korea as a whole. The S. Koreans who work for us get about four dollars a month pay. They do not get any time off and they work over 12 hours a day. The price of their own food and clothing is terribly high and all the workers are so thin and sickly looking. We scream at them in English and then get furious when they don't understand.

Source: Lisa Grunwald and Stephen Adler, eds., *Women's Letters: America from the Revolutionary War to the Present* (New York: Dial Press, 2005), 608–9.

Interpret the Evidence

- What is Stevenson's attitude about her work in Korea and about the war?
- Why would South Koreans have considered the United States to be an occupying power rather than a liberator?

Put It in Context

What impact did the Korean War have on the Cold War?

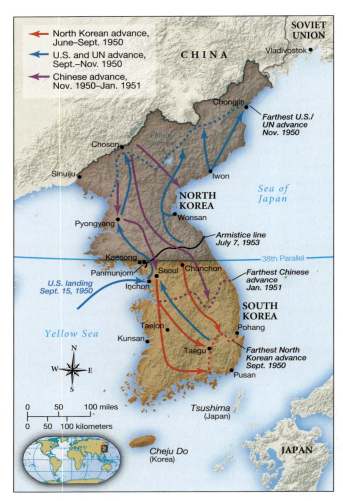

MAP 24.2   The Korean War, 1950–1953

Considered a "police action" by the United Nations, the Korean War cost the lives of nearly 37,000 U.S. troops. Approximately one million Koreans were killed, wounded, or missing. Each side pushed deep into enemy territory, but neither could achieve victory. When hostilities ceased in 1953, a demilitarized zone near the original boundary line separated North and South Korea.

the 38th parallel into North Korea. Within three weeks, UN troops marched through the country until they reached the Yalu River, which bordered China. With the U.S. military massed along their southern perimeter, the Chinese warned that they would send troops to repel the invaders if the Americans crossed the Yalu. Both General MacArthur and Secretary of State Acheson, based on faulty CIA intelligence, discounted this threat, figuring that the Chinese Communists did not want to fight another war so recently after winning their revolution. They were wrong. Truman approved MacArthur's plan to cross the Yalu, and on November 27, 1950, China sent more than 300,000 troops south into North Korea. This proved disastrous for the United States; within two months, Communist troops regained control of North Korea, allowing them once again to invade South Korea. On

January 4, 1951, the South Korean capital of Seoul fell to Chinese and North Korean troops (Map 24.2).

By the spring of 1951, the war had degenerated into a stalemate. UN forces succeeded in recapturing Seoul and repelling the Communists north of the 38th parallel. This time, with the American public anxious to end the war and with the presence of the Chinese promising an endless, bloody predicament, the president sought to replace combat with diplomacy. The American objective would be containment, not Korean unification.

Truman's change of heart infuriated General MacArthur, who was willing to risk an all-out war with China and to use nuclear weapons to win. After MacArthur spoke out publicly against Truman's policy by remarking, "There is no substitute for victory," the president removed him from command on April 11, 1951. However, even with the change in strategy and leadership, the war dragged on for two more years until July 1953, when a final armistice agreement was reached. By this time, Truman's term of office had ended.

The Korean War cost the United States 54,000 lives and $54 billion. This sacrifice of human lives and economic resources made the war unpopular among the American people. Few understood what good, if any, was accomplished. If American soldiers had to die and suffer, many Americans questioned why the Truman administration was satisfied with containment and not the expulsion of communism from Asia once and for all. When MacArthur returned to the United States, he was greeted as a hero, reflecting public dissatisfaction with a war in which fighting to a draw was represented as a victory.

The War and the Imperial Presidency

The Korean War boosted the imperial presidency by allowing the president to bypass Congress and the Constitution to initiate wars in the name of "police actions." The war allowed Truman to expand his powers as commander in chief and augmented the strength of the national security state over which he presided. As a result of the Korean conflict, the military draft became a regular feature of American life for young men over the next two decades. The expanded peacetime military was active around the globe, operating bases in Europe, Asia, and the Middle East. During the war, the military budget rose from $13.5 billion to $50 billion, strengthening the connection between economic growth and permanent mobilization to fight the Cold War. The war also permitted President Truman to reshape foreign policy along the lines sketched in NSC-68, including the extension of U.S. influence in Southeast Asia. Consequently, he authorized economic aid to support the French against Communist revolutionaries in Vietnam.

Yet the power of the imperial presidency did not go unchecked. Congress deferred to Truman on key issues of

Steel Strike, 1952

In this photograph, steelworkers in Gary, Indiana, listen to a speech by CIO president Philip Murray, given on June 22, 1952. Murray promised to lead the union on strike and get a contract for its members. Five years earlier, Congress had passed the Taft-Hartley Act, which hampered union organizing. Before the steel strike could begin, President Truman seized the steel plants and placed them under federal control, an action the Supreme Court soon reversed. © Bettmann/CORBIS

military policy, but on one important occasion the Supreme Court stepped in to restrain him. The central issue grew out of a labor dispute in the steel industry. In 1952 the United Steel Workers of America threatened to go on strike for higher wages, which would have had a serious impact on war production as well as the economy in general. On May 2, after the steel companies refused the union's demands, Truman announced the government seizure and operation of the steel mills to keep them running. He argued that as president he had the "inherent right" to take over the steel plants.

The steel companies objected and brought the matter before the Supreme Court. On June 2, 1952, the Court ruled against Truman. It held that the president did not have the intrinsic authority to seize private property, even during wartime. For the time being, the Supreme Court affirmed some limitations on the unbridled use of presidential power even during periods of war.

REVIEW & RELATE

What were the causes and consequences of the militarization of the containment strategy in the late 1940s and early 1950s?

How did the Korean War contribute to the centralization of power in the executive branch?

LEARNINGCurve bedfordstmartins.com/hewittlawson/LC

Peacetime Challenges, 1945–1948

As the Cold War heated up overseas, at home Americans faced numerous challenges posed by the reconversion of the economy from a war footing to peacetime. Consumers experienced shortages and high prices; businesses complained about tight regulations; and labor unions sought higher wages and a greater voice in companies' decision making. African Americans attempted to build on the gains they had achieved during World War II and to secure new civil rights victories at home. The return to peace also occasioned debates about whether married women, especially those with children, should continue to work outside the home. Even as the Cold War created new anxieties, Americans tried to achieve the peace and prosperity that had eluded them for the past two decades.

Coming Home

In August 1945, 12 million troops, two-thirds of all men between the ages of eighteen and thirty-four, were in uniform. One year later, 9 million had returned to the United States. Some wanted to continue their education, most wanted jobs, and all sought to reunite with their families. They came home to a changed world. The Great Depression was over, but industries still needed to shift to peacetime production before consumers could enjoy the fruits of the new prosperity. In the meantime, consumers faced shortages and high prices. Indeed, there was no guarantee that, with the booming war industries dismantled, the depression would not return.

World War II had also exerted pressures on traditional family life. During the war, millions of women had left their homes and worked jobs that their husbands, sons, and boyfriends had vacated (see chapter 23). Most of the 150,000 women who served in the military received their discharge, and like their male counterparts they hoped to obtain employment. Many other women who had tasted the benefits of wartime employment also wanted to keep working and were reluctant to give up their positions to men.

The war disrupted other aspects of family life as well. During the war, husbands and wives had spent long periods of time apart, resulting in marital tensions and an increased divorce rate. The relaxation of parental authority during the war led to a rise in juvenile delinquency, which added to the anxieties of adults. In 1948 the noted psychiatrist William C. Menninger observed, "While we alarm ourselves with talk of . . . atom bombs, we are complacently watching the disintegration of our family life." Some observers worried that the very existence of the traditional American family was in jeopardy. These fears proved unfounded, as the baby boom of the postwar decades would dramatically demonstrate.

Economic Conversion and Labor Discontent

Before the Cold War became the focus of U.S. foreign policy in 1947, Americans worried more about economic security than about fighting communism. In the absence of war-driven production and with the return of millions of veterans to the job market, Americans feared massive unemployment and another depression. Many families had managed to save money during the war with rationing in place, and they looked forward to spending it on consumer goods. Instead, they found shortages of manufactured items and foodstuffs as the economy moved slowly to peacetime production. Workers who had remained on the home front enjoyed rising incomes from overtime pay, but they worried about holding on to their increased earnings in peacetime.

Even before the war ended, the U.S. government took some steps to meet postwar economic challenges. In 1944, for example, Congress passed the **Servicemen's Readjustment Act**, commonly known as the GI Bill, which offered veterans educational opportunities and financial aid as they adjusted to civilian life. Overall, however, the Truman administration did not handle the economic problems of reconversion well. In the face of shortages and high prices for available commodities, the president wavered between retaining World War II price controls to benefit consumers and eliminating them to help corporate industrialists. He satisfied neither. Nor did the Employment Act of 1946 improve matters. Contrary to its name, the legislation did not guarantee jobs but merely recommended using tax policies to make adjustments to the economy and created a three-member Council of Economic Advisors to make suggestions to the president.

The president also ran into serious difficulty with labor unions. In the years immediately following the war, real incomes fell, undermined by inflation and reduced overtime hours. As corporate profits rose, workers in the steel, automobile, and fuel industries struck for higher wages and a greater voice in company policies. Truman responded harshly. Labor had been one of Franklin Roosevelt's strongest allies, but his successor put that relationship in jeopardy. In 1946 the federal government took over railroads and threatened to draft workers into the military until they stopped striking. Truman took a tough stance, but in the end union workers received a boost in pay, though it did little to relieve inflation.

Political developments forced Truman to change course. In the 1946 midterm elections, Republicans won control of the Eightieth Congress (1947–1949). Stung by this defeat, Truman sought to repair the damage his anti-union policies had done to the Democratic Party coalition. In 1947 Congress passed the **Taft-Hartley Act**. The act hampered the ability of unions to organize and limited their power to go on strike if larger, national interests were seen to be at stake. Seeking to regain labor's support, Truman vetoed the measure. Congress, however, overrode the president's veto, and the Taft-Hartley Act became law.

Veterans Return Home

After World War II, many veterans returned home, married, and started families. They went to school with funds provided by the GI Bill. This twenty-four-year-old former soldier, a student at the University of Iowa, tries to study while holding his baby daughter on his lap as his wife irons in their cramped house trailer.   Time & Life Pictures/Getty Images

The Postwar Civil Rights Struggle

With the war against Nazi racism and tyranny over, African Americans expected to win first-class citizenship in the United States. During World War II, A. Philip Randolph, a black activist and union leader, had led a successful effort to pressure the federal government to tackle discrimination. New organizations such as the **Congress of Racial Equality (CORE)** had emerged to attack racial exclusion in public accommodations, and older groups such as the National Association for the Advancement of Colored People (NAACP) had flourished by attracting new members and leading the legal battle against racial inequality. African American veterans returned home to the South determined to build on these victories, especially by extending the right to vote. "A Voteless citizen is a Voiceless citizen" became the slogan of campaigns throughout the South. Yet African Americans found that most whites resisted demands for racial equality.

Violence surfaced as the most visible evidence of many white people's determination to preserve the traditional racial order. In 1946 a race riot erupted in Columbia, Tennessee, in which blacks were killed and

black businesses were burned down. In February 1946 in South Carolina, Isaac Woodard, a black veteran still in uniform and on his way home on a bus, got into an argument with the white bus driver. When the local sheriff arrived, he pounded Woodard's face with a club, permanently blinding the ex-GI. Five months later, the Ku Klux Klan in Monroe, Georgia, shot a black veteran and three members of his family to death for "acting uppity." In Mississippi, Senator Theodore Bilbo, running for reelection in the Democratic primary, told his white audiences that they could keep blacks from voting "by seeing them the night before" the election. Groups such as the NAACP and the National Association of Colored Women demanded that the president take action to combat this reign of terror.

In December 1946, after meeting with a delegation of concerned African Americans, Truman issued an executive order creating the President's Committee on Civil Rights to investigate the situation and report back to him. Truman's response reflected moral concerns and good politics: It provided the opportunity to increase Democratic Party support among African Americans, which Roosevelt had

Journey of Reconciliation, 1947

Members of the interracial Congress of Racial Equality embarked on a Journey of Reconciliation (known later as freedom rides) to desegregate interstate bus transportation in the Upper South. They met resistance and were arrested several times. In this photograph, some members of CORE appear in front of their lawyer's office in Richmond, Virginia. Bayard Rustin, an important leader of the civil rights movement, stands fourth from the right.   Used with permission of the Fellowship of Reconciliation (http://forusa.org)

first succeeded in gaining in 1936. In April 1947, while the President's Committee on Civil Rights conducted its work, Jackie Robinson achieved a milestone by becoming the first black baseball player to enter the major leagues. This accomplishment proved to be a sign of changes to come.

After extensive deliberations, the committee, which consisted of blacks and whites, northerners and southerners, issued its report, **To Secure These Rights**, on October 29, 1947. The document placed the problem of what it called "civil rights shortcomings" within the context of the Cold War, arguing that racial inequality and unrest could only aid the Soviets in their global anti-American propaganda efforts. "The United States is not so strong," the committee asserted, "the final triumph of the democratic ideal not so inevitable that we can ignore what the world thinks of us or our record." A far-reaching document, the report called for racial desegregation in the military, interstate transportation, and education, as well as extension of the right to vote. The following year, in the midst of the presidential election and once again pressured by A. Philip Randolph, the president signed an executive order to desegregate the armed forces.

Explore

See Document 24.5 for an excerpt from *To Secure These Rights.*

The Election of 1948

By supporting civil rights measures recommended by his presidential committee, Truman alienated white southern segregationists, a significant force in the Democratic Party. On the president's political right, Strom Thurmond, the governor of South Carolina, mounted a presidential challenge by heading up the States' Rights Party, known as the Dixiecrats, which threatened to take away traditional southern Democratic voters from Truman.

At the same time, Truman's conduct of foreign affairs brought criticism from the left wing of his party. Former vice president Henry Wallace ran on the Progressive Party ticket, backed by disgruntled liberals living mainly in the North who opposed Truman's hard-line Cold War policies. Besides these two independent candidates, Truman also faced the popular Republican governor of New York, Thomas E. Dewey. Under these circumstances, political pundits and public opinion polls predicted that Truman would lose the 1948 presidential election.

Truman confounded these voices of gloom by winning the election. His victory resulted from a number of factors, including his vigorous campaign style; the complacency of his Republican opponent, who placed too much faith in opinion polls; and his success in winning over many potential Thurmond and Wallace voters. Much of his victory, however, depended on the continuing power of the New Deal coalition. Truman succeeded in holding together the winning alliance that Franklin Roosevelt had first put together. He did this by stitching together a coalition of labor, minorities, farmers, and liberals and won enough votes in the South to come out ahead despite long odds. In the four-candidate race, Truman did very well in winning slightly less than 50 percent of the popular vote. Democrats also regained control of Congress.

Having won election as president in his own right and armed with a Democratic majority in Congress, Truman still faced tough opposition in his second term. A coalition of southern Democrats and conservative Republicans blocked passage of civil rights proposals and Truman's so-called Fair Deal programs, including national health insurance, federal aid to education, and agricultural reform. The president did manage to obtain budget increases for New Deal measures such as Social Security, minimum wages, and public housing.

By this time, many liberals, as a result of their experience during World War II, had made peace with cooperative corporate executives and relied on the federal government to produce prosperity by tinkering

DOCUMENT 24.5

To Secure These Rights, 1947

In 1946 President Truman appointed a committee to investigate racial discrimination and segregation in the United States. In response to the committee's lengthy report released the following year, Truman issued executive orders to desegregate federal employment and the armed services in 1948. The following excerpt from the report explains the international conditions that prompted a change in American race relations.

Explore

Why does the committee emphasize the fact that America is a nation of immigrants?

The people of the United States stem from many lands. Other nations and their citizens are naturally intrigued by what has happened to their American "relatives." Discrimination against, or mistreatment of, any racial, religious, or national group in the United States is not only seen as our internal problem. The dignity of a country, a continent, or even a major portion of the world's population, may be outraged by it. A relatively few individuals here may be identified with millions of people elsewhere, and the way in which they are treated may have world-wide repercussions. We have fewer than half a million American Indians; there are 30 million more in the Western Hemisphere. Our Mexican American and Hispano groups are not large; millions in Central and South America consider them kin. We number our citizens of Oriental descent in the hundreds of thousands; their counterparts overseas are numbered in hundreds of millions. Throughout the Pacific, Latin America, Africa, the Near, Middle, and Far East, the treatment which our Negroes receive is taken as a reflection of our attitudes toward all dark-skinned peoples.

What impact does racial prejudice in the United States have worldwide?

In the recent war, citizens of a dozen European nations were happy to meet Smiths, Cartiers, O'Haras, Schultzes, di Salvos, Cohens, and Sklodowskas and all the others in our armies. Each nation could share in our victories because its "sons" had helped win them. How much of this good feeling was dissipated when they found virulent prejudice among some of our troops is impossible to say.

Who does the report imply is behind the global dissemination of negative descriptions of American race relations?

We cannot escape the fact that our civil rights record has been an issue in world politics. The world's press and radio are full of it. This Committee has seen a multitude of samples. We and our friends have been, and are, stressing our achievements. Those with competing philosophies have stressed—and are shamelessly distorting—our shortcomings. They have not only tried to create hostility toward us among specific nations, races, and religious groups. They have tried to prove our democracy an empty fraud, and our nation a consistent oppressor of underprivileged people. This may seem ludicrous to Americans, but it is sufficiently important to worry our friends.

Source: *To Secure These Rights: The Report of the President's Committee on Civil Rights* (Washington, D.C.: Government Printing Office, 1947), 147.

Put It in Context

What impact did the Cold War have on shaping the civil rights movement?

with the economy through tax and monetary adjustments; these liberals no longer supported the more radical approaches of income redistribution or reducing corporate concentration. They practiced what historian Arthur Schlesinger Jr. labeled **vital center liberalism**, avoiding what they considered the ideological dogmatism of the extreme political left and right. Militantly anti-Stalinist, centrist liberals supported civil rights, the prosecution of Communists through due process of law, and the expansion of New Deal social welfare programs. In the end, however, preoccupation with fighting the Cold War in Europe and the hot war in Korea diverted Truman's attention from aggressively pursuing a truly liberal political agenda in Congress.

REVIEW & RELATE

What social and economic challenges did America face as it made the transition from war to peace?

Why did Truman have only limited success in implementing his domestic agenda?

 LEARNINGCurve bedfordstmartins.com/hewittlawson/LC

The Anti-Communist Consensus, 1945–1954

For most of Truman's second administration, fear of Communist subversion within the United States consumed domestic politics. This focus on anticommunism did not emerge abruptly; rather it carried over from policies the president had employed in fighting the Cold War during his first term in office. There was a consensus within the Truman administration that Soviet-sponsored Communists were attempting to infiltrate American society and that such efforts constituted a grave threat to capitalist and democratic values and institutions. This consensus turned into an anti-Communist obsession, as evidence of Soviet espionage came to light. In an atmosphere of fear, lawmakers and judges blurred the distinction between actual Soviet spies and political radicals who were merely attracted to Communist beliefs. In the process, these officials trampled on individual constitutional freedoms.

Loyalty and Americanism

The postwar fear of communism echoed earlier anti-Communist sentiments. The government had initiated the repressive Palmer raids during the Red scare following World War I, which led to the deportation of immigrants sympathetic to the Communist doctrines of the Russian Revolution (see chapter 21). In 1938 conservative congressional opponents of the New Deal established the **House Committee on Un-American Activities (HUAC)** to investigate domestic communism, which they tied to the Roosevelt administration. Much of anticommunism, however, was bipartisan. In 1940 Roosevelt signed into law the **Smith Act**, which prohibited teaching or advocating the "duty, necessity, desirability, or propriety of overthrowing or destroying any government in the United States by force or violence" or belonging to any group with that aim. At the same time, President Roosevelt secretly authorized the FBI to monitor and wiretap individuals suspected of violating the act.

The Cold War produced the second Red scare. Just two weeks after his speech announcing the Truman Doctrine in March 1947, the president signed an executive order creating the **Federal Employee Loyalty Program**. Under this program, a board investigated federal employees to see if "reasonable grounds [existed] to suspect disloyalty." The attorney general compiled a list of suspect organizations to assist the board. Soviet espionage was, in fact, a cause for legitimate concern. Spies operated in both Canada and the United States during and after World II, and they had infiltrated the Manhattan Project. The Venona papers, declassified intercepts of Soviet intelligence communications first released in 1995, suggest that a cadre of government officials and federal employees worked for Soviet intelligence during the 1930s and 1940s.

The loyalty board, however, did not focus on espionage. Rather, it concentrated its attention on individuals who espoused dissenting views on a variety of political, social, and economic issues. It failed to uncover a single verifiable case of espionage or find even one actual Communist in public service. This lack of evidence did not stop the board from dismissing 378 government employees for their political beliefs and personal behavior. People lost jobs because they did not satisfactorily answer such questions as "Do you believe in racial integration?" or "Do you listen to the records of Paul Robeson?" (Robeson was an African American singer and actor who had close ties to Communists and the Soviet Union.) Some employees were dismissed because they were homosexuals and considered susceptible to blackmail by foreign agents. (Heterosexual men and women who were having extramarital affairs were not treated in the same manner.) The accused rarely faced their accusers and at times did not learn the nature of the charges against them. This disregard for due process of law spread as loyalty boards at state and municipal levels questioned and fired government employees, including public school teachers and state university professors.

Paul Robeson

Standing at a microphone and surrounded by supporters, Paul Robeson, an African American singer and a left-wing political activist, sings during a benefit concert at an abandoned golf course near Peekskill, New York, on September 4, 1949. A large group of war veterans chanting anti-Communist and racist slogans attacked members of the audience, resulting in some 140 injuries.   AP Photo

Congress also investigated communism in the private sector, especially in industries that shaped public opinion. In 1947 HUAC broadened the anti-Red probe from Washington to Hollywood. Convinced that the film industry had come under Communist influence and threatened to poison the minds of millions of moviegoers, HUAC conducted hearings that attracted much publicity. HUAC cited for contempt ten witnesses, among them directors and screenwriters, for refusing to answer questions about their political beliefs and associations. These and subsequent hearings assumed the form of a ritual. The committee already had information from the FBI about the witnesses; HUAC really wanted the accused to confess their Communist heresy publicly and to show contrition by naming their associates. Those who did not comply were considered "unfriendly" witnesses and were put on an industry **blacklist** that deprived them of employment. **See Document Project 24: McCarthyism and the Hollywood Ten, page 780.**

HUAC grabbed even bigger headlines in 1948. With Republicans in charge of the committee, they launched a probe of Alger Hiss, a former State Department official in the Roosevelt administration who had accompanied the president to the Yalta Conference. The hearings resulted from charges brought by former Soviet spy Whittaker Chambers that Hiss had passed him classified documents. Hiss denied the allegations, and President Truman dismissed them as a distraction. In fact, Democrats viewed the charges as a politically motivated attempt by Republicans to characterize the Roosevelt and Truman administrations as having been riddled with Communists.

The Democrats' concerns proved well founded. Following Truman's victory in the 1948 presidential election, first-term Republican congressman Richard M. Nixon kept the Hiss affair alive. A member of HUAC, Nixon went to Chambers's farm and discovered a cache of documents that Chambers had stored for safekeeping in a hollowed-out pumpkin. Armed with these "Pumpkin Papers," Nixon reopened the case. Hiss never wavered in maintaining his innocence, and the statute of limitations for espionage from the 1930s had expired. Nonetheless, the federal government had enough evidence to prosecute him for perjury. One trial produced a hung jury, but a second convicted Hiss; he was sentenced to five years in prison.

Hiss's downfall tarnished the Democrats, as Republicans charged them with being "soft on communism." It did not matter that Truman was a cold warrior who had advanced the doctrine of containment to stop Soviet expansionism or that he had instituted the federal loyalty program to purge Communists from government. In fact, in 1949 Truman tried to demonstrate his cold warrior credentials by authorizing the Justice Department to prosecute twelve high-ranking officials of the Communist Party for violating the Smith Act. In 1951 the Supreme Court upheld the conviction of the Communist leaders on the grounds that they posed a "clear and present danger" to the United States by advocating the violent overthrow of the government. Despite the presence of some 43,000 Communists, nearly all of them known to the FBI, out of a total population of 150 million and with no evidence of immediate danger, in *Dennis v. United States* the justices decided that "the gravity of the [Communist] evil" was enough to warrant conviction under the Smith Act.

In 1950 the Truman administration also prosecuted Julius and Ethel Rosenberg. Unlike the *Dennis* case, which involved political beliefs, the Rosenbergs were charged with espionage. When the Russians successfully tested an atomic bomb in 1949, anyone accused of helping them obtain this weapon became "Public Enemy Number One." The outbreak of the Korean War the following year, in which tens of thousands of soldiers died, made the Rosenbergs appear as conspirators to murder. After a lengthy trial in 1951, the couple received the death penalty, rather than a possible thirty-year sentence, undoubtedly because they refused to confess and because the trial took place during the war. The presiding judge, Irving Kaufman, admitted as much. In sentencing them to death, he told the Rosenbergs that their actions "caused . . . the Communist aggression in Korea, with the resultant casualties exceeding 50,000 and who knows what millions more innocent people may pay the price of your treason. Indeed, by your betrayal, you undoubtedly have altered the course of history to the disadvantage of our country."

By 1950 the anti-Communist crusade included Democrats and Republicans, liberals and conservatives. Liberals had the most to lose because conservatives could easily brand them as ideologically tainted. In his successful campaign to become a U.S. senator from California in 1950, Richard Nixon had accused his opponent, the liberal Democrat Helen Gahagan Douglas, of being "pink down to her underwear," not quite a Red but close enough. Liberal civil rights and civil liberties groups as well as labor unions were particularly vulnerable to such charges and rushed to rid their organizations of suspected Communists. Such efforts did nothing, however, to slow down conservative attacks. The conservative Republican chairman of HUAC, Harold Velde, linked the anti-Communist issue to traditional Republican fiscal policy in the slogan "Get the Reds out of Washington and Washington out of the red." In 1950 Republicans supported legislation proposed by Senator Pat McCarran, a conservative Democrat from Nevada, which

required Communist organizations to register with the federal government, established detention camps to incarcerate radicals during national emergencies, and denied passports to American citizens suspected of Communist affiliations. (As a result, singer Paul Robeson lost his right to travel abroad.) The severity of the entire measure proved too much for President Truman, and he vetoed it. Reflecting the bipartisan consensus on the issue, the Democratic-controlled Congress overrode the veto.

McCarthyism

Joseph Raymond McCarthy, a Republican senator from Wisconsin, did not create the phenomenon of postwar anticommunism, which was already in full swing from 1947 to 1950, but he served as its most public and feared voice from 1950 until 1954. Senator McCarthy used his position as the head of the Permanent Investigation Subcommittee of the Committee on Government Operations to harass current and former government officials and employees who, he claimed, collaborated with the Communist conspiracy. He had plenty of assistance from members of his own party who considered McCarthy a potent weapon in their battle to reclaim the White House. Robert A. Taft, the respected conservative Republican senator from Ohio, told McCarthy "to keep talking and if one case doesn't work [you] should proceed with another." The press also courted the young senator by giving his charges substantial coverage on the front pages of daily newspapers and then shifting the story to the back pages when McCarthy's claims turned out to be false. McCarthy bullied people, exaggerated his military service, drank too much, and did not pull his punches in making speeches—but he was not a maverick. He did seek publicity, but his anti-Communist tirades fit into mainstream Cold War politics.

Aware of the power of the Communists-in-government issue, McCarthy gave a speech in February 1950 at a Republican women's club in Wheeling, West Virginia. Waving sheets of paper in his hand, the senator announced that he had "the names of 205 men known to the Secretary of State as being members of the Communist Party and who nevertheless are still working and shaping the policy of the State Department," a claim that was based on old information. McCarthy cared more about the message than about the truth. As he continued campaigning for Republican congressional candidates across the country, he kept changing the number of alleged Communists in the government. When Senator Millard Tydings of Maryland, a Democrat who headed the Senate Foreign Relations Committee, launched an investigation of McCarthy's charges, he concluded that they were irresponsible and unfounded.

This finding did not stop McCarthy; if anything, it emboldened him to go further. He accused Tydings of being

Fighting Communism in the Movies

As part of a series of movies alerting audiences to the insidious dangers of communism, Hollywood produced *I Married a Communist* (1949). Although the story revolved around a shipping executive with a Communist past, the poster features a woman who uses her beauty to serve "a mob of terror" intent on destroying America.   Courtesy Everett Collection

"soft on communism" and campaigned against his reelection in 1952. Tydings's defeat in the election helped give McCarthy a reputation of political invincibility and scared off many critics from openly confronting him. McCarthy won reelection to the Senate, and when Republicans once again captured a majority in Congress, he became chair of the Permanent Investigations Subcommittee. Not only did he make false accusations and smear witnesses with anti-Communist allegations, but he also dispatched two aides to travel to Europe and purge what they considered disreputable books from the shelves of overseas libraries sponsored by the State Department.

McCarthy stood out among anti-Communists not for his beliefs but for his tactics. His name became synonymous with anticommunism as well as with manipulating the truth. At once jovial and sneering, McCarthy publicly hurled charges so astounding, especially coming from a U.S. senator, that people thought there must be something to them. He specialized in the "multiple untruth," a concoction of allegations so complex and convoluted that it was

impossible to refute them simply or quickly. By the time the accusations could be discredited, the damage was already done. The senator bullied and badgered witnesses, called them names, and if necessary furnished phony documents and doctored photographs linking them to known Communists.

In 1954 McCarthy finally went too far. After one of his aides got drafted and the army refused to give him a special commission, McCarthy accused the army of harboring Communists at Camp Kilmer and Fort Monmouth in New Jersey. To sort out these charges and to see whether the army had acted appropriately, McCarthy's own Senate subcommittee conducted an investigation, with the Wisconsin senator stepping down as chair. For two months, the relatively new medium of television broadcast live the army-McCarthy hearings, during which the cameras showed many viewers for the first time how reckless McCarthy had become. As his public approval declined, the Senate decided that it could no longer tolerate McCarthy's outrageous behavior and that he was making anticommunism look ridiculous at home and abroad. The famous television journalist Edward R. Murrow ran an unflattering documentary on McCarthy on his evening program on CBS, which further cast doubt on the senator's character and veracity. In December 1954, the Senate voted to censure McCarthy for conduct unbecoming a senator, having violated senatorial decorum by insulting colleagues who criticized him. McCarthy retained his seat on the subcommittee and all his Senate prerogatives, but he never again wielded substantial power. In 1957 he died from acute hepatitis, a disease related to alcoholism.

The anti-Communist consensus did not end with the execution of the Rosenbergs in 1953 or the censure of Joseph McCarthy in 1954 and his death three years later. Even J. Robert Oppenheimer, "the father of the atomic bomb" (see chapter 23), came under scrutiny. In 1954 the Atomic Energy Commission revoked Oppenheimer's security clearance for suspected, though unproven, Communist affiliations. That same year, Congress passed the Communist Control Act, which required "Communist infiltrated" groups to register with the federal government. Federal, state, and municipal governments required employees to take a loyalty oath affirming their allegiance to the United States and disavowing support for any organization that advocated the overthrow of the government. In addition, the blacklist continued in Hollywood throughout the rest of the decade. In the South, anticommunism actually flourished following the Senate's punishment of McCarthy. After the Supreme Court declared racial segregation in public schools unconstitutional in 1954, a number of southern states, including Florida and Louisiana, set up committees to investigate Communist influence in the civil rights movement. In a case concerning civil liberties, the Supreme Court still upheld HUAC's authority to investigate communism and to require witnesses who came before it to answer questions about their affiliations. Yet the Court did put a stop to the anti-Communist momentum. In 1957 the high court dealt a severe blow to enforcement of the Smith Act by ruling in *Yates v. United States* that the Justice Department could not prosecute someone for merely advocating an abstract doctrine favoring the violent overthrow of the government. In response, Congress tried, but failed, to limit the Supreme Court's jurisdiction in cases of this sort.

Even without the presence of Senator Joseph McCarthy, many Americans would have fallen victim to anti-Communist hysteria. J. Edgar Hoover and the FBI did more to fuel the second Red scare than did the Wisconsin senator. Hoover and his bureau did greater damage than McCarthy because they provided the information that Communist-hunters used throughout the government. The FBI was involved in criminal prosecutions in the *Dennis* and *Rosenberg* cases, supplied evidence to congressional committees and loyalty boards, and wiretapped suspected targets and used undercover agents to monitor and harass them. Historian Ellen Schrecker has suggested that because of the FBI's prominent role in the anti-Communist crusade we should call the attacks on suspected radicals during this period not **McCarthyism** but Hooverism.

REVIEW & RELATE

Why did fear of Communists in positions of influence escalate in the late 1940s and early 1950s?

Why was McCarthyism much more powerful than Joseph McCarthy?

LEARNINGCurve bedfordstmartins.com/hewittlawson/LC

Conclusion: The Cold War and Anticommunism

Anticommunism remained a potent weapon in political affairs as long as the Cold War operated in full force. When George Kennan designed the doctrine of containment in 1946 and 1947, he had no idea that it would lead to permanent military alliances such as NATO or to a war in Korea. He viewed the Soviet Union as an unflinching ideological enemy, but he believed that it should be contained through economic rather than military means, along the lines of the Marshall Plan. When the Korean War ended in 1953, the Truman administration had already put into operation around the world the heightened military plans called for by NSC-68. Hard-line Cold War rhetoric portrayed the struggle as a battle between good and evil, summed up in the phrase "I'd rather be dead than Red." Casting the conflict in apocalyptic terms did little justice to the nature of its origins. Born out of different perceptions of national interests and mutual misunderstandings of the other side's actions, the Cold War became frozen in the language of competing moralistic assumptions and self-righteousness. Within this context, though some Americans rallied to obtain clemency for the Rosenbergs, most considered that they got just what they deserved.

The Cold War remained the backdrop for life during the 1950s. Americans accepted it and took it for granted as part of the hazard of modern everyday life. Occasionally, overseas crises riveted their attention on the perilous possibilities of atomic brinkmanship with the Soviets, but for the most part Americans focused their attention on pursuing their economic dreams and raising their families. They could not avoid the Cold War, but they would try to work around it.

Chapter Review

LEARNINGCurve
Check what you know.
bedfordstmartins.com/hewittlawson/LC

Online Study Guide ▶ bedfordstmartins.com/hewittlawson

KEY TERMS

Truman Doctrine (p. 762)
Marshall Plan (p. 763)
imperial presidency (p. 764)
National Security Council (NSC) (p. 764)
Berlin airlift (p. 765)
North Atlantic Treaty Organization (NATO) (p. 765)
NSC-68 (p. 766)
Servicemen's Readjustment Act (p. 770)
Taft-Hartley Act (p. 770)
Congress of Racial Equality (CORE) (p. 771)
To Secure These Rights (p. 772)
vital center liberalism (p. 774)
House Committee on Un-American Activities (HUAC)
   (p. 774)
Smith Act (p. 774)
Federal Employee Loyalty Program (p. 774)
blacklist (p. 775)
McCarthyism (p. 778)

REVIEW & RELATE

1. Why did American policymakers believe that containing Communist expansion should be the foundation of American foreign policy?

2. What role did mutual misunderstandings and mistrust play in the emergence of the Cold War?

3. What were the causes and consequences of the militarization of the containment strategy in the late 1940s and early 1950s?

4. How did the Korean War contribute to the centralization of power in the executive branch?

5. What social and economic challenges did America face as it made the transition from war to peace?

6. Why did Truman have only limited success in implementing his domestic agenda?

7. Why did fear of Communists in positions of influence escalate in the late 1940s and early 1950s?

8. Why was McCarthyism much more powerful than Joseph McCarthy?

TIMELINE OF EVENTS

1938	House Committee on Un-American Activities (HUAC) established
1944	Servicemen's Readjustment Act (GI Bill) passed
1945	Potsdam Conference
1946	George Kennan sends telegram outlining containment strategy
	Winston Churchill delivers "iron curtain" speech
1947	Truman Doctrine articulated
	Taft-Hartley Act passed
	National Security Act passed; Central Intelligence Agency (CIA) established
	Truman creates Federal Employee Loyalty Program
	President's Committee on Civil Rights issues *To Secure These Rights*
	Jackie Robinson becomes the first black baseball player to enter the major leagues
1948–1949	Berlin blockade and airlift
	Alger Hiss affair
1948	Truman orders desegregation of the military
	Congress approves Marshall Plan
1949	National Security Agency established
	Communists win Chinese civil war
	North Atlantic Treaty Organization (NATO) formed
	Soviet Union successfully tests atomic weapon
1950–1953	Korean War
1950–1954	Senator Joseph McCarthy carries out anti-Communist crusade
1950	NSC-68 issued
1952	Truman administration seizes steel mills; Supreme Court reverses the action
1953	Julius and Ethel Rosenberg executed for espionage

McCarthyism and the Hollywood Ten

In 1947 the House Committee on Un-American Activities (HUAC) began a headline-grabbing investigation of Hollywood, hoping to expose Communist influence in the Screen Writers Guild and pro-Communist messages in films. HUAC first called a number of "friendly" witnesses, such as actors Ronald Reagan and Gary Cooper; writer Ayn Rand; and movie studio heads Walt Disney and Jack Warner. These witnesses affirmed the presence of Communists in the film industry, though they were careful to also affirm their own anti-Communist beliefs. HUAC then called ten "unfriendly" witnesses who were suspected of being Communists. They invoked the First Amendment's protection of free speech (or the right not to speak) and free association and refused to answer the committee's questions. The "Hollywood Ten," as they became known, included one director and nine writers, and all were held in contempt of Congress and given fines and jail sentences.

Over the next ten years, thousands of writers, actors, directors, producers, and technicians lost their jobs. Although some were able to continue working under pseudonyms (especially writers), others had to leave the United States to find work; many were forced to look for employment outside the entertainment industry. There were personal consequences, too: Some marriages and families broke apart from the strain, and a few individuals were even driven to suicide.

The following documents shed light on the nature of HUAC's inquiries into communism in the entertainment industry. In studying the documents, consider some of the larger issues and questions raised by McCarthyism and the treatment of the Hollywood Ten. Was McCarthyism an aberration or part of a larger and older force in American society? Why did so few people challenge McCarthy, HUAC, and other organizations involved in anti-Communist investigations? Why were the film and other entertainment industries investigated so extensively?

DOCUMENT 24.6

Ronald Reagan | Testimony before HUAC, 1947

Ronald Reagan's acting career began in the late 1930s and included numerous starring roles, mostly in B movies. During World War II, he served in the Public Relations Unit of the Army Air Corps, where he helped to produce hundreds of training films. Reagan was the president of the Screen Actors Guild during HUAC's Hollywood investigations, and he testified before the committee. Robert Stripling was the committee's chief investigator.

MR. STRIPLING   Mr. Reagan, what is your feeling about what steps should be taken to rid the motion-picture industry of any Communist influences, if they are there?

MR. REAGAN   Well, sir . . . 99 percent of us are pretty well aware of what is going on, and I think within the bounds of our democratic rights, and never once stepping over the rights given us by democracy, we have done a pretty good job in our business of keeping those people's activities curtailed. After all, we must recognize them at present as a political party. On that basis we have exposed their lies when we came across them, we have opposed their propaganda, and I can certainly testify that in the case of the Screen Actors Guild we have been eminently successful in preventing them from, with their usual tactics, trying to run a majority of an organization with a well organized minority.

So that fundamentally I would say in opposing those people that the best thing to do is to make democracy work. In the Screen Actors Guild we make it work by insuring everyone a vote and by keeping everyone informed. I believe that, as Thomas Jefferson put it, if all the American people know all of the facts they will never make a mistake.

Whether the party should be outlawed, I agree with the gentlemen that preceded me that that is a matter for the Government to decide. As a citizen I would hesitate, or not like, to see any political party outlawed on the basis of its political ideology. We have spent 170 years in this country on the basis that democracy is strong enough to stand up and fight against the inroads of any ideology. However, if it is proven that an organization is an agent of a power, a foreign power, or in any way not a legitimate political party, and I think the Government is capable of proving that, if the proof is there, then that is another matter.

I do not know whether I have answered your question or not. I . . . would like at this moment to say I happen to be very proud of the industry in which I work; I happen to be very proud of the way in which we conducted the fight. I do not believe the Communists have ever at any time been able to use the motion-picture screen as a sounding board for their philosophy or ideology. I think that will continue as long [as] the people in Hollywood continue as they are, which is alert, conscious of it, and fighting.

Source: House Committee on Un-American Activities, *Hearings Regarding the Communist Infiltration of the Motion Picture Industry*, 80th Cong., 1st sess. (Washington, D.C.: Government Printing Office, 1947), 216–17.

John Howard Lawson | Testimony before HUAC, 1947

Playwright and screenwriter John Howard Lawson was a founding member of the Screen Writers Guild. He was also a member of the American Communist Party and served as the party's cultural commissar in Hollywood, and many of his films included leftist political themes. In 1947 Lawson appeared before HUAC. The following selection shows several attempts by the committee to force Lawson's compliance. Like the other Hollywood Ten, Lawson was imprisoned and blacklisted for refusing to answer HUAC's questions or detail his political affiliations.

MR. LAWSON   I am glad you have made it perfectly clear that you are going to threaten and intimidate the witnesses, Mr. Chairman. (The chairman pounding gavel.)

MR. LAWSON   I am an American and I am not at all easy to intimidate, and don't think I am. (The chairman pounding gavel.)

MR. STRIPLING   Mr. Lawson, I repeat the question. Have you ever held any position in the Screen Writers Guild?

MR. LAWSON   I have stated that the question is illegal. But it is a matter of public record that I have held many offices in the Screen Writers Guild. I was its first president, in 1933, and I have held office on the board of directors of the Screen Writers Guild at other times. . . .

MR. STRIPLING   Mr. Lawson, are you now, or have you ever been a member of the Communist Party of the United States?

MR. LAWSON   In framing my answer to that question I must emphasize the points that I have raised before. The question of communism is in no way related to this inquiry, which is an attempt to get control of the screen and to invade the basic rights of American citizens in all fields.

MR. McDOWELL   Now, I must object—

MR. STRIPLING   Mr. Chairman— (The chairman pounding gavel.)

MR. LAWSON   The question here relates not only to the question of my membership in any political organization, but this committee is attempting to establish the right— (The chairman pounding gavel.)

MR. LAWSON (continuing)   Which has been historically denied to any committee of this sort, to invade the rights and privileges and immunity of American citizens, whether they be Protestant, Methodist, Jewish, or Catholic, whether they be Republicans or Democrats or anything else.

THE CHAIRMAN (pounding gavel)   Mr. Lawson, just quiet down again. Mr. Lawson, the most pertinent question that we can ask is whether or not you have ever been a member of the Communist Party. Now, do you care to answer that question?

MR. LAWSON   You are using the old technique, which was used in Hitler Germany in order to create a scare here—

THE CHAIRMAN (pounding gavel)   Oh—

MR. LAWSON   In order to create an entirely false atmosphere in which this hearing is conducted— (The chairman pounding gavel.)

MR. LAWSON   In order that you can then smear the motion-picture industry, and you can proceed to the press, to any form of communication in this country.

THE CHAIRMAN   You have learned—

MR. LAWSON   The Bill of Rights was established precisely to prevent the operation of any committee which could invade the basic rights of Americans. . . .

THE CHAIRMAN (pounding gavel)   We are going to get the answer to that question if we have to stay here for a week. Are you a member of the Communist Party, or have you ever been a member of the Communist Party?

MR. LAWSON   It is unfortunate and tragic that I have to teach this committee the basic principles of American—

THE CHAIRMAN (pounding gavel)   That is not the question. That is not the question. The question is: Have you ever been a member of the Communist Party?

MR. LAWSON   I am framing my answer in the only way in which any American citizen can frame his answer to a question which absolutely invades his rights.

THE CHAIRMAN   Then you refuse to answer that question; is that correct?

MR. LAWSON   I have told you that I will offer my beliefs, affiliations, and everything else to the American public, and they will know where I stand.

THE CHAIRMAN (pounding gavel)   Excuse the witness—

MR. LAWSON   As they do from what I have written.

THE CHAIRMAN (pounding gavel)   Stand away from the stand—

MR. LAWSON   I have written Americanism for many years, and I shall continue to fight for the Bill of Rights, which you are trying to destroy.

THE CHAIRMAN   Officers, take this man away from the stand—(Applause and boos.)

THE CHAIRMAN (pounding gavel)   There will be no demonstrations. No demonstrations, for or against. Everyone will please be seated.

Source: House Committee on Un-American Activities, *Hearings Regarding the Communist Infiltration of the Motion Picture Industry*, 80th Cong., 1st sess. (Washington, D.C.: Government Printing Office, 1947), 292–95.

DOCUMENT 24.8

Herblock | "Fire!" 1949

Editorial cartoonist Herbert Lawrence Block, who wrote under the name "Herblock," was a fierce critic of McCarthyism—both the man and the movement—and coined the term *McCarthyism* in March 1950, weeks after Senator McCarthy's first anti-Communist speech in Wheeling, West Virginia. The cartoon "Fire!" was published in June 1949 by the *Washington Post*.

"Fire!"

A 1949 Herblock Cartoon, © The Herb Block Foundation

DOCUMENT 24.9
Lillian Hellman | Letter to HUAC, 1952

Playwright Lillian Hellman, who was known for her devotion to leftist causes, was called to testify before HUAC in May 1952. Before her appearance, Hellman wrote the following letter to John Wood, the chairman of HUAC, explaining her willingness to answer questions about herself as long as she was not asked to testify against anyone else. Her request was denied. Hellman was blacklisted after invoking the Fifth Amendment during her HUAC appearance.

Dear Mr. Wood:

As you know, I am under subpoena to appear before your committee on May 21, 1952.

I am most willing to answer all questions about myself. I have nothing to hide from your committee and there is nothing in my life of which I am ashamed. I have been advised by counsel that under the fifth amendment I have a constitutional privilege to decline to answer any questions about my political opinions, activities, and associations, on the grounds of self-incrimination. I do not wish to claim this privilege. I am ready and willing to testify before the representatives of our Government as to my own opinions and my own actions, regardless of any risks or consequences to myself.

But I am advised by counsel that if I answer the committee's questions about myself, I must also answer questions about other people and that if I refuse to do so, I can be cited for contempt. My counsel tells me that if I answer questions about myself, I will have waived my rights under the fifth amendment and could be forced legally to answer questions about others. This is very difficult for a layman to understand. But there is one principle that I do understand: I am not willing, now or in the future, to bring bad trouble to people who, in my past association with them, were completely innocent of any talk or any action that was disloyal or subversive. I do not like subversion or disloyalty in any form and if I had ever seen any I would have considered it my duty to have reported it to the proper authorities. But to hurt innocent people whom I knew many years ago in order to save myself is, to me, inhuman and indecent and dishonorable. I cannot and will not cut my conscience to fit this year's fashions, even though I long ago came to the conclusion that I was not a political person and could have no comfortable place in any political group.

I was raised in an old-fashioned American tradition and there were certain homely things that were taught to me: To try to tell the truth, not to bear false witness, not to harm my neighbor, to be loyal to my country, and so on. In general, I respected these ideals of Christian honor and did as well with them as I knew how. It is my belief that you will agree with these simple rules of human decency and will not expect me to violate the good American tradition from which they spring. I would, therefore, like to come before you and speak of myself.

I am prepared to waive the privilege against self-incrimination and to tell you everything you wish to know about my views or actions if your committee will agree to refrain from asking me to name other people. If the committee is unwilling to give me this assurance, I will be forced to plead the privilege of the fifth amendment at the hearing.

A reply to this letter would be appreciated.

Sincerely yours,
Lillian Hellman

Source: House Committee on Un-American Activities, *Hearings Regarding Communist Infiltration of the Hollywood Motion-Picture Industry*, 82nd Cong., 2nd sess. (Washington, D.C.: Government Printing Office, 1952), 3545–46.

DOCUMENT 24.10

Arthur Miller | Reflections on HUAC, 2000

Playwright Arthur Miller was called before HUAC in June 1956. Though he testified about his own political activities, Miller refused to implicate anyone else associated with leftist causes, for which he was cited for contempt of Congress. Miller was fined, was sentenced to prison for thirty days, and was blacklisted in Hollywood. Four years earlier, Miller had written *The Crucible*, an allegorical play about the 1692 Salem witchcraft trials that had clear references to McCarthyism. In the following reflection, Miller describes the paranoia that swept America in the 1950s and the connections he drew between the witchcraft trials and McCarthyism.

I refer to the anti-communist rage that threatened to reach hysterical proportions and sometimes did. I can't remember anyone calling it an ideological war, but I think now that that is what it amounted to. I suppose we rapidly passed over anything like a discussion or debate, and into something quite different, a hunt not just for subversive people, but for ideas and even a suspect language. The object was to destroy the least credibility of any and all ideas associated with socialism and communism, whose proponents were assumed to be either knowing or unwitting agents of Soviet subversion. . . .

The heart of the darkness was the belief that a massive, profoundly organized conspiracy was in place and carried forward mainly by a concealed phalanx of intellectuals, including labor activists, teachers, professionals, sworn to undermine the American government. And it was precisely the invisibility of ideas that was frightening so many people. How could a play deal with this mirage world?

Paranoia breeds paranoia, but below paranoia there lies a bristling, unwelcome truth, so repugnant as to produce fantasies of persecution to conceal its existence. The unwelcome truth denied by the right was that the Hollywood writers accused of subversion were not a menace to the country, or even bearers of meaningful change. They wrote not propaganda but entertainment, some of it of a mildly liberal cast, but most of it mindless, or when it was political, as with [directors] Preston Sturges or Frank Capra, entirely and exuberantly un-Marxist.

As for the left, its unacknowledged truth was more important for me. If nobody was being shot in our ideological war but merely vivisected by a headline, it struck me as odd, if understandable, that the accused were unable to cry out passionately their faith in the ideals of socialism. There were attacks on the HUAC's right to demand that a citizen reveal his political beliefs; but on the idealistic canon of their own convictions, the defendants were mute. The rare exception, like Paul

Robeson's declaration of faith in socialism as a cure for racism, was a rocket that lit up the sky.

On a lucky afternoon I happened upon *The Devil in Massachusetts*, by Marion Starkey, a narrative of the Salem witch-hunt of 1692. I knew this story from my college reading, but in this darkened America it turned a completely new aspect toward me: the poetry of the hunt. Poetry may seem an odd word for a witch-hunt but I saw there was something of the marvelous in the spectacle of a whole village, if not an entire province, whose imagination was captured by a vision of something that wasn't there.

In time to come, the notion of equating the red-hunt with the witch-hunt would be condemned as a deception. There were communists and there never were witches. The deeper I moved into the 1690s, the further away drifted the America of the 50s, and, rather than the appeal of analogy, I found something different to draw my curiosity and excitement.

Anyone standing up in the Salem of 1692 and denying that witches existed would have faced immediate arrest, the hardest interrogation, and possibly the rope. Every authority not only confirmed the existence of witches but never questioned the necessity of executing them. It became obvious that to dismiss witchcraft was to forgo any understanding of how it came to pass that tens of thousands had been murdered as witches in Europe. To dismiss any relation between that episode and the hunt for subversives was to shut down an insight into not only the similar emotions but also the identical practices of both officials and victims. . . .

. . . Part of the surreality of the anti-left sweep was that it picked up people for disgrace who had already turned away from a pro-Soviet past but had no stomach for naming others who had merely shared their illusions. But the hunt had captured some significant part of the American imagination and its power demanded respect.

Source: Arthur Miller, "Are You Now or Were You Ever?," *The Guardian/The Observer* (online), June 17, 2000.

Interpret the Evidence

1. According to Ronald Reagan (Document 24.6), what threats did communism pose to American society? Why was Communist influence in entertainment seen as particularly dangerous? How should the Communist threat be handled?

2. How did the Herblock cartoon (Document 24.8) connect anti-Communist hysteria to the extinguishing of constitutional rights? Why did he see McCarthyism as a threat to American society?

3. Compare the testimonies of John Howard Lawson and Lillian Hellman (Documents 24.7 and 24.9). What were their chief objections to testifying before HUAC?

4. In what ways does Arthur Miller criticize both the right and the left (Document 24.10)?

5. In what different ways would HUAC and the witnesses appearing before it have defined "Un-American"? What gave HUAC so much power in the 1940s and 1950s?

Put It in Context

● Compare the Red scare following World War I with McCarthyism.

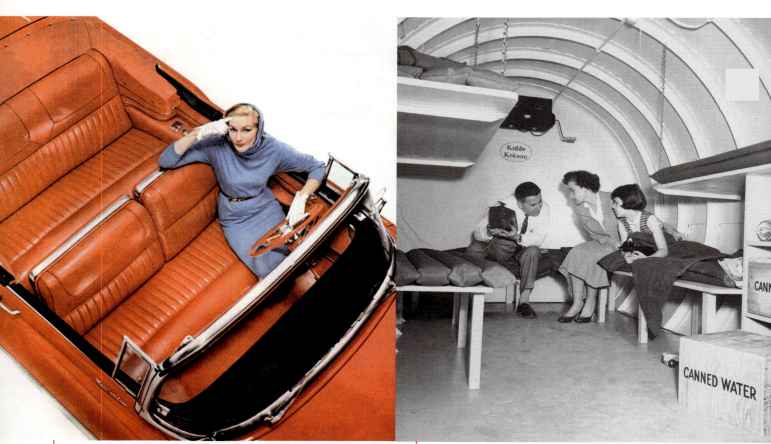

Rue des Archives/The Granger Collection, New York

© Bettmann/CORBIS

Buick advertisement, 1955.

Backyard bomb shelter, Garden City, New York, 1955.

25

Troubled Innocence

1950–1961

ullstein bild/The Granger Collection, New York

Teenage girl practicing with a hula hoop, 1958.

Alan Freed shook up American youth culture in the 1950s by rebranding existing black music and making it popular with white teenagers. *Rock 'n' roll* was a slang term among African Americans for sexual intercourse, but Freed turned it into an expression of musical rebellion. In 1951, at the age of twenty-nine, Aldon (Alan) James Freed was spinning records as a disc jockey, or "deejay," at a Cleveland, Ohio, radio station. He started out playing classical music but switched to rhythm and blues, an African American music style considered "race music." Freed began calling himself Moondog, howling like a dog, and using sound effects to rattle his radio listeners. Although he initially appealed mainly to a black audience, Freed's radio show and live concerts of music he dubbed rock 'n' roll soon attracted white teenagers.

In 1954 Freed moved to New York City radio station WINS, where his evening rock 'n' roll broadcast became a number one hit. Three years later at the height of his popularity, he hosted a nationally televised rock 'n' roll program, but only briefly. The American Broadcasting Company canceled Freed's show after four telecasts because of outrage from affiliate stations in the South after the black singer Frankie Lymon was shown dancing with a white girl.

The television incident was only the start of Freed's professional problems. In 1960 Freed was brought before a congressional committee investigating "payola," a common practice among deejays of receiving gifts from record companies in exchange for playing their records. His career sank further when Freed was indicted in 1962 for commercial

789

**Alan Freed
and Grace Metalious**

bribery by New York State. He was found guilty, was fined $300, and received a six-month suspended jail sentence. Freed never regained his earlier stature. Impoverished and struggling with alcoholism, Freed died in 1965 at the age of forty-three.

Like Alan Freed, Grace Metalious sent shock waves through American popular culture in the 1950s. Metalious grew up in poverty in a small mill town in southern New Hampshire. In 1943, while still a teenager, she married George Metalious and became a mother and housewife. In 1956 Metalious published her first novel, *Peyton Place*. Based on her hometown, the book sold more than three million copies the first year and unsettled the literary world. Considered provocative and racy because of its discussion of sex, rape, and incest, the novel punctured myths about the straitlaced life of small-town America. It criticized small-minded conformity that enforced a double standard of sexual behavior on women.

Despite the book's popularity, which inspired a toned-down Hollywood film and a television series, Metalious was never seen as a serious writer. Detractors described her as an untalented author who disseminated filth. In response to such allegations, she countered, "If I'm a lousy writer, then an awful lot of people have lousy taste." Metalious could not reconcile her success with the criticism she received and, like Alan Freed, increasingly turned to alcohol for comfort. She wrote other novels, but they never achieved the success that *Peyton Place* had. In 1964, a year before Freed's death and just eight years after publication of *Peyton Place*, she died at age thirty-nine of cirrhosis of the liver. Both Metalious and Freed challenged notions of conventional taste, and both found their lives upended by the conservative backlash their work inspired.

photos: Michael Ochs Archives/Getty Images; Courtesy Everett Collection

RONICALLY, THE AMERICAN HISTORIES of Alan Freed and Grace Metalious, both of whom attacked conformity, were made possible by the emergence of a mass-consumption economy fueled by technological innovation. The production of inexpensive paperback books enabled *Peyton Place* to reach a broad market. The development of low-cost records made rock 'n' roll songs widely available, and the creation of handheld transistor radios allowed teenagers to listen to music—played by deejays like Alan Freed—away from their parents' supervision. Young people were not the only ones to challenge their parents' culture. Writers and musicians experimented with freer forms of artistic expression and attacked the conformity they associated with mainstream America. African Americans challenged racial segregation directly in the Supreme Court and through powerful community protests. The Cold War remained the chief feature of foreign affairs and, despite wide-ranging

prosperity, continued to generate fears for the safety and security of all Americans.

The Boom Years

The notoriety of Grace Metalious and Alan Freed came at a time of renewed economic growth and prosperity in the United States. With more disposable income than they had enjoyed in decades, American consumers responded enthusiastically to the wide range of products that advertisers promised would make their lives easier and more enjoyable. The search for the good life propelled middle-class families from cities to the suburbs. At the same time, a postwar baby boom added millions of children to the population and created a market to supply them with goods from their infancy and childhood to their teenage years.

Economic Boom

The United States emerged from World War II in strong financial shape. The gross national product (GNP) soared 250 percent between 1945 and 1960, and per capita income (total income divided by the population) grew 35 percent. During this fifteen-year period, the average real income (actual purchasing power) for American workers increased by as much as it had during the fifty years preceding World War II. Equally striking, 60 percent of Americans achieved middle-class status, and the number of salaried office workers rose 61 percent. Factory workers also experienced gains. Union membership leaped to the highest level in U.S. history, reaching nearly 17 million. In the mid-1950s, the American Federation of Labor (AFL) and the Congress of Industrial Organizations (CIO) merged to increase labor union bargaining power, and the new AFL-CIO concentrated on improving its members' income.

The affluence of the 1950s was much more equally distributed than the prosperity of the 1920s had been. As the middle class grew, the top 5 percent of wealthy families dropped in the percentage of total income they earned from 21.3 percent to 19 percent. Though poverty remained a persistent problem, the rate of poverty decreased, falling from 34 percent in 1947 to 22.1 percent in 1960 (Figure 25.1). A college education served as a critical marker of entry into the middle class. Traditionally, colleges and universities had been accessible only to the upper class. That began to change in the postwar era. Between 1940 and 1960, the number of high school students who went on to college more than doubled, with the percentage of Americans who went to college vastly exceeding that of the British and the French.

In addition to purchasing paperbacks, transistor radios, and rock 'n' roll records, consumers bought televisions. TV sets became a household staple in the 1950s, and by 1960, 87 percent of Americans owned a television. Americans also continued to purchase automobiles—75 percent owned a car, most likely one produced by General Motors, Ford, or Chrysler. With gas supplies plentiful and the price per gallon less than 30 cents, automakers concentrated on size, power, and style to compete for buyers. With more cars on the road, motels built by chains such as Holiday Inn sprang up along the highways. Fast-food establishments proliferated to feed motorists

and their families. McDonald's hamburger restaurants, which first appeared in 1940 in San Bernardino, California, became the prototypical franchise chain for roadside fast food.

Baby Boom

In 1955 Illinois governor Adlai Stevenson told the graduating class of women at Smith College that they could do their part to maintain a free society as wives and mothers. Educated women had an important role to play in maintaining a household that boosted their husband's morale. "It is home work," Stevenson declared. "You can do it in the living-room with a baby in your lap or in the kitchen with a can opener in your hand . . . while you're watching television!" The mothers of these college graduates had suffered through the Great Depression, a time when the birthrate was 40 percent lower than in the 1950s. This was soon about to change.

In the 1950s, the average age at marriage was younger than it had been in the 1930s. On average, men married for

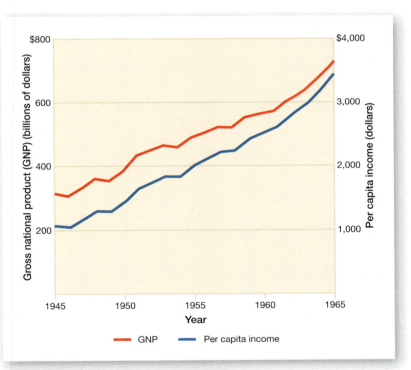

FIGURE 25.1   Economic Growth, 1945–1965

As industries shifted from war equipment to consumer goods, productivity remained high. More Americans entered the middle class in the two decades following World War II, while rising union membership ensured higher incomes for the working class. As a result, the purchasing power of most Americans increased in the immediate postwar period.

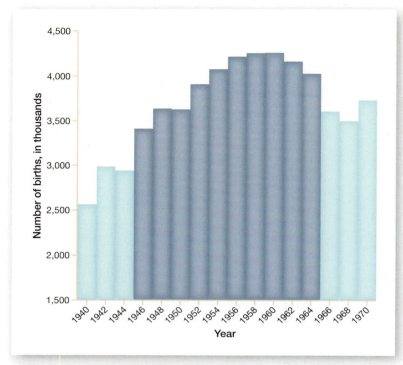

FIGURE 25.2   The Baby Boom, 1946–1964

The U.S. population increased dramatically in the postwar decades. Economic prosperity made it easier to support large families, women's early age at marriage contributed to high fertility, and improved health care led to the survival of more children.

vaccinations against diphtheria, whooping cough, and tuberculosis before they entered school. The most serious illness affecting young children remained the crippling disease of polio, or infantile paralysis. Each year, usually around summertime, parents and children feared a renewed outbreak of the polio virus, which they believed was spread through contact at crowded swimming pools and beaches. An outbreak of polio in 1952 and 1953 infected 93,000 people nationwide. In 1955 Dr. Jonas Salk developed a successful injectable vaccine against the disease. On April 12, 1955, news bulletins interrupted scheduled television programs to announce Salk's breakthrough, and, as one writer recalled, "citizens rushed to ring church bells and fire sirens, shouted, clapped, sang, and made every kind of joyous noise they could." Dr. Albert Sabin later developed a more convenient oral vaccine, and by the mid-1960s polio was no longer a public health menace in the United States.

the first time at the age of just under twenty-three, and 49 percent of women married at nineteen. Couples also produced children at an astonishing rate. In the 1950s, the growth rate in the U.S. population approached that of India, a country with one of the highest birthrates in the world (Figure 25.2).

Marriage and parenthood reflected a culture that increasingly emphasized early marriages and large families. The Cold War spurred this development. In the Atomic Age, public officials and the media urged young American men and women to build nuclear families in which the father held a paying job and the mother stayed at home and raised her growing family. Doing so would strengthen the moral fiber of the United States in its battle to contain Soviet communism. Religious leaders echoed this message. "The family that prays together stays together" became a popular refrain and served as an inducement to encourage marital fertility alongside spiritual fidelity.

Parents could also look forward to their children surviving childhood diseases that had resulted in many childhood deaths in the past. In the 1950s, children received

Suburban Boom

In 1948 real estate developer William Levitt remarked: "No man who owns his own house and lot can be a Communist. He has too much to do." Levitt did not invent the suburbs, but he promoted them as no one before him had. The economic and demographic booms encouraged migration out of the cities so that growing families could have their own homes, greater space, and a healthier environment. By 1960 nearly 60 million people, one-third of the nation's population, lived in suburbs. Residential communities outside New York City drew some 1.5 million people, and around Los Angeles the population tripled in size.

No section of the nation expanded faster than the West and the South. Attracted by the mild climate and jobs in the defense, petroleum, and chemical industries, transplanted Americans swelled the populations of California and Texas. The proliferation of air-conditioning in residences and businesses made the hot summer temperatures of these and other southern states more livable. California's population increased the most, adding nearly six million new residents between 1940 and 1960. In 1957, in a sign of the times, New York City lost two of its baseball teams, the New York Giants and the Brooklyn Dodgers, to San Francisco and Los Angeles. Retirees also flocked to California, and many others headed to Florida and Arizona. In Miami alone, the population jumped around 80 percent in the three decades after World War II. This migration to the **Sun Belt**, as the southern and western states would be called, transformed the political and social landscapes of the nation.

The extraordinary housing demand following World War II drove the suburban boom. The available housing stock could not accommodate returning veterans who married and started families. Many sought escape from crowded cities and a chance to achieve a piece of the American dream: a home with a front lawn, a backyard, and plenty of fresh air. To meet this demand, private enterprise and the federal government provided veterans and civilians opportunities to purchase their own homes.

William Levitt, a thirty-eight-year-old veteran from Long Island, New York, devised the formula for attracting home buyers to the suburbs. After World War II, Levitt, his father, and his brother saw their opportunity in the housing crunch and pioneered the idea of adapting Henry Ford's mass-production principles to the housing industry. To build his subdivision of **Levittown** in Hempstead, Long Island, twenty miles from Manhattan, he bulldozed 4,000 acres of potato fields and brought in trucks that dumped piles of building materials at exact intervals of sixty feet. Specialized crews then moved from pile to pile, each performing their assigned job. In July 1948, Levitt's workers constructed 180 houses a week, or 36 a day, in two shifts. These simple houses, placed on 60-by-100-foot lots, contained a living room, a kitchen, two bedrooms, and one bathroom. Levitt originally sold the homes for an affordable $7,990 and threw in a free television and washing machine. Mass-production methods kept prices low, and Levitt quickly sold his initial 17,000 houses and soon built other subdivisions in Pennsylvania and New Jersey. With Levitt leading the way, the production of new single-family homes nearly doubled from 937,000 in 1946 to 1.7 million in 1950.

Levitt and his fellow builders received a good deal of public help in making suburbia possible. The Federal Housing Administration, created in the 1930s, provided long-term mortgages to qualified buyers at low interest rates. After the war, the Veterans Administration offered even lower mortgage rates and did not require substantial down payments for ex-GIs to purchase a home. The federal government also cooperated by building roads that allowed drivers to commute to and from the suburbs. In 1956 the **National Interstate and Defense Highway Act** provided funds for the construction of 42,500 miles of roads throughout the country. In fashioning this policy of highway construction, Congress gave a tremendous boost not only to the development of the suburbs but also to the automobile industry. Between 1945 and 1960, the number of cars in the United States more than doubled. For many families living in suburban housing tracts, purchasing a second car became a necessity as husbands traveled by automobile to nearby cities and wives drove cars to go on errands and chauffeur their children to after-school activities.

Although millions of Americans took advantage of opportunities to move to the suburbs, millions of others could not. Levitt closed his subdivisions to African Americans. Many whites moved out of the cities because they did not want to live near the growing number of southern blacks who migrated north during World War II and the influx of Puerto Ricans who came to the United States after the war, and they did not welcome these minorities to their new communities. Levitt defended his racist exclusionary policy on business rather than on racial grounds. "I have come to know," he declared, "that if we sell one house to a Negro family, then 90 or 95 percent of our white customers will not buy into the community." Levitt was not alone in his discriminatory practices. Residents of many communities in the North purchased homes with restrictive covenants, which prohibited resale to blacks and members of other minority groups, including Hispanics, Jews, and Asian Americans. Although the Supreme Court outlawed restrictive covenants in *Shelley v. Kraemer* (1948), housing discrimination remained prevalent in urban and suburban neighborhoods. Real estate brokers steered minority buyers away from white communities, and banks refused to lend money to black purchasers who sought to move into white locales, an illegal policy called redlining.

Explore

See Documents 25.1 and 25.2 for two glimpses of 1950s suburban life.

REVIEW & RELATE

What factors contributed to the economic and population growth of the 1950s?

How did economic and demographic trends in the 1950s contribute to the growth of suburbs?

LEARNINGCurve bedfordstmartins.com/hewittlawson/LC

Living the Suburban Dream: Two Views

The postwar suburban boom eased housing shortages and gave millions the benefits of home ownership. In the 1950s, William Levitt built low-cost homes in the suburbs of New York City and Philadelphia. The following publicity photo for Levittown, Pennsylvania, just northeast of Philadelphia, is targeted at blue-collar workers. However, suburban developments largely excluded African Americans and other minorities. The restrictive covenant reprinted here is from Innis Arden, a suburban development created by the aircraft manufacturer William E. Boeing outside of Seattle, Washington. This restriction, written in 1941, remained in effect for several decades.

Explore

25.1 Levittown Advertisement, 1950s

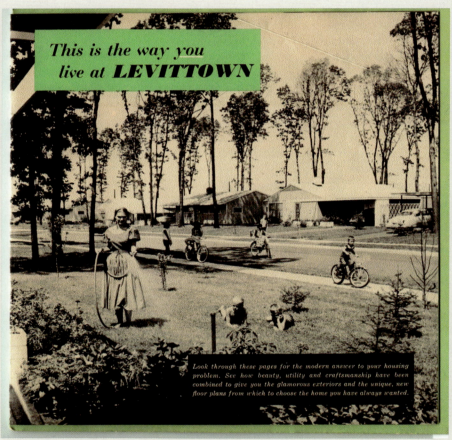

This is the way you live at LEVITTOWN

Look through these pages for the modern answer to your housing problem. See how beauty, utility and craftsmanship have been combined to give you the glamorous exteriors and the unique, new floor plans from which to choose the home you have always wanted.

Courtesy of The State Museum of Pennsylvania, Pennsylvania Historical and Museum Commission

The Culture of the 1950s

In the 1950s, popular culture developed as the United States confronted difficult political, diplomatic, and social issues. Amid this turmoil, television played a large role in shaping people's lives, reflecting their desire for success, and depicting the era as a time of innocence. The rise of teenage culture as a powerful economic force also influenced this portrayal of the 1950s. Teenage tastes, including rock 'n' roll, and consumption patterns reinforced the impression of a simpler and more carefree time. Religion painted a similar picture, as attendance at houses of worship rose. Still, the decade held a more complex social reality. Cultural rebels—writers, actors, and musicians—emerged to challenge mainstream values. Even women did not always act the suburban parts that television and society assigned them, and religion seemed

25.2 Restrictive Covenant for Innis Arden, Seattle, 1941

RACIAL RESTRICTIONS. No property in said addition shall at any time be sold, conveyed, rented, or leased in whole or in part to any person or persons not of the White or Caucasian race. No person other than one of the White or Caucasian race shall be permitted to occupy any property in said addition or portion thereof or building thereon except a domestic servant actually employed by a person of the White or Caucasian race where the latter is an occupant of such property.

ANIMALS. No hogs, cattle, horses, sheep, goats, or similar livestock shall be permitted or maintained on said property at any time. Chicken hens, pigeons, rabbits, and other similar small livestock not exceeding a total of twenty-five in number, shall be permitted but must be kept on the premises of the owner. Not more than one dog and cat may be kept for each building site.

Source: "Segregated Seattle," Seattle Civil Rights and Labor History Project, http://depts.washington.edu/civilr/segregated.htm.

Interpret the Evidence

- According to the advertisement, what would life in Levittown be like for potential buyers?
- Under what circumstances were nonwhites allowed to live in Innis Arden?

Put It in Context

How do these contrasting impressions of suburban life reflect home-purchasing opportunities in the 1950s?

to serve more of a communal, social function than an individual, spiritual one.

The Rise of Television

Few postwar developments had a greater impact on American society and politics than the advent of television. The first commercial TV broadcast occurred in 1939, but television sets did not become widely available until after World War II. The three major television networks—the Columbia Broadcasting System (CBS), the National Broadcasting Company (NBC), and the American Broadcasting Company (ABC)—offered programs nationwide that appealed to mainstream tastes while occasionally challenging the public with serious drama, music, and documentaries. During the 1950s, congressional investigations became a staple of television, and none provided a better morality tale than

their teenage audience after 1954 to rock 'n' roll, with its heavy downbeat and lyrics evoking teenage passion and sexuality. Black artists such as Chuck Berry, Little Richard, and Antoine "Fats" Domino and groups such as the Platters, the Channels, the Chords, the Chantels, and the Teenagers popularized the sound of classic, up-tempo rock and its soaring, harmonic variation known as doo-wop.

Although blacks pioneered the sound, the music entered the mainstream largely through white artists who added rural flavor to rhythm and blues. Elvis Presley was not the first white man to sing rock 'n' roll, but he became the most famous. Born in Tupelo, Mississippi, and living in Memphis, Tennessee, Elvis adapted the fashion and sensuality of the black performers he encountered to his own style. Elvis's snarling singing and wild pelvic gyrations excited young people, both black and white, while upsetting their parents. In an era when matters of sex remained private or were not discussed at all and when African Americans were still treated as second-class citizens, a

white man singing "black" music and shaking his body to the frenetic tempo of the music caused alarm. When Elvis sang on the popular *Ed Sullivan Show* in 1956, cameras were allowed to show him only from the waist up to uphold standards of decency. Four years later while Elvis was in the army, Congress targeted rock 'n' roll through its investigation of payola and the notorious deejay Alan Freed.

The Lives of Women

Throughout the 1950s, movies, women's magazines, mainstream newspapers, and medical and psychological experts informed women that only by embracing domesticity could they achieve personal fulfillment. Dr. Benjamin Spock's best-selling *Common Sense Book of Baby and Child Care* (1946) advised mothers that their children would reach their full potential only if wives stayed at home and watched over their offspring. In another best seller, *Modern Women: The Lost Sex* (1947), Ferdinand

Women in the Home and in the Workplace

In the 1950s, married women were encouraged to stay at home. Modern appliances like this refrigerator (right) supposedly made housework less difficult, but wives had to spend a great deal of time keeping it fully stocked and attending to other household chores. With all the new devices at their disposal, wives were expected to keep the home neat and spotless, while caring for their children. But not all married women stayed at home and tended the family. Senator Margaret Chase Smith (above) was an influential Republican senator from Maine who took on Senator Joseph McCarthy in Congress and challenged his harsh anti-Communist methods. Here she is engaged in serious deliberations with Democratic Majority Leader Lyndon B. Johnson at a Senate hearing in 1957. above: Time & Life Pictures/Getty Images; right: Hulton/Archive/Getty Images

Lundberg and Marynia Farnham called the independent woman "a contradiction in terms." A 1951 study of corporate executives found that most businessmen viewed the ideal wife as one who devoted herself to her husband's career. College newspapers described female undergraduates as distraught if they did not become engaged by their senior year. Certainly many women professed to find such lives fulfilling, but not all women were so content. Many experienced anxiety and depression, and, in their despair, some turned to alcohol and tranquilizers. Far from satisfied, these women suffered from what the social critic Betty Friedan would later call "a problem that has no name," a malady that derived not from any personal failing but from the unrewarding roles women were expected to play.

Not all women fit the stereotype, however. Although most married women with families did not work during the 1950s, the proportion of working wives doubled from 15 percent in 1940 to 30 percent in 1960, with the greatest increase coming in women over the age of thirty-five. Married women were more likely to work if they were African American or came from working-class immigrant families. Moreover, women's magazines did not offer readers a unified message of domesticity. Alongside articles about and advertisements directed at stay-at-home mothers, these periodicals profiled career women who served in politics, such as Maine senator Margaret Chase Smith, the African American educator Mary McLeod Bethune, and sports figures such as the golf and tennis great Babe (Mildred) Didrikson Zaharias. At the same time, working women played significant roles in labor unions, where they formulated plans to reduce disparities between men's and women's income and to provide a wage for housewives, recognizing the unpaid work they did at home in maintaining the family. Many other women joined women's clubs and organizations like the Young Women's Christian Association (YWCA), where they engaged in charitable and public service activities. Some participated in political organizations, such as Henry Wallace's Progressive Party, and peace groups, such as the Women's International League for Peace and Freedom, to campaign against the violence caused by racial discrimination at home and Cold War rivalries abroad.

Religious Revival

Along with marriage and the family, religion experienced a revival in the postwar United States. The arms race between the United States and the Soviet Union heightened the dangers of international conflict for ordinary citizens, and the social and economic changes that accompanied the Cold War intensified personal anxiety. Churchgoing underscored the contrast between the United States, a nation of religious worship, and the "godless" communism of the Soviet Union. The link between religion and Americanism prompted Congress in 1954 to add "under God" to the pledge of allegiance and to make "In God We Trust" the national motto. Even President Dwight D. Eisenhower joined a church for the first time in his life.

Americans turned in great numbers to religious worship. Between 1940 and 1950, church and synagogue membership rose by 78 percent, and more than 95 percent of the population professed a belief in God. Yet religious affiliation appeared to reflect a greater emphasis on togetherness than on specific doctrinal beliefs. Theologian Will Herberg wrote that this religious revival constituted "religiousness without religion." It offered a way to overcome isolation and embrace community in an increasingly alienating world. "The people in the suburbs want to feel psychologically secure, adjusted, at home in their environment," Herberg explained. "Being religious and joining a church is . . . a fundamental way of 'adjusting' and 'belonging.'"

Television also helped spread religiosity into millions of homes. The Catholic bishop Fulton J. Sheen spoke to a weekly television audience of ten million and alternated his message of "a life worth living" with attacks on atheistic Communists. The Methodist minister Norman Vincent Peale, also a popular TV figure, combined traditional religious faith with self-help remedies prescribed in his best-selling book *The Power of Positive Thinking* (1952). The Reverend Billy Graham, a preacher from Charlotte, North Carolina, who became the greatest evangelist of his era, was a traveling minister who blended his call for Americans to accept Jesus Christ into their hearts with fervent anticommunism. Graham used his considerable oratorical powers to preach at huge outdoor crusades in baseball parks and large arenas, which were broadcast on television. Religious Americans derived a variety of meanings from their religious experiences, but they embraced Americanism as their national religion. A good American, one magazine proclaimed, could not be "un-religious."

Explore

See Document 25.3 for Billy Graham's interpretation of America's problems in the 1950s.

DOCUMENT 25.3

Billy Graham | What's Wrong with Our World? 1958

Billy Graham, the most famous preacher of his generation, began speaking to packed auditoriums in the late 1940s. Known for his huge revival-style meetings, or crusades, Graham used mass media to reach national and international audiences through radio programs, television specials, movies, and newspaper columns. This excerpt from a 1958 speech shows Graham as a social critic. He laments Americans' unhappiness despite their high standard of living, and he locates the problem in personal sin rather than in economic and political institutions.

Explore

As a nation, as a human race, what's wrong with our world? . . . Our crime rate is increasing in city after city across the nation.

What causes those problems? What is back of it? Why cannot we solve our problems?

We in America have the highest standard of living in the world.

We are a prosperous nation. We have educational advantages. We have everything, and yet something is wrong.

We are not a happy people.

We have more boredom per square inch in this country than any country in the world.

Our divorce rate is the highest, indicating our homes are basically unhappy. . . .

We're facing problems within ourselves. Many people today are searching for happiness. They're searching for peace of mind. They're searching for joy, and they're not finding it. They've tried money, they've tried other things in life, but they haven't been able to find the peace, the relaxation, the joy, that they want.

What's wrong? What's happened? What's wrong with Man? What's wrong with the world in which we live?

I believe that the "United Nations" is doing the best it can, but I believe the "United Nations" is only dealing with symptoms of something deeper that is wrong with the world.

. . . I think all over the world men want peace, but somehow peace doesn't come.

We put out a fire in the Middle East and it breaks out again in the Far East. We put it out in the Far East and it breaks out again somewhere else. And it seems we're jumping from fire to fire. We're trying to solve the problems of the world but we make the mistake of treating symptoms!

The race problem is a symptom. War is a symptom. Crime is a symptom. The sociological problem is a symptom. Something deeper is wrong. . . .

What is the cause? The Bible has an answer. Jesus had an answer. Jesus said, "All these evil things come from within" and they devour the individual and they devour the society.

The Bible teaches that something is wrong with human nature. Something is wrong with Man himself. What is that something?

The Bible says that man has a disease and that disease is called S-I-N—"sin."

Now, ladies and gentlemen, that is what is wrong with the world tonight.

Source: Billy Graham, "What's Wrong with Our World?," *The Charlotte Observer*, September 28, 1958, 10.

Interpret the Evidence

- Why does Graham believe that Americans are unhappy?
- How does Graham's belief that "human nature" is the cause of the problem limit the solutions he might recommend?

Put It in Context

Why might Graham's message about personal sin as the source of war and social tensions have appealed to his audience during the 1950s?

Beats and Other Nonconformists

As many Americans migrated to the suburbs, spent money on leisure and entertainment, and cultivated religion, a small group of young poets, writers, intellectuals, musicians, and artists attacked mainstream politics and culture. Known as **beats** (derived from "beaten down"), they attacked white middle-class society with stinging critiques of what they considered the sterility and conformity of American life. In 1956 Allen Ginsberg began his epic poem *Howl* with the line "I saw the best minds of my generation destroyed by madness, starving hysterical naked." In his novel *On the Road* (1957), Jack Kerouac, a friend of Ginsberg's, praised the individual who pursued authentic experiences and mind-expanding consciousness through drugs, sexual experimentation, and living in the moment. At a time when whiteness was not just a skin color but a standard of beauty and virtue, the beats and authors such as Norman Mailer looked to African Americans as cultural icons, embracing jazz music and the spontaneity and coolness they attributed to inner-city blacks. The beats formed their own artistic enclaves in New York City's Greenwich Village and San Francisco's North Beach and Haight-Ashbury districts. Wherever they lived, they provided a lifestyle that a younger generation of political and cultural rebels would adopt in the 1960s.

The beat writers frequently read their poems and prose to the rhythms of jazz, reflecting both their affinity with African American culture and the innovative explorations taking place in music. From the big bands of the 1930s and 1940s, postwar jazz musicians formed smaller trios, quartets, and quintets and experimented with sounds more suitable for serious listening than for dancing. The bebop rhythms of trumpeter Dizzy Gillespie and alto saxophonist Charlie Parker revolutionized jazz and reflected the accompanying black rebellion against white supremacy. Trumpeter Miles Davis and tenor saxophonist John Coltrane experimented with more complex and textured forms of this music and took it to new heights. Like rock 'n' roll musicians, these black artists broke down racial barriers as their music crossed over to white audiences.

Homosexuals also attempted to live nonconformist sexual lifestyles, albeit clandestinely. According to studies by researcher Dr. Alfred Kinsey of Indiana University, homosexuals made up approximately 10 percent of the adult population. During World War II, gay men and

Recording *1958 Miles*

Jazz underwent great changes in the 1950s and became a soundtrack to the literary rebels of the beat generation. This 1958 recording session features four of the greatest jazz musicians of their era. From left to right, John Coltrane plays the tenor saxophone, Nat "Cannonball" Adderley the alto saxophone, Miles Davis (the leader) the trumpet, and Bill Evans the piano. Rue des Archives/The Granger Collection, New York lesbians had the opportunity to meet other homosexuals in the military and in venues that attracted gay soldiers. Though homosexuality remained taboo and public displays of it were a crime, politically radical gay men organized against homophobia after the war. In 1951 they formed the Mattachine Society in Los Angeles, which then spread to the East Coast. In 1954 a group of lesbians founded the Daughters of Bilitis in San Francisco. Because of police harassment, most homosexuals refused to reveal their sexual orientation, which made sense practically but reduced their ability to counter antihomosexual discrimination.

Alfred Kinsey also shattered myths about conformity in the private conduct of heterosexuals. In *Sexual Behavior in the Human Female* (1953), Kinsey revealed that many women rejected the double standard that allowed men, but not women, to lose their virginity before marriage. Fifty percent of the women he interviewed had had sexual intercourse before marriage, and 25 percent had had extramarital affairs. Kinsey's findings were supported by other data. Between 1940 and 1960, the frequency of out-of-wedlock births among all women rose from 7.1 newborns to 21.6 newborns per thousand women of childbearing age. The tawdry relations that Grace Metalious depicted in *Peyton Place* merely reflected what many Americans practiced but did not talk about. The brewing sexual revolution further went public in 1953 with the publication of *Playboy* magazine, founded by Hugh Hefner. Through a combination of serious articles and photographs of nude women, the magazine provided its chiefly male readers with a guide to pursuing sexual pleasure and a sophisticated lifestyle.

Like Metalious, many writers denounced the conformity and shallowness they found in suburban America. Novelist Sloan Wilson wrote about the alienating experience of suburban life in *The Man in the Gray Flannel Suit* (1955). "Without talking about it much," Wilson wrote of his fictional suburban couple, "they both began to think of the house as a trap, and they no more enjoyed refurbishing it than a prisoner would delight in shining up the bars of his cell." In J. D. Salinger's novel *Catcher in the Rye* (1951), the young protagonist, Holden Caulfield, mocks the phoniness of the adult world while ending up in a mental institution. Journalists and scholars joined in the criticism. Such critics often overstated the conformity that characterized the suburbs by minimizing the ethnic, religious, and political diversity of their residents. Yet they tapped into a growing feeling, especially among a new generation of young people, of the dangers of a mass culture based on standardization, compliance, and bureaucratization.

REVIEW & RELATE

What trends in American popular culture did the television shows and popular music of the 1950s reflect?

How did artists, writers, and social critics challenge the mainstream politics and culture of the 1950s?

The Civil Rights Movement

African Americans wanted what most other Americans desired after World War II—the opportunity to make a decent living, buy a nice home, raise a healthy family, and get the best education for their children. Yet blacks faced much greater obstacles than did whites in obtaining these dreams, particularly in the South, where African Americans attended separate and unequal schools, faced discrimination if not outright exclusion from public accommodations, were not permitted to vote, and encountered vigilante violence. Determined to eliminate these injustices, black Americans mounted a campaign against white supremacy in the decades after World War II. African Americans increasingly viewed their struggle as part of an international freedom movement of black people in Africa and other nonwhites in the Middle East and Asia to obtain their freedom from Western colonial rulers.

School Segregation and the Supreme Court

Led by the National Association for the Advancement of Colored People (NAACP), African Americans launched a prolonged assault on school segregation. Pursuing a strategy designed in the 1930s by its chief lawyer, Charles Hamilton Houston, the association filed lawsuits against states that excluded blacks from publicly funded law schools and universities. After victories in Missouri and Maryland, Houston's successor, Thurgood Marshall, convinced the Supreme Court in 1950 to disband the separate law school that Texas had set up for blacks and to allow them to attend the University of Texas Law School. At the same time, the Court also eliminated separate facilities for black students at the University of Oklahoma graduate school and ruled against segregation in interstate rail transportation.

Before African Americans could attend college, they had to obtain a first-class education in public schools. All-black schools typically lacked the resources provided to white schools. The NAACP understood that without federal intervention southern officials would never live up to the "separate but equal doctrine" asserted in *Plessy v. Ferguson* (1896). African Americans sought to integrate schools not because they wanted their children to sit next to white students in classrooms and adopt their ways, but because they believed that integration offered the best and quickest way to secure quality education.

In fighting segregated education, the NAACP drew on grassroots organizing techniques in southern communities. In the late 1940s, black families in towns throughout the South joined together to pressure white officials to provide buses to transport children to school, to raise the salaries of black teachers, and to furnish classrooms with critical supplies. Led by black activists in South Carolina and Virginia, the NAACP filed lawsuits seeking to overturn *Plessy*. The association added cases from Delaware and Kansas, where a measure of segregation persisted, as well as from Washington, D.C., where the federal government was responsible for maintaining segregated schools in the nation's capital.

On May 17, 1954, in **Brown v. Board of Education of Topeka, Kansas**, the Supreme Court overturned *Plessy*. In a unanimous decision read by Chief Justice Earl Warren, the Court concluded that "in the field of public education the doctrine of 'separate but equal' has no place. Separate educational facilities are inherently unequal." This ruling undercut the legal foundation for segregation and officially placed the law on the side of those who sought racial equality. Nevertheless, the ruling did not end the controversy; in fact, it led to more battles over segregation. In 1955 the Court issued a follow-up opinion calling for implementation with "all deliberate speed." But, it left enforcement of *Brown* to federal district courts in the South, which consisted mainly of white southerners who espoused segregationist views. As a result, southern officials emphasized "deliberate" rather than "speed" and slowed the implementation of the *Brown* decision.

Montgomery Bus Boycott, 1956

Two months after African American residents of Montgomery, Alabama, began their boycott of the city buses to protest segregation and mistreatment, the black community kept up its boycott despite violence and intimidation. Black women had made up the majority of bus riders, and this photograph, taken on February 1, 1956, shows many of them walking to work or going shopping. Time & Life Pictures/Getty Images

The Montgomery Bus Boycott

The *Brown* decision encouraged African Americans to protest against other forms of racial discrimination. In 1955 in Montgomery, Alabama, the Women's Political Council, a group of middle-class and professional black women, petitioned the city commission to improve bus service for black passengers. Among other things, they wanted blacks not to have to give up their seats to white passengers who boarded the bus after black passengers did. Their requests went unheeded until December 1, 1955, when Rosa Parks, a black seamstress and an NAACP activist, refused to give up her seat to a white man. Parks's arrest rallied civic, labor, and religious groups around her and sparked a bus boycott that involved nearly the entire black community. Instead of

riding buses, black commuters walked to work or joined car pools. One elderly woman reportedly declined a ride and insisted on walking, explaining, "My feet are tired, but my soul is rested." White officials refused to capitulate and fought back by arresting leaders of the **Montgomery Improvement Association,** the organization that coordinated the protest. Other whites hurled insults at blacks and engaged in violence. After more than a year of conflict, the Supreme Court ruled in favor of the complete desegregation of Montgomery's buses.

Out of this landmark struggle, Martin Luther King Jr. emerged as the civil rights movement's most charismatic leader. The son of a prominent Atlanta minister, King had graduated from the historically black Morehouse College and received a doctorate in theology from Boston University.

Twenty-six years old at the time of Parks's arrest, King was a recent arrival in Montgomery and the pastor of the prestigious Dexter Avenue Baptist Church. He did not seek to lead the boycott, but instead he had it thrust upon him. In Dr. King, Montgomery's blacks had found a man whose personal courage and power of oratory could inspire nearly all segments of the African American community. Though King was familiar with the nonviolent methods of the Indian revolutionary Mohandas Gandhi and the civil disobedience of the nineteenth-century writer Henry David Thoreau, he drew his inspiration and commitment to these principles mainly from the black church and secular leaders such as A. Philip Randolph and Bayard Rustin. King understood how to convey the goals of the civil rights movement to sympathetic white Americans, but his vision and passion grew out of black communities. At the outset of the Montgomery bus boycott, King noted proudly the achievement of African Americans: "When the history books are written in future generations, the historians will have to pause and say 'There lived a great people—a Black people—who injected new meaning and dignity into the veins of civilization.'"

The Montgomery bus boycott made King a national civil rights leader, but it did not guarantee him further success. In 1957 King and a like-minded group of southern black ministers formed the **Southern Christian Leadership Conference (SCLC)** to spread nonviolent protest throughout the region, but except in a few cities, such as Tallahassee, Florida, bus boycott spinoffs did not take hold.

White Resistance to Desegregation

Segregationists responded forcefully to halt black efforts to eliminate Jim Crow. In 1956, 101 southern congressmen issued a manifesto declaring the 1954 *Brown* opinion "a clear abuse of judicial power" and pledging to resist its implementation through "lawful means." Other southerners went beyond the law, as events in Little Rock, Arkansas, showed. In 1957 a federal court approved a plan submitted by the Little Rock School Board to integrate Central High School. However, the governor of Arkansas, Orval Faubus, obstructed the court ruling by sending the state National Guard to keep out nine black students chosen to attend Central High. Faced with blatant state resistance to federal authority, President Eisenhower, a lukewarm supporter of school desegregation, placed the National Guard under federal control and sent in the 101st Airborne Division to restore order after a mob blocked the students from entering the school. The black students, who became known as the **Little Rock Nine**, attended classes for the year under the protection of the National Guard but still encountered considerable harassment from white pupils inside the school. In June 1958, one of the black students, Ernest Green, graduated, but Governor Faubus and the state legislature shut down the school for a year until the Supreme Court in 1959 ordered its reopening. In defiance of the

high court, other school districts, such as Prince Edward County, Virginia, chose to close their public schools rather than desegregate. By the end of the decade, public schools in the South remained mostly segregated, and only a token number of black students in a handful of states attended school with whites.

The white South used other forms of violence and intimidation to preserve segregation. The third incarnation of the Ku Klux Klan (KKK) appeared after World War II to strike back at growing African American challenges to white supremacy. This terrorist group threatened, injured, and killed those blacks they considered "uppity." Following the *Brown* decision, segregationists also formed the White Citizens' Council (WCC). The WCC drew members largely from businessmen and professionals. Rather than condoning murder and violent confrontation, the WCC generally relied on intimidating blacks by threatening to fire them from jobs or denying them credit from banks. In Alabama, WCC members launched a campaign against radio stations playing the kind of rock 'n' roll music that Alan Freed popularized in New York City because they believed that it fostered close interracial contact. Reflecting much of the sentiment in the region, an Alabama segregationist called rock 'n' roll "the basic, heavy beat music of Negroes," which, if left unchecked, would result in the downfall of "the entire moral structure . . . the white man has built."

The WCC and the KKK created a racial climate in the deep South that encouraged whites to believe they could get away with murder to defend white supremacy. In the summer of 1955, Emmett Till, a fourteen-year-old from Chicago who was visiting his great-uncle in Mississippi, was killed because he allegedly flirted with a white woman in a country store. Although the two accused killers were brought to trial, an all-white jury quickly acquitted them. Elsewhere in Mississippi that same year, an NAACP official, George Lee, was killed for organizing voter registration drives; the crime was never prosecuted.

The Sit-Ins

With boycotts petering out and white violence rising, African Americans, especially high school and college students, developed new techniques to confront discrimination, including sit-ins, in which protesters seat themselves in a strategic spot and refuse to move until their demands are met or they are forcibly evicted. In 1958 the NAACP organized a sit-in against segregated lunch counters in Oklahoma City, and in 1959 the Congress of Racial Equality (CORE) did the same in Miami. However, mass demonstrations did not really get off the ground until February 1960, when four students at North Carolina A&T University in Greensboro waged sit-ins at the whites-only lunch counters in Woolworth and Kress department stores. Their protests sparked similar efforts throughout the Southeast, expanding to more than two hundred cities within a year (Map 25.1).

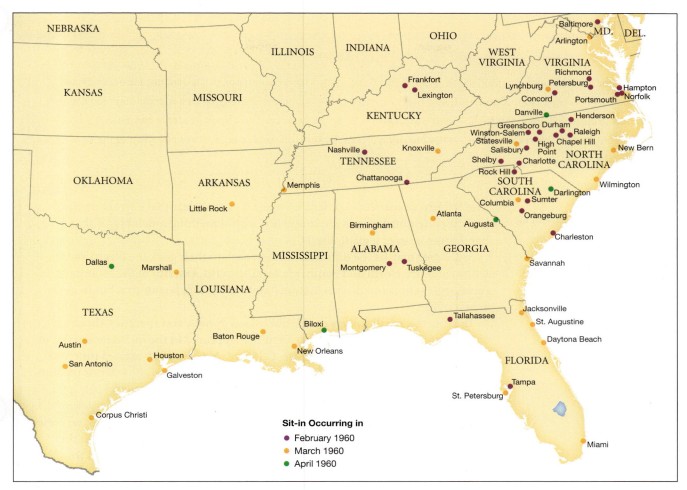

MAP 25.1 Lunch Counter Sit-Ins, February–April 1960

After starting slowly in the late 1950s, lunch counter sit-ins exploded in 1960 following a sit-in by college students in Greensboro, North Carolina. Within three months, sit-ins erupted in fifty-eight cities across the South. The participation of high school and college students revitalized the civil rights movement and led to the formation of the Student Nonviolent Coordinating Committee in April 1960.

A few months after the sit-ins began, a number of their participants formed the **Student Nonviolent Coordinating Committee (SNCC)**. The organization's young members sought not only to challenge racial segregation in the South but also to create interracial communities based on economic equality and political democracy. This generation of black and white sit-in veterans came of age in the 1950s at a time when the democratic rhetoric of America's role in the Cold War and the Supreme Court's decision in the *Brown* case raised their expectations for racial equality. Yet these young activists often saw their hopes dashed by numerous examples of southern segregationist resistance, including the 1955 murder of Emmett Till, an incident that both horrified and helped mobilize them to fight for black equality. "Emmett Till was only three years older than me and I identified with him," recalled Cleveland Sellers, a SNCC staff member from

South Carolina. "I tried to put myself in his place and imagine what he was thinking when those white men took him from his home that night. . . . I couldn't get over the fact that the men who were accused of killing him had not been punished at all."

Explore

See Document 25.4 for more on SNCC's core goals.

REVIEW & RELATE

What strategies did African Americans adopt in the 1950s to fight segregation and discrimination?

How and why did white southerners resist efforts to end segregation?

 LEARNINGCurve bedfordstmartins.com/hewittlawson/LC

DOCUMENT 25.4

Ella Baker | Bigger Than a Hamburger, 1960

Soon after the first lunch counter sit-ins, activist Ella Baker called for a conference of student organizers at Shaw University in Raleigh, North Carolina. Baker had fought for black rights and equality for decades through local and national groups, including the NAACP and SCLC. At the Shaw conference, she helped students establish the Student Nonviolent Coordinating Committee. In the following article, Baker summarizes an address she gave at the conference on SNCC's goals.

Explore

What is the significance of the article's title?

The Student Leadership Conference made it crystal clear that current sit-ins and other demonstrations are concerned with something much bigger than a hamburger or even a giant-sized Coke.

Whatever may be the difference in approach to their goal, the Negro and white students, North and South, are seeking to rid America of the scourge of racial segregation and discrimination—not only at lunch counters, but in every aspect of life.

In reports, casual conversations, discussion groups, and speeches, the sense and the spirit of the following statement that appeared in the initial newsletter of the students at Barber-Scotia College, Concord, N.C., were re-echoed time and again: "We want the world to know that we no longer accept the inferior position of second-class citizenship. We are willing to go to jail, be ridiculed, spat upon, and even suffer physical violence to obtain First Class Citizenship."

By and large, this feeling that they have a destined date with freedom, was not limited to a drive for personal freedom, or even freedom for the Negro in the South. Repeatedly it was emphasized that the movement was concerned with the moral implications of racial discrimination for the "whole world" and the "Human Race."

This universality of approach was linked with a perceptive recognition that "it is important to keep the movement democratic and to avoid struggles for personal leadership."

It was further evident that desire for supportive cooperation from adult leaders and the adult community was also tempered by apprehension that adults might try to "capture" the student movement. The students showed willingness to be met on the basis of equality, but were intolerant of anything that smacked of manipulation or domination.

What concerns did students cite about cooperating with adults?

According to Baker, what problems do "leader-centered groups" seem to create?

This inclination toward group-centered leadership, rather than toward a leader-centered group pattern of organization, was refreshing indeed to those of the older group who bear the scars of the battle, the frustrations and the disillusionment that come when the prophetic leader turns out to have heavy feet of clay.

Source: Ella Baker, "Bigger Than a Hamburger," *Southern Patriot*, June 1960, 4.

Put It in Context

How did SNCC's goals as expressed here represent a change from earlier efforts to achieve racial equality?

The Eisenhower Era

Despite the existence of civil rights protesters, rock 'n' roll upstarts, intellectual dissenters, and sexual revolutionaries, the 1950s seemed to many a tranquil, even dull period—one commentator referred to it as "the bland leading the bland." This impression owes a great deal to the leadership of President Dwight D. Eisenhower. Serving two terms from 1953 to 1961, Eisenhower, or "Ike" as he was affectionately called, convinced the majority of Americans that their country was in good hands regardless of political turbulence at home and heated international conflicts abroad.

Modern Republicanism

President Eisenhower, a World War II hero, radiated strength and trust, qualities the American people found very attractive as they rebuilt their lives and established families in the 1950s. Nominated by the Republican Party in 1952, the sixty-two-year-old Eisenhower shrewdly balanced his ticket by choosing as his running mate California senator Richard M. Nixon, a man twenty-three years his junior who had risen in politics by attacking Democrats as soft on communism. On election day, Eisenhower coasted to victory, winning 55 percent of the popular vote and 83 percent of the electoral vote. Despite Eisenhower's personal popularity, the Republicans managed to win only slim majorities in the Senate and the House. Within two years, they had lost even this slight edge in both houses, and the Democrats regained control of Congress.

With a limited electoral mandate, the president adopted what one of his speechwriters called **Modern Republicanism**, which tried to fit the traditional Republican Party ideals of individualism and fiscal restraint within the broad framework of Franklin Roosevelt's New Deal. With Democrats in control of Congress after 1954, Republicans agreed to raise Social Security benefits and to include coverage for some ten million additional workers. Congress and the president retained another New Deal mainstay, the minimum wage, and increased it from 75 cents to $1 an hour. Departing from traditional Republican criticism of big government, the Eisenhower administration added the Department of Health, Education, and Welfare to the cabinet in 1953. The president justified expanding the federal government in domestic matters as part of fighting the Cold War. In 1958 Eisenhower signed into law the National Defense Education Act, which provided aid for instruction in science, math, and foreign languages and graduate fellowships and loans for college students. He portrayed the new law as a way to catch up with the Soviets, who the previous year had successfully launched the first artificial satellite, called *Sputnik*, into outer space.

Eisenhower and the Cold War

In foreign affairs, Eisenhower perpetuated Truman's containment doctrine while at the same time espousing the contradictory principle of "rolling back" communism in Eastern Europe. However, when Hungarians rose up against their Soviet-backed regime in 1956, the U.S. government did little more than offering encouragement and allowing approximately eighty thousand Hungarian refugees to enter the country. Rather than pushing back communism, the Eisenhower administration expanded the doctrine of containment around the world by entering into treaties to establish regional defense pacts. In 1954 the Southeast Asia Treaty Organization was formed to protect Australia, France, Great Britain, New Zealand, Pakistan, the Philippines, and Thailand from Communist assault. In 1959 the Central Treaty Organization brought Iraq, Iran, Turkey, and once again Pakistan within the U.S. defense perimeter.

Eisenhower's commitment to fiscal discipline had a profound effect on his foreign policy. The president worried that the alliance among government, defense contractors, and research universities—which he dubbed "the military-industrial complex"—would bankrupt the economy and undermine individual freedom. With this in mind, he implemented the **New Look** strategy, which placed a higher priority on building a nuclear arsenal and delivery system than on the more expensive task of maintaining and deploying armed forces on the ground throughout the world. Nuclear missiles launched from the air by U.S. air force bombers or fired from submarines would give the United States, as Secretary of Defense Charles Wilson asserted, "a bigger bang for the buck." With the nation now armed with nuclear weapons, the Eisenhower administration threatened "massive retaliation" in the event of Communist aggression.

The New Look may have saved money and slowed the rate of defense spending, but it had serious flaws. First, it placed a premium on "brinksmanship," taking Communist enemies to the precipice of nuclear destruction, risking the death of millions, and hoping the other side would back down. Second, massive retaliation did not work for small-scale conflicts. For instance, in the event of a confrontation in Berlin, would the United States launch nuclear missiles toward Germany and expose its European allies in West Germany and France to nuclear contamination? Third, the buildup of nuclear warheads provoked an arms race by encouraging the Soviet Union to do the same. Peace depended on the superpowers terrifying each other with the threat of nuclear annihilation—that is, if one country attacked the other, retaliation was guaranteed to result in shared obliteration. This strategy was known as **mutually assured destruction**, and its acronym—**MAD**—summed up its nightmarish qualities. As each nuclear power increased its capacity to destroy the other many times over, the

both of the Cold War protagonists. Nonetheless, they were often drawn into East-West conflicts.

Such was the case in Egypt, which achieved independence from Great Britain in 1952. Two years later under General Gamal Abdel Nasser, the country sought to modernize its economy by building the hydroelectric Aswan Dam on the Nile River. Nasser welcomed financial backing from the United States and the Soviet Union, but the Eisenhower administration refused to contribute so long as the Egyptians accepted Soviet assistance. In 1956 Nasser, falling short of funds, sent troops to take over the Suez Canal, the waterway run by Great Britain and through which the bulk of Western Europe's oil was shipped. He intended to pay for the dam by collecting tolls from canal users. In retaliation, Britain and France, the two European powers most affected by the seizure, invaded Egypt on October 29, 1956. Locked in a struggle with Egypt and other Arab nations since its creation in 1948, Israel joined in the attack. The invading forces—all U.S. allies—had not warned the Eisenhower administration of their plans. Coming at the same time as the Soviet crackdown against the Hungarian revolution, the British-French-Israeli assault placed the United States in the difficult position of condemning the Soviets for intervening in Hungary while its anti-Communist partners waged war in Suez. Instead, Eisenhower cooperated with the United Nations to negotiate a cease-fire and engineer a pullout of the invading forces in Egypt. Ultimately, the Soviets proved the winners in this Cold War skirmish. The Suez invasion revived memories of European imperialism and fueled anti-Western sentiments and pan-Arab nationalism (a sense of unity among Arabs across national boundaries), which worked to the Soviets' advantage. Nasser obtained financial assistance from the Soviets and built the Aswan Dam.

The Eisenhower administration soon moved to counter growing Soviet power in the region. In 1957, fearing increasing Communist influence in the oil-rich Middle East, Congress approved the **Eisenhower Doctrine**, which gave the president a free hand to use U.S. military forces in the Middle East "against overt armed aggression from any nation controlled by International Communism," as he remarked to Congress. In effect, the Eisenhower administration was more concerned with protecting access to oil fields from hostile Arab nationalist leaders than with any Communist incursion. In 1958, when an anti-American, non-Communist regime came to power in Iraq, the president sent fourteen thousand marines to neighboring Lebanon to prevent a similar outcome there. A military realist, Eisenhower made his choice for intervention carefully—the invasion required limited force and allowed a speedy exit without any fatalities.

Just before Eisenhower left office in January 1961, his administration intervened in a civil war in the newly independent Congo. This former colony of Belgium held valuable mineral resources, which Belgium and the United States still coveted. After the Congo's first prime minister, Patrice Lumumba, stated his intentions to remain neutral in the Cold War, President Eisenhower and CIA Director Allen Dulles declared him unreliable in the conflict with the Soviet Union. With the support of Belgian military troops and encouragement from the United States, the resource-rich province of Katanga seceded from the Congo in 1960. After the Congolese military, under the leadership of Joseph Mobuto, overthrew Lumumba's government, the CIA launched an operation that culminated in the execution of Lumumba on January 17, 1961. Several years later, Mobuto became president of the country, changed its name to Zaire, and allied with the West. The Eisenhower administration had extended the Cold War to central Africa in a covert, but nonetheless bloody, manner.

Early U.S. Intervention in Vietnam

Eisenhower's intervention in Vietnam would have profound, long-term consequences for the United States. By the 1950s, Vietnamese revolutionaries (the Vietminh) had been fighting for independence from the French for decades. They were led by Ho Chi Minh, a revolutionary who had studied Communist doctrine in the Soviet Union but was not controlled by the Soviets. In fact, he modeled his 1945 Vietnamese Declaration of Independence on that of the United States. Ho's overriding objective was the liberation of Vietnam along socialist principles. In 1954 the Vietminh defeated the French at the Battle of Dien Bien Phu. With the backing of the United States, the Soviet Union, and China, both sides agreed to divide Vietnam at the seventeenth parallel and hold free elections to unite the country in 1956.

President Eisenhower believed that if Vietnam fell to the Communists, the rest of Southeast Asia and Japan would "go over very quickly" like "a row of dominoes," threatening American strategic power in the Far East as well as free access to Asian markets. Convinced that Ho Chi Minh and his followers would win free elections, the Eisenhower administration installed the anti-French, anti-Communist Ngo Dinh Diem to lead South Vietnam and then supported his regime's refusal to hold national elections in 1956. The anti-Communist interests of the United States had trumped its democratic promises. With the country now permanently divided, Eisenhower funneled economic aid to Diem to undertake needed land reforms that would strengthen his government and weaken

The Battle of Dien Bien Phu

This photograph shows Vietnamese soldiers resting in a trench at Dien Bien Phu, site of the pivotal battle at which French colonial forces were defeated. Fighting began on March 13, 1954, and ended on May 7, when French troops surrendered. This photo, like most of those taken of the battle, was restaged shortly after the action, mainly for propaganda purposes. AFP/Getty Images

the appeal of Ho Chi Minh. The president also dispatched CIA agents and military advisers to help the South Vietnamese government set up security forces, train military units, and extend educational opportunities. However, Diem used most of the money to consolidate his power rather than implement reforms, which only widened opposition to his regime from Communists and non-Communists alike. This prompted Ho Chi Minh in 1959 to support the creation in the South of the National Liberation Front, or **Vietcong**, to wage a military insurgency against Diem. By the end of the decade, the Eisenhower administration had created a major diplomatic problem with no clear plan for its resolution.

The Election of 1960

Even after experiencing eight years of dramatic challenges in both foreign and domestic affairs, Eisenhower remained popular. In 1956 voters had returned Eisenhower to the

White House with greater support than in 1952. Once again, Eisenhower's personal popularity did not carry over to the Republican Party, as Democrats increased their control over Congress. Eisenhower, however, could not run for a third term, barred by the Twenty-second Amendment (1951), and Vice President Richard M. Nixon ran as the Republican candidate for president in 1960. Unlike Eisenhower, Nixon was not universally liked or respected. His manipulation of the anti-Communist issue and his reputation for unsavory political combat drew the scorn of Democrats, especially liberals. Moreover, Nixon had to fend off charges that Republicans, as embodied in the seventy-year-old Eisenhower, were out-of-date and out of new ideas.

Running as the Democratic candidate for president in 1960, Senator John F. Kennedy of Massachusetts promised to instill renewed "vigor" in the White House and get the country moving again. Yet Kennedy did not differ much from his Republican rival on domestic and foreign policy issues. Kennedy's willingness to employ a rhetoric of high-minded change did not seem to be dampened by the fact that he had not compiled a distinguished or courageous record in the Senate, that his family's fortune had paved the way for his political career, and that he had earned a well-justified reputation in Washington as a playboy and womanizer.

The outcome of the 1960 election turned on several factors. The country was experiencing a slight economic recession, reviving memories in older voters of the Great Depression, which had begun with the Republican Hoover in power. In addition, presidential candidates faced off on television for the first time, participating in four televised debates. As the leading medium for information, TV emphasized visual style and presentation. With Nixon having just recovered from a stay in the hospital and looking haggard, Kennedy in the first debate convinced a majority of television viewers that he possessed the presidential bearing for the job. Nixon performed better in the next three debates, but the damage had been done. Still, Kennedy had to overcome considerable religious prejudice to win the election. No Catholic had ever won the presidency, and the prejudices of Protestants,

especially in the South, threatened to divert critical votes from Kennedy's Democratic base. While many southern Democrats did support Nixon, Kennedy balanced out these defections by gaining votes from the nation's Catholics, especially in northern states rich in electoral votes (Map 25.2).

Race also exerted a critical influence. Nixon and Kennedy had similar records on civil rights, and if anything, Nixon's was slightly stronger. However, on October 19, 1960, when Atlanta police arrested Martin Luther King Jr. for participating in a restaurant sit-in, Kennedy sprang to his defense, whereas Nixon kept his distance. Kennedy telephoned the civil rights leader's wife to offer his sympathy and used his influence to get King released from jail. As a result, King's father, a Protestant minister who had intended to vote against the Catholic Kennedy, switched his position and endorsed the Democrat. In addition to the elder King, Kennedy won back for Democrats 7 percent of black voters who had supported Eisenhower in 1956. Kennedy won by a margin of less than 1 percent of the popular vote, underscoring the importance of the African American electorate.

REVIEW & RELATE

- Why did Eisenhower adopt a moderate domestic agenda? What were his most notable accomplishments?

- How did Eisenhower use the CIA and covert actions to protect and expand American influence around the world?

✓ LEARNINGCurve bedfordstmartins.com/hewittlawson/LC

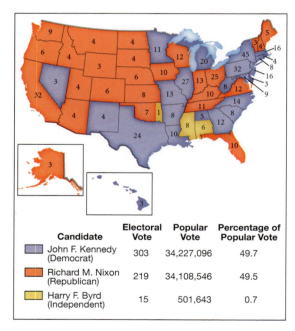

MAP 25.2   The Election of 1960

Candidate	Electoral Vote	Popular Vote	Percentage of Popular Vote
John F. Kennedy (Democrat)	303	34,227,096	49.7
Richard M. Nixon (Republican)	219	34,108,546	49.5
Harry F. Byrd (Independent)	15	501,643	0.7

The 1960 presidential candidates differed little on major policy issues. John F. Kennedy gained the White House by winning back black voters who had supported Eisenhower, gaining crucial support from Catholic voters across the country, and appearing more presidential on the first televised debate in history. Still his margin of victory was razor thin.

Conclusion: Cold War Politics and Culture

Following the end of World War II, the return of peace and prosperity fostered a baby boom that sent families scrambling for new housing and increasingly away from the cities. Suburbs grew as housing developers such as William Levitt built affordable, mass-produced homes in the suburbs and as the federal government provided new highways that allowed suburban residents to commute to their jobs in the cities. With increased income, consumers purchased the latest models in automobiles as well as newly introduced televisions, reshaping how they spent their leisure time. As the baby boom generation entered their teenage years, their sheer numbers and general affluence helped make them a significant economic and cultural force. They poured their dollars into clothes, music, and other forms of entertainment, which reinforced their identity as teenagers and set them apart from adults.

The increasingly distinct teenage culture owed a great deal to African Americans, who contributed to the development of rock 'n' roll and revolutionized jazz, thereby providing a standard for teenage rebellion and attacks on mainstream values by the beats. Yet African Americans remained most focused on tearing down the legal and institutional foundations of white supremacy. First in the courts and then in the streets, they confronted segregation and disfranchisement in the South. By the end of the 1950s, African Americans had persuaded the Supreme Court to reverse the doctrine of "separate but equal" that buttressed Jim Crow; they also won significant victories in desegregating buses in Montgomery, schools in Little Rock, and lunch counters in Greensboro. Black teenagers reinvigorated the civil rights movement through their boldness and energy, opening the path for even greater racial changes in the coming decade.

In addition to struggles over racial equality, the 1950s witnessed serious tensions at home and overseas. Teenage cultural rebellion; sexual revolution; McCarthyite witch-hunts; a bloody war in Korea; foreign crises in the Middle East, Eastern Europe, and Southeast Asia; clandestine operations in Iran, Guatemala, and the Congo—all of these confronted the citizens of Alan Freed's and Grace Metalious's America. Nevertheless, the popular image of the 1950s as a tranquil and innocent period persists, mainly because of the presence of President Dwight Eisenhower as a symbol for the age. A cheerful, grandfatherly patriarch, Eisenhower in this version of historical memory reflects a kinder and gentler time. The Republican Eisenhower provided moderate leadership that helped the country adjust to the changes it was undergoing. His critics complained that the nation had lost its spirit of adventure, had misplaced its ability to distinguish between community and conformity, had failed to live up to ideals of racial and economic justice, and had relinquished its primary place in the world. Nevertheless, most Americans emerging from decades of depression and war felt satisfied with the new lives they were building. Despite upheavals at home and abroad, they still liked Ike.

When Eisenhower left office in 1961, a new decade began with a Democratic president in charge. Yet the challenges that Eisenhower had faced and the diplomatic, social, and cultural forces that propelled them continued to confront his successors. During the following years, many of the teenagers and young people who had benefited from the peace and prosperity of the 1950s would lead the way in questioning the role of the United States in world affairs and its commitment to democracy, freedom, and equality at home.

LEARNINGCurve
Check what you know.
bedfordstmartins.com/hewittlawson/LC

Chapter Review

Online Study Guide ▶ bedfordstmartins.com/hewittlawson

KEY TERMS

Sun Belt (p. 793)

Levittown (p. 793)

National Interstate and Defense Highway Act (p. 793)

beats (p. 801)

Brown v. Board of Education of Topeka, Kansas (p. 803)

Montgomery Improvement Association (p. 803)

Southern Christian Leadership Conference (SCLC) (p. 804)

Little Rock Nine (p. 804)

Student Nonviolent Coordinating Committee (SNCC) (p. 805)

Modern Republicanism (p. 807)

New Look (p. 807)

mutually assured destruction (MAD) (p. 807)

Eisenhower Doctrine (p. 810)

Vietcong (p. 811)

REVIEW & RELATE

1. What factors contributed to the economic and population growth of the 1950s?

2. How did economic and demographic trends in the 1950s contribute to the growth of suburbs?

3. What trends in American popular culture did the television shows and popular music of the 1950s reflect?

4. How did artists, writers, and social critics challenge the mainstream politics and culture of the 1950s?

5. What strategies did African Americans adopt in the 1950s to fight segregation and discrimination?

6. How and why did white southerners resist efforts to end segregation?

7. Why did Eisenhower adopt a moderate domestic agenda? What were his most notable accomplishments?

8. How did Eisenhower use the CIA and covert actions to protect and expand American influence around the world?

TIMELINE OF EVENTS

1940–1960	Migration to Sun Belt swells region's population
1945–1960	U.S. gross national product soars 250 percent; 60 percent of Americans achieve middle-class status; union membership reaches new high
1951–1954	Alan Freed promotes rock 'n' roll with radio show and concerts
1953	CIA coup puts Shah Mohammad Reza Pahlavi in power in Iran
1954–1958	Eisenhower adopts Modern Republicanism and expands domestic programs
1954	CIA plot results in a military takeover of Guatemala
	Brown v. Board of Education of Topeka, Kansas Supreme Court ruling
1955–1956	Montgomery bus boycott
1955	Jonas Salk develops polio vaccine
	Emmett Till murdered
1956	Grace Metalious publishes *Peyton Place*
	National Interstate and Defense Highway Act passed
	U.S. begins supporting anti-Communist government of South Vietnam
1957	Martin Luther King Jr. and other black ministers form Southern Christian Leadership Council (SCLC)
	Eisenhower uses federal troops to enforce school desegregation in Little Rock, Arkansas
	Soviet Union launches *Sputnik*
	Congress approves Eisenhower Doctrine
1958	Eisenhower sends U.S. marines into Lebanon
1959	Fidel Castro takes power in Cuba
1960	U-2 spy plane shot down over Soviet Union
	Student Nonviolent Coordinating Committee (SNCC) formed
1960–1961	U.S. intervenes in civil war in Congo

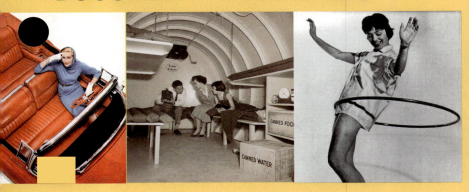

Teenagers in Postwar America

"There are many different opinions about just what is the most exclusive club in America these days," observed Dick Clark in his book *Your Happiest Years* (1959). But for Clark, the most exclusive and important club was the one he called "Teenagers of America, Inc." Clark's appraisal of American society in 1959 may have been self-serving—after all, his career hinged largely on appealing to teen audiences—but he was not alone in his belief in the significance of teenagers in postwar American society.

Even now, pop culture often portrays the 1950s as a simpler time when girls wore poodle skirts and swooned over Elvis Presley while boys raced hot-rod cars and took their dates to the malt shop. In this vision, teens were concerned with little more than increasing their popularity, "going steady," and watching *American Bandstand*. As the following documents illustrate, there is much to support this interpretation of postwar teen culture. Young people made rock 'n' roll into an enduring and lucrative entertainment industry, shaped the advertising and manufacture of products, and were the focus of numerous television shows and movies.

But there are other, more complicated images of teen life in this era. For one, juvenile delinquency was seen by many as a serious problem. Actor James Dean's *Rebel without a Cause* competed with singer Pat Boone's squeaky-clean haircut and white shoes. In 1959 actor Sandra Dee portrayed both a perky Malibu surfer in *Gidget* and an unwed pregnant teen in *A Summer Place*. Teens also grew up under the looming threat of the Cold War, the Korean War, and McCarthyism. African Americans helped popularize rock 'n' roll, but in Little Rock, Arkansas, and elsewhere in the South black teenagers risked their lives to desegregate public schools.

The following sources consider different aspects of teen life and postwar culture in the 1950s. They provide examples of the importance of teenagers as consumers and reveal some of the concerns adults expressed about their interests and desires. They also offer illustrations of teenagers in the 1950s who had more on their mind than just dating and having a good time.

DOCUMENT 25.5

Dick Clark | *Your Happiest Years*, 1959

By 1959 Dick Clark was a nationally popular disc jockey and host of television's *American Bandstand*. Always seen in a suit and tie, Clark, with his clean-cut good looks, projected a more wholesome vision of rock 'n' roll than did many of his contemporaries, such as Alan Freed. Clark's advice book for teenagers includes instruction on manners, makeup, and getting along with parents and other teens, as well as advice on romantic relationships.

We've mentioned before that it is very important to build a wide circle of friends, both fellows and girls. There are two reasons for this, but one is basic to dating. That is, the more fellows or girls you meet, the better the possibility that one or two might consider you what we called "date bait." The other reason, and it's a long shot, is that having a wide circle of friends, you meet more different types of people and learn how to adjust to them. This pays off after the teen years are past and you are either at work or away at school. But in order to get yourself into this teenage world of dating, let's just say you'll grow very lonely if you lock yourself away from eligible fellows or girls.

You've joined the staff of the school paper, or you are a member of a crowd of fellows that seem to attract a liberal following of the fair sex to your athletic contests. Or, on the distaff [female] side, you've a fine collection of girl friends—they're especially fine if they have at least one or two brothers of dating age. If you haven't quite reached that stage of teenage paradise yet, there are such events as community dances, or mixed school or church activities, that bring manly blips on your radarscope. In other words, you've gotten out of your shell and into the teenage swim. Don't be shy. You know that all the other fellows and girls your own age feel the same way you do. Remember, no self-pity. Braces on your teeth can't dim the glow of a sparkling personality, and neither can a shortage of new dresses or suits be an alibi for what is really a lack of effort on your part. Your fellow teenagers are eager to find sincere friends, and if you can prove that you are one then you definitely classify as "date bait." There is a phrase that I heard from General Carlos P. Romulo, the Philippines' famed patriot and Ambassador to the United States, and I think it applies here. "A stranger," the General said, "is a friend that I haven't met." It's a wonderful application of the Golden Rule, and it's one sentence that can carry a teenager through a lot of embarrassing uncertainty.

Accepting your fellow teenagers as friends, known or unknown, is another step toward that all-important phone call or whispered conference in the hall at school. You know the one I mean. It may begin, "Uh, Margie . . . uh, this Saturday night . . . uh, well, some of us were . . ." And a date is born.

Source: Dick Clark, *Your Happiest Years* (New York: Random House, 1959), 100–101.

DOCUMENT 25.6

Richard Gehman | The Nine Billion Dollars in Hot Little Hands, 1957

In the 1950s, teenagers were identified for the first time as a distinct and important consumer market. Advertising agencies and manufacturers studied teen spending habits on products such as movies, clothes, and records, and as the following article suggests, teenagers influenced purchases and popular culture well beyond their own experiences.

WHOLE INDUSTRIES are devoted exclusively to pleasing teenagers. Relatively untalented performers have become the highest-paid stars in the country simply because teenagers idolize them. Our eating habits have changed drastically; many families now eat the way teenagers do—from trays, in front of the TV set.

Currently there are three organizations in New York devoted exclusively to polling teenagers, discovering their opinions and tastes, and selling this information to manufacturers and advertising agencies. . . .

One watch company, whose products had not been striking the fancy of the nation's youth, designed a whole new line of wrist watches. Before long, word got around that this company's watches were *the* ones to have, and sales began to rise—even, to the manufacturer's surprise, in its adult line.

"The adults heard the kids talking about the watches and decided they must be pretty good," one dealer explains.

This illustrates another huge factor in the teens' influence. Kids are better-educated, better-informed, and, in the majority of cases, more alert today than at any previous time in history.

Also, they are more articulate. Schools encourage them to express their opinions and preferences. Consequently, adults respect them more, and listen when they talk about new inventions and products. A manufacturer of farm equipment tells of a salesman who visited a farmer to try to interest him in buying a tractor. The farmer said that if his teenaged son approved of the tractor, he would buy it. "This is going to be a cinch," the salesman thought—but to his surprise, the boy's reaction was negative. "That tractor of yours just won't do the work we need to do," he said. No sale.

Many of the innovations in Detroit-produced cars in recent years have come about as a result of the teenagers' interest in hot rods, says a publisher of motor magazines. "Four-barrel carburetors, twin exhausts, and the so-called 'power packages' found in many new models stem directly from hot rod activity," the publisher says.

Home design, too, is directly influenced by what teenagers want and don't want. A New Jersey contractor last year decided to build himself the house he had always wanted. It was to cost $200,000 and include all the ultra-modern features a house can possibly have. He hired an architect and set men to work on the foundation. Then one day his daughter came home from high school in tears. "Daddy," she said, "is it true we're going to have the biggest house in town? Everybody'll think we're snobs and climbers!" Then and there the contractor abandoned his plans for the house.

Nowadays, that contractor and hundreds of his contemporaries build houses with teenagers uppermost in their minds. They provide separate entrances to bedroom wings, so that the children won't track mud through the main part of the house; they build in special playrooms. The furniture manufacturers follow suit with special pieces that are sturdy enough to withstand teenage sprawling and covered with dirt-resistant fabrics. "There is no question about it," says one builder; "teenagers have taken over the house." He might well have carried it a few steps further. They've taken over everything.

Source: Richard Gehman, "The Nine Billion Dollars in Hot Little Hands," *Cosmopolitan*, November 1957, 72, 77–78.

DOCUMENT 25.7

Chevrolet Advertisement, 1954

Automobile manufacturers did not design cars specifically with teenagers in mind, but they did target the teen market for sales. Colorful, powerful, and sleek models were especially appealing to teenagers who considered cars a central part of their dating experience. The phrase "You're only young twice" appealed not only to youths but also to adults who wanted to stay young. As the previous document indicates, teenagers often influenced the purchases their parents made, and this advertisement appears to be aware of this influence.

Ever see a prettier car than the Chevrolet Bel Air Sport Coupe? And this is just one of a great line of Chevrolet beauties. Best choice in the field.

You're only young **twice**!

Once when you take your first battered old jalopy to your heart . . . and once again when you put your first brand-new Chevrolet on parade! After that—your motoring life is young for good! You've discovered the Fountain of Youth on wheels.

WHAT'S CHEVROLET GOT THAT YOUNG PEOPLE GO FOR?

First of all: It's smooth! Real cool! It looks as a car ought to look that's loaded with youngsters who love the feel of a spirited pick-up and the power of broad-shouldered brakes. Chevrolet is the _only_ low-priced car in the world with a Fisher Body.

And what a pleasant surprise to discover that you can run the new Chevrolet with the kind of money that fits a young man's budget. And, of course, everybody knows that Chevrolet's original cost is less than any other line in the low-price field.

It's the only low-priced car with a full length box-girder frame for _extra safety._

And if you're interested in those new automatic power features a family car ought to have, you'll find that Chevrolet offers them all—optional at extra cost if you want them.

YOUR MONEY'S WORTH IN FUN, TOO!

When you put your money in a Chevrolet you're putting it into the closest thing there is to a savings bank on wheels! You'll get your money's worth in fun all its long life, and a trade-in value that will make you realize all over again that nothing—no, nothing—has ever topped Chevrolet for VALUE.

Why don't you drop around to your dealer's and take a ride in a new Chevrolet? . . . Chevrolet Division of General Motors, Detroit 2, Michigan.

SAFER STOPPING, TOO! The going's great and so is the stopping! Those broad-shouldered Chevrolet brakes are actually the largest in the low-price field. That's to give you easier stops and safer control-anywhere, any time!

YEAR AFTER YEAR MORE PEOPLE BUY CHEVROLETS THAN ANY OTHER CAR!

SYMBOL OF SAVINGS
CHEVROLET
EMBLEM OF EXCELLENCE

DOCUMENT 25.8

Charlotte Jones | Letter on Elvis, 1957

Nothing highlighted the growing generation gap more than rock 'n' roll. When Elvis Presley burst onto the music scene in the mid-1950s, adults criticized his music and gyrating hips, while teenage boys dressed to imitate his style, and teenage girls screamed and fainted at his concerts. In 1957 Charlotte Jones, an admiring fan, wrote the following letter to the conservative newspaper columnist George Sokolsky in response to Sokolsky's criticism of Presley's popularity.

There are too many people saying that Elvis is going to die out. When Elvis dies out is when the sun quits burning.

You say everybody is forgotten that is once great; George Washington has never been forgotten and nobody can be as great a president or as long remembered as he. Nobody can ever take his place or do what he did. Well, it's the same with Elvis. He'll always be remembered and nobody has ever [done] or ever will do the same thing as Elvis has.

Elvis is the king of popularity and we (teens of America) love him and we'll see he lives forever. Not his body but his name. Adults won't admit he's so great, because they're jealous! They know that their top singers weren't as great as Elvis. They're mad because their taste isn't quite as good as ours.

Look at James Dean, been dead for a year and he's bigger now than he ever was.

God gifted Elvis to us and you oughta thank him, not tear down the greatest thing the world has ever known: Elvis Presley!!!!!!

Scornfully yours,
Charlotte Jones

P.S.: And if you're over 30, you're old. You're certainly not young.

Source: George E. Sokolsky, "Teenager Puts Rap on Suggestion Elvis on Way Out," *Milwaukee Sentinel*, March 11, 1957, 5.

DOCUMENT 25.9

Todd Gitlin | Reflections on the 1950s, 1987

Todd Gitlin was born in 1943 and grew up in the Bronx, where he attended the prestigious Bronx High School of Science in the late 1950s. By the end of the decade, Gitlin had started questioning American domestic and foreign policies and began moving in the direction of the radicalism that he would embrace in the 1960s. In this excerpt from his book on the 1960s, Gitlin recalls the political disillusionment he was beginning to feel as a teenager.

On New Year's Eve, as 1958 slipped into 1959, I wasn't especially aware I was living in the dead, dreary Fifties. I was a high school senior about to turn sixteen. I had little sense of living in any kind of "Fifties" at all; I wasn't old enough to think in decades. I was simply living my life: striving for grades, wondering about sex, matching my exploits against those—real and imagined—of my rivals, watching the tides of adolescence rip through me. The only threshold I thought about was the one I would cross later that year, on the way to college. I was not living in history, but in biography.

Which is not to say I was devoid of political interests. I read *The New York Times* and my parents were liberal. I stayed up late on election nights and rooted for Democrats almost as passionately as I followed the New York Giants baseball team (until they broke my heart by running off to San Francisco in 1958). I thought President Dwight David Eisenhower was a genial deadhead, a semiliterate fuddy-duddy who deserved to be chastised almost as much for excessive golfing and tangled sentences as for embracing *Generalísimo* Franco [Spanish dictator Francisco Franco]. I thought Richard Nixon was sinister. I delighted in Jules Feiffer's [a cartoonist and writer] worldly spoofs of Eisenhower's syntax, the phone company's arrogance, and the middle class's clichés. I liked Herblock's liberal cartoons, including one in which [presidential adviser] Bernard Baruch said that Eisenhower's stinginess with the military budget would make the United States "the richest man in the graveyard." A friend introduced me to H. L. Mencken's tilts at the philistine American "booboisie," and when I wrote the valedictory speech at the Bronx High School of Science later that year, the only quotation was from Mencken: "We live in a land of abounding quackeries."

My closest friends, the children of Jewish civil servants and skilled workers, held similar opinions. As we celebrated the coming of 1959, around midnight, in a fragment of news squeezed into Guy Lombardo's orchestral schmaltz, we saw the black-and-white footage of bearded Cubans wearing fatigues, smoking big cigars, grinning big grins to the cheers of throngs deliriously happy at the news that Batista had fled; and we cheered too. The overthrow of a brutal dictator, yes. But more, on the faces of the striding, strutting *barbudos* [bearded men] surrounded by adoring crowds we read redemption—a revolt of young people, underdogs, who might just cleanse one scrap of earth of the bloodletting and misery we had heard about all our lives. From a living room in the Bronx we saluted our unruly champions.

Source: Todd Gitlin, *The Sixties: Years of Hope, Days of Rage* (New York: Bantam, 1987), 1–2.

DOCUMENT 25.10

The Desegregation of Central High School, 1957

In 1957 nine black teenagers attempted to desegregate Central High School in Little Rock, Arkansas, pursuant to a federal court order. This photograph captures fifteen-year-old Elizabeth Eckford, one of the Little Rock Nine, surrounded by an angry white crowd on the first day of school. The photo also shows an enraged white student, Hazel Bryan, shouting at her to go home. Neither Eckford nor the other black students managed to attend school that day, but they entered Central High after President Eisenhower sent in federal troops to protect them.

Lloyd Dinkins/The Commercial Appeal/Landov

Interpret the Evidence

1. What information in these documents confirms commonly held beliefs about teenagers in the 1950s?

2. What information in these documents challenges the conventional wisdom about teenagers in the 1950s?

3. Documents 25.5 and 25.7 speak specifically to teenagers. How do they differ, either in tone or in content, from those written *about* teens (Document 25.6) or *by* teens (Document 25.8)?

4. What do Documents 25.6 and 25.8 tell us about generational differences?

5. How much do these documents tell us about racial differences among teenagers in the postwar era?

6. What do Documents 25.5 and 25.10 reveal about gender roles and expectations within teenage culture in the 1950s?

Put It in Context

How do these documents show the way teenagers shaped the larger post–World War II society?

background photo: page 819, Library of Congress

LEARNING*Curve*
Check what you know.
bedfordstmartins.com/hewittlawson/LC

Robert Abbott Sengstacke/Getty Images

Santi Visalli Inc./Getty Images

Demonstrators carry American flags on the march from Selma to Montgomery to support voters' rights, 1965.

Protester at the Miss America Pageant at Atlantic City, New Jersey, 1969.

26

The Liberal Consensus and Its Challengers

1960–1973

Dirck Halstead / Time & Life Pictures/Getty Images

U.S. military adviser with a South Vietnamese soldier of the 5th Airborne Brigade, 1972.

AMERICAN HISTORIES

How did a Republican politician who advocated the internment of Japanese Americans during World War II end up presiding over the most liberal Supreme Court in U.S. history? As attorney general of California at the outset of World War II, Earl Warren helped convince President Franklin D. Roosevelt to order the relocation of 110,000 Japanese Americans. After the war, as governor, he continued to fight against perceived threats to national security by joining the anti-Communist crusade. In 1953 President Dwight D. Eisenhower appointed Warren to be chief justice of the Supreme Court, a choice that many observers saw as a safe conservative pick by a safe conservative president.

As chief justice, however, Warren defied expectations and instead led the Court in a liberal direction. In 1954 Warren wrote the landmark opinion ordering school desegregation in *Brown v. Board of Education of Topeka, Kansas.* Departing from his own strong anti-Communist record, Warren upheld the rights of political dissenters and extended the boundaries of free speech. The Warren Court did not shrink from controversy, and its rulings expanding the rights of accused criminals, banning prayer in public school classrooms, and upholding birth control as a right of privacy evoked harsh criticism from the police, religious fundamentalists, and conservative politicians.

Unlike Earl Warren, Bayard Rustin worked outside of regular political and social channels to achieve change. Raised by his Quaker grandparents in Pennsylvania, Rustin began his career as an activist for social justice in

1937 when he moved to New York City to work as a youth organizer. He joined the Young Communist League because of its commitment to economic justice, racial equality, and international peace, but the pacifist Rustin quit the organization in 1941 when the party supported U.S. intervention in World War II and retreated on its fight against racial discrimination during the war.

In 1942 Rustin helped found the Congress of Racial Equality (CORE), an interracial organization that pioneered nonviolent, direct-action protests against racial bias. A committed pacifist, Rustin was imprisoned from 1943 to 1946 for declining to perform alternative service after he refused to register for the military draft. Prison strengthened his determination to challenge racial injustice through unconventional means. After his release, he continued to push for racial equality, and in 1947 Rustin helped plan and lead the Journey of Reconciliation, which challenged segregation on interstate buses in the South (see chapter 24). In the 1950s and 1960s, he became an adviser to Martin Luther King Jr. and a major strategist in the civil rights movement in his own right.

Rustin remained active in various causes throughout his life. One of his last efforts was perhaps his most personal: the struggle against antigay prejudice. As a homosexual, Rustin had to conceal his sexual identity at a time when the public and his political allies rejected homosexuals. Rustin often had to work behind the scenes to avoid unfavorable publicity, and even Dr. King on occasion kept his distance from him. In the 1980s, as the gay liberation movement grew more vocal, Rustin spoke out for tolerance and equality until his death in 1987. ●

THE AMERICAN HISTORIES of Earl Warren and Bayard Rustin demonstrate the complexity of social change. The federal government had the power to encourage social movements by interpreting the Constitution, enacting legislation, and enforcing the law in a manner that eliminated barriers to racial, sexual, and political equality. Yet federal action likely would not have happened without the pressure applied by activists like Rustin. At the same time, efforts to promote equality and social justice produced a strong reaction from conservatives who feared that their political and social values were under assault. By the end of the 1960s, liberal reformers had achieved many of their objectives, but they had also triggered a stiff challenge from conservative opponents who sought to roll back those gains and pursue their own policies of small government, low taxes, and self-help.

The Politics of Liberalism

In 1960 the liberal agendas of Presidents Franklin Roosevelt and Harry Truman remained unfinished. Hoping to build on the legacy of the New Deal, liberals sought to increase the role of the federal government in the economy, education, and health care. Most liberals supported a staunchly anti-Communist foreign policy, differing with Republicans more over means than over ends. Indeed, when Democrats recaptured the White House in 1960, they seized opportunities in Cuba and Southeast Asia to vigorously challenge the expansion of Soviet influence.

Kennedy's New Frontier

With victory in World War II and the revival of economic prosperity, liberal thinkers regained confidence in capitalism. Many saw the postwar American free-enterprise system as different from the old-style capitalism that had existed before Franklin Roosevelt's New Deal. In their view, this new "reform capitalism," or democratic capitalism, created abundance for all and not just for a few elites. Rather than pushing for the redistribution of wealth, liberals now called on the government to help create conditions conducive to economic growth and increased productivity. In this context, the liberal economist John Kenneth Galbraith argued in *The Affluent Society* (1958) that increased public investments in education, research, and development were the key to American prosperity and progress.

These ideas guided the thinking of Democratic politicians such as Senator John F. Kennedy of Massachusetts. Elected president in 1960, the forty-three-year-old Kennedy brought good looks, charm, a beautiful wife, and young children to the White House—presenting a public image that matched the kind of nuclear family that Americans tuned in to watch on their television sets during the 1950s. Yet this was no ordinary family. The Kennedy family had numerous estates, and the president's father had used his fortune to bankroll his son John's political ambitions, first as a Massachusetts congressman, then as a U.S. senator, and finally as president. As president, John Kennedy pledged a **New Frontier** to battle "tyranny, poverty, disease, and war," but lacking strong majorities in Congress, he contented himself with making small gains on the New Deal foundation established by Franklin Roosevelt. Congress expanded unemployment benefits, increased the minimum wage, extended Social Security benefits, and raised appropriations for public housing, but Kennedy's caution disappointed many liberals.

The Kennedy administration showed greater zeal in fighting the Cold War abroad. The president believed that the same reform capitalism that had worked well in the United States should become a global model, especially in newly developing nations in Asia, Africa, and the Middle East. Communism, like fascism before it, posed a fundamental threat to American interests and to other countries' ability to emulate the economic miracle of the United States. The faith of liberals in American ingenuity, willpower, technological superiority, and moral righteousness encouraged them to reshape the "free world" in America's image.

President Kennedy's first Cold War battle took place in Cuba. During the 1960 campaign, Kennedy criticized the Eisenhower administration for allowing Fidel Castro to establish a Communist dictatorship in Cuba—despite Kennedy's knowledge of a secret CIA plan, devised by the Eisenhower administration, to topple Castro from power. After becoming president, Kennedy approved the scheme that Eisenhower had already set in motion.

The operation ended disastrously. On April 17, 1961, the invasion force of between 1,400 and 1,500 Cuban exiles, trained by the CIA, landed by boat at the Bay of Pigs on Cuba's southwest coast. Kennedy refused to provide backup military forces for fear of revealing America's role in the attack. After three days of fighting, Castro's troops defeated the insurgents. CIA planners had underestimated Cuban popular support for Castro, falsely believing that the invasion would inspire a national uprising against the Communist regime. The Kennedy administration had blundered its way into a bitter foreign policy defeat.

Two months later, Kennedy met Soviet leader Nikita Khrushchev at a summit meeting in Vienna. At the conference, Khrushchev took advantage of the president's embarrassing defeat in Cuba to press his own demands. The confrontational summit meeting increased tensions between the superpowers. Returning from Vienna, Kennedy persuaded Congress to increase the defense budget, dispatch additional troops to Europe, and bolster civil defense. In August, the Soviets responded by constructing a wall through Berlin, making it more difficult for refugees to flee from East Berlin to West Berlin, but they did not close off U.S. access to West Berlin. After the building of the Berlin Wall, tensions seemed to subside for a time, only to spike again the following year in a confrontation over Cuba that brought the world to the brink of nuclear disaster.

Following the Bay of Pigs disaster, the United States continued its efforts to topple the Castro regime. Such attempts were uniformly unsuccessful, but a wary Castro decided to invite the Soviet Union to install short- and intermediate-range missiles in his country to protect against further U.S. incursion. On October 22, 1962, Kennedy went on national television to inform the American people that Soviet missile sites were under construction in Cuba. The Kennedy administration decided to blockade Cuba to prevent Soviet ships from supplying the deadly missile warheads that would make the missiles fully operational. If this effort failed and Soviet ships defied the blockade, the president would order air strikes on Cuba. Ordinary Americans, particularly those within striking distance of Cuban-based Soviet missiles, nervously contemplated the very real possibility of nuclear destruction.

On the brink of nuclear war, both sides decided to compromise. Khrushchev agreed to remove the missiles, and Kennedy pledged not to invade Cuba and secretly promised to dismantle U.S. missile sites in Turkey that were aimed at the Soviet Union. The outcome did not please everyone. Castro, who still feared U.S. intervention, remained disappointed, as did Soviet hard-line leaders who believed that Khrushchev had displayed weakness. (Two years later, they deposed him.) The rest of the world breathed a sigh of relief, and Kennedy and Khrushchev, having stepped back from the edge of nuclear holocaust, worked to ease tensions further. In 1963 they signed a Partial Nuclear Test Ban Treaty—which prohibited atmospheric but not underground testing—and installed an electronic "hot line" to ensure swift communications between Washington and Moscow.

Explore

See Document 26.1 for one cartoonist's commentary on the Soviet removal of missiles from Cuba.

DOCUMENT 26.1

Edmund Valtman | The Cuban Missile Crisis, 1962

For thirteen days in October 1962, the world held its breath while President Kennedy and Soviet premier Khrushchev traded threats over the presence of nuclear weapons in Cuba. Khrushchev eventually backed down and removed the missiles. Two days after the crisis ended, the following cartoon by Edmund Valtman appeared in the *Hartford Times*.

Explore

Why might Khrushchev tell Castro, "This hurts me more than it hurts you!"?

What does the placement of the missiles suggest about their importance to Cuba?

What does the position of both characters suggest about the power relationship between Castro and Khrushchev?

Library of Congress

Put It in Context

How did the Cuban missile crisis affect Kennedy's and Khrushchev's thinking about the Cold War?

Containment in Southeast Asia

In addition to Cuba, Kennedy inherited the policy of containing communism in Southeast Asia. He shared his predecessors' belief that the Soviet Union was behind wars of national liberation throughout the third world. Like Eisenhower, Kennedy believed that if Communists toppled one regime in Asia it would produce a "domino effect," with one country after another falling to the Communists. Kennedy, a World War II veteran, also believed that aggressive nations that attacked weaker ones threatened world peace unless they were challenged.

Kennedy's containment efforts ran into difficulty in Vietnam because the United States did not control the situation on the ground. After supporting Ngo Dinh Diem as president of South Vietnam in 1955, the United States poured more than $1 billion into the country to implement land reform and create a stable government capable of withstanding Communist opposition from the Vietcong and North Vietnamese leader Ho Chi Minh's Communist forces in North Vietnam. However, Diem spent the money on building up military and personal security forces to suppress all political opposition. In 1961 Kennedy sent military advisers to help the South Vietnamese fight the Communists, but the situation deteriorated in 1963 when the Catholic Diem prohibited the country's Buddhist majority from holding religious celebrations. In protest, Buddhist monks committed suicide by setting themselves on fire, a grisly display captured on television news programs in the United States. With political opposition mounting against Diem's oppressive regime and the war going poorly, the Kennedy administration endorsed a military coup to replace the Diem government with one more capable of fighting Communists. On November 1, 1963, the coup leaders removed Diem from office, assassinated the deposed president and key members of his regime, and installed a military government.

Diem's death, however, did little to improve the worsening war against the Communists. The Vietcong had more support in the rural countryside than did the South Vietnamese government because the rebels promised land reform and recruited local peasants disturbed by the corruption and ruthlessness of the Diem regime. The Kennedy administration committed itself to supporting Diem's successor, but by late November 1963 Kennedy seemed ambivalent about what to do next. He was torn between sending more American troops and finding a way to negotiate a peace.

This ambivalence was reflected in Kennedy's more general effort to balance his hard-line anti-Communist policies with new outreach efforts to inspire developing nations to follow a democratic path. The Peace Corps program sent thousands of volunteers to teach and advise developing nations, and Kennedy's Alliance for Progress supplied economic aid to emerging democracies in Latin America. In June 1963, Kennedy announced his departure from his earlier militant Cold War stance in a commencement address at American University. Instead of describing a bipolar world of good and evil, Kennedy envisioned a "world safe for diversity. For in the final analysis, our most basic common link is that we all inhabit this small planet. We all breathe the same air. We all cherish our children's future and we are all mortal."

On November 22, 1963, three weeks after the assassination of Diem, Lee Harvey Oswald murdered Kennedy as he rode in an open motorcade in Dallas, Texas. The fatal shots from the assassin's rifle brought the nation to a standstill and prompted an outpouring of public grief not seen since President Roosevelt died in office in 1945. In death, Kennedy achieved immense popularity, and many Americans viewed him as a martyr. Yet Kennedy had left many problems unresolved. His legislative agenda, including civil rights, remained unfulfilled, and at the time of his death there were 16,000 American military advisers in Vietnam.

Johnson Escalates the War in Vietnam

Kennedy's successor, Lyndon B. Johnson, faced a difficult decision about Vietnam. Privately, the new president harbored reservations about fighting in Vietnam, but he was fearful of being considered soft on communism and was concerned that a demonstration of weakness would jeopardize congressional support for his domestic plans. Although President Johnson eventually concluded that more U.S. forces had to be sent to Vietnam, he hesitated to act immediately. Instead, he waited for the right moment to rally Congress and the American public behind an escalation of the war.

That moment came in August 1964. On August 2, North Vietnamese gunboats sixty miles off the North Vietnamese coast in the Gulf of Tonkin attacked an American spy ship. Two days later, another U.S. destroyer reported coming under torpedo attack, but because of stormy weather this second ship was not certain that it had actually been fired on. Neither ship suffered any damage. In fact, when informed of the assaults, the president responded: "For all I know, our navy might have been shooting at whales out there." Despite the considerable uncertainty about what actually happened, Johnson seized the opportunity to prompt Congress to authorize military action. On August 7, with only two dissenting votes, Congress passed the **Gulf of Tonkin Resolution**, which empowered the president to "repel any armed attacks against the forces of the United States and to prevent further aggression." In effect, Congress provided Johnson with unlimited power to make military decisions regarding Vietnam.

After winning election in 1964, President Johnson stepped up U.S. military action. In March 1965, with North Vietnamese forces flooding into the South, the president initiated Operation Rolling Thunder, a massive bombing campaign over North Vietnam and infiltration routes into the South along the Vietnamese borders with Cambodia and Laos, known as the Ho Chi Minh Trail. For more than three years, American planes dropped a million tons of bombs on North Vietnam, more than the total amount the United States used in World War II. Despite this massive firepower, the operation proved ineffective. A largely agricultural country, North Vietnam did not have the type of industrial targets best suited for air attacks. It stored its vital military resources underground, and the North Vietnamese were able to reconstruct rudimentary bridges and roads to maintain the flow of troops into the South within hours after U.S. bombers had pounded them.

Responding to the need to protect American air bases and the persistent ineffectiveness of the South Vietnamese government and military, Johnson deployed ever-increasing numbers of ground troops to Vietnam. In 1963, when Johnson became president, 16,000 American troops were serving in Vietnam; this number grew to 380,000 in 1966, to 485,000 in 1967, and to 536,000 in 1968, with Johnson hoping that each new infusion would be the last. An estimated 200,000 North Vietnamese reached draft age annually, and Hanoi replenished its troops to counter the U.S. escalation. The U.S. military also deployed napalm bombs, which spewed burning jellied gasoline, and Agent Orange, a chemical defoliant that denuded the Vietnamese countryside and produced long-term adverse health effects for those who came in contact with it, including American soldiers. These attacks added to the resentment of the South Vietnamese peasants living in the countryside and helped the Vietcong gain new recruits.

The United States confronted a challenging guerrilla war in Vietnam. The Vietcong fought at night and blended in during the day as ordinary residents of cities and villages. They did not provide a visible target, and they recruited women and men of all ages, making it difficult for U.S. ground forces to distinguish friend from foe. To meet this challenge, the military, under the direction of General William C. Westmoreland, established "strategic hamlets" to separate the Vietcong from noncombatants. Troops moved residents out of their villages to a new location, set up a defense perimeter

My Lai Massacre, 1968
On March 16, 1968, U.S. army soldiers killed hundreds of unarmed civilians—most of them women, children, and the elderly—in the village of My Lai. The soldiers left bodies piled in ditches that ran around the village. The massacre became public in 1969, but only one soldier was convicted by a military tribunal.   Time & Life/Getty Images

around it, and assumed that anyone found outside this zone must be the enemy. Westmoreland then instituted "search and destroy" missions throughout the countryside to defeat the Vietcong. In the end, these policies did little to advance the U.S. military effort and alienated the population they were designed to safeguard.

Explore

> See Document 26.2 for one American soldier's experience in Vietnam.

On the ground, frustration also bred racism, as many American soldiers could not relate to the Vietnamese way of life and dismissed the enemy as "gooks." Lieutenant Philip Caputo later admitted that he could order his men to burn the thatch and bamboo shacks the Vietnamese lived in because to him a "home had brick or frame walls, a window, a lawn, a TV antenna on the roof." This attitude pushed some of the troops over the line between legitimate wartime practices and murder. Frustrated by rising casualties from an enemy they could not see, some American soldiers indiscriminately burned down villages and killed noncombatant civilians. Such disreputable behavior peaked in March 1968 with the My Lai massacre, when an American platoon murdered between 347 and 504 unarmed Vietnamese civilians in the village of My Lai.

DOCUMENT 26.2

George Olsen | Letter Home from Vietnam, 1969

George Olsen sent the following letter to his girlfriend shortly after he was sent to Vietnam in August 1969. The previous year, more than 16,000 American soldiers were killed, the largest one-year total of the war. By the time Olsen arrived in Vietnam, many Americans believed that the United States should withdraw its troops, and antiwar protests in America had escalated dramatically. Olsen was killed in action in March 1970.

Explore

31 Aug '69

Dear Red,

Last Monday I went on my first hunter-killer operation. . . . The frightening thing about it all is that it is so very easy to kill in war. There's no remorse, no theatrical "washing of the hands" to get rid of nonexistent blood, not even any regrets. When it happens, you are more afraid than you've ever been in your life—my hands shook so much I had trouble reloading. . . . You're scared, really scared, and there's no thinking about it. You kill because that little SOB is doing his best to kill you and you desperately want to live, to go home, to get drunk or walk down the street on a date again. And suddenly the grenades aren't going off any more, the weapons stop and, unbelievably fast it seems, it's all over. . . .

I have truly come to envy the honest pacifist who honestly believes that no killing is permissible and can, with a clear conscience, stay home and not take part in these conflicts. I wish I could do the same, but I can't see letting another take my place and my risks over here. . . . The only reason pacifists such as the Amish can even live in an orderly society is because someone—be they police or soldiers—is taking risks to keep the wolves away. . . . I guess that's why I'm over here, why I fought so hard to come here, and why, even though I'm scared most of the time, I'm content to be here.

Source: Bernard Edelman, ed., *Dear America: Letters Home from Vietnam* (New York: Pocket Books, 1985), 204–5.

Interpret the Evidence

- According to Olsen, why is it both easy and difficult to kill in wartime?
- Why does Olsen think it is important for him to fight?

Put It in Context

Why did Americans become disillusioned with the war in Vietnam?

On January 31, 1968, the Buddhist New Year of Tet, some 67,000 Communist forces mounted a surprise offensive throughout South Vietnam that targeted major population centers (Map 26.1). For six hours, a suicide squadron of Vietcong surrounded the U.S. Embassy in Saigon. U.S. forces finally repelled the **Tet Offensive**, but the battle proved psychologically costly to the United States. Following the Tet Offensive, the most revered television news anchor of the era, Walter Cronkite of CBS, turned against the war and expressed the doubts of a growing number of viewers when he announced: "To say that we are mired in stalemate seems the only reasonable, yet unsatisfactory conclusion."

Tet marked the beginning of the end of the war's escalation. On March 31, 1968, President Johnson ordered a halt to the bombing campaign and called for peace negotiations. He also stunned the nation by announcing that he would not seek reelection. By the time he left the White House in 1969, peace negotiations had stalled and some 36,000 Americans had died in combat, along with 52,000 South Vietnamese troops.

REVIEW & RELATE

How did President Kennedy's domestic agenda reflect the liberal political ideology of the early 1960s?

How and why did the United States escalate its role in the Vietnam War?

LEARNINGCurve bedfordstmartins.com/hewittlawson/LC

MAP 26.1   The Vietnam War, 1968
The United States wielded vastly more military personnel and weaponry than the Vietcong and North Vietnamese but faced a formidable challenge in fighting a guerrilla war in a foreign country. Massive American bombing failed to defeat the North Vietnamese or stop their troop movements and supply lines along the Ho Chi Minh Trail. The 1968 Tet Offensive demonstrated the shortcomings in the U.S. strategy.

Civil Rights

Back home, the most critical issue facing the nation in the early 1960s was the intensification of the civil rights movement. As a candidate, Kennedy had promised vigorous action on civil rights, but as president he did little to follow through on his promises. With southern Democrats occupying key positions in Congress and threatening to block any civil rights proposals, Kennedy hesitated to upset this critical component of his political base. Following Kennedy's death in 1963, President Johnson succeeded in breaking the legislative logjam and signed into law three major pieces of civil rights legislation. He did so under considerable pressure from the civil rights movement.

Freedom Rides

The Congress of Racial Equality took the offensive on May 4, 1961. Similar to Bayard Rustin's efforts in the 1940s, CORE mounted racially integrated **Freedom Rides** to test whether facilities in the South, from Virginia to Louisiana, were complying with the 1960 Supreme Court ruling that outlawed segregated bus and train stations serving passengers who were traveling interstate. CORE had alerted the Justice Department and the FBI of its plans, but the riders received no protection when Klan-dominated mobs in Anniston and Birmingham, Alabama, attacked two buses containing activists, seriously wounding several passengers.

Freedom Rides, 1961

On May 4, 1961, two buses of black and white riders left Washington, D.C., and headed for New Orleans to desegregate bus terminal facilities along the route. When one of the buses arrived in Anniston, Alabama, it was attacked and burned by white mobs, forcing the passengers to flee for safety. Despite the violence, the Freedom Rides continued and grew in scope.   Library of Congress

After safety concerns forced CORE to forgo the rest of the trip, members of the Student Nonviolent Coordinating Committee (SNCC) rushed to Birmingham to continue the bus rides. The Kennedy administration urged them to reconsider, but Diane Nash, a SNCC founder, explained that although the group realized the peril of resuming the journey, "we can't let them stop us with violence. If we do, the movement is dead." When the replenished busload of riders reached Montgomery on May 20, they were brutally assaulted by a mob. Dr. Martin Luther King Jr., who supported the rides but had not participated in them, subsequently held a rally in a Montgomery church, which became the target of renewed white attacks that threatened the lives of King and the Freedom Riders inside the building. Faced with the prospect of serious bloodshed, the Kennedy administration dispatched federal marshals to the scene and persuaded the governor to call out the Alabama National Guard to ensure the safety of everyone in the church.

The president and his brother, Attorney General Robert Kennedy, worked out a compromise to let the rides

continue with minimal violence and publicity; at the same time, Robert Kennedy petitioned the Interstate Commerce Commission (ICC) to issue an order prohibiting segregated transportation facilities, which went into effect in November 1961. Despite the ICC declaration, many southern communities refused to comply. When Freedom Riders encountered opposition in Albany, Georgia, in the fall of 1961, SNCC workers remained in Albany and helped local leaders organize residents of the town against segregation and other forms of racial discrimination. Even with the assistance of Dr. King and the Southern Christian Leadership Conference (SCLC), the Albany movement stalled, as the Kennedy administration refused to provide support.

The Government Responds on Civil Rights

Despite the setback in Albany, the civil rights movement kept up pressure on other fronts. In September 1962, Mississippi governor Ross Barnett tried to thwart the registration of James Meredith as an undergraduate at the

University of Mississippi. Barnett's obstruction precipitated a riot on campus, and as Eisenhower had done at Little Rock, President Kennedy dispatched army troops and federalized the Mississippi National Guard to restore order, but not before two bystanders were killed.

The following year, King and the SCLC joined the Reverend Fred Shuttlesworth's freedom movement in Birmingham, Alabama, in its battle against employment discrimination, segregation in public accommodations, and police brutality. With the white supremacist Eugene "Bull" Connor in charge of law enforcement, civil rights protesters, including children ranging in age from six to sixteen, encountered violent resistance, the use of vicious police dogs, and high-powered water hoses. Connor ordered mass arrests, including Dr. King's, prompting the minister to write his famous "Letter from Birmingham Jail," in which he justified the use of nonviolent direct action. Seeking to defuse the crisis and concerned about America's image abroad, President Kennedy sent an emissary in early May 1963 to negotiate a peaceful solution that granted concessions to Birmingham blacks and ended the demonstrations. On Sunday, September 15, 1963, however, a few months after the successful end of the conflict, the Ku Klux Klan dynamited Birmingham's Sixteenth Street Baptist Church, a freedom movement staging ground. The blast killed four young girls attending services.

Meanwhile, after several years of caution, the president finally decided to speak out about the nation's duty to guarantee equal rights regardless of race. On June 11, 1963, shortly after negotiating the Birmingham agreement, Kennedy delivered a nationally televised address. He acknowledged that the country faced a "moral crisis" heightened by the events in Birmingham, and he noted the difficulty of preaching "freedom around the world" while "this is a land of the free except for Negroes." He proposed congressional legislation to end segregation in public accommodations, increase federal power to promote school desegregation, and broaden the right to vote.

Events on the day Kennedy delivered his powerful speech reinforced the need for swift action. Earlier that morning, Alabama governor George C. Wallace, a segregationist, had stood in front of the administration building at the University of Alabama to block the entrance of two black undergraduates. To uphold the federal court decree ordering their admission, Kennedy deployed federal marshals and the Alabama National Guard, and Wallace, having dramatized his point, stepped aside. Victory soon turned into tragedy. Later that evening, the president learned of the killing of Medgar Evers, the head of the NAACP in Mississippi, who was shot in the driveway of his Jackson home by the white supremacist Byron de la Beckwith. (Following two trials, de la Beckwith remained free until 1994, when he was retried and convicted for Evers's murder.)

Nonetheless, Congress was still unwilling to act. To increase pressure on lawmakers, civil rights organizations held a **March on Washington for Jobs and Freedom** on August 28, 1963, carrying out an idea first proposed by A. Philip Randolph in 1941 (see chapter 23). With Randolph as honorary chair, his associate Bayard Rustin directed the proceedings, delivering 250,000 black and white peaceful protesters to a rally in front of the Lincoln Memorial. Two speakers in particular caught the attention of the crowd. John Lewis, the chairman of SNCC, expressed the frustration of militant blacks with both the Kennedy administration and Congress. "The revolution is at hand. . . . We will not wait for the President, nor the Justice Department, nor Congress," Lewis asserted. "But we will take matters into our own hands." In a more conciliatory tone, King delivered a speech expressing his dream for racial and religious brotherhood. Still, King issued a stern warning to "those who hope that the Negro needed to blow off steam and will now be content. . . . There will be neither rest nor tranquility in America until the Negro is granted his citizenship rights. The whirlwinds of revolt will continue to shake the foundations of our nation until the bright day of justice emerges."

Freedom Summer and Voting Rights

Following Kennedy's death and three months after the March on Washington, President Johnson took charge of the pending civil rights legislation. Under Johnson's leadership, a bipartisan coalition turned back a southern filibuster (a tactic that delays or prevents action in Congress) in the Senate and passed the **Civil Rights Act of 1964**. The law prohibited discrimination in public accommodations, increased federal enforcement of school desegregation and the right to vote, and created the Community Relations Service, a federal agency authorized to help resolve racial conflicts. The act also contained a final measure to combat employment discrimination on the basis of race and sex.

Yet even as President Johnson signed the 1964 Civil Rights Act into law on July 2, black freedom forces launched a new offensive to secure the right to vote in the South. The 1964 act contained a voting rights provision but did little to address the main problems of the discriminatory use of literacy tests and poll taxes and the biased administration of voter registration procedures that kept the majority of southern blacks from voting. Three years earlier, the Kennedy administration had brokered a deal to secure private funding for voter registration drives in the South directed by the Atlanta-based Voter Education Project. Civil rights workers believed that the Justice

Freedom Schools, 1964

In Mileston, Mississippi, summer volunteer Martha Honey teaches a freedom school class that included Eddie Carthan (far left), who later became mayor of nearby Tchula. Because the state provided black students a limited education, these schools, staffed by volunteers, offered an opportunity to learn basic reading, writing, and arithmetic skills as well as African American history and culture.   © Matt Heron/Take Stock/The Image Works

Department would provide federal protection for voter drives, but the Kennedy and Johnson administrations let them down. Beatings, killings, arson, and arrests became a routine response to voting rights efforts. Although the Justice Department filed lawsuits against recalcitrant voter registrars and police officers, the government refused to send in federal personnel or instruct the FBI to safeguard vulnerable civil rights workers.

To focus national attention on this problem, SNCC, CORE, the NAACP, and the SCLC launched the **Freedom Summer** project in Mississippi. They assigned eight hundred volunteers from around the nation, mainly white college students, to work on voter registration drives and in "freedom schools" to improve education for rural black youngsters stuck in inferior, segregated schools. White supremacists fought back against what they perceived as an enemy invasion. In late June 1964, the Ku Klux Klan, in collusion with local law enforcement officials, killed three civil rights workers. This tragedy brought national attention, and President Johnson pressed the usually uncooperative FBI to find the culprits, which it did. However, civil rights workers continued to encounter white violence and harassment throughout Freedom Summer. **See Document Project 26: Freedom Summer, page 849.**

One outcome of the Freedom Summer project was the creation of the **Mississippi Freedom Democratic Party (MFDP)**. Because the regular all-white state Democratic Party excluded blacks, the civil rights coalition formed an alternative Democratic Party open to everyone. In August 1964, the mostly black MFDP sent a delegation to the Democratic National Convention meeting in Atlantic City, New Jersey, to challenge the seating of the all-white delegation from Mississippi. One of the MFDP delegates, Fannie Lou Hamer, who had lost her job on a Mississippi plantation for her voter registration activities, offered passionate testimony broadcast on television. To avoid a bruising political fight, Johnson hammered out a compromise that gave the MFDP two general at-large seats, imposed a loyalty oath on members of the regular delegation to support the Democratic presidential ticket, and prohibited racial discrimination in the future by any state Democratic Party. Although both sides rejected the compromise, four years later an integrated delegation, which included Hamer, represented Mississippi at the Democratic National Convention in Chicago.

Freedom Summer highlighted the problem of disfranchisement, but it took further demonstrations in Selma, Alabama, to resolve it. After state troopers shot and killed a black voting rights demonstrator in February 1965, Dr. King called for a march from Selma to the capital of Montgomery to petition Governor George Wallace to end the violence and allow blacks to vote. Local law enforcement officials answered their peaceful protests with arrests and beatings. On Sunday, March 7, as black and white marchers left Selma, the sheriff's forces sprayed them with tear gas, beat them, and sent them running for their lives

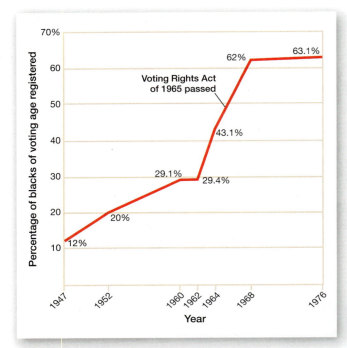

FIGURE 26.1 **Black Voter Registration in the South, 1947–1976**

After World War II, the percentage of black adults registered to vote in the South slowly but steadily increased, largely as a result of grassroots voting drives. Despite the Kennedy administration's support for voter registration drives, a majority of southern blacks remained prohibited from voting in 1964. The passage of the 1965 Voting Rights Act removed barriers such as literacy tests and poll taxes, strengthened the federal government's enforcement powers, and enabled more than 60 percent of southern blacks to vote by the late 1960s. Source: Data from David Garrow, *Protest at Selma* (New Haven: Yale University Press, 1978), and U.S. Department of Commerce, Bureau of the Census, *Statistical Abstract of the United States*, 1976.

back to town. A few days later, a white clergyman who had joined the protesters was killed on the streets of Selma by a group of white thugs. On March 21, following another failed attempt to march to Montgomery, King led protesters on the fifty-mile hike to the state capital, where they arrived safely four days later. Tragically, after the march, the Ku Klux Klan murdered a white female marcher from Michigan.

Events in Selma prompted President Johnson to take action. On March 15, he addressed a joint session of Congress and told lawmakers and a nationally televised audience that the black "cause must be our cause too. Because it is not just Negroes, but really it is all of us, who must overcome the crippling legacy of bigotry and injustice." In the words of the civil rights movement anthem, Johnson added, "And we shall overcome." On August 6, 1965, the president signed the **Voting Rights Act**, which banned the use of literacy tests for voter registration,

authorized a federal lawsuit against the poll tax (which succeeded in 1966), empowered federal officials to register disfranchised voters, and required seven southern states to submit any voting changes to Washington before they went into effect. With strong federal enforcement of the law, by 1968 a majority of African Americans and nearly two-thirds of black Mississippians could vote in the South (Figure 26.1).

REVIEW & RELATE

- What role did the federal government play in advancing the cause of racial equality in the early 1960s?

- How did civil rights activists pressure state and federal government officials to enact their agenda?

LEARNINGCurve bedfordstmartins.com/hewittlawson/LC

Reforming the Social Order

President Johnson carried liberal reform to its greatest heights, drawing on Kennedy's legacy and his own considerable political skills to win passage of the most important items on the liberal agenda. While Johnson pressed ahead in the legislative arena, Chief Justice Earl Warren's Supreme Court issued rulings that extended social justice to minorities and the economically oppressed and favored those who believed in a firm separation of church and state, in free speech, and in a right to privacy.

The Great Society

In an address at the University of Michigan on May 22, 1964, President Johnson sketched out his dream for the **Great Society**, one that "rests on abundance and liberty for all. It demands an end to poverty and racial justice, to which we are totally committed in our time. But that is just the beginning." According to Johnson, increasing the power and wealth of America was not enough. He saw the Great Society as "a place where the city of man serves not only the needs of the body and the demands of commerce but the desire for beauty and the hunger for community." Besides poverty and race, he outlined three broad areas in need of reform: education, the environment, and cities.

Johnson did not hesitate to approve plans to develop Kennedy's unfinished fight against poverty. Kennedy had persuaded lawmakers to provide federal aid to poor regions such as Appalachia. In designing the Economic Opportunity Act of 1964, Johnson wanted to offer the poor "a hand up, not a handout." His program provided job training, remedial education (later to include the preschool program Head Start), a domestic Peace Corps called Volunteers in Service to America (VISTA), and a Community Action Program that empowered the poor to shape policies affecting their own communities. The antipoverty program helped reduce the proportion of poor people from 20 percent in 1963 to 13 percent five years later, and it helped reduce the rate of black poverty from 40 percent to 20 percent during this same period.

Johnson intended to fight the War on Poverty through the engine of economic growth. In 1962 Congress had passed the Revenue Act, which gave more than $1 billion in tax breaks to businesses. Kennedy had agreed to the targeted tax reduction because he believed it would encourage businesses to plow added savings into new investments and to expand production, thereby creating new jobs. Johnson's tax cut, which applied across the board, stimulated the economy and sent the gross national product soaring from $591 billion in 1963 to $977 billion by the end of the decade. Thus the logic of economic expansion rather than redistribution guided Johnson's War on Poverty.

Despite considerable success, Johnson's program failed to meet liberal expectations. It would have taken an annual appropriation of about $11 billion to lift every needy person above the poverty line. To reduce opposition from cost-minded legislators who wanted to starve his programs if they could not stop them, Johnson asked Congress for just under $1 billion a year. Because the president refused to

press lawmakers harder for money, his ability to fight the War on Poverty was severely limited.

Whatever the limitations, Johnson campaigned on his antipoverty and civil rights record in his bid to recapture the White House in 1964. His Republican opponent, Senator Barry M. Goldwater of Arizona, personified the conservative right wing of the Republican Party and rejected the Modern Republicanism identified with President Eisenhower (see chapter 25). The Arizona senator condemned big government, supported states' rights, and accused liberals of not waging the Cold War forcefully enough. His aggressive conservatism appealed to his grassroots base in small-town America, especially in southern California, the Southwest, and the South. His tough rhetoric, however, scared off moderate Republicans, resulting in a landslide for Johnson on election day, as well as considerable Democratic majorities in Congress.

Flush with victory, Johnson moved quickly and achieved impressive results. To cite only a few examples, the Eighty-ninth Congress (1965–1967) provided federal aid to public schools; subsidized health care for the elderly and the poor by creating Medicare and Medicaid; expanded voting rights for African Americans in the South; authorized funds to cities for housing, jobs, education, mass transportation, crime prevention, and recreation; raised the minimum wage; created national endowments for the fine arts and humanities; and adopted regulations to preserve clean air and water supplies. The 1965 Immigration Act

The Johnson Treatment

At six feet four inches tall, Lyndon Johnson towered over most of his colleagues. As Senate majority leader, he became famous for putting pressure on lawmakers and cajoling them into submission. This 1963 photograph shows President Johnson leaning over his former Senate mentor, Richard B. Russell of Georgia, and firmly making his point in pursuit of his legislative agenda. LBJ Library photo by Yoichi Okamoto

TABLE 26.1   Major Great Society Measures, 1964–1968

Year	Legislation or Order	Purpose
1964	Civil Rights Act	Prohibited discrimination in public accommodations, education, and employment
	Economic Opportunity Act	Established War on Poverty agencies: Head Start, VISTA, Job Corps, and Community Action Program
1965	Elementary and Secondary Education Act	Federal funding for elementary and secondary schools
	Medical Care Act	Provided Medicare health insurance for citizens 65 years and older and Medicaid health benefits for the poor
	Voting Rights Act	Banned literacy tests for voting, authorized federal registrars to be sent into seven southern states, and monitored voting changes in these states
	Executive Order 11246	Required employers to take affirmative action to promote equal opportunity and remedy the effects of past discrimination
	Immigration and Nationality Act	Abolished quotas on immigration that reduced immigration from non-Western and southern and eastern European nations
	Water Quality Act	Established and enforced federal water quality standards
	Air Quality Act	Established air pollution standards for motor vehicles
	National Arts and Humanities Act	Established National Endowment of the Humanities and National Endowment of the Arts to support the work of scholars, writers, artists, and musicians
1966	Model Cities Act	Approved funding for the rehabilitation of inner cities
1967	Executive Order 11375	Expanded affirmative action regulations to include women
1968	Civil Rights Act	Outlawed discrimination in housing

repealed discriminatory national origins quotas established in 1924, resulting in a shift of immigration from Europe to Asia and Central and South America (Table 26.1).

The Warren Court

The Warren Court reflected this high tide of liberalism. The Court affirmed the constitutionality of the Voting Rights Act and struck down the poll tax as a voting requirement in 1966. A year later, the justices overturned state laws prohibiting interracial marriages. And in 1968, fourteen years after the *Brown* school desegregation decision, they ruled that school districts in the South could no longer maintain racially exclusive schools and must desegregate immediately. In a series of cases, the Warren Court ensured fairer legislative representation for blacks and whites by removing the disproportionate power that rural districts had held over urban districts.

The Supreme Court's most controversial rulings dealt with the criminal justice system, religion, and private sexual practices, all of which involved liberal interpretations of the individual freedoms guaranteed by the Bill of Rights. Strengthening the rights of criminal

defendants, the justices ruled in *Gideon v. Wainwright* (1963) that states had to provide indigents accused of felonies with an attorney, and in *Miranda v. Arizona* (1966) they ordered the police to advise suspects of their constitutional rights.

The Court also moved into new, controversial territory concerning school prayer, contraception, and pornography. In 1962 the Court outlawed a nondenominational Christian prayer recited in New York State schools as a violation of the separation of church and state guaranteed by the First Amendment. Three years later, in *Griswold v. Connecticut*, the justices struck down a state law that banned the sale of contraceptives because such laws, they contended, infringed on an individual's right to privacy. In a 1966 case reversing Massachusetts's ban of an erotic novel, the Supreme Court ruled that states could not prohibit what they deemed pornographic material unless it was "utterly without redeeming social value," a standard that opened the door for the dissemination of sexually explicit books, magazines, and films. These verdicts unleashed a firestorm of criticism, especially from religious groups that accused the Warren Court of undermining traditional values of faith and decency.

REVIEW & RELATE

What problems and challenges did Johnson's Great Society legislation target?

In what ways did the Warren Court's rulings advance the liberal agenda?

✓ *LEARNINGCurve* bedfordstmartins.com/hewittlawson/LC

Challenges to the Liberal Center

Even at its peak in the 1960s, liberalism faced major challenges from both the left and the right. A generation of young activists, mainly in colleges and universities, became impatient with what they saw as the slow pace of social progress and were increasingly disturbed by the escalation of the Vietnam War. At the same time, the right contended that liberals had instituted reforms that diminished individual initiative and benefited racial minorities at the expense of the white middle class. They disparaged liberals for not winning the Vietnam War and depicted the left as unpatriotic and out of step with mainstream American values. By 1969 liberalism and the left were in retreat, and Richard M. Nixon, a political conservative, had captured the White House.

Movements on the Left

The civil rights movement had inspired many young people to activism. Combining ideals of freedom, equality, and community with direct-action protest, civil rights activists offered a model for those seeking to address a variety of problems, including the Cold War threat of nuclear devastation, the loss of individual autonomy in a corporate society, racism, poverty, sexism, and the poisoning of the environment. The formation of SNCC in 1960 illuminated the possibilities for personal and social transformation and offered a movement culture founded on democracy.

Tom Hayden helped apply the ideals of SNCC to predominantly white college campuses. After spending the summer of 1961 registering voters in Mississippi and Georgia, the University of Michigan graduate student returned to campus eager to recruit like-minded students who questioned America's commitment to democracy. "Beyond lunch counter demonstrations," Hayden wrote, "there are more serious evils which must be ripped out by any means: exploitation, socially destructive capital, evil political and legal structure, and myopic liberalism which is anti-revolutionary."

Hayden became an influential leader of the **Students for a Democratic Society (SDS)**, which advocated the formation of a "New Left." They considered the "Old Left," which revolved around the Communist Party, as autocratic and no longer relevant. In its **Port Huron Statement** (1962), SDS condemned mainstream liberal politics, Cold War foreign policy, racism, and research-oriented universities that cared little for their undergraduates. It called for the adoption of "participatory democracy," which would return power to the people. SDS argued that the age of the military-industrial complex, with its mega-universities and giant corporations, had created a new educated class of alienated white-collar workers and college students perfectly suited to lead the revolution.

The New Left never consisted of one central organization such as SDS; after all, many protesters challenged the very idea of centralized authority. In fact, SDS did not initiate the New Left's most dramatic, early protest. In 1964 the University of California at Berkeley banned political activities just outside the main campus entrance in response to CORE protests against racial bias in local hiring. When CORE defied the prohibition, campus police arrested its leader, prompting a massive student uprising. The university's prohibition also spurred students to form the **Free Speech Movement (FSM)**, which held rallies in front of the administration building, culminating in a nonviolent, civil rights–style sit-in to assert their right to participate in such activities. When California governor Edmund "Pat" Brown dispatched a large force of state and county police to evict the demonstrators, students and faculty joined together in protest and forced the university administration to yield to FSM's demands for amnesty and reform. By the end of the decade, hundreds of demonstrations had erupted on campuses throughout the nation, culminating in 1968 in a bloody confrontation at Columbia University between students and New York City police. Unlike protests in the South aimed at reactionary white supremacists, campus revolts targeted liberals, dismissing them as obstacles to genuine social change.

The Vietnam War accelerated student radicalism, and college campuses provided a strategic setting for antiwar activities. Like most Americans in the mid-1960s, undergraduates had only a dim awareness of U.S. activity in Vietnam. Yet all college men were eligible for the draft once they graduated and lost their student deferment. As more troops were sent to Vietnam, student concern intensified.

Protests escalated in 1966 as President Johnson authorized an additional 250,000-troop buildup in Vietnam. This mobilization required higher draft calls, which began to affect more college men. With induction into the military a looming possibility, student protesters engaged in a variety of activities. Some burned draft cards; disrupted attempts by outside firms, such as the CIA and Dow Chemical Company (which made napalm), to recruit on campus; or

The Berkeley Free Speech Movement

Mario Savio, a student leader at the University of California at Berkeley and a Freedom Summer volunteer, stands among demonstrators sitting in at Sproul Hall on December 3, 1964, to protest university curbs on free speech. A day earlier, Savio had declared: "There's a time when the operation of the machine becomes so odious . . . you've got to put your bodies upon the gears . . . and you've got to make it stop."   AP Photo/Robert Houston

campaigned against the presence on campus of Reserve Officers' Training Corps (ROTC), which prepared future military leaders. Others resisted the draft by fleeing to Canada, and still others engaged in various forms of civil disobedience. Most college students, however, were not activists—between 1965 and 1968, only 20 percent of college students attended demonstrations. Nevertheless, the activist minority received wide media attention and helped raise awareness about the difficulty of waging the Vietnam War abroad and maintaining domestic tranquillity at home.

By the end of 1967, as the number of troops in Vietnam approached half a million, protests increased. Antiwar sentiment had spread to faculty, artists, writers, business people, and elected officials. Earlier that year in April, Martin Luther King Jr. delivered a powerful antiwar address at Riverside Church in New York City. "The world now demands," King declared, ". . . that we admit that we have been wrong from the beginning of our adventure in Vietnam, that we have been detrimental to the life of the Vietnamese people." In 1968 SDS split into factions, with the most prominent of them, the **Weathermen**, going underground and adopting violent tactics.

The New Left's challenge to liberal politics attracted many students, and the **counterculture**'s rejection of conventional middle-class values of work, sexual restraint, and faith in reason captivated even more. Cultural rebels emphasized living in the present, immediate gratification, authenticity of feelings, and reaching a higher consciousness through mind-altering drugs like marijuana and LSD. These youth rebels, popularly called "hippies," mocked their elders in the slogan "Don't trust anyone over thirty." Despite differences in approach, both the New Left and the counterculture expressed concerns about modern technology, bureaucratization, and the possibility of nuclear annihilation and sought new means of creating political, social, and personal liberation.

Rock 'n' roll became the soundtrack of the counterculture. In 1964 Bob Dylan's song "The Times They Are A-Changin'" became an anthem for youth rebellion, just as his "Blowin' in the Wind" did for the civil rights movement. In 1964 the Beatles, a British quartet influenced by 1950s black and white rock 'n' rollers, came to the United States and revolutionized popular music. Originally singing tuneful compositions of teenage love and angst, the Beatles embraced the counterculture and began writing songs

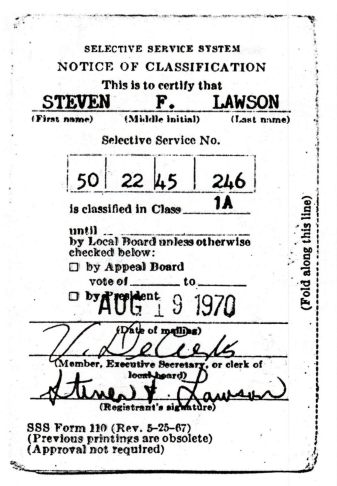

Draft Card

In 1963 Steven F. Lawson reached the age of eighteen and registered with his draft board, but as a college undergraduate he received a student deferment (II-S). With draft calls climbing due to the escalation of the Vietnam War, Lawson like many others was reclassified to I-A status—"available for military service." When a draft lottery was introduced in 1969, he drew a high number and was not drafted.   Courtesy of Steven F. Lawson

about alienation and politics, flavoring them with the drug-inspired sounds of psychedelic music. The Beatles launched a "British invasion," which also brought the Rolling Stones, who offered a harder-edged and raunchier sound than did the Beatles. Although most of the songs that reached the top ten on the record charts did not undermine traditional values, the music of groups like the Beatles, the Rolling Stones, the Who, the Grateful Dead, Jefferson Airplane, and the Doors spread counterculture messages of youth rebellion. At the same time, young black and white rebels embraced "soul music," black dance music popularized through the African American–owned Motown Records in Detroit and the white-owned Stax Records in Memphis.

The counterculture viewed the elimination of sexual restrictions as essential for transforming personal and social behavior. The 1960s generation did not invent sexual freedom, but it did a great deal to shatter time-honored moral codes of monogamy, fidelity, and moderation. Promiscuity—casual sex, group sex, extramarital affairs, public nudity—and open-throated vulgarity tested public tolerance. Yet within limits, the popular culture reflected these changes. The Broadway production of the musical *Hair* showed frontal nudity, the movie industry adopted ratings of "X" and "R" that made films with nudity and profane language available to a wider audience, and new television comedy shows featured sketches including risqué content and double entendres. With a nod from the Warren Court's easing definitions of pornography, counterculture writers assaulted the boundaries of "good taste."

With sexual conduct in flux, society had difficulty maintaining the double standard of behavior that privileged men over women. The counterculture gave many women a chance to pursue and enjoy sexual pleasure that had long been denied to them. The availability of birth control pills for women, introduced in 1960, made much of this sexual freedom possible. Although sexual liberation still carried more risks for women than for men, increased openness in discussing sexuality allowed many women to gain greater control over their bodies and their relationships.

Women's Liberation

Struggles in the 1960s for racial equality, peace, economic justice, and cultural and sexual freedom helped revive the fight for women's emancipation. Despite passage of the Nineteenth Amendment in 1920, which gave women the right to vote (see chapter 19), women did not have equal access to employment and education or control over reproduction. Nor did they have sufficient political power to remove the remaining obstacles to full equality. By 1960 nearly 40 percent of all women held jobs—representing one-third of the labor force—and women made up 35 percent of college enrollments. Subsequently, the social movements of the 1960s—civil rights, the New Left, and the counterculture—included large numbers of women and provided them with experience, connections, principles, and grievances that would lead women to create their own movement for liberation.

The federal government played a significant role in addressing gender discrimination. In 1961 President Kennedy appointed the **Commission on the Status of Women**. The commission's report, *American Women*, issued in 1963, reaffirmed the primary role of women in raising the family but cataloged the inequities women faced in the workplace. In 1963 Congress passed the Equal Pay Act, which required employers to give men and women equal pay for equal work. The following year, the 1964 Civil Rights Act opened up further opportunities when it prohibited sexual bias in employment and created the Equal Employment Opportunity Commission (EEOC). However, women remained divided over the need for the Equal Rights Amendment (ERA), first proposed in 1923 by suffragist Alice Paul. The Commission on the Status of Women refused to endorse it largely because labor union women believed that adopting the ERA would eliminate laws that specifically protected women workers with respect to hours, wages, and safety conditions.

In 1963 Betty Friedan published a landmark work in the history of the women's rights movement, *The Feminine Mystique*, a book that questioned society's prescribed gender roles. In *The Feminine Mystique*, she described the isolation and alienation experienced by her female friends and associates, raising the consciousness of many women, particularly college graduates and professionals. However, not all women saw themselves reflected in Friedan's book. Many working-class women from African American and other minority families had not had the opportunity to attend college and had to work to help support their families, and younger women had not yet experienced the burdens of domestic isolation.

Nevertheless, in October 1966, Betty Friedan and like-minded women formed the **National Organization for Women (NOW)**. With Friedan as president, NOW dedicated itself to moving society toward "true equality for all women in America, and toward a fully equal partnership of the sexes." NOW also called on the EEOC to enforce women's employment rights more vigorously and favored passage of the ERA, maternity leave rights in employment, the establishment of child care centers, and reproductive rights. Although NOW advocated job training programs and assistance for impoverished women, it attracted a mainly middle-class white membership. Some blacks were among its charter members, but most African American women chose to concentrate on first eliminating racial barriers that affected black women and men alike. Some union women also continued to

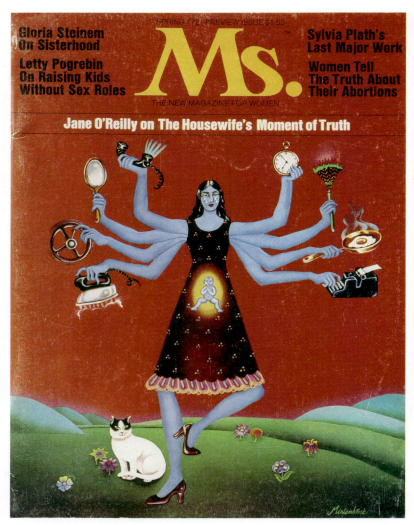

The Feminist Movement

In 1972 Gloria Steinem, a founder of NOW, established *Ms.* magazine in hope of attracting readers from across the feminist political spectrum. In this premiere issue, women's art and poetry appear alongside articles on sisterhood, child rearing, and abortion. The cover illustrates the demands on housewives who juggle domestic chores with paid employment and the pressure to remain attractive. The Granger Collection, New York

oppose the ERA, and antiabortion advocates wanted to steer clear of NOW's support for reproductive rights. Despite these concerns, between 1966 and 1971 NOW's membership increased dramatically from 1,000 to 15,000.

Supporters of women's equality drew lessons from the black freedom struggle. SNCC empowered women staff through community-organizing projects, but even within the civil rights movement women had not always been treated equally, often being assigned clerical duties. Women came up against even greater discrimination in the antiwar movement. Men held a higher status in such groups because women were not eligible for the draft. Ironically, men's claims of moral advantage justified many of them in seeking sexual favors. "Girls say yes to guys who say no," quipped draft-resisting men who sought to put women in their traditional sexual place.

As a result of these experiences, radical women formed their own, mainly local organizations. They created "consciousness-raising" groups that allowed them to share their experiences of oppression in the household, the workplace, the university, and movement organizations. These women's liberationists went beyond NOW's emphasis on legal equality and attacked male domination, or patriarchy, as the primary source of women's subordination. They criticized the nuclear family and cultural values that glorified women as the object of male sexual desires, and they protested creatively against discrimination. In 1968 radical feminists picketed the popular Miss America contest in Atlantic City, New Jersey, the epitome of male conceptions of female beauty, and set up a "Freedom Trash Can" into which they threw undergarments and cosmetics. Radical groups such as the Redstockings condemned all men as oppressors and formed separate female collectives to affirm their identities as women.

In 1973 feminists won a major battle in the Supreme Court over a woman's right to control reproduction. In *Roe v. Wade*, the high court ruled that states could not prevent a woman from obtaining an abortion in the first three months of pregnancy but could impose some limits in the next two trimesters. In furthering the constitutional right of privacy for women, the justices classified abortion as a private medical issue between a patient and her doctor. This decision marked a victory for a woman's right to choose to terminate her pregnancy, but it also stirred up a fierce reaction from women and men who considered abortion to be the murder of an unborn child. Although the basic principle of the right to an abortion has remained intact, legal and cultural battles have raged to the present day.

Power to the People

In addition to stimulating feminist consciousness, the civil rights movement emboldened other oppressed groups to emancipate themselves. African Americans led the way in influencing the liberationist struggles of Latinos, Indians, and gay men and women.

Malcolm X shaped the direction that many African Americans would take in seeking independence and power. Born Malcolm Little, he had engaged in a life of crime, which landed him in prison. Inside jail, he converted to the Nation of Islam, a religious sect based partly on Muslim teachings and partly on the belief that white people were

devils (not a doctrine associated with orthodox Islam). After his release from jail, Malcolm rejected his "slave name" and substituted the letter X to symbolize his unknown African forebears. A charismatic leader, Minister Malcolm helped convert thousands of disciples in black ghettos by denouncing whites and encouraging blacks to embrace their African cultural heritage and beauty as a people. Favoring self-defense over nonviolence, he criticized civil rights leaders for failing to protect their women, their children, and themselves. After 1963, Malcolm X broke away from the Nation of Islam, visited the Middle East and Africa and accepted the teachings of traditional Islam, moderated his rhetoric against all whites as devils, but remained committed to black self-determination. He had already influenced the growing number of disillusioned young black activists when, in 1965, members of the Nation of Islam murdered him, apparently in revenge for challenging the organization.

Black militants, echoing Malcolm X's ideas, further challenged the liberal consensus on race. They renounced King's and Rustin's ideas, rejecting their principles of integration and nonviolence in favor of black power and self-defense. Instead of welcoming whites within their organizations, black radicals believed that African Americans had to assert their independence from white America. In 1966 SNCC decided to expel whites and create an all-black organization. That same year, Stokely Carmichael, SNCC's chairman, proclaimed the rallying cry of "black power" as the central goal of the freedom struggle, linking the cause of African American freedom to revolutionary conflicts in Cuba, Africa, and Vietnam.

Black power seemed menacing to most whites. Its emergence in the midst of riots in black ghettos, which erupted across the nation starting in the mid-1960s, underscored the concern. Few white Americans understood the horrific conditions that led to riots in Harlem and Rochester, New York, in 1964; in Los Angeles in 1965; and in Cleveland, Chicago, Detroit, Newark, and Tampa in the following two years. Black northerners still faced problems of high unemployment, dilapidated housing, and police mistreatment, which civil rights legislation had done nothing to correct. While whites perceived the ghetto uprisings solely as an exercise in criminal behavior, many blacks viewed the violence as an expression of political discontent—as rebellions, not riots. The Kerner Commission, appointed by President Johnson to assess urban disorders and chaired by Governor Otto Kerner of Illinois, concluded in 1968 that white racism remained at the heart of the problem: "Our nation is moving toward two societies, one black, one white—separate and unequal."

New groups emerged to take up the cause of black power. In 1966 Huey P. Newton and Bobby Seale, two black college students in Oakland, California, formed the **Black Panther Party**. Like Malcolm X and Stokely Carmichael, the Panthers linked their cause to revolutionary movements around the world. Dressed in black leather, sporting black berets, and carrying guns, the Panthers appealed mainly to black men. They did not, however, rely on armed confrontation and bravado alone. The Panthers established day care centers and health facilities, which gained the admiration of many in their communities. Much of this good work was overshadowed by violent confrontations with the police, which led to the deaths of Panthers in shootouts and the imprisonment of key party officials. By the early 1970s, local and federal government crackdowns on the Black Panthers had destabilized the organization and reduced its influence.

Black militants were not the only African Americans to clash with the government. After 1965, King increasingly criticized the Johnson administration for waging war in Vietnam and failing to fight the War on Poverty more vigorously at home. In 1968 he prepared to mount a massive Poor People's March on Washington when he was shot and killed by James Earl Ray in Memphis, where he was supporting demonstrations for striking sanitation workers. The death of King furthered black disillusionment. In the wake of his murder, riots again erupted in hundreds of cities throughout the country. Little noticed amid the fiery turbulence, President Johnson signed into law the 1968 Fair Housing Act, the final piece of civil rights legislation of his term.

The African American freedom movement inspired Latinos struggling for equality and advancement. During the 1960s, the size of the Spanish-speaking population in the United States tripled from three million to nine million. Hispanic Americans were a diverse group who hailed from many countries and backgrounds. In the 1950s, Cesar Chavez had emerged as the leader of oppressed Mexican farmworkers in California. In seeking the right to organize a union and gain higher wages and better working conditions, Chavez shared King's nonviolent principles. In 1962 Chavez formed the National Farm Workers Association, and in 1965 the union called a strike against California grape growers, one that attracted national support and lasted five years before reaching a successful settlement.

Younger Mexican Americans, especially those in cities such as Los Angeles and other western *barrios* (ghettos), supported Chavez's economic goals but challenged older political leaders who sought cultural assimilation. Borrowing from the Black Panthers,

Mexican Americans formed the Brown Berets, a self-defense organization. As a sign of their increasing militancy and independence, in 1969 some 1,500 activists gathered in Denver and declared themselves *Chicanos*, a term that expressed their cultural pride and identity, instead of Mexican Americans. Chicanos created a new political party, **La Raza Unida (The United Race)**, to promote their interests, and the party and its allies sponsored demonstrations to fight for jobs, bilingual education, and the creation of Chicano studies programs in colleges. Chicano and other Spanish-language communities also took advantage of the protections of the Voting Rights Act, which, in 1975, was amended to include sections of the country—from New York to California to Florida and Texas—where Hispanic literacy in English and voter registration were low.

American Indians also joined the upsurge of

Explore

See Document 26.3 for a statement on Chicano self-identity.

activism and ethnic nationalism. By 1970 some 800,000 people identified themselves as American Indians, many of whom lived in poverty on reservations. They suffered from inadequate housing, high alcoholism rates, low life expectancy, staggering unemployment, and lack of education. Conscious of their heritage before the arrival of white people, determined to halt their continued deterioration, and seeking to assert "red" pride, they established the **American Indian Movement (AIM)** in 1968. The following year, AIM protesters occupied the abandoned prison island of Alcatraz in San Francisco Bay, where they remained until 1971. In 1972 AIM occupied the headquarters of the Federal Bureau of Indian Affairs in Washington, D.C., where protesters presented twenty demands, ranging from reparations for treaty violations to abolition of the bureau. AIM demonstrators also seized the village of Wounded Knee, South Dakota, the scene of the 1890 massacre of the Sioux residents by the U.S. army (see chapter 15), to dramatize the impoverished living conditions on the reservation. They held on for more than seventy days with eleven hostages until a shootout with the FBI ended the confrontation, killing one protester and wounding another.

The results of the red power movement proved mixed. Demonstrations focused media attention on the plight of American Indians but did little to halt their downward spiral. Nevertheless, courts became more sensitive to Indian claims and protected mineral and fishing rights on reservations. Still, in the early 1970s the

DOCUMENT 26.3

Chicano Student Movement of Aztlán, 1969

In April 1969, a group of students met at the University of California at Santa Barbara and formed the *Movimiento Estudiantil Chicano de Aztlán* (MEChA; Chicano Student Movement of Aztlán). MEChA organizers drafted "El Plan de Santa Barbara," excerpted below, which set out their basic philosophy and objectives. Their goals included using the term *Chicano* instead of *Mexican American* as a sign of cultural nationalism and political consciousness, creating Chicano studies departments at colleges and universities, and organizing other MEChA groups in the United States.

Explore

For decades Mexican people in the United States struggled to realize the "American Dream." And some—a few—have. But the cost, the ultimate cost of assimilation, required turning away from *el barrio* [one's neighborhood] and *la colonia* [one's community]. In the meantime, due to the racist structure of this society, to our essentially different life style, and to the socioeconomic functions assigned to our community by Anglo-American society—as suppliers of cheap labor and a dumping ground for the small-time capitalist entrepreneur— the *barrio* and *colonia* remained exploited, impoverished, and marginal.

As a result, the self-determination of our community is now the only acceptable mandate for social and political action; it is the essence of Chicano commitment. Culturally, the word *Chicano*, in the past a pejorative and class-bound adjective, has now become the root idea of a new cultural identity for our people. It also reveals a growing solidarity and the development of a common social praxis [customary conduct]. The widespread use of the term *Chicano* today signals a rebirth of pride and confidence. *Chicanismo* simply embodies an ancient truth: that man is never closer to his true self as when he is close to his community.

Chicanismo draws its faith and strength from two main sources: from the just struggle of our people and from an objective analysis of our community's strategic needs. We recognize that without a strategic use of education, an education that places value on what we value, we will not realize our destiny. Chicanos recognize the central importance of institutions of higher learning to modern progress, in this case, to the development of our community. But we go further: we believe that higher education must contribute to the information of a complete man who truly values life and freedom.

Source: Carlos Muñoz Jr., *Youth, Identity, Power: The Chicano Movement* (London: Verso, 1989), 191–92.

Interpret the Evidence

- Why does MEChA focus on the use of the term *Chicano*, and what does it hope to gain by its usage?
- Why did MEChA reject, at least in part, the goal of assimilation into mainstream American society?

Put It in Context

What connections does MEChA make between cultural awareness and political activism?

average annual income of American Indian families hovered around $1,500.

Unlike African Americans, Chicanos, and American Indians, homosexuals were not distinguished by the color of their skin. Estimated at 10 percent of the population, gays and lesbians remained invisible to the rest of society. Homosexuals were a target of repression during the Cold War, and the government treated them harshly and considered their sexual identity a threat to the American way of life. In the 1950s, gay men and women created their own political and cultural organizations and frequented bars and taverns outside mainstream commercial culture, but most lesbians and gay men like Bayard Rustin hid their identities. It was not

Native American Power

Drawing on the civil rights movement, this group of Native Americans occupied the former prison at Alcatraz Island on November 25, 1969. Among their demands, they offered to buy the island for $24 in beads and cloth—a reference to the purchase of Manhattan Island in 1626—and turn it into an Indian educational and cultural center.   AP Photo

The Revival of Conservatism

These diverse social movements did a great deal to change the political and cultural landscapes of the United States, but they did not go unchallenged. Many mainstream Americans worried about black militancy, opposed liberalism, and were even more dismayed by the radical offshoots they spawned. Generally overshadowed by more colorful protests for progressive causes, conservatives soon attracted support from many Americans who did not see change as progress. Many believed that the political leadership of the nation did not speak for them about what constituted a great society.

Conservatism had suffered a severe political blow with the ascendancy of Franklin Roosevelt's New Deal liberalism. Yet as conservatives lost political influence, they joined together to keep alive and publicize their beliefs. The brand of conservatism that emerged in the 1960s united libertarian support for a laissez-faire political economy and opposition to social welfare policies with moralistic concerns for defeating communism and defending religious devotion, moral decency, and family values. Unlike earlier conservatives, the new generation believed that the United States had to escalate the struggle against the evil of godless communism anywhere it posed a threat in the world, but they opposed internationalism as represented in the United Nations.

Conservative religious activists who built grassroots organizations to combat liberalism joined forces with political and intellectual conservatives such as William F. Buckley, the founder of the *National Review*, an influential journal of conservative ideas. The Reverend Billy Joe Hargis's Christian Crusade and Dr. Frederick Charles Schwartz's Christian Anti-Communist Crusade, both formed in the early 1950s, spun conspiracy theories about how the eastern liberal establishment intended to sell the country out to the Communists by supporting the United Nations, foreign aid, Social Security, and civil rights. The John Birch Society, named after a Baptist missionary and U.S. military intelligence officer killed during World War II by Communists in China, packaged these ideas in periodicals and radio broadcasts throughout the country and urged readers and listeners to remain vigilant to attacks against their freedom.

In the late 1950s and early 1960s, the conservative revival grew, mostly unnoticed, at the grassroots level in the

until 1969 that they took a giant step toward asserting their collective grievances in a very visible fashion. Police regularly cracked down on the **Stonewall Tavern** in New York City's Greenwich Village, but gay patrons battled back on June 27 in a riot that the *Village Voice* called "a kind of liberation, as the gay brigade emerged from the bars, back rooms, and bedrooms of the Village and became street people." In the manner of black power and the New Left, homosexuals organized the Gay Liberation Front, voiced pride in being gay, and demanded equality of opportunity regardless of sexual orientation.

As with other oppressed groups, gays achieved victories slowly and unevenly. In the decades following the 1960s, homosexuals faced discrimination in employment, could not marry or receive domestic benefits, and were subject to violence for public displays of affection.

suburbs of southern California and the Southwest. Bolstered by the postwar economic boom that centered around the military research and development of the Cold War, these towns in the Sun Belt attracted college-educated engineers, technicians, managers, and other professionals from the Midwest (or Rust Belt) seeking new economic opportunities. These migrants brought with them Republican loyalties as well as traditional conservative political and moral values. Women played a large part in conservative causes, especially in protesting against public school curricula that they believed encouraged secularism over religion, sex education over abstinence, and anti-Americanism over patriotism. Young housewives built an extensive network of conservative study groups.

In addition, the conservative revival, like the New Left, found fertile recruiting ground on college campuses. In October 1960, some ninety young conservatives met at William Buckley's estate in Sharon, Connecticut, to draw up a manifesto of their beliefs. The Sharon Statement affirmed the conservative doctrines of states' rights, the free market, and anticommunism. Participants at the conference formed the **Young Americans for Freedom (YAF)**, which six months later boasted 27,000 members on one hundred college campuses, far more than were in SDS in 1960. The *National Review* became its bible as subscriptions to Buckley's journal tripled to more than 90,000 by 1964. In 1962 the YAF filled Madison Square Garden to listen to a speech by the one politician who excited them: Republican senator Barry M. Goldwater of Arizona.

Explore

> See Documents 26.4 and 26.5 to compare Johnson's ideas on the Great Society with a statement from the Young Americans for Freedom.

Goldwater's book *The Conscience of a Conservative* (1960) attacked New Deal liberalism and advocated abolishing Social Security; dismantling the Tennessee Valley Authority, the government-owned public power utility; and eliminating the progressive income tax. His firm belief in states' rights put him on record against the ruling in *Brown v. Board of Education of Topeka, Kansas* and prompted him to vote against the Civil Rights Act of 1964, positions that won him increasing support from conservative white southerners. However, Goldwater's advocacy of small government did not prevent him from supporting increased military spending to halt the spread of communism abroad. The senator may have anticipated growing concerns of government excess, but he was ahead of his time. His defeat to Lyndon Johnson by a landslide in the 1964 presidential election indicated that most voters perceived Goldwater's brand of conservatism as too extreme and were not yet ready to support it.

The election of 1964 also brought George C. Wallace onto the national stage as a leading architect of the conservative revival. As Democratic governor of Alabama, the segregationist Wallace had supported states' rights and opposed federal intervention to reshape social and political affairs. Wallace began to attract white northerners fed up with rising black militancy, forced busing to promote school integration, and open housing laws to desegregate their neighborhoods. Running in the Democratic presidential primaries in 1964, the Alabama governor had no chance to win, but he garnered 34 percent of the votes in Wisconsin, 30 percent in Indiana, and 43 percent in Maryland.

More so than Goldwater, Wallace united a populist message against the political establishment with concern for working-class Americans. Wallace voters identified with the governor as an "outsider," despised by liberal elites as uncouth, uncultured, and unrespectable. Many of them also backed Wallace for attacking privileged college students who, he claimed, mocked patriotism, violated sexual taboos, and looked down on hardworking, churchgoing, law-abiding Americans. How could "all those rich kids—from the fancy suburbs," one father wondered, "[avoid the draft] when my son has to go over there and maybe get his head shot off?" Each in his own way, George Wallace and Barry Goldwater waged political campaigns against liberals for undermining the economic freedom of middle- and working-class whites and coddling what they considered "racial extremists" and "countercultural barbarians."

REVIEW & RELATE

- How did organizations on the left challenge social, cultural, and economic norms in the 1960s?
- What groups were attracted to the 1960s conservative movement? Why?

 LEARNINGCurve bedfordstmartins.com/hewittlawson/LC

Conclusion: Liberalism and Its Discontents

The presidencies of John Kennedy and Lyndon Johnson marked the high point of liberal reform. Kennedy's New Frontier and Johnson's Great Society expanded the power of the national state to provide both compassionate government and bureaucratic regulation. Liberalism permitted greater freedom for racial, ethnic, and sexual minorities; expanded educational opportunities for the disadvantaged; reduced poverty; extended health care; and began to clean up the environment. However, liberalism imposed a degree of federal oversight that seemed too restrictive and expensive to many Americans. Johnson's escalation of the Vietnam War weakened many of these accomplishments and fractured the liberal consensus of the 1960s.

Kennedy and Johnson did not achieve liberal triumphs by themselves. The civil rights movement, with unsung heroes like Bayard Rustin, forced the federal government into action by creating crises and raising the stakes for preserving domestic tranquillity. In addition, Earl Warren's Supreme Court affirmed the constitutionality of major

pieces of reform legislation and charted a new course for expanding the guarantees of the Bill of Rights.

Although the Vietnam War tarnished liberalism, the struggles of African Americans, women, Chicanos, Indians, and gays continued. Indeed, the civil rights movement spurred other exploited groups to seek greater freedom, and they flourished in the late 1960s and early 1970s despite the waning of the liberal consensus. Even the counterculture, which lost its most extreme elements to drugs and

DOCUMENTS 26.4 AND 26.5

Liberalism and Conservatism: Two Views

President Johnson's major domestic initiative, the Great Society, was designed to address the problems of poverty and discrimination in postwar America and rally the nation's youth behind it, as he expressed in a 1964 commencement address at the University of Michigan. His social vision reflected the major principles of liberalism in the 1960s. In 1960, at a gathering in Sharon, Connecticut, young conservatives presented their own ideas on how to tackle the social and moral problems affecting the country and its future.

Explore

26.4 Lyndon B. Johnson | The Great Society, 1964

The Great Society rests on abundance and liberty for all. It demands an end to poverty and racial injustice, to which we are totally committed in our time. But that is just the beginning.

The Great Society is a place where every child can find knowledge to enrich his mind and to enlarge his talents. It is a place where leisure is a welcome chance to build and reflect, not a feared cause of boredom and restlessness. It is a place where the city of man serves not only the needs of the body and the demands of commerce but the desire for beauty and the hunger for community.

It is a place where man can renew contact with nature. It is a place which honors creation for its own sake and for what it adds to the understanding of the race. It is a place where men are more concerned with the quality of their goals than the quantity of their goods. . . .

So I want to talk to you today about three places where we begin to build the Great Society—in our cities, in our countryside, and in our classrooms. . . .

The solution to these problems does not rest on a massive program in Washington, nor can it rely solely on the strained resources of local authority. They require us to create new concepts of cooperation, a creative federalism, between the National Capital and the leaders of local communities. . . .

So, will you join in the battle to give every citizen the full equality which God enjoins and the law requires, whatever his belief, or race, or the color of his skin?

Will you join in the battle to give every citizen an escape from the crushing weight of poverty?

Will you join in the battle to make it possible for all nations to live in enduring peace—as neighbors and not as mortal enemies?

Will you join in the battle to build the Great Society, to prove that our material progress is only the foundation on which we will build a richer life of mind and spirit?

There are those timid souls who say this battle cannot be won; that we are condemned to a soulless wealth. I do not agree. We have the power to shape the civilization that we want.

Source: *Public Papers of the Presidents of the United States: Lyndon B. Johnson, 1963–1964* (Washington, D.C.: Government Printing Office, 1965), 1:704, 706.

overindulgence, saw its styles, music, and attitudes toward pleasure blended into mainstream consumer culture.

Liberalism produced unparalleled accomplishments but planted the seeds for its own unraveling. During the 1960s, liberal policies and programs generated powerful counterattacks from radicals and conservatives alike. Indeed, over the next twenty-five years conservatives mobilized the American electorate and gained power by attacking liberal political, economic, and cultural values.

The liberal ascendancy proved short-lived, but its impact on the United States has had a lasting effect.

Rather than encompassing any one political and social philosophy, the decade of the 1960s was a time when reform, revolution, and reaction intermingled. Although the era remains known for radicalism and excess, it also saw the revival of conservatism as a force that would dominate politics for the rest of the twentieth century and into the beginning of the next millennium.

Explore

26.5 The Sharon Statement, 1960

In this time of moral and political crises, it is the responsibility of the youth of America to affirm certain eternal truths.

We, as young conservatives, believe:

That foremost among the transcendent values is the individual's use of his God-given free will, whence derives his right to be free from the restrictions of arbitrary force;

That liberty is indivisible, and that political freedom cannot long exist without economic freedom;

That the purpose of government is to protect those freedoms through the preservation of internal order, the provision of national defense, and the administration of justice;

That when government ventures beyond these rightful functions, it accumulates power, which tends to diminish order and liberty;

That the Constitution of the United States is the best arrangement yet devised for empowering government to fulfill its proper role, while restraining it from the concentration and abuse of power;

That the genius of the Constitution—the division of powers—is summed up in the clause that reserves primacy to the several states, or to the people, in those spheres not specifically delegated to the Federal government;

That the market economy, allocating resources by the free play of supply and demand, is the single economic system compatible with the requirements of personal freedom and constitutional government, and that it is at the same time the most productive supplier of human needs;

That when government interferes with the work of the market economy, it tends to reduce the moral and physical strength of the nation; that when it takes from one man to bestow on another, it diminishes the incentive of the first, the integrity of the second, and the moral autonomy of both.

Source: Young Americans for Freedom, "The Sharon Statement," *National Review*, September 1960, 173.

Interpret the Evidence

- What does Johnson see as the major responsibility of government?
- What do the authors of the Sharon Statement see as the major responsibility of government?

Put It in Context

What do these documents reveal about the major differences between liberal and conservative political philosophies in the 1960s?

Chapter Review

Online Study Guide ▶ bedfordstmartins.com/hewittlawson

KEY TERMS

New Frontier (p. 825)
Gulf of Tonkin Resolution (p. 827)
Tet Offensive (p. 830)
Freedom Rides (p. 830)
March on Washington for Jobs and Freedom (p. 832)
Civil Rights Act of 1964 (p. 832)
Freedom Summer (p. 833)
Mississippi Freedom Democratic Party (MFDP) (p. 833)
Voting Rights Act (p. 834)
Great Society (p. 834)
Students for a Democratic Society (SDS) (p. 837)
Port Huron Statement (p. 837)
Free Speech Movement (FSM) (p. 837)
Weathermen (p. 838)
counterculture (p. 838)
Commission on the Status of Women (p. 839)
National Organization for Women (NOW) (p. 840)
Roe v. Wade (p. 841)
Black Panther Party (p. 842)
La Raza Unida (The United Race) (p. 842)
American Indian Movement (AIM) (p. 842)
Stonewall Tavern (p. 844)
Young Americans for Freedom (YAF) (p. 845)

REVIEW & RELATE

1. How did President Kennedy's domestic agenda reflect the liberal political ideology of the early 1960s?

2. How and why did the United States escalate its role in the Vietnam War?

3. What role did the federal government play in advancing the cause of racial equality in the early 1960s?

4. How did civil rights activists pressure state and federal government officials to enact their agenda?

5. What problems and challenges did Johnson's Great Society legislation target?

6. In what ways did the Warren Court's rulings advance the liberal agenda?

7. How did organizations on the left challenge social, cultural, and economic norms in the 1960s?

8. What groups were attracted to the 1960s conservative movement? Why?

TIMELINE OF EVENTS

1960	Young Americans for Freedom founded; Sharon Statement issued
1961	Kennedy sends military advisers to South Vietnam
	Cuban exile invasion force lands at Bay of Pigs
	CORE mounts Freedom Rides
	Soviets build Berlin Wall
1962	Students for a Democratic Society (SDS) issues Port Huron Statement
	Cuban missile crisis
1963–1968	U.S. troop levels in Vietnam rise from 16,000 to 536,000
1963	Betty Friedan publishes *The Feminine Mystique*
	U.S. and Soviet Union agree to Partial Nuclear Test Ban Treaty
	March on Washington for Jobs and Freedom
	John F. Kennedy assassinated by Lee Harvey Oswald; Lyndon B. Johnson becomes president
1964–1966	Great Society domestic programs enacted
1964	Civil Rights Act of 1964 passed
	Freedom Summer project in Mississippi
	Congress passes Gulf of Tonkin Resolution
1965	Operation Rolling Thunder begins
	Voting Rights Act passed
	Griswold v. Connecticut Supreme Court decision
1966	Black Panther Party formed
	National Organization for Women (NOW) formed
1968	American Indian Movement (AIM) founded
	Martin Luther King Jr. assassinated
	Tet Offensive begins in Vietnam
1969	Gays fight police at Stonewall Tavern
1973	*Roe v. Wade* Supreme Court decision

DOCUMENT PROJECT 26

Freedom Summer

In June 1964, white college students gathered at the Western College for Women in Oxford, Ohio, to train for a massive voter registration project in Mississippi. Freedom Summer, as it was called, was organized by the Student Nonviolent Coordinating Committee, the Congress of Racial Equality, the National Association for the Advancement of Colored People, and the Southern Christian Leadership Conference. Working under an umbrella organization, the Congress of Federated Organizations (COFO), the project focused on political rights, particularly the right to vote. COFO set up freedom schools, which taught voter literacy, organizing techniques, and basic reading and writing skills. The decision to use white volunteers was a deliberate one to put more activists on the ground and, more important, draw national attention to the cause. The activities of Freedom Summer volunteers provoked violence and resistance. Perhaps the most well-known acts of violence were the murders of three civil rights workers: James Chaney, a local black activist; and Michael Schwerner and Andrew Goodman, two northern whites.

Also, black activists formed the interracial Mississippi Freedom Democratic Party (MFDP), which sent its own delegates to the Democratic National Convention in Atlantic City, New Jersey, and sought official recognition by the convention to replace the all-white delegation. Offered a compromise, the MFDP refused it and returned home but supported Lyndon Johnson's election.

Although few black Mississippians successfully registered to vote and the MFDP was denied official recognition at the Democratic National Convention, Freedom Summer did publicize the plight of black communities in Mississippi and throughout the South, and this publicity contributed to the passage of the Voting Rights Act of 1965. As you examine the following documents, consider whether you think the campaign was a success.

DOCUMENT 26.6

Prospectus for Mississippi Freedom Summer, 1964

Civil rights organizers carefully prepared for Freedom Summer, knowing that such a large campaign against intransigent disfranchisement in Mississippi would require extensive planning and coordination. The following selection is from an internal document of the Student Nonviolent Coordinating Committee that summarizes the purpose and strategies of Freedom Summer. It highlights the goals of voter registration and freedom schools.

It has become evident to the civil rights groups involved in the struggle for freedom in Mississippi that political and social justice cannot be won without the massive aid of the country as a whole, backed by the power and authority of the federal government. Little hope exists that the political leaders of Mississippi will steer even a moderate course in the near future (Governor Johnson's [Mississippi governor Paul Johnson] inaugural speech notwithstanding); in fact, the contrary seems true: as the winds of change grow stronger, the threatened political elite of Mississippi becomes more intransigent and fanatical in its support of the status quo. The closed society of Mississippi is, as Professor [James] Silver asserts, without the moral resources to reform itself. And Negro efforts to win the right to vote cannot succeed against the extensive legal weapons and police powers of local and state officials without a nationwide mobilization of support.

A program is planned for this summer which will involve the massive participation of Americans dedicated to the elimination of racial oppression. Scores of college students, law students, medical students, teachers, professors, ministers, technicians, folk artists, and lawyers from all over the country have already volunteered to work in Mississippi this summer—and hundreds more are being recruited. . . .

Why this summer?

Mississippi at this juncture in the movement has received too little attention—that is, attention to what the state's attitude really is—and has presented COFO with a major policy decision. Either the civil rights struggle has to continue, as it has for the past few years, with small projects in selected communities with no real progress on any fronts, or [there must be a] task force of such a size as to force either the state and the municipal governments to change their social and legal structures, or the Federal Government to intervene on behalf of the constitutional rights of its citizens.

Since 1964 is an election year, the clear-cut issue of voting rights should be brought out in the open. Many SNCC and CORE workers in Mississippi hold the view that Negroes will never vote in large numbers until Federal marshals intervene. At any rate, many Americans must be made to realize that the voting rights they so often take for granted involve considerable risk for Negroes in the South. In the larger context of the national civil rights movement, enough progress has been made during the last year that there can be no turning back. Major victories in Mississippi, recognized as the stronghold of racial intolerance in the South, would speed immeasurably the breaking down of legal and social discrimination in both North and South. . . .

Direction of the Project . . .

Voter Registration: This will be the most concentrated level of activity. Voter registration workers will be involved in an intensive summer drive to encourage as many Negroes as possible to register. They will participate in COFO's Freedom Registration, launched in early February, to register over 400,000 Negroes on Freedom Registration books. These books will be set up in local Negro establishments and will have simplified standards of registration (the literacy test and the requirement demanding an interpretation of a section of the Mississippi Constitution will be eliminated).

Freedom Registration books will serve as the basis of a challenge of the official books of the state and the validity of "official" elections this fall. Finally, registration workers will assist in the campaigns of Freedom candidates who are expected to run for seats in all five of the State's congressional districts and for the seat of Senator John Stennis, who is up for re-election.

Freedom Schools:

1. *General Description.* About 25 Freedom Schools are planned, of two varieties: day schools in about 20–25 towns (commitments still pending in some communities) and one or two boarding, or residential, schools on college campuses. Although the local communities can provide school buildings, some furnishings, and staff housing (and, for residential schools, student housing), all equipment, supplies, and staff will have to come from outside. A nationwide recruitment program is underway to find and train the people and solicit the equipment needed. In the schools, the typical day will be hard study in the morning, an afternoon break (because it's too hot for an academic program), and less formal evening activities.

Source: Prospectus for the Mississippi Freedom Summer, Miller (Michael J.) Civil Rights Collection, McCain Library and Archives, University of Southern Mississippi.

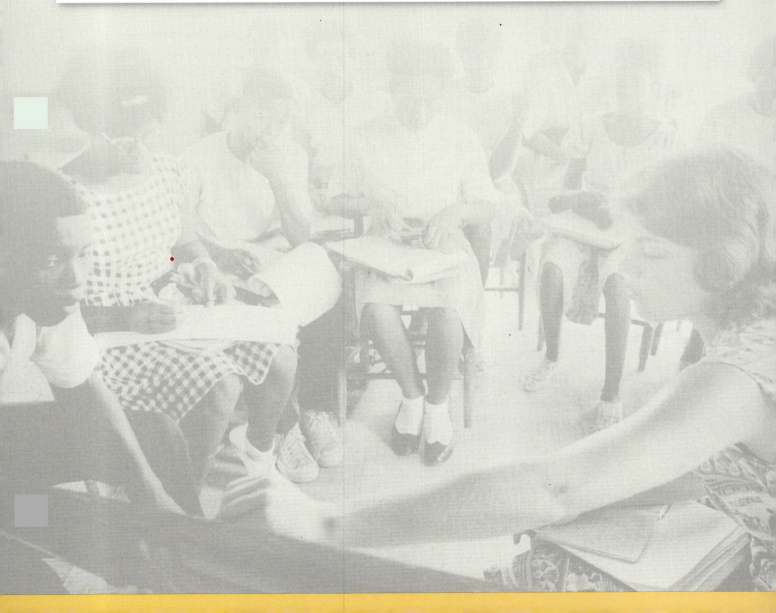

DOCUMENT 26.7

Nancy Ellin | Letter Describing Freedom Summer, 1964

Setting up freedom schools throughout Mississippi was a key project of Freedom Summer. The schools in Hattiesburg were staffed by many northern white volunteers, including Nancy and Joseph Ellin. Both originally from New York City, Nancy and Joseph met at Yale University, where Joseph received his doctorate in philosophy in 1962. At the time of Freedom Summer, Joseph was a philosophy professor at Western Michigan University. The following selection is from a letter written by Nancy to Joseph's parents shortly after they arrived in Mississippi.

June 30

Dear Dr. and Mrs. Ellin,

It was nice to get your letter today; we hope you will write often. I'm sure Joe will write to you any minute now, but I thought I might as well, too.

We got here OK, though we were frightened most of the way, quite unnecessarily. It was the people who came down in integrated cars who had the unpleasant time—refused service, cars following them, etc. We came down with a very nice girl who just graduated from Smith [College] and who did quite a bit of driving.

We are currently hard at work getting the Freedom Schools organized. Joe and another boy have everyone typing up stencils of the Constitution, the Declaration of Independence, etc. The school enrollment is over 150; we are having official registration Thursday. The philosophy is to take everyone who comes; we will be teaching adults in the evening. There are 10 teachers, 8 more expected from New York City on Thursday. We also intend to recruit a few local people.

I, too, am sorry things came to such a pass. We felt terrible about causing you all such anguish, but we felt the decision was ours to make, and though we were very afraid and doubtful at Oxford [in Ohio], we made the decision to come. You must know that you were not the only parents who were worried, and some kids did drop out, one from our group, in fact, who was underage and couldn't get his parents' consent. Now that we are here we feel more than ever that coming here was the right thing to do. Even if we don't teach a single child (and I think the odds are heavily against that) we still will have accomplished something in showing the people of Hattiesburg that they should not hate whites. Even our own group leaders, Carolyn and Arthur Reese, who are Detroit Negroes (schoolteachers), were very anti-white until Oxford, Ohio. (Carolyn has been extremely frightened much of the time we have been here.) The people of Hattiesburg are militant and eager; our landlady told us last night about a woman who had attempted to register to vote 17 times before she made it.

Things here are pretty horrible. The Negro section, where we are, smells and looks more than a little like India. The house we are staying in (free) is pretty good-sized but very dilapidated—creaky floors, etc. It has a bathroom—some don't. Our landlady is registered; her husband has tried but hasn't made it yet. Everyone agrees that things here would be much worse right this minute if it weren't for our presence and the pressure exerted on the govt. on our behalf by our rich Northern parents. Negroes in the movement tend to lose their jobs. We feel—rightly or wrongly—that our place is here, in the heart of the struggle. No man is an island . . .

Otherwise, there isn't much news. We have been to one mass meeting and are cutting another one tonight to make stencils. Another job we have before us is organizing the library—there are tremendous quantities of books. We haven't had much contact yet, aside from smiles and handshakes, with the regular Negro community, so I haven't much else to report. The leaders we have met are terrific.

Thank Mary and everyone for praying for us.

Love,
Nancy

Source: Letter from Joseph and Nancy Ellin to Dr. and Mrs. Ellin, Joseph and Nancy Ellin Freedom Summer Collection, McCain Library and Archives, University of Southern Mississippi.

DOCUMENT 26.8

Letter from a Freedom Summer Volunteer, 1964

The following letter is from an unknown Freedom Summer volunteer in Meridian, Mississippi. Written the day after the FBI discovered the bodies of slain civil rights activists James Chaney, Michael Schwerner, and Andrew Goodman, the letter describes how the local community remembered "Mickey" Schwerner and "Jimmy" Chaney.

Meridian, August 5

At the Freedom school and at the community center, many of the kids had known Mickey and almost all knew Jimmy Chaney. That day we asked the kids to describe Mickey and Jimmy because we had never known them.

"Mickey was a big guy. He wore blue jeans all the time." . . . I asked the kids, "What did his eyes look like?" and they told me they were "friendly eyes" "nice eyes" ("nice" is a lovely word in a Mississippi accent). "Mickey was a man who was at home everywhere and with anybody," said the 17-year-old girl I stay with. The littlest kids, the 6, 7, 8 year olds, tell about how he played "Frankenstein" with them or took them for drives or talked with them about Freedom. Many of the teenage boys were delinquents until Mickey went down to the bars and jails and showed them that one person at least would respect them if they began to fight for something important. . . . And the grown-ups too, trusted him. The lady I stay with tells with pride of how Mickey and Rita [his wife] came to supper at their house, and police cars circled around the house all during the meal. But Mickey could make them feel glad to take the risk.

People talk less about James Chaney here, but feel more. The kids describe a boy who played with them—whom everyone respected but who never had to join in fights to maintain this respect—a quiet boy but very sharp and very understanding when he did speak. Mostly we know James through his sisters and especially his 12-year-old brother, Ben. Today Ben was in the Freedom School. At lunchtime the kids have a jazz band (piano, washtub bass, cardboard boxes and bongos as drums) and tiny Ben was there leading it all even with his broken arm, with so much energy and rhythm that even Senator Eastland [Senator James Eastland of Mississippi] would have had to stop and listen if he'd been walking by.

Source: Elizabeth Sutherland, ed., *Letters from Mississippi* (New York: McGraw-Hill, 1965), 190.

DOCUMENT 26.9

White Southerners Respond to Freedom Summer, 1964

As Freedom Summer activists began arriving in Mississippi, newspapers throughout the South ran editorials and articles condemning the volunteers. The following article appeared in a South Carolina newspaper and is representative of the ways in which white southerners characterized Freedom Summer. It mentions the National Council of Churches, a federation of white and black Christian churches that supported many civil rights and peace causes in the postwar era, including Freedom Summer.

This week the vanguard of a youthful army left the rolling hill country of southwestern Ohio, where volunteers had spent several weeks being indoctrinated and incensed, for the flat Delta land of Mississippi. The Summer Project, a joint effort of the Student Non-Violent Coordinating Committee (SNICK) and the National Council of Churches, was on the march. . . .

"The real aim of SNICK and the other more extreme Negro organizations is to secure the military occupation of Mississippi by federal troops." This is not the expressed judgment of Mississippi Governor Paul Johnson or even of Senator James Eastland. The words are those of Joseph Alsop, the liberal columnist [from the *Washington Post*]. Mr. Alsop, however much he may desire civil rights for Negroes, knows that no good can come from this Summer Project, controlled as it is by the most militant of the many civil rights groups and the one whose ranks include, according to Mr. Alsop, more than a few dedicated Communists.

It would be comforting to believe that the young persons involved in this project understand something of what is going on behind the scenes. It would be much easier then to dismiss their possible fate from the mind. But the facts will not allow such optimism.

"Last summer I went back to London for three months and did nothing," one recruit told a *Washington Post* reporter. "It was unhealthy. This summer I want to do something."

Another young recruit said he didn't think he could live with himself if he didn't do something about Mississippi. A third, a young lady studying theology, said she was going because of her belief that "the SNICK people are living a life that is relevant to the New Testament." Just how accurate is this rosy view?

The crusade leaders say publicly that the main thrust of the summer invasion will be directed at voter discrimination in Mississippi, where only 6.6 percent of Negroes of voting age are registered to vote. Such an effort, conducted with forbearance and directed at helping the Negro improve himself, might produce some good. Judging by the record, however, SNICK is short on forbearance and uncommonly long on making trouble. Nor is the National Council of Churches likely to provide much in the way of restraint.

The Council has invested $260,000 in this project, and it wants more out of that investment than a handful of votes. At a Baltimore meeting last February, during which the Summer Project was under discussion, Council members talked of "social redevelopment" in Mississippi, of applying "corrective treatment" to the Delta region.

"The main problem at this point," the Council's own report of the Baltimore meeting said, "is the concentration of wealth among the few, e.g., on an average, 5 percent of the farms control 50 percent of all the farmland."

Voting? This has nothing to do with voting. The Council is speaking of agrarian reform of the sort that socialists promote.

From this, the goals of the Summer Project appear to be two-fold: first, indoctrination in socialist economics; second, military occupation of Mississippi if that can be arranged. This is no longer a struggle of black and white. If the reports of even the most liberal observers are to be believed, the Reds predominate and the nation can anticipate a long, hot summer indeed.

Source: "'Freedom' to the Delta," *Charleston Post*, June 24, 1964.

DOCUMENT 26.10

Fannie Lou Hamer | Address to the Democratic National Convention Credentials Committee, 1964

At the 1964 Democratic National Convention, Mississippi Freedom Democratic Party (MFDP) members attempted to unseat the official all-white Mississippi delegation. Several MFDP members testified before the convention's credentials committee, including Fannie Lou Hamer. Hamer's testimony began in front of a national television audience, but that coverage ended when President Johnson quickly held a press conference to divert attention from the controversy. On the evening news, however, the major networks carried stories about Hamer and the MFDP. Though the MFDP was not recognized in 1964, four years later Hamer led the party's official delegation at the Democratic National Convention. In the following selection, Hamer tells of her arrest in Winona, Mississippi, as she traveled home from a voter registration workshop.

I was carried to the county jail and put in the booking room. They left some of the people in the booking room and began to place us in cells. I was placed in a cell with a young woman called Miss Euvester Simpson. After I was placed in the cell, I began to hear sounds of licks and screams. I could hear the sounds of licks and horrible screams. And I could hear somebody say, "Can you say, 'yes, sir,' nigger? Can you say 'yes, sir'?" And they would say other horrible names.

She would say, "Yes, I can say 'yes, sir.'"

"So, well, say it."

She said, "I don't know you well enough." They beat her, I don't know how long. And after a while she began to pray, and asked God to have mercy on those people.

And it wasn't too long before three white men came to my cell. One of these men was a state highway patrolman and he asked me where I was from. And I told him Ruleville. He said, "We are going to check this." And they left my cell and it wasn't too long before they came back. He said, "You's from Ruleville all right," and he used a curse word. And he said, "We are going to make you wish you was dead."

I was carried out of that cell into another cell where they had two Negro prisoners. The state highway patrolmen ordered the first Negro to take the blackjack [police baton]. The first Negro prisoner ordered me, by orders from the state highway patrolman, for me to lay down on a bunk bed on my face.

And I laid on my face and the first Negro began to beat. And I was beat by the first Negro until he was exhausted. I was holding my hands behind me at that time on my left side, because I suffered from polio when I was six years old. After the first Negro had beat until he was exhausted, the state highway patrolman ordered the second Negro to take the blackjack. The second Negro began to beat and I began to work my feet, and the state highway patrolman ordered the first Negro [who] had beat me to sit on my feet—to keep me from working my feet. I began to scream and one white man got up and began to beat me in my head and tell me to hush.

One white man—my dress had worked up high—he walked over and pulled my dress, I pulled my dress down, and he pulled my dress back up.

I was in jail when Medgar Evers was murdered.

All of this is on account of we want to register, to become first-class citizens. And if the Freedom Democratic Party is not seated now, I question America. Is this America, the land of the free and the home of the brave, where we have to sleep with our telephones off of the hooks because our lives be threatened daily, because we want to live as decent human beings, in America? Thank you.

Source: Megan Parker Brooks and David W. Houck, eds., *The Speeches of Fannie Lou Hamer: To Tell It like It Is* (Jackson: University Press of Mississippi, 2011), 44–45.

DOCUMENT 26.11

Lyndon B. Johnson | Monitoring the MFDP Challenge, 1964

President Johnson feared that the MFDP challenge at the 1964 Democratic National Convention would prove divisive and lessen his chances of winning the South in the upcoming election. To maintain unity, he instructed Senator Hubert Humphrey of Minnesota, a respected liberal and civil rights supporter, to work out a compromise. In this telephone conversation on August 9, 1964, with Walter Reuther, the head of the United Auto Workers and a power broker at the convention, an irritated Johnson explains his reasoning for working out a deal.

JOHNSON   If you and Hubert Humphrey have got any leadership, you'd get Joe Rauh [MFDP lawyer] off that damn television. The only thing that can really screw us good is to seat that group of challengers from Mississippi. . . . He said he's going to take it to the convention floor. Now there's not a damn vote that we get by seating these folks. What we want to do is elect some Congressmen to keep 'em from repealing this [1964 Civil Rights] act. And who's seated at this convention don't amount to a damn. Only reason I would let Mississippi [all-white delegation] come in is because I don't want to run off fourteen border states, like Oklahoma and Kentucky. . . . Incidentally this Governor [Mississippi governor Paul Johnson] has done everything I've asked him to do in Mississippi. We've broken that case [the Chaney, Schwerner, and Goodman murders]. I talk to him two or three times a week. Now he's not for [me]. But I can't say that he hasn't listened to us and he hasn't cooperated.

REUTHER   Exactly. . . . We'll lose Mississippi, but the impact on the other Southern states—

JOHNSON   That's all I'm worried about. . . . I've got to carry Georgia. . . . I've got to carry Texas. . . . We don't want to cut off our nose to spite our face. If they give us four years, I'll guarantee the Freedom delegation somebody representing views like that will be seated four years from now. But we can't do it all before breakfast.

Source: Michael R. Beschloss, ed., *Taking Charge: The Johnson White House Tapes, 1963–1964* (New York: Simon and Schuster, 1997), 510–11.

Interpret the Evidence

1. What did local blacks think of white volunteers in the Freedom Summer project (Documents 26.7 and 26.8)? What were the advantages and disadvantages of bringing white volunteers to Mississippi?

2. Why were voter registration and political organizing the focus of Freedom Summer (Document 26.6)? Why did the project also include freedom schools?

3. What arguments did the *Charleston Post* (Document 26.9) make to discredit Freedom Summer?

4. How did Fannie Lou Hamer use the testimony of her experience in a Mississippi jail (Document 26.10) to gain support for the Mississippi Freedom Democratic Party?

5. Do you think President Johnson's views toward seating the MFDP delegation (Document 26.11) were consistent with his vision of the Great Society? Explain.

Put It in Context

- In what ways did Freedom Summer succeed? In what ways did it fail?

Time & Life Pictures/Getty Images

Time & Life Pictures/Getty Images

Political activist Phyllis Schlafly and other women at a government hearing on the Equal Rights Amendment in Kansas City, Missouri, 1976.

Line of cars waiting for gas during a fuel shortage, 1979.

27
The Conservative Ascendancy

1968–1992

Spencer Grant/Getty Images

Attendants observe a moment of prayer during the New England Rally for God, Family, and Country in Boston, Massachusetts, 1970.

Allan Bakke was not a political ideologue or an activist. He had always played by the rules. Born in Minnesota in 1940, Bakke grew up in a white middle-class family, earned a degree in mechanical engineering, and served in Vietnam. When his tour of duty was over, Bakke returned home, found an engineering job in Sunnyvale, California, and received a master's degree from Stanford University. However, he had not satisfied his great ambition—to become a physician.

In 1972 Bakke applied to two California medical schools and was turned down, probably because at age thirty-two he was considered too old. The next year, he applied to twelve schools but was rejected by all of them, including the University of California at Davis. Bakke learned that of the one hundred available spaces in the incoming class, the university awarded sixteen spots to minority group members, consisting mainly of African Americans, Chicanos, and Asian Americans. Contending that the policy amounted to reverse discrimination, he sued the University of California at Davis for violating his constitutional rights. In his challenge to the university's admission policy, Bakke complained: "I realize that the rationale for these quotas is that they attempt to atone for past racial discrimination, but insisting on a new racial bias in favor of minorities is not a just situation." In 1978 the U.S. Supreme Court ruled in his favor, and Bakke successfully completed his studies and graduated with a medical degree.

Like Allan Bakke, Anita Faye Hill did not seek celebrity, yet like Bakke she, too, would gain notoriety in a cause not of her own making. Born in Oklahoma in 1956, Hill grew up in a large family whose ancestors included Creek Indians and former slaves. Like other African Americans in the state, she encountered racial segregation when she attended school, but her parents encouraged her to work hard and abide by strong religious and moral values.

A bookish and determined young woman, Hill graduated from Yale Law School in 1980. The following year, she went to work in the Office of Civil Rights at the Department of Education. Her boss, Clarence Thomas, was an African American supporter of President Ronald Reagan. When Thomas moved to the Equal Employment Opportunity Commission in May 1982, Hill transferred as well. Although a pragmatic moderate who privately favored affirmative action, she tried not to make waves and defended the positions that the conservative Thomas implemented to further reduce the scope of affirmative action in the aftermath of the *Bakke* case.

Anita Hill would have remained an obscure public servant had President George H. W. Bush not nominated Thomas to the Supreme Court in 1991. During the course of Thomas's Senate confirmation hearing, Hill testified before the Senate Judiciary Committee and a nationally televised audience that Thomas had made unwanted sexual advances to her on and off the job. Disturbed by Thomas's harassment and sexual impropriety, Hill had quit her job in 1983 and returned to Oklahoma to teach at a law school. It was difficult for this usually shy black woman to publicly describe these embarrassing moments concerning a high-ranking black man, but her courage was not rewarded. Black and white conservatives defended Thomas and attacked Hill's credibility, and Thomas won confirmation by a 52–48 vote. Nevertheless, she became a hero for many working women who faced similar incidents of sexual bias and harassment. ●

ALLAN BAKKE and Anita Hill were not engaged in politics in the usual sense of the word. Nonetheless, their American histories took on profound political importance in the larger context of the rise and ascendancy of conservatism in the late twentieth century. Scoring their first national victory with the election of Richard Nixon in 1968, conservatives became the dominant force on the political landscape with the election of Ronald Reagan in 1980. Reagan led a New Right coalition that meshed the traditional economic conservatism of lower taxes, deregulation, and anti-unionism with the concerns of religious conservatives over abortion and family values. By 1992 conservatives had built upon the judicial victory of Allan Bakke and brushed back the complaint of Anita Hill in reshaping the nation's political priorities. Still, they had neither silenced their progressive critics nor eliminated the impact of liberal achievements from the 1960s.

Richard M. Nixon, War, and Politics, 1969–1974

Richard Nixon won the presidency in 1968 by forging a conservative coalition behind him, blaming liberals for the radical excesses of the 1960s. While continuing to fight Communists in Vietnam, Nixon improved relations with the Soviet Union and China, creating a thaw in the Cold War. At home, Nixon mixed conservatism with pragmatic politics, supporting some liberal measures while defending the virtues of limited government and traditional values. Nixon won reelection in 1972 by a landslide, but his victory was short-lived. In an effort to ensure electoral success, the Nixon administration engaged in illegal activities that subsequently came to light in the Watergate scandal. Nixon was forced to resign, and the conservative movement suffered a temporary setback.

The Election of President Nixon

The year 1968 was a turbulent one. In February, police shot indiscriminately into a crowd gathered for civil rights protests at South Carolina State University in Orangeburg, killing three students in the so-called Orangeburg massacre. The following month, student protests at Columbia University led to a violent confrontation with the New York City police. On April 4, the murder of Martin Luther King Jr. sparked an outburst of rioting by blacks in more than one hundred cities throughout the country (see chapter 26). The assassination of Democratic presidential aspirant Robert Kennedy in June further heightened the mood of despair. Adding to the unrest, demonstrators gathered in Chicago in August at the Democratic National Convention to press for an antiwar plank in the party platform. Thousands of protesters were beaten and arrested by Chicago police officers, who violently released their frustrations on the crowds. Many Americans watched in horror as television networks broadcast the bloody clashes, but a majority of viewers sided with the police rather than the protesters.

Similar protests occurred around the world. In early 1968, university students outside of Paris protested educational policies and what they perceived as their second-class status. When students at the Sorbonne in Paris joined them in the streets, police attacked them viciously. In June, French president Charles de Gaulle sent in tanks to break up the strikes but also instituted political and economic reforms. Protests erupted during the spring in Prague, Czechoslovakia, as well. President Alexander Dubček, vowing to reform the Communist regime by initiating "socialism with a human face," lifted press censorship, guaranteed free elections, and encouraged artists and writers to express themselves freely. Unaccustomed to such dissent and fearful it would spread to other nations within its imperial orbit, the Soviet Union sent its military into Prague in August 1968 to crush the reforms. Czechoslovakian protesters were no match for Soviet forces, and the brief experiment in freedom remembered as the "Prague Spring" came to a violent end. During the same year, student-led demonstrations erupted in Yugoslavia, Poland, West Germany, Italy, Spain, Japan, and Mexico.

It was against this backdrop of protest, violence, and civil unrest that Richard Nixon ran for president against the Democratic nominee Hubert H. Humphrey, who was Johnson's vice president, and the independent candidate, George C. Wallace, the segregationist governor of Alabama and a popular archconservative. To outflank Wallace on the right, Nixon appealed to disaffected Democrats as well as traditional Republicans. He declared himself the "law and order" candidate, a phrase that became a code for reining in black militancy. To win southern supporters, he pledged to ease up on enforcing federal civil rights legislation and opposed forced busing to achieve racial integration in schools. He criticized antiwar protesters and promised to end the Vietnam War with honor (without disclosing exactly how he would achieve this goal). Seeking to portray the Democrats as the party of social and cultural radicalism, Nixon geared his campaign message to the "silent majority" of voters—what one political analyst characterized as "the unyoung, the unpoor, and unblack."

Although Nixon won 301 electoral votes, 110 more than Humphrey, none of the three candidates received a majority of the popular vote (Map 27.1). Yet Nixon and Wallace together received about 57 percent of the popular vote, a dramatic shift to the right compared with Johnson's landslide victory just four years earlier. Nixon's election ushered in more than two decades of Republican presidential rule, interrupted only by scandal. The New Left, which had captured the imagination of many of America's young people, would give way to the **New Right**, an assortment of old and new conservatives, overwhelmingly white, who were determined to contain, if not roll back, the Great Society.

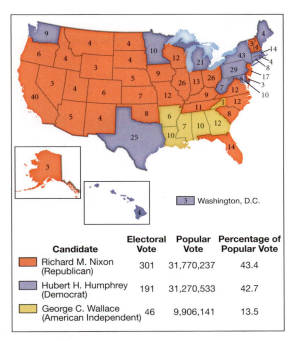

Candidate	Electoral Vote	Popular Vote	Percentage of Popular Vote
Richard M. Nixon (Republican)	301	31,770,237	43.4
Hubert H. Humphrey (Democrat)	191	31,270,533	42.7
George C. Wallace (American Independent)	46	9,906,141	13.5

MAP 27.1   The Election of 1968

Democratic presidential candidate Hubert Humphrey lost across the South as white voters turned to Republican Richard Nixon or segregationist George Wallace. Many working-class whites in the North and West also shifted their allegiance to these "law and order" candidates, rejecting the civil rights and antipoverty agendas promoted by President Johnson and blaming Democrats for the turmoil over the Vietnam War.

The Failure of Vietnamization

Vietnam plagued Nixon as it had his Democratic predecessor. Despite intimations during the campaign that he had a secret plan to end the war, Nixon's approach to Vietnam turned out to look much the same as Johnson's. Henry Kissinger, who served first as national security adviser and then as secretary of state, continued peace talks with the North Vietnamese, which had been initiated by Johnson. Over the next four years, Nixon and Kissinger devised a strategy that removed U.S. ground forces and turned over greater responsibility for the fighting to the South Vietnamese army, a process called **Vietnamization**.

Vietnamization did not, however, mean an end to U.S. belligerence in the region. In 1969, at the same time that American troop levels were being drawn down, the president ordered secret bombing raids in Cambodia, a neutral country adjacent to South Vietnam that contained enemy forces and parts of the Ho Chi Minh Trail. Meant to pressure the North Vietnamese into accepting U.S. peace terms, the bombing accomplished little in the mountainous jungle. In April 1970, Nixon ordered the invasion of Cambodia, which destabilized the country and eventually brought to power the Communist Khmer Rouge, who later slaughtered two million Cambodians. In 1971 the United States sponsored the South Vietnamese invasion of Laos, another neutral neighbor that harbored North Vietnamese troops and supply lines, which again yielded no battlefield gains. Finally, in December 1972, shortly before Christmas, the United States carried out a massive eleven-day bombing campaign of targets in North Vietnam meant to force the North Vietnamese government to come to a peace accord.

The intense bombing of North Vietnam did end formal U.S. involvement in the war. An agreement signed on January 27, 1973, stipulated that the United States would remove all American troops, the North Vietnamese would return captured U.S. soldiers, and North and South Vietnam would strive for peaceful national unification. Nixon and Kissinger could now claim that they had

The Fall of Saigon, 1975

On April 29, 1975, the day before Communist troops took control of Saigon, crowds of South Vietnamese, many of whom had supported the United States, scramble to climb the wall of the U.S. Embassy. They were making a desperate attempt to get to evacuation helicopters, but with space limited on available aircraft, many of these people were left behind. AP Photo/Neal Ulevich achieved "peace with honor," ending U.S. involvement in Vietnam without compromising America's credibility with its anti-Communist allies around the world. In fact, peace had not been achieved, and the United States had failed in its stated goal of preventing a Communist takeover of South Vietnam. The war in Vietnam continued, and in 1975 North Vietnamese and Vietcong forces captured Saigon, resulting in a Communist victory. This outcome came at a terrible cost. Some 58,000 American soldiers, 215,000 South Vietnamese soldiers, 1 million North Vietnamese and Vietcong soldiers, and an estimated 4 million South and North Vietnamese civilians were killed in the conflict.

The Nixon administration's war efforts generated great controversy at home. In 1969 the president eliminated most draft deferments and introduced an impartial lottery system. This procedure was more equitable, but it exposed a wider range of young men to the draft. More important, the invasion of Cambodia touched off widespread campus demonstrations in May 1970. At Kent State University in Ohio, four student protesters were shot and killed by the National Guard. Large crowds of antiwar demonstrators descended on Washington in 1969 and 1971, though the president refused to heed their message. Nevertheless, the American public, and not just radicals, had turned against the war. By 1972 more than 70 percent of those polled believed that the Vietnam War was a mistake, and 31 percent disapproved of Nixon's handling of it. Growing numbers of Vietnam veterans also spoke out against the war. Contributing to this disillusionment, in 1971 the *New York Times* and the *Washington Post* published a classified report known as the **Pentagon Papers**. This document, leaked by former Defense Department analyst Daniel Ellsberg, confirmed that the Kennedy and Johnson administrations had misled the public about the origins and nature of the Vietnam War. The Nixon administration tried, unsuccessfully, to block its publication. Congress reflected growing disapproval for the war by repealing the Gulf of Tonkin Resolution in 1970 after the Cambodian invasion. In 1973 Congress passed the **War Powers Act**, which required the president to consult with Congress within forty-eight hours of deploying military forces and to obtain a declaration of war from Congress if troops remained on foreign soil beyond sixty days. That same year, as the U.S. combat mission in Vietnam drew to a close, President Nixon disbanded the draft and created an all-volunteer military.

Cold War Realism and Détente

As Nixon maneuvered to end the Vietnam War, he embarked on a parallel effort to improve relations with his Cold War Communist enemies. Nixon had begun his political career as a fierce anti-Communist, but he also considered himself a realist in foreign affairs. He was concerned less about promoting abstract ideals of democracy than about fashioning a stable world order based on a balance of power. With this in mind, Nixon and Secretary of State Kissinger worked to establish closer relations with both the People's Republic of China and the Soviet Union, hoping each power could be persuaded to pressure the North Vietnamese to accept an American peace settlement and end the war quickly. In addition, with the Soviet Union and China competing for influence in Asia, Nixon sought to exploit this conflict to keep these nuclear powers divided.

Nixon and Kissinger's plans succeeded in many ways. Their efforts to use great-power diplomacy to pressure the North Vietnamese into concessions failed, but their greatest triumph came in easing tensions with the country's Cold War adversaries. Through secret maneuvering, Kissinger prepared the way for Nixon to make the bold move of visiting mainland China in 1972, the first president to do so since the Cold War began. The meeting set in motion a new relationship between the capitalist and Communist nations. After blocking the People's Republic of China's admission to the United Nations for twenty-two years, the United States announced that it would no longer oppose China's entry to the world organization. This cautious renewal of relations between the two countries benefited both. It opened up possibilities of American access to the huge China market, and for the Chinese it promised trade with the United States.

Shaken by the movement toward closer relations between China and the United States, Soviet premier Leonid Brezhnev invited President Nixon to Moscow in May 1972, the first time an American president had visited the Soviet Union since 1945. The main topic of discussion concerned arms control, and with the Soviet Union eager to make a deal in the aftermath of Nixon's trip to China, the two sides worked out the historic **Strategic Arms Limitation Treaty (SALT I)**, the first to curtail nuclear arms production during the Cold War. The pact restricted the number of antiballistic missiles that each nation could deploy and froze the number of intercontinental ballistic missiles and submarine-based missiles for five years, with each side agreeing to pursue nuclear "sufficiency" rather than "superiority."

Nixon's diplomatic initiatives failed to resolve festering problems in the Middle East, an area of strategic concern to both the United States and the Soviet Union. Since its victory in the Six-Day War of 1967, Israel had occupied territory once controlled by Egypt and Syria as well as the former Palestinian capital of East Jerusalem. On October 6, 1973, during the start of the Jewish High Holidays of Yom Kippur, Egyptian and Syrian troops, fortified with Soviet arms, caught the Israelis off guard and quickly managed to recapture territory lost in 1967. An Israeli counterattack, reinforced by a shipment of $2 billion of American weapons, repelled Arab forces, and the Israeli military stood ready to destroy the Egyptian army. To avoid a complete breakdown in the balance of power, the United States and the Soviet Union agreed to broker a cease-fire that left the situation the same as before the war.

U.S. involvement in the struggle between Israel and its Arab enemies exacerbated economic troubles at home. On October 17, 1973, in the midst of the Yom Kippur War, the Arab-dominated **Organization of Petroleum Exporting Countries (OPEC)** imposed an oil embargo on the United States as punishment for its support of Israel. As a result of the embargo, the price of oil skyrocketed, and reduced oil supplies produced long lines at the gas pumps. The effect of high oil prices rippled through the economy, leading to increased inflation and unemployment, which rose from 5 to 7 percent. The embargo also affected America's allies in Western Europe, which imported 80 percent of its oil supply from Arab states, compared with 12 percent for the United States. The crisis lasted until May 1974, when OPEC lifted its embargo following six months of diplomacy by Kissinger.

The United States preferred to support stability over democracy when its strategic or economic interests were at stake. Under Nixon's leadership, the United States supported repressive regimes in Nicaragua, South Africa, the Philippines, and Iran. In Chile, the United States overthrew the democratically elected socialist president Salvador Allende, who was murdered in a CIA-backed operation in 1973. The coup brought nearly two decades of dictatorial rule to that country.

Pragmatic Conservatism at Home

On the domestic front, Nixon had pledged during his 1968 campaign to "reverse the flow of power and resources from the states and communities to Washington" and redirect "power and resources" back to the American people, a key objective of conservatism. He kept his promise by dismantling Great Society social programs, cutting funds for the War on Poverty, and eliminating the Office of Economic Opportunity. In 1972 the president adopted a program of revenue sharing, which transferred federal tax revenues to the states to use as they wished. Hoping to rein in the liberal Warren Court, Nixon nominated conservative justices, such as William Rehnquist and Lewis Powell, to the Supreme Court.

However, in several areas Nixon departed from conservatives who favored limited government. In 1970 he persuaded Congress to pass the Environmental Protection Act, which strengthened federal oversight of environmental programs throughout the country. In 1972 the federal government increased its responsibility for protecting the health and safety of American workers through the creation of the Occupational Safety and Health Administration (OSHA). The Consumer Products Safety Commission was established to provide added safety for the buying public. The president also signed a law banning cigarette advertising on radio and television because of the link between smoking and cancer.

Nixon applied this pragmatic conservatism to racial issues. The president proposed legislation that prevented the use of busing to promote school desegregation, which the Democratic Congress rejected. In general, he supported "benign neglect" concerning the issue of race

Gas Shortages, 1973

A gas station owner in Perkasie, Pennsylvania, lets his customers know he is out of gas. OPEC's 1973 oil embargo during the Yom Kippur War caused gas shortages and soaring prices in the United States. Motorists scrambling to find available supplies at gas stations created long lines.   AP Photo and therefore rejected new legislative attempts to remove the vestiges of racial discrimination. In this way, Nixon courted southern conservatives in an attempt to deter George Wallace from mounting another third-party challenge in 1972. Still, Nixon moved back to the political center with efforts that furthered civil rights. Expanding **affirmative action** programs begun under the Johnson administration, he adopted plans that required construction companies and unions to recruit minority workers according to their percentage in the local labor force. His support of affirmative action was part of a broader approach to encourage "black capitalism," a concept designed to convince African Americans to seek opportunity within the free-enterprise system. Moreover, in 1970 Nixon signed the extension of the 1965 Voting Rights Act, thereby renewing the law that had provided suffrage to the majority of African Americans in the South. The law also lowered the voting age from twenty-one to eighteen for national elections. In 1971 the Twenty-sixth Amendment was ratified to lower the voting age for state and local elections as well.

The Nixon administration also veered away from the traditional Republican free market philosophy by resorting to wage and price controls to curb rising inflation brought on, for the most part, by increased military spending during the Vietnam War. In 1971 the president declared a ninety-day freeze on wages and prices, placed a temporary 10 percent surtax on imports, and let the value of the dollar drop on the international market, leading to increased U.S. exports. Taken together, these measures stabilized consumer prices, reduced unemployment, and boosted the gross national product. Although these proved to be only short-term gains, they improved Nixon's prospects for reelection.

The Nixon Landslide and Disgrace, 1972–1974

By appealing to voters across the political spectrum, Nixon won a monumental victory in 1972. The president invigorated the "silent majority" by demonizing his opponents and encouraging Vice President Spiro Agnew to aggressively pursue Nixon's strategy of polarization. Agnew called protesters "kooks" and "social misfits" and attacked the media and Nixon critics with heated rhetoric. As Nixon had hoped, George Wallace rejected a third-party bid and ran in the Democratic primaries. Wallace won impressive victories in North Carolina, Florida, Tennessee, Maryland, and Michigan, but his campaign ended after an assassination attempt left him paralyzed. With Wallace out of the race, the Democrats helped Nixon look more centrist by nominating George McGovern, a liberal antiwar senator from South Dakota, who ran a generally inept campaign.

The election marked the personal triumph of Richard Nixon. Winning in a landslide, he captured more than

60 percent of the popular vote and nearly all of the electoral votes. Democrats retained control of Congress but were trounced in their bid for the White House. However, Nixon would have little time to savor his victory, for within the next two years his conduct in the campaign would come back to destroy his presidency.

In the early hours of June 17, 1972, five men broke into Democratic Party headquarters in the Watergate apartment complex in Washington, D.C. What appeared initially as a routine robbery turned into the most infamous political scandal of the twentieth century. It was eventually revealed that the break-in had been authorized by the Committee for the Re-Election of the President in an attempt to steal documents from the Democrats.

Whether President Nixon knew about the break-in in advance and approved it remains in dispute, but he did authorize a cover-up of his administration's involvement. Nixon ordered his chief of staff, H. R. Haldeman, to get the CIA and FBI to back off from a thorough investigation of the incident by claiming that it would breach national security. To silence the burglars at their trials, the president promised them $400,000 and hinted at a presidential pardon after their conviction.

Nixon embarked on the cover-up to protect himself from revelations of his administration's other illegal activities. Several of the Watergate burglars belonged to a secret band of operatives known as "the plumbers," which had been formed in 1971 and authorized by the president. Their mission was to find and plug up unwelcome information leaks from government officials. On their first secret operation, the plumbers broke into the office of Daniel Ellsberg's psychiatrist to look for embarrassing personal information with which to discredit Ellsberg, who had leaked the *Pentagon Papers*. The president had other unsavory matters to hide. In an effort to contain leaks about the administration's secret bombing of Cambodia in 1969, the White House had illegally wiretapped its own officials and members of the press.

Watergate did not become a major scandal until after the election. The trial judge forced one of the burglars to reveal their backers. This revelation led two *Washington Post* reporters, Bob Woodward and Carl Bernstein, to doggedly investigate the link between the administration and the plumbers. With the help of Mark Felt, a top FBI official whose identity long remained secret and whom the reporters called "Deep Throat," Woodward and Bernstein succeeded in exposing the true nature of the crime. With the president still denying any knowledge of the offense, the Senate created a special committee in February 1973 to investigate the scandal. Televised hearings absorbed the public. White House counsel John Dean, whom Nixon had fired, testified about discussing the cover-up with the president and his

The New Right also benefited by the defection of disillusioned liberals. Labeled **neoconservatives**, intellectuals such as Irving Kristol, Norman Podhoretz, and Nathan Glazer reversed course and condemned the Great Society programs that they had originally supported. They believed that federal policies had aggravated rather than improved the problems government planners intended to solve. Of particular concern to many neoconservatives were affirmative action programs, the domination of campus debate and discourse by New Left radicals, and left-wing criticism of the use of American military and economic might to advance U.S. interests overseas.

Perhaps the greatest spark igniting the New Right came from socially conservative religious believers, mainly evangelical Christians and Catholics. Phyllis Schlafly—a Catholic, a former Goldwater supporter, and an ERA opponent—played a major role in connecting the political conservatism of the 1960s with the social conservatism of the following decade. Yet evangelical Christians most often provided the leadership and core support for this political movement. Evangelicals considered themselves to have been "born again"—literally experiencing Jesus Christ's saving presence inside of them. By the end of the 1970s, evangelical Christians numbered around 50 million, about a quarter of the population. The Christian Right opposed abortion, gay rights, and sex education; attacked Supreme Court rulings banning prayer in the public schools; denounced Darwin's theory of evolution in favor of divine creationism; and supported the traditional role of women as mothers and homemakers. Certainly not all evangelical Christians held all of these beliefs; for example, President Jimmy Carter, a born-again Christian, did not. Still, conservative Christians believed that the liberals and radicals of the 1960s had spread the secular creed of individual rights and personal fulfillment at the expense of traditional Christian values.

Social conservatives worried that the traditional nuclear family was in danger, as households consisting of married couples with children declined from 30 percent in the 1970s to 23 percent thirty years later, and the divorce rate soared. The number of unmarried couples living together doubled over the last quarter of the twentieth century, and the percentage of children born to single mothers jumped from 18 in 1980 to 40 in 2007. This increase was part of a trend in developed countries worldwide, and among these nations the United States ranked in the middle between Iceland at the top and Japan at the bottom.

Since the 1950s, Billy Graham, a charismatic Southern Baptist evangelist from North Carolina, had used television to conduct nationwide crusades that attracted millions of followers. Television became an even greater instrument in the hands of New Right Christian preachers in the 1970s and 1980s. The Reverend Pat Robertson of Virginia founded the Christian Broadcasting Network, and ministers such as

Jerry Falwell used the airwaves to great effect. What distinguished Falwell and Robertson from earlier evangelists like Graham was their fusion of religion and electoral politics. In 1979 Falwell founded the Moral Majority, an organization that backed political candidates who supported a "family values" social agenda. Within two years of its creation, the Moral Majority counted four million members who were eager to organize in support of New Right politicians. The alliance of economic, intellectual, and religious conservatives offered a formidable challenge to liberalism.

Explore

See Document 27.2 for a statement from Jerry Falwell.

The Triumph of Ronald Reagan

Ronald Reagan's presidential victory in 1980 consolidated the growing New Right coalition and reshaped American politics for a generation to come. The former movie actor had transformed himself from a New Deal Democrat into a conservative Republican politician when he ran for governor of California in 1966. As governor, he implemented conservative ideas of free enterprise and small government and denounced Johnson's Great Society for threatening private property and individual liberty. "Government," Reagan

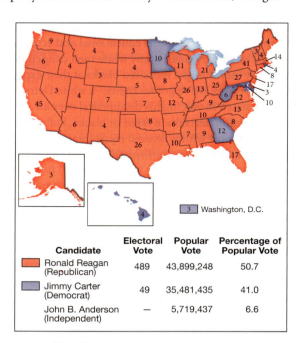

Candidate	Electoral Vote	Popular Vote	Percentage of Popular Vote
Ronald Reagan (Republican)	489	43,899,248	50.7
Jimmy Carter (Democrat)	49	35,481,435	41.0
John B. Anderson (Independent)	—	5,719,437	6.6

MAP 27.3 The Election of 1980

Ronald Reagan won 50.7 percent of the popular vote in the 1980 election, but his margin of victory over Jimmy Carter was much greater in the electoral vote. Reagan won the votes of the South and many disaffected Democrats in the urban North. A third-party candidate, John Anderson of Illinois, won 6.6 percent of the popular vote, demonstrating significant disapproval with both major parties.

DOCUMENT 27.2

Jerry Falwell | We Must Return to Traditional Religious Values, 1980

Socially conservative evangelical Christians opposed the feminist movement, abortion rights, gay rights, and other forces they believed contributed to the secularization of American society. Southern Baptist preacher Jerry Falwell was one of the Christian Right's most powerful leaders. He founded the Thomas Road Baptist Church and Liberty University, in Lynchburg, Virginia, as well as the Moral Majority political organization. The following selection illustrates Falwell's merging of religious beliefs with a conservative political agenda.

Explore

We must reverse the trend America finds herself in today. Young people between the ages of twenty-five and forty have been born and reared in a different world than Americans of years past. The television set has been their primary baby-sitter. From the television set they have learned situation ethics and immorality—they have learned a loss of respect for human life. They have learned to disrespect the family as God has established it. They have been educated in a public-school system that is permeated with secular humanism. They have been taught that the Bible is just another book of literature. They have been taught that there are no absolutes in our world today. They have been introduced to the drug culture. They have been reared by the family and by the public school in a society that is greatly void of discipline and character-building. These same young people have been reared under the influence of a government that has taught them socialism and welfarism. They

have been taught to believe that the world owes them a living whether they work or not. . . .

It is now time to take a stand on certain moral issues, and we can only stand if we have leaders. We must stand against the Equal Rights Amendment, the feminist revolution, and the homosexual revolution. We must have a revival in this country. . . .

As a preacher of the Gospel, I not only believe in prayer and preaching, I also believe in good citizenship. If a labor union in America has the right to organize and improve its working conditions, then I believe that the churches and the pastors, the priests, and the rabbis of America have a responsibility, not just the right, to see to it that the moral climate and conscience of Americans is such that this nation can be healed inwardly. If it is healed inwardly, then it will heal itself outwardly.

Source: Jerry Falwell, *Listen America!* (New York: Doubleday, 1980), 17–18.

Interpret the Evidence

- According to Falwell, what are the biggest problems facing American society?
- What solutions does Falwell propose?

Put It in Context

What contribution did Falwell make in expanding the base of the New Right?

observed, "is like a baby, an alimentary canal with a big appetite at one end and no sense of responsibility at the other." His winning combination of support for conservative economic and social issues carried him to the presidency.

Reagan triumphed over Jimmy Carter and John Anderson, a moderate Republican who ran as an independent candidate (Map 27.3). The high unemployment and inflation of the late 1970s worked in Reagan's favor. Reagan appealed to a coalition of conservative Republicans

and disaffected Democrats, promising to cut taxes and reduce spending, to relax federal supervision over civil rights programs, and to end what was left of expensive Great Society measures and affirmative action. Finally, he energized members of the religious right, who flocked to the polls to support Reagan's demands for voluntary prayer in the public schools, defeat of the Equal Rights Amendment, and a constitutional amendment to outlaw abortion.

DOCUMENTS 27.3 AND 27.4

Morning in America: Two Views

In the 1980s, as the nation reeled in the aftermath of Watergate and the Vietnam War as well as the more immediate crises of oil shortages and stagflation, Ronald Reagan promised voters that better times were coming. In his first inaugural address, Reagan reasserted his pledges to lower taxes, reduce the size of the federal government, and restore American pride. By 1984 Reagan and his supporters were ready to claim victory, seeing in the return of economic growth vindication of their ideas and optimism. New York governor Mario Cuomo's keynote address at the Democratic National Convention, however, portrays a very different picture.

Explore

27.3 Ronald Reagan | First Inaugural Address, January 20, 1981

The business of our nation goes forward. These United States are confronted with an economic affliction of great proportions. We suffer from the longest and one of the worst sustained inflations in our national history. It distorts our economic decisions, penalizes thrift, and crushes the struggling young and the fixed-income elderly alike. It threatens to shatter the lives of millions of our people.

Idle industries have cast workers into unemployment, human misery, and personal indignity. Those who do work are denied a fair return for their labor by a tax system which penalizes successful achievement and keeps us from maintaining full productivity. . . .

In this present crisis, government is not the solution to our problem; government is the problem. From time to time, we've been tempted to believe that society has become too complex to be managed by self-rule, that government by an elite group is superior to government for, by, and of the people.

Well, if no one among us is capable of governing himself, then who among us has the capacity to govern someone else? All of us together, in and out of government, must bear the burden. The solutions we seek must be equitable, with no one group singled out to pay a higher price. . . .

It is my intention to curb the size and influence of the Federal establishment and to demand recognition of the distinction between the powers granted to the Federal Government and those reserved to the States or to the people. All of us need to be reminded that the Federal Government did not create the States; the States created the Federal Government.

Now, so there will be no misunderstanding, it's not my intention to do away with government. It is rather to make it work—work with us, not over us; to stand by our side, not ride on our back. Government can and must provide opportunity, not smother it; foster productivity, not stifle it.

Source: Michael Waldman, ed., *My Fellow Americans: The Most Important Speeches of America's Presidents, from George Washington to George W. Bush* (Naperville, IL: Sourcebooks, 2003), 247–49.

AIDS was a plague visited on sexual deviants by an angry God. "The poor homosexuals," mocked Pat Buchanan, a Reagan adviser. "They have declared war on nature and now nature is exacting an awful retribution." As the epidemic spread beyond the gay community, mainly through blood transfusions and illegal intravenous drug use, gay rights organizers and their heterosexual allies raised research money and public awareness. By the early 1990s, medical advances had begun to extend the lives of AIDS patients and manage the disease.

Increased immigration also troubled social conservatives as another reflection of the general societal breakdown. The number of immigrants to the United States rose dramatically in the 1970s and 1980s following the relaxation of foreign quota restrictions after 1965 (Figure 27.1). During these decades, immigrants came mainly from

Explore

27.4 Mario Cuomo | Speech to the Democratic National Convention, July 16, 1984

Ten days ago, President Reagan admitted that although some people in this country seemed to be doing well nowadays, others were unhappy, and even worried, about themselves, their families, and their futures.

The president said he didn't understand that fear. He said, "Why, this country is a shining city on a hill."

The president is right. In many ways we *are* "a shining city on a hill."

But the hard truth is that not everyone is sharing in this city's splendor and glory.

A shining city is perhaps all the president sees from the portico of the White House and the veranda of his ranch, where everyone seems to be doing well.

But there's another part of the city, the part where some people can't pay their mortgages and most young people can't afford one, where students can't afford the education they need and middle-class parents watch the dreams they hold for their children evaporate.

In this part of the city there are more poor than ever, more families in trouble, more and more people who need help but can't find it.

Even worse: there are elderly people who tremble in the basements of the houses there.

There are people who sleep in the city's streets, in the gutter, where the glitter doesn't show. . . .

In fact, Mr. President, this nation is more a "Tale of Two Cities" than it is a "shining city on a hill."

Maybe if you visited more places, Mr. President, you'd understand.

Maybe if you went to Appalachia, where some people still live in sheds, and to Lackawanna, where thousands of unemployed steel workers wonder why we subsidized foreign steel while we surrender their dignity to unemployment and welfare checks. . . .

Maybe, Mr. President.

But I'm afraid not.

Because, the truth is, this is how we were warned it would be.

President Reagan told us from the very beginning that he believed in a kind of social Darwinism. Survival of the fittest. "Government can't do everything," we were told. "So it should settle for taking care of the strong and hope that economic ambition and charity will do the rest. Make the rich richer and what falls from their table will be enough for the middle class and those trying to make it into the middle class."

Source: Mario Cuomo, *More Than Words: The Speeches of Mario Cuomo* (New York: St. Martin's Press, 1993), 21–23.

Interpret the Evidence

- How do Reagan's and Cuomo's views of American society and the role of government differ?
- What are Cuomo's chief criticisms of Reagan?

Put It in Context

Why do you think Reagan's views triumphed politically over Cuomo's?

Mexico, Central America, the Caribbean, and eastern and southern Asia and tended to settle in California, Florida, Texas, New York, and New Jersey. Like those who came nearly a century before, most sought economic opportunity, political freedom, and escape from wars; and like their predecessors, they brought with them foreign languages, their native cultural practices, and poverty. By 1990 one-third of Los Angeles's and New York City's populations were foreign-born, figures similar to the high numbers of European immigrants at the turn of the twentieth century.

As happened during previous immigration waves, many Americans whose ancestors had immigrated to the United States generations earlier expressed hostility toward the new immigrants. The New Right provoked traditional fears that immigrants took away jobs and depressed wages, and

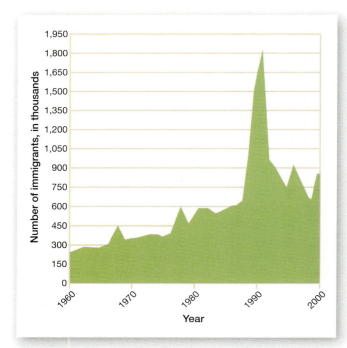

FIGURE 27.1   Immigrant Arrivals to the United States, 1960–2000

Following the relaxation of foreign quota restrictions after 1965, immigration to the United States rose dramatically in the 1970s and 1980s, peaking in the early 1990s. Between 1970 and 2000, nearly 21 million immigrants arrived in the United States, mainly from Mexico, Central America, the Caribbean, and eastern and southern Asia.   Source: Data from *2000 Statistical Yearbook of the Immigration and Naturalization Service.*

questioned whether these culturally diverse people could assimilate into American society. Cities and states, led by California, enacted laws making English their official language. The migration of illegal immigrants intensified the controversy. In 1985 the Reagan administration, with bipartisan congressional support, fashioned a compromise that extended amnesty to undocumented aliens residing in the United States for a specified period and allowed them to acquire legal status. At the same time, the act penalized employers who hired new illegal workers. The measure allowed Reagan and the Republicans to appeal to Latino voters in the Sun Belt states while convincing the New Right that the administration intended to halt further undocumented immigration.

The Presidency of George H. W. Bush

After Reagan left office, his two-term vice president, George H. W. Bush, carried on his legacy. The son of a former senator from Connecticut, Bush made a fortune in the Texas oil business and began his political career as a member of Congress in the mid-1960s. After losing the Republican nomination to Reagan in 1980, Bush joined the ticket as vice president. In doing so, he abandoned his moderate Republican political views and became a loyal follower of Reaganomics. In his 1988 presidential campaign against Michael Dukakis, the Democratic governor of Massachusetts, Bush defended conservative principles when he promised: "Read my lips: No new taxes." The Republican candidate attacked Dukakis for his liberal positions and accused him of being soft on crime. Bush also affirmed his own opposition to abortion and support for gun rights and the death penalty. At the same time, however, he also called for a "kinder, gentler nation" in dealing with social justice and the environment.

Once in office, George Bush had to deal with problems that he inherited from his predecessor. Reagan's economic programs and military spending had left the nation with a mounting federal budget deficit, which reached nearly $300 billion in 1992 and slowed economic growth, resulting in another recession in 1990. Unemployment reached 7 percent, and state and local governments had difficulty paying for the educational, health, and social services that the Reagan and Bush administrations had transferred to them. To reverse the downward spiral, Bush abandoned his "no new taxes" pledge. In 1990 he supported a deficit reduction package that included more than $130 billion in new taxes, which failed to solve the economic problems and angered Reagan conservatives who had never fully trusted Bush. He also departed from anti-Washington conservatives when he signed the Americans with Disabilities Act (1990), extending an assortment of protections to some 40 million Americans with physical and mental handicaps.

Bush had a mixed record on the environment. In 1989 he continued supporting oil drilling after the oil tanker *Exxon Valdez* struck a reef off the coast of Alaska, dumping nearly 11 million gallons of oil into Prince William Sound. By contrast, in 1990 the president signed the Clean Air Act, which reduced emissions from automobiles and power plants. Two years later, however, the president opposed international efforts to limit carbon dioxide emissions, greenhouse gases that contribute to climate change.

Bush also courted conservatives in his nomination of Clarence Thomas to fill the Supreme Court vacancy left by Justice Thurgood Marshall, the first African American justice. Thomas belonged to a rising group of conservative blacks who shared Republican views supporting private enterprise and the free market system and opposing affirmative action. As chief of the Equal Employment Opportunity Commission under Reagan, Thomas had generally weakened the agency's enforcement of racial and gender equality in the workplace. He also opposed abortion and denounced welfare. Anita Hill's charges of sexual harassment did not stop his advancement. Following his confirmation battle in 1991, Thomas became one of the most conservative members of the Court.

ACT UP Protest, 1989

Amid the AIDS epidemic in the gay community, the militant group ACT UP (AIDS Coalition to Unleash Power) campaigned for better funding of programs to fight the disease. In this 1989 photo, a protester falls to the ground as police break up a demonstration in New York City.   Chester Higgins Jr./The New York Times/Redux

Despite Bush's overtures to conservatives, his popularity plummeted to 34 percent in 1992 based largely on his inability to revive the sagging economy. He ran for reelection against Governor William Jefferson (Bill) Clinton of Arkansas, a candidate skilled in the art of political maneuvering. Learning from the mistakes of Michael Dukakis, Clinton ran as a centrist Democrat who promised to reduce the federal deficit by raising taxes on the wealthy and who supported conservative social policies such as the death penalty, tough measures against crime, and welfare reform. Though he did pledge to extend health care and opposed discrimination against homosexuals, Clinton relied on his mainstream southern Democratic credentials to deflect any claims that he was a liberal. Bush also faced a challenge from the independent candidate Ross Perot, a wealthy self-made businessman from Texas, whose campaign against rising government deficits won 19 percent of the popular vote, mostly at Bush's expense. In turn, Clinton defeated the incumbent by a two-to-one electoral margin.

REVIEW & RELATE

What was Reaganomics, and what were its most important long-term consequences?

How did conservative ideas shape the social, cultural, and political landscape of the 1980s and 1990s?

✓ *LEARNINGCurve* bedfordstmartins.com/hewittlawson/LC

Conclusion: The Conservative Legacy

The defeat of George Bush in 1992 did not signal the end of the conservative political consensus of the previous twenty years. The Nixon-Reagan-Bush era had succeeded in dismantling most of Lyndon Johnson's Great Society, and what it did not disassemble these Republican administrations starved by underfunding. President Reagan managed to reorient the political discourse in the country by turning liberalism into an outmoded idea and a pejorative label. The conservatism that Reagan had rallied behind in the unsuccessful Goldwater campaign of 1964 now provided the political instrument with which Republicans defeated Democrats. The Democratic presidential administration of Jimmy Carter acknowledged the conservative notions of limited government and a deregulated market economy while embracing key conservative social values, such as faith in God and prayer. Both Carter and Bill Clinton, who won in 1992, departed from conservatives on some key issues concerning the economy, race, and gender, but neither of them portrayed himself as the heir of the liberal ideals promoted by Franklin Roosevelt, Harry Truman, and Lyndon Johnson.

The movement toward conservatism had been slow and sporadic. Nixon's pragmatic course and his downfall following the Watergate scandal stalled the march toward greater conservatism, and indeed his expediency angered many conservatives to his political right. Reagan represented the triumph of the New Right and transformed the politics of resentment toward the excesses of the 1960s into the politics of revivalism, convincing many that traditional values once again might guide the nation. In constructing this winning coalition, Reagan tapped into the political awakening of the Christian Right, led by evangelicals and Catholics.

The conservative political ascendancy, however, did not stifle dissent. For much of the 1970s and 1980s, Democrats controlled Congress and tried to restrain conservative presidents. The Supreme Court shifted in a more conservative direction, but the Court did not reject the precedents established by the Warren Court. Conservative justices limited controversial decisions on affirmative action and abortion but did not overturn their constitutional foundations. Civil rights reformers, feminists, environmentalists, and antinuclear activists continued to press their concerns and achieve victories.

The New Right bestowed a mixed legacy. Although the Reagan administration reduced inflation and revived economic growth, it burdened the country with unsupportable budget deficits that damaged economic growth and international trade. Tax and spending cuts further enriched the wealthy but hurt the poor and the middle class. Fiscal and monetary policies encouraged widespread speculation on Wall Street and increased the power of giant corporations over political and economic life. Americans learned about the dangers to the environment, took some measures to correct them, but generally refused to alter their lifestyles. African Americans and women broke through barriers that denied them equal access to education and politics, but they confronted white male opposition to further progress.

Yet ordinary people of all backgrounds still made a difference. Allan Bakke was not a conservative ideologue, but his desire to go to medical school helped reshape affirmative action and stimulate a controversy that lasted far beyond his graduation from medical school. Anita Hill rode the conservative wave that brought Reagan to power. However, when she was subjected to sexual harassment, she broke ranks with conservatives and testified against the nomination of Clarence Thomas. Her assertions failed to derail his appointment to the Supreme Court, but her testimony encouraged more women to challenge sexual harassment.

Conservative successes on the home front did not take place in a vacuum. The rise of conservatism coincided with political shifts taking place in the United Kingdom and West Germany. Moreover, conservatives came to power amid major changes occurring in foreign affairs, most notably the proliferation and then the cessation of the Cold War.

Chapter Review

Online Study Guide ▶ bedfordstmartins.com/hewittlawson

KEY TERMS

New Right (p. 861)
Vietnamization (p. 862)
Pentagon Papers (p. 863)
War Powers Act (p. 863)
Strategic Arms Limitation Treaty (SALT I) (p. 863)
Organization of Petroleum Exporting Countries
    (OPEC) (p. 864)
affirmative action (p. 865)
Watergate (p. 865)
Equal Rights Amendment (ERA) (p. 869)
Environmental Protection Agency (EPA) (p. 871)
neoconservatives (p. 874)
Reaganomics (p. 876)
acquired immune deficiency syndrome (AIDS) (p. 877)

REVIEW & RELATE

1. Who made up the New Right coalition that brought Nixon to power? How did Nixon appeal to the New Right?

2. How did Nixon's pragmatism shape both his foreign and domestic policies?

3. What issues and trends shaped the presidency of Jimmy Carter?

4. How and why did the social and cultural developments of the 1960s continue to create conflict and controversy in the 1970s?

5. What was Reaganomics, and what were its most important long-term consequences?

6. How did conservative ideas shape the social, cultural, and political landscape of the 1980s and 1990s?

TIMELINE OF EVENTS

1970	Nixon orders invasion of Cambodia
	Four students shot by National Guardsmen at Kent State University
	Congress repeals Gulf of Tonkin Resolution
1971	Environmental Protection Agency (EPA) created
	New York Times and *Washington Post* publish the *Pentagon Papers*
1972	Nixon visits China
	U.S. and Soviet Union sign the Strategic Arms Limitation Treaty (SALT I)
	Watergate break-in
1973	Endangered Species Act passed
	Congress passes the War Powers Act
	U.S. supports Israel in Yom Kippur War
	U.S. agrees to withdraw from Vietnam
1973–1974	OPEC oil embargo against the United States creates gas shortages
1974	Nixon resigns
1975	North Vietnam defeats South Vietnam
1977	Department of Energy created
1978	Proposition 13 passed in California
	Allan Bakke wins his affirmative action case
1979	Divorce rate peaks at 23 divorces per 1,000 married couples
	Moral Majority founded
	Three Mile Island nuclear accident
1981	Reagan fires striking air traffic controllers
	Reagan survives assassination attempt
1982	Ratification period expires for Equal Rights Amendment
1991	Senate confirmation hearing for Clarence Thomas

AP Photo/Ira Schwartz

© Owen Franken/CORBIS

President Ronald Reagan greets a baby held by Soviet leader Mikhail Gorbachev during a visit to Moscow, 1988.

A worker tests a camera at a joint Chinese-German plant in Qingdao, China, 1985.

28
Ending the Cold War
1977–1991

Boston Globe via Getty Images

A boy waves to soldiers on the Berlin Wall, 1989.

AMERICAN HISTORIES

As secretary of state, George Pratt Shultz presided over the end of the Cold War. A skilled mediator, Shultz believed in the brand of hard-nosed diplomacy practiced by Henry Kissinger during the Nixon administration, asserting that "negotiations are a euphemism for capitulation if the shadow of power is not cast across the bargaining table." After graduating from Princeton with an economics degree in 1942, the twenty-two-year-old Shultz joined the Marine Corps and served in the Pacific during World War II. Three years later, Captain Shultz returned home, got married, and earned a Ph.D. in industrial economics. Shultz taught at the Massachusetts Institute of Technology and the University of Chicago and published several books on labor and wage issues. In 1955 he joined President Eisenhower's Council of Economic Advisors, the first of many government posts he would fill.

Known for his judicious temperament and bipartisanship, Shultz, a Republican, served under Democratic presidents John F. Kennedy and Lyndon B. Johnson, as well as Republican president Richard Nixon, who appointed him secretary of labor. With Nixon's resignation in 1974, Shultz left government for the corporate world.

In 1982 Shultz returned to Washington to serve as President Ronald Reagan's secretary of state. Like Reagan, Shultz believed that the United States needed to reassert itself as a global power and rebound from the insecurity and self-doubt that followed the Vietnam War. The president believed that a tough approach would bring peace, and he revived the fiery rhetoric and military preparedness of the darkest days of the Cold War. As a seasoned economist, Shultz doubted that the Soviet Union was financially able to sustain its military strength, and his predictions proved correct. Faced with an escalating arms race, a fresh group of Soviet leaders decided to pursue peaceful relations, a decision that had great repercussions for the internal structure of the Soviet Union and the nations subject to its control.

While President Reagan and Secretary of State Shultz advocated confrontation with the Soviet Union, Barbara Deming challenged their efforts and devoted her life to promoting peace in a far different manner. She was born in 1917, three years earlier than Shultz, to a middle-class family living in New York City. Deming attended Quaker schools before graduating from Bennington College with a degree in theater and literature. She became an outspoken proponent of nuclear disarmament, feminism, civil rights, and pacifism. Her radical political beliefs and her recognition that she was a lesbian at the age of sixteen placed her outside the social and cultural mainstream. She lived in a women's commune and mobilized heterosexual and gay women to demonstrate for peaceful coexistence with the Soviet Union.

In the 1980s, Deming applied her nonviolent, pacifist beliefs against Reagan and Shultz's muscular approach to fighting the Cold War. "We can put *more* pressure on the antagonist for whom we show human concern," Deming argued. As part of a worldwide campaign against the deployment of nuclear weapons, she joined the Women's Encampment for a Future of Peace and Justice, which opened in western New York in 1983 next to an army depot that stored nuclear missiles. On July 30, 1983, Deming led a march of seventy-five women from the camp into the small town of Waterloo. "Four miles into our walk," she recalled, "our way was blocked by several hundred townspeople brandishing American flags and chanting, 'Commies, go home!'" The marchers then sat down in the style of nonviolent protest and engaged their opponents in dialogue to no avail, as the police arrested Deming and fifty-three other protesters. Demonstrations continued throughout the rest of the summer, inspiring protests in other American communities and throughout Europe. •

THE AMERICAN HISTORIES of George Shultz and Barbara Deming were shaped in profound ways by decades of conflict between the United States and the Soviet Union. Both Shultz and Deming believed that the conflict was one of the defining issues of their times, and both were convinced that their approach was the best way to achieve lasting global peace.

The Cold War that Shultz and Deming were dedicated to ending underwent significant changes in the decades following the Nixon administration's reduction of tensions with the Soviet Union. In the late 1970s, President Jimmy Carter emphasized the moralistic diplomacy of human rights, but by the end of his term he had increased the size of the U.S. military in response to Soviet aggression in Afghanistan. His successor, Ronald Reagan, employed harsher rhetoric and accelerated the military buildup begun under Carter. However, Reagan would have been far less successful had it not been for the willingness of Soviet leader Mikhail Gorbachev to join him in ending the Cold War. With the ultimate collapse of the Soviet Union and its empire, the United States became the world's sole superpower. At the same time, the United States had to operate in an increasingly globalized world. Embracing new challenges, the United States tested its strength in Central America, the Middle East, and the Persian Gulf.

Carter's Diplomacy, 1977–1980

Drawing on the foreign policies of Gerald Ford and Richard Nixon, President Jimmy Carter sought to negotiate with the Soviets over arms reduction while at the same time challenging them to do more to protect human rights. In practice, Carter found this balancing act difficult to sustain, and despite his desire to find ways to cooperate with the Soviets, relations between the superpowers deteriorated over the course of his term in office. Trouble in the Persian Gulf also added to the Carter administration's woes.

The Perils of Détente

Carter made human rights a cornerstone of his foreign policy, and he was vocal in his criticism of the Soviet Union for violating the human rights requirements of the Helsinki accords that President Ford and Soviet leader Leonid Brezhnev had signed in 1975. His emphasis on human rights extended to other regimes as well. Unlike previous presidents who had supported dictatorial governments as long as they were anti-Communist, Carter intended to hold such regimes to a higher moral standard. Thus the Carter administration cut off military and economic aid to repressive regimes in Argentina, Uruguay, and Ethiopia. Still, Carter was not entirely consistent in his application of moral standards to diplomacy. Important U.S. allies around the world such as

the Philippines, South Korea, and South Africa were hardly models of democracy, but national security concerns kept the president from severing ties with them.

One way that Carter tried to set an example of responsible moral leadership was by signing an agreement to return control of the Panama Canal Zone to Panama at the end of 1999. The treaty that President Theodore Roosevelt negotiated in 1903 gave the United States control over this ten-mile piece of Panamanian land forever (see chapter 20). Panamanians resented this affront to their sovereignty, and Carter considered the occupation as a vestige of colonialism. Conservative critics viewed the transfer of land as a sign of weakness, but after extended debate the Senate ratified the treaty to relinquish the canal.

The president's pursuit of **détente**, or the easing of tensions, with the Soviet Union was less successful. In 1978 the Carter administration extended full diplomatic recognition to the People's Republic of China. Abandoning the United States' traditional ally of Taiwan, Carter sought to drive a greater wedge between China and the Soviet Union. Nevertheless, Carter did not give up on cooperation with the Soviets. In June 1979, Carter and Brezhnev signed **SALT II**, a new strategic arms limitation treaty. Six months later, however, the Soviet Union invaded Afghanistan to bolster its pro-Communist Afghan regime. President Carter viewed this action as a violation of international law and a threat to Middle East oil supplies and persuaded the Senate to drop consideration of SALT II. To counter Soviet aggression in Afghanistan, Carter obtained from Congress

Afghan Mujahideen, January 1980

On December 25, 1979, Soviet troops invaded Afghanistan in order to suppress mujahideen guerrillas who were trying to overthrow the nation's secular, pro-Soviet regime. These rebel forces were among the guerrillas who defeated the Soviets after a decade of warfare and eventually established an Islamic theocracy. © Pascal Manoukian/Sygma/Corbis a 5 percent increase in military spending. The Carter administration also reduced grain sales to the USSR and led a boycott of the 1980 Olympic Games in Moscow to punish the Soviet Union for its invasion of Afghanistan.

Of perhaps the greatest long-term importance was President Carter's decision to authorize the CIA to provide covert military and economic assistance to Afghan rebels resisting the Soviet invasion. Chief among these groups were the *mujahideen*, or warriors who wage jihad. Although portrayed as freedom fighters, these Islamic fundamentalists (including a group known as the Taliban) did not support democracy in the Western sense, and many of them were dedicated to creating a theocratic Islamic nation in Afghanistan. Among the mujahideen who received assistance from the United States was Osama bin Laden, a Saudi Arabian Islamic fundamentalist.

In ordering these CIA operations, Carter ignored recent revelations about questionable intelligence practices. Responding to presidential excesses stemming from the Vietnam War and the Watergate scandal, the Senate had held hearings in 1975 into clandestine CIA and FBI activities at home and abroad. Led by Frank Church of Idaho, the Senate Select Committee to Study Governmental Operations with Respect to Intelligence Activities (known as the Church Committee) issued reports revealing that both intelligence agencies had illegally spied on Americans and that the CIA had fomented revolution abroad, contrary to the provisions of its charter. Despite the Church Committee's findings, Carter revived some of these murky practices to combat the Soviets in Afghanistan.

Challenges in the Middle East

Before President Carter attempted to restrain the Soviet Union in Afghanistan, he did have some notable diplomatic successes. Five years after the 1973 Yom Kippur War (see chapter 27), with relations between Israel and its Arab neighbors in a deadlock, Carter invited the leaders of Israel and Egypt to the United States. Following two weeks of discussions in September 1978 at the presidential retreat at Camp David, Maryland, Israeli prime minister Menachem Begin and Egyptian president Anwar Sadat reached an agreement on a "framework for peace." For the first time in its history, Egypt would extend diplomatic recognition to Israel in exchange for Israel's agreement to return the Sinai peninsula to Egypt, which Israel had captured and occupied since 1967. Carter facilitated Sadat's acceptance of the **Camp David accords** by promising to extend foreign aid to Egypt. The treaty, however, left unresolved controversial issues between Israelis and Arabs concerning the establishment of a Palestinian state and control of Jerusalem.

Whatever success Carter had in promoting peace in the Middle East suffered a serious setback in the Persian Gulf nation of Iran. In 1953 the CIA helped overthrow Iran's democratically elected president, replacing him with a monarch and staunch ally, Mohammad Reza Pahlavi, the shah of Iran. For more than two decades, the shah ruled Iran with U.S. support, seeking to construct a modern, secular state allied with the United States. In doing so, he used repressive measures against Islamic fundamentalists, deploying his secret police to imprison, torture, and exile dissenters. The shah's lavish lifestyle stood in contrast to the poverty of most Iranians, and in 1979 revolutionary forces headed by Ayatollah Ruholla Khomeini, an Islamic fundamentalist exiled by the shah, overthrew his government. Khomeini intended to end the growing secularism in Iran and reshape the nation according to strict Islamic law.

When the deposed shah needed treatment for terminal cancer, President Carter invited him to the United States for medical assistance as a humanitarian gesture, despite warnings from the Khomeini government that it would consider this invitation a hostile action. On November 4, 1979, the ayatollah ordered fundamentalist Muslim students to seize the U.S. Embassy in Tehran and hold its fifty-two occupants hostage until the United States returned the shah to Iran to stand trial. Rather than submit to this violation of international law, President Carter retaliated by freezing all Iranian assets in American banks, breaking off diplomatic relations, and imposing a trade embargo. Carter's response did nothing to free the hostages, and the cutoff of Iranian oil shipments contributed to a 130 percent increase in the price of gasoline in the United States. For most Americans, the oil embargo meant shortages and high gas prices. In response, Khomeini incited Iranian nationalism by denouncing the United States as "the Great Satan." As the impasse dragged on and with the presidential election of 1980 fast approaching, Carter became desperate. After a failed U.S. rescue attempt, Khomeini's guards separated the hostages, making any more rescue efforts impossible. Further humiliating the president, Khomeini released the hostages on January 20, 1981, the inauguration day of Carter's successor, Ronald Reagan.

> **Explore**
>
> See Document 28.1 to read about one hostage's experience.

Despite good intentions and some notable achievements, Jimmy Carter left office with many of his foreign policy objectives unfulfilled. His administration was inconsistent in its approach to the Soviet Union, with attempts at improving relations, as evidenced in the SALT II talks, undermined by moral outrage at the Soviets for invading Afghanistan. The Camp David accords marked a high point of Carter's diplomatic efforts; however, his policies satisfied neither liberals nor conservatives in the

DOCUMENT 28.1

Robert Ode | Iran Hostage Diary, 1979–1980

In November 1979, Iranian students stormed the U.S. Embassy in Tehran and held fifty-two Americans hostage for 444 days. Their demands included the surrender of the recently deposed shah, who was in the United States for medical care. At the time of his capture, American hostage Robert Ode was a retired diplomat who was on special assignment in Tehran. He was released in January 1981 along with the other hostages. While he was in captivity, Ode kept a diary, which included the following entries.

Explore

November 4, 1979
We were taken back to the Compound, being pushed and hurried along the way and forced to put our hands above our heads and then marched to the Embassy residence. After arriving at the residence I had my hands tied behind my back so tightly with nylon cord that circulation was cut off. I was taken upstairs and put alone in a rear bedroom and after a short time was blindfolded. After protesting strongly that the cord was too tight the cord was removed and the blindfold taken off when they tried to feed me some dates and I refused to eat anything I couldn't see. I strongly protested the violation of my diplomatic immunity, but these protests were ignored. I then was required to sit in a chair facing the bedroom wall. Then another older student came in and when I again protested the violation of my diplomatic immunity he confiscated my U.S. Mission Tehran I.D. card. My hands were again tied and I was taken to the Embassy living room on the ground floor where a number of other hostages were gathered. Some students attempted to talk with us, stating how they didn't hate Americans—only our U.S. Government, President Carter, etc. We were given sandwiches and that night I slept on the living room floor. We were not permitted to talk to our fellow hostages and from then on our hands were tied day and night and only removed while we were eating or had to go to the bathroom. . . .

April 28, 1980
Nothing special has happened since my being moved to the new (less desirable room) except that I forgot to mention that about a week or 10 days ago we had hasps [metal fasteners] applied to the doors of our room and are now padlocked in the room as an extra security precaution! So with the bars on our windows and our doors being padlocked, it is more like a prison than ever!

[*A year later, the hostages were still in captivity.*]
October 21, 1980 (353rd Day!!!!)
Still no more mail today. Thirty-three days with only one letter from my wife and only 10 others from other family members, friends, and strangers. Every day is exactly the same as the one before and the one after. Mohsen came in Monday, October 20 and said we could take showers. However, I have decided not to go through the hassle anymore of being blindfolded, put into a car, stumbling around, and then have to shower in a filthy bathroom used by countless student-terrorists. I am just going to make my daily sponge baths do even though it is cold water.

Source: Robert Ode, "Iran Hostage's Diary," 1979–1980, Jimmy Carter Library, http://www.jimmycarterlibrary.gov/documents/r_ode/index.phtml.

Interpret the Evidence

- How does Ode react when he is initially taken hostage? How does he describe the Iranian students?
- Based on this entry, do you think that Ode grew resigned to his captivity over time? Why or why not?

Put It in Context

How did the hostage crisis expose the weakness in the United States' ability to defend its interests throughout the world?

United States, and the Iran fiasco helped ensure Carter's defeat in 1980 (see chapter 27).

REVIEW & RELATE

How did Carter's foreign policy differ from that of Ford and Nixon?

How did events in Afghanistan and Iran undermine the Carter administration?

LEARNINGCurve bedfordstmartins.com/hewittlawson/LC

Reagan's Cold War Policy, 1981–1988

Ronald Reagan entered the White House determined to offer a direct challenge to the Soviets. Reagan and Secretary of State George Shultz believed that détente would become feasible only after the United States achieved military supremacy over the Soviet Union. Reagan also took strong measures to fight communism around the globe, from Central America to the Middle East. Yet military superiority alone would not defeat the Soviet Union. A shift of leadership within the USSR, as well as a worldwide protest movement for nuclear disarmament, involving people like Barbara Deming, helped bring an end to the Cold War and prepare the way for the dissolution of the Soviet empire.

"The Evil Empire"

In running for president in 1980, Reagan wrapped his hard-line anti-Communist message in the rhetoric of peace. "I've called for whatever it takes to be so strong that no other nation will dare violate the peace," he told the Veterans of Foreign Wars Convention on August 18, 1980. Still, he made it clear that he did not intend to pursue peace at any price; it "must not be a peace of humiliation and gradual surrender." Once in the White House, Reagan left no doubt about his anti-Communist stance. He called the Soviet Union "the evil empire," regarding it as "the focus of evil in the modern world." The president planned to confront that evil with both words and deeds, backing up his rhetoric with a massive military buildup.

In a show of moral and economic might, Reagan proposed the largest military budget in American history. Under the Reagan administration, the defense budget grew about 7 percent per year, increasing from $157 billion in 1981 to around $282 billion in 1988. Reagan clearly intended to win the Cold War by outspending the Soviets, even if it meant running up huge deficits that greatly burdened the U.S. economy (see chapter 27).

The president sought to expand the Cold War by developing new weapons to be deployed in outer space. He proposed a Strategic Defense Initiative (SDI), or "Star Wars," as it was dubbed, to create an orbiting shield of antiballistic missiles, which even Secretary of State Shultz privately called "lunacy." Seeming more like a page out of science fiction, the SDI was never carried out, though the government spent $17 billion on research.

Reagan was unyielding in his initial dealings with the Soviet Union, and negotiations between the superpowers moved slowly and unevenly. The Reagan administration's initial "zero option" proposal called for the Soviets to dismantle all of their intermediate-range missiles in exchange for the United States agreeing to refrain from deploying any new medium-range missiles. The administration presented this option merely for show, expecting the Soviets to reject it. However, in 1982, after the Soviets accepted the principle of "zero option," Reagan sent negotiators to begin Strategic Arms Reduction Talks (START). Influenced by antinuclear protests in Europe, which had a great impact on European governments, the Americans proposed shelving the deployment of 572 Pershing II and cruise missiles in Europe in return for the Soviets' dismantling of Eastern European–based intermediate-range ballistic missiles that were targeted at Western Europe. The Soviets viewed this offer as perpetuating American nuclear superiority and rejected it.

Relations between the two superpowers deteriorated in September 1983 when a Soviet fighter jet shot down a South Korean passenger airliner, killing 269 people. The Soviets charged that the plane had veered off course and violated their airspace on a trip from Anchorage, Alaska, to Seoul, South Korea. Although the disaster resulted mainly from Soviet mistakes, Reagan chose to condemn this attack as further proof of the malign intentions of the USSR, and country singer Lee Greenwood wrote the patriotic song "God Bless the USA" in support of the country and of Reagan. The United States sent additional missiles to bases in West Germany, Great Britain, and Italy; in response, the Soviets abandoned the disarmament talks and replenished their nuclear arsenal in Czechoslovakia and East Germany. More symbolically, the Soviets boycotted the 1984 Olympic Games in Los Angeles, in retaliation for the U.S. boycott of the Olympics in Moscow four years earlier. As the two adversaries swung from peace talks to threats of nuclear confrontation, one European journalist observed: "The second Cold War has begun."

Human Rights and the Fight against Communism

The Reagan administration extended its firm Cold War position throughout the world, emphasizing anticommunism often at the expense of human rights. The president saw threats of Soviet intervention in Central America and the Middle East, and he aimed to contain them. As had former presidents John Kennedy, Lyndon Johnson, and Richard Nixon, Reagan exploited the fear of communism in Central America and the Caribbean, where for nearly a century the United States had guarded its sphere of influence. During the 1980s, the United States continued its economic isolation of Cuba via the trade embargo, and it sought to prevent other Communist or leftist governments from emerging in Central America and the Caribbean. In doing so, the Reagan administration interfered in the internal affairs of small nations struggling to lift themselves from the poverty caused by decades of oppressive rule that had benefited private companies and commercial interests in the United States.

In the late 1970s, Nicaraguan revolutionaries, known as the National Liberation Front or Sandinistas, had overthrown the tyrannical government of General Anastasio Somoza, a brutal dictator who had suppressed dissent and tortured opponents. President Jimmy Carter, who had originally supported Somoza's overthrow, halted all aid to Nicaragua in 1980 after the Sandinistas began nationalizing foreign companies and drawing closer to Cuba. In the early years of the Reagan administration, Secretary of State Shultz suggested a U.S. invasion of Nicaragua, reflecting the administration's belief that the Sandinistas were "Soviet proxies" and that the revolution in Nicaragua had been sponsored by Moscow. Rather than invade, Reagan adopted a more indirect but no less violent approach. In 1982 he authorized the CIA to train approximately two thousand guerrilla forces outside the country, known as Contras (Counterrevolutionaries), to overthrow the Sandinista government. Although Reagan praised the Contras as "the moral equivalent of our Founding Fathers," the group consisted of pro-Somoza reactionaries as well as anti-Marxist democrats who blew up bridges and oil dumps, burned crops, and killed civilians. In 1982 Congress, unwilling to support such actions, passed the **Boland Amendment**, which prohibited direct aid to the Contras, thereby limiting the president's ability to aid the anti-Sandinista forces.

Proponents of the Boland Amendment drew on the lessons of the Vietnam War. Recalling that President Johnson had manipulated Congress and the public to support intervention in a civil war conducted by guerrillas, supporters of the amendment sought to prevent Reagan from producing another disaster of this kind. Members of the Reagan administration viewed Vietnam differently. They believed that the United States had to restore its honor and credibility following the defeat in Vietnam, especially in fighting Communists in its own backyard. In the face of congressional opposition, Reagan and his advisers came up with a plan that would secretly fund the efforts of their military surrogates in Nicaragua.

Elsewhere in Central America, the Reagan administration supported a corrupt right-wing government in El Salvador that, in an effort to put down an insurgency,

sanctioned military death squads and killed forty thousand people during the 1980s. Despite the failings and abuses of the El Salvadoran government, Reagan insisted that Communist regimes in Nicaragua and Cuba were behind the Salvadoran insurgents. The United States sent more than $5 billion in aid to El Salvador and trained its military leaders to combat guerrilla forces.

While many Americans supported Reagan's strong anti-Communist stance, others opposed to the president's policy mobilized protests. Marches, rallies, and teach-ins were organized in cities and college campuses nationwide. U.S.-sponsored wars also drove many people to flee their danger-ous, poverty-stricken countries and seek asylum in the United States. Between 1984 and 1990, 45,000 Salvadorans and 9,500 Guatemalans applied for asylum in the United States, but because the United States supported the established govern-ments in those two nations, nearly all requests for refugee status were denied. Approximately five hundred American churches and synagogues established a sanctuary movement to provide safe haven for those fleeing Central American civil wars. Other Americans, especially in California and Texas, began to view the influx of refugees from Central America with alarm. This immigration, both legal and illegal, meant an increase in medical and educational costs for state and local communities, which taxpayers considered a burden.

In addition to financing secret wars in Central America, on October 25, 1983, Reagan sent 7,000 marines to invade the tiny 133-square-mile Caribbean island of Grenada. After a coup toppled the leftist government of Maurice Bishop, who had received Cuban and Soviet aid, the United States stepped in, ostensibly to protect American medical school students in Grenada from political instability following the coup. A swift victory in Grenada boosted Reagan's popular-ity and installed a pro-American government.

In Reagan's worldview, securing human rights was less important than fighting communism. Thus Reagan sup-ported repressive governments in the Middle East, Asia, Latin America, and Africa without reservations. Reagan embraced the distinction made by his ambassador to the United Nations, Jeane Kirkpatrick, between non-Communist "authoritarian" nations, which were acceptable, and Commu-nist "totalitarian" regimes, which were not. The difference remained fuzzy in practice, particularly in South Africa, where a white totalitarian government ruled over the black majority. Reagan considered the South African government an example of an acceptable authoritarianism, even though it practiced apartheid (white supremacy and racial separation) and torture. The fact that the South African Communist Party had joined the fight against apartheid reinforced Reagan's desire to support the white-minority, anti-Communist government. Interested in the country's vast mineral wealth, Reagan opted for what he called "constructive engagement"

Antiapartheid Protest, Cornell University

In 1986 students on college campuses such as Cornell protested apartheid in South Africa. They constructed shantytowns to highlight the poverty of nonwhite South Africans. Their immediate goal was to persuade their universities to remove their investments in companies that did business in South Africa.   David Lyons

with South Africa, meaning that the United States would maintain and expand trade with a nation whose government had been condemned by the United Nations for its racist practices. The Reagan administration did so even as protesters across the United States and the world spoke out against South Africa's repressive white-minority government and campaigned for divestment of public and corporate funds from South African companies.

As early as 1977, the Reverend Louis Sullivan, an African American clergyman from Philadelphia and a board member of General Motors, convinced the company, the largest employer of blacks in South Africa, to treat its employees equally and in a nonsegregated manner. Supporters of this approach campaigned to persuade other companies doing business in South Africa to adopt what became known as the Sullivan Principles and to get investment funds to withdraw their portfolios from the apartheid nation. In the mid-1980s, students on U.S. college campuses nationwide joined the **divestment movement** by building "shantytowns" to protest the squalid, segregated living conditions of black South Africans. They also conducted demonstrations to demand that universities remove investments in South Africa from their endowment funds. Antiapartheid forces staged similar protests against municipal and state governments. At the same time, numerous African American officials and their allies conducted sit-ins at the South African Embassy in Washington, D.C. These efforts were largely successful. Between 1984 and 1988, the number of colleges and universities divesting either partially or fully from South Africa tripled from 53 to 155. In 1986 Congress passed the Comprehensive

Anti-Apartheid Act, which prohibited new trade and investment in South Africa. President Reagan vetoed it, but in testimony to the strength of this popular grassroots movement, Congress overrode the president's veto.

Fighting International Terrorism

Two days before the Grenada invasion in 1983, the U.S. military suffered a grievous blow halfway around the world. In the tiny country of Lebanon, wedged between Syrian occupation on its northern border and the Palestine Liberation Organization's (PLO) fight against Israel to the south, a civil war raged between Christians and Muslims. Reagan believed that stability in the region was in America's national interest. With this in mind, in 1982 the Reagan administration sent 800 marines, as part of a multilateral force that included French and Italian troops, to keep the peace, but fighting continued in Beirut between Christian and Muslim militias. On October 23, 1983, a suicide bomber drove a truck into a marine barracks, killing 241 soldiers. Reagan withdrew the remaining troops.

The removal of troops did not end threats to Americans in the Middle East. Terrorism had become an ever-present danger, especially since the Iranian hostage crisis in 1979–1980. In 1985, 17 American citizens were killed in terrorist assaults, and 154 were injured. In June 1985, Shi'ite Muslim extremists hijacked a TWA airliner in Athens with 39 Americans on board and flew it to Beirut. The Israeli government acceded to the hijackers' demands to release Shi'ite prisoners in its jails, and the crisis ended safely for the hostages. That same year, PLO members hijacked an

Bombing of Marine Barracks, Lebanon, 1983

On October 23, 1983, an Islamic terrorist group ignited two truck bombs that blasted U.S. marine barracks in Beirut, killing 241. Here rescuers search for survivors in the wreckage of the U.S. marine command. The troops were part of a multilateral peacekeeping force during the Lebanese civil war. President Reagan removed American forces after the bombings.   AP Photo/Zouki

Italian cruise ship in the Mediterranean. Before the dangerous situation was resolved, an elderly American man in a wheelchair was killed and his body dumped in the sea.

In response, the Reagan administration targeted the North African country of Libya for retaliation. Its military leader, Muammar al-Qaddafi, supported the Palestinian cause and provided sanctuary for terrorists. In 1981 a squadron of Libyan planes attacked a U.S. naval flotilla conducting maneuvers off Libyan shores, and American pilots shot down two enemy planes. The Reagan administration placed a trade embargo on Libya, and Secretary of State Shultz remarked: "We have to put Qaddafi in a box and close the lid." In 1986, after the bombing of a nightclub in West Berlin killed 2 American servicemen and injured 230, Reagan charged that Qaddafi was responsible. In late April, the United States retaliated by sending planes to bomb the Libyan capital of Tripoli. The military strongman survived, but one of his daughters perished in the attack. Following the bombing, Qaddafi took a much lower profile against the

United States. Reagan had demonstrated his nation's military might despite the retreat in Lebanon (Map 28.1).

The Reagan administration's efforts to fight communism in Central America and terrorism in the Middle East continued unabated. Despite passage of the Boland Amendment in 1982 and its extension in 1984, the president continued to support the Nicaraguan Contras. By 1985 the Contras numbered somewhere between 10,000 and 20,000 troops and relied almost entirely on U.S. assistance. Barred from providing direct military or economic aid to the Contras, Reagan ordered the CIA and the National Security Council (NSC) to raise money from anti-Communist leaders abroad and wealthy conservatives at home. This effort, called "Project Democracy," raised millions of dollars. In violation of federal law, CIA director William Casey also authorized his agency to continue training the Contras in assassination techniques and other methods of subversion.

In the meantime, the situation in Lebanon remained critical as the strife caused by civil war led to the seizing of

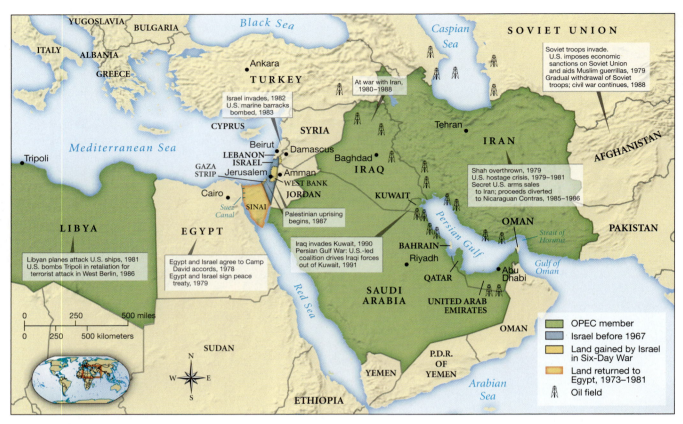

MAP 28.1   The United States in the Middle East, 1978–1991

The United States has historically needed access to the rich oil reserves of the Middle East. From the 1970s to the 1990s, both Democratic and Republican administrations were committed to the security of Israel, supportive of Afghan rebels fighting Soviet invaders, and opposed to the rising power of Islamic regimes. These principles often led to contradictory policies that further embroiled the United States in Middle East affairs.

American hostages. By mid-1984, seven Americans, including the CIA bureau chief in Beirut, had been kidnapped by Shi'ite Muslims financed by Iran. Since 1980, Iran, a Shi'ite nation, had been engaged in a protracted war with Iraq, which was ruled by military leader Saddam Hussein and his Sunni Muslim party, the chief rival to the Shi'ites. With relations between the United States and Iran having deteriorated in the aftermath of the 1979 coup, the Reagan administration backed Iraq in this war. The fate of the hostages, however, motivated Reagan to make a deal with Iran. In late 1985, Reagan's national security adviser Robert McFarlane negotiated secretly with an Iranian intermediary for the United States to sell antitank missiles to Iran in exchange for the Shi'ite government using its influence to induce the Muslim kidnappers to release the hostages. This covert bargain produced mixed success. Two Americans were freed by the end of 1986, but by then another three had been captured.

Had the matter ended there, the secret deal might never have come to light. However, NSC aide Lieutenant Colonel Oliver North developed a plan to transfer the proceeds from

the arms-for-hostages deal to fund the Contras and circumvent the Boland Amendment. Despite opposition from Secretary of State Shultz, Reagan liked North's plan, although the president seemed vague about the details, and some $10 million to $20 million of Iranian money flowed into the hands of the Contras.

In 1986 information about the **Iran-Contra** connection came to light. **See Document Project 28: The Iran-Contra Scandal, page 918.** Not since the Watergate scandal had a presidential administration received such intense media scrutiny. In the summer of 1987, televised Senate hearings exposed much of the tangled, covert dealings with Iran. In 1988 a special federal prosecutor indicted NSC adviser Vice Admiral John Poindexter (who had replaced McFarlane), North, and several others on charges ranging from perjury to conspiracy to obstruct justice. However, Reagan did not suffer the same fate or disgrace as had Nixon. Certainly the president knew what had been going on and had even approved it, but what he said publicly about his responsibility was circumscribed: "A few months ago, I told the American people I did not trade arms for hostages. My heart and best intentions still tell me that is true, but the facts and the evidence tell me it is not."

The Nuclear Freeze Movement

Despite his tough talk and military buildup, Reagan was not immune to public pressure. Rising protests against nuclear weapons in the United States and Europe in the early 1980s revealed a public increasingly anxious about the possibility of nuclear confrontation with the Soviet Union. At the end of the Carter administration, the United States had promised NATO that it would station new missiles in England, Italy, West Germany, and Belgium. Coupled with his confrontational stance against the Soviet Union, Reagan's decision to implement this policy sparked enormous protest. The campaign for nuclear disarmament included men and women, but women played a particularly strong leadership role in opposing nuclear proliferation. In 1981 peace activists set up camp at Greenham Common in England outside of one of the military bases prepared to house the arriving missiles. With twenty such camps in England, the disarmament forces organized nonviolent protests, including marches and sit-ins. The peace camp at Greenham Common became the model for the Women's Encampment for a Future of Peace and Justice at Seneca Falls, where Barbara Deming and other activists staged demonstrations. Protesters engaged in various forms of nonviolent expression, including singing, dancing, and performing skits to affirm women's solidarity for peace. As the participation of Deming as well as those at Greenham Common showed, women came together not only to promote disarmament but also to empower themselves and create communities based on mutual respect, trust, equality, and nonviolence.

These activities were part of a larger **nuclear freeze movement** that began in 1980. Its proponents called for a "mutual freeze on the testing, production, and deployment of nuclear weapons and of missiles and aircraft designed primarily to deliver nuclear weapons." Grassroots activists also held town meetings throughout the United States to mobilize ordinary citizens to speak out against nuclear proliferation. In 1982 some 750,000 people rallied in New York City's Central Park, the largest demonstration of its kind, to support a nuclear freeze resolution presented at the United Nations. Despite opposition from the United States and its NATO allies, measures favoring the freeze easily passed in the UN General Assembly. In the 1982 elections, peace groups placed nonbinding, nuclear freeze referenda on local ballots, which passed with wide majorities. The nuclear freeze movement's momentum carried over to Congress, where the House of Representatives narrowly rejected an "immediate freeze" by only two votes. Catholic bishops in the United States sent a pastoral letter to their parishioners condemning the spread of nuclear armaments. Even hard-line anti-Communists like Republican senator and former presidential candidate Barry Goldwater of Arizona joined the critics. "I'm not one of those freeze-the-nukes nuts," he explained in opposing new missile production, "but I think we have enough."

Explore

See Documents 28.2 and 28.3 to read about two nuclear freeze efforts.

Women's Peace Encampment Vigil

On October 24, 1983, protesters from the Women's Encampment for a Future of Peace and Justice held a candlelight vigil outside the Seneca Army Depot in Romulus, New York. Originally organized by feminist women, the protests also drew men. Together they campaigned to shut down the base, which was used as a munitions storage and disposal facility. In 1995 the military closed the depot.　AP Photo

Demonstrations in the United States and in Europe influenced Reagan. According to a 1982 public opinion poll, 57 percent of Americans favored an immediate nuclear freeze. Reflecting this sentiment, a 1983 television drama, *The Day After*, graphically portrayed the devastating horror of a nuclear attack on America. Reagan acknowledged that he was more inclined to reconsider deploying missiles abroad because European leaders felt pressure from protesters in their home countries. Ironically, the president credited Europeans' sentiments on the matter while claiming to ignore widespread efforts of domestic opponents such as Barbara Deming. However, the freeze movement inside and outside the United States created a favorable climate in which the president and Soviet leaders could negotiate a genuine plan for nuclear disarmament by the end of the decade.

The Road to Nuclear De-escalation

As frightening as this massive arms buildup was and despite the continuation of peace protests, Ronald Reagan won reelection in 1984 by a landslide (see chapter 27). Following his enormous victory, the popular Reagan softened his militant stance and became more amenable to negotiating with the USSR. Like Nixon, Reagan came to office with a well-deserved reputation as a fervent anti-Communist and left the White House having eased tensions between the

---

DOCUMENTS 28.2 AND 28.3

The Nuclear Freeze Movement: Two Views

In 1982, 30 percent of American voters considered nuclear freeze referenda in ten states and thirty-seven cities and counties. The nuclear freeze movement called on the United States and the Soviet Union to mutually halt the production, testing, and deployment of nuclear weapons. A nonbinding referendum in New Jersey passed overwhelmingly in every county. In addition to initiating ballot measures, the nuclear freeze campaign won the support of the Catholic Church, which issued a pastoral letter in 1983.

Explore

28.2 New Jersey Referendum on Nuclear Freeze, 1982

Public Question No. 1: Freeze on Nuclear Arms Escalation

Do you support a mutual United States–Soviet Union nuclear weapons "freeze" and urge the government of the United States:

(1) to propose to the government of the Soviet Union that both countries immediately agree to a mutual, verifiable halt of all further testing, production, and deployment of nuclear warheads, missiles, and delivery systems as a first step toward mutual, balanced reduction, and

(2) to apply the money saved to human needs and tax reduction?

Interpretive Statement

"This non-binding referendum, if approved by the public, would demonstrate the voters' support of a nuclear weapons freeze and would direct the Secretary of State to transmit the results of these voters' opinions on this question to the President of the United States, the Speaker of the House of Representatives, and President of the United States Senate no later than twenty (20) days after the conclusion of the election."

Source: "New Jersey Nuclear Freeze Ballot," 1982, http://www.initiativeforchange.org/ProtestOnBallot.htm.

United States and the Soviet Union. It took a president with impeccable credentials in fighting communism to reduce Cold War conflicts. Had a liberal or even a moderate Democratic president copied Reagan's actions, he would have been seen as a traitor for succumbing to what many considered the godless Soviet villains. Reagan, even more than Nixon, espoused conservative principles during his presidency, but he refused to let rigid dogma interfere with more pragmatic considerations to foster peace. Notwithstanding his aggressive, moralistic rhetoric, he perceived the limits of America's power in the post-Vietnam era, as evidenced by his decision to invade a very weak Grenada rather than Cuba, Nicaragua, or El Salvador, and he quickly withdrew U.S. marines from Lebanon rather than risk a wider war. By the time President Reagan left office, little remained of the Cold War.

In the mid-1980s, powerful changes were sweeping through the Soviet Union, which helped bring the Cold War to a close. In September 1985, Mikhail Gorbachev became general secretary of the Communist Party and head of the Soviet Union. The first Soviet chief of state born after the 1917 Bolshevik Revolution, Gorbachev introduced a program of economic and political reform. Through *glasnost* (openness) and *perestroika* (restructuring), the Soviet leader hoped to reduce massive state control over the declining economy and to extend democratic elections and

Explore

28.3 United States Conference of Catholic Bishops | Pastoral Letter on War and Peace, 1983

What are we saying? Fundamentally, we are saying that the decisions about nuclear weapons are among the most pressing moral questions of our age. While these decisions have obvious military and political aspects, they involve fundamental moral choices. In simple terms, we are saying that good ends (defending one's country, protecting freedom, etc.) cannot justify immoral means (the use of weapons which kill indiscriminately and threaten whole societies). We fear that our world and nation are headed in the wrong direction. More weapons with greater destructive potential are produced every day. More and more nations are seeking to become nuclear powers. In our quest for more and more security we fear we are actually becoming less and less secure. . . .

On Promoting Peace

1. We support immediate, bilateral verifiable agreements to halt the testing, production, and deployment of new nuclear weapons systems. This recommendation is not to be identified with any specific political initiative.

2. We support efforts to achieve deep cuts in the arsenals of both superpowers; efforts should concentrate first on systems which threaten the retaliatory forces of either major power.

3. We support early and successful conclusion of negotiations of a comprehensive test ban treaty.

4. We urge new efforts to prevent the spread of nuclear weapons in the world, and to control the conventional arms race, particularly the conventional arms trade.

5. We support, in an increasingly interdependent world, political and economic policies designed to protect human dignity and to promote the human rights of every person, especially the least among us.

Source: "The Challenge of Peace: God's Promise and Our Response," United States Conference of Catholic Bishops, 1983.

Interpret the Evidence

- What did voters in New Jersey hope to accomplish with a nonbinding referendum? Do you think the nonbinding nature of the measure made much difference to the outcome of the vote?
- Why did the Catholic Church take such a strong position in support of the nuclear freeze? How do their goals compare with those of the New Jersey referendum?

Put It in Context

What impact did the nuclear freeze movement have on the Cold War?

freedom of speech and freedom of the press. Gorbachev understood that the success of his reforms depended on reducing Cold War tensions with the United States and slowing the arms escalation that was bankrupting the Soviet economy. Gorbachev's *glasnost* brought the popular American musical performer Billy Joel to the Soviet Union in August 1987, staging the first rock concert in the country.

The changes that Gorbachev brought to the internal affairs of the Soviet Union carried over to the international arena. From 1986 to 1988, the Soviet leader negotiated in person with the American president, something that had not happened during Reagan's first term. In 1986 at a summit in Reykjavik, Iceland, the two leaders agreed to cut the number of strategic nuclear missiles in half. Gorbachev even proposed to eliminate his nation's entire nuclear stockpile of weapons if Reagan terminated the SDI program, an offer Reagan declined. Despite widespread skepticism in the scientific community about the practicality of the SDI, Reagan sincerely believed that it offered the best hope of preventing nuclear warfare. In 1987 the two sides negotiated an Intermediate Nuclear Forces Treaty, which provided for the destruction of existing intermediate-range missiles and on-site inspections to ensure compliance. The height of détente came in December 1987, when Gorbachev traveled to the United States to take part in the treaty-signing ceremony. Reagan no longer referred to the USSR as "the evil empire," and Gorbachev impressed Americans with his personal charm and by demonstrating the media savvy associated with American politicians. The following year, Reagan flew to the Soviet Union and hugged his new friend Mikhail at Lenin's Tomb and told reporters, "They've changed," referring to the once and not-so-distant "evil empire." Citizens of the two adversarial nations breathed a collective sigh of relief; at long last, the Cold War appeared to be winding down.

REVIEW & RELATE

- How did anticommunism shape Ronald Reagan's foreign policy?
- What role did ordinary citizens play in prompting the superpowers to move toward nuclear de-escalation?

LEARNINGCurve **bedfordstmartins.com/hewittlawson/LC**

The Fall of the Iron Curtain

When George H. W. Bush, Reagan's vice president and successor, took office in January 1989, he encountered a very different Soviet Union from the one Ronald Reagan had faced a decade earlier. The USSR was undergoing an internal revolution, one that allowed Bush and the United States to take on a new role in a world that was no longer divided between capitalist and Communist nations and their allies. The United States led the formation of new global partnerships that included the former Soviet Union. Globalization became the hallmark of the post–Cold War era, replacing previously dualistic economic and political systems, with mixed consequences. Following the collapse of the old world order, local and regional conflicts long held in check by the Cold War broke out along religious, racial, and ethnic lines.

The Breakup of the Soviet Union

Bush's first year in office coincided with upheavals in the Soviet-controlled Communist bloc, with Poland leading the way. In 1980 Polish dockworker Lech Walesa organized **Solidarity**, a trade union movement that conducted a series of popular strikes that forced the Communist government to recognize the group. Solidarity had ten million members and attracted various opponents of the Communist regime, including working-class democrats, Catholics, and nationalists who favored breaking ties with the Soviet Union. In 1981 Soviet leaders, disturbed by Solidarity's growing strength, forced the Polish government to crack down on the organization, arrest Walesa, and ban Solidarity. However, in 1989 Walesa and Solidarity were still alive and seized on the changes ushered in by Mikhail Gorbachev's *glasnost* in the USSR to press their demands for democracy in Poland. This time, with Gorbachev in command, the Soviets refused to intervene, and Poland conducted its first free elections since the beginning of the Cold War, electing Lech Walesa as president of the country. In July 1989, Gorbachev further broke from the past and announced that the Soviet Union would respect the national sovereignty of all the nations in the Warsaw Pact, which the Soviet Union had controlled since the late 1940s. "There is no universal road toward socialism," the Soviet chief declared.

Explore

See Document 28.4 for Gorbachev's statement to the United Nations on *glasnost* and *perestroika*.

Gorbachev's proclamation spurred the end of communism throughout Eastern Europe. Within the next year, Soviet-sponsored regimes fell peacefully in Hungary and Czechoslovakia, and elected governments replaced them. In Bulgaria, government officials dropped the word *Communist* from their party's name and held free elections, which brought reformers to power. Only in Romania did Communist rulers put up a fight. There, it took a violent popular uprising to topple the brutal dictator Nicolae Ceausescu. The pent-up animosity was so great that Romanian revolutionaries executed Ceausescu and his wife in 1989. The Baltic states of Latvia, Lithuania, and Estonia, which

Mikhail Gorbachev | Speech to the United Nations, 1988

Soviet leader Mikhail Gorbachev instituted two major reform movements, called *glasnost* and *perestroika*. *Glasnost* was meant to transform the Soviet political system by creating more governmental openness and transparency, while *perestroika* referred to the restructuring of the Soviet economy. In December 1988, Gorbachev stunned the world when he discussed these changes at the United Nations and outlined plans to reduce Soviet military units in Eastern Europe.

Explore

What does Gorbachev's statement about constructing a state based on the rule of law imply about conditions in the Soviet Union prior to *glasnost*?

We have gone substantially and deeply into the business of constructing a socialist state based on the rule of law. A whole series of new laws has been prepared or is at a completion stage. Many of them come into force as early as 1989, and we trust that they will correspond to the highest standards from the point of view of ensuring the rights of the individual. Soviet democracy is to acquire a firm, normative base. This means such acts as the Law on Freedom of Conscience, on glasnost, on public associations and organizations, and on much else. There are now no people in places of imprisonment in the country who have been sentenced for their political or religious convictions. It is proposed to include in the drafts of the new laws additional guarantees ruling out any form or persecution on these bases. . . . We intend to expand the Soviet Union's participation in the monitoring mechanism on human rights in the United Nations and within the framework of the pan-European process. We consider that the jurisdiction of the International Court in The Hague with respect to interpreting and applying agreements in the field of human rights should be obligatory for all states.

What new possibilities did a free exchange of information represent for Soviet citizens?

Within the Helsinki process, we are also examining an end to jamming of all the foreign radio broadcasts to the Soviet Union. On the whole, our credo is as follows: Political problems should be solved only by political means, and human problems only in a humane way. . . . Now about the most important topic, without which no problem of the coming century can be resolved: disarmament. . . .

What impact would the withdrawal of Soviet troops from the USSR's satellite nations have on those countries?

Today I can inform you of the following: The Soviet Union has made a decision on reducing its armed forces. In the next two years, their numerical strength will be reduced by 500,000 persons, and the volume of conventional arms will also be cut considerably. These reductions will be made on a unilateral basis. . . . By agreement with our allies in the Warsaw Pact, we have made the decision to withdraw six tank divisions from the GDR [East Germany], Czechoslovakia, and Hungary, and to disband them by 1991. Assault landing formations and units, and a number of others, including assault river-crossing forces, with their armaments and combat equipment, will also be withdrawn from the groups of Soviet forces situated in those countries.

Source: "Address by Mikhail Gorbachev at the 43rd U.N. General Assembly Session," December 7, 1988, http://legacy.wilsoncenter.org/coldwarfiles/index-34441.html.

Put It in Context

What is Gorbachev's vision of the future of the Soviet Union? What role did he hope a reformed Soviet Union would play in the world?

the Soviets had incorporated into the USSR at the outset of World War II, also regained their independence, signaling the geographical breakup of the Soviet Union itself.

Perhaps the most striking symbolism in the dismantling of the Soviet empire came in Germany, a country that had been divided between East and West states since 1945 and had been the scene of confrontations between the two superpowers throughout the Cold War (see chapters 24 and 26). With Communist governments collapsing around them, East Germans demonstrated against the regime of Erich Honecker. With no Soviet help forthcoming, Honecker decided to open the border between East and West Germany. On November 9, 1989, East and West Germans flocked to the Berlin Wall and jubilantly joined workers in knocking down the concrete barricade that divided the city. A year later, East and West Germany merged under the democratic, capitalist Federal Republic of Germany, the nation that the United States and its anti-Communist allies had set up after World War II.

Gorbachev also brought an end to the costly nine-year Soviet-Afghan War. More than 14,000 Soviet troops had died in the war, and more than 450,000 suffered from wounds and diseases. The war cost the Soviets more than $20 billion, which severely strained their already ailing economy. When the Soviets withdrew their last troops on February 15, 1989, they left Afghanistan in shambles. One million Afghans had perished, and another 5 million fled the country for Pakistan and Iran, resulting in the political destabilization of Afghanistan. Following a civil war, the Taliban, a group of Sunni Muslim fundamentalists, came to power in the mid-1990s and established a theocratic regime that, among other things, strictly regulated what women could wear in public and denied them educational and professional opportunities. The Taliban also provided sanctuary for many of the mujahideen rebels who had fought against the Soviets, including Osama bin Laden, who would use the country as a base for his al-Qaeda organization to promote terrorism against the United States.

Meanwhile, the Soviet Union disintegrated. Free elections were held in 1990, which ironically threatened Gorbachev's own power by bringing non-Communists to local and national political offices. Although an advocate of economic reform and political openness, Gorbachev remained a Communist and was committed to preserving the USSR. Challenges to Gorbachev came from both ends of the political spectrum. Boris Yeltsin, his former protégé, led the non-Communist forces that wanted Gorbachev to move more quickly in adopting capitalism; on the other side, hard-line generals in the Soviet army disapproved of Gorbachev's reforms and his cooperation with the United States. On August 18, 1991, a group of conspirators from the army, the Communist Party, and the KGB (the Soviet intelligence agency) staged a coup against Gorbachev,

placed him under house arrest, and surrounded the parliament building with troops. Yeltsin, the president of the Russian Republic, rallied fellow legislators and Muscovites against the plotters and brought the uprising to a peaceful end. After Gorbachev was set free, he resigned in December 1991. Following the official dissolution of the Soviet Union, Yeltsin engineered the formation of the Commonwealth of Independent States (CIS), consisting of the Russian Federation and eleven of fifteen former Soviet republics (the Baltic states of Latvia, Lithuania, and Estonia did not join). Later that month, the CIS removed the hammer and sickle, the symbol of communism, from its flag. With the Soviet Union dismantled, Yeltsin, as head of the Russian Federation and the CIS, expanded the democratic and free market reforms initiated by Gorbachev (Map 28.2).

Despite his fall from power, Gorbachev deserves a great deal of credit for ending the Cold War. In bringing economic and political reforms to the Soviet Union, he opened the way for greater dialogue with the United States on arms control. His refusal to intervene when communism collapsed in Eastern Europe ensured that the nations in the region would follow their own course toward independence and democracy. He paid a high price for his efforts to restructure his country, as the reforms he set in motion ultimately led to his overthrow and the breakup of the Soviet Union. Yet he must be recognized as one of the prime movers in bringing the Cold War to an end.

Before Gorbachev left office, he completed one last agreement with the United States to curb nuclear arms. In mid-1991, just before conspirators staged their abortive coup, Gorbachev met with President Bush, who had traveled to Moscow to sign a strategic arms reduction treaty. Under this pact, each side agreed to reduce its bombers and missiles by one-third and to trim its conventional military forces. This accord led to a second strategic arms reduction treaty, signed in 1993. Gorbachev's successor, Boris Yeltsin, met with Bush in January 1993, and the two agreed to destroy their countries' stockpile of multiple-warhead intercontinental missiles within a decade.

Globalization and the New World Order

With the end of the Cold War, cooperation replaced economic and political rivalry between capitalist and Communist nations in a new era of **globalization**—the extension of economic, political, and cultural relationships among nations, through commerce, migration, and communication. In 1976 the major industrialized democracies had formed the Group of Seven (G7). Consisting of the United States, the United Kingdom, France, West Germany, Italy, Japan, and Canada, the G7 nations met annually to discuss common problems related to issues of global concern, such

MAP 28.2   The Fall of Communism in Eastern Europe and the Soviet Union, 1989–1991

The collapse of Communist regimes in eastern Europe was due in part to political and economic reforms initiated by Soviet Premier Mikhail Gorbachev, including agreements with the United States to reduce nuclear arms. These changes inspired demands for free elections that were supported by popular uprisings, first in Poland and then in other former Soviet satellites.

as trade, health, energy, the environment, and economic and social development. After the fall of communism, Russia joined the organization, which became known as G8. This group of countries represented only 14 percent of the globe's population but produced 60 percent of the world's economic output. Four of the G8 members—the United States, the United Kingdom, Russia, and France—controlled more than 95 percent of the nuclear weapons in the world.

The United States took an active lead in promoting the World Trade Organization (WTO). The WTO emerged from the General Agreement on Tariffs and Trade, a multilateral agreement fashioned after World War II to encourage tariff reductions and free trade. Created in 1995, the WTO consists of more than 150 nations and seeks "to ensure that trade flows as smoothly, predictably and freely as possible." The policies of the WTO generally benefit wealthier nations, such as the United States. From 1978 to 2000, the value of U.S. exports and imports jumped from 17 percent to 25 percent of the gross national product.

Globalization was accompanied by the extraordinary growth of **multinational (or transnational) corporations**— companies that operate production facilities or deliver services in more than one country. Between 1970 and 2000, the number of such firms soared from 7,000 to well over 60,000. By 2000 the 500 largest corporations in the world generated more than $11 trillion in revenues, owned more than $33 trillion in assets, and employed 35.5 million people. American companies left their cultural and social imprint on the rest of the world. Walmart greeted shoppers in more than 1,200 stores outside the United States, and McDonald's changed global eating habits with its more than 1,000 fast-food restaurants worldwide. Traveling abroad, American tourists marveled at local inhabitants in Europe, Asia, and Africa wearing T-shirts and baseball caps with the logos of American companies. As American firms penetrated other countries with their products, foreign companies changed the economic landscape of the United States. For instance, by the twenty-first century Japanese automobiles, led by Toyota and Honda, captured a major share of the American market, surpassing Ford and General Motors, once the hallmark of the country's superior manufacturing and salesmanship.

Globalization also affected popular culture. In the 1990s, reality shows, many of which originated in Europe, became a staple of American television. British imports included the hugely popular *American Idol*. At the same time, American programs were shown as reruns all over the world. As cable channels proliferated, American viewers of Hispanic or Asian origin could watch programs in their native languages. The Cable News Network (CNN), the British Broadcasting Corporation (BBC), and Al Jazeera, an Arabic-language television channel, competed for viewers with specially designed international broadcasts.

Globalization also had some negative consequences. Organized labor in particular suffered a severe blow. By 2004 union membership in the United States had dropped to 12.5 percent of the industrial workforce. Fewer and fewer consumer goods bore the label "Made in America," as multinational companies shifted manufacturing jobs to low-wage workers in third world countries in Central America, East Asia, and Southeast Asia. Many of these foreign workers earned more than the prevailing wages in their countries, but by Western standards their pay was extremely low. There were few or no regulations governing working conditions or the use of child labor, and many foreign factories resembled the sweatshops of early-twentieth-century America. Not surprisingly, workers in the United States could not compete in this market. Furthermore, China, which by 2007 had become a prime source for American manufacturing, failed to regulate the quality of its products closely. Chinese-made toys, including the popular Thomas the Train, showed up in U.S. stores with excessive lead paint and had to be returned before endangering millions of children.

Globalization also posed a danger to the world's environment. As poorer nations sought to take advantage of the West's appetite for low-cost consumer goods, they industrialized rapidly and chaotically, with little concern for the excessive pollution that accompanied their efforts. The landscapes of some countries were transformed beyond recognition. The desire for wood products and the expansion of large-scale farming eliminated one-third of Brazil's rain forests. The health of indigenous people suffered wherever globalization-related manufacturing appeared. In Taiwan and China, chemical by-products of factories and farms turned rivers into polluted sources of drinking water and killed the rivers' fish and plants.

The older, industrialized nations added their share to the environmental damage. Besides using nuclear power, Americans consumed electricity and gas produced overwhelmingly from coal and petroleum. Gas-guzzling automobiles, and particularly sport-utility vehicles (SUVs) beginning in the 1990s, further harmed the environment. The burning of fossil fuels by cars and factories released greenhouse gases, which has raised the temperature of the atmosphere and the oceans and contributed to the phenomenon known as global warming. Most scientists believe that global warming has led to the melting of the polar ice

Globalization, 1980s

Following the efforts of Presidents Nixon, Ford, and Carter to normalize relations with Communist China, companies established commercial enterprises there, including American fast-food chain restaurants. Here a soldier, standing beside a replica of Colonel Sanders, picks up his order at the bike ride-up window of a Kentucky Fried Chicken restaurant.   © Dave Bartruff/CORBIS caps and threatens the existence of human and animal survival on the planet. However, after the industrialized nations of the world signed the Kyoto Protocol in 1998 to curtail greenhouse-gas emissions, the U.S. Senate refused to ratify it. Critics of the agreement maintained that it did not address the newly emerging industrial countries that polluted heavily and thus was unfair to the United States.

Globalization also highlighted health problems such as the AIDS epidemic. By the outset of the twenty-first century, approximately 33.2 million people worldwide suffered from the disease, though the number of new cases diagnosed annually had dropped to 2.5 million from more than 5 million a few years earlier. Africa remained the continent with the largest number of AIDS patients and the center of the epidemic. Initially concentrated in gay men, intravenous drug users, and sex workers, AIDS constituted a continual though diminished threat. Increased education and the development of more effective pharmaceuticals to treat the illness reduced cases and prolonged the lives of those affected by the disease. Though treatments were more widely available in prosperous countries like the United States, agencies such as the United Nations and the World Health Organization, together with nongovernmental groups such as Partners in Health, were instrumental in offering relief in developing countries.

Globalization did not mean the end of regional cooperation. To boost their economic might, western European nations formed the **European Union (EU)** in 1993, and by 2007 twenty-seven countries had joined the EU. The EU allowed people to move freely by abolishing passport control and customs checks for residents traveling from one member state to another. The organization encouraged free trade and investment. In 1999 the EU introduced a common currency, the euro, which has been adopted by thirteen nations. In 2007 the EU had representation in the G8, contained a population of 500 million, and accounted for approximately 31 percent of the world's output of goods and services.

To strengthen its trading position, the United States formed its own regional economic partnership in North America. In 1993, together with the governments of Mexico and Canada, the U.S. Congress ratified the **North American Free Trade Agreement (NAFTA)**, and it went into effect the following year. The agreement removed tariffs and other obstacles to commerce and investment among the three countries to encourage trade. NAFTA produced noteworthy gains: Between 1994 and 2004, trade among NAFTA nations increased nearly 130 percent. Although income disparity remains large between Mexico and the United States, Mexico has seen a significant drop in poverty rates and a rise in real income. At the same time, NAFTA has harmed workers in the United States. From 1994 to 2007, net manufacturing jobs dropped by 3,654,000, as U.S. companies outsourced their production to plants in Mexico, taking advantage of the low wage and benefits structure.

Managing Conflict after the Cold War

The end of the Cold War left the United States as the only remaining superpower. Though Reagan's Cold War defense spending had created huge deficits (see chapter 27), the United States emerged from the Cold War with its economic and military strength intact. With the power vacuum created by the breakup of the Soviet Union, the question remained how the United States would use its strength to preserve world order and maintain peace.

In several areas of the globe, the move toward democracy that had begun in the late 1980s proceeded peacefully into the 1990s. The oppressive, racist system of apartheid fell in South Africa, and antiapartheid activist Nelson Mandela was released after twenty-seven years in prison to become president of the country in 1994. In 1990 Chilean dictator Augusto Pinochet stepped down as president of Chile and ceded control to a democratically elected candidate. That same year, the pro-Communist Sandinista government lost at the polls in Nicaragua, and in 1992 the ruling regime in El Salvador signed a peace accord with the rebels.

The end of the Cold War allowed President Bush to turn his attention to explosive issues in the Middle East. The president brought the Israelis and Palestinians together to sign an agreement providing for eventual Palestinian self-government in the Gaza Strip and the West Bank. In doing so, the United States for the first time officially recognized Yasser Arafat, the head of the PLO, whom both the Israelis and the Americans had considered a terrorist.

Before Bush left the White House in 1993, he had deployed military forces in both the Caribbean and the Persian Gulf, confident that the United States could exert its influence without a challenge from the former Soviet Union. During the 1980s, the United States had developed a precarious relationship with Panamanian general Manuel Noriega. Noriega played the United States against the Soviet Union in this region that was vital to American security. Although he channeled aid to the Contras with the approval and support of the CIA, he angered the Reagan administration by maintaining close ties with Cuba. Noriega cooperated with the U.S. Drug Enforcement Agency in halting shipments of cocaine from Latin America headed for the United States at the same time that he collaborated with Latin American drug kingpins to elude U.S. agents and launder the drug lords' profits. In 1988 two Florida grand juries indicted the Panamanian leader on charges of drug smuggling and bribery, pressuring President Reagan to cut off aid to Panama and to ask Noriega to resign. Not only did Noriega refuse to step down, but he also nullified the results of the 1989 presidential election in Panama and declared himself the nation's "maximum leader."

After the United States tried unsuccessfully to foment an internal coup against Noriega, in 1989 the Panamanian leader proclaimed a "state of war" between the United States and his country. The situation worsened in mid-December when a U.S. marine was killed on his way home from a restaurant, allegedly by Panamanian defense forces. On December 28, 1989, President Bush launched Operation Just Cause, sending some 27,000 marines to invade Panama. Bush justified the invasion as necessary to protect the Panama Canal and the lives of American citizens, as well as to halt the drug traffic promoted by Noriega. In reality, the main purpose of the mission was to overthrow and capture the Panamanian dictator. In Operation Just Cause, the United States easily defeated a much weaker enemy. The U.S. government installed a new regime, and the marines captured Noriega and sent him back to Florida to stand trial on the drug charges. In 1992 he was found guilty and sent to prison.

Flexing military muscle in Panama was more feasible than doing so in China. President Bush believed that the acceleration of trade relations that followed full U.S. diplomatic recognition of Communist China in 1978 would prompt the kind of democratic reforms that swept through the Soviet Union in the 1980s. His expectation proved far too optimistic. In May 1989, university students in Beijing and other major cities in China held large-scale protests to demand political and economic reforms in the country. Some 200,000 demonstrators consisting of students, intellectuals, and workers gathered in the capital city's huge Tiananmen Square, where they constructed a papier-mâché figure resembling the Statue of Liberty and sang songs borrowed from the African American civil rights movement. Deng Xiaoping, Mao Zedong's successor, cracked down on the demonstrations by declaring martial law and dispatching the army to disperse the protesters. Peaceful activists were mowed down by machine guns and stampeded by tanks. Rather than displaying the toughness he showed in Panama, Bush merely issued a temporary ban on sales of weapons and nonmilitary items to China. When outrage over the Tiananmen Square massacre subsided, the president restored normal trade relations.

By contrast, the Bush administration's most forceful military intervention came in Iraq. Maintaining a steady flow of oil from the Persian Gulf was vital to U.S. strategic interests. During the prolonged Iraq-Iran War in the 1980s, the Reagan administration had switched allegiance from one belligerent to the other to ensure that neither side emerged too powerful. Though the administration had orchestrated the arms-for-hostages deal with Iran, it had also courted the Iraqi dictator Saddam Hussein. U.S. support for Hussein ended in 1990, after Iraq sent 100,000 troops to invade the small oil-producing nation of Kuwait, on the southern border of Iraq.

President Bush responded aggressively. He compared Saddam Hussein to Adolf Hitler and warned the Iraqis that their invasion "will not stand." Oil was at the heart of the matter. Hussein needed to revitalize the Iraqi economy, which was devastated after a decade of war with Iran. In conquering Kuwait, which held huge oil reserves, Hussein would control one-quarter of the world output of the "black gold." Bush feared that the Iraqi dictator would also attempt to overrun Kuwait's neighbor Saudi Arabia, an American ally, thereby giving Iraq control of half of the world's oil supply. Bush was also concerned that an emboldened Saddam Hussein would then upset the delicate balance of power in the Middle East and pose a threat to Israel by supporting the Palestinians. The Iraqis were rumored to be quickly developing nuclear weapons, which Hussein could use against Israel.

Rather than act unilaterally, President Bush organized a multilateral coalition against Iraqi aggression. Secretary of State James Baker persuaded the United Nations—including the Soviet Union and China, the United States' former Cold War adversaries—to adopt a resolution calling for Iraqi withdrawal from Kuwait and imposing economic sanctions. Thirty-eight nations, including the Arab countries of Egypt, Saudi Arabia, Syria, and Kuwait, contributed 160,000 troops, roughly 24 percent of the 700,000 allied forces that were deployed in Saudi Arabia in preparation for an invasion if Iraq did not comply. Hussein's bellicosity against an Islamic nation won him few allies in the Middle East.

With military forces stationed in Saudi Arabia, Bush gave Hussein a deadline of January 15, 1991, to withdraw from Kuwait or else risk attack. However, the president faced serious opposition at home against waging a war for oil. Demonstrations occurred throughout the nation, and most Americans supported the continued implementation of economic sanctions, which were already causing serious hardships for the Iraqi people. In the face of widespread opposition, the president requested congressional authorization for military operations against Iraq. Lawmakers were also divided, but after long debate they narrowly approved Bush's request.

Saddam Hussein let the deadline pass. On January 16, **Operation Desert Storm** began when the United States launched air attacks on Baghdad and other key targets in Iraq. After a month of bombing, Hussein still refused to capitulate, so a ground offensive was launched on February

Gulf War Protests, 1991

The United States gave Iraq a January 15, 1991, deadline to withdraw from Kuwait or face military force. Protesters at the University of South Florida in Tampa favored continued diplomatic efforts. They carry signs that refer to the January 15 deadline, which also is the birthday of Martin Luther King Jr., a critic of U.S. militarism.   Courtesy of Steven Lawson and Nancy Hewitt

24, 1991. Under the command of General Norman H. Schwarzkopf, more than 500,000 allied troops moved into Kuwait and easily drove Iraqi forces out of that nation; they then moved into southern Iraq. Although Hussein had confidently promised that the U.S.-led military assault would encounter the "mother of all battles," the vastly outmatched Iraqi army, worn out from its ten-year war with Iran, was quickly defeated. Desperate for help, Hussein ordered the firing of Scud missiles on Israel to provoke it into war, which he hoped would drive a wedge between the United States and its Arab allies. Despite sustaining some casualties, Israel refrained from retaliation. The ground war ended within one hundred hours, and Iraq surrendered. An estimated 100,000 Iraqis died; by contrast, 136 Americans perished (see Map 28.1 on page 904).

With the war over quickly, President Bush resisted pressure to march to Baghdad and overthrow Saddam Hussein. Bush's stated goal had been to liberate Kuwait; he did not wish to fight a war in the heart of Iraq. The administration believed that such an expedition would involve house-to-house, urban guerrilla warfare. Marching on Baghdad would also entail battling against Hussein's elite Republican Guard, not the weaker conscripts who had put up little resistance in Kuwait. Bush's Arab allies opposed expanding the war, and the president did not want to risk losing their support. Finally, getting rid of Hussein might make matters worse by leaving Iran and its Muslim fundamentalist rulers the dominant power in the region.

For these reasons, President Bush held Schwarzkopf's troops in place.

The Gulf War preserved the U.S. lifeline to oil in the Persian Gulf. President Bush and his supporters concluded that the United States had the determination to make its military presence felt throughout the world. Bush and the chairman of the Joint Chiefs of Staff, General Colin Powell, understood that the United States had succeeded because it had pieced together a genuine coalition of nations, including Arab ones, to coordinate diplomatic and military action. Military leaders had a clear and defined mission— the liberation of Kuwait—as well as adequate troops and supplies. When they carried out their purpose, the war was over. However, American withdrawal later allowed Saddam Hussein to slaughter thousands of Iraqi rebels, including Kurds and Shi'ites, to whom Bush had promised support. In effect, the Bush administration had applied the Cold War policy of limited containment in dealing with Hussein. The end of the Cold War and peaceful relations with former adversaries in Moscow and Beijing made possible the largest and most successful U.S. military intervention since the war in Vietnam.

REVIEW & RELATE

What led to the end of Communist rule in Eastern Europe and the breakup of the Soviet Union?

How did the end of the Cold War contribute to the growth of globalization?

Conclusion: Farewell to the Cold War

The Cold War between the United States and the Soviet and Chinese Communists occupied the attention of two generations of Americans from 1945 to 1991. Citizens in these nations faced the nightmare of nuclear holocaust caused by even small missteps between the adversaries. But some unlikely people were responsible for ending the Cold War. Ronald Reagan, a militant anti-Communist crusader, together with his pragmatic and steady secretary of state, George Shultz, guided the United States through a policy of heightened military preparedness in order to push the Soviet Union toward peace. It was a dangerous gambit, but it worked; diplomacy rather than armed conflict prevailed. Reagan's Cold War strategy succeeded largely because during the 1980s an enlightened leader, Mikhail Gorbachev, governed the Soviet Union. He envisioned the end of the Cold War as a means of bringing political and economic reform to his beleaguered and bankrupt nation. What Gorbachev began, his successor, Boris Yeltsin, finished: the dismantling of the Soviet Union and its empire, and the infusion of democracy and capitalism into Russia.

The activism of ordinary people around the world also helped transform the relationship between the superpowers. Antinuclear protesters in Western Europe and the United States, including Barbara Deming and her feminist cadre at the Seneca Falls Women's Encampment, kept up pressure on Western leaders to make continued nuclear expansion unacceptable. In Eastern Europe, Polish dockworker Lech Walesa and other fighters for democracy broke from the Soviet orbit and tore down the bricks and barbed-wire fences of the iron curtain. Who won the Cold War? Clearly, the United States did, thereby gaining dominance as the world's sole superpower. Yet this did not necessarily guarantee peace. In assuming this preeminent role, the United States faced new threats to international security from governments and insurgents seeking to rebuild nations along ethnic and religious lines in the Balkans, the Middle East, the Persian Gulf, and Africa. Ironically, the bipolar Cold War in some ways had meant a more stable and manageable world presided over by the two superpowers. The collapse of the Soviet empire created a power vacuum that would be filled by a variety of unchecked and combustible local and regional forces intent on challenging the political and economic dominance of the United States and, even more sweeping, the values of Western civilization. At the same time, as globalization and digital technology shrank the world economically and culturally, the United States became the chief target of those who wanted to contain the spread of Western values. Terrorism, which transcended national borders, replaced communism as the leading enemy of the United States and its allies.

LEARNINGCurve
Check what you know.
bedfordstmartins.com/hewittlawson/LC

Chapter Review

Online Study Guide ▶ **bedfordstmartins.com/hewittlawson**

KEY TERMS

détente (p. 897)
SALT II (p. 897)
mujahideen (p. 898)
Camp David accords (p. 898)
Boland Amendment (p. 901)
divestment movement (p. 902)
Iran-Contra (p. 904)
nuclear freeze movement (p. 905)
glasnost (p. 907)
perestroika (p. 907)
Solidarity (p. 908)
globalization (p. 910)
multinational (or transnational) corporations (p. 911)
European Union (EU) (p. 913)
North American Free Trade Agreement (NAFTA) (p. 913)
Operation Desert Storm (p. 914)

REVIEW & RELATE

1. How did Carter's foreign policy differ from that of Ford and Nixon?

2. How did events in Afghanistan and Iran undermine the Carter administration?

3. How did anticommunism shape Ronald Reagan's foreign policy?

4. What role did ordinary citizens play in prompting the superpowers to move toward nuclear de-escalation?

5. What led to the end of Communist rule in Eastern Europe and the breakup of the Soviet Union?

6. How did the end of the Cold War contribute to the growth of globalization?

TIMELINE OF EVENTS

1975 — U.S. and USSR sign Helsinki accords

1978 — Camp David accords between Israel and Egypt

1979 — U.S. Embassy staff in Tehran taken hostage

U.S. and USSR sign SALT II; Congress does not ratify

Soviet Union invades Afghanistan

1980 — Solidarity founded in Poland

1982 — Boland Amendment passed

750,000 attend nuclear freeze rally in New York City's Central Park

1983 — Suicide bomb attack in Lebanon kills 241 U.S. soldiers

U.S. invasion of Grenada

1985 — Reagan administration sells arms to Iran for release of hostages and to fund Nicaraguan Contras

Mikhail Gorbachev assumes leadership of the Soviet Union

1987 — Senate hearings on Iran-Contra affair

U.S. and Soviet Union sign Intermediate Nuclear Forces Treaty

1989 — Tiananmen Square protests and crackdown in China

Fall of the Berlin Wall

1990–1991 — Soviet Union dismantled

1991 — U.S. pushes Iraq out of Kuwait

1993 — European Union (EU) formed

1994 — North Atlantic Free Trade Agreement (NAFTA) goes into effect

The Iran-Contra Scandal

On November 3, 1986, the Lebanese maga-zine *Ash-Shiraa* revealed a secret arms-for-hostages deal between the United States and Iran. As the scandal unfolded, it was revealed that the profits from these arms sales had been illegally diverted to aid anti-Sandinista rebels (called Contras) in Nicaragua. For the next year, the Iran-Contra scandal, as it was known, played out in the press as questions of governmental conspiracy, abuse of power, and a White House cover-up swirled around the Reagan administration.

Since the early 1980s, the Central Intelligence Agency had been funding, arming, and training groups of dissident forces opposing the leftist Nicaraguan government. After Congress passed the Boland Amendment, which prohibited further aid to the Contras, the Reagan administration then looked for other ways to continue its support for the rebels, eventually funneling sales from the Iranian arms sales.

Less than a month after the story broke, President Reagan appointed a three-person committee to investigate the allegations. The Tower Commission—named after commission member John Tower, a Republican senator from Texas—spent several months calling witnesses and poring over classified documents. Unsatisfied with the Tower Commission's work, the U.S. Senate and House of Represen-tatives established their own joint investigative committee and held hearings in the summer of 1987. Both the Tower Commission and the congressional committee concluded that neither Reagan nor Vice President George H. W. Bush was aware of the illegal funding of the Contras, though Reagan was sharply criticized as a poor administrator who needed to exert more control over his staff.

Several of Reagan's top officials were eventually indicted on a variety of felony accounts, including lying to Congress, destroying evidence, and obstructing justice. In all, eleven men were convicted or pleaded guilty. In late 1992, then President George H. W. Bush pardoned six men indicted or convicted as part of the Iran-Contra scandal.

DOCUMENT 28.5

The Boland Amendment, 1982

Alarmed at the CIA's involvement in the Nicaraguan civil war, Congress passed a measure in 1982 to limit funding and support for these activities. Offered by Edward Boland, a Democratic representative from Massachusetts, the Boland Amendment prohibited the CIA or any government agency from providing military aid or advice to the Contra rebels.

Amendment to H.R. 7355, Offered December 8, 1982

A substitute amendment to the Harkin amendment [which also prohibited support of military activity in Nicaragua] to prohibit the CIA or Defense Department to use funds of the bill to furnish military equipment, military training or advice, or other support for military activities, to any group or individual, not part of a country's armed forces, for the purpose of overthrowing the government of Nicaragua or provoking a military exchange between Nicaragua and Honduras. The Harkin amendment has prohibited support of any military activity in Nicaragua.

Source: House Amendment 974, 97th Congress (1981–1982).

DOCUMENT 28.6

CIA Freedom Fighter's Manual, 1983

The CIA's support for the Contras included training in sabotage to disrupt Nicaraguan government and society. In 1983 the CIA prepared a Freedom Fighter's Manual and air-dropped thousands of pamphlets over Nicaragua. Promising "minimal risk for the combatant," the manual's advice ranged from passive and mundane techniques—such as showing up late for work, spreading false rumors, and plugging up toilets with sponges—to more aggressive methods of sabotage, shown here.

PUT NAILS ON ROADS AND HIGHWAYS

PUT DIRT INTO GASOLINE TANKS

PUT NAILS NEXT TO THE TIRES OF PARKED VEHICLES

PUT WATER IN GASOLINE TANKS

DOCUMENT 28.7

Tower Commission Report, 1987

As the scandal unfolded, President Reagan appointed a three-member commission to investigate the allegations. In addition to Senator Tower, the Tower Commission included Edmund Muskie, a former secretary of state, and Brent Scowcroft, a former national security adviser to President Ford. More than seventy witnesses testified, and Reagan appeared before the commission in December 1986. At the center of the scandal was Lieutenant Colonel Oliver North, a marine assigned to the National Security Council and the professed coordinator of the arms sales and the diversion of funds to the Contras. When the commission released its report in February 1987, it concluded that while Reagan should have been more directly aware of the actions of his advisers, he was not aware of the illegal diversion of funds to the Contras.

The President's management style is to put the principal responsibility for policy review and implementation on the shoulders of his advisors. Nevertheless, with such a complex, high-risk operation and so much at stake, the President should have insured that the N.S.C. [National Security Council] system did not fail him. He did not force his policy to undergo the most critical review of which the N.S.C. participants and the process were capable. At no time did he insist upon accountability and performance review. Had the President chosen to drive the N.S.C. system, the outcome could well have been different. As it was, the most powerful features of the N.S.C. system—providing comprehensive analysis, alternatives, and follow-up—were not utilized. . . .

The board found considerable reason to question the actions of Lt. Col. North in the aftermath of the disclosure. The board has no evidence to either confirm or refute that Lt. Col. North destroyed documents on the initiative in an effort to conceal facts from threatened investigations. The board found indications that Lt. Col. North was involved in an effort, over time, to conceal or withhold important information. The files of Lt. Col. North contained much of the historical documentation that the board used to construct its narrative. Moreover, Lt. Col. North was the primary U.S. Government official involved in the details of the operation. The chronology he produced has many inaccuracies. These "histories" were to be the basis of the "full" story of the Iran initiative. These inaccuracies lend some evidence to the proposition that Lt. Col. North, either on his own or at the behest of others, actively sought to conceal important information.

Out of concern for the protection of classified material, [CIA] Director [William] Casey and [National Security Adviser Vice Admiral (VADM) John] Poindexter were to brief only the Congressional intelligence committees on the "full" story; [Casey] before the committees and VADM Poindexter in private sessions with the chairmen and vice chairmen. [Casey] and VADM Poindexter undertook to do this on November 21, 1986. It appears from the copy of [Casey's] testimony and notes of VADM Poindexter's meetings that they did not fully relate the nature of events as they had occurred. The result is an understandable perception that they were not forthcoming.

The board is also concerned about various notes that appear to be missing. VADM Poindexter was the official note taker in some key meetings, yet no notes for the meetings can be found. The reason for the lack of such notes remains unknown to the board. If they were written, they may contain very important information. We have no way of knowing if they exist.

Source: President's Special Review Board, *The Tower Commission Report* (New York: New York Times Books, 1987), 84–86.

DOCUMENT 28.8

Ronald Reagan | Speech on Iran-Contra, 1987

A few weeks after the Tower Commission released its report, President Reagan went on television and spoke about the Iran-Contra scandal. Although he had appeared on television during the commission's hearings, this was the first time he spoke directly to the American people about the scandal. He discussed the Tower Commission report as well as the steps he was taking to address the problems it identified about his administration and management style.

I've studied the Board's report. Its findings are honest, convincing, and highly critical; and I accept them. And tonight I want to share with you my thoughts on these findings and report to you on the actions I'm taking to implement the Board's recommendations.

First, let me say I take full responsibility for my own actions and for those of my administration. As angry as I may be about activities undertaken without my knowledge, I am still accountable for those activities. As disappointed as I may be in some who served me, I'm still the one who must answer to the American people for this behavior. And as personally distasteful as I find secret bank accounts and diverted funds—well, as the Navy would say, this happened on my watch.

Let's start with the part that is the most controversial. A few months ago I told the American people I did not trade arms for hostages. My heart and my best intentions still tell me that's true, but the facts and the evidence tell me it is not. As the Tower board reported, what began as a strategic opening to Iran deteriorated, in its implementation, into trading arms for hostages. This runs counter to my own beliefs, to administration policy, and to the original strategy we had in mind. There are reasons why it happened, but no excuses. It was a mistake. . . .

Now, another major aspect of the Board's findings regards the transfer of funds to the Nicaraguan contras. The Tower board wasn't able to find out what happened to this money, so the facts here will be left to the continuing investigations of the court-appointed Independent Counsel and the two congressional investigating committees. I'm confident the truth will come out about this matter, as well. As I told the Tower board, I didn't know about any diversion of funds to the contras. But as President, I cannot escape responsibility.

Much has been said about my management style, a style that's worked successfully for me during 8 years as Governor of California and for most of my Presidency. The way I work is to identify the problem, find the right individuals to do the job, and then let them go to it. I've found this invariably brings out the best in people. They seem to rise to their full capability, and in the long run you get more done. . . .

I'm taking action in three basic areas: personnel, national security policy, and the process for making sure that the system works. First, personnel—I've brought in an accomplished and highly respected new team here at the White House. They bring new blood, new energy, and new credibility and experience. . . .

Now, what should happen when you make a mistake is this: You take your knocks, you learn your lessons, and then you move on. That's the healthiest way to deal with a problem. This in no way diminishes the importance of the other continuing investigations, but the business of our country and our people must proceed. I've gotten this message from Republicans and Democrats in Congress, from allies around the world, and—if we're reading the signals right—even from the Soviets. And of course, I've heard the message from you, the American people. You know, by the time you reach my age, you've made plenty of mistakes. And if you've lived your life properly—so, you learn. You put things in perspective. You pull your energies together. You change. You go forward.

Source: "Address to the Nation on the Iran Arms and Contra Aid Controversy," March 4, 1987, http://www.pbs.org/wgbh/americanexperience/features/primary-resources/reagan-iran-contra.

DOCUMENT 28.9

Oliver North | Testimony to Congress, July 1987

As the Iran-Contra scandal intensified, Lieutenant Colonel Oliver North appeared before the joint congressional committee in the summer of 1987 and admitted his role as a chief operator in the Iran-Contra affair. He also admitted that he had lied to Congress and had shredded incriminating documents, but he defended himself as a soldier in service to his country. North was eventually indicted and convicted on three felony counts, though his conviction was overturned on appeal.

QUESTION: Is it correct to say that following the enactment of the Boland Amendment, our support for the war in Nicaragua did not end and that you were the person in the United States Government who managed it?

Answer: Starting in the spring of 1984, well before the Boland proscription of no appropriated funds made available to the D.O.D. [Department of Defense] and the C.I.A. etc., I was already engaged in supporting the Nicaraguan resistance and the democratic outcome in Nicaragua. I did so as part of a covert operation. It was carried out starting as early as the spring of '84, when we ran out of money and people started to look in Nicaragua, in Honduras and Guatemala, El Salvador, and Costa Rica for some sign of what the Americans were really going to do, and that that help began much earlier than the most rigorous of the Boland proscriptions. And yes, it was carried out covertly, and it was carried out in such a way as to insure that the heads of state and the political leadership in Nicaragua—in Central America—recognized the United States was going to meet the commitments of the President's foreign policy.

And the President's foreign policy was that we are going to achieve a democratic outcome in Nicaragua and that our support for the Nicaraguan freedom fighters was going to continue, and that I was given the job of holding them together in body and soul. And it slowly transitioned into a more difficult task as time went on and as the C.I.A. had to withdraw further and further from that support, until finally we got to the point in October when I was the only person left talking to them. . . .

Question: Do you know whether or not the President was aware of your activities seeking funds and operational support for the contras, from third countries?

Answer: I do not know.

Question: Were you ever—

Answer: I assumed that he did.

Question: . . . What was the basis of your assumption?

Answer: Just that there was a lot going on and it was very obvious that the Nicaraguan resistance survived—I sent forward innumerable documents, some of which you've just shown us as exhibits, that demonstrated that I was keeping my superiors fully informed, as to what was going on.

Source: "Iran-Contra Hearings: 'I Came Here to Tell You the Truth'; The Colonel States His Case: Country and Orders above All," *New York Times*, July 8, 1987, A8.

DOCUMENT 28.10

George Mitchell | Response to Oliver North, 1987

Maine senator George Mitchell joined the joint House and Senate committee investigating the Iran-Contra affair in 1987. During Oliver North's testimony, Mitchell listened to North's characterization of his activities and support for the Contras as the true patriotic course of action. In Mitchell's response to North, he discusses the meaning of patriotism in a democratic society.

My time is nearly up and I want to make some closing observations, because you have, as I indicated, expressed several points of view with respect to which there are other points of view, and I think they ought to be expressed, and I would like to do that now.

You have talked here often and eloquently about the need for a democratic outcome in Nicaragua. There is no disagreement on that. There is disagreement as how best to achieve that objective. Many Americans agree with the President's policy; many do not. Many patriotic Americans, strongly anti-Communist, believe there's a better way to contain the Sandinistas, to bring about a democratic outcome in Nicaragua and to bring peace to Central America.

And many patriotic Americans are concerned that in the pursuit of democracy abroad we not compromise it in any way here at home. You and others have urged consistency in our policies, you have said repeatedly that if we are not consistent our allies and other nations will question our reliability. That is a real concern. But if it's bad to change policies, it's worse to have two different policies at the same time: one public policy and an opposite policy in private. It's difficult to conceive of a greater inconsistency than that. It's hard to imagine anything that would give our allies more cause to consider us unreliable than that we say one thing in public and secretly do the opposite. And that's exactly what was done when arms were sold to Iran and arms were swapped for hostages.

Now, you have talked a lot about patriotism and the love of our country. Most nations derive from a single tribe, a single race; they practice a single religion. Common racial, ethnic, religious heritages are the glue of nationhood for many. The United States is different; we have all races, all religions, we have a limited common heritage. The glue of nationhood for us is the American ideal of individual liberty and equal justice. The rule of law is critical in our society. It's the great equalizer, because in America everybody is equal before the law. We must never allow the end to justify the means where the law is concerned. However important and noble an objective, and surely democracy abroad is important and is noble, it cannot be achieved at the expense of the rule of law in our country. And our diversity is very broad.

You talked about your background and it was really very compelling, and is obviously one of the reasons why the American people are attracted to you.

Let me tell you a story from my background. Before I entered the Senate, I had the great honor of serving as a federal judge. In that position I had great power. The one I most enjoyed exercising was the power to make people American citizens. From time to time I presided at what we call naturalization ceremonies; they're citizenship ceremonies. These are people who came from all over the world, risked their lives, sometimes left their families and their fortunes behind to come here. They had gone through the required procedures, and I, in the final act, administered to them the oath of allegiance to the United States, and I made them American citizens. To this moment, to this moment it was the most exciting thing I've ever done in my life.

Ceremonies were always moving for me because my mother was an immigrant, my father the orphan son of immigrants. Neither of them had any education, and they worked at very menial tasks in our society. But because of the openness of America, because of equal justice under law in America, I sit here today a United States Senator. And after every one of these ceremonies I made it a point to speak to these new Americans, I asked them why they came, how they came, and their stories, each of them, were inspiring. I think you would be interested and moved by them given the views you have expressed on this country.

And when I asked them why they came they said several things, mostly two. The first is they said we came because here in America everybody has a chance, opportunity. And they also said over and over again, particularly people from totalitarian societies, we came here because here in America you can criticize the government without looking over your shoulder. Freedom to disagree with the government.

Now, you have addressed several pleas to this committee, very eloquently. None more eloquent than last Friday when in response to a question by Representative [Richard] Cheney you asked that Congress not cut off aid to the Contras for the love of God and for the love of country. I now address a plea to you. Of all the qualities which the American people find compelling about you, none is more impressive than your obvious deep devotion to this country. Please remember that others share that devotion and recognize that it is possible for an American to disagree with you on aid to the Contras and still love God and still love this country just as much as you do.

Although he's regularly asked to do so, God does not take sides in American politics. And in America, disagreement with the policies of the government is not evidence of lack of patriotism.

I want to repeat that: in America, disagreement with the policies of the Government is not evidence of lack of patriotism.

Indeed, it is the very fact that Americans can criticize their government openly and without fear of reprisal that is the essence of our freedom, and that will keep us free.

Now, I have one final plea. Debate this issue forcefully and vigorously as you have and as you surely will, but, please, do it in a way that respects the patriotism and the motives of those who disagree with you, as you would have them respect yours.

Source: Iran-Contra Investigation, Joint Hearings Part II, July 10, 13, and 14, 1987: Continued Testimony of Oliver L. North and Robert C. McFarlane, 31–46.

Interpret the Evidence

1. What was the goal of the Boland Amendment (Document 28.5), and was its wording sufficient to meet that goal? Why or why not?

2. What, if anything, surprises you about the Freedom Fighter's Manual (Document 28.6)? Why would it focus on these specific activities, and do you think they were effective?

3. What does the Tower Commission conclude about Ronald Reagan's management style (Document 28.7)? How does Reagan respond (Document 28.8)?

4. Why did Oliver North assume that President Reagan knew about his activities (Document 28.9)? How does his testimony compare with what Reagan says he knew (Document 28.8)? Can they both be right?

5. Why does George Mitchell focus on the rule of law in his speech (Document 28.10)? How does he relate that idea to patriotism?

Put It in Context

- Compare the Iran-Contra scandal with Watergate (chapter 27). How did Reagan's presidency survive such a scandal when Nixon's did not?

background photo: page 919, Library of Congress

LEARNINGCurve
Check what you know.
bedfordstmartins.com/hewittlawson/LC

Robert Nickelsberg/Getty Images

Matthew Craig/The Commercial Appeal / Landov

One of many demonstrators of all faiths marching against the House Committee on Homeland Security's hearings on the radicalization of American Muslims, 2011.

A mother and daughter watch the inauguration of President Barack Obama at the National Civil Rights Museum in Memphis, Tennessee, 2009.

29

The Challenges of a New Century

1993 to the present

Joe Raedle/Getty Images

A girl sits on her father's shoulders at an Occupy Miami protest in Miami, Florida, 2011.

William Henry Gates III started tinkering with computers at age thirteen. At that time in the late 1960s, computers were big, bulky machines that filled entire rooms. As a teenager in 1969, the enterprising Gates and some of his friends set up a business to make computerized traffic counters to gauge the speed of automobiles and other vehicles, for which they earned $20,000.

His brilliant mathematical mind and entrepreneurial inclinations led Gates to enroll at Harvard, where those same qualities soon led him to drop out. He spent more time at the university's computer center than he did in class, and in 1974 he became interested in microcomputers as an alternative to large conventional computers. A year later, Gates went to Albuquerque, New Mexico, and formed a computer software company called Microsoft (an amalgam of *microcomputer* and *software*). He envisioned the microcomputer on every office desktop and in homes throughout America. Gates actively pursued the lucrative financial rewards that microcomputers would bring, in contrast to other microcomputer pioneers who did not seek commercial gain and shared information and software with one another freely and unconditionally.

Bill Gates succeeded beyond all expectations. In 1980 Microsoft, now headquartered in Bellevue, Washington, collaborated with International Business Machines (IBM) to create a software package for IBM's new line of personal computers. Additional technological breakthroughs came rapidly. Microsoft joined the financial boom of the 1980s and in 1986 became a publicly traded company on the New York Stock Exchange. Within a

927

decade, Gates became the richest man in America, and like other industrial titans a century earlier, he has donated generously to fund philanthropic activities worldwide.

Despite the enormous benefits of computer technology, the digital revolution has had unforeseen consequences. The terrorists who attacked the World Trade Center and the Pentagon on September 11, 2001, communicated through e-mail and cell phones and trained on computerized flight simulators. They belonged to al-Qaeda, an international terror network that spread its ideology and raised and transferred money over the Internet.

Kristen Breitweiser was a young housewife and mother living in suburban New Jersey on September 11, 2001 (9/11). Her husband, Ron, a senior vice president at an investment management service, worked in Tower Two of the World Trade Center. When one of the planes commandeered by terrorists crashed into the building, her husband died in the fiery collapse of the building, leaving her a widow with a two-year-old daughter. Breitweiser's loss transformed her from a grieving victim and a stay-at-home mother into a political activist.

She started attending meetings of the Victim Compensation Fund established by the federal government following 9/11. She met Mindy Kleinberg, Lorie Van Auken, and Patty Casazza, widows like herself living in New Jersey. The "Jersey Girls," as they became known, addressed concerns over victims' compensation but soon confronted larger political issues. Seeking more than financial compensation for their losses, they

Bill Gates and Kristen Breitweiser

demanded to know how the 9/11 attacks could have happened and what the federal government might have done to prevent them. Breitweiser and her colleagues favored an investigation by an independent commission to gather information about what had occurred and to make recommendations to prevent other attacks. However, they found themselves in opposition to President George W. Bush, who initially resisted the creation of such a commission.

Undeterred, the four women mounted a vigorous campaign to pressure the White House and Congress to form a national commission. Breitweiser testified before the Joint Congressional Intelligence Committee to garner support. The women's perseverance paid off: In November 2002, Congress established a bipartisan commission that President Bush signed into law.

However, the commission's final report in 2004 disappointed Breitweiser. She called the report "hollow" and criticized President Bush for not fully and openly cooperating with the investigation. Although Breitweiser had voted for Bush in the 2000 election and considered herself a conservative, her rapid political education since 9/11 turned her against his candidacy in 2004. She also spoke out against the Iraq War, which the administration had initiated in 2003 in response to the 9/11 attacks. Breitweiser continued her political activism as a blog writer for *The Huffington Post*. In this way, this housewife from New Jersey shared her views with millions of people through technology that Bill Gates's generation had developed. •

THE AMERICAN HISTORIES of Bill Gates and Kristen Breitweiser were deeply affected by the twin forces of digital technology and terror that dominated life in the United States and throughout the world at the start of the twenty-first century. Computers, the Internet, and cell phone technology reformulated commerce and social relations, fostering the globalization that emerged after the Cold War (see chapter 28). Google, the Web, Facebook, and Twitter became household words and broke down domestic and global barriers that twentieth-century technology had not yet demolished. Computer technology revolutionized political communication and organization, mobilized ordinary citizens into action, and expanded opportunities for disgruntled and oppressed citizens of foreign countries to overthrow despotic rulers. Driven by new computer models for trading in financial securities, the stock market grew highly volatile, and downturns in the economy became greater in intensity and scope. At the same time, the threat of terrorism continued to preoccupy the United States and its allies around the world, and their governments used the latest technologies to monitor suspected terrorists. Ordinary people paid for this increased surveillance each time they boarded an airplane and were subjected to intimate security searches.

Transforming American Society

The decade of the 1990s was a period of great economic growth and technological advancement in the United States. Computers stood at the center of the technological revolution of the late twentieth and early twenty-first centuries, allowing both small and large businesses to reach new markets and transform the workplace. Digital technology also altered the personal habits of individuals in the way they worked, purchased goods and services, communicated, and spent their leisure time. As the Internet and World Wide Web connected Americans to the rest of the world, corporate leaders embraced globalization as the key to economic prosperity. They put together business mergers so that their companies could operate more powerfully in the international market. Government officials generally supported their efforts by reducing regulations on business and financial practices, thus encouraging greater risk taking and easing the way for freer trade overseas. Globalization not only thrust American business enterprises outward but also brought a new population of immigrants to the United States.

The Computer Revolution

The first working computers were developed for military purposes during World War II and the Cold War and were enormous in size and cost. Engineers began to resolve the size issue with the creation of transistors. Invented by Bell Laboratories in the late 1940s, these silicon pieces of equipment came into widespread use in running computers during the 1960s. As companies manufactured smaller and smaller silicon chips, computers became faster, cheaper, and more reliable. The design of integrated circuits in the 1970s led to the production of microcomputers in which a silicon chip the size of a nail head did the work once

performed by huge computers. Bill Gates was not the only one to recognize the potential market of microcomputers for home and business use. Steve Jobs, like Gates a college dropout, founded Apple Computer Company in 1976. By 1980 the company had become a publicly traded corporation, turning its founder into a multimillionaire.

Microchips and digital technology found a market beyond home and office computers. Beginning in the 1980s, computers replaced the mechanical devices that ran household appliances such as washing machines, dishwashers, and refrigerators. Over the next twenty years, computers operated everything from standard appliances such as televisions and telephones, to new electronic gadgets such as VCR and CD players, fax machines, cell phones, and iPods. Computers controlled traffic lights on the streets and air traffic in the skies. They changed the leisure patterns of youth: Many young people preferred to play video games at home, rather than engage in outside activities. Consumers purchased goods online, and companies such as Amazon sold merchandise through cyberspace without any actual retail stores. Computers became the stars of movies such as *The Matrix* (1999), *A.I. Artificial Intelligence* (2001), and *Iron Man* (2008). In 2010 *The Social Network* became a hit in portraying the life of Mark Zuckerberg, the primary developer of the social media Web site Facebook, which in 2012 had 900 million users worldwide.

The Internet—an open, global series of interconnected computer networks that transmit data, information, electronic mail, and other services—made social networking possible. The Internet grew out of military research in the 1970s, when the Department of Defense constructed a system of computer servers connected to one another throughout the United States. The main objective of this network was to preserve military communications in the event of a Soviet nuclear attack. At the end of the Cold War, the Internet was repurposed for nonmilitary use, and it now links government, academic, business, and organizational systems. In 1991 the World Wide Web came into existence as a way to access the Internet and share documents and images. Search engines like Google and Yahoo were developed to allow computer users to "surf the Net" and gain access to Web pages. Consumers could shop online as they once had in stores, and researchers could find information previously available only in libraries. Politicians learned how to use the Internet to raise campaign funds and spread their messages to voters more widely and more quickly than they had been able to do in person or on television. Terrorist groups, such as al-Qaeda, also went online. In 2010 around 75 percent of people in the United States used the Internet, as did nearly 2 billion people worldwide, about a quarter of the globe's population.

The Digital Revolution

Digital technology revolutionized business and personal communications. Introduced in the 1990s, smartphones combine the functions of cell phones with those of a computer, and they appeal to users of all ages. Using their smartphones, this family can make phone calls, send text messages, take photos and videos, listen to music, surf the Web, and download applications. Compassionate Eye Foundation/Jetta Productions/ Getty Images

Digital communication revolutionized globalization. Bill Gates's computer software programs, along with the Internet and World Wide Web, dramatically reduced the time it took for trading partners around the world to converse and make business decisions. Consumers in the United States called customer service operators stationed in India and other remote sites. E-mail largely replaced postal mail, allowing Americans to instantly contact relatives, friends, or professional and business associates around the country or the world.

Business Consolidation

The incredible growth of the computer industry led to increased business consolidation, making it possible for large firms to communicate instantly within the United States and throughout the world and to keep control over their far-flung operations. In addition, the federal government aided the merger process by relaxing financial regulation. Media companies took the greatest advantage of this situation. In 1990 the giant Warner Communications merged with Time Life to create an entertainment empire that included a film studio (Warner Brothers), a television cable network (Home Box Office), a music company (Atlantic Records), a baseball team (the Atlanta Braves), and several magazines (*Time, Sports Illustrated*, and *People*). Before Warner Communications combined with the Internet service provider America Online (AOL) in

2001, it had topped $21 billion annually in sales. Several other media conglomerates formed during this period as well. The Australian-born Rupert Murdoch, who already owned considerable holdings in his home country and in Great Britain, moved his operations to the United States. Murdoch soon purchased the Fox Broadcasting Company to go along with a satellite dish company; a movie studio; a variety of newspapers, including the *New York Post* and the *Wall Street Journal*; and thirty television stations. Media mergers mirrored the trend in the rest of the economy. The estimated number of business mergers rose dramatically from 1,529 in 1991 to 4,500 in 1998. The market value of these transactions in 1998 was approximately $2 trillion, compared with $600 billion for 1989, the previous peak year for consolidation.

Corporate consolidation brought corporate malfeasance, as some chief executives of major companies abused their power by expanding their companies too quickly and making risky financial deals, which put workers and stockholders in jeopardy. Such practices led to a number of scandals, including one involving Enron. Enron was the product of a merger in 1985 between Houston Natural Gas and InterNorth, a gas company headquartered in Omaha, Nebraska. Operating out of Houston, Texas, Enron benefited from the deregulation of the gas and electric industry in the 1990s, which brought exorbitant profits and encouraged corporate greed. As Enron thrived, its prices shot up and its stock soared, earning the company more than

$50 billion in 2001. In October of that year, information began to trickle out about insider trading, faulty business deals, and questionable accounting practices. As these revelations mounted, Enron's stock and its credit rating plunged, jeopardizing the solvency of the company. In December 2001, the once mighty Enron filed for bankruptcy and fired four thousand employees; its top two executives were subsequently convicted on charges of criminal fraud. This scandal affected companies beyond Enron, leading to the conviction of executives from Enron's accounting firm, Arthur Andersen, and another Andersen client, WorldCom.

The Changing American Population

At the same time as the technological revolution helped transform the U.S. economy and society, an influx of immigrants began to greatly alter the composition of the American population. Since passage of the Immigration Act of 1965 (see chapter 26), the country had experienced a wave of immigration comparable to that at the turn of the twentieth century. As the population of the United States grew from 202 million to 300 million between 1970 and 2006, immigrants accounted for some 28 million of the increase. They came to live in the United States for much the same reasons as those who had journeyed before: to seek economic opportunity and to find political and religious freedom.

Most newcomers who came in the 1980s and 1990s arrived from Latin America and South and East Asia; relatively few Europeans (approximately 2 million) moved to the United States, though their numbers increased after the collapse of the Soviet empire in the early 1990s. Poverty and political unrest pushed migrants out of Mexico, Central America, and the Caribbean. The prizewinning film *El Norte* (1983) dramatized the plight of undocumented Guatemalan Indians who traveled through Mexico to settle in California. Yet most others took advantage of a provision in the 1965 act that permitted them to join family members already settled in the United States. At the beginning of the twenty-first century, Latinos (35 million) had surpassed African Americans (34 million) as the nation's largest minority group. However, with the arrival of Caribbean

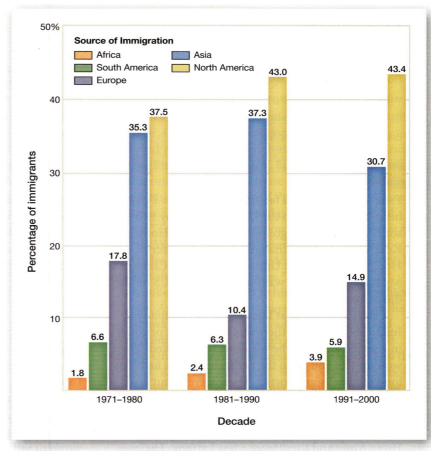

FIGURE 29.1   Immigrant Growth by Home Region, 1971–2000

In the late twentieth century, immigration to the United States increased significantly, especially from North America (which in this figure includes Mexico, Central America, and the Caribbean). Residents of East and South Asia formed the second largest group of immigrants while Africans arrived in small but growing numbers.   Source: Data from *2000 Statistical Yearbook of the Immigration and Naturalization Service.*

and African immigrants, black America was also becoming more diverse in this period.

Explore

See Document 29.1 for one immigrant's experience in low-wage factory work.

In addition to the 16 million immigrants who came from south of the U.S. border, another 9 million headed eastward from Asian nations, including China, South Korea, and the Philippines, together with refugees from the Vietnam War and Cambodia. By 2007 an estimated 1.6 million Indians from South Asia had immigrated to the United States, most arriving after the 1960s. Indian Americans became the third-largest Asian American group behind Chinese and Filipinos. Another 1 to 2 million people came from predominantly Islamic nations such as Pakistan, Lebanon, Iraq, and Iran (Figure 29.1).

Clinton tried to appeal to voters across the political spectrum on other issues. He signed a tough anticrime law that funded the recruitment of an additional 100,000 police officers to patrol city streets, while supporting gun control legislation. Managing to overcome the powerful lobby of the National Rifle Association, in 1993 Clinton signed the Brady Bill (named after Ronald Reagan's aide who was shot in the attempted assassination of the president in 1981), which imposed a five-day waiting period to check the background of gun buyers.

The president achieved even greater success in promoting racial diversity. He appointed African Americans to high-level positions in his cabinet—his selection of four African Americans at one time was unprecedented. His "rainbow administration" welcomed women and minorities to other important posts. Born in the segregated South, Clinton had become a strong advocate of affirmative action and did what he could to protect it from conservative challenges in the states and the courts.

Clinton's fiscal policies ushered in a period of economic growth and prosperity, which ended the recession of the early 1990s. With congressional support, the president reduced domestic and defense spending by $500 billion, while raising taxes on wealthy individuals and corporations. By the end of the 1990s, the Clinton administration had eliminated the deficit, the gross domestic product was rising 3 percent annually, unemployment dropped from 6 percent to 4 percent, and the stock market reached record highs.

President Clinton's accomplishments aroused fierce opposition from conservatives. Right-wing talk radio hosts criticized the president and his wife, Hillary Rodham Clinton, a lawyer and leader in the effort to reform health care. Conservatives blamed Clinton for all they considered wrong in society—feminism, abortion, affirmative action, and secularism. Rush Limbaugh, a popular conservative talk-show host, donned the self-proclaimed mantle of the "angry white male." His rhetoric respected few boundaries, even on publicly owned airwaves, where he uttered comments such as "Feminism was established to allow unattractive women access to mainstream society." Clinton's personal life also provided ammunition for his opponents. Rumors of marital infidelity hounded him, and questions about his and his wife's pre-presidential dealings in a controversial real estate development project known as Whitewater prompted the appointment in 1994 of a special prosecutor to investigate allegations of impropriety.

Facing conservative opposition, the president and the Democratic Party fared poorly in the 1994 congressional elections. Republicans, led by House Minority Leader Newt Gingrich of Georgia, championed the **Contract with America**. This document embraced conservative principles of a constitutional amendment for a balanced budget, reduced welfare spending, lower taxes, and term limits for lawmakers. Democrats lost fifty-four seats in the House, and for the first time since 1952 Republicans captured a majority of both houses of Congress. This election also underscored the increasing electoral influence of white evangelical Christians, who turned out to vote in large numbers for Republican candidates.

Stung by this defeat, Clinton tried to outmaneuver congressional Republicans by shifting rightward politically and championing welfare reform. In 1996 he signed the **Personal Responsibility and Work Opportunity Reconciliation Act**, which abolished the Aid to Families with Dependent Children provision of the Social Security law, the basis for welfare in the United States since the New Deal. The measure required adults on the welfare rolls to find work within two years or lose the benefits provided to families earning less than $7,700. Welfare had provided Republicans with a wedge issue to divide the Democratic electorate, and Clinton diminished its effect by supporting reform. Also in 1996, the president approved the Defense of Marriage Act, which denied married same-sex couples the federal benefits granted to heterosexual married couples, including Social Security survivor's benefits.

In adopting such positions as deficit reduction, welfare reform, and antigay legislation, Clinton ensured his reelection in 1996. Running against Republican senator Robert Dole of Kansas, a military veteran of World War II, and the independent candidate Ross Perot, Clinton captured 49 percent of the popular vote and 379 electoral votes. Dole received 41 percent of the vote, and Perot came in a distant third with 8 percent, a sharp decline from the 19 percent he had received four years earlier (see chapter 27).

Global Challenges and Economic Renewal

Clinton faced numerous foreign policy challenges during his two terms in office. As the first president elected to office in the post–Cold War era, Clinton could approach trouble spots without the rigid anti-Communist views of his predecessors. Increasingly, the problems facing the United States did not result from customary military aggression by one nation against another; rather, the greatest threats came from the implosion of national governments into factionalism and genocide, as well as the dangers posed by Islamic extremists.

At first, the Clinton administration acted cautiously. During a civil war in the African nation of Rwanda, Hutu extremists dispatched armed militias to exterminate the ethnic Tutsi population. The United States watched from the sidelines, along with most of the rest of the world. The slaughter of more than 800,000 Tutsis and moderate Hutus brought condemnation but little action other than the United Nations' attempt to evacuate refugees from the massacre. Following this tragedy, Hollywood told the story of this genocide in the movie *Hotel Rwanda* (2004), which occasioned sympathy for the plight of the Rwandan victims, if not shame for the inaction of the United States.

By contrast, Clinton responded boldly to violence in the Balkans, an area considered more vital to U.S. national security than Rwanda. Along with the collapse of Eastern European regimes in 1989, Yugoslavia splintered into religious and ethnic pieces after the crumbling of the ruling Communist regime. The predominantly Roman Catholic states of Slovenia and Croatia declared their independence from the largely Russian Orthodox Serbian population in Yugoslavia. In 1992 the mainly Muslim territory of Bosnia-Herzegovina also broke away, much to the chagrin of its substantial Serbian population (Map 29.1). This unleashed a civil war between Serb and Croatian minorities and the Muslim-dominated Bosnian government. Supported by Slobodan Milošević, the leader of the neighboring province of Serbia, Bosnian Serbs wrested control of large parts of the region and slaughtered tens of thousands of Muslims through what they euphemistically called **ethnic cleansing**.

MAP 29.1   The Breakup of Yugoslavia, 1991–2008
With the collapse of Communist control of Yugoslavia in 1989, the country splintered along ethnic and religious lines, eventually forming seven separate nations. A civil war between Serbia and Croatia ended in 1995, but Serbs then attacked Muslims in Bosnia and Kosovo.

In 1995, following three years of violence, Clinton sponsored NATO bombing raids against the Serbs and dispatched 20,000 American troops as part of a multilateral peacekeeping force. At the same time, the president brokered a peace agreement, known as the **Dayton Peace Accords**, among Serbia, Croatia, and Bosnia at a conference in Dayton, Ohio. In 1999 renewed conflict erupted when Milošević's Serbian government attacked the province of Kosovo to eliminate its Albanian Muslim residents. Clinton and NATO responded by initiating air strikes against the Serbs and placing troops on the ground, actions that preserved Kosovo's independence. (Milošević was later brought before the World Court to face trial for war crimes but died before the court reached a verdict.)

The United States faced an even graver danger from Islamic extremists intent on waging a religious struggle (jihad) of terror against their perceived enemies and establishing a transnational Muslim government, or caliphate. Former presidents Jimmy Carter in Iran and Ronald Reagan in Lebanon had experienced the wrath of radical Muslims (see chapter 28). The United States' close relationship with Israel placed it high on the list of terrorist targets, along with pro-American Muslim governments in Egypt, Pakistan, and Indonesia. In 1993 Islamic militants orchestrated the bombing of the World Trade Center's underground garage, which killed six people and injured more than one thousand. Five years later, terrorists blew up American embassies in the African nations of Kenya and Tanzania, killing hundreds and injuring thousands of local workers and residents. In retaliation, Clinton ordered air strikes against terrorist bases in Sudan and Afghanistan. However, the danger persisted. In 2000 al-Qaeda terrorists blew a gaping hole in the side of the USS *Cole*, a U.S. destroyer anchored in Yemen, killing seventeen American sailors.

International terrorism did not lead to the undoing of President Clinton, but more mundane, sexual indiscretions nearly brought him down. Starting in 1995, Clinton had engaged in consensual sexual relations with Monica Lewinsky, a twenty-two-year-old White House intern. Clinton denied these charges under oath and before a national television audience, but when Lewinsky testified about the details of their sexual encounters, the president recanted his earlier statements that he had never had "sexual relations with *that* woman." After an independent prosecutor concluded that Clinton had committed perjury and obstructed justice, the Republican-controlled House voted to impeach the president on December 19, 1998, the first time it had done so in 130 years (see chapter 14). However, on February 12, 1999, Republicans in the Senate failed to muster the necessary two-thirds vote to convict Clinton on the impeachment charges.

Despite his impeachment, Clinton left the country in more prosperous shape than he had found it. At the height of the sex scandal in 1998, the unemployment rate fell to 4.3 percent, the lowest level since the early 1970s. The rate of home ownership reached a record-setting nearly 67 percent. As the "misery index"—a compilation of unemployment and inflation—fell, the gross domestic product grew by more than $250 billion. By 1999 the stock market's Dow Jones average reached a historic 10,000 points, up 2,000 points from just two years before. The Clinton administration boasted that its economic policies had succeeded in canceling the Reagan-Bush budget deficit, yielding a surplus of $230 billion for the fiscal year 2000. This boom, however, did not affect everyone equally. African Americans and Latinos lagged behind whites economically. The gap between rich and poor widened, as the wealthiest 13,000 American families earned as much income as the poorest 20 million. Despite these shortcomings, most Americans seemed pleased with the economic renaissance of the Clinton years.

REVIEW & RELATE

How did conflicts between Democrats and Republicans affect President Clinton's accomplishments?

How did the end of the Cold War shape President Clinton's foreign policies?

 LEARNING*Curve* bedfordstmartins.com/hewittlawson/LC

The New Millennium

Following the prosperous but turbulent Clinton years, Americans looked forward to celebrating the new millennium with hope for the future. Yet this did not happen. Within two years, the country endured a bruising presidential election, experienced unprecedented terrorism at home, and engaged in two wars abroad. The second baby boomer president, George W. Bush, left the country as politically divided as had his predecessor.

George W. Bush and Compassionate Conservatism

In the first presidential election of the new century, the Democratic candidate, Vice President Al Gore, ran against George W. Bush, the Republican governor of Texas and son of the forty-first president. This election marked the first contest between members of the baby boom generation, but in many ways politics remained the same. Candidates began

to use the latest technology—the Internet and sophisticated phone banks to mobilize voters—but they rehashed issues stemming from the Clinton years. Gore ran on the coattails of the Clinton prosperity, endorsed affirmative action, was pro-choice on women's reproductive rights, and warned of the need to protect the environment. Presenting himself as a "compassionate conservative," Bush opposed abortion, gay rights, and affirmative action while at the same time supporting faith-based reform initiatives in education and social welfare. Also in the race was Ralph Nader, an anticorporate activist who ran under the banner of the Green Party, a party formed in 1991 in support of grassroots democracy, environmentalism, social justice, and gender equality. According to Nader, Gore and Bush were "Tweedledee and Tweedledum—they look and act the same, so it doesn't matter who you get." Despite this claim, Nader appealed to much the same constituency as did Gore.

Nader's candidacy drew votes away from Gore, but fraud and partisanship hurt the Democrats even more. Gore won a narrow plurality of the popular vote (48.4 percent) compared with 47.8 percent for Bush and 2.7 percent for Nader. However, Bush won a slim majority of the electoral votes: 271 to 267. The key state in this Republican victory was Florida, where Bush outpolled Gore by fewer than 500 popular votes. Counties with high proportions of African Americans and the poor encountered the greatest difficulty and outright discrimination in voting, and in these areas voters were more likely to support Gore. A subsequent recount of the vote might have benefited Bush because Republicans controlled the state government. (Jeb Bush, the Republican candidate's younger brother, was Florida's governor, and Republicans held a majority in the legislature.) Eventually, litigation over the recount reached the U.S. Supreme Court, and on December 12, 2000, more than a month after the election, the Court proclaimed Bush the winner in a decision that clearly reflected the preferences of the conservative justices appointed by Ronald Reagan and George H. W. Bush.

George W. Bush did not view his slim, contested victory cautiously. Rather, he intended to appeal mainly to his conservative political base and govern as boldly as if he had received a resounding electoral mandate. Republicans still controlled the House, whereas a Republican defection in the Senate gave the Democrats a one-vote majority. According to the veteran political reporter Ronald Brownstein, Bush and his congressional leaders "would rather pass legislation as close as possible to his preferences on a virtual party-line basis than make concessions to reduce political tensions or broaden his support among Democrats."

The president promoted the agenda of the evangelical Christian wing of the Republican Party. He spoke out against gay marriage, abortion, and federal support for stem cell impulse for building large-scale organizations, the same passion for size as could be seen in corporate consolidations. Between 1970 and 2005, the number of megachurches jumped from 50 to more than 1,300, with California, Texas, and Florida taking the lead. The establishment of massive churches was part of a worldwide movement, with South Korea home to the largest congregation. Joel Osteen—the evangelical pastor of Lakewood Church in Houston, Texas, the largest megachurch in the United States—drew average weekly audiences of 43,000 people, with sermons available in English and Spanish. Preaching in a former professional basketball arena and using the latest technology, Osteen stood under giant video screens that projected his image. He and other pastors of megachurches have earned enormous wealth from preaching and writing, which their followers consider justified. "Many preachers tell us that God loves us, but Osteen makes us believe that God loves us. And this is why he is so successful," one observer reflected.

While courting such people of faith, Bush did not neglect economic conservatives. The Republican Congress gave the president tax-cut proposals to sign in 2001 and 2003, measures that favored the wealthiest Americans. Yet to maintain a balanced budget, the cardinal principle of fiscal conservatism, these tax cuts would have required a substantial reduction in spending, which Bush and Congress chose not to do. Furthermore, continued deregulation of business encouraged unsavory and harmful activities that resulted in corporate scandals and risky financial practices.

At the same time, Bush showed the compassionate side of his conservatism. Like Clinton's cabinet appointments, Bush's appointments reflected racial, ethnic, and sexual diversity. They included African Americans as secretary of state (Colin Powell), national security adviser (Condoleezza Rice, who later succeeded Powell as secretary of state), and secretary of education (Rod Paige). In addition, the president chose women to head the Departments of Agriculture, Interior, and Labor and also appointed one Latino and two Asian Americans to his cabinet.

In 2002 the president signed the No Child Left Behind Act, which raised federal appropriations for the education of students in primary and secondary schools, especially in underprivileged areas. The law imposed federal criteria for evaluating teachers and school programs, relying on standardized testing to do so. Another display of compassionate conservatism came in the 2003 passage of the Medicare Prescription Drug, Improvement, and Modernization Act. The law was projected to cost more than $400 billion over a ten-year period to lower the cost of prescription drugs to some 40 million senior citizens under the 1965 Medicare Act and received support from the American Association of Retired Persons (AARP).

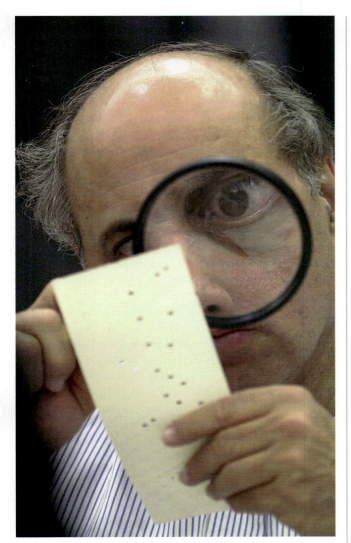

Hanging Chads and the 2000 Presidential Election
The outcome of the 2000 presidential election between George W. Bush and Al Gore hinged on who won Florida. The closeness of the vote required a recount, and election officials, including this one in Broward County, had to scrutinize ballots closely to figure out the intentions of voters who left a hanging chad (paper fragment) on the punch-card ballot.   AP Photo/Alan Diaz

research, a scientific procedure that used discarded embryos to find cures for diseases. The president created a special office in the White House to coordinate faith-based initiatives, programs that provided religious institutions with federal funds for social service activities without violating the First Amendment's separation of church and state.

At the turn of the twenty-first century, a growing number of churchgoers were attending **megachurches**. These congregations, mainly Protestant, each contained 2,000 or more worshippers and reflected the American

The United States at War

President Bush ultimately spent little of his presidency focusing on domestic issues because events originating from abroad vaulted him into the role of wartime president. To make up for his lack of experience in foreign affairs, Bush relied heavily on Vice President Richard (Dick) Cheney, Secretary of Defense Donald Rumsfeld, and Condoleezza Rice. In running for election in 2000, Bush had pledged: "I would be very careful about using our troops as nation builders. I believe the role of the military is to fight and win war and therefore prevent war from happening in the first place." However, Bush's closest advisers had other ideas and sought to reshape critical parts of the post–Cold War world through preemptive force, most notably in the Persian Gulf.

After the attacks on the World Trade Center and the Pentagon on September 11, 2001, the president abandoned his campaign promise to use U.S. troops cautiously and followed the counsel of his advisers. The violence that killed Kristen Breitweiser's husband and thousands of others on that day changed the direction of U.S. foreign and domestic policies. The country undertook a war on terror, one that led to protracted and costly conflicts in Afghanistan and Iraq and the erosion of civil liberties at home. As part of that effort, in 2002 Congress created a cabinet-level superagency, the Department of Homeland Security,

responsible for developing a national strategy against further terrorist threats. Congress also enacted into law a key recommendation of the national commission that Breitweiser and the Jersey Girls pressured the government to establish. In 2004 Congress created the Office of the Director of National Intelligence to coordinate the work of security agencies more effectively.

In the immediate aftermath of the September 11 terrorist attacks, Bush acted decisively. The president dispatched U.S. troops to Afghanistan, whose Taliban leaders refused to turn over Osama bin Laden and other terrorists operating training centers in the country. A combination of anti-Taliban warlords and U.S. military special forces, backed up by American aircraft, toppled the Taliban regime and installed a pro-American government; however, the United States did not immediately capture the elusive bin Laden, who escaped somewhere in the remote territory of Pakistan.

On the home front, the war on terror prompted passage of the **Patriot Act** in October 2001. The measure eased restrictions on domestic and foreign intelligence gathering and expanded the authority of law enforcement and immigration officials in detaining and deporting immigrants suspected of terrorism-related acts. The act gave law enforcement agencies nearly unlimited authority to wiretap telephones, retrieve e-mail messages, and search the medical, financial, and library borrowing records of

President Bush at Ground Zero

On September 14, 2001, President George W. Bush toured the wreckage of the destroyed World Trade Center. Standing on a pile of rubble, he heard firefighters, police officers, and other rescuers shout, "USA, USA." He responded: "I can hear you. The rest of the world hears you. And the people who knocked these buildings down will hear all of us soon." Reuters/ Win McNamee/Landov

individuals, including U.S. citizens, suspected of involvement in terrorism overseas or at home. The computer age had provided terrorist networks like al-Qaeda with the means to communicate quickly through electronic mail and cell phones across national boundaries and to raise money and launder it into safe bank accounts online. Computer technology also gave U.S. intelligence agencies ways to monitor these communications and transactions.

Amid rising anti-Muslim sentiments, the overwhelming majority of Americans supported the Patriot Act. In the weeks and months following September 11, some people committed acts of violence against mosques, Arab American community centers and businesses, and individual Muslims and people thought to be Muslims (such as Sikhs). Near Chicago, a crowd of about three hundred anti-Arab youths waved flags, shouted "USA, USA," and attempted to march on a mosque. In this atmosphere, some critics complained about the harsh provisions of the Patriot Act, comparing them to the measures restricting civil liberties during the Red scare following World War I (see chapter 21). Nevertheless, in 2006 Congress renewed the act with only minor changes.

President Bush and his advisers, particularly Vice President Cheney and Secretary of Defense Rumsfeld, did not believe that the defeat of the Taliban in Afghanistan had ended the war on terror. Rather, they saw it as part of a larger plan to reshape the politics of the Middle East and Persian Gulf regions along pro-American lines. In doing so, the United States and its European allies would ensure the flow of cheap oil in order to satisfy the energy demands of consumers in these countries. Furthermore, by replacing authoritarian regimes with democratic governments in places like Iraq and Afghanistan, the Bush administration envisioned a domino effect that would lead to the toppling of reactionary leaders throughout the region. The establishment of pro-American, democratic nations, according to this strategy, would defeat extremist Islamic powers, thereby paving the way for resolving deep-seated, ongoing conflicts between Arabs and Israelis. In crafting this strategy, the Bush administration departed from the well-established, post–World War II policy of containing enemies short of going to war. Instead, the **Bush Doctrine** proposed undertaking preemptive war against despotic governments deemed a threat to U.S. national security, even if that danger was not imminent.

Following this doctrine, President Bush declared in January 2002 that Iraq was part of an "axis of evil," along with Iran and North Korea. Although the United States had supported Saddam Hussein in Iraq's war against Iran in the 1980s, Bush considered the Iraqi dictator to be in the same terrorist camp with Osama bin Laden. Little had changed in Iraq since the 1980s, but President Bush sought to complete the job that his father had started and then retreated from in the 1991 Gulf War—removing Hussein from power. The Iraqi leader was considered too undependable to protect U.S. oil interests in the region. Removing him would also open a path to overthrowing the radical Islamic government of neighboring Iran, which had embarrassed the United States in 1979 and remained its sworn enemy (see chapter 28).

Over the next two years, Bush convinced Congress and a majority of the American people that Iraq presented an immediate danger to the security of the United States in its effort to fight global terrorism. He did so by falsely connecting Saddam Hussein to the 9/11 al-Qaeda terrorists. The president also accused Iraq of being well along the way to building and stockpiling "weapons of mass destruction." Even after UN inspectors examined alleged nuclear and chemical weapons facilities in Iraq and found nothing harmful, the Bush administration remained adamant. Further, the government manipulated questionable intelligence information to defend its claims. In a speech to the United Nations based on dubious and inaccurate information, Secretary of State Powell charged that intelligence services had gathered direct evidence that Iraq was working on a nuclear device. **See Document Project 29: The Uses of September 11, page 952.**

Challenging the Bush administration's assumptions and allegations about Iraq, antiwar critics staged mass demonstrations in major cities throughout the country, but with little success. Most Americans gave the president the benefit of the doubt. At the very least, they agreed with Bush that Saddam Hussein was "evil" and that his removal was justified. Thus in March 2003, after a congressional vote of approval, U.S. military aircraft unleashed massive bombing attacks on Baghdad as part of the Bush-Rumsfeld strategy of "shock and awe." Unlike the 1991 Gulf War, in which the first President Bush had responded to the Iraqi invasion of Kuwait and led a broad coalition of nations, including Arab countries (see chapter 28), the United States did not wait for any overt act of aggression and created merely a nominal alliance of nations, with only Great Britain supplying significant combat troops. Nevertheless, within weeks Hussein went into hiding, prompting Bush to declare that "major combat operations" had ended in Iraq.

This triumphant declaration proved premature, although Hussein was captured several months later. Despite the presence of 130,000 U.S. and 30,000 British troops, the war dragged on. More American soldiers (more than 4,000) died after the president proclaimed victory than had died during the invasion. The perception of the United States as an occupying power destabilized Iraq, leading to a civil war between the country's Shi'ite Muslim majority, which had been persecuted under Saddam Hussein, and its Sunni minority, which Hussein represented. In the northern part of the nation, the Kurdish majority, another group brutalized by Hussein, also battled Sunnis. Moreover, al-Qaeda forces, which previously had been absent from the country, joined the fray.

Explore

See Document 29.2 for one reporter's description of life in war-torn Iraq.

The U.S. occupation and attempts at nation building, something that Bush during the 2000 campaign vowed he would not support, caused serious problems. American soldiers staffing jails containing Iraqi war prisoners, such as Abu Ghraib, were caught in photographs abusing their captives. The reconstituted Iraqi army and police lacked experience and harbored rebels within their ranks. Absent a military draft, Bush could not put sufficient active-duty troops into Iraq without exhausting them through extended tours of duty. In 2004 the military began relying on National Guard units to meet troop requirements, and they eventually constituted about 40 percent of the U.S. armed forces in Iraq. To make up for staffing shortages, the Pentagon outsourced to private companies jobs that would normally be performed by military personnel. American companies profited immensely from construction projects; from supplying troops with housing, meals, and uniforms; and from providing security for high-ranking military and diplomatic personnel. The Defense Department awarded contracts without competitive bidding to companies such as Halliburton, which had close ties to Vice President Cheney.

Amid a protracted war in Iraq, President Bush won reelection in 2004 by promising to finish the course of action he had started in Iraq. Bush argued that to do less would encourage terrorists, subvert burgeoning democracy in Iraq and Afghanistan, and dishonor the troops who had been killed and wounded. Although the Democratic presidential candidate, Senator John Kerry of Massachusetts, criticized Bush's handling of Iraq, Bush eked out a victory; however, this time, unlike four years before, the president won a majority of the popular vote (50.7 percent).

Bush's Second Term

Bush won reelection, but over the next four years his credibility suffered. Several issues—the continued presence of sectarian violence in Iraq, the lack of progress in training Iraqi troops and police to safeguard civilians, the mounting death tolls, and the failure of the U.S.-supported Iraqi government to work out a political solution to the country's problems—turned the majority of Americans against the

war. Even when in 2007 the president ordered an increase of 30,000 troops, known as "the surge," which succeeded in reducing mayhem in Baghdad and its vicinity, many Americans had had enough. In 2008 polls showed that 54 percent of Americans considered the invasion of Iraq a mistake, and 49 percent wanted U.S. troops to return home (compared with 47 percent who opposed withdrawal).

However, the president seemed impervious to criticism. The Bush administration continued to enforce the Patriot Act with little concern for the protection of privacy and civil liberties, and it justified its actions on the belief that in a time of war the president had few limits on his power. Bush also refused to back down from the policy of incarcerating suspected al-Qaeda rebels in the U.S. military base in Guantánamo, Cuba. The facility housed more than six hundred men classified as "enemy combatants," who were subject to extreme interrogation and were deprived of legal counsel. This policy changed somewhat when the Supreme Court, in *Hamdan v. Rumsfeld* (2006), ruled that the military tribunals established by the president to prosecute Guantánamo prisoners were unconstitutional. Shortly after, Congress passed legislation providing a small measure of protection for the four hundred prisoners who remained in Guantánamo.

As Bush's handling of the Iraq War generated rising disapproval, his management of a major natural disaster further diminished his popularity. On August 29, 2005, **Hurricane Katrina** slammed into the Gulf coast states of Louisiana and Mississippi. This powerful storm devastated New Orleans, a city with a population of nearly 500,000, a majority of whom were African American. A thirty-foot flood surge caused poorly maintained levees to break, placing large areas of the city underwater. Despite the evacuation of hundreds of thousands of people from New Orleans before the hurricane struck, approximately 50,000 residents remained trapped by the flood. Not only did local and state officials respond slowly and ineptly, but so, too, did the federal government in providing assistance to those trapped in the city.

In the days after the storm hit, chaos reigned in New Orleans. Evacuees were housed in the Superdome football stadium and a municipal auditorium without adequate food, water, and sanitary conditions, and the scenes of despair were broadcast on national television. The flooding killed at least 1,800 residents of the Gulf coast, New Orleans's population dropped by around 130,000 residents, and critics blamed the president for his lack of leadership and slow response to the disaster. Some argued that just as Bush had failed to manage the war in Iraq, he also lacked the ability to handle the Katrina catastrophe. Overall, Hurricane Katrina was just as much a human-made disaster as a natural one.

Farnaz Fassihi | Report from Baghdad, 2004

After U.S. forces ousted Saddam Hussein in 2003, civil war broke out between rival religious sects of Sunni and Shi'ite Muslims. Many Iraqis viewed the United States as an occupying power despite efforts to reconstruct the war-torn nation and promote free elections. In an e-mail to friends in the United States, *Wall Street Journal* correspondent Farnaz Fassihi presents a frank assessment of the deteriorating conditions in Baghdad in September 2004.

Explore

Being a foreign correspondent in Baghdad these days is like being under virtual house arrest. Forget about the reasons that lured me to this job: a chance to see the world, explore the exotic, meet new people in far away lands, discover their ways, and tell stories that could make a difference.

Little by little, day-by-day, being based in Iraq has defied all those reasons. I am house bound. I leave when I have a very good reason to and a scheduled interview. I avoid going to people's homes and never walk in the streets. I can't go grocery shopping any more, can't eat in restaurants, can't strike a conversation with strangers, can't look for stories, can't drive in anything but a full armored car, can't go to scenes of breaking news stories, can't be stuck in traffic, can't speak English outside, can't take a road trip, can't say I'm an American, can't linger at checkpoints, can't be curious about what people are saying, doing, feeling. And can't and can't. There has been one too many close calls, including a car bomb so near our house that it blew out all the windows. So now my most pressing concern every day is not to write a kick-ass story but to stay alive and make sure our Iraqi employees stay alive. In Baghdad I am a security personnel first, a reporter second. . . .

How do conditions in Baghdad affect Fassihi's ability to report on the war?

Iraqis like to call this mess "the situation." When asked "how are things?" they reply: "the situation is very bad."

What they mean by situation is this: the Iraqi government doesn't control most Iraqi cities, there are several car bombs going off each day around the country killing and injuring scores of innocent people, the country's roads are becoming impassable and littered by hundreds of landmines and explosive devices aimed to kill American soldiers, there are assassinations, kidnappings, and beheadings. The situation, basically, means a raging barbaric guerilla war. In four days, 110 people died and over 300 got injured in Baghdad alone. The numbers are so shocking that the ministry of health—which was attempting an exercise of public transparency by releasing the numbers—has now stopped disclosing them.

Why do the Iraqis think the war is going badly?

Insurgents now attack Americans 87 times a day. . . . As for reconstruction: firstly it's so unsafe for foreigners to operate that almost all projects have come to a halt. After two years, of the $18 billion Congress appropriated for Iraq reconstruction only about $1 billion or so has been spent and a chunk has now been reallocated for improving security, a sign of just how bad things are going here. . . .

What are some of the challenges of rebuilding Iraq?

Source: Lisa Grunwald and Stephen J. Adler, eds., *Women's Letters: America from the Revolutionary War to the Present* (New York: Dial Press, 2005), 758–60.

Put It in Context

How does this document challenge the Bush administration's views on the Iraq War?

Two Perceptions of New Orleans Looting

Some members of the media were guilty of racial profiling in their reporting of the aftermath of Hurricane Katrina. Compare the original caption for the photo on the left ("A young man walks through chest-deep floodwater after looting a grocery store in New Orleans") with the one on the right ("Two residents wade through chest-deep water after finding bread and soda from a local grocery store after Hurricane Katrina came through the area in New Orleans"). Racial identity appears to be the only distinction between who was "looting" and who was "finding."   left: AP Photo/ Dave Martin; right: Chris Graythen/Getty Images

Displeased with the Bush administration, voters elected a Democratic majority to the House and Senate in 2006, yet little changed. American troops remained in Iraq and Afghanistan. Mobilization for the war on terror had become a permanent part of life in the United States, much like the growth of the national security state during the Cold War (see chapter 24). However, not all Americans experienced the war equally. With military enlistments at low levels, the men and women who served in Iraq and Afghanistan were disproportionately poor and from minority communities. At the same time, Osama bin Laden remained alive and in hiding, and al-Qaeda had regrouped in Pakistan and Yemen. The Bush administration did little to address the perennial problem of Israeli-Palestinian relations, one of the chief elements that fueled terrorism and Islamic radicalism. Making the situation even more combustible, in 2006 Hamas (the Islamic Resistance Movement), which the United States considered an anti-Semitic, terrorist organization, won Palestinian parliamentary elections and posed a new threat to peace in the Middle East.

With turmoil continuing in the Middle East and the Persian Gulf, the threat of nuclear proliferation grew. Iraq did not have nuclear weapons, but Iran sought to develop nuclear capabilities. Iranian leaders claimed that they wanted nuclear technology for peaceful purposes, but the Bush administration believed that Iran's real purpose was to build nuclear devices to attack Israel and establish its supremacy in the region. The election in 2005 of Mahmoud Ahmadinejad, an avowed enemy of Israel, as president of Iran reinforced Bush's fears. Pakistan, a country that already had nuclear weapons, also proved troublesome. Although an ally of the United States, Pakistan was largely ineffective in removing al-Qaeda and Taliban forces from their bases along the country's border with Afghanistan. Equally disturbing, a high-ranking nuclear scientist in Pakistan had previously sold information to North Korea, one of the states in Bush's "axis of evil." North Korea, a totalitarian nation and one of the few remaining Communist dictatorships left from the Cold War era, conducted underground nuclear tests in 2006.

REVIEW & RELATE

How did President Bush put compassionate conservatism into action?

How did the war on terror prompt U.S. leaders to rethink America's position in the world?

LEARNINGCurve bedfordstmartins.com/hewittlawson/LC

Challenges Ahead

The changes brought by the digital technology of Bill Gates and the war on terror following September 11 had become firmly embedded in the United States and throughout an interconnected, globalized world. In 2008 a new concern emerged with the arrival of the worldwide Great Recession. At the same time, many Americans rallied behind the presidential candidacy of Barack Obama with renewed hope. Obama's election reflected sweeping demographic changes in the United States and brought reform, but Obama's victory did not eliminate the deep political and cultural divisions in the nation or eradicate pervasive economic and social inequality.

The Great Recession

In 2008 the boom times of the early years of the twenty-first century came to a sudden halt. The stock market's Dow Jones average, which had hit a high of 14,000, fell 6,000 points, the steepest percentage drop since 1931. Americans who had invested their money in the stock market lost trillions of dollars. The stock market crash plunged investment firms into crisis. Lehman Brothers, a financial services firm founded in 1850, lost more than $2 billion and went bankrupt. The gross domestic product fell by about 6 percent, a loss too great for the economy to absorb quickly. Americans lost their jobs as consumer spending decreased, and many forfeited their homes when they could no longer afford to pay their mortgages. Unemployment jumped from 4.9 percent in January 2008 to 7.6 percent a year later. Confronted by this spiraling disaster, President Bush approved a $700 billion bailout plan to rescue the nation's largest banks and brokerage houses.

The causes of the **Great Recession** were many and had developed over a long period. Since the Reagan presidency, the federal government had relaxed regulation of the financial industry. The Clinton administration supported repeal of the Glass-Steagall Act (see chapter 22). This measure, enacted during the New Deal, had separated commercial and investment banking to protect small business people and American families and to avoid the intense financial speculation that preceded the stock market crash of 1929 and the Great Depression. The Federal Reserve Bank encouraged excessive borrowing through keeping interest rates very low and relaxed its oversight of Wall Street practices that placed ordinary investors' money at risk. Investment houses developed elaborate computer models that produced new and risky kinds of financial instruments, which went unregulated and whose complex nature few people understood. Insurance companies such as American International Group marketed so-called credit default swaps as protection for risky securities, exacerbating the financial crisis. In addition, some financial managers engaged in corrupt practices. One of the most notorious, securities broker Bernard Madoff, swindled investors out of billions of dollars through phony securities dealings.

The Housing Bubble Bursts

The housing bubble of the early twenty-first century burst in 2006. By 2007 the owners of this Miami home could no longer afford to pay their mortgage, and like millions around the country they lost their home. Risky lending practices, including subprime mortgages and real estate speculation, triggered the housing collapse. California, Florida, Michigan, and Nevada posted the highest rates of foreclosures.   Joe Raedle/Getty Images

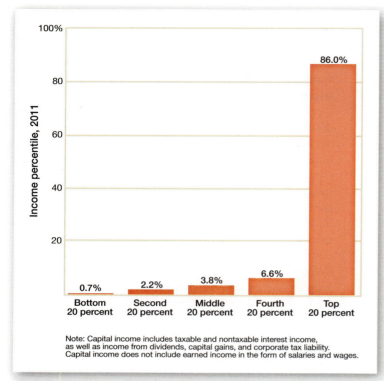

FIGURE 29.2   Wealth Inequality (Capital Income), 2011

The decline of American manufacturing and the expansion of the low-wage service sector, combined with the rise of high-tech industries and unregulated investment banking, led to growing disparities of wealth in the early twenty-first century. Disparities exist even within the top 20 percentile, as the top 1 percent controlled more than half of all capital income in 2011.

securities industry and greater economic equality to bolster consumer spending. But this was not the case. Wealth remained concentrated in relatively few hands. In 2007 the top 1 percent of households owned 34.6 percent of all privately held wealth, and the next 19 percent held 50.5 percent. Thus 80 percent of Americans owned only 15 percent of the wealth, and the gap between rich and poor widened further. The poverty rate stood at around 13 percent (and as high as 20 percent for those under eighteen years of age). This maldistribution of wealth made it extremely difficult to support an economy that required ever-expanding purchasing power and produced steadily rising personal debt (Figure 29.2).

In the age of globalization, the Great Recession spread rapidly throughout the world. Great Britain's banking system teetered on the edge of collapse. Some of the other nations in the European Union (EU)—most notably Greece and Spain, which were the most heavily in debt—verged on bankruptcy and had to be rescued by stronger EU nations. Ireland, whose economy had leaped in the early years of the twenty-first century, abruptly fell on hard times. In providing financial assistance to its member states, the EU required countries such as Greece to slash spending for government services and to lower minimum wages. Even in China, where the economy had boomed as a result of globalization, businesses shut down and unemployment rose as consumer demand for its products declined in the wake of worldwide recession.

Consumers also shared some of the blame. Many took advantage of the easy mortgage policies that had been devised to allow buyers to purchase homes beyond their means. Known as **subprime mortgages**, these loans appealed to borrowers with low incomes or poor credit ratings, especially minorities, who historically had had difficulty obtaining mortgages and personal loans. On the surface, subprime mortgages appeared to make possible the American dream of home ownership. However, when the housing market collapsed, they turned into the nightmare of home foreclosure as many homeowners ended up owing banks and mortgage companies much more than their homes were worth. Investment banks, which had bundled risky mortgages together for speculative purposes, made the situation even worse. Enticed by the easy availability of credit, consumers also went heavily into personal debt to finance purchases of new technology-driven goods, such as personal computers, smartphones, and larger and larger digital televisions.

The economy might have experienced a less severe downturn if there had been stricter regulation of the

The Rise of Barack Obama

In the midst of the Great Recession, the United States held the 2008 presidential election. The Republican candidate, John McCain, was a Vietnam War hero and a longtime senator from Arizona. His Democratic opponent was Barack Obama, who was a young boy during the Vietnam War and had served a mere four years in the Senate from Illinois. For their vice presidential running mates, McCain chose Sarah Palin, the first-term governor of Alaska, and Obama selected Joseph Biden, the senior senator from Delaware. Whoever won would represent a break with tradition. If McCain triumphed, for the first time a woman would serve as vice president. An Obama victory would place an African American in the White House for the first time in history.

In the end, Obama overcame lingering racial prejudices in the country by speaking eloquently about his background as an interracial child, the son of an immigrant from Kenya and the grandson of a World War II veteran from Kansas. He also refuted charges that he was a Muslim (he is a Christian), that he was not born in the United States (he was born in Hawaii), and that he associated with terrorists (in the 1990s, he had participated in a few Chicago civic engagements with a past 1960s radical). The former community organizer succeeded in building a nationwide, grassroots political movement through digital technology. He raised an enormous amount of campaign money from ordinary donors through the Internet and used Web sites and text messaging to mobilize his supporters. Obama won the presidential election most of all because the public blamed the Bush administration for the recession, and Obama offered hope—"Yes we can" was his campaign slogan—for economic recovery. Obama captured 53 percent of the popular vote, obtaining a majority of votes from African Americans, Latinos, women, and the young, who turned out in record numbers, and a comfortable 365 electoral votes. The Democrats also scored big victories in the House and Senate.

Yet the election of President Obama did not erase the impact of generations of racism from the United States or usher in what some have called a "postracial" America. From 1975 to 2002, the number of black elected officials in the United States increased from around 3,500 to more than 9,000. African Americans had also made significant economic progress as a result of antidiscrimination laws and affirmative action, expanding the size of the black middle class. However, the racial gap in wealth, education, and rates of incarceration remained wide. In 2006 the median income for blacks was $32,132, compared with $50,673 for whites. About 75 percent of whites owned their home, compared with slightly less than 50 percent for blacks, a reflection of the continued disparity in wealth between the races. By 2008 approximately 24 percent of African Americans (compared with 8 percent of whites) lived in poverty, nearly double the national poverty rate of 12.7 percent. The percentage of whites who received a bachelor's degree was almost double that for blacks. More than 28 percent of black men were expected to be imprisoned during their lifetime, compared with 4 percent for whites. More than half the prison population in the United States is black and another quarter

Latino, far out of proportion with their percentages among the total U.S. population.

Despite the persistence of racism, President Obama achieved notable victories during his first term in office. He continued the Bush administration's bailout of collapsing banks and investment firms and expanded it to include American automobile companies, which within three years bounced back, became profitable again, and began paying back the government for the bailout. The president supported passage of an economic stimulus plan that provided federal funds to state and local governments to create jobs and keep their employees, including teachers, on the public payroll. Congress also extended the period of unemployment insurance benefits. More controversially, President Obama pushed Congress to pass a health care

The Election of Barack Obama
On the evening of November 4, 2008, after Barack Obama won the 2008 presidential election, he gave his victory speech at Grant Park in his home city of Chicago, Illinois, before a crowd of approximately 240,000 people. The first African American to be elected president, Obama echoed the words in speeches by Martin Luther King Jr. and Abraham Lincoln.   AP Photo/David Guttenfelder

reform measure, which mandated that all Americans had to obtain health insurance and that no one could be denied coverage for a preexisting condition. He also signed into law repeal of the "don't ask, don't tell" policy, which discriminated against gays in the military. Although the Supreme Court in 2003 had declared unconstitutional a Texas law making homosexual acts a crime, the issue of same-sex marriage remained unresolved. Initially Obama supported civil unions rather than gay marriage, but in 2012 he declared his support for same-sex marriage.

In foreign affairs, the president appointed Hillary Clinton, the former First Lady and a senator from New York, as secretary of state. The U.S. military increased combat troop withdrawals from Iraq and turned over security for the country to the newly elected Iraqi government. At the same time, the Obama administration stepped up the war in Afghanistan by increasing U.S. troop levels, which led to a rise in casualties. Still, the president pledged withdrawal of combat soldiers by 2014. His most dramatic success came in 2011, when U.S. special forces killed Osama bin Laden in his hideout in Pakistan. The Obama administration also persuaded the Senate to approve the renewal of a nuclear disarmament treaty with Russia.

President Obama continued to encounter vigorous political opposition. Most Republican lawmakers refused to support his economic stimulus and health care reform bills. A group of Republican conservatives formed the **Tea Party movement**, which they named after colonial Americans who sought to topple British rule. Its followers attacked the president as a "socialist" for what they perceived as an effort to expand federal control over the economy and diminish individual liberty with passage of the health care act. The Fox News media empire, owned by Rupert Murdoch, backed this movement and its leaders, such as Sarah Palin and talk-show host Glenn Beck.

Obama encountered growing political difficulties because the economy remained stagnant. The president did save the financial system from collapse, and the stock market had rebounded by 2012, but unemployment remained over 8 percent (a drop from its high of 10.2 percent). As millions of people remained out of work, a resurgent Wall Street rewarded its managers and employees with big financial bonuses. Large corporations earned millions of dollars in profits but did not create new jobs. The 2010 midterm elections illustrated the growing dissatisfaction of American voters, as Republicans regained control of the House and the Democratic majority in the Senate narrowed. The Tea Party flexed its electoral muscle in successfully campaigning for Republican congressional and gubernatorial candidates who supported its positions. Exit polls showed that 41 percent of the voters endorsed the Tea Party movement. Governor Scott Walker of Wisconsin, backed by the Tea Party, took aim at public employee unions in his state and signed into law a measure limiting

Same-Sex Marriage

A lesbian couple from St. Louis, Missouri, gets married on May 1, 2009, in Iowa City, Iowa. Joining them on what they called the "Show Me Marriage Equality Bus," another sixteen same-sex couples from Missouri also rode to Iowa City to get married. By June 2012, Connecticut, Iowa, Massachusetts, New Hampshire, New York, Vermont, Washington, and Washington, D.C., had authorized same-sex marriage. Photo copyright The Cedar Rapids, Iowa, Gazette

collective bargaining. (In 2012 his opponents failed to win a recall election to remove him from office.)

Dissent also came from the left. In 2011 protesters in cities around the nation launched the **Occupy Wall Street** movement, which attacked corporate greed, economic inequality, and the inability of the federal government to relieve the widespread suffering. Many in the movement were inspired to act by massive cuts in education spending, crippling state budget deficits and declining tax revenues that slashed social services, decaying infrastructure, and crushing student loan debts. These and other Americans continued to be concerned about environmental issues, including dependence on foreign oil, global warming, and air and water pollution.

With unemployment remaining high, economic growth moving at a slow pace, and a number of European economies still in recession and unable to pay mounting debts, the economy loomed as the top issue in the 2012 presidential election. The Republican nominee, Mitt Romney, the former governor of Massachusetts, appealed to conservative voters by opposing Obama's economic programs, including health care reform, and by embracing the social agenda of the Christian Right. Although admitting that much remained

to be done, Obama defended his record on creating new jobs, reducing unemployment, and rescuing the automobile industry. He also criticized economic inequality in the country and promised to raise taxes on the rich. Despite the slower-than-expected economic recovery, Barack Obama won reelection by holding together his coalition of African American, Latino, female, young, and lower-income voters.

Explore

See Documents 29.3 and 29.4 for testimonies from the Great Recession.

An Unfinished Agenda

The United States will continue to face serious tests to its international leadership in the twenty-first century. Terrorism remains a potent threat. Iraq has yet to prove that it can survive as a stable nation in the absence of a strong American military presence, and the outcome of the war against al-Qaeda and the Taliban in Afghanistan

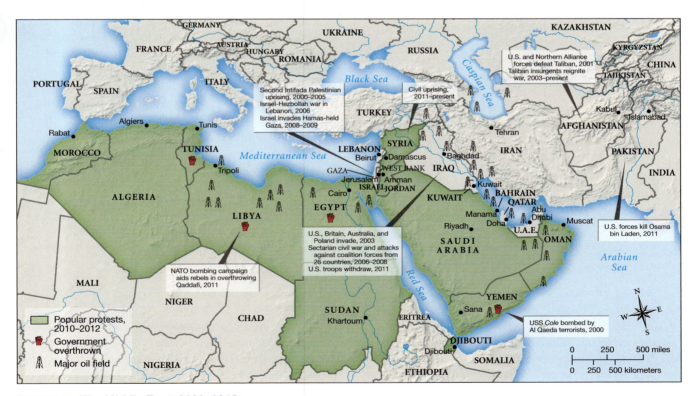

MAP 29.2   The Middle East, 2000–2012

Since 2000, the Middle East has been marked by both terrorism and democratic uprisings. After 9/11 the United States tried to transform Iraq and Afghanistan by military might, which led to prolonged wars. Yet popular rebellions in 2011, led by young people and fueled by new technology, created hope that change was possible. However, as of 2012 the most brutal government repression of the uprisings continued in Syria.

DOCUMENTS 29.3 AND 29.4

The Great Recession: Two Views

For generations of Americans, education has provided an opportunity for upward mobility. During the Great Recession, many people with college degrees found themselves deep in debt with few job opportunities. Prospects for people without degrees were even worse, as these two selections show. The first tells the story of Alice, who was born in Korea and has a bachelor's degree in architecture. She was interviewed by Melissa K. McDonough, who transcribed and edited the conversation for the blog RecessionGrads. The second entry, from a different blog, is by an anonymous navy veteran and substitute schoolteacher.

Explore

29.3 Alice | RecessionGrads Interview, April 21, 2011

I thought I would get a job, right after college. I graduated college, I have a degree, I should get a job. But that wasn't the case. And my parents thought I would get a job, be independent and those kind of things. But I moved in with my parents and my parents were *very* . . . upset, in a way, and very disappointed. They didn't say it, but, because I was the oldest kid, they were expecting a lot more. . . .

And [my job search] lasted more than six months. And, then your parents start to say, you know, you shouldn't just look for planning and architecture, why are you just doing that? You should just work somewhere else. And they just kind of keep telling you. And it's kind of annoying. *She laughs.* Because I do have a goal to get some experience in planning and eventually get a full time job. It was very, very stressful. And, you know, you have your younger siblings with you too. It's kind of like . . . they're looking at me like I'm a bad example, you know? . . .

I thought, you go to elementary, middle school, high school, college and get a job. I thought that was the whole thing and you don't really have to *try* to do it. I thought if you get good grades in college then you automatically get a job, but that wasn't the case. I'm a pretty positive, optimistic person, so I was like, 2 to 3 months, I'll get a job. You know? I'll get a job. I was pretty optimistic. And then that kind of diminishes every month. *She laughs.*

There weren't many full time positions opening. Most of the positions were either internship or part time or temporary positions. So it was really difficult, but even if it was just internship, part time, temporary positions, competition was amazing. Like, I apply for [assistant planner] and they call me for an interview and I went there, there were like, 20, 30 people waiting for the interview. If you think about how many people already applied and they selected those people to interview, I was awed. I was awed.

Source: http://recessiongrads.blogspot.com/2011_04_01_archive .html.

remains questionable. Despite Osama bin Laden's death, al-Qaeda in Yemen still poses a serious danger, and U.S.-trained Afghan forces must demonstrate that they can maintain control once the U.S. military withdraws. If Iran succeeds in developing nuclear weapons, it will present an even greater threat, as will the continuing stalemate between the Israeli government and the Palestinians in reaching agreement over issues of peace and land that have been unresolved since 1967.

In 2011 great changes swept across the Middle East, as young people, armed mainly with cell phones and connected through social media networks, peacefully toppled pro-Western but despotic governments in Egypt and Tunisia. In Libya, armed rebels succeeded in overthrowing the government of the dictator Muammar al-Qaddafi. Elsewhere, a hostile North Korea has developed nuclear weapons. Prolonged instability in the Middle East, the Persian Gulf, and Asia is harmful to U.S. security

29.4 Anonymous | We Are the 99 Percent Blog, November 5, 2011

I am 36 years old. I have a husband and two children, ages 13 and 11, and live in an apartment on a university campus.

I have an extruded disc in my back that presses on my sciatic nerve and leaves me in constant pain, making me unable to stand for more than 20 minutes at a time. My husband and I are both veterans of the US Navy, having served our country honorably and proudly. We are unable to afford medical insurance so we use the VA [Veterans Administration]. We don't qualify for dental insurance through them and both have several missing and broken teeth, as well as numerous abscesses.

Our children have healthcare through the state's medical insurance for needy families. We rely on housing assistance to be able to afford our apartment. We only qualify for food stamps because of our children as adults cannot qualify without steady 32+ hours per week jobs.

We were raised to believe that a college education would make you more successful and able to achieve the American Dream. I have a bachelor's degree and am certified to teach elementary education and middle school science and social studies. I will graduate in a month with a master's degree in educational technology and over $70,000 in debt. My husband has two bachelor's degrees and is working toward a master's and his debt is equivalent to mine.

He works as an adjunct professor at a university because he cannot find regular, steady employment. I am a substitute teacher in the local school district because I am "overqualified" for other work and cannot find a full time teaching position.

We both work at the whim of our employers on an as needed basis. We are literally living paycheck to paycheck, unable to have savings of any sort. My family and I are the 99%.

Source: "We Are the 99 Percent," http://wearethe99percent.tumblr .com/page/30.

Interpret the Evidence

- How has each woman pursued economic advancement?
- What challenges does each woman face in overcoming her economic problems?

Put It in Context

What effect has the Great Recession had on the middle class?

interests and to achieving lasting peace in these regions (Map 29.2).

Whatever happens in the war on terror, the United States still faces challenges of globalization. China, a nation of 1.3 billion people, is contesting American economic supremacy. As China flourishes economically, American workers have lost jobs, and the Chinese have amassed a nearly $200 billion trade surplus with the United States. China also owns a substantial portion of America's national

debt, a situation that further alters the balance of economic power between the two nations. In addition, the growth of manufacturing and the market economy in China has resulted in the rising consumption of oil and gasoline, thereby adding to soaring fuel prices in the United States.

Along with the United States and China, the rest of the world faces the problem of climate change and ultimately the survival of the planet. Global warming during the twentieth century resulted mainly from emissions of greenhouse gases into the atmosphere and the erosion of the ozone layer. As temperatures climb, they cause a rise in the sea level, the melting of glaciers, extreme fluctuations of weather, and famines. Powerful hurricanes such as Katrina have been attributed to rising temperatures in the Atlantic Ocean and Caribbean. Disruptions in industrial production caused by storms and the subsequent expense of rebuilding have a negative impact on the U.S. and world economies.

As the twenty-first century unfolds, immigration will continue to arouse considerable political controversy. Immigration restrictionists, particularly in Arizona and California, support such policies as building a fence along the U.S.-Mexican border and strengthening the administration of immigration laws. Supporters of immigration reform favor amnesty for illegal residents who have lived in this country for a designated period and have jobs, opening up a path to citizenship. At the heart of this issue is the question that has always existed during periods of intense foreign immigration, especially from non-English-speaking nations: Do the nation's vitality and character still depend on welcoming a new generation of foreigners to make their living and their home in the United States? Whatever the answer, by the end of the twenty-first century the population of the United States will look much different. The percentage of Latinos and Asian Americans will increase, while that of whites and blacks will decline. In 2012 the U.S. Census Bureau reported that nonwhite babies made up the majority of births for the first time. If present trends continue, the country's racial and ethnic composition will become much more mixed through intermarriage. In 2010 the Census Bureau reported that one of seven new marriages, or 14.6 percent, was interracial or interethnic. In 1961, when Barack Obama was born, the figure for interracial marriages was less than one in a thousand. And, as for the institution of marriage, we can expect its legal recognition to expand to gays, although in 2012 voters approved state referenda that rejected same-sex marriage.

REVIEW & RELATE

What were the causes and consequences of the Great Recession?

What effects did the election and presidency of Barack Obama have on American politics and society?

✔ *LEARNINGCurve* bedfordstmartins.com/hewittlawson/LC

Conclusion: Technology and Terror in a Global Society

Since 1993, Americans have faced new forms of globalization, new technologies, and new modes of warfare. The computer revolution that Bill Gates helped initiate

changed the way Americans gather information, communicate ideas, purchase goods, and conduct business. It has also shaped national and international conflicts. The September 11, 2001, attacks on the World Trade Center and the Pentagon demonstrated that terrorists could use computers and digital equipment to wreak havoc on the most powerful nation in the world. At the same time, Kristen Breitweiser used the Internet to mobilize public support for the families of 9/11 victims. And Barack Obama's 2008 presidential campaign, protesters demonstrating against various Middle East dictatorships, and the leaders of the Tea Party and Occupy Wall Street movements also used technology to inspire men and women to join their causes.

Along with the computer revolution, globalization has encouraged vast economic transformation throughout the world. Presidents as politically different as Bill Clinton and George W. Bush supported deregulation, free trade, and other policies that fostered corporate mergers that allowed businesses to reach beyond U.S. borders for cheap labor, raw materials, and markets in new and more profitable ways. While the 1990s witnessed the fruits of the new global economy, by 2008 the dangers of financial speculation and intertwined national economies became striking in the onset of the Great Recession. This economic collapse has underscored the inequalities of wealth that continue to exist and grow larger, aggravated by racial, ethnic, and gender disparities. Gripped by ongoing partisan deadlock, U.S. lawmakers have been unable to address the troublesome problems of unemployment, budget deficits, health care, global warming, immigration reform, energy consumption, and the protection of civil liberties.

Throughout its history, the United States has shown great strength in developing and adapting to new technology, with the computers of Bill Gates and other digital pioneers only the latest. At the same time, the nation has incorporated diverse populations into its midst, redefined old cultural identities and created new ones, expanded civil rights and civil liberties, extended economic opportunities, and joined other nations to fight military aggression and address common international concerns. The election of Barack Obama in 2008 shows that the nation has progressed significantly from the Reconstruction era to the present. Still, many problems remain before the United States achieves the "more perfect union" that the Founders and their successors envisioned. Ordinary Americans such as Kristen Breitweiser and many others who came before her have tried to make this country live up to its principles. The United States will have to draw on the many histories of its diverse peoples if it expects to continue to exert leadership in the world and maintain its greatness into the twenty-first century.

Chapter Review

Online Study Guide ▶ bedfordstmartins.com/hewittlawson

KEY TERMS

"don't ask, don't tell" (p. 933)

Contract with America (p. 934)

Personal Responsibility and Work Opportunity
Reconciliation Act (p. 934)

ethnic cleansing (p. 935)

Dayton Peace Accords (p. 935)

megachurches (p. 937)

Patriot Act (p. 938)

Bush Doctrine (p. 939)

Hurricane Katrina (p. 940)

Great Recession (p. 943)

subprime mortgages (p. 944)

Tea Party movement (p. 946)

Occupy Wall Street (p. 947)

REVIEW & RELATE

1. How have computers changed life in the United States?

2. How has globalization affected business consolidation and immigration?

3. How did conflicts between Democrats and Republicans affect President Clinton's accomplishments?

4. How did the end of the Cold War shape President Clinton's foreign policies?

5. How did President Bush put compassionate conservatism into action?

6. How did the war on terror prompt U.S. leaders to rethink America's position in the world?

7. What were the causes and consequences of the Great Recession?

8. What effects did the election and presidency of Barack Obama have on American politics and society?

TIMELINE OF EVENTS

1975	Microsoft formed
1976	Apple Computer Company formed
1980–1990s	Immigration surges from Mexico, Central America, the Caribbean, and South and East Asia
1991	World Wide Web comes into existence
1993–2011	"Don't ask, don't tell" policy enacted
1994	Contract with America announced; Republicans win control of Congress
1995	Dayton Peace Accords
1996	Personal Responsibility and Work Reconciliation Act reforms welfare
	Defense of Marriage Act
1998	President Clinton impeached
2000	al-Qaeda bombs USS *Cole* in Yemen
	Supreme Court rules in favor of George W. Bush in contested presidential election
2001	September 11 al-Qaeda attacks on World Trade Center and Pentagon
	U.S. troops invade Afghanistan; Patriot Act passed
2002	No Child Left Behind Act passed
2003–2011	War in Iraq
2005	Hurricane Katrina hits Gulf coast
2008	Great Recession begins
	Barack Obama elected president
	Tea Party movement formed
2009	Congress passes health care reform act
2011	Osama bin Laden killed by U.S. special forces
	Occupy Wall Street movement formed
2012	U.S. Census Bureau reports majority of nonwhite births for first time in U.S. history

The Uses of September 11

The terrorist attacks on the morning of September 11, 2001, killed three thousand people and left the American nation reeling. Millions spent that morning and the days that followed glued to their television sets, watching repeated images of the World Trade Center, the Pentagon, and scattered wreckage in Pennsylvania. Police and firefighters flocked to the Pentagon and Ground Zero to aid in rescue and recovery efforts. Rumors began circulating immediately about various terrorist groups or nations that might be responsible, and it was quickly discovered that the terrorist organization al-Qaeda, under the direction of Osama bin Laden, had carried out the attacks.

Americans reacted to the events in various ways, and official responses were immediate. The Bush administration launched the war on terror, which included the creation of the Department of Homeland Security, passage of the Patriot Act, and the invasion of Afghanistan. In the aftermath of the attacks, more than eighty thousand Arabs and Muslims living in the United States were fingerprinted and registered with the federal government. President Bush, believing that Saddam Hussein was linked to both the terrorism and al-Qaeda, launched an American invasion of Iraq in the spring of 2003.

Individuals and communities nationwide responded with an outpouring of grief. Throughout the nation, communities held ceremonies, candlelight vigils, and marches. Impromptu memorials appeared in New York City and Washington, D.C., and photos of the missing filled subway stations and parks. Many businesses and individuals prominently displayed American flags as people searched for ways to find meaning in the attacks.

The following documents present different responses to September 11, from official responses to cultural commentary on the events. As you read these documents, consider how the authors understand the attacks in the larger international context. How do the authors' different backgrounds influence their responses? In what ways do these documents speak to one another?

DOCUMENT 29.5

George W. Bush | The Axis of Evil, 2002

Four months after the September 11 attacks, President Bush delivered his annual State of the Union message, in which he expressed the lingering shock and outrage that many Americans felt and discussed his administration's actions, particularly the war in Afghanistan. He also issued a warning to those nations he deemed "an axis of evil"—North Korea, Iran, and Iraq. He accused Iraq of developing weapons of mass destruction, a charge that he used to support the American invasion of Iraq in 2003.

While the most visible military action is in Afghanistan, America is acting elsewhere. We now have troops in the Philippines, helping to train that country's armed forces to go after terrorist cells that have executed an American and still hold hostages. Our soldiers, working with the Bosnian Government, seized terrorists who were plotting to bomb our Embassy. Our Navy is patrolling the coast of Africa to block the shipment of weapons and the establishment of terrorist camps in Somalia.

My hope is that all nations will heed our call and eliminate the terrorist parasites who threaten their countries and our own. Many nations are acting forcefully. Pakistan is now cracking down on terror, and I admire the strong leadership of President [Pervez] Musharraf. But some governments will be timid in the face of terror. And make no mistake about it: If they do not act, America will.

Our second goal is to prevent regimes that sponsor terror from threatening America or our friends and allies with weapons of mass destruction. Some of these regimes have been pretty quiet since September the 11th, but we know their true nature.

North Korea is a regime arming with missiles and weapons of mass destruction, while starving its citizens.

Iran aggressively pursues these weapons and exports terror, while an unelected few repress the Iranian people's hope for freedom.

Iraq continues to flaunt its hostility toward America and to support terror. The Iraqi regime has plotted to develop anthrax and nerve gas and nuclear weapons for over a decade. This is a regime that has already used poison gas to murder thousands of its own citizens, leaving the bodies of mothers huddled over their dead children. This is a regime that agreed to international inspections, then kicked out the inspectors. This is a regime that has something to hide from the civilized world.

States like these and their terrorist allies constitute an axis of evil, arming to threaten the peace of the world. By seeking weapons of mass destruction, these regimes pose a grave and growing danger. They could provide these arms to terrorists, giving them the means to match their hatred. They could attack our allies or attempt to blackmail the United States. In any of these cases, the price of indifference would be catastrophic.

We will work closely with our coalition to deny terrorists and their state sponsors the materials, technology, and expertise to make and deliver weapons of mass destruction. We will develop and deploy effective missile defenses to protect America and our allies from sudden attack. And all nations should know: America will do what is necessary to ensure our Nation's security.

We'll be deliberate, yet time is not on our side. I will not wait on events while dangers gather. I will not stand by as peril draws closer and closer. The United States of America will not permit the world's most dangerous regimes to threaten us with the world's most destructive weapons.

Source: "Address before a Joint Session of the Congress on the State of the Union, January 29, 2002," *Weekly Compilation of Presidential Documents*, vol. 38, no. 5 (Washington, D.C.: Government Printing Office, Monday, February 4, 2002), 135.

DOCUMENT 29.6

Diana Hoffman | "The Power of Freedom," 2002

The September 11 attacks inspired thousands of poems, essays, and songs that expressed sorrow for the victims and resolve that the tragedy would make America a stronger nation. The following poem by Diana Hoffman, which reflects these sentiments, appeared on a memorial Web site in 2002.

I know you're celebrating
what your evil deeds have wrought
But with the devastation
something else you've also brought

For nothing is more powerful
than Americans who unite
Who put aside their differences
and for freedom fight

Each defenseless victim whose
untimely death you caused
And every fallen hero
whose brave life was lost

Has only served to strengthen
our national resolve
Each freedom-loving citizen
will surely get involved

You've galvanized our nation
into a force so strong
We'll end your reign of terror
although the fight is long

For every heart that's broken
ten million will stand tall
and every tear that's falling
is the mortar for it all

And when this war is over
one thing I know is sure
Our country will be greater
and our freedom will endure

Source: Diana Hoffman, "The Power of Freedom,"
http://911neverforget.tripod.com/neverforgotten/id3.html.

DOCUMENT 29.7

Daniel Harris | The Kitschification of September 11, 2001

Amid the outpouring of September 11 cultural and artistic expression, writer Daniel Harris criticized much of it as empty kitsch, or art that is considered overly sentimental and tasteless. His article on the "kitschification" of September 11 appeared on *Salon.com*, an online news and entertainment magazine.

Within minutes after the collapse of the World Trade Center, inspirational songs, propagandistic images designed to feed the fires of patriotic fury, and poetry commemorating the victims began to proliferate on radio, television, and the Internet. The Dixie Chicks performed an a cappella rendition of "The Star Spangled Banner"; car-window decals appeared featuring a lugubrious poodle with a glistening tear as large as a gum drop rolling mournfully down its cheek; refrigerator magnets of Old Glory flooded the market ("buy two and get a third one FREE!"); and the unofficial laureates of the World Wide Web brought the Internet to a crawl by posting thousands of elegies with such lyrics as "May America's flag forever fly unfurled, / May Heaven be our perished souls' 'Windows on the World'!" Gigabytes of odes to the lost firemen and celebrations of American resolve turned the information superhighway into a parking lot:

My Daddy's Flag

Arriving home from work and a trip to the store,

My 5 year old daughter greeted me at the door.

"Hi daddy!" she smiled, "what's in the bag?"

"Well, daddy has brought home the American flag."

With a puzzled look she asked "What does it do?"

I answered, "it's our country's colors, red, white, and blue.

This flag on our house will protect you my dear,

It has magical powers to keep away fear."

　　Does an event as catastrophic as this one require the rhetoric of kitsch to make it less horrendous? Do we need the overkill of ribbons and commemorative quilts, haloed seraphim perched on top of the burning towers, and teddy bears in firefighter helmets waving flags, in order to forget the final minutes of bond traders, restaurant workers, and secretaries screaming in elevators filling with smoke, standing in the frames of broken windows on the 90th floor waiting for help, and staggering down the stairwells covered in third-degree burns? Perhaps saccharine images of sobbing Statues of Liberty

(continued on page 956)

and posters that announce "we will never forget when the Eagle cried" make the incident more palatable, more "aesthetic" in a sense, decorated with the mortician's reassuringly familiar stock in trade. Through kitsch, we avert our eyes from tragedy, transforming the unspeakable ugliness of diseases, accidents, and wars into something poetic and noble, into pat stories whose happy endings offer enduring lessons in courage and resilience.

And yet while kitsch may serve to anesthetize us to the macabre spectacle of perfectly manicured severed hands embedded in the mud and charred bodies dropping out of windows, it may conceal another agenda. The strident sentimentality of kitsch makes the unsaid impermissible and silences dissenting opinions, which cannot withstand the emotional vehemence of its rhetoric. It not only beautifies ghoulish images, it whitewashes the political context of the attack which, when portrayed as a pure instance of gratuitous sadism, of inexpiable wickedness, appears to have had no cause, no ultimate goal. Four months to Bush's "crusade," despite clear successes, we remain far from certain about what, in the long run, we hope to achieve.

Source: Daniel Harris, "The Kitschification of September 11," in *Afterwords: Stories and Reports from 9/11 and Beyond*, compiled by the Editors of *Salon.com* and David Talbot (New York: Washington Square Press, 2002), 203–5.

DOCUMENT 29.8

Khaled Abou El Fadl | Response to September 11, 2001

Arab Americans and Muslims became targets of violence, racial profiling, surveillance, and even deportation in the wake of the September 11 attacks. Khaled Abou El Fadl is a law professor at the University of California at Los Angeles and a leading expert on Islamic law. In the following reflection, he recalls how he felt on September 11 and how being a Muslim shaped his response to the attacks.

My reaction very soon after it happened was anguished hope that Muslims were not involved in this. And actually I remember very distinctly sort of a degree of feeling ashamed about having that hope, because you would like to respond to something like this at a human and universal level. You would like to feel like, Muslim or not Muslim, this is just terrible, period. It's really irrelevant who has done this. But because of what I knew, what it's going to mean for Muslims, I knew that the sort of hyphenation of whether a Muslim did this or not was going to make a big difference for me, for my friends, for my family, for my son. That's a reality. And the agony of it has not subsided because the worst fears, that this is going to open a door of much suffering for many human beings, has fully materialized. . . .

The word *fear* describes everything. There is fear of fellow citizens being killed. There is fear that you yourself will be the subject of a terrorist attack. Terrorism doesn't have an exemption clause for Arabs or Muslims. If I was on that plane that day, the fact that I was Arab or Muslim wouldn't have made an iota of difference. So you run the risk of being the victim of a terrorist attack as much as any other member of society. But you now also run the risk of being blamed for it, just simply by the fact that you're Arab or Muslim. . . .

We belong on this plane and on our seat, you don't. You're here because we allow you to be here. It's as if it's a privilege. You're different, it's a privilege that you are allowed on this plane. And when I started wearing suits and ties consistently, regardless of how long or short the flight is, I've noticed that the treatment has gotten better. But it's always anxiety producing, not just for the normal security concerns, but because it's an unknown sum. You just don't know whether you're going to run into someone who's going to say something rude, something hurtful, whether you're going to sit next to someone who asks to change seats, which has happened to me, because they don't feel comfortable sitting next to you. Every time you pick up something from your travel bag, or you take out a magazine, or take out a book, they look like they're going to have a heart attack. Or constantly staring at you. It's just, it's an extremely anxiety producing experience and the irony of it is that if, God forbid, there is a terrorist attack, and I am on a plane, I'm just like everyone else, I die just like everyone else.

Source: "Face to Face: Stories from the Aftermath of Infamy," ITVS Interactive, http://archive.itvs.org/facetoface/stories/khaled.html.

DOCUMENT 29.9

Anti-Muslim Discrimination, 2011

The terrorist attacks on September 11 incited anti-Muslim sentiment among many Americans. Although President Bush made it clear that the enemy was al-Qaeda and not Muslims in general, the passage of the Patriot Act and the roundup and deportation of Arab and Muslim immigrants reflected an underlying hostility to Muslim Americans. This cartoon, which appeared in a Florida newspaper, compares discrimination against Muslims to the prejudice that Japanese Americans experienced during World War II.

DOCUMENT 29.10

Brian Gallagher | Hundred-Mile Marine, 2012

In 2006 construction began on the National September 11 Memorial and Museum, located on the former site of the World Trade Center. The memorial was dedicated on the tenth anniversary of the attacks and has been visited by millions of people. Brian Gallagher, who grew up in New York City and served in the Marine Corps, explains his plan to honor the memory and sacrifices of those who died in the attacks and the servicemembers who fought in Iraq and Afghanistan. On May 26, 2012, he achieved his goal of running one hundred miles around the World Trade Center site.

At the time of its completion, One World Trade Center, or what is commonly known as the Freedom Tower, will soon scrape the New York City skyline at 1,776 feet. The height of the tower symbolically represents the year that [the] Continental Congress formally adopted the Declaration of Independence, charting a path of freedom for this great nation.

For centuries, we've enjoyed the fruits of liberty, which was due in large part to brave men and women who proudly serve in our military forces. Freedom is not, nor shall ever be, free. Protecting it bears a price. The price paid is not in currency, but in sacrifice. Sacrifice from the few, selfless warriors whose actions speak volumes—their dedication without reserve. They are the sons and daughters of our nation who risk their lives to protect ours and the freedoms we enjoy.

They come home wounded, forever changed. As these wounded warriors return home, many face difficult times. Their fight continues long after their time in service.

What do you do for those service members who provided the blanket of freedom that protects us and has been physically or mentally injured? How do you ensure their sacrifices do not fade from our memory?

(continued on page 960)

I asked myself the same questions and created an event to help spread awareness to the actions of our heroes.

On May 26, [2012] this Memorial Day weekend, I will execute a one-man, 100-mile run under 30 hours, circling around the World Trade Center to support wounded warriors and their families and to honor the sacrifices of our heroes who have shown the courage, commitment, and dedication that has been the hallmark and strength of our nation.

The height of the One World Trade Center symbolically represents the birth of America. It is my hope that my 100-mile journey is the first step to raise funds for the National September 11 Memorial & Museum and two other organizations that help assist our wounded warriors and their families.

As former Pres. Ronald Reagan once said, "Freedom is never more than one generation away from extinction. We didn't pass it to our children in the bloodstream. It must be fought for, protected, and handed on for them to do the same."

Please help me support those who have fought for and protected our freedom. Together, we can show these great warriors the enduring respect they deserve.

Source: "Marine Runs 100 Miles in Support of Memorial, Wounded Service Members," *The Memo Blog*, http://www.911memorial.org/blog/marine-runs-100-miles-support-911-memorial-and-wounded-military.

Interpret the Evidence

1. Of the three nations that George W. Bush characterizes as "an axis of evil" (Document 29.5), why do you think his administration chose to invade Iraq?

2. What do you think of Daniel Harris's assessment of September 11 responses as kitsch (Document 29.7)? What purposes does kitsch serve? What might Harris say about Diana Hoffman's poem (Document 29.7)?

3. How does being a Muslim shape Khaled Abou El Fadl's reaction to September 11 (Document 29.8)?

4. Why does the cartoonist in Document 29.9 compare the Muslim experience following September 11 to that of Japanese-Americans interned in World War II camps?

5. How does Brian Gallagher draw on history to memorialize September 11 (Document 29.10)? How might his memories of September 11 differ from those of El Fadl?

Put It in Context

- Compare the treatment of Muslim Americans after September 11 with the experience of German Americans during World War I and Japanese Americans during World War II.

- How did the attacks on September 11 change America?

background photo: page 956, Library of Congress

The Declaration of Independence

In Congress, July 4, 1776.

The unanimous Declaration of the thirteen united States of America,

When in the course of human events, it becomes necessary for one people to dissolve the political bands which have connected them with another, and to assume, among the powers of the earth, the separate and equal station to which the laws of nature and of nature's God entitle them, a decent respect to the opinions of mankind requires that they should declare the causes which impel them to the separation.

We hold these truths to be self-evident, that all men are created equal; that they are endowed by their Creator with certain unalienable rights; that among these, are life, liberty, and the pursuit of happiness. That, to secure these rights, governments are instituted among men, deriving their just powers from the consent of the governed; that, whenever any form of government becomes destructive of these ends, it is the right of the people to alter or to abolish it, and to institute a new government, laying its foundation on such principles, and organizing its powers in such form, as to them shall seem most likely to effect their safety and happiness. Prudence, indeed, will dictate that governments long established, should not be changed for light and transient causes; and, accordingly, all experience hath shown, that mankind are more disposed to suffer, while evils are sufferable, than to right themselves by abolishing the forms to which they are accustomed. But, when a long train of abuses and usurpations, pursuing invariably the same object, evinces a design to reduce them under absolute despotism, it is their right, it is their duty, to throw off such government and to provide new guards for their future security. Such has been the patient sufferance of these colonies, and such is now the necessity which constrains them to alter their former systems of government. The history of the present King of Great Britain is a history of repeated injuries and usurpations, all having, in direct object, the establishment of an absolute tyranny over these States. To prove this, let facts be submitted to a candid world: He has refused his assent to laws the most wholesome and necessary for the public good.

He has forbidden his governors to pass laws of immediate and pressing importance, unless suspended in their operation till his assent should be obtained; and, when so suspended, he has utterly neglected to attend to them.

He has refused to pass other laws for the accommodation of large districts of people, unless those people would relinquish the right of representation in the legislature; a right inestimable to them, and formidable to tyrants only.

He has called together legislative bodies at places unusual, uncomfortable, and distant from the depository of their public records, for the sole purpose of fatiguing them into compliance with his measures.

He has dissolved representative houses repeatedly for opposing, with manly firmness, his invasions on the rights of the people.

He has refused, for a long time after such dissolutions, to cause others to be elected; whereby the legislative powers, incapable of annihilation, have returned to the people at large for their exercise; the state remaining in the mean-time exposed to all the danger of invasion from without, and convulsions within.

He has endeavoured to prevent the population of these States; for that purpose, obstructing the laws for naturalization of foreigners, refusing to pass others to encourage their migration hither, and raising the conditions of new appropriations of lands.

He has obstructed the administration of justice, by refusing his assent to laws for establishing judiciary powers.

He has made judges dependent on his will alone, for the tenure of their offices, and the amount and payment of their salaries.

He has erected a multitude of new offices, and sent hither swarms of officers to harass our people, and eat out their substance.

He has kept among us, in times of peace, standing armies, without the consent of our legislature.

He has affected to render the military independent of, and superior to, the civil power.

He has combined, with others, to subject us to a jurisdiction foreign to our Constitution, and unacknowledged by our laws; giving his assent to their acts of pretended legislation:

For quartering large bodies of armed troops among us:

For protecting them by a mock trial, from punishment, for any murders which they should commit on the inhabitants of these States:

For cutting off our trade with all parts of the world:

For imposing taxes on us without our consent:

For depriving us, in many cases, of the benefit of trial by jury:

For transporting us beyond seas to be tried for pretended offences:

For abolishing the free system of English laws in a neighboring province, establishing therein an arbitrary government, and enlarging its boundaries, so as to render it at once an example and fit instrument for introducing the same absolute rule into these colonies:

For taking away our charters, abolishing our most valuable laws, and altering, fundamentally, the powers of our governments:

For suspending our own legislatures, and declaring themselves invested with power to legislate for us in all cases whatsoever.

He has abdicated government here, by declaring us out of his protection, and waging war against us.

He has plundered our seas, ravaged our coasts, burnt our towns, and destroyed the lives of our people.

He is, at this time, transporting large armies of foreign mercenaries to complete the works of death, desolation, and tyranny, already begun, with circumstances of cruelty and perfidy scarcely paralleled in the most barbarous ages, and totally unworthy the head of a civilized nation.

He has constrained our fellow citizens, taken captive on the high seas, to bear arms against their country, to become the executioners of their friends, and brethren, or to fall themselves by their hands.

He has excited domestic insurrections amongst us, and has endeavored to bring on the inhabitants of our frontiers, the merciless Indian savages, whose known rule of warfare is an undistinguished destruction of all ages, sexes, and conditions.

In every stage of these oppressions, we have petitioned for redress; in the most humble terms; our repeated petitions have been answered only by repeated injury. A prince, whose character is thus marked by every act which may define a tyrant, is unfit to be the ruler of a free people.

Nor have we been wanting in attention to our British brethren. We have warned them, from time to time, of attempts made by their legislature to extend an unwarrantable jurisdiction over us. We have reminded them of the circumstances of our emigration and settlement here. We have appealed to their native justice and magnanimity, and we have conjured them, by the ties of our common kindred, to disavow these usurpations, which would inevitably interrupt our connections and correspondence. They, too, have been deaf to the voice of justice and consanguinity. We must, therefore, acquiesce in the necessity which denounces our separation, and hold them as we hold the rest of mankind, enemies in war, in peace, friends.

We, therefore, the representatives of the United States of America, in general Congress assembled, appealing to the Supreme Judge of the world for the rectitude of our intentions, do, in the name, and by authority of the good people of these colonies, solemnly publish and declare, that these united colonies are, and of right ought to be, free and independent states: that they are absolved from all allegiance to the British Crown, and that all political connection between them and the state of Great Britain is, and ought to be, totally dissolved; and that, as free and independent states, they have full power to levy war, conclude peace, contract alliances, establish commerce, and to do all other acts and things which independent states may of right do. And, for the support of this declaration, with a firm reliance on the protection of Divine Providence, we mutually pledge to each other our lives, our fortunes, and our sacred honor.

The foregoing Declaration was, by order of Congress, engrossed, and signed by the following members:

JOHN HANCOCK

New Hampshire
Josiah Bartlett
William Whipple
Matthew Thornton

Massachusetts Bay
Samuel Adams
John Adams
Robert Treat Paine
Elbridge Gerry

Rhode Island
Stephen Hopkins
William Ellery

Connecticut
Roger Sherman
Samuel Huntington
William Williams
Oliver Wolcott

New York
William Floyd
Phillip Livingston
Francis Lewis
Lewis Morris

New Jersey
Richard Stockton
John Witherspoon
Francis Hopkinson

John Hart
Abraham Clark

Pennsylvania
Robert Morris
Benjamin Rush
Benjamin Franklin
John Morton
George Clymer
James Smith
George Taylor
James Wilson
George Ross
Caesar Rodney
George Read
Thomas M'Kean

Maryland
Samuel Chase
William Paca
Thomas Stone
Charles Carroll, of Carrollton

North Carolina
William Hooper
Joseph Hewes
John Penn

South Carolina
Edward Rutledge
Thomas Heyward, Jr.
Thomas Lynch, Jr.
Arthur Middleton

Virginia
George Wythe
Richard Henry Lee
Thomas Jefferson
Benjamin Harrison
Thomas Nelson, Jr.
Francis Lightfoot Lee
Carter Braxton

Georgia
Button Gwinnett
Lyman Hall
George Walton

Resolved, That copies of the Declaration be sent to the several assemblies, conventions, and committees, or councils of safety, and to the several commanding officers of the continental troops; that it be proclaimed in each of the United States, at the head of the army.

The Articles of Confederation and Perpetual Union

Agreed to in Congress, November 15, 1777. Ratified March 1781.

Between the states of New Hampshire, Massachusetts Bay, Rhode Island and Providence Plantations, Connecticut, New York, New Jersey, Pennsylvania, Delaware, Maryland, Virginia, North Carolina, South Carolina, Georgia.*

Article 1

The stile of this confederacy shall be "The United States of America."

Article 2

Each State retains its sovereignty, freedom and independence, and every power, jurisdiction, and right, which is not by this confederation expressly delegated to the United States, in Congress assembled.

Article 3

The said states hereby severally enter into a firm league of friendship with each other for their common defence, the security of their liberties and their mutual and general welfare; binding themselves to assist each other against all force offered to, or attacks made upon them, or any of them, on account of religion, sovereignty, trade, or any other pretence whatever.

Article 4

The better to secure and perpetuate mutual friendship and intercourse among the people of the different states in this union, the free inhabitants of each of these states, paupers, vagabonds, and fugitives from justice excepted, shall be entitled to all privileges and immunities of free citizens in the several states; and the people of each State shall have free ingress and regress to and from any other State, and shall enjoy therein all the privileges of trade and commerce, subject to the same duties, impositions, and restrictions, as the inhabitants thereof respectively; provided, that such restrictions shall not extend so far as to prevent the removal of property, imported into any State, to any other State of which the owner is an inhabitant; provided also, that no imposition, duties, or restriction, shall be laid by any State on the property of the United States, or either of them. If any person guilty of, or charged with treason, felony, or other high misdemeanor in any State, shall flee from justice and be found in any of the United States, he shall, upon demand of the governor or executive power of the State from which he fled, be delivered up and removed to the State having jurisdiction of his offence. Full faith and credit shall be given in each of these states to the records, acts, and judicial proceedings of the courts and magistrates of every other State.

Article 5

For the more convenient management of the general interests of the United States, delegates shall be annually appointed, in such manner as the legislature of each State shall direct, to meet in Congress, on the 1st Monday in November in every year, with a power reserved to each State to recall its delegates, or any of them, at any time within the year, and to send others in their stead for the remainder of the year.

No State shall be represented in Congress by less than two, nor by more than seven members; and no person shall be capable of being a delegate for more than three years in

*This copy of the final draft of the Articles of Confederation is taken from the Journals, 9:907–925, November 15, 1777.

any term of six years; nor shall any person, being a delegate, be capable of holding any office under the United States, for which he, or any other for his benefit, receives any salary, fees, or emolument of any kind.

Each State shall maintain its own delegates in a meeting of the states, and while they act as members of the committee of the states.

In determining questions in the United States, in Congress assembled, each State shall have one vote.

Freedom of speech and debate in Congress shall not be impeached or questioned in any court or place out of Congress: and the members of Congress shall be protected in their persons from arrests and imprisonments, during the time of their going to and from, and attendance on Congress, except for treason, felony, or breach of the peace.

Article 6

No State, without the consent of the United States, in Congress assembled, shall send any embassy to, or receive any embassy from, or enter into any conference, agreement, alliance, or treaty with any king, prince, or state; nor shall any person, holding any office of profit or trust under the United States, or any of them, accept of any present, emolument, office or title, of any kind whatever, from any king, prince, or foreign state; nor shall the United States, in Congress assembled, or any of them, grant any title of nobility.

No two or more states shall enter into any treaty, confederation, or alliance, whatever, between them, without the consent of the United States, in Congress assembled, specifying accurately the purposes for which the same is to be entered into, and how long it shall continue.

No state shall lay any imposts or duties which may interfere with any stipulations in treaties entered into by the United States, in Congress assembled, with any king, prince, or state, in pursuance of any treaties already proposed by Congress to the courts of France and Spain.

No vessels of war shall be kept up in time of peace by any State, except such number only as shall be deemed necessary by the United States, in Congress assembled, for the defence of such State or its trade; nor shall any body of forces be kept up by any State, in time of peace, except such number only as, in the judgment of the United States, in Congress assembled, shall be deemed requisite to garrison the forts necessary for the defence of such State; but every State shall always keep up a well regulated and disciplined militia, sufficiently armed and accoutred, and shall provide, and constantly have ready for use, in public stores, a due number of field pieces and tents, and a proper quantity of arms, ammunition and camp equipage.

No State shall engage in any war without the consent of the United States, in Congress assembled, unless such State be actually invaded by enemies, or shall have received certain advice of a resolution being formed by some nation of Indians to invade such State, and the danger is so imminent as not to admit of a delay till the United States, in Congress assembled, can be consulted; nor shall any State grant commissions to any ships or vessels of war, nor letters of marque or reprisal, except it be after a declaration of war by the United States, in Congress assembled, and then only against the kingdom or state, and the subjects thereof, against which war has been so declared, and under such regulations as shall be established by the United States, in Congress assembled, unless such State be infested by pirates, in which case vessels of war may be fitted out for that occasion, and kept so long as the danger shall continue, or until the United States, in Congress assembled, shall determine otherwise.

Article 7

When land forces are raised by any State for the common defence, all officers of or under the rank of colonel, shall be appointed by the legislature of each State respectively, by whom such forces shall be raised, or in such manner as such State shall direct; and all vacancies shall be filled up by the State which first made the appointment.

Article 8

All charges of war and all other expences, that shall be incurred for the common defence or general welfare, and allowed by the United States, in Congress assembled, shall be defrayed out of a common treasury, which shall be supplied by the several states, in proportion to the value of all land within each State, granted to or surveyed for any person, as such land and the buildings and improvements thereon shall be estimated according to such mode as the United States, in Congress assembled, shall, from time to time, direct and appoint.

The taxes for paying that proportion shall be laid and levied by the authority and direction of the legislatures of the several states, within the time agreed upon by the United States, in Congress assembled.

Article 9

The United States, in Congress assembled, shall have the sole and exclusive right and power of determining on peace and war, except in the cases mentioned in the 6th article; of sending and receiving ambassadors; entering into treaties and alliances, provided that no treaty of commerce shall be made, whereby the legislative power of the respective states shall be restrained from imposing such imposts and duties on foreigners as their own people are subjected to, or from prohibiting the exportation or importation of any species of goods or commodities whatsoever; of establishing rules for deciding, in all cases, what captures on land or water shall be legal, and in what manner prizes, taken by land or naval forces in the service of the United States, shall be divided or appropriated; of granting letters of marque and reprisal in times of peace; appointing courts for the trial of piracies and felonies committed on the high seas, and establishing courts for receiving and determining, finally, appeals in all cases of captures; provided, that no member of Congress shall be appointed a judge of any of the said courts.

The United States, in Congress assembled, shall also be the last resort on appeal in all disputes and differences now subsisting, or that hereafter may arise between two or more states concerning boundary, jurisdiction or any other cause whatever; which authority shall always be exercised in the manner following: whenever the legislative or executive authority, or lawful agent of any State, in controversy with another, shall present a petition to Congress, stating the matter in question, and praying for a hearing, notice thereof shall be given, by order of Congress, to the legislative or executive authority of the other State in controversy, and a day assigned for the appearance of the parties by their lawful agents, who shall then be directed to appoint, by joint consent, commissioners or judges to constitute a court for hearing and determining the matter in question; but, if they cannot agree, Congress shall name three persons out of each of the United States, and from the list of such persons each party shall alternately strike out one, the petitioners beginning, until the number shall be reduced to thirteen; and from that number not less than seven, nor more than nine names, as Congress shall direct, shall, in the presence of Congress, be drawn out by lot; and the persons whose names shall be so drawn, or any five of them, shall be commissioners or judges to hear and finally determine the controversy, so always as a major part of the judges who shall hear the cause shall agree in the determination; and if either party shall neglect to attend at the day appointed, without shewing reasons which Congress shall judge sufficient, or, being present, shall refuse to strike, the Congress shall proceed to nominate three persons out of each State, and the secretary of Congress shall strike in behalf of such party absent or refusing; and the judgment and sentence of the court to be appointed, in the manner before prescribed, shall be final and conclusive; and if any of the parties shall refuse to submit to the authority of such court, or to appear or defend their claim or cause, the court shall nevertheless proceed to pronounce sentence or judgment, which shall, in like manner, be final and decisive, the judgment or sentence and other proceedings begin, in either case, transmitted to Congress, and lodged among the acts of Congress for the security of the parties concerned: provided, that every commissioner, before he sits in

judgment, shall take an oath, to be administered by one of the judges of the supreme or superior court of the State where the cause shall be tried, "well and truly to hear and determine the matter in question, according to the best of his judgment, without favour, affection, or hope of reward:" provided, also, that no State shall be deprived of territory for the benefit of the United States.

All controversies concerning the private right of soil, claimed under different grants of two or more states, whose jurisdictions, as they may respect such lands and the states which passed such grants, are adjusted, the said grants, or either of them, being at the same time claimed to have originated antecedent to such settlement of jurisdiction, shall, on the petition of either party to the Congress of the United States, be finally determined, as near as may be, in the same manner as is before prescribed for deciding disputes respecting territorial jurisdiction between different states.

The United States, in Congress assembled, shall also have the sole and exclusive right and power of regulating the alloy and value of coin struck by their own authority, or by that of the respective states; fixing the standard of weights and measures throughout the United States; regulating the trade and managing all affairs with the Indians not members of any of the states; provided that the legislative right of any State within its own limits be not infringed or violated; establishing and regulating post offices from one State to another throughout all the United States, and exacting such postage on the papers passing through the same as may be requisite to defray the expences of the said office; appointing all officers of the land forces in the service of the United States, excepting regimental officers; appointing all the officers of the naval forces, and commissioning all officers whatever in the service of the United States; making rules for the government and regulation of the said land and naval forces, and directing their operations.

The United States, in Congress assembled, shall have authority to appoint a committee to sit in the recess of Congress, to be denominated "a Committee of the States," and to consist of one delegate from each State, and to appoint such other committees and civil officers as may be necessary for managing the general affairs of the United States, under their direction; to appoint one of their number to preside; provided that no person be allowed to serve in the office of president more than one year in any term of three years; to ascertain the necessary sums of money to be raised for the service of the United States, and to appropriate and apply the same for defraying the public expences; to borrow money or emit bills on the credit of the United States, transmitting, every half year, to the respective states, an account of the sums of money so borrowed or emitted; to build and equip a navy; to agree upon the number of land forces, and to make requisitions from each State for its quota, in proportion to the number of white inhabitants in such State; which requisitions shall be binding; and thereupon, the legislature of each State shall appoint the regimental officers, raise the men, and cloathe, arm, and equip them in a soldier-like manner, at the expence of the United States; and the officers and men so cloathed, armed, and equipped, shall march to the place appointed and within the time agreed on by the United States, in Congress assembled; but if the United States, in Congress assembled, shall, on consideration of circumstances, judge proper that any State should not raise men, or should raise a smaller number than its quota, and that any other State should raise a greater number of men than the quota thereof, such extra number shall be raised, officered, cloathed, armed, and equipped in the same manner as the quota of such State, unless the legislature of such State shall judge that such extra number cannot be safely spared out of the same, in which case they shall raise, officer, cloathe, arm, and equip as many of such extra number as they judge can be safely spared. And the officers and men so cloathed, armed, and equipped, shall march to the place appointed and within the time agreed on by the United States, in Congress assembled.

The United States, in Congress assembled, shall never engage in a war, nor grant letters of marque and reprisal in time of peace, nor enter into any treaties or alliances, nor coin money, nor regulate the value thereof, nor ascertain the sums and expences necessary for the defence and welfare of the United States, or any of them: nor emit bills, nor borrow money on the credit of the United States, nor appropriate money, nor agree upon the number of vessels of war to be built or purchased, or the number of land or sea forces to be raised, nor appoint a commander in chief of the army or navy, unless nine states assent to the same; nor shall a question on any other point, except for adjourning from day to day, be determined, unless by the votes of a majority of the United States, in Congress assembled.

The Congress of the United States shall have power to adjourn to any time within the year, and to any place within the United States, so that no period of adjournment be for a longer duration than the space of six months, and shall publish the journal of their proceedings monthly, except such parts thereof, relating to treaties, alliances or military operations, as, in their judgment, require secrecy; and the yeas and nays of the delegates of each State on any question shall be entered on the journal, when it is desired by any

delegate; and the delegates of a State, or any of them, at his, or their request, shall be furnished with a transcript of the said journal, except such parts as are above excepted, to lay before the legislatures of the several states.

Article 10

The committee of the states, or any nine of them, shall be authorized to execute, in the recess of Congress, such of the powers of Congress as the United States, in Congress assembled, by the consent of nine states, shall, from time to time, think expedient to vest them with; provided, that no power be delegated to the said committee, for the exercise of which, by the articles of confederation, the voice of nine states, in the Congress of the United States assembled, is requisite.

Article 11

Canada acceding to this confederation, and joining in the measures of the United States, shall be admitted into and entitled to all the advantages of this union; but no other colony shall be admitted into the same, unless such admission be agreed to by nine states.

Article 12

All bills of credit emitted, monies borrowed and debts contracted by, or under the authority of Congress before the assembling of the United States, in pursuance of the present confederation, shall be deemed and considered as a charge against the United States, for payment and satisfaction whereof the said United States and the public faith are hereby solemnly pledged.

Article 13

Every State shall abide by the determinations of the United States, in Congress assembled, on all questions which, by this confederation, are submitted to them. And the articles of this confederation shall be inviolably observed by every State, and the union shall be perpetual; nor shall any alteration at any time hereafter be made in any of them, unless such alteration be agreed to in a Congress of the United States, and be afterwards confirmed by the legislatures of every State.

These articles shall be proposed to the legislatures of all the United States, to be considered, and if approved of by them, they are advised to authorize their delegates to ratify the same in the Congress of the United States; which being done, the same shall become conclusive.

The Constitution of the United States*

Agreed to by Philadelphia Convention, September 17, 1787. Implemented March 4, 1789.

Preamble

We the people of the United States, in order to form a more perfect union, establish justice, insure domestic tranquility, provide for the common defense, promote the general welfare, and secure the blessings of liberty to ourselves and our posterity, do ordain and establish this Constitution for the United States of America.

Article I

Section 1. All legislative powers herein granted shall be vested in a Congress of the United States, which shall consist of a Senate and a House of Representatives.

Section 2. The House of Representatives shall be composed of members chosen every second year by the people of the several States, and the electors in each State shall have the qualifications requisite for electors of the most numerous branch of the State Legislature.

No person shall be a Representative who shall not have attained to the age of twenty-five years, and been seven years a citizen of the United States, and who shall not, when elected, be an inhabitant of that State in which he shall be chosen.

Representatives and direct taxes shall be apportioned among the several States which may be included within this Union, according to their respective numbers, *which shall be determined by adding to the whole number of free persons, including those bound to service for a term of years and excluding Indians not taxed, three-fifths of all other persons.* The actual enumeration shall be made within three years after the first meeting of the Congress of the United States, and within every subsequent term of ten years, in such manner as they shall by law direct. The number of Representatives shall not exceed one for every thirty thousand, but each State shall have at least one Representative; and until such enumeration shall be made, *the State of New Hampshire shall be entitled to choose three, Massachusetts eight, Rhode Island and Providence Plantations one, Connecticut five, New York six, New Jersey four, Pennsylvania eight, Delaware one, Maryland six, Virginia ten, North Carolina five, South Carolina five, and Georgia three.*

When vacancies happen in the representation from any State, the Executive authority thereof shall issue writs of election to fill such vacancies.

*Passages no longer in effect are in italic type.

The House of Representatives shall choose their Speaker and other officers; and shall have the sole power of impeachment.

Section 3. The Senate of the United States shall be composed of two Senators from each State, *chosen by the legislature thereof,* for six years; and each Senator shall have one vote.

Immediately after they shall be assembled in consequence of the first election, they shall be divided as equally as may be into three classes. The seats of the Senators of the first class shall be vacated at the expiration of the second year, of the second class at the expiration of the fourth year, and of the third class at the expiration of the sixth year, so that one-third may be chosen every second year; and if vacancies happen by resignation or otherwise, during the recess of the legislature of any State, the Executive thereof may make temporary appointments until the next meeting of the legislature, which shall then fill such vacancies.

No person shall be a Senator who shall not have attained to the age of thirty years, and been nine years a citizen of the United States, and who shall not, when elected, be an inhabitant of that State for which he shall be chosen.

The Vice-President of the United States shall be President of the Senate, but shall have no vote, unless they be equally divided.

The Senate shall choose their other officers, and also a President pro tempore, in the absence of the Vice-President, or when he shall exercise the office of President of the United States.

The Senate shall have the sole power to try all impeachments. When sitting for that purpose, they shall be on oath or affirmation. When the President of the United States is tried, the Chief Justice shall preside: and no person shall be convicted without the concurrence of two-thirds of the members present.

Judgment in cases of impeachment shall not extend further than to removal from the office, and disqualification to hold and enjoy any office of honor, trust or profit under the United States: but the party convicted shall nevertheless be liable and subject to indictment, trial, judgment and punishment, according to law.

Section 4. The times, places and manner of holding elections for Senators and Representatives shall be prescribed in each State by the legislature thereof; but the Congress may at any time by law make or alter such regulations, except as to the places of choosing Senators.

The Congress shall assemble at least once in every year, and such meeting *shall be on the first Monday in December, unless they shall by law appoint a different day.*

Section 5. Each house shall be the judge of the elections, returns and qualifications of its own members, and a majority of each shall constitute a quorum to do business; but a smaller number may adjourn from day to day, and may be authorized to compel the attendance of absent members, in such manner, and under such penalties, as each house may provide.

Each house may determine the rules of its proceedings, punish its members for disorderly behavior, and with the concurrence of two-thirds, expel a member.

Each house shall keep a journal of its proceedings, and from time to time publish the same, excepting such parts as may in their judgment require secrecy; and the yeas and nays of the members of either house on any question shall, at the desire of one fifth of those present, be entered on the journal.

Neither house, during the session of Congress, shall, without the consent of the other, adjourn for more than three days, nor to any other place than that in which the two houses shall be sitting.

Section 6. The Senators and Representatives shall receive a compensation for their services, to be ascertained by law and paid out of the treasury of the United States. They shall in all cases except treason, felony and breach of the peace, be privileged from arrest during their attendance at the session of their respective houses, and in going to and returning from the same; and for any speech or debate in either house, they shall not be questioned in any other place.

No Senator or Representative shall, during the time for which he was elected, be appointed to any civil office under the authority of the United States, which shall have been created, or the emoluments whereof shall have been increased, during such time; and no person holding any office under the United States shall be a member of either house during his continuance in office.

Section 7. All bills for raising revenue shall originate in the House of Representatives; but the Senate may propose or concur with amendments as on other bills.

Every bill which shall have passed the House of Representatives and the Senate, shall, before it become a law, be presented to the President of the United States; if he approve he shall sign it, but if not he shall return it with objections to that house in which it shall have originated, who shall enter the objections at large on their journal, and proceed to reconsider it. If after such reconsideration two-thirds of that house shall agree to pass the bill, it shall be sent, together with the objections, to the other house, by which it shall likewise be reconsidered, and, if approved by two-thirds of that house, it shall become a law. But in all such cases the votes of both houses shall be determined by yeas and nays, and the names of the persons voting for and against the bill shall be entered on the journal of each house respectively. If any bill shall not be returned by the President within ten days (Sundays excepted) after it shall have been presented to him, the same shall be a law, in like manner as if he had signed it, unless the Congress by their adjournment prevent its return, in which case it shall not be a law.

Every order, resolution, or vote to which the concurrence of the Senate and House of Representatives may be necessary (except on a question of adjournment) shall be presented to the President of the United States; and before the same shall take effect, shall be approved by him, or being disapproved by him, shall be repassed by two-thirds of the Senate and House of Representatives, according to the rules and limitations prescribed in the case of a bill.

Section 8. The Congress shall have power

To lay and collect taxes, duties, imposts, and excises, to pay the debts and provide for the common defense and general welfare of the United States; but all duties, imposts and excises shall be uniform throughout the United States;

To borrow money on the credit of the United States;

To regulate commerce with foreign nations, and among the several States, and with the Indian tribes;

To establish an uniform rule of naturalization, and uniform laws on the subject of bankruptcies throughout the United States;

To coin money, regulate the value thereof, and of foreign coin, and fix the standard of weights and measures;

To provide for the punishment of counterfeiting the securities and current coin of the United States;

To establish post offices and post roads;

To promote the progress of science and useful arts by securing for limited times to authors and inventors the exclusive right to their respective writings and discoveries;

To constitute tribunals inferior to the Supreme Court;

To define and punish piracies and felonies committed on the high seas and offences against the law of nations;

To declare war, grant letters of marque and reprisal, and make rules concerning captures on land and water;

To raise and support armies, but no appropriation of money to that use shall be for a longer term than two years;

To provide and maintain a navy;

To make rules for the government and regulation of the land and naval forces;

To provide for calling forth the militia to execute the laws of the Union, suppress insurrections and repel invasions;

To provide for organizing, arming, and disciplining the militia, and for governing such part of them as may be employed in the service of the United States, reserving to the States respectively the appointment of the officers, and the authority of training the militia according to the discipline prescribed by Congress;

To exercise exclusive legislation in all cases whatsoever, over such district (not exceeding ten miles square) as may, by cession of particular States, and the acceptance of Congress, become the seat of the government of the United States, and to exercise like authority over all places purchased by the consent of the legislature of the State, in which the same shall be, for erection of forts, magazines, arsenals, dock-yards, and other needful buildings;—and

To make all laws which shall be necessary and proper for carrying into execution the foregoing powers, and all other powers vested by this Constitution in the government of the United States, or in any department or officer thereof.

Section 9. *The migration or importation of such persons as any of the States now existing shall think proper to admit shall not be prohibited by the Congress prior to the year one thousand eight hundred and eight; but a tax or duty may be imposed on such importation, not exceeding ten dollars for each person.*

The privilege of the writ of habeas corpus shall not be suspended, unless when in cases of rebellion or invasion the public safety may require it.

No bill of attainder or ex post facto law shall be passed.

No capitation, or other direct, tax shall be laid, unless in proportion to the census or enumeration herein before directed to be taken.

No tax or duty shall be laid on articles exported from any State.

No preference shall be given by any regulation of commerce or revenue to the ports of one State over those of another; nor shall vessels bound to, or from, one State be obliged to enter, clear, or pay duties in another.

No money shall be drawn from the treasury, but in consequence of appropriations made by law; and a regular statement and account of the receipts and expenditures of all public money shall be published from time to time.

No title of nobility shall be granted by the United States: and no person holding any office of profit or trust under them, shall, without the consent of the Congress, accept of any present, emolument, office, or title, of any kind whatever, from any king, prince, or foreign state.

Section 10. No State shall enter into any treaty, alliance, or confederation; grant letters of marque and reprisal; coin money; emit bills of credit; make anything but gold and silver coin a tender in payment of debts; pass any bill of attainder, ex post facto law, or law impairing the obligation of contracts, or grant any title of nobility.

No State shall, without the consent of Congress, lay any imposts or duties on imports or exports, except what may be absolutely necessary for executing its inspection laws: and the net produce of all duties and imposts, laid by any State on imports or exports, shall be for the use of the treasury of the United States; and all such laws shall be subject to the revision and control of the Congress.

No State shall, without the consent of Congress, lay any duty of tonnage, keep troops, or ships of war in time of peace, enter into any agreement or compact with another State, or with a foreign power, or engage in war, unless actually invaded, or in such imminent danger as will not admit of delay.

Article II

Section 1. The executive power shall be vested in a President of the United States of America. He shall hold his office during the term of four years, and, together with the Vice-President, chosen for the same term, be elected as follows:

Each State shall appoint, in such manner as the legislature thereof may direct, a number of electors, equal to the whole number of Senators and Representatives to which the State may be entitled in the Congress; but no Senator or Representative, or person holding an office of trust or profit under the United States, shall be appointed an elector.

The electors shall meet in their respective States, and vote by ballot for two persons, of whom one at least shall not be an inhabitant of the same State with themselves. And they shall make a list of all the persons voted for, and of the number of votes for each; which list they shall sign and certify, and transmit sealed to the seat of government of the United States, directed to the President of the Senate. The President of the Senate shall, in the presence of the Senate and House of Representatives, open all the certificates, and the votes shall then be counted. The person having the greatest number of votes shall be the President, if such number be a majority of the whole number of electors appointed; and if there be more than one who have such majority, and have an equal number of votes, then the House of Representatives shall immediately choose by ballot one of them for President; and if no person have a majority, then from the five highest on the list said house shall in like manner choose the President. But in choosing the President the votes shall be taken by States, the representation from each State having one vote; a quorum for this purpose shall consist of a member or members from two-thirds of the States, and a majority of all the States shall be necessary to a choice. In every case, after the choice of the President, the person having the greatest number of votes of the electors shall be the Vice-President. But if there should remain two or more who have equal votes, the Senate shall choose from them by ballot the Vice-President.

The Congress may determine the time of choosing the electors, and the day on which they shall give their votes; which day shall be the same throughout the United States.

No person except a natural-born citizen, *or a citizen of the United States at the time of the adoption of this Constitution,* shall be eligible to the office of President; neither shall any person be eligible to that office who shall not have attained to the age of thirty-five years, and been fourteen years a resident within the United States.

In cases of the removal of the President from office or of his death, resignation, or inability to discharge the powers and duties of the said office, the same shall devolve on the Vice-President, and the Congress may by law provide for the case of removal, death, resignation, or inability, both of the President and Vice-President, declaring what officer shall then act as President, and such officer shall act accordingly, until the disability be removed, or a President shall be elected.

The President shall, at stated times, receive for his services a compensation, which shall neither be increased nor diminished during the period for which he shall have been elected, and he shall not receive within that period any other emolument from the United States, or any of them.

Before he enter on the execution of his office, he shall take the following oath or affirmation:—"I do solemnly swear (or affirm) that I will faithfully execute the office of the President of the United States, and will to the best of my ability preserve, protect and defend the Constitution of the United States."

Section 2. The President shall be commander in chief of the army and navy of the United States, and of the militia of the several States, when called into the actual service of the United States; he may require the opinion, in writing, of the principal officer in each of the executive departments, upon any subject relating to the duties of their respective offices, and he shall have power to grant reprieves and pardons for offenses against the United States, except in cases of impeachment.

He shall have power, by and with the advice and consent of the Senate, to make treaties, provided two-thirds of the Senators present concur; and he shall nominate, and by and with the advice and consent of the Senate, shall appoint ambassadors, other public ministers and consuls, judges of the Supreme Court, and all other officers of the United States, whose appointments are not herein otherwise provided for, and which shall be established by law: but Congress may by law vest the appointment of such inferior officers, as they think proper, in the President alone, in the courts of law, or in the heads of departments.

The President shall have power to fill up all vacancies that may happen during the recess of the Senate, by granting commissions which shall expire at the end of their next session.

Section 3. He shall from time to time give to the Congress information of the state of the Union, and recommend to their consideration such measures as he shall judge necessary and expedient; he may, on extraordinary occasions, convene both houses, or either of them, and in case of disagreement between them, with respect to the time of adjournment, he may adjourn them to such time as he shall think proper; he shall receive ambassadors and other public ministers; he shall take care that the laws be faithfully executed, and shall commission all the officers of the United States.

Section 4. The President, Vice-President and all civil officers of the United States shall be removed from office on impeachment for, and on conviction of, treason, bribery, or other high crimes and misdemeanors.

Article III

Section 1. The judicial power of the United States shall be vested in one Supreme Court, and in such inferior courts as the Congress may from time to time ordain and establish. The judges, both of the Supreme and inferior courts, shall hold their offices during good behavior, and shall, at stated times, receive for their services a compensation which shall not be diminished during their continuance in office.

Section 2. The judicial power shall extend to all cases, in law and equity, arising under this Constitution, the laws of the United States, and treaties made, or which shall be made, under their authority;—to all cases affecting ambassadors, other public ministers and consuls;—to all cases of admiralty and maritime jurisdiction;—to controversies to which the United States shall be a party;—to controversies between two or more States;—between a State and citizens of another State;—between citizens of different States;—between citizens of the same State claiming lands under grants of different States, and between a State, or the citizens thereof, and foreign states, citizens or subjects.

In all cases affecting ambassadors, other public ministers and consuls, and those in which a State shall be party, the Supreme Court shall have original jurisdiction. In all the other cases before mentioned, the Supreme Court shall have appellate jurisdiction, both as to law and fact, with such exceptions, and under such regulations, as the Congress shall make.

The trial of all crimes, except in cases of impeachment, shall be by jury; and such trial shall be held in the State where said crimes shall have been committed; but when not committed within any State, the trial shall be at such place or places as the Congress may by Law have directed.

Section 3. Treason against the United States shall consist only in levying war against them, or in adhering to their enemies, giving them aid and comfort. No person shall be convicted of treason unless on the testimony of two witnesses to the same overt act, or on confession in open court.

The Congress shall have power to declare the punishment of treason, but no attainder of treason shall work corruption of blood, or forfeiture except during the life of the person attainted.

Article IV

Section 1. Full faith and credit shall be given in each State to the public acts, records, and judicial proceedings of every other State. And the Congress may by general laws prescribe the manner in which such acts, records, and proceedings shall be proved, and the effect thereof.

Section 2. The citizens of each State shall be entitled to all privileges and immunities of citizens in the several States.

A person charged in any State with treason, felony, or other crime, who shall flee from justice, and be found in another State, shall on demand of the executive authority of the State from which he fled, be delivered up, to be removed to the State having jurisdiction of the crime.

No Person held to service or labor in one State, under the laws thereof, escaping into another, shall, in consequence of any law or regulation therein, be discharged from such service or labor, but shall be delivered up on claim of the party to whom such service or labor may be due.

Section 3. New States may be admitted by the Congress into this Union; but no new State shall be formed or erected within the jurisdiction of any other State; nor any State be formed by the junction of two or more States, or parts of States, without the consent of the legislatures of the States concerned as well as of the Congress.

The Congress shall have power to dispose of and make all needful rules and regulations respecting the territory or other property belonging to the United States; and nothing in this Constitution shall be so construed as to prejudice any claims of the United States, or of any particular State.

Section 4. The United States shall guarantee to every State in this Union a republican form of government, and shall protect each of them against invasion; and on application of the legislature, or of the executive (when the legislature cannot be convened), against domestic violence.

Article V

The Congress, whenever two-thirds of both houses shall deem it necessary, shall propose amendments to this Constitution, or, on the application of the legislatures of two-thirds of the several States, shall call a convention for proposing amendments, which, in either case, shall be valid to all intents and purposes, as part of this Constitution, when ratified by the legislatures of three-fourths of the several States, or by conventions in three-fourths thereof, as the one or the other mode of ratification may be proposed by the Congress; *provided that no amendments which may be made prior to the year one thousand eight hundred and eight shall in any manner affect the first and fourth clauses in the ninth section of the first article;* and that no State, without its consent, shall be deprived of its equal suffrage in the Senate.

Article VI

All debts contracted and engagements entered into, before the adoption of this Constitution, shall be as valid against the United States under this Constitution, as under the Confederation.

This Constitution, and the laws of the United States which shall be made in pursuance thereof; and all treaties made, or which shall be made, under the authority of the United States, shall be the supreme law of the land; and the judges in every State shall be bound thereby, anything in the Constitution or laws of any State to the contrary notwithstanding.

The Senators and Representatives before mentioned, and the members of the several State legislatures, and all executive and judicial officers, both of the United States and of the several States, shall be bound by oath or affirmation to support this Constitution; but no religious test shall ever be required as a qualification to any office or public trust under the United States.

Article VII

The ratification of the conventions of nine States shall be sufficient for the establishment of this Constitution between the States so ratifying the same.

Done in convention by the unanimous consent of the States present, the seventeenth day of September in the year of our Lord one thousand seven hundred and eighty-seven and of the Independence of the United States of America the twelfth. In witness whereof we have hereunto subscribed our names.

GEORGE WASHINGTON, President and Deputy from Virginia

New Hampshire
John Langdon
Nicholas Gilman

Massachusetts
Nathaniel Gorham
Rufus King

Connecticut
William Samuel
  Johnson
Roger Sherman

New York
Alexander Hamilton

New Jersey
William Livingston
David Brearley
William Paterson
Jonathan Dayton

Pennsylvania
Benjamin Franklin
Thomas Mifflin
Robert Morris
George Clymer
Thomas FitzSimons
Jared Ingersoll
James Wilson
Gouverneur Morris

Delaware
George Read
Gunning Bedford, Jr.
John Dickinson
Richard Bassett
Jacob Broom

Maryland
James McHenry
Daniel of St. Thomas Jenifer
Daniel Carroll

Virginia
John Blair
James Madison, Jr.

North Carolina
William Blount
Richard Dobbs Spaight
Hugh Williamson

South Carolina
John Rutledge
Charles Cotesworth Pinckney
Charles Pinckney
Pierce Butler

Georgia
William Few
Abraham Baldwin

Amendments to the Constitution
(including six unratified amendments)

Amendment I
[Ratified 1791]

Congress shall make no law respecting an establishment of religion, or prohibiting the free exercise thereof; or abridging the freedom of speech, or of the press; or the right of the people peaceably to assemble, and to petition the government for a redress of grievances.

Amendment II
[Ratified 1791]

A well-regulated militia being necessary to the security of a free State, the right of the people to keep and bear arms shall not be infringed.

Amendment III
[Ratified 1791]

No soldier shall, in time of peace, be quartered in any house without the consent of the owner, nor in time of war, but in a manner to be prescribed by law.

Amendment IV
[Ratified 1791]

The right of the people to be secure in their persons, houses, papers, and effects, against unreasonable searches and seizures, shall not be violated, and no warrants shall issue but upon probable cause, supported by oath or affirmation, and particularly describing the place to be searched, and the persons or things to be seized.

Amendment V
[Ratified 1791]

No person shall be held to answer for a capital, or otherwise infamous crime, unless on a presentment or indictment of a grand jury, except in cases arising in the land or naval forces, or in the militia, when in actual service in time of war or public danger; nor shall any person be subject for the same offence to be twice put in jeopardy of life or limb; nor shall be compelled in any criminal case to be a witness against himself, nor be deprived of life, liberty, or property, without due process of law; nor shall private property be taken for public use without just compensation.

Amendment VI
[Ratified 1791]

In all criminal prosecutions, the accused shall enjoy the right to a speedy and public trial, by an impartial jury of the State and district wherein the crime shall have been committed, which district shall have been previously ascertained by law, and to be informed of the nature and cause of the accusation; to be confronted with the witnesses against him; to have compulsory process for obtaining witnesses in his favor, and to have the assistance of counsel for his defence.

Amendment VII
[Ratified 1791]

In suits at common law, where the value in controversy shall exceed twenty dollars, the right of trial by jury shall be preserved, and no fact tried by a jury shall be otherwise reexamined in any court of the United States, than according to the rules of the common law.

Amendment VIII
[Ratified 1791]

Excessive bail shall not be required, nor excessive fines imposed, nor cruel and unusual punishments inflicted.

Amendment IX
[Ratified 1791]

The enumeration in the Constitution, of certain rights, shall not be construed to deny or disparage others retained by the people.

Amendment X
[Ratified 1791]

The powers not delegated to the United States by the Constitution, nor prohibited by it to the States, are reserved to the States respectively, or to the people.

Unratified Amendment
[Reapportionment Amendment (proposed by Congress September 25, 1789, along with the Bill of Rights)]

After the first enumeration required by the first article of the Constitution, there shall be one Representative for every thirty thousand, until the number shall amount to one hundred, after which the proportion shall be so regulated by Congress, that there shall be not less than one hundred Representatives, nor less than one Representative for every forty thousand persons, until the number of Representatives shall amount to two hundred; after which the proportion shall be so regulated by Congress, that there shall not be less than two hundred Representatives, nor more than one Representative for every fifty thousand persons.

Amendment XI
[Ratified 1798]

The judicial power of the United States shall not be construed to extend to any suit in law or equity, commenced or prosecuted against one of the United States by citizens of another State, or by citizens or subjects of any foreign state.

Amendment XII
[Ratified 1804]

The electors shall meet in their respective States, and vote by ballot for President and Vice-President, one of whom, at least, shall not be an inhabitant of the same State with themselves; they shall name in their ballots the person voted for as President, and in distinct ballots the person voted for as Vice-President, and they shall make distinct lists of all persons voted for as President, and of all persons voted for as Vice-President, and of the number of votes for each, which lists they shall sign and certify, and transmit sealed to the seat of government of the United States, directed to the President of the Senate;—the President of the Senate shall, in the presence of the Senate and House of Representatives, open all the certificates and the votes shall then be counted;—the person having the greatest number of votes for President shall be the President, if such number be a majority of the whole number of electors appointed; and if no person have such majority, then from the persons having the highest numbers not exceeding three on the list of those voted for as President, the House of Representatives shall choose immediately, by ballot, the President. But in choosing the President, the votes shall be taken by States, the representation from each State having one vote; a quorum for this purpose shall consist of a member or members from two-thirds of the States, and a majority of all the States shall be necessary to a choice. And if the House of Representatives shall not choose a President whenever the right of choice shall devolve upon them, before *the fourth day of March* next following, then the Vice-President shall act as President, as in the case of the death or other constitutional disability of the President.

The person having the greatest number of votes as Vice-President shall be the Vice-President, if such number be a majority of the whole number of electors appointed; and if no person have a majority, then from the two highest numbers on the list the Senate shall choose the Vice-President; a quorum for the purpose shall consist of two-thirds of the whole number of Senators, and a majority of the whole number shall be necessary to a choice. But no person constitutionally ineligible to the office of President shall be eligible to that of Vice-President of the United States.

Unratified Amendment
[Titles of Nobility Amendment (proposed by Congress May 1, 1810)]

If any citizen of the United States shall accept, claim, receive or retain any title of nobility or honor or shall, without the consent of Congress, accept and retain any present, pension, office or emolument of any kind whatever, from any emperor, king, prince or foreign power, such person shall cease to be a citizen of the United States, and shall be incapable of holding any office of trust or profit under them or either of them.

Unratified Amendment

[Corwin Amendment (proposed by Congress March 2, 1861)]

No amendment shall be made to the Constitution which will authorize or give to Congress the power to abolish or interfere, within any State, with the domestic institutions thereof, including that of persons held to labor or service by the laws of said State.

Amendment XIII

[Ratified 1865]

Section 1. Neither slavery nor involuntary servitude, except as a punishment for crime whereof the party shall have been duly convicted, shall exist within the United States, or any place subject to their jurisdiction.

Section 2. Congress shall have power to enforce this article by appropriate legislation.

Amendment XIV

[Ratified 1868]

Section 1. All persons born or naturalized in the United States, and subject to the jurisdiction thereof, are citizens of the United States and of the State wherein they reside. No State shall make or enforce any law which shall abridge the privileges or immunities of citizens of the United States; nor shall any State deprive any person of life, liberty, or property, without due process of law; nor deny to any person within its jurisdiction the equal protection of the laws.

Section 2. Representatives shall be appointed among the several States according to their respective numbers, counting the whole number of persons in each State, excluding Indians not taxed. But when the right to vote at any election for the choice of Electors for President and Vice-President of the United States, Representatives in Congress, the executive and judicial officers of a State, or the members of the legislature thereof, is denied to any of the *male* inhabitants of such State, being *twenty-one* years of age and citizens of the United States, or in any way abridged, except for participation in rebellion, or other crime, the basis of representation therein shall be reduced in the proportion which the number of such male citizens shall bear to the whole number of *male* citizens *twenty-one* years of age in such State.

Section 3. No person shall be a Senator or Representative in Congress, or Elector of President and Vice-President, or hold any office, civil or military, under the United States, or under any State, who, having previously taken an oath, as a member of Congress, or as an officer of the United States, or as a member of any State legislature, or as an executive or judicial officer of any State, to support the Constitution of the United States, shall have engaged in insurrection or rebellion against the same, or given aid or comfort to the enemies thereof. Congress may, by a vote of two-thirds of each house, remove such disability.

Section 4. The validity of the public debt of the United States, authorized by law, including debts incurred for payment of pensions and bounties for services in suppressing insurrection or rebellion, shall not be questioned. But neither the United States nor any State shall assume or pay any debt or obligation incurred in aid of insurrection or rebellion against the United States, or any claim for the loss or emancipation of any slave; but all such debts, obligations, and claims shall be held illegal and void.

Section 5. The Congress shall have power to enforce, by appropriate legislation, the provisions of this article.

Amendment XV

[Ratified 1870]

Section 1. The right of citizens of the United States to vote shall not be denied or abridged by the United States or by any State on account of race, color, or previous condition of servitude.

Section 2. The Congress shall have power to enforce this article by appropriate legislation.

Amendment XVI

[Ratified 1913]

The Congress shall have power to lay and collect taxes on incomes, from whatever source derived, without apportionment among the several States, and without regard to any census or enumeration.

Amendment XVII

[Ratified 1913]

Section 1. The Senate of the United States shall be composed of two Senators from each State, elected by the people thereof, for six years; and each Senator shall have one vote. The electors in each State shall have the qualifications requisite for electors of [voters for] the most numerous branch of the State legislatures.

Section 2. When vacancies happen in the representation of any State in the Senate, the executive authority of such State shall issue writs of election to fill such vacancies: Provided, that the Legislature of any State may empower the executive thereof to make temporary appointments until the people fill the vacancies by election as the Legislature may direct.

Section 3. *This amendment shall not be so construed as to affect the election or term of any Senator chosen before it becomes valid as part of the Constitution.*

Amendment XVIII
[Ratified 1919; repealed 1933 by Amendment XXI]

Section 1. *After one year from the ratification of this article the manufacture, sale, or transportation of intoxicating liquors within, the importation thereof into, or the exportation thereof from the United States and all territory subject to the jurisdiction thereof, for beverage purposes, is hereby prohibited.*

Section 2. *The Congress and the several States shall have concurrent power to enforce this article by appropriate legislation.*

Section 3. *This article shall be inoperative unless it shall have been ratified as an amendment to the Constitution by the legislatures of the several States, as provided by the Constitution, within seven years from the date of the submission thereof to the States by the Congress.*

Amendment XIX
[Ratified 1920]

Section 1. The right of citizens of the United States to vote shall not be denied or abridged by the United States or by any State on account of sex.

Section 2. Congress shall have the power to enforce this article by appropriate legislation.

Unratified Amendment
[Child Labor Amendment (proposed by Congress June 2, 1924)]

Section 1. *The Congress shall have power to limit, regulate, and prohibit the labor of persons under eighteen years of age.*

Section 2. *The power of the several States is unimpaired by this article except that the operation of State laws shall be suspended to the extent necessary to give effect to legislation enacted by Congress.*

Amendment XX
[Ratified 1933]

Section 1. The terms of the President and Vice-President shall end at noon on the 20th day of January, and the terms of Senators and Representatives at noon on the 3rd day of January, of the years in which such terms would have ended if this article had not been ratified; and the terms of their successors shall then begin.

Section 2. The Congress shall assemble at least once in every year, and such meeting shall begin at noon on the 3rd day of January, unless they shall by law appoint a different day.

Section 3. If, at the time fixed for the beginning of the term of the President, the President-elect shall have died, the Vice-President-elect shall become President. If a President shall not have been chosen before the time fixed for the beginning of his term, or if the President-elect shall have failed to qualify, then the Vice-President-elect shall act as President until a President shall have qualified; and the Congress may by law provide for the case wherein neither a President-elect nor a Vice-President-elect shall have qualified, declaring who shall then act as President, or the manner in which one who is to act shall be selected, and such person shall act accordingly until a President or Vice-President shall have qualified.

Section 4. The Congress may by law provide for the case of the death of any of the persons from whom the House of Representatives may choose a President whenever the right of choice shall have devolved upon them, and for the case of the death of any of the persons from whom the Senate may choose a Vice-President whenever the right of choice shall have devolved upon them.

Section 5. Sections 1 and 2 shall take effect on the 15th day of October following the ratification of this article.

Section 6. This article shall be inoperative unless it shall have been ratified as an amendment to the Constitution by the Legislatures of three-fourths of the several States within seven years from the date of its submission.

Amendment XXI
[Ratified 1933]

Section 1. The eighteenth article of amendment to the Constitution of the United States is hereby repealed.

Section 2. The transportation or importation into any State, Territory, or Possession of the United States for delivery or use therein of intoxicating liquors, in violation of the laws thereof, is hereby prohibited.

Section 3. This article shall be inoperative unless it shall have been ratified as an amendment to the Constitution by conventions in the several States, as provided in the Constitution, within seven years from the date of the submission thereof to the States by the Congress.

Amendment XXII
[Ratified 1951]

Section 1. No person shall be elected to the office of the President more than twice, and no person who has held the office of President, or acted as President, for more than two years of a term to which some other person was elected President shall be elected to the office of President more than once. But this article shall not apply to any person holding the office of President when this Article was proposed by the Congress, and shall not prevent any person who may be holding the office of President, or acting as President, during the term within which this Article becomes operative from holding the office of President or acting as President during the remainder of such term.

Section 2. This article shall be inoperative unless it shall have been ratified as an amendment to the Constitution by the legislatures of three-fourths of the several States within seven years from the date of its submission to the States by the Congress.

Amendment XXIII
[Ratified 1961]

Section 1. The District constituting the seat of Government of the United States shall appoint in such manner as the Congress may direct: A number of electors of President and Vice-President equal to the whole number of Senators and Representatives in Congress to which the District would be entitled if it were a State, but in no event more than the least populous State; they shall be in addition to those appointed by the States, but they shall be considered for the purposes of the election of President and Vice-President, to be electors appointed by a State; and they shall meet in the District and perform such duties as provided by the twelfth article of amendment.

Section 2. The Congress shall have the power to enforce this article by appropriate legislation.

Amendment XXIV
[Ratified 1964]

Section 1. The right of citizens of the United States to vote in any primary or other election for President or Vice-President, for electors for President or Vice-President, or for Senator or Representative in Congress, shall not be denied or abridged by the United States or any State by reason of failure to pay any poll tax or other tax.

Section 2. The Congress shall have the power to enforce this article by appropriate legislation.

Amendment XXV
[Ratified 1967]

Section 1. In case of the removal of the President from office or of his death or resignation, the Vice-President shall become President.

Section 2. Whenever there is a vacancy in the office of the Vice-President, the President shall nominate a Vice-President who shall take office upon confirmation by a majority vote of both Houses of Congress.

Section 3. Whenever the President transmits to the President pro tempore of the Senate and the Speaker of the House of Representatives his written declaration that he is unable to discharge the powers and duties of his office, and until he transmits to them a written declaration to the contrary, such powers and duties shall be discharged by the Vice-President as Acting President.

Section 4. Whenever the Vice-President and a majority of either the principal officers of the executive departments or of such other body as Congress may by law provide, transmit to the President pro tempore of the Senate and the Speaker of the House of Representatives their written declaration that the President is unable to discharge the powers and duties of his office, the Vice-President shall immediately assume the powers and duties of the office as Acting President.

Thereafter, when the President transmits to the President pro tempore of the Senate and the Speaker of the House of Representatives his written declaration that no inability exists, he shall resume the powers and duties of his office unless the Vice-President and a majority of either the principal officers of the executive department[s] or of such other body as Congress may by law provide, transmit within four days to the President pro tempore of the Senate and the Speaker of the House of Representatives their written declaration that the President is unable to discharge the powers and duties of his office. Thereupon Congress shall decide the issue, assembling within forty-eight hours for that purpose if not in session. If the Congress, within twenty-one days after receipt of the latter written declaration, or, if Congress is not in session, within twenty-one days after Congress is required to assemble, determines by two-thirds vote of both Houses that the President is unable to discharge the powers and duties of his office, the Vice-President shall continue to discharge the same as Acting President; otherwise, the President shall resume the powers and duties of his office.

Amendment XXVI
[Ratified 1971]

Section 1. The right of citizens of the United States, who are eighteen years of age or older, to vote shall not be denied or abridged by the United States or by any State on account of age.

Section 2. The Congress shall have power to enforce this article by appropriate legislation.

Unratified Amendment
[Equal Rights Amendment (proposed by Congress March 22, 1972; seven-year deadline for ratification extended to June 30, 1982)]

Section 1. *Equality of rights under the law shall not be denied or abridged by the United States or by any State on account of sex.*

Section 2. *The Congress shall have the power to enforce, by appropriate legislation, the provisions of this article.*

Section 3. *This amendment shall take effect two years after the date of ratification.*

Unratified Amendment
[D.C. Statehood Amendment (proposed by Congress August 22, 1978)]

Section 1. *For purposes of representation in the Congress, election of the President and Vice-President, and article V of this Constitution, the District constituting the seat of government of the United States shall be treated as though it were a State.*

Section 2. *The exercise of the rights and powers conferred under this article shall be by the people of the District constituting the seat of government, and as shall be provided by Congress.*

Section 3. *The twenty-third article of amendment to the Constitution of the United States is hereby repealed.*

Section 4. *This article shall be inoperative, unless it shall have been ratified as an amendment to the Constitution by the legislatures of three-fourths of the several states within seven years from the date of its submission.*

Amendment XXVII
[Ratified 1992]

No law, varying the compensation for the services of the Senators and Representatives, shall take effect, until an election of Representatives shall have intervened.

Admission of States to the Union

State	Year of Admission	State	Year of Admission
Delaware	1787	Michigan	1837
Pennsylvania	1787	Florida	1845
New Jersey	1787	Texas	1845
Georgia	1788	Iowa	1846
Connecticut	1788	Wisconsin	1848
Massachusetts	1788	California	1850
Maryland	1788	Minnesota	1858
South Carolina	1788	Oregon	1859
New Hampshire	1788	Kansas	1861
Virginia	1788	West Virginia	1863
New York	1788	Nevada	1864
North Carolina	1789	Nebraska	1867
Rhode Island	1790	Colorado	1876
Vermont	1791	North Dakota	1889
Kentucky	1792	South Dakota	1889
Tennessee	1796	Montana	1889
Ohio	1803	Washington	1889
Louisiana	1812	Idaho	1890
Indiana	1816	Wyoming	1890
Mississippi	1817	Utah	1896
Illinois	1818	Oklahoma	1907
Alabama	1819	New Mexico	1912
Maine	1820	Arizona	1912
Missouri	1821	Alaska	1959
Arkansas	1836	Hawaii	1959

Presidents of the United States

President	Term	President	Term
George Washington	1789–1797	Benjamin Harrison	1889–1893
John Adams	1797–1801	Grover Cleveland	1893–1897
Thomas Jefferson	1801–1809	William McKinley	1897–1901
James Madison	1809–1817	Theodore Roosevelt	1901–1909
James Monroe	1817–1825	William H. Taft	1909–1913
John Quincy Adams	1825–1829	Woodrow Wilson	1913–1921
Andrew Jackson	1829–1837	Warren G. Harding	1921–1923
Martin Van Buren	1837–1841	Calvin Coolidge	1923–1929
William H. Harrison	1841	Herbert Hoover	1929–1933
John Tyler	1841–1845	Franklin D. Roosevelt	1933–1945
James K. Polk	1845–1849	Harry S. Truman	1945–1953
Zachary Taylor	1849–1850	Dwight D. Eisenhower	1953–1961
Millard Fillmore	1850–1853	John F. Kennedy	1961–1963
Franklin Pierce	1853–1857	Lyndon B. Johnson	1963–1969
James Buchanan	1857–1861	Richard M. Nixon	1969–1974
Abraham Lincoln	1861–1865	Gerald R. Ford	1974–1977
Andrew Johnson	1865–1869	Jimmy Carter	1977–1981
Ulysses S. Grant	1869–1877	Ronald Reagan	1981–1989
Rutherford B. Hayes	1877–1881	George H. W. Bush	1989–1993
James A. Garfield	1881	Bill Clinton	1993–2001
Chester A. Arthur	1881–1885	George W. Bush	2001–2009
Grover Cleveland	1885–1889	Barack Obama	2009–

Glossary of Key Terms

acquired immune deficiency syndrome (AIDS) Immune disorder that reached epidemic proportions in the United States in the 1980s. (p. 877)

affirmative action Programs meant to overcome historical patterns of discrimination against minorities and women in education and employment. By establishing guidelines for hiring and college admissions, the government sought to advance equal opportunities for minorities and women. (p. 865)

Agricultural Adjustment Act New Deal legislation that raised prices for farm produce by paying farmers subsidies to reduce production. Large farmers reaped most of the benefits from the act. The Supreme Court declared it unconstitutional in 1936. (p. 697)

America First Committee Isolationist organization founded by Senator Gerald Nye in 1940 to keep the United States out of World War II. (p. 724)

American Equal Rights Association Group of black and white women and men formed in 1866 to promote gender and racial equality. The organization split in 1869 over support for the Fifteenth Amendment. (p. 438)

American Federation of Labor (AFL) Trade union federation founded in 1886. Led by its first president, Samuel Gompers, the AFL sought to organize skilled workers into trade-specific unions. (p. 534)

American Indian Movement (AIM) An American Indian group, formed in 1968, that promoted "red power" and condemned the United States for its continued mistreatment of Native Americans. (p. 842)

American Plan Voluntary program initiated by businesses in the early twentieth century to protect worker welfare. The American Plan was meant to undermine the appeal of labor unions. (p. 658)

American Protective League (APL) An organization of private citizens that cooperated with the Justice Department and the Bureau of Investigation during World War I to spy on German residents suspected of disloyal behavior. (p. 639)

American Woman Suffrage Association Organization founded in 1869 to support ratification of the Fifteenth Amendment. (p. 438)

Anti-Imperialist League An organization founded in 1898 to oppose annexation of the Philippines. Some feared that annexation would bring competition from cheap labor; others considered Filipinos racially inferior and the Philippines unsuitable as an American territory. (p. 628)

Atlantic Charter August 1941 agreement between Franklin Roosevelt and Winston Churchill that outlined potential war aims and cemented the relationship between the United States and Britain. (p. 725)

Battle of the Little Big Horn 1876 battle in the Montana Territory in which Lieutenant Colonel George Armstrong Custer and his troops were massacred by Lakota Sioux. (p. 466)

beats A small group of young poets, writers, intellectuals, musicians, and artists who attacked mainstream American politics and culture in the 1950s. (p. 801)

Berlin airlift During the Berlin blockade by the Soviets from 1948 to 1949, the U.S. and British governments dispatched their air forces to transport food and supplies to West Berlin. (p. 765)

black codes Racial laws passed in the immediate aftermath of the Civil War by southern legislatures. The black codes were intended to reduce free African Americans to a condition as close to slavery as possible. (p. 432)

Black Panther Party Organization founded in 1966 by Huey P. Newton and Bobby Seale to advance the black power movement in black communities. (p. 842)

Black Tuesday October 29, 1929, crash of the American stock market. The 1929 stock market crash marked the beginning of the Great Depression. (p. 674)

blacklist Informal list of individuals barred from employment in the entertainment industry in the late 1940s and early 1950s as a result of their suspected Communist connections. (p. 775)

Boland Amendment 1982 act of Congress prohibiting direct aid to the Nicaraguan Contra forces. (p. 901)

Bonus Army World War I veterans who marched on Washington, D.C., in 1932 to demand immediate payment of their service bonuses. President Hoover refused to negotiate and instructed the U.S. army to clear the capital of protesters, leading to a violent clash. (p. 695)

boss Leader of a political machine. Men like "Boss" George Washington Plunkitt of New York's Tammany Hall wielded enormous power over city life. (p. 577)

Brown v. Board of Education of Topeka, Kansas Landmark 1954 Supreme Court case that overturned the "separate but equal" principle established by *Plessy v. Ferguson* and applied to public schools. Few schools in the South were racially desegregated for more than a decade. (p. 803)

buffalo soldiers African American cavalrymen who fought in the West against the Indians in the 1870s and 1880s and served with distinction. (p. 466)

bully pulpit Term used by Theodore Roosevelt to describe the office of the presidency. Roosevelt believed that the president should use his office as a platform to promote his programs and rally public opinion. (p. 607)

Bush Doctrine President George W. Bush's proposal to engage in preemptive war against despotic governments, such as Iraq, deemed to threaten U.S. national security, even if the danger was not imminent. (p. 939)

Californios Spanish and Mexican residents of California. Before the nineteenth century, Californios made up California's economic and political elite. Their position, however, deteriorated after the conclusion of the Mexican-American War in 1848. (p. 479)

Camp David accords 1978 peace accord between Israel and Egypt facilitated by the mediation of President Jimmy Carter. (p. 898)

carpetbaggers Derogatory term for white Northerners who moved to the South in the years following the Civil War. Many white Southerners believed that such migrants were intent on exploiting their suffering. (p. 440)

Chinese Exclusion Act 1882 act that banned Chinese immigration into the United States and prohibited those Chinese already in the country from becoming naturalized American citizens. (p. 481)

civic housekeeping Idea promoted by Jane Addams for urban reform by using women's traditional skills as domestic managers; caregivers for children, the elderly, and the needy; and community builders. (p. 594)

Civil Rights Act of 1964 Wide-ranging civil rights act that, among other things, prohibited discrimination in public accommodations and employment and increased federal enforcement of school desegregation. (p. 832)

Civilian Conservation Corps (CCC) New Deal work program that hired young, unmarried men to work on conservation projects. The CCC employed about 2.5 million men and lasted until 1942. (p. 699)

collective bargaining The process of negotiation between labor unions and employers. (p. 532)

Commission on the Status of Women Commission appointed by President Kennedy in 1961. The commission's 1963 report, *American Women*, highlighted employment discrimination against women and recommended legislation requiring equal pay for equal work regardless of sex. (p. 839)

Committee on Public Information (CPI) Committee established in 1917 to create propaganda and promote censorship in order to generate enthusiasm for World War I and stifle antiwar dissent. (p. 639)

Compromise of 1877 Compromise between Republicans and southern Democrats that resulted in the election of Rutherford B. Hayes. Southern Democrats agreed to support Hayes in the disputed presidential election in exchange for his promise to end Reconstruction. (p. 446)

Comstock Lode Massive silver deposit discovered in the Sierra Nevada in the late 1850s. (p. 469)

Congress of Racial Equality (CORE) Civil rights organization, founded in 1942, that fought against racial exclusion in public accommodations. The emergence of organizations like CORE signaled a new phase in the civil rights struggle. (p. 771)

conservative coalition Alliance of southern Democrats and conservative northern Republicans in Congress that thwarted passage of New Deal legislation after 1938. (p. 707)

Contract with America A document that called for reduced welfare spending, lower taxes, term limits for lawmakers, and a constitutional amendment for a balanced budget. In preparation for the 1994 midterm congressional elections, Republicans, led by Representative Newt Gingrich, drew up this proposal. (p. 934)

convict lease The system used by southern governments to furnish mainly African American prison labor to plantation owners and industrialists and to raise revenue for the states. In practice, convict labor replaced slavery as the means of providing a forced labor supply. (p. 497)

corporation A form of business ownership in which the liability of shareholders in a company is limited to their individual investments. The formation of corporations in the late nineteenth century greatly stimulated investment in industry. (p. 499)

counterculture Young cultural rebels of the 1960s who rejected conventional moral and sexual values and used drugs to reach a higher consciousness. These so-called hippies bonded together in their style of clothes and taste in rock 'n' roll music. (p. 838)

court-packing plan Proposal by President Franklin Roosevelt in 1937 to increase the size of the Supreme Court and reduce its opposition to New Deal legislation. Congress failed to pass the measure, and the scheme increased resentment toward Roosevelt. (p. 707)

Coxey's army 1894 protest movement led by Jacob Coxey. Coxey and five hundred supporters marched from Ohio to Washington, D.C., to protest the lack of government response to the depression of 1893. (p. 544)

Cuba Libre Vision of Cuban independence developed by José Martí, who hoped that Cuban independence would bring with it greater social and racial equality. (p. 626)

D Day June 6, 1944, invasion of German-occupied France by Allied forces. The D Day landings opened up a second front in Europe and marked a major turning point in World War II. (p. 728)

Dawes Act 1887 act that ended federal recognition of tribal sovereignty and divided Indian land into 160-acre parcels to be distributed to Indian heads of household. The act dramatically reduced the amount of Indian-controlled land and undermined Indian social and cultural institutions. (p. 467)

Dayton Peace Accords 1995 peace agreement ending the war in Bosnia that emerged from a conference hosted by President Bill Clinton in Dayton, Ohio. (p. 935)

depression of 1893 Severe economic downturn triggered by railroad and bank failures. The severity of the depression, combined with the failure of the federal government to offer an adequate response, led to the realignment of American politics. (p. 544)

détente An easing of tense relations with the Soviet Union during the Cold War. This process moved unevenly through the 1970s and early 1980s but accelerated when Soviet leader Mikhail Gorbachev came to power in the mid-1980s. (p. 897)

divestment movement 1980s campaign against apartheid by ending investments by U.S. corporations, universities, and municipalities in South Africa. (p. 902)

dollar diplomacy Term used by President Taft to describe the economic focus of his foreign policy. Taft hoped to use economic policies and the control of foreign assets by American companies to influence Latin American nations. (p. 633)

"don't ask, don't tell" The official policy toward gays in the U.S. military established by President Bill Clinton in 1993. The policy prohibited discrimination against homosexuals as long as they did not reveal their sexual identity, but it banned openly gay men and women from serving in the armed forces. It was repealed by President Barack Obama in 2011. (p. 933)

Eisenhower Doctrine A doctrine guiding intervention in the Middle East. In 1957 Congress granted President Dwight Eisenhower the power to send military forces into the Middle East to combat Communist aggression. Eisenhower sent U.S. marines into Lebanon in 1958 under this doctrine. (p. 810)

Enola Gay American B-29 bomber that dropped an atomic bomb on Hiroshima on August 6, 1945. The dropping of a second bomb on Nagasaki three days later led to Japan's surrender. (p. 732)

Environmental Protection Agency (EPA) Federal agency established by Richard Nixon in 1971 to regulate activities that resulted in pollution or other environmental degradation. (p. 871)

Equal Rights Amendment (ERA) A proposed amendment that prevented the abridgment of "equality of rights under law . . . by the United States or any State on the basis of sex." Not enough states had ratified the amendment by 1982, when the ratification period expired, so it was not adopted. (p. 869)

Espionage Act 1917 act that prohibited antiwar activities, including opposing the military draft. It punished speech critical of the war as well as deliberate actions of sabotage and spying. (p. 639)

ethnic cleansing Ridding an area of a particular ethnic minority in order to achieve ethnic homogeneity. In the civil war between Serbs and Croatians in Bosnia from 1992 to 1995, the Serbian military attempted to eliminate the Croatian population through murder, rape, and expulsion. (p. 935)

eugenics The pseudo-science of producing genetic improvement in the human population through selective breeding. Proponents of eugenics often saw ethnic and racial minorities as genetically "undesirable" and inferior. (p. 570)

European Union (EU) Organization formed by European nations in 1993 to boost their economic and political power. Member nations took steps to facilitate free trade, investment, and migration among EU states. (p. 913)

Exodusters Blacks who migrated from the South to Kansas in 1879 seeking land and a better way of life. (p. 441)

Fair Employment Practice Committee (FEPC) Committee established in 1941 to help African Americans gain a greater share of wartime industrial jobs. (p. 740)

Fair Labor Standards Act 1938 law that provided a minimum wage of 40 cents an hour and a forty-hour workweek for employees in businesses engaged in interstate commerce. (p. 707)

Farmers' Alliances Regional organizations formed in the late nineteenth century to advance the interests of farmers. The most prominent of these organizations were the Northwestern Farmers' Alliance, the Southern Farmers' Alliance, and the Colored Farmers' Alliance. (p. 540)

Federal Employee Loyalty Program Program established by President Truman in 1947 to investigate federal employees suspected of disloyalty. (p. 774)

Fifteenth Amendment Amendment to the Constitution prohibiting the abridgment of a citizen's right to vote on the basis of "race, color, or previous condition of servitude." From the 1870s on, southern states devised numerous strategies for circumventing the Fifteenth Amendment. (p. 438)

fireside chats Radio addresses by Franklin Roosevelt during the depression. Roosevelt's addresses boosted morale and informed the public about government efforts to help ease their difficulties. (p. 697)

Fourteen Points The core principles President Wilson saw as the basis for lasting peace, including freedom of the seas, open diplomacy, and self-determination for colonial peoples. (p. 639)

Fourteenth Amendment Amendment to the Constitution defining citizenship and protecting individual civil and political rights from abridgment by the states. Adopted during Reconstruction, the Fourteenth Amendment overturned the *Dred Scott* decision. (p. 436)

Free Speech Movement (FSM) Movement protesting policies instituted by the University of California at Berkeley that restricted free speech. In 1964 students at Berkeley conducted sit-ins and held rallies against these policies. (p. 837)

Freedmen's Bureau Federal agency created in 1865 to provide ex-slaves with economic and legal resources. The Freedmen's Bureau played an active role in shaping black life in the postwar South. (p. 427)

Freedom Rides Integrated bus rides through the South organized by CORE in 1961 to test compliance with Supreme Court rulings on segregation. (p. 830)

Freedom Summer 1964 civil rights project in Mississippi launched by SNCC, CORE, the SCLC, and the NAACP. Some eight hundred volunteers, mainly white college students, worked on voter registration drives and in freedom schools to improve education for rural black youngsters. (p. 833)

ghettos Neighborhoods dominated by a single ethnic, racial, or class group. (p. 565)

Ghost Dance Religious ritual performed by the Paiute Indians in the late nineteenth century. Following a vision he received in 1888, the prophet Wovoka believed that performing the Ghost Dance would cause whites to disappear and allow Indians to regain control of their lands. (p. 468)

Gilded Age Term coined by Mark Twain and Charles Dudley Warner to describe the late nineteenth century. The term referred to the opulent and often ostentatious lifestyles of the era's superrich. (p. 505) *glasnost* Policy of political "openness" initiated by Soviet leader Mikhail Gorbachev in the 1980s. Under *glasnost*, the Soviet Union extended democratic elections, freedom of speech, and freedom of the press. (p. 907)

globalization The extension of economic, political, and cultural relationships among nations, through commerce, migration, and communication. Globalization expanded in the late twentieth century because of free trade agreements and the relaxation of immigration restrictions. (p. 910)

"The Gospel of Wealth" 1889 essay by Andrew Carnegie in which he argued that the rich should act as stewards of the wealth they earned, using their surplus income for the benefit of the community. (p. 504)

Grangers Members of an organization founded in 1867 to meet the social and cultural needs of farmers. Grangers took an active role in the promotion of the economic and political interests of farmers. (p. 539)

great migration Population shift of more than 400,000 African Americans who left the South beginning in 1917–1918 and headed north and west hoping to escape poverty and racial discrimination. During the 1920s another 800,000 blacks left the South. (p. 657)

Great Plains Semiarid territory in central North America. (p. 461)

Great Recession The severe economic decline in the United States and throughout the world that began in 2008, leading to bank failures, high unemployment, home foreclosures, and large federal deficits. (p. 943)

Great Society President Lyndon Johnson's vision of social, economic, and cultural progress in the United States. (p. 834)

Gulf of Tonkin Resolution 1964 congressional resolution giving President Lyndon Johnson wide discretion in the use of U.S. forces in Vietnam. The resolution followed reported attacks by North Vietnamese gunboats on two American destroyers. (p. 826)

Haymarket Square Site of 1886 rally and violence. In the aftermath of the events in Haymarket Square, the union movement in the United States went into temporary decline. (p. 533)

Hetch Hetchy valley Site of a controversial dam built to supply San Francisco with water and power in the aftermath of the 1906 earthquake. The dam was built over the objections of preservationists such as John Muir. (p. 606)

Homestead Act 1862 act that established procedures for distributing 160-acre lots to western settlers, on condition that they develop and farm their land, as an incentive for western migration. (p. 474)

Homestead strike 1892 strike by steelworkers at Andrew Carnegie's Homestead steel factory. The strike collapsed after a failed assassination attempt on Carnegie's plant manager, Henry Clay Frick. (p. 534)

Hoovervilles Shantytowns that sprang up in the years following the 1929 stock market crash. Many Americans believed that President Hoover did not do enough to relieve the suffering that accompanied the Great Depression. (p. 690)

horizontal integration The ownership of as many firms as possible in a given industry by a single owner. John D. Rockefeller pursued a strategy of horizontal integration when he bought up rival oil refineries. (p. 499)

House Committee on Un-American Activities (HUAC) House committee established in 1938 to investigate domestic communism. After World War II, HUAC conducted highly publicized investigations of Communist influence in government and the entertainment industry. (p. 774)

Hull House Settlement house established in 1889 by Jane Addams and Ellen Starr. Hull House inspired a generation of young women to work directly in immigrant communities. (p. 594)

Hurricane Katrina 2005 storm that hit the Gulf coast states of Louisiana, Mississippi, and Alabama. The hurricane caused massive flooding in New Orleans after levees broke. Federal, state, and local government responses to the storm were inadequate and highlighted racial and class inequities. (p. 940)

imperial presidency Term used to describe the growth of presidential powers during the Cold War, particularly with respect to war-making powers and the conduct of national security. (p. 764)

Indian Reorganization Act (IRA) 1934 act that ended the Dawes Act, authorized self-government for those living on reservations, extended tribal landholdings, and pledged to uphold native customs and language. (p. 706)

Industrial Workers of the World (IWW) Organization that grew out of the activities of the Western Federation of Miners in the 1890s and formed by Eugene V. Debs. The IWW attempted to unite all skilled and unskilled workers in an effort to overthrow capitalism. (p. 536)

internment The relocation of persons seen as a threat to national security to isolated camps during World War II. Nearly all people of Japanese descent living on the West Coast were forced to sell or abandon their possessions and relocate to internment camps during the war. (p. 743)

Interstate Commerce Commission (ICC) Regulatory commission established by Congress in 1887. The commission investigated interstate shipping, required railroads to make their rates public, and could bring lawsuits to force shippers to reduce "unreasonable" fares. (p. 539)

Iran-Contra Reagan administration scandal involving the funneling of funds from an illegal arms-for-hostages deal with Iran to the Nicaraguan Contras in the mid-1980s. (p. 904)

Jim Crow Late-nineteenth-century statutes that established legally defined racial segregation in the South. Jim Crow legislation helped ensure the social and economic inferiority of southern blacks. (p. 509)

jingoists Superpatriotic supporters of the expansion and use of military power. Jingoists such as Theodore Roosevelt longed for a war in which they could demonstrate America's strength and prove their own masculinity. (p. 624)

Joint Electoral Commission Commission created by Congress to resolve the disputed presidential election of 1876. The commission consisted of five senators, five House members, and five Supreme Court justices—seven Republicans, seven Democrats, and one independent. The commission sided with the Republican presidential candidate, Rutherford B. Hayes. (p. 446)

Knights of the Ku Klux Klan (KKK) Organization formed in 1865 by General Nathan Bedford Forrest to enforce prewar racial norms. Members of the KKK used threats and violence to intimidate blacks and white Republicans. (p. 443)

La Raza Unida (The United Race) A Chicano political party, formed in 1969, that advocated job opportunities for Chicanos, bilingual education, and Chicano cultural studies programs in universities. (p. 842)

laissez-faire French for "let things alone." Advocates of laissez-faire believed that the marketplace should be left to regulate itself, allowing individuals to pursue their own self-interest without any government restraint or interference. (p. 503)

League of Nations The international organization proposed by Woodrow Wilson after the end of World War I to ensure world peace and security in the future through mutual agreement. The United States failed to join the league because Wilson and his opponents in Congress could not work out a compromise. (p. 640)

Lend-Lease Act March 1941 law permitting the United States to lend or lease military equipment and other commodities to Great Britain and its allies. Its passage marked the end of American neutrality before the U.S. entered World War II. (p. 725)

Levittown Suburban subdivision built in Long Island, New York, in the 1950s in response to the postwar housing shortage. Subsequent Levittowns were built in Pennsylvania and New Jersey. (p. 793)

Liberal Republicans Political group organized to challenge the reelection of President Grant in 1872. The Liberal Republicans called for an end to federal efforts at Reconstruction in the South. (p. 445)

Little Rock Nine Nine African American students who, in 1957, became the first black students to attend Central High School in Little Rock, Arkansas. Federal troops were required to overcome the resistance of white officials and to protect the students. (p. 804)

Long Drive Cattle drive from the grazing lands of Texas to rail depots in Kansas. Once in Kansas, the cattle were shipped eastward to slaughterhouses in Chicago. (p. 471)

Lost Generation A term used by the writer Gertrude Stein to describe the writers and artists disillusioned with the consumer culture of the 1920s. (p. 664)

Manhattan Project Code name for the secret program to develop an atomic bomb. The project was launched in 1942 and directed by the United States with the assistance of Great Britain and Canada. (p. 731)

March on Washington for Jobs and Freedom August 28, 1963, rally by civil rights organizations in Washington, D.C., that brought increased national attention to the movement. (p. 832)

Marshall Plan Post–World War II European economic aid package developed by Secretary of State George Marshall. The plan helped rebuild Western Europe and served American political and economic interests in the process. (p. 763)

McCarthyism Term used to describe the harassment and persecution of suspected political radicals. Senator Joseph McCarthy was one of many prominent government figures who helped incite anti-Communist hysteria in the early 1950s. (p. 778)

megachurches Mainly Protestant congregations containing at least two thousand members. The number of megachurches in the United States increased dramatically during the 1980s and 1990s. (p. 937)

melting pot Popular metaphor for immigrant assimilation into American society. According to this ideal, all immigrants underwent a process of Americanization that produced a homogeneous society. (p. 570)

Mexican revolution 1911 revolution in Mexico, which led to nearly a decade of bloodshed and civil war. (p. 634)

military-industrial complex The government-business alliance related to the military and national defense that developed out of World War II and that greatly influenced future development of the U.S. economy. (p. 734)

Mississippi Freedom Democratic Party (MFDP) Political party formed in 1964 to challenge the all-white state Democratic Party for seats at the 1964 Democratic presidential convention and run candidates for public office. Although unsuccessful in 1964, MFDP efforts led to subsequent reform of the Democratic Party and the seating of an interracial, convention delegation from Mississippi in 1968. (p. 833)

Modern Republicanism The political approach of President Dwight Eisenhower that tried to fit traditional Republican Party ideals of individualism and fiscal restraint within the broad framework of the New Deal. (p. 807)

Montgomery Improvement Association Organization founded in Montgomery, Alabama, in 1955 to coordinate the boycott of city buses by African Americans. (p. 803)

Mormons Religious sect that migrated to Utah to escape religious persecution; also known as the Church of Jesus Christ of Latter-Day Saints. (p. 478)

muckrakers Investigative journalists who specialized in exposing corruption, scandal, and vice. Muckrakers helped build public support for progressive causes. (p. 593)

mujahideen Religiously inspired Afghan rebels who resisted the Soviet invasion of Afghanistan in 1979. (p. 898)

multinational (or transnational) corporations Companies that operate production facilities or deliver services in more than one country. Between 1970 and 2000, the number of such firms increased ninefold. (p. 911)

mutual aid societies Voluntary associations that provide a variety of economic and social benefits to their members. (p. 565)

mutually assured destruction (MAD) Defense strategy built around the threat of a massive nuclear retaliatory strike. Adoption of the doctrine of mutually assured destruction contributed to the escalation of the nuclear arms race during the Cold War. (p. 807)

National Association for the Advancement of Colored People (NAACP) Organization founded by W. E. B. Du Bois, Ida B. Wells, Jane Addams, and others in 1909 to fight for racial equality. The NAACP strategy focused on fighting discrimination through the courts. (p. 602)

National Interstate and Defense Highway Act 1956 act that provided funds for construction of 42,500 miles of roads throughout the United States. (p. 793)

National Labor Relations Act 1935 act (also known as the Wagner Act) that created the National Labor Relations Board (NLRB). The NLRB protected workers' right to organize labor unions without owner interference. (p. 704)

National Organization for Women (NOW) Feminist organization formed in 1966 by Betty Friedan and like-minded activists. (p. 840)

National Origins Act 1924 act establishing immigration quotas by national origin. The act was intended to severely limit immigration from southern and eastern Europe as well as prohibit all immigration from East Asia. (p. 668)

National Recovery Administration (NRA) New Deal agency established in 1933 to create codes to regulate production, prices, wages, hours, and collective bargaining. The NRA failed to produce the intended results and was eventually ruled unconstitutional. (p. 698)

National Security Council (NSC) Council created by the 1947 National Security Act to advise the president on military and foreign affairs. The NSC consists of the national security adviser and the secretaries of state, defense, the army, the navy, and the air force. (p. 764)

National War Labor Board (NWLB) Government agency created in 1918 to settle labor disputes. The NWLB consisted of representatives from unions, corporations, and the public. (p. 638)

National War Labor Board Board established in 1942 to oversee labor-management relations during World War II. The board regulated wages, hours, and working conditions and authorized the government to take over plants that refused to abide by its decisions. (p. 736)

National Woman Suffrage Association Organization founded in 1869 to support women's voting rights. Founders Susan B. Anthony and Elizabeth Cady Stanton objected to the Fifteenth Amendment because it did not provide suffrage for women. (p. 438)

nativism The belief that foreigners pose a serious danger to a nation's society and culture. Nativist sentiment rose in the United States as the size and diversity of the immigrant population grew. (p. 568)

neoconservatives Disillusioned liberals who condemned the Great Society programs they had originally supported. Neoconservatives were particularly concerned about affirmative action programs, the domination of campus discourse by New Left radicals, and left-wing criticism of the use of American military and economic might to advance U.S. interests overseas. (p. 874)

Neutrality Acts Legislation passed between 1935 and 1937 to make it more difficult for the United States to become entangled in overseas conflicts. The Neutrality Acts reflected the strength of isolationist sentiment in 1930s America. (p. 723)

New Deal The policies and programs that Franklin Roosevelt initiated to combat the Great Depression. The New Deal represented a dramatic expansion of the role of government in American society. (p. 697)

New Freedom Term used by Woodrow Wilson to describe his limited-government, progressive agenda. Wilson's New Freedom was offered as an alternative to Theodore Roosevelt's New Nationalism. (p. 610)

New Frontier President Kennedy's domestic agenda. Kennedy promised to battle "tyranny, poverty, disease, and war," but, lacking strong majorities in Congress, he achieved relatively modest results. (p. 825)

New Look The foreign policy strategy implemented by President Dwight Eisenhower that emphasized the development and deployment of nuclear weapons in an effort to cut military spending. (p. 807)

New Nationalism Agenda articulated by Theodore Roosevelt in his 1912 presidential campaign. Roosevelt called for increased regulation of large corporations, a more active role for the president, and the extension of social justice using the power of the federal government. (p. 610)

New Negro 1920s term for the second generation of African Americans born after emancipation and who stood up for their rights. (p. 665)

New Right The conservative coalition of old and new conservatives, as well as disaffected Democrats. The New Right came to power with the election of Ronald Reagan in 1980. (p. 861)

New South Term popularized by newspaper editor Henry Grady in the 1880s, a proponent of the modernization of the southern economy. Grady believed that industrial development would lead to the emergence of a "New South." (p. 497)

new woman 1920s term for the modern, sexually liberated woman. The new woman, popularized in movies and magazines, flouted traditional morality. (p. 664)

Noble Order of the Knights of Labor Labor organization founded in 1869 by Uriah Stephens. The Knights sought to include all workers in one giant union. (p. 532)

North American Free Trade Agreement (NAFTA) Free trade agreement approved in 1993 by the United States, Canada, and Mexico. (p. 913)

North Atlantic Treaty Organization (NATO) Cold War military alliance intended to enhance the collective security of the United States and Western Europe. (p. 765)

NSC-68 April 1950 National Security Council document that advocated the intensification of the policy of containment both at home and abroad. (p. 766)

nuclear freeze movement 1980s protests calling for a mutual freeze on the testing, production, and deployment of nuclear weapons and of missiles and aircraft designed primarily to deliver nuclear weapons. (p. 905)

Occupy Wall Street A loose coalition of progressive and radical forces that emerged in 2011 in New York City and around the country to protest corporate greed and federal policies that benefit the very wealthy. (p. 947)

Open Door 1899 policy in which Secretary of State John Hay informed the nations occupying China that the United States had the right of equal trade in China. (p. 631)

Operation Desert Storm Code name of the 1991 allied air and ground military offensive that pushed Iraqi forces out of Kuwait. (p. 914)

Organization of Petroleum Exporting Countries (OPEC) Organization formed by oil-producing countries to control the price and supply of oil on the global market. (p. 864)

Palmer raids Government roundup of some 6,000 suspected alien radicals in 1919–1920, ordered by Attorney General A. Mitchell Palmer and his assistant J. Edgar Hoover. The raids resulted in the deportation of 556 immigrants. (p. 656)

Patriot Act 2001 law passed in response to the September 11 terror attacks. It eased restrictions on domestic and foreign intelligence gathering and expanded governmental power to deport immigrants. (p. 938)

Pendleton Civil Service Reform Act 1883 act that required federal jobs to be awarded on the basis of merit through competitive exams rather than through political connections. (p. 579)

Pentagon Papers Classified report on U.S. involvement in Vietnam leaked to the press in 1971. The report confirmed that the Kennedy and Johnson administrations had misled the public about the origins and nature of the Vietnam War. (p. 863)

perestroika Policy of economic "restructuring" initiated by Soviet leader Mikhail Gorbachev. Gorbachev hoped that by reducing state control he could revive the Soviet economy. (p. 907)

Personal Responsibility and Work Opportunity Reconciliation Act 1996 act reforming the welfare system in the United States. The law required adults on the welfare rolls to find work within two years or lose their welfare benefits. (p. 934)

Platt Amendment 1901 act of Congress limiting Cuban sovereignty. American officials pressured Cuban leaders to incorporate the amendment into the Cuban constitution. (p. 628)

Plessy v. Ferguson 1896 Supreme Court ruling that upheld the legality of Jim Crow legislation. The Court ruled that as long as states provided "equal but separate" facilities for whites and blacks, Jim Crow laws did not violate the equal protection clause of the Fourteenth Amendment. (p. 509)

political machine Urban political organizations that dominated many late-nineteenth-century cities. Machines provided needed services to the urban poor, but they also fostered corruption, crime, and inefficiency. (p. 577)

Populists The People's Party of America, formed in 1892. The Populists sought to appeal to both farmers and industrial workers. (p. 541)

Port Huron Statement Students for a Democratic Society manifesto written in 1962 that condemned liberal politics, Cold War foreign policy, racism, and research-oriented universities. It called for the adoption of "participatory democracy." (p. 837)

pragmatism Philosophy that holds that truth can be discovered only through experience and that the value of ideas should be measured by their practical consequences. Pragmatism had a significant influence on the progressives. (p. 593)

Proclamation of Amnesty and Reconstruction 1863 proclamation that established the basic parameters of President Lincoln's approach to Reconstruction. Lincoln's plan would have readmitted the South to the Union on relatively lenient terms. (p. 431)

Progressive Party Third party formed by Theodore Roosevelt in 1912 to facilitate his candidacy for president. Nicknamed the "Bull Moose Party," the Progressive Party split the Republican vote, allowing Democrat Woodrow Wilson to win the election. (p. 610)

Pullman strike 1894 strike by workers against the Pullman railcar company. When the strike disrupted rail service nation-wide, threatening the delivery of the mail, President Cleveland ordered federal troops to get the railroads moving again. (p. 535)

Reaganomics Ronald Reagan's economic policies based on the theories of supply-side economists and centered on tax cuts and cuts to domestic programs. (p. 876)

Red scare The fear of Communist-inspired radicalism in the wake of the Russian Revolution. The Red scare following World War I culminated in the Palmer raids on suspected radicals. (p. 655)

Redeemers White, conservative Democrats who challenged and overthrew Republican rule in the South during Reconstruction. (p. 443)

Roe v. Wade The 1973 Supreme Court opinion that affirmed a woman's constitutional right to abortion. (p. 841)

Roosevelt Corollary 1904 addition to the Monroe Doctrine that affirmed the right of the United States to intervene in the internal affairs of Caribbean and Latin American countries to preserve order and protect American interests. (p. 631)

Sacco and Vanzetti case 1920 case in which Nicola Sacco and Bartolomeo Vanzetti were convicted of robbery and murder. The trial centered on the defendants' foreign birth and political views, rather than the facts pertaining to their guilt or innocence. (p. 668)

SALT II 1979 strategic arms limitation treaty agreed on by President Jimmy Carter and Soviet leader Leonid Brezhnev. After the Soviet Union invaded Afghanistan, Carter persuaded the Senate not to ratify the treaty. (p. 897)

scalawags Derisive term for white Southerners who supported Reconstruction. (p. 440)

Scottsboro Nine Nine African American youths convicted of raping two white women in Scottsboro, Alabama, in 1931. The Communist Party played a key role in defending the Scottsboro Nine and in bringing national and international attention to their case. (p. 692)

second front Beginning in 1942, Stalin wanted an immediate invasion by U.S., British, and Canadian forces into German-occupied France to take pressure off the Soviet forces fighting the Germans on the eastern front. The attack in western Europe did not begin until 1944, fostering resentment in Stalin. (p. 728)

second industrial revolution Revolution in technology and productivity that reshaped the American economy in the early twentieth century. (p. 660)

Sedition Act 1918 act appended to the Espionage Act. It punished individuals for expressing opinions deemed hostile to the U.S. government, flag, or military. (p. 639)

Servicemen's Readjustment Act 1944 act that offered educational opportunities and financial aid to veterans as they readjusted to civilian life. Known as the GI Bill, the law helped millions of veterans build new lives after the war. (p. 770)

settlement houses Community centers established by urban reformers in the late nineteenth century. Settlement house organizers resided in the institutions they created and were often female, middle-class, and college educated. (p. 579)

Share Our Wealth Plan devised by Senator Huey Long of Louisiana to provide families with a $5,000 homestead and a guaranteed annual income of $2,000. These results would be achieved by taxing the wealthy. (p. 702)

sharecropping A system that emerged as the dominant mode of agricultural production in the South in the years after the Civil War. Under the sharecropping system, sharecroppers received tools and supplies from landowners in exchange for a share of the eventual harvest. (p. 441)

Sherman Antitrust Act 1890 act that outlawed monopolies that prevented free competition in interstate commerce. (p. 500)

sit-down strike A strike in which workers occupy their place of employment. In 1937 the United Auto Workers conducted sit-down strikes in Flint, Michigan, against General Motors to gain union recognition, higher wages, and better working conditions. The union won its demands. (p. 704)

skilled workers Workers with particular training and skills. Skilled workers were paid more and were more difficult for owners to replace than unskilled workers. (p. 529)

skyscrapers Buildings more than ten stories high that first appeared in U.S. cities in the late nineteenth century. Urban crowding and high prices for land stimulated the drive to construct taller buildings. (p. 573)

Smith Act 1940 act that prohibited teaching or advocating the violent overthrow of the U.S. government or belonging to any group with that aim. (p. 774)

social gospel Religious movement that advocated the application of Christian teachings to social and economic problems. The ideals of the social gospel inspired many progressive reformers. (p. 593)

Social Security Act Landmark 1935 act that created retirement pensions for most Americans, as well as unemployment insurance. (p. 703)

Solidarity Polish trade union movement led by Lech Walesa. During the 1980s, Solidarity played a central role in ending Communist rule in Poland. (p. 908)

Southern Christian Leadership Conference (SCLC) Organization founded in 1957 by Martin Luther King Jr. and other black ministers to encourage nonviolent protests against racial segregation and disfranchisement in the South. (p. 804)

Stonewall Tavern The gay bar in Greenwich Village in New York City where, in 1969, its patrons fought the police in response to harassment. This encounter helped launch the gay liberation movement. (p. 844)

Strategic Arms Limitation Treaty (SALT I) 1972 agreement between the United States and Soviet Union to curtail nuclear arms production during the Cold War. The pact froze for five years the number of antiballistic missiles (ABMs), intercontinental ballistic missiles (ICBMs), and submarine-based missiles that each nation could deploy. (p. 863)

Student Nonviolent Coordinating Committee (SNCC) Civil rights organization that grew out of the sit-ins of 1960. The organization focused on taking direct action and political organizing to achieve its goals. (p. 805)

Students for a Democratic Society (SDS) Student activist organization formed in the early 1960s that advocated the formation of a "New Left" that would overturn the social and political status quo. (p. 837)

subprime mortgages Mortgages that are normally made out to borrowers with lower credit ratings. During the early twenty-first century, banks and mortgage companies devised lenient lending policies to allow buyers to purchase homes beyond their means. (p. 944)

subtreasury system A proposal by the Farmers' Alliances in the 1880s for the federal government to extend loans to farmers and store their crops in warehouses until prices rose and they could buy back and sell their crops to repay their debts. (p. 541)

suffragists Supporters of voting rights for women. Campaigns for women's's suffrage gained strength in the late nineteenth and early twentieth centuries and culminated in ratification of the Nineteenth Amendment in 1920. (p. 596)

Sun Belt The southern and western part of the United States. After World War II, millions of Americans moved to the Sun Belt, drawn by the region's climate and jobs in the defense, petroleum, and chemical industries. (p. 793)

sweatshops Small factories or shops in which workers toiled under adverse conditions. Business owners, particularly in the garment industry, turned tenement apartments into sweatshops. (p. 575)

Taft-Hartley Act 1947 law that curtailed unions' ability to organize. It prevented unions from barring employment to non-union members and authorized the federal government to halt a strike for eighty days if it interfered with the national interest. (p. 770)

Tea Party movement A loose coalition of conservative and libertarian forces that arose around 2008. Generally working within the Republican Party, the Tea Party advocates small government, low taxes, and reduced federal deficits. (p. 946)

Teapot Dome scandal Oil and land scandal during the Harding administration that highlighted the close ties between big business and the federal government in the early 1920s. (p. 659)

Teller Amendment Amendment to the 1898 declaration of war against Spain stipulating that Cuba should be free and independent. The amendment was largely ignored in the aftermath of America's victory. (p. 628)

tenements Multifamily apartment buildings that housed many poor urban dwellers at the turn of the twentieth century. Tenements were crowded, uncomfortable, and dangerous. (p. 574)

Tennessee Valley Authority (TVA) New Deal agency that brought low-cost electricity to rural Americans and redeveloped the Tennessee River valley through flood-control projects. The agency built, owned, and supervised a number of power plants and dams. (p. 698)

Tenure of Office Act Law passed by Congress in 1867 to prevent President Andrew Johnson from removing cabinet members sympathetic to the Republican Party's approach to congressional Reconstruction without Senate approval. Johnson was impeached, but not convicted, for violating the act. (p. 437)

Tet Offensive January 31, 1968, offensive mounted by Vietcong and North Vietnamese forces against population centers in South Vietnam. The offensive was turned back, but it shocked many Americans and increased public opposition to the war. (p. 830)

Thirteenth Amendment Amendment to the Constitution abolishing slavery. The Thirteenth Amendment was passed in January 1865 and sent to the states for ratification. (p. 431)

To Secure These Rights Report issued by President Truman's Committee on Civil Rights in 1947 that advocated extending racial equality. Among its recommendations was the desegregation of the military, which Truman instituted by executive order in 1948. (p. 772)

transcontinental railroad A railroad linking the East and West Coasts of North America. Completed in 1869, the transcontinental railroad facilitated the flow of migrants and the development of economic connections between the West and the East. (p. 462)

Treaty of Fort Laramie 1851 treaty that sought to confine tribes on the northern plains to designated areas in an attempt to keep white settlers from encroaching on their land. In 1868, the second Treaty of Fort Laramie gave northern tribes control over the "Great Reservation" in parts of present-day Montana, Wyoming, North Dakota, and South Dakota. (p. 465)

Triangle Shirtwaist Company Site of an infamous industrial fire in New York City in 1911. Inadequate fire safety provisions in the factory led to the deaths of 146 workers. (p. 575)

Truman Doctrine U.S. pledge to contain the expansion of communism around the world. Based on the idea of containment, the Truman Doctrine was the cornerstone of American foreign policy throughout the Cold War. (p. 762)

Tuskegee Institute African American educational institute founded in 1881 by Booker T. Washington. Following Washington's philosophy, the Tuskegee Institute focused on teaching industrious habits and practical job skills. (p. 599)

unions Groups of workers seeking rights and benefits from their employers through their collective efforts. (p. 532)

Universal Negro Improvement Association (UNIA) Organization founded by Marcus Garvey in 1914 to promote black self-help, pan-Africanism, and racial separatism. (p. 666)

unskilled workers Workers with little or no specific expertise. Unskilled workers, many of whom were immigrants, made up the vast majority of the late-nineteenth-century industrial workforce. (p. 529)

vertical integration The control of all elements in a supply chain by a single firm. For example, Andrew Carnegie, a vertically integrated steel producer, sought to own suppliers of all the raw materials used in steel production. (p. 499)

Vietcong The popular name for the National Liberation Front (NLF) in South Vietnam, which was formed in 1959. The Vietcong waged a military insurgency against the U.S.-backed president, Ngo Dinh Diem, and received support from Ho Chi Minh, the leader of North Vietnam. (p. 811)

Vietnamization President Richard Nixon's strategy of turning over greater responsibility for the fighting of the Vietnam War to the South Vietnamese army. (p. 862)

vital center liberalism Political ideology of Harry Truman supporters who took a middle political ground between the extreme right and left. Vital center liberals supported the Cold War, favored civil rights measures and federal government support for public housing and medical care, and opposed McCarthyism while supporting domestic anticommunism efforts. (p. 774)

Voting Rights Act 1965 act that eliminated many of the obstacles to African American voting in the South and resulted in dramatic increases in black participation in the electoral process. (p. 834)

War Industries Board (WIB) Government commission created in 1917 to supervise the purchase of military supplies and oversee the conversion of the economy to meet wartime demands. The WIB embodied a government-business partnership that lasted beyond World War I. (p. 637)

War Powers Act 1973 act that required the president to consult with Congress within forty-eight hours of deploying military forces and to obtain a declaration of war from Congress if troops remained on foreign soil beyond sixty days. (p. 863)

War Production Board Board established in 1942 to oversee the economy during World War II. The War Production Board was part of a larger effort to convert American industry to the production of war materials. (p. 735)

Watergate Scandal and cover-up that forced the resignation of Richard Nixon in 1974. The scandal revolved around a break-in at Democratic Party headquarters in 1972 and subsequent efforts to conceal the administration's involvement in the break-in. (p. 865)

Weathermen A group advocating the use of revolutionary violence, formed in 1968 by dissident members of Students for a Democratic Society (SDS). The Weathermen went underground to avoid criminal prosecution. (p. 838)

white-collar workers Managerial, clerical, and technical workers. The creation of large numbers of white-collar jobs in the late nineteenth century was the key factor in the expansion of the American middle class. (p. 506)

Woman's Christian Temperance Union (WCTU) Organization founded in 1874 to campaign for a ban on the sale and consumption of alcohol. In the late nineteenth century, under Frances Willard's leadership, the WCTU supported a broad social reform agenda. (p. 602)

Works Progress Administration (WPA) New Deal agency established in 1935 to put unemployed Americans to work on public projects ranging from construction to the arts. (p. 702)

Yalta Agreement Agreement negotiated at the 1945 Yalta Conference by Roosevelt, Churchill, and Stalin about the fate of postwar eastern Europe. The Yalta Agreement did little to ease growing tensions between the Soviet Union and its Western allies. (p. 730)

yellow journalism Sensationalist news accounts meant to provoke an emotional response in readers. Yellow journalism contributed to the growth of public support for American intervention in Cuba in 1898. (p. 627)

Young Americans for Freedom (YAF) A group of young conservatives from college campuses formed in 1960 in Sharon, Connecticut. It favored free market principles, states' rights, and anticommunism. (p. 845)

Zimmermann telegram 1917 telegram in which Germany offered Mexico an alliance in the event that the United States entered World War I. The telegram's publication in American newspapers helped build public support for war. (p. 635)

zoot suit riots Series of riots in 1943 in Los Angeles, California, sparked by white hostility toward Mexican Americans. White sailors attacked Mexican American teenagers who dressed in zoot suits—suits with long jackets with padded shoulders and baggy pants tapered at the bottom. (p. 742)

Chapter 15

Document 15.4: "Letter from a Homesteader" from *Frontier Mother: The Letters of Gro Svendsen,* edited by Pauline Farseth and Theodore Blegen. Norwegian-American Historical Association. Used by permission.

Chapter 17

Document 17.2: "Reflections on the Homestead Strike" from *Living My Life* by Emma Goldman, Alfred Knopf, Inc. 1931, reprinted 1970, Dover edition. Used by permission of Dover Publications, Inc.

Chapter 18

Document 18.1: Anzia Yezierska, excerpts from *Bread Givers*, pp. 21–22. Copyright 1925 by Doubleday & Co., Inc., renewed 1952 by Anzia Yezierska. Reprinted with the permission of Persea Books, Inc (New York), www.perseabooks.com.

Chapter 22

Document 22.1: From *The Nation*, August 7, 1937. ©1937 The Nation Company, LLC. All rights reserved. Used by permission and protected by the Copyright Laws of the United States. The printing, copying, redistribution, or retransmission of this Content without express written permission is prohibited.

Document 22.5: Reprinted from *Dust Bowl Diary* by Ann Marie Low by permission of the University of Nebraska Press. Copyright 1984 by the University of Nebraska Press.

Document 22.8: From *The Harvest Gypsies: On the Road to the Grapes of Wrath* by John Steinbeck, originally published in *The San Francisco News*, October 7, 1936. Reprinted by permission of Heyday.

Document 22.9: From *The Nation*, December 19, 1936. © 1936 The Nation Company, LLC. All rights reserved. Used by permission and protected by the Copyright Laws of the United States. The printing, copying, redistribution, or retransmission of this Content without express written permission is prohibited.

Chapter 23

Document 23.1: "Letter to Her Parents," December 22, 1941, by Monica Conter. Reprinted by permission.

Document 23.2: From *Nisei Daughter* by Monica Sone. Copyright 1953 and renewed © 1981 by Monica Sone. Used by permission of Little, Brown and Company.

Document 23.5: From *Taps for a Jim Crow Army: Letters from Black Soldiers in World War II*, edited by Philip McGuire. Copyright © 1983 by Philip McGuire. Reprint copyright © by The University Press of Kentucky. Reprinted by permission of The University Press of Kentucky.

Chapter 24

Document 24.1: Reproduced with permission of Curtis Brown, London on behalf of the Beneficiaries of the Estate of Winston S. Churchill. Copyright © The Beneficiaries of the Estate of Winston S. Churchill.

Document 24.2: "The Way to Peace" by Henry Wallace, from the Papers of Henry A. Wallace, University of Iowa Libraries, Iowa City, Iowa. Used by permission.

Document 24.4: "Letter from Korea, 30 April 1951" by Helen Stevenson. Meyner Papers, Special Collections & College Archives, Skillman Library, Lafayette College. Used by Permission.

Document 24.10: From "Are You Now or Were You Ever?" by Arthur Miller, from *The Guardian/The Observer* (online), June 17, 2000. Copyright Guardian News & Media Ltd 2000. Used by permission.

Chapter 25

Document 25.2: Courtesy of Seattle Civil Rights and Labor History Project, University of Washington. http://depts.washington.edu/civilr/InnisArden.htm.

Document 25.3: From *The Charlotte Observer,* September 9, 1958 © 1958 McClatchy. All rights reserved. Used by permission and protected by the Copyright Laws of the United States. The printing, copying, redistribution, or retransmission of this Content without express written permission is prohibited.

Document 25.6: "The Nine Billion Dollars in Hot Little Hands" by Richard Gehman, from *Cosmopolitan*, November 1957. Courtesy of Christian Gehman.

Document 25.8: From George E. Sokolsky, "Teenager Puts Rap on Suggestion Elvis on Way Out," *Milwaukee Sentinel,* March 11, 1967.

Document 25.9: Excerpt(s) from *The Sixties: Years of Hope and Rage* by Todd Gitlin, copyright © 1987 by Todd Gitlin. Used by permission of Bantam Books, an imprint of Random House, a division of Penguin Random House LLC. All rights reserved. Any third party use of this material, outside of this publication, is prohibited. Interested parties must apply directly to Penguin Random House LLC for permission.

Chapter 26

Document 26.2: From *Dear America: Letters Home from Vietnam*, edited by Bernard Edelman for the New York Vietnam Veterans Memorial Commission; W. W. Norton & Company, 1985. Used by permission of Bernard Edelman.

Document 26.5: From "The Sharon Statement," 1960. Courtesy of Young America's Foundation.

Document 26.6: From "Prospectus for Mississippi Freedom Summer," the Michael J. Miller Civil Rights Collection. Courtesy of Archives and Special Collections, The University of Mississippi.

Document 26.7: "Letter from Joseph and Nancy Ellin to Dr. and Mrs. Ellin," June 30, 1964. Used by permission of David Ellin.

Document 26.8: Excerpt from *Letters from Mississippi*, edited by Elizabeth Sutherland Martínez. Original edition copyright © 1965 and renewed 1993 by Elizabeth Sutherland Martínez. New edition copyright © 2002 by Elizabeth Sutherland Martínez. Reprinted with the permission of The Permissions Company, Inc., on behalf of Zephyr Press, www.zephyrpress.org.

Document 26.9: From "'Freedom' to the Delta," *Charleston Post*, June 26, 1964.

Chapter 27

Document 27.1: From *Capitalist Patriarchy and the Case for Socialist Feminism*, edited by Zillah R. Eisenstein. Reprinted with permission of the Monthly Review Foundation.

A **Note about the Index:** Names of individuals appear in boldface. Letters in parentheses following page numbers refer to documents (*d*), figures (*f*), illustrations (*i*), maps (*m*), and tables (*t*).

second Red scare and, 774–778
Soviet, 710
in Vietnam, 810, 863
Communist Control Act (1954), 778
Communist Party
in Great Depression, 695, 701
labor unions and, 695
prosecutions of, 776
Rosenbergs and, 758
Scottsboro Nine defended by, 692, 695
Communists
Hitler and, 723
Nazis and, 733
in Vietnam, 827
after World War I, 655–656
in World War II, 743
Communities
African American urban, 572–573
immigrant, 565–566
Community Action Program, 835
Community Relations Service, 832
Compassionate conservatism, 936–937
Competition
in cattle ranching, 474
industrial consolidation and, 498, 499
industrialists and, 504
Comprehensive Anti-Apartheid Act (1986), 902
Comprehensive Environmental Response, Compensation, and Liability Act (Superfund), 871
Compromise of 1877, 446
Compulsory Sterilization Law (Indiana, 1907), 617(d)
Computer revolution, 929–930
Computers
digital technology and, 927–929
Microsoft and, 927–928
Comstock Lode, 469, 470
Concentration camps, Nazi, 733, 733(i)
Coney Island, 537
"Confessions of a Political Boss" (Plunkett), 579(d)
Conflict. See also specific battles and wars
management after Cold War, 913–915
Conformity, in 1950s, 790, 802
Conglomerates, media, 930
Congo, civil war in, 810
Congreso de Pueblos de Habla Española, El, 688
Congress (U.S.). See also House of Representatives; Senate
1876 elections and, 446
1994 elections and, 934
2006 elections and, 942
2010 elections and, 946

Eightieth, 770
ex-Confederates elected to, 432, 433, 445
Fortieth, 437
gridlock in, 510–511
inaction and, 511–513
Johnson, Andrew, and, 432, 433–437, 438
nuclear freeze movement and, 905
women in, 869
Congressional Medal of Honor, to African American, 466
Congressional Reconstruction, 437–438
southern resistance to, 441–444
Congress of Federated Organizations (COFO), 849
Congress of Industrial Organizations (CIO), 688, 704, 769(i), 791
Congress of Racial Equality (CORE), 740, 771, 772(i), 804, 824, 830
Freedom Summer and, 849
Conkling, Roscoe, 514
Connor, Eugene "Bull," 832
Conscience of a Conservative (Goldwater), 845
"Consciousness-raising" groups, 841
Conscription. See Military draft
Conservation, 869–871
Pinchot and, 591–592, 673–674
preservation and, 605–606, 607
Taft and, 609
Conservative coalition, 707, 860
Conservatives and conservatism
in 1950s, 790
in 1960s, 844–845, 847
of Bush, George W., 937
Clinton opposed by, 934
in Great Depression, 701
immigration and, 878–879
movement toward, 882
New Right and, 873–874
of Nixon, 837
under Reagan, 877–880
of Supreme Court, 877
Consolidation
industrial, 498–499
of railroads, 495
Constitution(s)
of Cuba, 628
Hawaiian, 644
Reconstruction state, 441
Constitution (U.S.), 503
male inserted in, 438
Reconstruction amendments and, 447
Constitutional conventions, during Reconstruction, 437

"Constructive engagement" policy, under Reagan, 901–902
Consumer economy. See Market economy
Consumer goods
in late 19th century, 508
mail-order catalogs and, 502
mass-produced, 571
production of (1921 and 1929), 660(f)
retail outlets and, 500–502
Consumer Products Safety Commission, 864
Consumers and consumerism
in 1920s, 660–661, 662(i)
in 1950s, 790, 817
in Cold War, 769–770
online purchasing by, 929
Containment, 757–758, 762, 778
economic, 762–763
Eisenhower and, 807
in Gulf War, 915
in Korea, 768
military, 764–769
NSC-68 and, 766
in Southeast Asia, 827
Conter, Monica, "Letter to Her Parents," 726(d)
Contraception. See Birth control
Contracts, 517
Contract with America, 934
Contras, in Nicaragua, 901, 903, 918
Convict lease system, 497
Conwell, Russell, 504, 580
"Acres of Diamonds" sermon of, 503
Coolidge, Calvin
1924 election and, 673(m)
on Boston police strike, 655
as president, 659
Cooperatives, farm, 539, 540
Coral Sea, Battle of the, 730
CORE. See Congress of Racial Equality
Corn (maize), 476–478
"Corn-hog cycle," in farming, 478
Corporate capitalism, 509
Corporate mergers. See Mergers
Corporations, 515. See also Business; specific companies
in 1920s, 661
growth of, 499–502
interlocking management of, 663
limited liability and, 500
malfeasance of, 930–931
managerial specialists in, 500
multinational, 911–912
trusts and, 500
Wilson and, 611

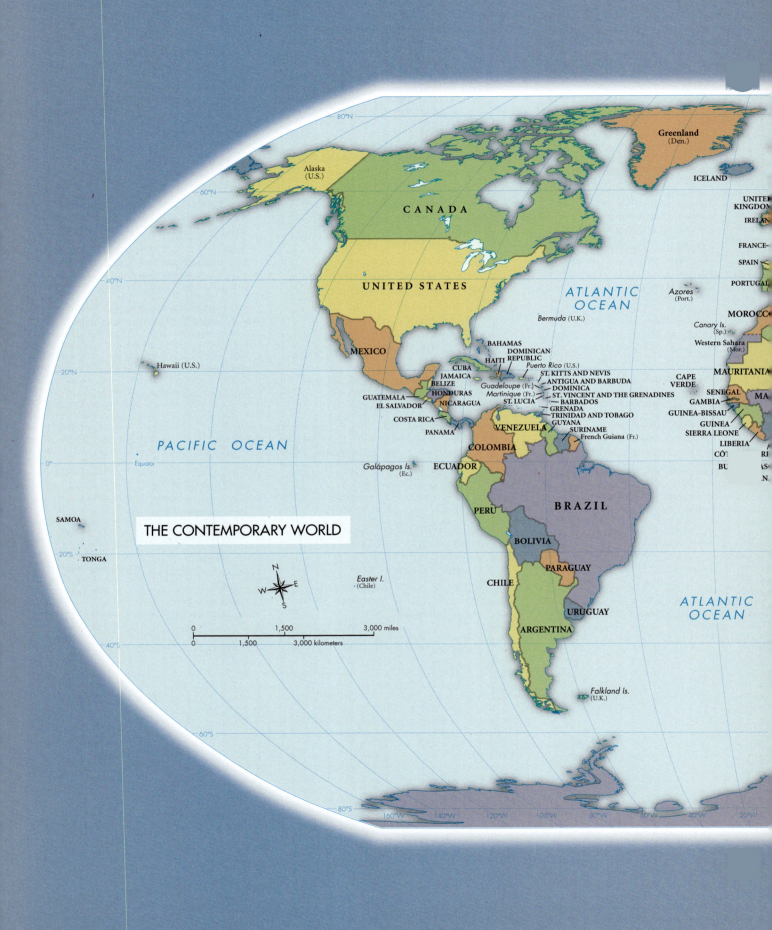

THE CONTEMPORARY WORLD

Alaska
(U.S.)

CANADA

UNITED STATES

Hawaii (U.S.)

MEXICO

GUATEMALA
EL SALVADOR

COSTA RICA

PANAMA

BAHAMAS
DOMINICAN
REPUBLIC
HAITI

CUBA
JAMAICA
BELIZE
HONDURAS
NICARAGUA

Puerto Rico (U.S.)
ST. KITTS AND NEVIS
ANTIGUA AND BARBUDA
Guadeloupe (Fr.) DOMINICA
Martinique (Fr.) ST. VINCENT AND THE GRENADINES
ST. LUCIA   BARBADOS
GRENADA
TRINIDAD AND TOBAGO
GUYANA
SURINAME
French Guiana (Fr.)

VENEZUELA

COLOMBIA

ECUADOR

Galápagos Is.
(Ec.)

PERU

BRAZIL

BOLIVIA

PARAGUAY

CHILE

URUGUAY

ARGENTINA

Falkland Is.
(U.K.)

ATLANTIC
OCEAN

Bermuda (U.K.)

Azores
(Port.)

Canary Is.
(Sp.)

Western Sahara
(Mor.)

Greenland
(Den.)

ICELAND

UNITED
KINGDOM

IRELAND

FRANCE

SPAIN

PORTUGAL

MOROCCO

MAURITANIA

CAPE
VERDE

SENEGAL

GAMBIA

GUINEA-BISSAU

GUINEA

SIERRA LEONE

LIBERIA

MALI

CÔTE

BU

PACIFIC OCEAN

Equator

SAMOA

TONGA

Easter I.
(Chile)

ATLANTIC
OCEAN

N
W   E
S

| 0 | 1,500 | 3,000 miles |
| 0 | 1,500 | 3,000 kilometers |

80°N

60°N

40°N

20°N

0°

20°S

40°S

60°S

80°S

160°W   140°W   120°W   100°W   80°W   60°W   40°W   20°W

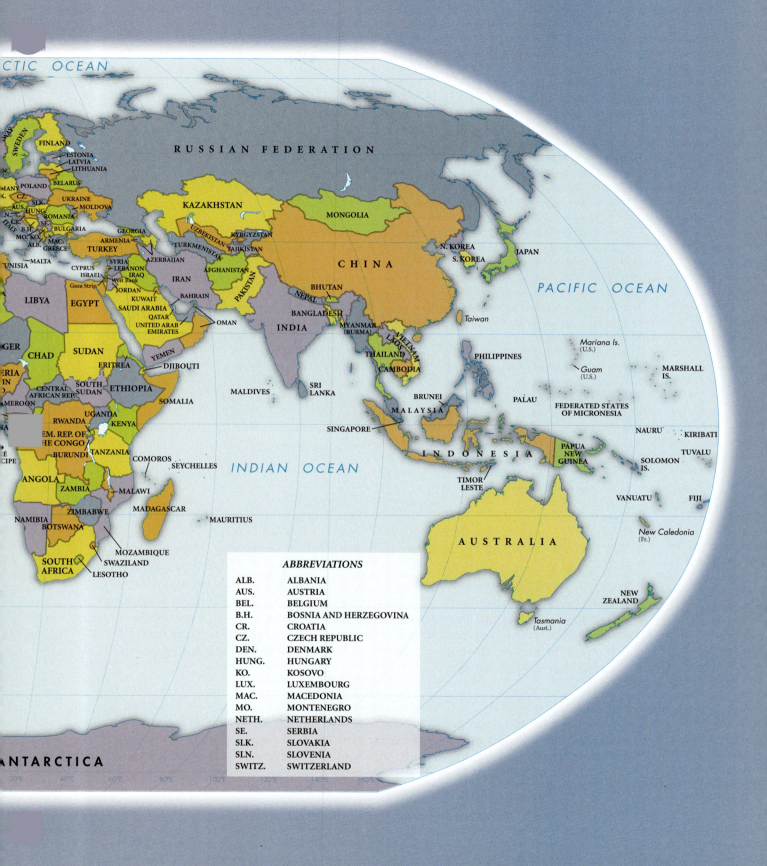

ARCTIC OCEAN

SWEDEN
FINLAND
ESTONIA
LATVIA
LITHUANIA
MANY POLAND BELARUS
CZ. UKRAINE
AUS. SLK. MOLDOVA
HUNG. ROMANIA
SE. BULGARIA
B.H. GEORGIA
MO. KO. GREECE TURKEY ARMENIA
ALB. MAC. AZERBAIJAN
TUNISIA MALTA
CYPRUS SYRIA LEBANON IRAQ
ISRAEL West Bank
Gaza Strip JORDAN
LIBYA EGYPT KUWAIT
SAUDI ARABIA
QATAR
UNITED ARAB
EMIRATES OMAN
GER CHAD SUDAN YEMEN
ERITREA DJIBOUTI
ERIA CENTRAL SOUTH
IN AFRICAN REP. SUDAN ETHIOPIA
MEROON SOMALIA
UGANDA
RWANDA KENYA
CIPE EM. REP. OF
THE CONGO BURUNDI TANZANIA COMOROS
ANGOLA SEYCHELLES
ZAMBIA MALAWI
ZIMBABWE MADAGASCAR
NAMIBIA
BOTSWANA
SOUTH MOZAMBIQUE
AFRICA SWAZILAND
LESOTHO MAURITIUS

RUSSIAN FEDERATION

KAZAKHSTAN MONGOLIA
UZBEKISTAN KYRGYZSTAN
TURKMENISTAN TAJIKISTAN
N. KOREA JAPAN
S. KOREA
IRAN AFGHANISTAN CHINA
PAKISTAN BHUTAN
BAHRAIN NEPAL Taiwan
BANGLADESH
INDIA MYANMAR VIETNAM
(BURMA) LAOS
THAILAND PHILIPPINES
CAMBODIA Mariana Is.
(U.S.)
MALDIVES SRI Guam MARSHALL
LANKA (U.S.) IS.
BRUNEI PALAU
FEDERATED STATES
OF MICRONESIA
SINGAPORE MALAYSIA NAURU KIRIBATI
TUVALU
INDONESIA PAPUA SOLOMON
NEW IS.
GUINEA VANUATU FIJI
TIMOR
LESTE New Caledonia
(Fr.)

PACIFIC OCEAN

INDIAN OCEAN

AUSTRALIA

NEW
ZEALAND

Tasmania
(Aust.)

ANTARCTICA

ABBREVIATIONS	
ALB.	ALBANIA
AUS.	AUSTRIA
BEL.	BELGIUM
B.H.	BOSNIA AND HERZEGOVINA
CR.	CROATIA
CZ.	CZECH REPUBLIC
DEN.	DENMARK
HUNG.	HUNGARY
KO.	KOSOVO
LUX.	LUXEMBOURG
MAC.	MACEDONIA
MO.	MONTENEGRO
NETH.	NETHERLANDS
SE.	SERBIA
SLK.	SLOVAKIA
SLN.	SLOVENIA
SWITZ.	SWITZERLAND

About the authors

Authors Steven F. Lawson and Nancy A. Hewitt outside the couple's home with their trusty consultant, Scooter.

Nancy A. Hewitt (Ph.D., University of Pennsylvania) is professor of history and of Women's and Gender Studies at Rutgers University. Her publications include *Southern Discomfort: Women's Activism in Tampa, Florida, 1880s–1920s,* for which she received the Julia Cherry Spruill Prize from the Southern Association of Women Historians; *Women's Activism and Social Change: Rochester, New York, 1822–1872*; and the edited volume *No Permanent Waves: Recasting Histories of U.S. Feminism.* She is currently working on a biography of the nineteenth-century radical activist Amy Post and a book that recasts the U.S. woman suffrage movement.

Steven F. Lawson (Ph.D., Columbia University) is professor emeritus of history at Rutgers University. His research interests include U.S. politics since 1945 and the history of the civil rights movement, with a particular focus on black politics and the interplay between civil rights and political culture in the mid-twentieth century. He is the author of many works, including *Running for Freedom: Civil Rights and Black Politics in America since 1941*; *Black Ballots: Voting Rights in the South, 1944–1969*; and *In Pursuit of Power: Southern Blacks and Electoral Politics, 1965–1982.*